The Paradox of Agrarian Change

The Paradox of Agrarian Change

Food Security and the Politics of
Social Protection in Indonesia

Edited by
*John F. McCarthy, Andrew McWilliam
and Gerben Nooteboom*

NUS PRESS
SINGAPORE

Published by:

NUS Press
National University of Singapore
AS3-01-02, 3 Arts Link
Singapore 117569

Fax: (65) 6774-0652
E-mail: nusbooks@nus.edu.sg
Website: http://nuspress.nus.edu.sg

ISBN 978-981-325-183-0 (paper)
ePDF ISBN 978-981-325-199-1

National Library Board, Singapore Cataloguing in Publication Data

Name(s): McCarthy, John F. (John Fitzgerald), 1964- editor. | McWilliam, Andrew, editor. | Nooteboom, Gerben, 1970- editor.
Title: The paradox of agrarian change : food security and the politics of social protection in Indonesia / edited by John F. McCarthy, Andrew McWilliam and Gerben Nooteboom.
Description: Singapore : NUS Press, [2023]
Identifier(s): ISBN 978-981-325-183-0 (paperback)
Subject(s): LCSH: Rural poor--Indonesia. | Food security--Indonesia. | Poverty--Government policy--Indonesia. | Economic assistance, Domestic--Indonesia.
Classification: DDC 339.4609598--dc23

Cover image: Warm sweet Indonesian tea served on a *lesehan* or a mat. Yogyakarta, Indonesia, 27 June 2020.
Photo by Ani Fathudin / Shutterstock.com
Photo ID: 1764445283

Typeset by: Ogma Solutions Pvt Ltd
Printed by: Integrated Books International

To the people of rural Indonesia, whose resilience, endurance and resourcefulness continue to inspire.

Contents

List of Figures

List of Tables

Acknowledgements

We undertook this project under an Australian Research Council grant entitled "Household Vulnerability, Food Security and the Politics of Social Protection in Indonesia" [DP140103828]. The project involved joint research with an international consortium of researchers from the Australian National University, the University of Western Sydney and Murdoch University in Australia; in Indonesia, we collaborated with the Gadjah Mada University Center for Population and Policy Studies (PSKK), the University of North Sumatra, the University of Syiah Kuala, Malikussaleh University and Almuslim University in Aceh and Halu Oleo University in Southeast Sulawesi. We also collaborated with the University of Amsterdam and Leiden University in the Netherlands. The Dutch Research Council (NWO/ Wotro—Science for Global Development) also contributed to research and travel costs. We thank them for their support and participation.

The research and analysis for this volume have also benefitted from the extensive discussions, insights and advice offered by a wide range of Indonesian policymakers and programme managers at national and regional levels of government, including village leaders and District field staff of the Ministry of Social Affairs. We thank them for their engagement and encouragement.

This consortium of six Indonesian, two Dutch and three Australian universities continues to collaborate on research and policy discussions related to agrarian change, vulnerability and food security. Yunita Winarto, Henri Sitorus, Pande Made Kutanegara, Vania Budianto and John McCarthy drew on the research conclusions from this study to produce a report entitled *COVID-19 and Food Systems in Indonesia* (2020) funded by the Australian Centre for International Research which has served as the basis for the epilogue.

Researchers presented earlier versions of these chapters at workshops hosted at Gadjah Mada University; at the regional planning office in Banda Aceh, the University of North Sumatra; at the ISEAS conference in Leiden, the Euroseas conferences in Oxford (2017) and Berlin (2019), and at the Australasian AID Conference in Canberra. Our work has also been disseminated and discussed in a series of policy discussions, blogs and webinars.

A heartfelt thanks to Pande Made Kutanegara of the Center for Population and Policy Studies at Gadjah Mada University for facilitating the project in Indonesia. We also thank all students and field assistants who joined data collection and all villagers, officials and assistants in the field. Thanks also to Rudy Purba and Ngoc Chu for their tireless assistance with the survey data. We are also very grateful to Sarah Cook, then at the Institute for Global Development, UNSW (formerly director UNRISD), for sharing her thoughts and insights and providing critical comments on an earlier draft of one of the social protection chapters.

We also express our thanks to our two anonymous reviewers and Bec Donaldson for her meticulous and timely copy-editing. We are also extremely grateful to Elspeth Thomson and others in the NUS Press editorial team for their patience and assiduous work.

Research material that fed into this book has also been published elsewhere, including:

McWilliam, A., N.I Wianti and Y. Taufik (2021), "Poverty and Prosperity among Sama Bajo Fishing Communities (Southeast Sulawesi, Indonesia)", *Singapore Journal of Tropical Geography* 42,1: 132–48;

McCarthy, J.F. and M. Sumarto (2018), "Distributional Politics and Social Protection in Indonesia: Dilemmas of Layering, Nesting and Social Fit in Jokowi's Poverty Policy", *Journal of Southeast Asian Economies* 35, 2: 223–36;

McCarthy, J.F. (2020), "The Paradox of Progressing Sideways: Food Poverty and Livelihood Change in the Rice Lands of Outer Island Indonesia", *Journal of Peasant Studies* 47, 5: 1077–97;

Nooteboom, G. (2019), "Understanding the Nature of Rural Change: The Benefits of Migration and the (Re)creation of Precarity for Men and Women in Rural Central Java, Indonesia", *TRaNS: Trans -Regional and -National Studies of Southeast Asia* 7, 1: 113–33;

Warren, C. and D.J. Steenbergen (2021), "Fisheries Decline, Local Livelihoods, and Conflicted Governance: An Indonesian Case", *Ocean and Coastal Management* 202: 1–13.

Acronyms and Glossary

Adat	Custom/customary
Bagi rata	To divide equally
Bagito (*Bagi roto*)	To divide equally
Balita	Toddlers/young children
Bappenas (*Badan Perencanaan Pembangunan Nasional*)	National Development Planning Board of the Republic of Indonesia
Beasiswa miskin	Scholarships for the poor
Bedah rumah	Housing for the poor
Beras	Unhusked rice
BPNT (*Bantuan Pangan Non-Tunai*)	Non-Cash Food Assistance programme, formerly Raskin
BLT (*Bantuan Langsung Tunai*)	Unconditional cash transfer programme
Bulog (*Badan Urusan Logistik*)	Indonesian Bureau of Logistics
Buruh sawah	Rural labourers (in padi fields)
Dana desa	Village fund
DTKS (*Data Terpadu Kesejahteraan Sosial*)	Integrated Social Welfare Data, the database of potential recipients
E-warung	Authorised grocery outlet(s) (payment by card)
Gagal melaut	Unable to go fishing due to the windy season
Jajan	Snacks/ sweets (usually sugar-rich snacks from the shop and less nutritious)
Janda migran	Migration widows

Jilbab	Long and loose-fit outer garment worn by some Muslim women to cover head to chest area
JKN (*Jaminan Kesehatan Nasional*)	National Health Insurance scheme
JPS (*Jaring Pengaman Sosial*)	Social Safety Net
Kartu Sakti	Power card. Since 2014, President Joko Widodo's administration promoted the combined benefit scheme comprising access to three critical support programmes (health, education and replacing Rastra rice distribution programmes with a non-cash food assistance)
Kartu Sembako	Staple Food Card, e.g. to purchase food at the *E-warung*
Kayu	Wood
Kemensos (*Kementerian Sosial*)	Ministry of Social Affairs of the Republic of Indonesia
KIP card (*Kartu Indonesia Pintar*)	Smart Indonesia Card, to access educational benefits
KIS (*Kartu Indonesia Sehat*)	Healthy Indonesia Card, to access health services
KKS card (*Kartu Keluarga Sejahtera*)	Prosperous Family Card, to access benefits of the conditional cash transfers programme
Krismon (*Krisis Moneter*)	Monetary Crisis in Indonesia (1998–2000s)
Ladang	Dry, non-irrigated fields
Miskin	(the) Poor
MPM (*Mekanisme Pemutakhiran Mandiri*)	Self-Updating Method
Musim paceklik	Scarcity season
Musim angin	Windy season

OPK (Operasi Pasar Khusus)	Special Market Operation; Market Operation for Sale of Subsidised Rice
Padi	Unhusked rice
Pas-pasan	Not less but also not more; just enough for unassuming life (generally about income). Has the same meaning as *cukupan*
PBDT (*Pemutakhiran Basis Data Terpadu*)	Unitary database; revising the social registry following a new community vetting of beneficiary lists, surveying and proxy means-testing to fix the problem
PNPM	Program Nasional Pemberdayaan Masyarakat/National Programme for Community Empowerment
Penanganan Fakir Miskin	Islamic care of the poor
Pendamping	Officer in charge of checking conditionalities recipients' conditional cash transfers (PKH)
Penerima zakat fitrah	Recipients of Islamic alms
Perlindungan sosial	Social protection
PKH (*Program Keluarga Harapan*)	Families of Hope programme, conditional cash transfers programme
Pusdatin (Pusat Data dan Informasi)	The Centre for Data and Information under the Ministry of Social Affairs (*Kemensos*)
Ramadan	Fasting month, the ninth month of the Muslim year, when Muslims do not eat between the rising and setting of the sun; celebrates the month that God first revealed the words of the Quran to Mohammed
Raskin (Beras Miskin)	Rice for the poor programme
Rastra (Beras untuk Keluarga Sejahtera)	Rice for Welfare Family, a rice subsidy programme
Reformasi	Reform era, post-Suharto (1998–2000s)

Sawah	Rice or paddy field
Sederhana	Simple but enough
Sembako	Essential staple food package provided by the government at subsidised prices
Sosialisasi	Awareness-raising (*socialisation*)
SBY	Susilo Bambang Yudhoyono, President of Indonesia, 2004–14
SoP	Stages of Progress
SUSENAS (*Survei Sosial Ekonomi Nasional*)	National Socioeconomic Survey
Tidak punya	Not having (*Ran Duwe* in Javanese)
TKI (*Tenaga Kerja Indonesia*)	Indonesian workers; Indonesian citizens that work in foreign countries outside of Indonesia
TKSK (*Tenaga Kesejahteraan Sosial Kecamatan*)	Social welfare field officer
TNP2K (*Tim Nasional Percepatan Penanggulangan Kemiskinan*)	National Team for the Acceleration of Poverty Reduction
Warung	Village kiosk/small food stall
Zakat	The Islamic system of informal cash distributions to the poor that is undertaken annually through an institution/an obligatory annual 2.5% tax on accumulated wealth practised in predominantly Islamic regions

"Well, the way of paradoxes is the way of truth".
Oscar Wilde

"For thence,—a paradox
Which comforts while it mocks".
Robert Browning

Part One

Agrarian Change and Social Protection

CHAPTER 1

Understanding Agrarian Change: Scenarios of Agricultural Development, Income Diversification, Food Poverty and Nutritional Insecurity in Indonesia

John F. McCarthy, Gerben Nooteboom and Andrew McWilliam

Introduction

Following strong economic growth in Asia, most of the world's extreme poor—an estimated 735 million—now live in middle-income countries (Yemtsov et al. 2018). In the process of economic and demographic growth and rapid urbanisation, until the onset of the COVID-19 pandemic we saw declining poverty—in both relative and absolute numbers—accompanying increasing social and regional inequality and persistent nutritional insecurity (FAO, IFAD and WFP 2015).

Indonesia fits the pattern: the statistics suggest that, before 2020, it had reduced extreme poverty to a remarkable extent, with official rates falling to less than 10 per cent by 2019, and Indonesia moving into the ranks of middle-income countries and joining the G20 (Setkab 2019).[1] Despite consistent economic growth prior to the COVID-19 pandemic, high levels of stunting (low height for age) persisted, indicating a continuing pattern of nutritional insecurity. An estimated 37 per cent of children under age five in Indonesia were stunted in 2015 (Beal et al. 2018: 2), falling to 30.8 per cent in 2018 (Kementerian Kesehatan 2020). This is "a stunting rate usually seen in low-income countries" (World Bank 2015a). These problems are more acute in rural Indonesia: here, poverty and stunting rates are considerably higher, indicating ongoing patterns of rural deprivation (see Chapter 15).[2] We have a paradox here, and this provides the start point for our enquiries: why has statistical poverty fallen substantially while nutritional insecurity remains high, especially in rural areas? How is poverty changing?

Inequality and highly concentrated asset ownership remain highly political issues. A World Bank (2015b) study suggested that the wealthiest one per cent of Indonesian citizens owns half of the country's wealth, the second-highest level after Russia from a selection of 38 countries. How has economic development benefited the approximately 120 million people still living in rural Indonesia?

Indonesia's experience of economic change appears to resonate with well-established ways of thinking about how development is established and spreads across rural landscapes. As the significance of agriculture for economic growth falls, and as people move out of rural work, optimists might well find signs of a structural transformation of the countryside: low-income societies for which "agriculture absorbs most labour and generates most economic output, become high-income societies characterised by a relatively smaller but more productive agricultural sector" (Barrett et al. 2017: i13). At the same time, with growing inequality and the persistence of high rates of nutritional insecurity amidst areas of relative deprivation, pessimists may well trace signs of a truncated agrarian transition, where many people who are leaving agriculture cannot find secure livelihoods (Fairbairn et al. 2014). How do the changes experienced in rural Indonesia fit current debates on agrarian transitions? Are there alternative narratives of agrarian change that better fit field realities? Moreover, how effectively do current social protection policies in Indonesia curb the adverse social effects of development and rural change?

We have witnessed the global rise of social cash transfers in academic and policy discussions from liberal and social democratic perspectives over the last decades. Social policies among international organisations and across the Global South have experimented with new programmes to address increasing disparities. The increasing emphasis on social protection, or social assistance, implies a paradigm shift in development policy. Social protection refers to a broad set of "public actions taken in response to levels of vulnerability, risk and deprivation deemed unacceptable within a given polity or society" (Conway, de Haan and Norton 2000: 5). In contrast, social assistance refers to a narrower set of programmes, specifically cash or in-kind benefits financed by the state and usually provided based on a means or income test (Howell 2001).

Development policy has come to the view that social inclusion and poverty reduction require the direct provision of cash to individuals, extending benefits to those excluded by social insurance and other schemes (Leisering 2009; Ferguson 2015). Indonesian policymakers have also taken up this policy approach in an ambitious way. Social cash transfers (defined here as non-contributory and non-repayable) and regular cash transfers to the poor and vulnerable have become a key policy instrument for dealing with poverty and inequality (Leisering 2009). So far, scholars have studied these changes separately. This book brings these developments together: it analyses the nature and social consequences of development and economic change processes in rural Indonesia in relation to the scope and effectiveness of Indonesia's new social assistance programmes.

These changes in social assistance policy amount to an "entitlements revolution" (Leisering 2009). For the first time, overlooked social groups, principally the rural poor and those in the informal sector, are considered worthy of direct public support through cash transfers. As the state constructs new social registries, previously invisible citizens are being made visible to their governments for the first time. The state bestowing welfare benefits onto previously overlooked social groups implies recognising people's legitimate social needs and moving towards their deeper integration into society. These changes have also opened up an aspirational space where a more comprehensive range of people can claim a share of material wealth, instituting what Ferguson (2015) calls "a new politics of distribution".

Increasingly, social cash transfers have become a critical feature of the new policy landscape in contemporary Indonesia. Since 2006, the Indonesian state has rolled out social cash transfer programmes; it has transformed non-conditional cash transfers (BLT) into conditional cash transfers (PKH), and remodelled in-kind assistance (rice for the poor programme, *Raskin-Rastra*) into a non-cash food assistance programme (BPNT) or an e-voucher system (*kartu sembako*).

These developments—persistent food poverty alongside sharper inequality and the rolling out of social cash transfers, with their attendant politics of distribution, participation and recognition—raise a new set of questions and suggest a reassessment of existing ways of thinking. New ways of explaining recent changes are required. How do we account for the persistence of nutritional insecurity and vulnerability in the countryside despite high economic growth and falling statistical poverty? Can we identify the agrarian transitions taking place? How to disentangle the links between agrarian transitions, their social consequences and food security? In contemporary Indonesia, who are the poor and vulnerable, why are they poor, what creates vulnerability and how do they experience the benefits of social assistance policies in these challenging circumstances?

Focus

This volume begins with the observation that in order to appreciate how social cash transfers and other forms of assistance might work in context we need to understand the processes that enable the poor to overcome poverty, cope, or which allow them to fall deeper into poverty. In other words, we need to understand changing poverty and (agrarian) structures and the drivers of food poverty to appreciate the implications of what the *New York Times* has described as "the most important government anti-poverty programme the world has ever seen" (Rosenberg 2011).

Previous research has pointed to weaknesses and gaps in diagnostic approaches to poverty and vulnerability, suggesting that a more robust focus on causality within poverty analysis is required (CPR 2009). Most interventions rely on available statistics and proxy indicators that enable statistically generalisable understandings of who are poor, how many are poor and where they exist, relative to quantifiable definitions of poverty. However, these interventions afford an inadequate knowledge of the causal drivers of poverty, mainly how situated dynamics interact with broader problems to generate vulnerability and insecurity (Hart 2009). The problem is that statistical generalisation may disguise the challenges facing the chronically poor, and therefore the nature of poverty may be insufficiently visible to those who research, make and implement policy. For understandable reasons, standardised blueprint approaches tend to dominate. However, the literature suggests that interventions to address poverty work better if tailored to specific conditions. Yet, to date, there has been limited understanding of vulnerability contexts. This indicates the need for a better understanding of poverty dynamics. This need is even more urgent in rural areas, where production, labour and consumption are entangled in complex ways. Without this understanding, it is unlikely that assistance programmes will be well designed (Krishna 2004; Krishna 2006).

In addition, over the last few years, there has also been renewed interest in processes of agrarian change in Southeast Asia (Li 2014; Borras 2009; Peluso and Purwanto 2018; Rigg and Vandergeest 2012; Hart, Turton and White 1989; Hirsch 2012; Kelly 2011; Neilson 2016; White and Wiradi 1989). Research using economic and agrarian political economy frameworks has studied how and under what conditions the rural poor transition into wage labour or take up commercial farming. Optimistic accounts point to the possibility of income diversification and migration providing people with the means to rise above poverty (World Bank 2007). Others suggest that the poor may be unable to progress through farming, given the inadequate prospects for an exit into the labour market (Bernstein 2010; Akram-Lodhi and Kay 2010; Li 2011). How apt are these characterisations of agrarian change today?

From the time of the East Asian economic crisis which began in July 1997, a large number of economic studies has focused on poverty in rural Indonesia (Manning and Sumarto 2011; Hill 2014), including the impact of high rice prices on the poor and the quality of their diet (Timmer 2004). There is also an extensive series of ethnographic studies on agrarian change (Koning and Hüsken 2006; Nooteboom 2015; Li 2014; Potter 2011). Researchers have yet to compare poverty experiences systematically among the different communities across archipelagic Indonesia, the largest nation in Southeast Asia.

This volume also focuses on social assistance, primarily on conditional cash transfers (CCTs). While CCTs are only one part of a full array of support programmes, they are the leading social assistance programmes in the communities we studied. It is crucial to understand how social assistance fits into the rural landscape. A set of critical questions can be asked concerning how or indeed whether the global CCT model (Leisering 2019)—with its econometric approach and material definition of poverty—is a good fit for the Indonesian context. Since social cash transfers have emerged as a dominant social assistance approach, extensive academic literature has focused on their global spread across Africa and Latin America (Cook and Kabeer 2010; Ellis, Devereux and White 2009; Holzmann and Sipos 2009). When these approaches extended to Asia, the Indonesian government rolled out Social Safety Net programmes as part of its structural adjustment programme, to lessen the effects of the crisis on the poor. As economists began to study these programmes, they highlighted the difficulty of targeting the poor (Dhanani and Islam 2002). Many agency reports focused on the technical aspects of social protection programme (SPP) development, the effectiveness of SPPs in dealing with poverty, the national level politics encompassing design and the challenges of implementation (Yemtsov et al. 2018).

However, despite these numerous reports, there remain few grounded ethnographic studies which have sought to understand the impacts on the poor in context. It remains to be seen whether or how these social assistance solutions work out: how effectively will they support the poor and vulnerable? What social consequences emerge during this encounter between the (global) social assistance schemes and local specificities? How do people experience the newly introduced social assistance programmes, and why is this solution attractive from a political point of view? While cash transfers to the poor offer an apparent means of reducing the poverty headcount, to what degree do SPPs address the structural causes of rural poverty or change the social, political and economic contexts that generate risk? How do social assistance schemes affect men and women, mothers and children, the elderly and young generations living in rural areas? Finally, how are these distributional programmes working out in the messy circumstances where the poor access benefits? The complex distributional politics and the impacts of local forms of vulnerability remain largely unstudied.

To sum up, this book has two broad sets of objectives. First, we consider what is driving vulnerability and insecurity in critical rural contexts and production systems in rural Indonesia. What are the defining livelihood trajectories in each agrarian context? Here, we systematically compare poverty dynamics and agrarian change scenarios across a set of purposively designed case studies, to provide a broader set of analytical generalisations about poverty dynamics. We aim to show what the existing forms of food insecurity are and what changes are taking place. We aim to provide a view "from below" that incorporates structural and locality specific analyses of poverty.

Secondly, we consider the social effects of social cash transfers and how they intersect with the social consequences of ongoing processes of agrarian change. What are their implications for vulnerability and rural livelihoods, and how do people make sense of them and experience them? Our aim here is to provide a view that is largely missing in the debates and econometric evaluations regarding the apparent success of poverty alleviation policies and CCT programmes in Indonesia before COVID-19. Using qualitative approaches, we analyse how the state implements these new models of social cash transfers. We provide an understanding of how relational and institutional processes shape outcomes, linking the experience of the poor in rural contexts with an analysis of CCT practices to understand more broadly where social cash transfers fit in.

Approach

Our study involved seven comparative case studies of rural communities across Indonesia. Researchers chose cases to illustrate forms of vulnerability associated with critical contexts and production systems. The project compared the "livelihood trajectories" of village households in seven distinctive agro-ecological locations: wet rice (Aceh and Java); smaller-scale fisheries (Bali and Southeast Sulawesi); upland vegetable farming (Central Java); dryland agriculture (Sumba); and oil palm (North Sumatra) (see Table 1.1 and Figure 1.1).[3]

Table 1.1 Research locations and major agro-ecological production systems

Province	District	Sub-District	Land Use	Authors
Aceh	Aceh Besar	*Simpang Tiga*	Wet rice	McCarthy, Shaummil Hadi, Nulwita Maliati
	Aceh Utara	*Sawang*	Wet rice and dryland	Idem
Sumatera Utara	Asahan	*B.P. Mandoge*	Oil Palm plantations	Sitorus & McCarthy
	Langkat	*Wampu*	Smallholder oil palm	Idem
Yogyakarta	Bantul	*Imogiri 1*	Mixed wet rice, dryland & migrant labour	Kutanegara & Nooteboom
		Imogiri 2	Mixed wet rice, dryland & migrant labour	Idem
Jawa Tengah	Wonosobo	*Kejajar*	Upland vegetable farming (high altitude)	Woodward
	Sleman	*Pakem*	Upland mixed agriculture	Idem
Bali	Jembrana	*Jembrana*	Fisheries (coastal)	Warren
Sulawesi Tenggara	Konawe	*Soropia 1*	Fisheries (coastal)	McWilliam, Wianti & Taufik
		Soropia 2	Fisheries (island)	Idem
Nusa Tenggara Timur	Sumba Timur	*Nggaha Oriangu*	Dry land	Vel & Makambombu
		Umalulu	Dry land, coastal	Idem
		Wula Waijelu	Dry land, irrigated rice, sugar cane investment	Idem

These cases represent the disparate patterns of growth and poverty found across the archipelago. Hill and Vidyattama (2014) distinguish the consistently non-poor provinces, with per capita incomes around one-quarter above or below the national average. In the case of Bali (studied by Warren, Chapter 9), the emergence of a labour-intensive tourism industry has spread benefits widely, with Bali moving from above-average poverty to below average (Ilmma and Wai-Poi 2014), leaving Bali with the lowest regional poverty rate alongside Jakarta. We also find North Sumatra in this group, studied by Sitorus and

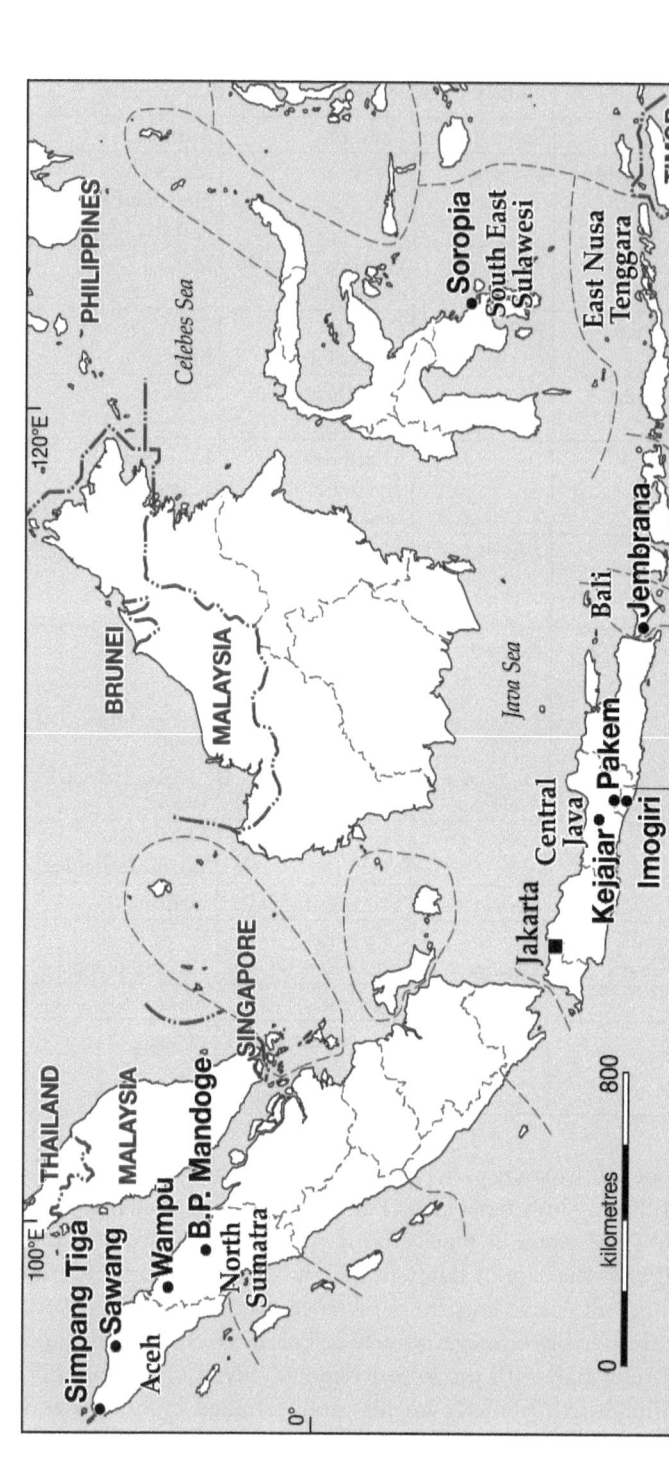

Figure 1.1 Location of research studies

© Australian National University CC BY SA 4.0
CartoGIS CAP 19-287_KP

Subdistrict
International boundary
Province boundary

McCarthy (Chapter 7). North Sumatra has a diversified and dynamic economy (Hill 2014): close to the national average relative income with plantation, estates manufacture and services industries, and proximity to Malaysia and Singapore working in its favour. Hill and Vidyattama (2014) also distinguish the more impoverished provinces, where per capita income is only 50–70 per cent of the national average. Such areas include Central Java (studied by Kutanegara and Nooteboom in Chapter 4) and Southeast Sulawesi (studied by McWilliam, Wianti and Taufik in Chapter 10), with the latter having 50 per cent of its population classified as poor (Ilmma and Wai-Poi 2014). The poorest provinces include East Nusa Tenggara (studied by Vel and Makambombu in Chapter 6), with less than half of the national average per capita income. While East Nusa Tenggara has seven of the ten poorest districts in Indonesia, Aceh (studied by McCarthy, Nuliani and Hadi in Chapter 5) has also fallen into the poor province category following conflict and the impact of the 2006 tsunami. On average, poverty rates in Aceh and Eastern Indonesia are more than double the national average (Ilmma and Wai-Poi 2014; Chapter 8).

Our research applies mixed methods. Each case analyses what is driving vulnerability and insecurity and considers the distinct livelihood trajectories. To this end, each case study combines the same diagnostic methodologies, namely:

1. A qualitative assessment is made of livelihood dynamics in the villages using an ethnographic approach.
2. A wealth ranking exercise and the stages of progress (SoP) approach are applied. This is a simple participatory tool that engages key village actors in exploring poverty dynamics and articulating local concepts of poverty (Krishna 2006). Village focus groups rank households against this emic concept of poverty and chart their movement vis-à-vis this definition.
3. We carried out a nutritional security analysis (using the FANTA Household Food Insecurity Access Scale [HFIAS]) to understand experimental aspects of food poverty (Coates, Swindale and Bilinsky 2007). We also applied systematic livelihood surveys to provide descriptive statistics. Chapter 15 compares this with official state statistics (e.g. regional stunting poverty and National Socio-Economic Household Survey [SUSENAS] data).
4. Each case study also reflects on social protection programmes (SPPs) active in the area. In one case (Chapter 13), we compared state targeting and benefit allocation with community poverty rankings, considering how effectively state-based and informal mechanisms work to address rural vulnerability.

5.   The case studies form the basis for the synthesis chapters (Chapters 2 and 3), drawing out patterns and conclusions and answering the critical research questions that frame the book.

By applying the same methodology in each case, the project aimed to develop a comparative approach to understanding the distinctive causal processes generating prosperity and poverty in rural Indonesia's main agricultural production landscapes.

Conceptualising Poverty: Our Study

There are various ways to conceptualise poverty. Given the multiple overlapping and interacting factors associated with the phenomena, no agreed theory can divide the poor from the non-poor in all contexts. We can usefully distinguish between at least three ways of approaching the problem. *Objectivist* concepts conceive poverty as a state of deficiency and scarcity, identifiable in quantitative terms relative to an objectively defined standard. In contrast, a *contextual* or *social* concept of poverty refers to the poor's inability to satisfy basic needs, their failure to meet the minimum acceptable standards of the communities living in the milieu studied. A third notion of poverty refers to a *social category*, defined as receiving public support according to a politico-administrative category (Leisering 2019). This third concept of poverty becomes visible in social assistance programmes (elaborated in Chapter 3).

All these approaches involve developing thresholds where poverty is conceptualised relative to a specific normative standard. Hence, behind the proliferation of definitions and poverty lines, as Fischer (2018: 51) notes, we are caught in the reality that "the specification of a standard is fundamentally a political exercise". There is no avoiding the implied question: "'insufficiency of what and according to whom?'" Many economic discussions are concerned with the technical problem of defining what satisfies basic needs, an important if interminable question. Both national and international poverty lines have been criticised for being arbitrary, set too low and not based on the real needs of human beings. Poverty measures have serious policy and political consequences. Given the implications for budgets and political promises to address poverty, politics often shapes how the poverty line is defined.

In this study, we first present state poverty data, applying "objectivist" statistical understandings of poverty. These are important to policymakers because they arguably provide a better basis for comparing cases than do social poverty constructs. The official poverty line is based on the SUSENAS survey, which records household expenditures. In 2018, the survey considered people to be below the poverty line if their average spending was around IDR 11,000 (USD 0.76) a day. Indonesian commentators have questioned this approach, arguing that Indonesia's official poverty line is set too low (Renaldi 2018). Even applying this low metric, almost one-fifth of farming households live below the national poverty line (FAO 2018), and as many as 25 per cent of fishing households (DPP KNTI 2020). In contrast, the World Bank has set the international poverty rate at USD 1.90 per day, a level which is also controversial (Ranjan 2017).[4] However, even these limitations fail to tell the whole story: poverty statistics typically fail to adequately enumerate elements of community livelihoods that are non-commodified, self-provisioned, extra-market exchanges; all local forms of social provision are central to rural communities.

In response to these statistical, monetary or social concepts of poverty, researchers have developed multidimensional measures of poverty or "ill-being". "Thin" measures of poverty are simple, and are directly comparable and have communicative power, whereas "thick" measures of poverty (qualitative and quantitative) tend to provide more complex understandings of the condition. For instance, the Multidimensional Poverty Index (MPI) attempts to capture severe deprivations that each person faces at the same time concerning education, health and living standards (Netivist n.d.). Critics have responded, arguing that these approaches are somewhat arbitrary and involve the relative determination of thresholds (Fischer 2018).[5]

In studying poverty dynamics, we need to recollect that poverty is a state in which people do not have enough of some key dimension of well-being (Pinstrup-Andersen 2009). These include attributes such as physical needs, the need for dignity, self-respect and social inclusion. Yet, there is no escaping the observation that "poverty is always shorthand for poverty in place x and time y", which means "having insufficient resources to meet what are typically seen as basic needs in that specific place and time" (Karelis 2007: 9). Consequently, complementing the objectivist framing of poverty, we are interested in discovering the ordinary (vernacular) understanding of poverty at a given time and place. We set out to understand how people in the places we study define poverty, by asking them directly. In other words, we wish to understand social and cultural concepts of poverty based on livelihood standards and norms conceptualised by local communities. As people also recognise non-physiological needs, including respect and social inclusion, some of our informants consider some people poor even if they obtain income above the official poverty line.

To explore the contextual or social aspects of poverty dynamics, we used Krishna's (2006) stages of progress (SoP) methodology, which involves asking key village informants to define what it means to be a poor household in local terms. In this respect, we seek to develop an emic or social understanding of poverty. This objective entailed identifying a socially constructed poverty cut-off, the point above which the community no longer considers a household poor. A group of local people then assessed the relative assets and capacities of households. Key informants ranked households into poor/non-poor categories according to village-based wealth criteria, and then labelled their status positions over time against this village-identified poverty cut-off. While wealth ranking exercises are challenging to do well, we found that they enabled us to rapidly develop a proportional randomly stratified sample, select a 40-household sample in each village and undertake a household-based livelihood survey.

Food or nutritional insecurity, like poverty, "is not a natural fact, but a social experience" (Green and Hulme 2005). Hence, we employed methods developed to capture experiential dimensions of food poverty (Maxwell 1996). Enumerators surveyed those experiencing difficulties using a food security survey instrument, the HFIAS methodology (Coates, Swindale and Bilinsky 2007). This provides a means of categorising households in terms of one of the main coping strategies, grouping them according to the extent that they reduced the varieties or quantities of food consumed (Coates, Swindale and Bilinsky 2007). Each team surveyed households who confirmed that they struggled to afford groceries, could not pay bills, or became indebted to provide necessities during periods of maximum vulnerability. This was a snapshot of the degree to which households were cutting back or taking recourse to unsustainable livelihood strategies.

In short, this study draws on fieldwork by experienced social science researchers concerned with understanding the drivers of vulnerability across Indonesia. It takes a novel approach by comparing experiences of communities in the major agricultural production systems of the country—stretching from the irrigated rice-producing plains and seasonal cropping in the uplands, to estate crop landscapes outside Java and the diverse fisheries sector—with intersecting social assistance policies. It develops a comparative analysis of what drives vulnerability and insecurity in these critical contexts and analyses each locality's distinct livelihood trajectories, while confronting this with the effectiveness of current social assistance programmes. Researchers focused on understanding the dynamic mechanisms and processes at work, the production and persistence of inequality, the occurrence of (seasonal) food insecurity, and the differential outcomes of social policies. Each case includes a view from below and aims to understand local ideas of poverty, the socio-cultural embeddedness of rural economies, local practices of mutual help and reciprocity, regional stunting figures and the targeting and effectiveness of the social assistance programmes, namely the "food for the poor" programme and conditional cash transfers.

Argument

Analysts acknowledge that economic change can come to the countryside in various ways; agrarian change can take many directions (Rigg and Vandergeest 2012). Yet the classic notion of the structural transformation of agrarian societies still frames a great deal of thinking about rural change (Timmer and Akkus 2008). Analysts have also pointed to the pathways out of poverty working through industrialisation, deagrarianisation, diversification and migration (Rigg 2006; World Bank 2007). Accordingly, in more prosperous developing countries, we expect to see an increase in income and improving living standards accompanying the development of farming enterprises and non-agricultural sectors in rural areas and urbanisation, as workers migrate to cities (Imai, Gaiha and Garbero 2014). On the other hand, some scholars have disputed this causal nexus, describing a "truncated agrarian transition" scenario where agriculture and labour fail to provide sufficient opportunities (Friedmann 2006; Li 2011). Here, rural change leads to land concentration, increasing inequality, dispossession and/or the formation of a rural underclass and other marginalising outcomes.

This volume develops the concept of *agrarian change scenarios* as a heuristic tool to describe and analyse socio-economic rural transitions (see Chapter 2) and presents a number of important findings. First, in contrast to broader narratives that focus on the global or national scale, we develop a scenario analysis to consider the particularities of socio-environmental change in specific production contexts. We apply this framework to compare the scenarios with the broad optimistic and pessimistic agrarian transition narratives mentioned above. A careful analysis of the patterns that our cases reveal places the structural transformation and truncated transition narratives within a more comprehensive range of patterns. Hence, by developing scenarios of agrarian change, we provide an understanding of critical processes working at finer scales that are overlooked by the global narratives. We find that this enriches our awareness of the ways in which structural mechanisms are inscribed on local contexts, opening up a more multidimensional vision of processes of agrarian change.

Second, by comparing our agrarian change scenarios with each other, we find an apparent paradox: in virtually all of the cases examined, global market integration has worked to provide many households with the means to move out of poverty. At the same time, it has created the conditions for increasing inequality, nutritional insecurity and ecological decline. This paradox enables us to understand why improvement occurs in terms of the statistical markers of poverty, even while many households remain nutritionally insecure.

Patterns of food poverty persist across Indonesia, despite a fall in poverty rates. While high-value farming, diversification and migration may offer a means of economic progress, for poor households there is limited accumulation. This is due to the way class, gender and power work in remote local contexts, and the fact that much surplus income is used for enhanced consumption and changing lifestyles. Hence, contrary to historical expectations of development, in most of our sites we find few signs of the classical structural transformation of the countryside considered to provide the pathway out of rural poverty. We do see much evidence of extensive food poverty and ongoing precarity. However, we do not see an out-and-out agrarian crisis.

Contrary to narratives of agrarian transformation, we find high-value farming, diversification and migration linked both to stagnation and indebtedness, and to survival and progress (cf. McCarthy 2020). As market integration often fails to lead households out of food poverty, the assumed links between poverty (measured by poverty surveys in terms of household consumption), income and welfare outcomes need to be re-examined. As poverty statistics and analyses that use proxy indicators hide critical trends, we argue that the analysis of scenarios can assist by revealing the underlying processes leading to livelihood trajectories, thus opening the possibility for addressing particular types of vulnerability.

Considering this puzzle, we argue for developing a more nuanced framework for understanding how scenarios of agrarian change are realised in specific contexts and for how broader process of change work. We can unpack the structural, contextual triggers and proximate elements leading to changing agrarian livelihoods by parsing how land ownership, agricultural production systems, social relations, labour opportunities, consumption patterns and access to food are negotiated in specific cases.

Third, while we find established health and nutrition-based framing of food security valuable, we argue that patterns of nutritional insecurity and stunting also need to be understood in relation to patterns of agrarian change. These patterns encompass the extension of the cash economy and the commodification of extensive areas of local life, the emergence of new social needs and cultural food preferences, in the context of ecological fragilities and climate change that make livelihoods ever more insecure. A key consideration here is how the social assistance programmes intersect with the scenarios of agrarian change and provide security in the face of the negative consequences of development.

This volume also studies the local and national impact of state social assistance (principally conditional cash transfers) in Indonesia as a travelling global discourse and its accompanying technologies (targeting, proxy means testing, algorithms). We note that the social assistance system could mark an essential step towards institutionalising social assistance and providing a social protection floor upon which most marginal people could depend. Moreover, the rolling out of social assistance programmes suggests that Indonesian society is now following an international trend towards *nationalisation, internationalisation* and *individualisation.* The experience of poverty has moved from being a local concern of families and communities to a responsibility of the state and international donors, contributing towards the formation of new forms of entitlements for the poor (Leisering 2019). Yet, the model relies on methods that see poverty as rooted in individuals and households' characteristics and circumstances (Devereux and McGregor 2014: 297). Depending upon methodological individualism, these technically sophisticated models tend to overlook local socio-cultural norms and sociality, not to mention broader politico-economic structural factors.

Indonesia's current approach to social protection is politically opportune. While programme evaluations are positive, the embrace of a liberal-residual concept of social assistance has raised all the questions and problems discussed elsewhere (Leisering 2019). With budgetary constraints in mind, the current approach proceeds on the principle that programmes prioritise those in the most need. The most effective way to do this is through econometric targeting amended by community input. We find little evidence that these interventions help the rural poor move into more productive livelihoods. As our surveys reveal, large numbers of households perceived as poor by local criteria are missing out on support. Our volume argues that the current methodology generates high inclusion and exclusion errors even while the breadth and depth of social assistance support remain insufficient for helping all those in needs of support. Hence, people of equivalent welfare status have different experiences with social assistance. As in many other models across the global south, this is an incomplete and categorically fragmented cash transfer regime (Leisering 2019). As Chapters 3, 12 and 13 of this volume show, it also generates a complex and messy politics of distribution in rural Indonesia. Our analysis suggests that social assistance will soften the experience of poverty. As some poor households gain the extra capacity to consume goods and services, this positively brings many people over the (very low) statistical poverty line. However, as other research has long observed, a broader approach is required that moves beyond smoothing consumption (managing fluctuating livelihoods to improve stability and predictability) among the poor, to promoting livelihood opportunities for accumulating assets and transforming the socio-economic factors that keep them poor (Barrientos, Hulme and Shepperd 2005; Devereux and Sabates-Wheeler 2004).

Our research shows substantial levels of mistargeting, high exclusion and inclusion errors, all of which relate directly to the technologies applied in Indonesia's social programmes (see Chapters 3, 11, 12 and 13). We also find that the poverty targeting system involves gross simplifications, and operates as a form of anti-politics, by rendering the poverty question into a technical problem (Li 2007; Ferguson 2015), while obscuring—among other things—the structural questions underpinning inequality in Indonesia. We see this at work through technologies such as the proxy means test, (e)banking for the poor and the household life skills workshop, which obscure poverty's structural (and political) dimensions. The criticisms raise the question of whether the predominant poverty technologies, along with the limited funding and resources provided for social assistance, are sufficient for dealing with the nature and structural dimensions of poverty: how well do they match rural Indonesia's relational socialities and economic dynamics?

This leads us to conclude that despite the contributions that current social assistance programmes make to reducing poverty headcounts and rural poverty, food insecurity and precarity are likely to persist (especially after the setback caused by the emergence of COVID-19) unless other redistributive policy settings and strategies are developed which shift the structural drivers of inequality and invest in the productive capacity of people to empower their futures.

Finally, we discuss possibilities for moving to a better system to provide vulnerable households with a "rightful share" of the benefits being distributed (Ferguson 2015). We support experimenting with other approaches that build on the views and logics of local social life (Chapter 15). As much research has demonstrated (e.g. Benda-Beckmann and Benda-Beckmann 1994: 2007), Indonesian societies have their own notions of social security, for the most part, embedded in social relationships, customary obligations and religion (e.g. *zakat*). Here, receiving assistance from welfare-related practices depends upon investing in social relations. The very poor are usually also impoverished in terms of their social relationships (or "social capital"), so they tend to receive less from their community. A liberal-residual approach to social cash transfers seeks to reach only the poorest of the poor; it provides social cash transfers to some while excluding others who may feel equally entitled. Such an approach transgresses local expectations of sharing that are tied into moral expectations of identity and membership in a local community. While the poorest can very much benefit from social cash transfers, for the very poor, exclusion and mistargeting are especially painful.

Outline of the Volume

Chapter 2 analyses and sums up our findings regarding the agrarian and rural development questions. The chapter develops scenario analysis as a heuristic to compare the socio-environmental change processes working in specific production contexts and to identify broader patterns. This approach provides new insights into processes that operate at finer scales and that do not map fully onto orthodox development thinking. Chapter 3 discusses the scope, significance and consequences of the social protection "revolution" for the rural poor.

The main section of the book presents a series of case studies. Each case considers the drivers of poverty and food insecurity, the (enabling) agrarian structures, the forms of rural poverty viewed through a food and consumption lens, and the impacts of social cash transfers. The chapters are grounded in an analysis of the critical production systems (rice land, upland, lowland and fisheries), with contrasting cases from outer and core areas of Indonesia. The book's final section presents a series of critical analyses of the emergence and development of current social assistance policies and programmes. Together, the chapters and sections aim to open up a more multidimensional vision of processes of rural change, and contribute new ways of thinking about (and addressing) the processes generating vulnerability. The volume argues for approaches that fit with the social expectations, institutions, cultures and logics of rural social life, generate sustained economic opportunities, and address the entrenched structural nature of social vulnerability and nutritional insecurity in rural Indonesia.

Notes

[1] The World Bank poverty line is 1.90 USD a day. Indonesia uses a low per capital income definition of just over IDR 400,000 per month (about IDR 11,000 or USD 0.76 per day) which is based on an aggregated food poverty line (2100 kcal / capita / day + non-essential food). Taking the World Bank definition of USD 1.90 per day would sharply increase the number of poor in Indonesia (Lingga 2018).

[2] In 2018, 13.2 per cent of rural people were considered as poor, compared to 7.02 per cent in urban areas. In rural areas in some regions, such as in Maluku, poverty rates are as high as 29.15 per cent (Lingga 2018).

[3] Bagchi et al. (1998), De Haan and Zoomers (2005) and Sallu, Twyman and Stringer (2010) use the term "livelihood trajectory" to describe and explain the direction and pattern of livelihoods, taking into account the effects of shocks, stresses and livelihood strategies that contribute to resilience and vulnerability.

[4] The World Bank (2019) has also estimated that 68 per cent of the Indonesian population is vulnerable to an economic shock.

[5] As Fischer (2018: 140) noted, poverty indexes involve the choice of variables and are developed at some distance from tangible social meaning. As they may aggregate identified dimensions or indicators, this can also obscure underlying dynamics. They also tend to reflect the priorities of those who develop them.

References

Akram-Lodhi, A.H. and C. Kay. 2010. "Surveying the Agrarian Question (Part 2): Current Debates and Beyond", *Journal of Peasant Studies* 37: 255–84.

Bagchi, D.K. et al. 1998. "Conceptual and Methodological Challenges in the Study of Livelihood Trajectories: Case-studies in Eastern India and Western Nepal", *The Journal of International Development* 10, 4: 453–68.

Barrett, C.B. et al. 2017. "On the Structural Transformation of Rural Africa", *Journal of African Economies* 26 (Supplement 1): i11–i35.

Barrientos, A., D. Hulme and A. Shepperd. 2005. "Can Social Protection Tackle Chronic Poverty?", *The European Journal of Development Research* 17, 1: 8–23.

Beal, T. et al. 2018. "A Review of Child Stunting Determinants in Indonesia", *Maternal & Child Nutrition* 14, 4: 1–10.

Benda-Beckmann, F. von and K. von Benda-Beckmann. 1994. "Coping with Insecurity", in *Coping with Insecurity. An "Underall" Perspective on Social Security in the Third World*, ed. F. von Benda-Beckmann, K. von Benda-Beckmann and Hans Marks. Pustaka Pelajar and Focal Foundation.

_____. 2007. *Social Security between Past and Future: Ambonese Networks of Care and Support*. Berlin: Hopf.

Bernstein, H. 2010. *Rural Livelihoods and Agrarian Change: Bringing Class Back In*. Hartford, CT.: Kumarian Press.

Borras, S.M. 2009. "Agrarian Change and Peasant Studies: Changes, Continuities and Challenges–An Introduction", *Journal of Peasant Studies* 36, 1: 5–31.

Coates, J., A. Swindale and P. Bilinsky. 2007. *Household Food Insecurity Access Scale (HFIAS) for Measurement of Food Access: Indicator Guide Version 3*. Washington, DC: Food and Nutrition Technical Assistance Project (FANTA). Available at https://www.fantaproject.org/monitoring-and-evaluation/household-food-insecurity-access-scale-hfias (accessed 26 Feb. 2022).

Conway, T., Arjaan de Haan and Andy Norton, eds. 2000. *Social Protection: New Directions of Donor Agencies*. London: Department for International Development.

Cook, S. and N. Kabeer. 2010. *Social Protection as Development Policy: Asian Perspectives*. London: Routledge.

CPR (Chronic Poverty Report). 2009. *Escaping Poverty Traps*. Available at https://www.odi.org/sites/odi.org.uk/files/odi-assets/publications-opinion-files/2566.pdf (accessed 20 Aug 2020).

De Haan, L.J. and A. Zoomers. 2005. "Exploring the Frontier of Livelihood Research", *Development and Change* 36, 1: 27–47.

Devereux, S. and J.A. McGregor. 2014. "Transforming Social Protection: Human Wellbeing and Social Justice", *The European Journal of Development Research* 26: 296–310.

Devereux, S. and R. Sabates-Wheeler. 2004. "Transformative Social Protection". IDS Working Paper. Institute of Development Studies, October. Available at https://www.ids.ac.uk/download.php?file=files/dmfile/Wp232.pdf (accessed 20 Aug. 2020).

Dhanani, S. and I. Islam. 2002. "Poverty, Vulnerability and Social Protection in a Period of Crisis: The Case of Indonesia", *World Development* 30, 7: 1211–31.

DPP KNTI (Indonesian Traditional Fisherfolk Union). 2020. *Covid-19 Outbreak: Socio-economic Impact on Small-scale Fisher and Aquaculture in Indonesia*. Available at https://focusweb.org/covid-19-outbreak-socio-economic-impact-on-small-scale-fisher-and-aquaculture-in-indonesia/ (accessed 12 June 2020).

EKONID Insight. 2020. "Covid-19 developments in Indonesia". Available at https://indonesien.ahk.de/en/infocenter/news/news-details/covid-19-developments-in-indonesia (accessed 5 Sept. 2020).

Ellis, F., S. Devereux and P. White. 2009. *Social Protection in Africa*. Northampton: Edward Elgar.

Fairbairn, M. et al. 2014. "Introduction: New Directions in Agrarian Political Economy", *The Journal of Peasant Studies* 41, 5: 653–66.

FAO (Food and Agriculture Organization of the United Nations). 2018. *Small Family Farms Country Factsheet*. Available at www.fao.org/3/i8881en/I8881EN.pdf (accessed 5 Sept. 2020).

FAO, IFAD (International Fund for Agricultural Development) and WFP (World Food Programme). 2015. *The State of Food Insecurity in the World*. Available at http://www.fao.org/3/a-i4646e.pdf (accessed 20 Aug. 2020).

Ferguson, J. 2015. *Give a Man a Fish: Reflections on the New Politics of Distribution*. Durham, NC: Duke University Press.

Fischer, A. 2018. *Poverty as Ideology: Rescuing Social Justice from Global Development Agendas*. London: Zed Books.

Friedmann, H. 2006. "Focusing on Agriculture: A Comment on Henry Bernstein's 'Is There an Agrarian Question in the 21st Century?'", *Canadian Journal of Development Studies* 4: 461–5.

Green, M. and D. Hulme. 2005. "From Correlates and Characteristics to Causes: Thinking About Poverty from a Chronic Poverty Perspective", *World Development* 33, 6: 867–79.

Hardjono, J., N. Akhmadi and S. Sumarto. 2010. *Poverty and Social Protection in Indonesia*. Singapore: Institute of Southeast Asian Studies.

Hart G., A. Turton and B. White. 1989. *Agrarian Transformations: Local Processes and the State in Southeast Asia*. Berkeley: University of California Press.

Hart, T. 2009. "Exploring Definitions of Food Insecurity and Vulnerability: Time to Refocus Assessments", *Agrekon* 48, 4: 362–83.

Hill, H., ed. 2014. *Regional Dynamics in a Decentralised Indonesia*. Singapore: Institute of Southeast Asian Studies.

Hill, H. and Y. Vidyattama. 2014. "Hares and Tortoises: Regional Development Dynamics in Indonesia", in *Regional Dynamics in a Decentralised Indonesia*, ed. H. Hill. Singapore: Institute of Southeast Asian Studies, pp. 68–97.

Hirsch, P. 2012. "Reviving Agrarian Studies in South-East Asia: Geography on the Ascendancy", *Geographical Research* 50, 4: 393–403.

Holzmann, R. and S. Sipos. 2009. "Social Protection and Labor at the World Bank: An Overview", in *Social Protection and Labor at the World Bank: 2000–2008*, ed. R. Holzmann. Washington, DC: World Bank, pp. 1–10.

Howell, F. 2001. "Social Assistance-Theoretical Background", in *Social Protection in the Asia and Pacific*, ed. I. Ortiz. Manila: Asian Development Bank.

Ilmma, A. and M. Wai-Poi. 2014. "Patterns of Regional Poverty in the New Indonesia", in *Regional Dynamics in a Decentralised Indonesia*, ed. Hal Hill. Singapore: Institute of Southeast Asian Studies, pp. 98–133.

Imai, K.S., R. Gaiha and A. Garbero. 2014. "Poverty Reduction during the Rural-Urban Transformation: Rural Development is Still More Important than Urbanisation?" BWI Working Paper. Brooks World Poverty Institute, 20 June.

Karelis, C. 2007. *The Persistence of Poverty: Why the Economics of the Well-off Can't Help the Poor*. New Haven and London: Yale University Press.

Kelly, P. 2011. "Migration, Agrarian Transition, and Rural Change in Southeast Asia", *Critical Asian Studies* 43, 4: 479–506.

Kementerian Kesehatan (Indonesian Ministry of Health). 2020. *Profil kesehatan Indonesia tahun 2019* [Health Profile for Indonesia, 2019]. Available at https://pusdatin.kemkes.go.id/resources/download/pusdatin/profil-kesehatan-indonesia/Profil-Kesehatan-indonesia-2019.pdf (accessed 12 June 2020).

Koning, J. and F. Hüsken, eds. 2006. *Ropewalking and Safety Nets: Local Ways of Managing Insecurities in Indonesia*. Leiden: Brill.

Krishna, A. 2004. "Escaping Poverty and Becoming Poor: Who Gains, Who Loses, and Why", *World Development* 31, 1: 121–36.

_____. 2006. "Pathways Out of and Into Poverty in 36 Villages of Andhra Pradesh, India", *World Development* 34, 2: 271–88.

Leisering, L. 2009. "Extending Social Security to the Excluded: Are Social Cash Transfers to the Poor an Appropriate Way of Fighting Poverty in Developing Countries?", *Global Social Policy* 2: 246–72.

_____. 2019. *The Global Rise of Social Cash Transfers: How States and International Organizations Constructed a New Instrument for Combating Poverty.* Oxford: Oxford University Press.

Li, T.M. 2007. *The Will to Improve: Governmentality, Development, and the Practice of Politics.* Durham, NC: Duke University Press

_____. 2011. "Centering Labor in the Land Grab Debate", *The Journal of Peasant Studies* 38: 281–98.

_____. 2014. *Land's End: Capitalist Relations on an Indigenous Frontier.* Durham, NC: Duke University Press.

Lingga, V. 2018. "Commentary: Reducing Inequality, Cracking Wealth Concentration in Indonesia", *Jakarta Post,* 2 Apr. 2018.

Manning, C. and S. Sumarto, eds. 2011. *Employment, Living Standards and Poverty in Contemporary Indonesia.* Singapore: Institute of Southeast Asian Studies.

Maxwell, S. 1996. "Food Security: A Post-modern Perspective", *Food Policy* 2, 1: 155–70.

McCarthy, J.F. 2010. "Processes of Inclusion and Adverse Incorporation: Oil Palm and Agrarian Change in Sumatra, Indonesia", *The Journal of Peasant Studies* 37, 4: 821–50.

_____. 2020. "The Paradox of Progressing Sideways: Food Poverty and Livelihood Change in the Rice Lands of Outer Island Indonesia", *The Journal of Peasant Studies* 47, 5: 1077–97.

Ministry of Finance, Indonesia. 2018. *2019 State Budget Indonesia: Realistic & Rising Focus on Social Spending.* Available at https://www.indonesia-investments.com/ news/todays-headlines/2019-state-budget-indonesia-realistic-rising-focus-on-social-spending/item8945 (accessed 20 Aug. 2020).

Neilson, J. 2016. "Agrarian Transformations and Land Reform in Indonesia", in *Land and Development in Indonesia: Searching for the People's Sovereignty,* ed. J.F. McCarthy and K. Robinson. Singapore: Institute of Southeast Asian Studies, pp. 245–64.

Netivist. n.d. *Measuring Poverty in the 21st century: Are "Thick" Measures Better than "Thin?".* Available at https://netivist.org/debate/measuring-poverty (accessed 23 Aug. 2020).

Nooteboom, G. 2015. *Forgotten People: Poverty, Risk and Social Security in Indonesia: The Case of the Madurese.* Leiden: Brill.

Peluso, N.L. and A.B. Purwanto. 2018. "The Remittance Forest: Turning Mobile Labor into Agrarian Capital", *Singapore Journal of Tropical Geography* 39, 1: 6–36.

Pinstrup-Andersen, P. 2009. "Food Security: Definition and Measurement", *Food Security* 1: 5–7.

Potter, L. 2011. "Agrarian Transitions in Kalimantan: Characteristics, Limitations and Accommodations", in *Borneo Transformed: Agricultural Expansion on the Southeast Asian Frontier*, ed. R. De Koninck, S. Bernard and J.F. Bisonnett. Singapore: NUS Press.

Ranjan, R. 2017. *Has the World Bank Got a Problem with its Poverty Figures?* Available at https://www2.monash.edu/impact/articles/economy/has-the-world-bank-got-a-problem-with-its-poverty-figures/ (accessed 20 Aug. 2020).

Renaldi, A. 2018. "Poverty isn't Decreasing, Indonesia's Official Poverty Line is Just Too Low". Available at https://www.vice.com/en/article/ev8z7w/poverty-isnt-decreasing-indonesias-official-poverty-line-is-just-too-low (accessed 20 Aug. 2020).

Rigg, J. 2006. "Land, Farming, Livelihoods and Poverty: Rethinking the Links in the Rural South", *World Development* 34, 1: 180–202.

Rigg, J. and P. Vandergeest. 2012. *Revisiting Rural Places: Pathways to Poverty and Prosperity in Southeast Asia*. Singapore: NUS Press.

Rosenberg, T. 2011. "To Beat Back Poverty, Pay the Poor", *The New York Times*, 3 Jan. 2011. Available at https://opinionator.blogs.nytimes.com/2011/01/03/to-beat-back-poverty-pay-the-poor/ (accessed 20 Aug. 2020).

Sallu, S.M., C. Twyman and L.C. Stringer. 2010. "Resilient or Vulnerable Livelihoods? Assessing Livelihood Dynamics and Trajectories in Rural Botswana", *Ecology and Society: a Journal of Integrative Science for Resilience and Sustainability*, 15, 4. Available at http://www.ecologyandsociety.org/vol15/iss4/art3/. ISSN 1708-3087 (accessed 12 June 2022).

Setkab (Cabinet Secretary of the Republic of Indonesia). 2019. *BPS: Poverty Rate in Indonesia Decreases*. Available at https://setkab.go.id/en/bps-poverty-rate-in-indonesia-decreases/ (accessed 20 Aug. 2020).

Timmer, C.P. 2004. "Food Security in Indonesia: Current Challenges and the Long-Run Outlook". Center for Global Development Working Paper. Center for Global Development, November 2004. Available at https://www.files.ethz.ch/isn/35741/2004_11_12.pdf.

Timmer, C.P. and S. Akkus. 2008. "The Structural Transformation as a Pathway out of Poverty: Analytics, Empirics and Politics". Center for Global Development Working Paper. Center for Global Development, July. Available at https://www.files.ethz.ch/isn/91306/wp150.pdf (accessed 12 June 2022).

White, B. and G. Wiradi. 1989. "Agrarian and Non-agrarian Bases of Inequality in Nine Javanese Villages", in *Agrarian Transformations: Local Processes and the State in Southeast Asia,* ed. G. Hart, A. Turton and B. White. Berkeley: University of California Press, pp. 266–302.

World Bank. 2007. *World Development Report 2008: Agriculture for Development.* Washington, DC: World Bank. Available at https://openknowledge.worldbank. org/bitstream/handle/10986/5990/WDR%202008%20-%20English. pdf?sequence=3&isAllowed=y (accessed 12 June 2022).

_____. 2015a. *Indonesia and World Bank Group to Join Forces to Reduce Child Stunting and Maternal Mortality.* Available at https://www.worldbank.org/en/news/press-release/2015/05/21/indonesia-and-world-bank-group-to-join-forces-to-reduce-child-stunting-and-maternal-mortality (accessed 20 Aug. 2020).

_____. 2015b. *Indonesia's Rising Divide.* November. Available at http://documents1. worldbank.org/curated/en/885651468180231995/pdf/101668-WP-PUBLIC-Box394818B-Executive-Summary-Indonesias-Rising-Divide-English.pdf (accessed 20 August 2020).

Yemtsov, R. et al. 2018. *Measuring the Effectiveness of Social Protection: Concepts and Applications.* Washington, DC: World Bank. Available at https://openknowledge. worldbank.org/handle/10986/29802 (accessed 12 June 2022).

CHAPTER 2

Agrarian Scenarios and Nutritional Security in Indonesia

John F. McCarthy, Gerben Nooteboom and Andrew McWilliam

Over the last few decades, prior to the COVID-19 pandemic, poverty rates in Indonesia had been declining. Within just one generation, tens of millions of people—both urban and rural poor—have improved their incomes, living conditions, infrastructure, education facilities and health care. This shift reflects the official poverty line statistics and local conceptualisations of poverty provided by our community wealth ranking exercises (discussed below). According to local criteria, at least 30 per cent of the inhabitants in half of our village studies transitioned out of more extreme forms of poverty. Yet, shifting standards of material welfare occur, alongside the persistence of poverty and nutritional insecurity in rural areas. The prevalence of high levels of stunting and ongoing deprivation (in local terms) indicates poverty's complexity and multi-dimensional nature, and invites a deeper investigation of the underlying processes.

The literature suggests that, before COVID-19, Indonesia was unexceptional. Several other middle-income countries shared this predicament of declining statistical poverty accompanied by persistent nutritional insecurity (Pritchard, Vicol and Jones 2017; FAO 2019). To understand this apparent contradiction, we explored why people are (or are not) poor, by asking a set of closely related questions concerning the structures and processes that lead to vulnerability and nutritional insecurity in Indonesia's main agricultural production systems. Why do rural poverty and stunting persist, even while statistical rates of extreme poverty are falling? What are the typical scenarios and trajectories of change that shape poverty, vulnerability and nutritional (in-)security? How is the nature of poverty shifting, and what are the implications of this analysis of food poverty—the inability to access nutritious meals throughout the year—for our understanding of agrarian change?

This chapter advances four sets of arguments. First, building on previous studies of rural change, and keeping in view the well-rehearsed problems of teleological approaches to the agrarian transition (Rigg et al. 2016; Du Toit and Neves 2014; Levien, Watts and Yan 2018), we advanced a different approach, which we call "agrarian change scenario analysis" to understand the coproduction processes shaping agrarian-ecological change. This heuristic provides us with a framework to analyse how proximate factors and contextual triggers work together with structural forces, particularly those related to the "routine functioning of the core institutions of the global market economy"(Du Toit and Neves 2014: 836), to constrain or enhance rural people's livelihoods. While the interaction between these contextual and structural mechanisms varies across space and time, generating specific scenarios of agrarian change, it is possible to identify particular patterns.

Second, based on case studies undertaken across Indonesia, we developed a set of agrarian change scenarios that point to a critical paradox: in virtually all the cases, global market integration provides households with the means of moving out of poverty. At the same time, however, market integration on adverse terms leads to nutritional insecurity, increasing economic inequality and deepening ecological degradation. While progress and development do take place, this usually favours only some, and is often precarious because the structural and productive changes often do not improve lives in ways that are sustainable over time. Even in successful scenarios of declining poverty, progress is thin, and, as demonstrated by the COVID-19 pandemic (see Chapter 17), in many cases, integration into markets is both insecure and conducted on adverse terms. Hence, alongside movements out of poverty, we also found the ongoing reproduction of poverty on a large scale, primarily where livelihoods depend more on agriculture and fisheries. In all but one of our scenarios, we found extensive evidence of nutritional insecurity and food poverty, and poor households facing continuing patterns of seasonal insecurity and scarcity.

In counterpoint to the predominant health and nutrition-based framing of food security, our third argument is that patterns of nutritional insecurity and stunting need to be understood in terms of agrarian change, the extension of the cash economy, increasing landlessness and the emergence of new social needs and cultural food practices. Exacerbated by ecological fragilities and climate changes, these patterns influence rural production choices and play a foundational role in the multidimensional forms of insecurity found across our scenarios.

Finally, concerning agrarian change, we found that even where high-value farming, diversification and migration seem to offer households the means to an upward economic trajectory, many poor households cannot save and end up treading water in livelihood terms. For these households, there is no positive effect of an agrarian transition. Contrary to notions of either an agrarian transition or a truncated transition (see Chapter 1), we found that farming, migration and diversification are simultaneously linked to stagnation and indebtedness, as well as to survival and progress (McCarthy 2020). Hence, the links between poverty levels (as measured by poverty surveys of household consumption), degrees of integration into the cash economy and nutritional outcomes are not clear cut. Where households become net-food purchasers and lose the ability to provide food for themselves, integration into the cash economy and higher cash incomes do not guarantee less nutritional insecurity. We conclude that poverty statistics mask critical trends and that the two predominant agrarian transition narratives only partially account for our observed changes.

These research findings emerge from 14 village case studies chosen to represent Indonesia's critical rural production systems (irrigated rice, oil palm plantations, fisheries and seasonal upland agriculture), all undertaken before the COVID-19 pandemic. To begin our analysis, we examine how poverty is conceptualised in the study and discuss our theoretical framework. We then set out, in summary, our empirical findings, before analysing their significance and meaning. As we show, the agrarian lens provides fresh understandings of the predominant experiences of livelihood progress, vulnerability and poverty, while offering new insights into nutritional insecurity and inequality. By understanding this set of transformative changes, we can explain forms of paradoxical progress: emergent prosperity in poverty statistics alongside enduring forms of insecurity.

Conceptual Considerations

Poverty and vulnerability are embedded in the structures and processes of change across rural landscapes. There is now substantial literature on rural change. Neo-classical and agrarian political economists dominate this literature, each providing a template for understanding the dynamics of change. But to what extent do these theories help us to understand contemporary vulnerability and nutritional insecurity?

Classical economists argue that the economic development of the countryside requires a structural transformation, where the relative role of agriculture in employment declines as the economy expands and absorbs labour elsewhere. By delinking livelihoods from old forms of farming, the future for rural populations, it has been argued, lies in off-farm livelihood diversification, labour migration and the adoption of high-value agricultural production (Naylor 2014; Rigg 2006; World Bank 2007). This optimistic view suggests that an agrarian transition is still available for dynamic market-orientated smallholders who integrate into high-value chains, diversify into wage labour or migrate into the nodes of industrial development.

Some agrarian political economists have argued that through accumulation, differentiation and dispossession, capitalist expansion results in rural people becoming more disconnected from their land-based livelihoods (Hebinck 2018), leading to inevitable depeasantisation (Bryceson 2000). However, many contemporary political economists are sceptical, arguing that debilitating social and economic change processes and adverse social relations entrap poor people living in the global south. From this perspective, "the poverty of certain categories of people is not just unimproved by growth or integration into (global) markets but deepened by it" (Mosse 2010: 1161). For those seeking to escape poor agricultural situations through wage labour and migration, opportunities are often scarce. The risk is that many seeking to move off the farm may find themselves stuck between agrarian livelihoods and employment in petty trade and services that do not support their needs (Akram-Lodhi and Kay 2010; Breman and Wiradi 2002). These populations become isolated from the industrial production system where their labour is of limited relevance to capital (Li 2011). As market integration has re-worked the nature of vulnerability, so many rural-based households keep a foot on the land due to "the precarity of much non-farm work, the absence of a well-woven social safety net, and a certain emotional attachment to natal homes" (Rigg, Salamanca and Thompson 2016: 131).

To what extent do these narratives help us to understand the changes transforming rural landscapes in Indonesia? As we will see, they are helpful up to a point, but even a cursory reading of our cases suggests that processes, mechanisms and outcomes are much more varied than these narratives suggest. In other words, we see a multi-modal and variable process (Van der Ploeg 2018) where there is no one agrarian transition but rather a "mosaic of directionalities" (De Koninck, Rigg and Vandergeest 2012). These general transition narratives thus only partially map onto contemporary livelihood landscapes in our scenarios. To complement this literature, we need to explore the cultural basis of production and consumption practices, food preferences and livelihood choices. We also need to account for networks of reciprocity, local moral economies and mutual help that, while not always working well, and sometimes reinforcing inequalities, provide continuing access to resources and opportunities. In some scenarios, people fall back onto common-pool resources (forests, coastal fisheries and rivers) that offer partial support as families engage in livelihood *bricolage*, a complex and flexible crafting together of various livelihood possibilities.

Our Approach

The mechanisms and processes which on the one hand generate opportunities for leaving poverty behind, and those on the other hand which produce vulnerability, vary across production systems and regional economies. While we need to move beyond studying rural changes in specific spaces, and identify a broader set of processes and structures that shape or block opportunities, we also need to avoid simplifying narratives. Building on the work of Sen (1981), Watts and Bohle (1993), Ribot and Peluso (2003), Scoones (2015), Devereux (2001), Li (2014), Ribot (2014) and others, we understand change in terms of a heuristic represented graphically in Figure 2.1. This figure shows how agrarian scenario analysis proceeds as an iterative process for unpacking the dynamically interrelated processes that jointly produce agrarian change.

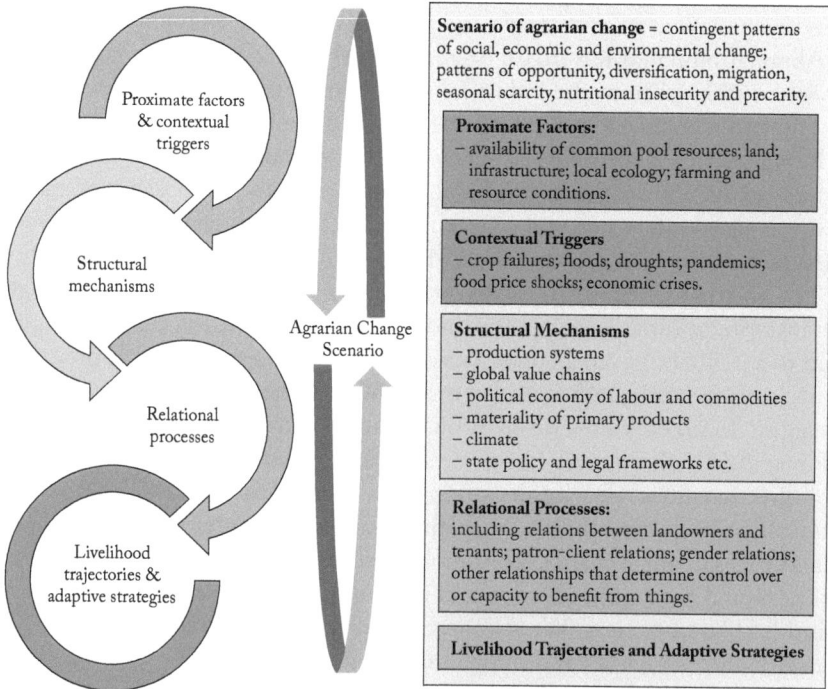

Figure 2.1   Heuristic for understanding agrarian change scenarios

This approach starts by analysing the *proximate factors* that are temporally and spatially close to the livelihood outcomes and agrarian change patterns and that appear to facilitate them directly. Proximate factors arise at the micro-level and are "actor-based and process orientated" (Schneider and Wagemann 2006). Examples include the history of local agricultural uses and resource exploitation practices, farm characteristics, local household and social-cultural characteristics, the availability of land, labour opportunities, common-pool resources, local ecological features and the local infrastructure (e.g. roads) prevalent in the immediate context. This extends to contextual triggers, for instance a contingent event such as a flood or drought that leads to entitlement failures and livelihood shocks (Devereux 2001). For example, the COVID-19 pandemic works as a contextual trigger, a contingent event that interacts with structural mechanisms and leads to differential responses and outcomes in various scenarios of change (see Epilogue) depending on structural, proximate and relational dynamics.

Behind the proximate factors stand underlying structural mechanisms that operate diffusely and shape the context. These include the long-term factors that are not readily influenced, either because of the time scale needed or because they are determined from outside the context. Examples include economic and social structures, climate change and technological progress, trade and investment patterns, the underlying political economy, production systems, global value chains and the materiality of primary products. Structural constraints, such as existing political arrangements and state policies, facilitate and impede the ability of individuals or organisations to pursue livelihoods, and are critical root causes of (under-)development.

We can distinguish a succession of underlying structural mechanisms moving from the immediate proximate processes to more far-reaching structural mechanisms, including those that work far beyond the immediate context (Blaikie and Brookfield 1987; Scheyvens and Shivakoti 2019). In other words, we avoid positing a simple proximate/structural binary. Rather, there is a spectrum extending from more proximate causes to more diffuse structural mechanisms. The main distinction here is that while proximate causes tend to be the close, immediate, or apparent reason for an outcome, underlying structural mechanisms are not integrally bound to specific places. Yet the latter are critical: they shape inequalities, as well as the rights and capacities of households to benefit from resources, and the functioning of labour and commodity markets within particular locales.[1] They also affect the opportunities and obstacles for accumulation, facilitating or impeding mobility amongst the poor. Global and regional structural mechanisms interlink across scale to produce structural poverty, affecting how actors access farm inputs, market chains and terms of trade, off-farm income opportunities and financial support services. Structural mechanisms influence the direction and pattern of livelihoods.

Poverty is the consequence of "historically developed economic and political relations" (Mosse 2010: 1156). Such *social relations* encompass relations of dependence and exploitation, the informal and formal power relations that shape people's actions and lead to relations of debt and dependency. These include class and gender relations and the power relations that underpin surplus extraction and appropriation, including patron-client and wider networks surrounding the local state, market and community actors who shape developments in particular places. While political and moral ties to landlords, employers, village patrons, solidarity networks and formal welfare institutions are critical to livelihoods, they can also be used, invested in and manipulated. These extend to the exchange relations that affect the ability of actors to command food or income in the market and lead to patterns of vulnerability and household disadvantage. Social relations affect the terms of socioeconomic inclusion, including the processes that keep people poor over time and those that provide capacities to leave poverty behind. Hence relational processes are both enabling and constraining: they make social navigation possible and are critical factors in poverty traps.

People's agency, identity and choice are critical as they use various strategies to respond to social, economic and environmental change (Scoones 2015). Within a broad spectrum of livelihood strategies, Dorward et al. (2009) suggest three general types of pathways pursued by rural people: "hanging in" to maintain livelihood levels, "stepping up" to improve livelihoods, and "stepping out", accumulating and then moving into different activities as well as "dropping out". Livelihood strategies depend upon the ability to grow food or forage from forests, rivers or the sea and upon the access to opportunities and assistance linked to kinship, village membership, religious affiliation and patron-client relationships. Individuals' strategic behaviour is embedded in livelihood trajectories (Bagchi and Kato 1998; De Haan and Zoomers 2005; Sallu, Twyman and Stringer 2010). Trajectories consist of embodied practices and households on the same livelihood trajectory experience the same forms of resilience and vulnerability.

An *agrarian change scenario* is an account of a sequence of developments setting out how specific proximate processes, contextual triggers, relational processes and structural mechanisms converge with people's aspirations, adaptive strategies and coping behaviours to coproduce contingent directions of social, economic and environmental change (Figure 2.1; Table 2.1). Each scenario accounts for how causal processes, relations, and logical sequences of

Table 2.1 Agrarian change scenarios overview

Scenario	Proximate factors and contextual triggers	Structural Mechanisms	Relational processes	Livelihood trajectories
Oil palm				
Smallholder development scenario	Well-integrated into provincial economy; extensive smallholder control of land; opportunities for labour and livelihood diversification	Ecology and seasonality of palm oil; limited opportunity for intercropping food crops; difficulty of replacing old tree stock leads to low production trap; insecure market	Open palm oil value chain governance; casualised labour relations under landowner control	Rising incomes for dynamic independent smallholders with access to land, finance and diversification opportunities; stagnation for small non-poor landowners; fragmentation of landholdings over time; casual labourers and marginal landholders face seasonal nutritional insecurity
Enclave plantation scenario	Isolation; poor opportunities for income diversification; insufficient labour opportunities; extensive plantation control of land; smallholder enclave	integration for casual labourers; low opportunities for casual work in off season	Village elite domination of value chains; exploitative plantation labour regimes; vulnerability for casual workers and higher risks for women	Affluent landowners control key value chains and develop client base of dependent households/casual labourers; stagnation and poverty for marginal smallholders and casual labourers; deeper seasonal nutritional insecurity for casual labourers, landless and marginal farmers

(cont'd overleaf)

Table 2.1 (*cont'd*)

Scenario	Proximate factors and contextual triggers	Structural Mechanisms	Relational processes	Livelihood trajectories
Irrigated Rice Production				
Sideways scenario	Limited opportunities for diversification or migration; insecure labour market integration; agriculture remains primary source of livelihood for rural households;	Large inequalities in land ownership; consumptive lifestyles; commodification of labour and inputs; high costs; high dependence on credit for agricultural inputs; structural inequalities holdback those without networks, finance or education	Tenant farming structures of landownership predominate; Poor are dependent on landholder storekeeper patrons	Successful households diversify out of agriculture and accumulate from renting out land, formal employment, or businesses; small landowners move sideways; tenant farmers lack control over rice surplus and subject to nutritional insecurity; vulnerability of those unable to diversify successfully; poor and small-scale farmer households and female-headed households especially vulnerable
Precarious, developmental scenario	infrastructure/means of transportation and labour markets provide significant opportunities for (male) migration and off-farm diversification, rising levels of education.		Increased dependence on low skilled and unstable labour opportunities in cities and urban areas; Young workers move away from agriculture; Decline of land-based power base of village elites.	Upward trajectories of migrant labour and diversifying households able to access income earning opportunities; agriculture has become part-time, feminine and grey; precarity of migrant labour and those dependent on insecure income, the ageing and ill. Mechanisms ensuring households' social welfare tend to be individualised due to migration, individualised government support and eroding, reciprocal networks of exchange and mutual help

Table 2.1 (*cont'd*)

Scenario	Proximate factors and contextual triggers	Structural Mechanisms	Relational processes	Livelihood trajectories
Community Fisheries Scenarios				
Fishing boom scenario	Resource frontier with significant fisheries stocks; lack of opportunities for livelihood diversification	Increasing global market integration and demand; new technologies; marked seasonality of fisheries; loose regulatory arrangements leading to over-fishing and habitat destruction	Strong patron–client ties structure credit and investment	Opportunistic trading into regional and international value chains generates wealth and material progress for aspirational fishers; Poor and small-scale fisher households especially female headed households face poverty, adverse incorporation, indebtedness and deep seasonal nutritional insecurity.
Resource degradation scenario	Deteriorating marine ecologies; large fishing fleets; precarious opportunities for diversification in construction and tourism sectors		Community practices of reciprocity act as bulwark against nutritional insecurity	Demand-driven overfishing leads to fishery collapse; commercial fleet now competing with near shore artisanal fishers; fishery dependent households move sideways or use reciprocal relations to avoid nutritional insecurity; households with education, capital and contacts find employment outside the village

(cont'd overleaf)

Table 2.1 (*cont'd*)

Scenario	Proximate factors and contextual triggers	Structural Mechanisms	Relational processes	Livelihood trajectories
Upland and Dryland Cropping Scenarios				
Boom crop, agrarian differentiation scenario	Strong consumer demand for horticultural commodities in Java leads to crop boom; proximity to trade, industry and government centres provides diversification opportunities	Insecure labour market; increasing climate variability; rising input costs and fluctuating producer prices; poor access to finance	Dependence on landlords and creditors	Entrepreneurial farmers with access to credit and labour pursue upwards trajectory; small landowners face rising costs and price squeezes, through diversified livelihoods and casual work tread water; vulnerable households move downwards and face nutritional insecurity
Subsistence-orientated scenario	Unfavourable agroecology; remoteness from markets, poor infrastructure, and poor access to credit; absence of labour opportunities outside farming; land relatively abundant; household labour relatively scarce.		Strong clan-based networks shape opportunities for education and migration and provide a bulwark against hunger	Some households progress through access to credit/projects, opening small enterprises, selling cash crops and becoming traders; Clan investment in education via urban–rural networks provides for upwards trajectory of a limited number of individuals who obtain a government job and contribute to expenses of village kin; with limited labour opportunities, and seasonal variability and frequent crop losses, large numbers of households face seasonal nutritional insecurity

events shape how agrarian change occurs. Scenarios represent the directional spectrum of choice and room to manoeuvre within which households face opportunities and limitations. We find specific combinations of structural and contextual processes shaping distinct household trajectories in each scenario. We can best consider these by focusing on both the choices people make and the specific contextual factors and structural mechanisms at work.

This volume uses this scenario heuristic to unpack the processes and mechanisms coproducing patterns of livelihood advancement, poverty, precarity and nutritional insecurity. We employ the concept to capture diversity and compare the array of processes taking place; we thereby gain insights into the disparate causes that prevail in variegated settings and circumstances, providing an alternative to linear and singular agrarian change models. The scenario heuristic helps to analyse ongoing processes that, although rooted in past agrarian change pathways (or conjunctures), continue in the present and, although the future does not repeat the past, (given path dependencies) are likely to proceed into the future.

As scenarios depict how change occurs, they also aid causal analysis of future developments. For, as Bradfield, Derbyshire and Wright (2016) suggest, by improving the knowledge of causal processes underlying events, scenario methods can uncover possible futures. By questioning established narratives, they can challenge conventional thinking and reframe understandings, informing policy discussions and improving decision-making. The emphasis here on casual pathways provides an orientation for policy-makers and scholars undertaking scenario planning because "without firstly orientating ourselves with an examination of the present and how it has come to be, our consideration of the future becomes rudderless" (Bradfield, Derbyshire and Wright 2016: 2). Scenario approaches provide "the context within which to think about the future and how it may differ from that present" (Bradfield, Derbyshire and Wright 2016: 10).

To sum up, the heuristic aims to provide an analytical approach for understanding the coproduction of agrarian change. This requires mapping how immediate, proximate factors at the micro-level, structural mechanisms (e.g. in the political economy), relational processes (e.g. class, gender, ethnicity, kinship), and people's agency interact with ecological change and meteorological forces to coproduce particular patterns of agrarian change. As noted in Chapter 1, agrarian transformation narratives tend to focus on understanding abstract patterns of agrarian change and are less helpful for understanding transitions working at intermediate scales in grounded settings. In contrast, "conjunctural" analysis captures how dynamic elements align and collide to shape livelihood change, connecting diverse social and material elements that shape change over time in particular cases (Li 2014). "Assemblage" approaches also focus on how heterogeneous elements come together purposively in specific contingent and singular arrangements (Buchanan 2015). As Moore (2022) notes, the former places change in world history and abstracts it from its local-historical context, while the latter privileges conjuncture and assemblage. Both approaches reveal essential truths. The heuristic used here aims to build on both insights, understanding together how rural change proceeds through messy, contingent variation and, working comparatively, to explore how more general patterns of agrarian change, livelihood transition and vulnerability production emerge. We present the salient scenarios revealed by applying this heuristic in the different case studies.

Plantation Scenarios

In our two North Sumatran oil palm field studies (Chapter 7), the two contexts have different histories of land enclosure and smallholder development. In Asahan, village leaders refused to allow a plantation-out grower or nucleus estate (*Perkebunan Inti Rakyat* or PIR) scheme, and most of the land remains under village control. With good road infrastructure and larger land endowments, Asahan smallholders have greater opportunities than villagers in the Langkat plantation enclave, particularly as the area is well integrated into the broader North Sumatran economy. In contrast, PIR schemes targeted the Langkat site very early. As the area was set aside for a PIR programme, smallholders faced land shortages and inclusion into plantation regimes when agribusiness enclosed the forest area before village settlement. Following a long history of plantation enclosure and the history of the specific nucleus estate scheme development in Langkat village, we saw extensive plantation control of land and widespread landlessness. Hence, in the two oil palm cases, such proximate factors had critical roles in producing two distinctly different agrarian change scenarios: rising incomes, less inequality and relatively lower levels of nutritional insecurity in Asahan; and relatively more stagnation and poverty in Langkat, given its isolation, greater degree of landlessness and poorer opportunities for income diversification.

Despite these proximate differences, we saw the same broad structures at work at both sites. These included various materialities of the crop, the ecology and seasonality of palm oil, the enclosure of land by investors (large landowners or plantations), the difficulty of replacing old tree stock and a significant reserve army of landless labour.

Relational factors affect labour regimes and the workings of value chains, shaping the markets for agricultural inputs and palm tree fruits. Social relations also function somewhat differently in each site: for instance, the comparative isolation and village elite domination of the local nodes in palm oil value chains and plasma oil palm land impact the Langkat site. These factors constrain farming and labour opportunities in Langkat. Compared to the elite capture found in Langkat, the Asahan case has a more open pattern of value chain governance. As a result, poverty levels, stunting and food insecurity among landless and labouring families were much higher in the Langkat Plantation Scenario than in the Asahan Smallholder Scenario. Further, given the gendered nature of labour regimes in the plantation sector, women face more significant risks as casual workers.

The two oil palm cases illustrate how structural mechanisms and relational processes come together with proximate processes in different ways, generating a *Smallholder development scenario* in Asahan and an *Enclave plantation scenario* in Langkat. Each of these scenarios leads to specific patterns of nutritional insecurity while offering distinct possibilities for improving livelihoods. As discussed in Chapter 7, although the structures persist, contextual and proximate factors work differently across the two sites. In each scenario, different percentages of the villagers follow one of three salient trajectories: accumulating capital and assets, muddling through by moving sideways, or becoming impoverished and nutritionally insecure. These agrarian change scenarios have social implications for the generation of wealth and poverty, stunting, vulnerability and food insecurity. In the Asahan Smallholder Development Scenario, a large cohort of smallholders moves out of poverty, and we see rising incomes, less inequality and relatively low levels of nutritional insecurity. In contrast, in the Langkat Enclave Plantation Scenario we found elite capture of marketing channels, plantation control of land and much deeper nutritional insecurity.

Irrigated Rice Production Scenarios

In lowland rice-producing Central Java (Chapter 4) and Aceh (Chapter 5), we saw similar broad structural features at work. The structures of land-ownership encompass significant inequalities, although the degree of disparity varies and in both scenarios, tenant farming encompasses large areas. Green revolution investments in agriculture have generated higher production but increased commodification of labour and inputs, leading to higher costs. These in turn produce new economic and ecological vulnerabilities. Yet the two contexts are distinct. Industrialisation and urban development in Java have generated labour markets that provide significant opportunities for migration and off-farm diversification. Hence, agriculture has largely become a part-time activity in Java, except for women and older people. In Aceh, regional labour markets provide very limited opportunities for integration into the broader economy and the Acehnese villagers have few options for diversification or migration. Here arable land remains the primary anchor for food-insecure households.

The structural mechanisms articulate with these distinct contexts in completely different ways and, combined with other proximate factors, this leads to different scenarios. In Java, there is a high demand for cheap unskilled labour in the cities, enabling large numbers of (often male) villagers to move out of farming. But Javanese households face stresses and shocks and readily fall back into poverty. Hence this is a *precarious, developmental scenario*, where poorer sections of the population, especially those dependent on a single insecure source of income, and also the ageing and ill, are vulnerable to livelihood and lifecycle shocks and economic crises. The sudden and massive job losses caused by the 1998 Asian financial crisis and the 2020–21 COVID-19 epidemic are cases in point. In Aceh, the combination of similar agricultural structures with attenuated labour opportunities leads to a *sideways scenario*, where many households diversify only to tread water. Hence, the predominant livelihood trajectory in each scenario is different: vulnerabilities and degrees of nutritional insecurity emerge in each case, but are of a different nature and are experienced differently.

Community Fisheries Scenarios

We found consistent structural patterns at work in both the fisheries scenarios (Chapters 9 and 10). With intensified domestic and international demand for seafood, even remote fisheries have integrated into the global market. Key actors have invested more in wild-caught and farmed production. The widespread availability of ice supplies and boat technologies facilitates fish harvesting and marketing success. But loose regulatory arrangements lead to over-fishing and habitat destruction, increased pressure on fishing stocks and declining yields, all of which undermine the future viability of the fishing sector and its importance to nutritional security across the Indonesian archipelago.

The Sama Bajo of Sulawesi have adapted to a dynamic marine context in which they have converted practices of subsistence seafood capture into opportunistic trading. A class of entrepreneurial fishers takes advantage of high value and seasonal fishing opportunities and prosperous fish traders enjoy solid links to investors and regional markets. While the Sama Bajo remain vulnerable to deteriorating marine ecologies, the fishing frontier has not yet closed and a *fishing boom scenario* is still very much in evidence, with significant numbers of households following a "stepping up" or "stepping out" trajectory.

Yet, despite so many moving out of poverty within this boom scenario, the predominant social relations also shape the impoverishment of subsistence incomes of fishers who suffer from annual seasonal downturns in fishing production. Local patron-client models for credit and investment in fishing enterprises predominate and adverse incorporation of the poor into these credit-trade arrangements leads to a period of nutritional insecurity for fishing crews who cannot save enough to tide them over the scarcity season (*paceklik*).

In the Bali fishing case, the same structural integration into the global market has occurred. The commercial sardine fleet initially brought small-scale subsistence fishers significant benefits from participation in a globally-linked commercial fishing sector. However, this context is distinctly different from the Sulawesi frontier: in Bali, large fishing fleets and large coastal communities live close to a large tourism industry. Villagers who accessed casual work in Bali's buoyant tourism economy, at least before its collapse due to COVID-19, could diversify their livelihoods and alleviate their vulnerability to some degree. At the same time, community practices of reciprocity involving strong relational networks also enable the Balinese coastal communities to ameliorate household risks to some degree.

In Bali, resource degradation due to overfishing and illegal, unreported and unregulated (IUU) practices have surpassed the effects of market-driven economic development. Over a few short years, demand-driven overfishing has caused the fishery to collapse, and with it, the fortunes of both the small-scale fishers and commercial operators. Within this *resource degradation scenario*, the long-term decline has taken the place of unsustainable "development". Casual labour opportunities outside fisheries and agriculture enable some diversification in low-income unskilled labour surplus sectors. For most villagers, this supports a "moving sideways" trajectory at best. During the COVID-19 period, declining fisheries and tourism income has led to additional large reductions in incomes.

Sulawesi's resource frontier scenario involves the generation of wealth and poverty and of material progress alongside stunting, vulnerability and food insecurity. In comparison, at least until COVID-19, the opportunities for diversification and the strong reciprocal relations found in coastal Bali worked against the generation of nutritional insecurity.

Upland and Dryland Cropping Scenarios

In the Java uplands (Chapter 8), the critical structural factor is the strong consumer demand for horticultural commodities across the island. This, along with the introduction of pesticides, fertilisers and credit, has led to a horticultural crop boom in the highlands. Unequal land ownership and insecure labour market integration are also key structural features. The climate powerfully shapes the horticultural context: heavy rains, high winds or prolonged dry seasons.

Here we see a *boom crop, agrarian differentiation* scenario. As commercially-orientated smallholders have engaged in entrepreneurial farming, better-positioned households have experienced an upwards trajectory, capitalising on their farming efforts. This has led to the emergence of a class of efficient farmers and successful entrepreneurs. Meanwhile, poorer farmers are caught in social relations that leave them dependent on landlords and creditors. Those who borrow for agricultural inputs face rising input costs and fluctuating producer prices. As these squeeze their livelihoods, many are left vulnerable and even nutritionally insecure. Those losing from this agrarian differentiation scenario move sideways or even downwards. The focus in this case study on the potential of education to provide a means for young people to leave poverty behind resounds across the other scenarios. Different contextual factors, such as proximity to trade, industry and government centres, accentuate the variable opportunities for the next generation to step out and up.

In Sumba (Chapter 6), structural constraints are distinct: climate variability and an unfavourable agroecology, with regular droughts, destructive winds, pests and disease, make it difficult to crop consistently. Together with remoteness, poor infrastructure and poor access to credit, these factors constrain agriculture, while the absence of labour opportunities outside farming limits opportunities for diversification. Here proximate factors differ: land is relatively abundant in this context while household labour is scarce. In this *subsistence-orientated scenario*, households are poorly integrated into the cash economy, and land-based livelihoods on their own cannot always provide secure livelihoods. Social relations, principally Sumba's strong clan-based semi-subsistence system, shape opportunities for education and migration. In Sumba, people invest in complex exchange networks to cope with periods of scarcity, so that while hunger is rare, stunting rates and nutritional insecurity remain.

In the agrarian production systems discussed above, we discuss how these different agrarian change scenarios unfold. By differentiating the structural, proximate and relational processes, we unpack the diversity of processes and outcomes, the changing nature of poverty and the emergence of old and new forms of vulnerabilities and food insecurities in different regions in rural Indonesia. In the next section, we discuss the livelihood outcomes produced in each agrarian change scenario in more detail.

Livelihood Outcomes: Findings of the Case Studies

In this section we discuss our findings regarding poverty, vulnerability and the livelihood opportunities available to people. This discussion relies on the data and cross-case comparisons set out in Chapter 15. We focus on the poverty and nutritional insecurity outcomes and the opportunity structure of different agrarian change scenarios. We elaborate according to the following sequence: first, we discuss the role of land, farming and fisheries in rural livelihoods, focusing on patterns of depeasantisation and deagrarianisation. In most scenarios we see the decline of subsistence agriculture and a reduction of the reliance on agriculture and fisheries within diversified livelihoods. Second, we discuss how households diversify their livelihoods through wage labour, off-farm employment and migration enabled by different agrarian change scenarios. Here we consider the degree to which occupations and livelihoods are diversifying, delocalised, spatially fractured, and/or remaining linked to productive land and natural resources. Third we consider food poverty patterns, specifically how households attain nutritional security (or not), and the persistence of seasonal periods of scarcity. Finally, we analyse the implications for the broader literature regarding the mechanisms and processes that enable people to progress, trap them in relentless poverty or cause them to fall into poverty.

The Role of Farming and Fisheries

According to the structural transformation narrative discussed earlier, the role of land and agriculture in livelihoods diminishes as the economic transformation from agricultural to non-agricultural sources of income takes hold. The palm oil study areas of Langkat and Asahan are rather exceptional given that the entire economy in plantation areas is focused a single commercial crop, which is firmly integrated into a trans-global commodity chain. In the Langkat plantation areas, people have limited access to land and few opportunities for alternative sources of income. Similarly, access to land remains critical to livelihoods across most of our scenarios, and we see little sign of the consolidation of landholdings as people move to the city. In Asahan, villagers control most land, and there are more opportunities for income diversification. The same applies to the rice lands of Java and Aceh. Better off landowners enjoy the benefits of high-production rice agriculture, accumulating a surplus within farming while diversifying and educating their children for livelihoods beyond the village. In upland and lowland Java, the poorest tend to be those with the least control over land who eke out livelihoods on tiny plots without successfully diversifying or migrating. In the Aceh *sideways scenario*, access to land remains critical to escaping nutritional insecurity, even while farming alone fails to provide a means of leaving poverty behind. In Asahan, Aceh and Java, livestock secures savings and acts as a buffer against sliding backwards during a crisis. Even though the productivist agenda of the green revolution succeeded in Aceh, without significant changes in labour markets, the intensification of agriculture has not resolved poverty.

In the oil palm *enclave scenario* (see Chapter 7), agriculture is linked to insecurity for different reasons. Here, plantation enclosures have led to marginalisation. Control of land remains critical: With agribusinesses controlling most of the landscape, most villagers have small oil palm plots and work as insecure day-labourers; this erodes the ability of villagers to live from combining farming and family labour. In the Sumba *semi-subsistence scenario*, agriculture remains linked to poverty. Although communities resort to complex exchange networks to survive periods of scarcity, land-based livelihoods alone tend to provide insecure livelihoods. Even though the poverty rate (measured in cash income) is comparatively low in the oil palm cases compared to dry-land Sumba, as most villagers in oil palm landscapes have little capacity to grow food (low subsistence capacity), stunting rates remain comparatively high.

As elsewhere in Asia, agriculture alone, even with productivist gains, is insufficient to provide sustainable livelihoods for most rural people in Indonesia unless secure labour absorption in the city has occurred, as it has in Java for many (Rigg et al. 2016). Nonetheless, wealth accumulation continues in most cases. We still saw landlords, money lenders, vendors and merchandisers of cheap snacks, motorbikes, mobile phones and other consumer goods profiting from the countryside: the countryside remains central to the accumulative strategies of a large cohort of actors.

In the Javanese lowland *developmental-precarity scenario*, the land provides a sense of security, identity and membership as people grow old. Similarly, in Bali and Sumba, the village remains vital for reproduction, identity, social security, kinship networks and schooling. The productive functions associated with agriculture and land-based livelihoods are "entwined within a wider livelihood web", with land serving as a basis for social reproduction, providing a bulwark of food (and by extension, livelihood) security through own production (Pritchard, Vicol and Jones 2017: 54).

While farms are "nested within pluriactive household economies" (Rigg et al. 2016: 120), in many of our cases, the implications are not always positive. In the lowland Java scenario, women bear a heavier burden as they balance social reproduction (raising and schooling children; cooking) and farm work while the men are away (Nooteboom 2019; Pattenden and Wastuti 2021). With insecure labour prospects in the city, people keep one foot (and the family) in the village. However, we also optimistically observed that in this lowland Java *developmental-precarity scenario*, there were large-scale shifts out of poverty as people migrated and worked off-farm, even if the non-agrarian livelihoods remained insecure. In this case, depending on one's perspective, non-farm work subsidises farming or farming underpins the labour market, with households retaining an anchor in the village for identity and reproduction purposes.

Some observers have noted that agrarianisation processes can accompany deagrarianisation, leading to a translocal peasantry rooted in the family farm and integrated into wage-labour relations. Hebinck (2018: 17) found this pattern remarkably resilient, paying tribute to the agency of rural people who carve out a living under such precarious conditions. Yet it is clear that agriculture plays a contradictory role in how households experience poverty and prosperity. Depending on contextual factors or how households are inserted into relational and structural processes, agriculture can play a part in helping families leave poverty behind or remaining within a poverty trap.

Diversification and Labour Migration[2]

Diversification, the involvement of rural households in other economic sectors and spaces, is seen as necessary for survival or progress (Hebinck 2018). Here, the reduction in agrarian and primary production livelihoods (*deagrarianisation*) is seen as a natural process that provides a possible upward livelihood trajectory. This, however, is problematic in some scenarios. With the delinking of livelihoods from old forms of farming, some argue that the future for rural populations lies in off-farm livelihood diversification, migration and the adoption of high-value agricultural production (Rigg 2006; World Bank 2007). A more pessimistic argument suggests however that the urban industrial sector offers insufficient opportunities to absorb rural labour for the surplus population displaced from the land (Li 2010).[3] We found evidence for both these arguments, supporting our conclusion that it is critical to study how contextual factors work with relational dynamics and structural forces within particular scenarios to determine outcomes.

Diversification was found to play a less significant role than expected in some scenarios. In the Sumba semi-subsistence scenario, while labour (rather than land) is scarce, returns on labour remain unsatisfactory. Faced with erratic rainfall and poor production, people may move elsewhere, as households have few opportunities to diversify locally. This occurs when clan groups send selected children to town to enrol in higher education, or support a son or daughter to go to Bali in search of a paid job. Most lack the means to do this and remain caught in an increasingly (environmentally) high-risk, low capital and low asset poverty trap. While the deagrarianisation dynamic is relatively weak, with strong ties to the place and social identity, villagers prefer to stay in place.

In Aceh's sideways scenario, even those who have diversified or attempted to migrate may stay insecure. Here, our surveys revealed that even among those who obtain more than 40 per cent of their income outside agriculture, 37 per cent cut back on food—typically protein—during the scarcity period. Given Aceh's position on the periphery of Indonesian industrial development, industries outside agriculture do not readily absorb Acehnese labour, with few jobs in small businesses, plantations or the service sector. Significant numbers of the unskilled Acehnese move away for periods. However, given the limited nature of Acehnese ethnic networks in urban centres outside Aceh, they struggle to find even low-wage, unskilled and precarious work in Java and Malaysia. For Acehnese, Rigg et al.'s (2016: 125) "extraordinary mobility revolution" is not working.

In the Sulawesi *fisheries boom scenario*, the Sama Bajo do not diversify much beyond the fishing sector. For the most part, they expand their settlements around the bay, or relocate to other prospective fishing locations in the region and do more of the same. Here limited diversification and some intensification occur, but all within the smallholder fisheries sector. There is a vital cultural component here, which may be slowly changing with more education.

In Bali (*marine resource degradation scenario*), however, diversification has, for the most part, provided a stop-gap, temporary solution. Here, developments in the fishing industry provided an initial boost to incomes until the Bali Strait sardine fishery collapsed in 2010. As overfishing and climate change have increasingly affected small-scale fishers, households have faced deterioration in the primary production sector. In response, households have diversified into low-value construction labour and domestic production, which, together with redistributive relations in this fishing community, have cushioned the impacts of seasonal variation and resource decline on food security. Given the low wages and casual nature of work in these sectors, only some households with better educated or well-connected members can find high-value employment outside the village and escape the precarity felt by the majority. Rising land values and new opportunities in tourism in other parts of the island (pre-COVID) have created the chance of some upward mobility. However, workers earning low wages in service occupations can send little back to their villages after paying rent and higher urban living costs. To be sure, households have pursued pluriactive strategies, the local economy has diversified, and we see temporary movement in and out of fishing and casual labour. This, alongside investment in reciprocal social relations and receipt of some small remittances, allows households to stay afloat. In this scenario, however, prospects seem bleak. Slow and relentless economic reversal has followed the improvements in technology and market access. Over-exploitation and climate change continue to squeeze living standards. Those left behind in fisheries find themselves on a path to deepening insecurity.

Hence, we need to be wary of overstating the significance of migration. In most scenarios, a limited number of households have families outside the village. From our 14 cases, only in four cases did we see more than 20 per cent of households having a family member living outside the village. The numbers of people sending remittances, and their amounts, are often small. Although surveys may well underestimate the sums sent home, reported remittance incomes ranged from 2.5 million rupiah (USD 185) to less than 500,000 rupiah (USD 37) per year across our 14 case studies (see Chapter 15).

In contrast, in the lowland Java *developmental-precarity scenario*, remittances are significant to village incomes. They improve the livelihoods of a large proportion of the households that used to be extremely poor. Even remitting relatively small sums can contribute significantly to the nutritional security of a household or dependent family member. There is a methodological problem at work here: households tend to count remittances as household income, and the quantity of remittances may be underestimated.[4] In the *development-precarity scenario*, labour movements are highly gendered, with men in some locations moving to work in the cities, even as in other contexts, women move overseas. Here, this is leading to the feminisation of agriculture and large numbers of female-headed households.[5]

Even in the most diversified scenario (lowland Java), deagrarianisation processes may provide only tentative livelihood solutions. Rural labour is still in demand; here we see market integration of labour into industrial and service sectors. Yet, the shift out of agriculture is insecure, as moving to the city is yet to offer reliable incomes. In reflecting on why households keep their base in the village, Rigg et al. (2016: 131) note that "the precarity of much non-farm work, the absence of a well-woven social safety net, and a certain emotional attachment to natal homes all play a role". This suggests that the "increasingly multi-spatial character of rural livelihoods" may at best only deliver partial solutions (Hebinck 2018: 230). In so many of these scenarios, households hedge their bets and move sideways, diversifying and engaging in livelihood *bricolage*, not for accumulation, but rather to hold on.[6]

Food Poverty

Our study triangulated stunting data and household food security surveys with qualitative work and community wealth rankings to gain insights into village food consumption patterns (Chapter 15), and to understand why, despite a fall in statistical poverty rates (before COVID-19), patterns of precarity, vulnerability and food poverty persist even where we saw material gain (such as Java and Bali). This progress tended to be thin or insecure. In most scenarios, large numbers of people remained subject to patterns of seasonal nutritional insecurity and scarcity. We investigate the reasons for this by analysing how the dynamic interactions between context-specific triggers and political, institutional, social-economic and environmental structures and processes constrain or enhance livelihoods.

A key factor here remains subsistence capacity: the ability of people to provide for their own food needs (Fischer 2008). Nowadays, rural people need to pay for hired labour and inputs, including fertilisers and mobile phones, motorbikes, school expenses, health costs and other necessities. They need to complement food crops with cash incomes, grow cash crops or hire out their own labour, for instance by migrating, which affects their subsistence capacity. Unless they retain some subsistence capacities in rural assets and production functions, or find sufficient income streams, they become increasingly dependent on purchasing food and can become more vulnerable to nutritional insecurity during periods of the year. However, as is occurring elsewhere in Southeast Asia, land development projects and the enclosure of community lands and common pool resources such as forests have undermined agricultural livelihoods and subsistence capacities (De Koninck, Rigg and Vandergeest 2012). With the move away from subsistence, we find a comprehensive set of structural changes occurring. Social needs have shifted, with more commodified or cash-dependent livelihoods. Changing markers of prestige and status and aspirations to a better life correspond with shifts in the things people need, desire or aspire to consume. Consequently, much of their surplus income now funds consumption and changing lifestyles.

Cultural food practices are critical here. Bottle feeding, fast foods and high carbohydrate diets ("food from nowhere") indicate rising consumption patterns. These also contribute to nutritional insecurity. With increasing expenditure on non-food items, and as calorie-rich foods became inexpensive, we see a nutritional transition as people buy cheap sugar-rich and carbohydrate-dense foods in the market. The marketing of ultra-processed food contributes to shifting diets away from traditional and wild foods (Pawera et al. 2020), towards higher consumption of sugar and vegetable oils (Nurhasan et al. 2021).

Families make difficult trade-offs between competing needs. While social needs such as transport and education must be met, families can cut back on protein. Households may reduce the quality of meals by cutting back on micronutrient-rich but more expensive foods such as fish. Hence growth or integration into (global) markets may deepen rather than improve the lives of specific categories of people (Mosse 2010).

An extensive literature provides health and nutrition-based understandings of the high rates of stunting and nutritional insecurity. Yet while nutritional and health conceptual frameworks may be "effective in identifying a broad range of stunting determinants", they do not provide an adequate understanding of the causal pathways leading to poor nutritional outcomes (Beal et al. 2018: 8). We need to understand how nutritional security emerges from a web of intersecting processes and practices to generate patterns of affluence and deprivation within particular agrarian scenarios. Rising consumption coincides with patterns of precarity, vulnerability and food poverty.

We see this working in specific ways in each scenario. For example, the most nutritionally insecure in Aceh's *sideways scenario* are those who have lost control over their rice production, with up to two-thirds of the rice harvest taken to pay land rent and debt. In the *fishing boom scenario*, fishing crews caught in debt arrangements remain the most vulnerable to nutritional insecurity. In contrast, in the *developmental-precarity scenario* (Java) those unable to hedge precarious migrant work with agricultural work in the village stay the most insecure. In each scenario, contextual and structural elements come together in specific ways to shape the "spaces of vulnerability" (Watts and Bohle 1993) where people are unable to access sufficient nutrition through putting together a diverse portfolio of farming, diversification, self-provision and forms of local assistance. While progress can occur in terms of the statistical markers of poverty, such as cash income, many households remain nutritionally insecure.

Climate

The impacts of climate change and environmental degradation have already taken hold of rural life. The significant achievements of the last half-century occurred during the post-1950s surge in growth rates across an extensive range of measures of human activity known as the "Great Acceleration" (Steffen et al. 2015). In the oil palm, fisheries and rice production scenarios, the intensification of production has relied on cheap fossil fuels. The fixation of nitrogen into fertilisers, and the use of petrol-powered harvesters, fishing boats and tractors, are fossil fuel dependent. The 2019 IPCC report on climate change and land outlines clearly how changes in land use, including those associated with the oil palm boom, have contributed to carbon emissions, creating feedback loops which further intensify harmful climate change (IPCC 2019).

In the fisheries scenarios, economic growth has involved over-exploitation of the resource and associated environmental degradation, with over-accumulation exposing ecological damage and losses that may well wash away the gains of recent decades. As this growth comes to an end, many elements of agrarian transition found in these scenarios are likely to be unsustainable and even reversed. This is particularly so in the context of the COVID-19 pandemic, and as climate change and other environmental impacts take hold.

An increasingly erratic climate threatens to tighten constraints on marginal farmers and smallholders. Farming activities are susceptible to variations in the pattern and distribution of rainfall, with shifts in seasons and periods of planting having significant implications for farm productivity (Sugihardjo et al. 2018). For instance, studies have estimated that a 30-day delay in the onset of the wet season in Indonesia decreases rice yields by 6.5–11 per cent, prolonging the "hunger season". This can increase the risks of harvest failures in the second planting season and delay the consecutive rice crop (GFDRR 2011; Netherlands Ministry of Foreign Affairs 2018). Climate-related events such as floods and droughts also exacerbate crop losses, and reduce soil fertility and the number of crop plantings per year (Fedele et al. 2016). Climate change compounds existing forms of nutritional and livelihood insecurity and the vulnerable conditions of many ecosystems, particularly for rural people dependent on agriculture, fisheries or who live on the forest fringe.

Soil management and other production difficulties exacerbate the economic squeeze felt by marginal and tenant farmers who borrow to repay debts for agricultural inputs related to rising input costs and fluctuating producer prices. For instance, though profitable in the short run, agriculture in the *horticultural boom scenario* (upland Java) may prove to be unsustainable. Applying technologies such as pesticides and fertilisers for thrice-yearly crops does not allow the land to rest sufficiently and places farmers on a treadmill of increasing inputs to sustain their yields (see Chapter 8).

From any perspective, humans are major actors in the modification of the environment: climate and other environmental forces are influenced by human social processes and are worked into social organisation. Agrarian change and climate change are coproduced, with no clear boundaries between climate and society (Taylor 2015). Biophysical processes, such as those related to climate change, work together with social processes to create observed patterns of environmental and social vulnerability. Climate vulnerability is socially differentiated: climate change risks and impacts tend to be more acute for marginalised people. The social-political mechanisms that render particular categories of people vulnerable also ensure that the consequences of climate change work out unequally.

Implications

Declining poverty statistics across rural Indonesia suggest that the rates of deprivation are falling, implying that relatively few households suffer from insecurity. Yet the raw stunting data (see Chapter 15 for our sites) indicate a persistent pattern of nutritional insecurity and the prevalence of vulnerability and food poverty across landscapes and production systems (Arif et al. 2020), a feature that triangulates with the emic concepts of poverty that our study has developed. For instance, a recent report estimated that 30.8 per cent of children were stunted (Kementerian Kesehatan [Ministry of Health] 2019). According to a 2018 report, Indonesia remains one of the three countries globally with the highest numbers of children suffering from wasting (Development Initiatives 2018). Stunting and food insecurity rates vary considerably across Indonesia. Yet our food security and stages of progress (SoP) analysis (Chapter 15) indicates that the experience of deprivation, food poverty and vulnerability is more widespread than suggested by poverty statistics. This analysis reveals the reality of insecure progress and nutritional insecurity, as too many households consume insufficiently-nutritious food and inadequate protein.

For at least three reasons, official poverty statistics may help us to grasp this reality only partially. First, poverty statistics can mask the dynamics of rural development. Falling poverty rates might reflect the inadequacy of how poverty is measured as much as changes in social needs and the experience of poverty. As Fischer (2018: 258) argues, "poverty statistics underestimate the reproduction of poverty over time". They depend upon concepts of basic need that are based on calculations of what households require for subsistence, which may be no longer valid given the structural transformation in rural livelihoods. As discussed in Chapter 15, basic social needs have changed, along with the minimum requirements for functioning in modern society.

Analysis needs to consider better the changing experience of poverty and the new social needs discussed earlier.

Second, as Fisher (2018) also notes, poverty statistics play an ideological role within an anti-politics of development. They involve making normative and political decisions regarding what constitutes poverty. These involve social and institutional processes that are veiled by highly technical methods.

Finally, statistical analysis may apply an objectivist approach that involves simplifications by conceptualising poverty "in a way that emphasises attributes and capabilities attached to individuals and influencing their life chances" (Mosse 2010: 1158). While sophisticated statistical methods can be applied to counting and identifying the most vulnerable, it is equally important to understand why people are vulnerable (Ribot 2014). We need both to keep in mind the more comprehensive socioeconomic and political processes that render people poor and to develop more nuanced ways of analysing patterns of vulnerability associated with land use categories, ecological-resource dependencies and labour relations. Hence, we argue that it is crucial to pursue scenario analyses that complement and move beyond statistical simplification.

Contribution of the Scenario Approach

The orthodox narratives of agrarian transition tend to work at a global or national scale. While these narratives have sustained global policy ideas regarding "pathways out of poverty", such as that advanced by the World Bank's *World Development Report* (2007), this involves a degree of abstraction from the lived experiences of rural people. A problem emerges if we assume that local processes somehow fit with the simplified logics of broadly-identified developmental narratives.

In contrast, we have developed our scenarios from the study of socio-environmental change in production systems at local and intermediate levels—in the specific places where people live. While keeping in sight the workings of the broader political economy, we use grounded social science understandings of rural change and local knowledge to appreciate local people's change experiences. This involves grasping how developmental forces shape livelihood landscapes, revealing who is vulnerable in specific contexts and why, acknowledging that poverty and vulnerability manifest in significantly different ways across space and time. By testing the assumptions of the grand narratives of change against regional and local variation, scenario analysis enriches the understanding of how broader structural mechanisms are inscribed at intermediate or local scales. We find that this approach opens possibilities for rethinking how (food) poverty is produced and how to address its most salient forms. The neo-classical and political economy narratives discussed earlier present an optimistic-pessimistic dualism. In contrast, our approach allows us to tease out and compare the causal processes and enabling contexts that enhance and constrain the ability of communities and households to overcome vulnerability and attain nutritional security. The approach allows us to identify more variegated outcomes and paradoxical processes that elude narratives that depend on broad-scale generalisations.

Researchers have used up a great deal of ink discussing "pathways out of poverty" related to diversification, farming and migration. These include narratives of structural change, agrarian transition, truncated transitions, or optimistic mobility narratives that suggest linear teleologies and transitions. A plethora of nominalisations ending in "-ation" (diversification, intensification, extensification, deagrarianisation, depeasantisation, commodification, repeasantisation, structural transformation, etc.) is central to most accounts of agrarian change processes.

Superficially, our scenarios may seem to fit with the patterns identified in the agrarian transformation literature. For example, Aceh's sideways scenario or Java's insecure deagarianisation scenarios resemble the truncated transition to a certain extent. Yet, rather than being surplus to the requirements of capital during a truncated transition, we find Javanese workers are still in much demand. In Aceh, workers appear to be surplus to accumulation processes in the market economy and left aside. However, we find the poor still provide a large market for agro-food, credit, mobile phones and motorcycles, and a large rice surplus is sucked out of this region to feed the industrial centre of nearby Medan. Farming, migration and diversification are linked to stagnation and indebtedness and survival and progress (McCarthy 2020). However, our scenario analysis shows that livelihoods are hybrid and too highly varied to map them onto simple change narratives.

To be sure, we find patterns of change; for example, diversification and deagrarianisation work across scenarios. However, the meaning, scale and significance of these processes are distinct to each scenario (and this is not caught by the predominant agrarian change narratives). For instance, in most areas, households aspire to follow migration pathways. Some families can do so, but not in the same ways or scale. For example, Vel and Makambombu argue (Chapter 6) that migration did provide a pathway for a small number of people in Sumba. Still, we may understand this pathway only in the context of Sumba's unseen reciprocity economy. Here, clan groups (rather than households *per se*) pursue the strategy of helping at least one child into secure employment—perhaps a civil servant's job—as a resource for the wider group. Hence, migration and deagrarianisation have a particular inflection. It remains difficult to envisage the vast majority following that path.

In contrast, deagrarianisation in Java follows the more familiar pattern of migration and off-farm work. The significance and meaning of deagrarianisation and migration (seen, for example, in the Aceh *sideways scenario*) depend upon how structural mechanisms interact with the context. The fieldwork of prominent scholars of agrarian change, such as Bernstein (2011), Li (2014) and Rigg (2006), provides rich understandings of processes of change, while our approach enables us to place these analytical narratives of change within a broader set of scenarios.

Scrutinising each scenario, we find dynamics of deagrarianisation and agrarianisation, adaptive diversity and rural stagnation working in ways that problematise the settled ideas (teleologies) provided by narratives of "structural transformation", "agrarian transitions" or "truncated transitions". We argue that reality is less determinate and much more open than agrarian change narratives suggest. Our scenario approach suggests we look at specific contexts: "what is happening" rather than "what is not" (Du Toit and Neves 2014). Hence, we conclude that agrarian studies need to build on and move beyond grand narratives that have dominated studies of agrarian change over recent decades.

This analysis has several implications. First, scenario analysis points to links between land enclosure and dispossession, precarious post-industrial work, ecological decline and emerging forms of precarity. Research suggests that both smallholder access to sufficient land and healthy ecological systems are linked to more diverse diets (Nurhasan et al. 2021). Land ownership and common pool resources can provide social protection (a buffer against vulnerability and nutritional insecurity). By avoiding natural resource extraction and landscape transformations that undermine livelihoods, development policy can reduce environmental pressures. If combined with upskilling and value-adding processing, such policy can work to support more sustainable fisheries, agroforestry and agricultural livelihoods.

Second, scenario analysis can indicate the processes that render people subject to the scarcity season and why. Insights into scarcity seasons can help to design specific development policies which address the structural mechanisms of exclusion and inequality. Policymakers could develop social assistance measures to address specific patterns of vulnerability by, for example, rolling out assistance precisely when local people are most insecure. Local authorities might provide employment schemes to the most vulnerable during the most challenging part of the year. District and provincial poverty measures could also be redesigned based on indigenous notions of vulnerability and poverty revealed by scenario analysis. Further, programmes could focus on vulnerable categories of people: the sharecroppers and landless in Aceh or fishers without assets in high debt during the off-season in Sulawesi. Programmes could assist the diversification of livelihoods and diets and (avoiding vulnerable monocultures) support measures to enhance the heterogeneity of agroforestry and production systems, including home gardens and cattle ownership, as well as efforts to prevent livestock epidemics and to protect the rural poor's capital (see Chapter 15).

Conclusion

This chapter advances a series of arguments elaborated in subsequent chapters. First, we have utilised a scenario analysis approach as a heuristic to analyse agrarian change. We used this approach to understand the multidimensional nature of rural poverty, nutritional insecurity and the diverse drivers of change shaping households' fortunes. Drawing on the extensive debates and literature around agrarian change, the *agrarian change scenarios* approach has highlighted the impact of different constraints and opportunities that enable some rural households to thrive and prosper while others struggle to overcome poverty, nutritional insecurity and entrenched inequality. The agrarian change scenarios approach enables us to distinguish and compare the specific contextual triggers, structural mechanisms and actor responses that emerge in different agro-ecological production contexts and shape contingent choices and directions of social, economic and environmental change. We suggest that this approach allows us to move beyond the simplifications of the grand narratives advanced by global studies of the agrarian transition.

Second, in seeking to explain why rural poverty and stunting persist while statistical rates of extreme poverty keep falling, we needed to analyse why, in virtually all our scenarios, global market integration has enabled many households to move out of poverty while this integration is also being associated with increasing inequality and persistent nutritional insecurity. This paradox is expressed in different ways across our scenarios. In Bali's *marine ecological degradation* and the Java *upland cropping scenarios*, livelihood progress occurred along with over-accumulation, as particular actors over-harvested or unsustainably mined natural resource bases, leading to subsequent environmental degradation and livelihood decline. In the Javanese *developmental but precarious scenario*, many households appeared to be doing better, progressing against crucial development indicators. Yet a closer analysis reveals that their progress depended upon precarious inclusion into labour markets, which is easily eroded or even reversed by market fluctuations, lifecycle crises or pandemics. Similarly, in the Acehnese *sideways scenario*, while ascending households diversified to various degrees to advance in statistical terms, most poor households diversified and progressed sideways without finding security. In the Sumba *subsistence-orientated scenario*, enduring subsistence capacities paradoxically provided nutritional security outcomes that were comparable to some of the more precarious market-orientated scenarios. For instance, economic indicators in the *plantation scenarios* suggested that integration into the booming oil palm economy led to economic progress. However, fieldwork and stunting data reveal the profound nutritional insecurity among many households in oil palm landscapes following a long history of plantation enclosures.

Our analysis shows that while the processes that render marginal groups vulnerable vary considerably, the symptoms are somewhat similar. Arif et al. (2020: 7) note that "poverty is highly correlated with food insecurity". Smallholder farmers, farmworkers and fishers constitute most of the food insecure (Valesova et al. 2017). Arif et al. (2020) conclude that carbohydrates continue to dominate the diets of most Indonesians, despite the continued increase of per capita income. As we note, commodified livelihoods and consumptive lifestyles have taken hold. With fast food and snack retailing and marketing penetrating remote villages, we see shifting social needs and changing food cultures. This, alongside ecological decline, leads to a loss of subsistence capacity, as households make trade-offs and substitute micro-nutrient rich food and proteins for carbohydrates.

Across these scenarios, agriculture plays a paradoxical role in the experience of poverty and prosperity. According to the structural transformation narrative discussed earlier, the role of land and agriculture in livelihoods is meant to diminish. Even with productivist gains from intensification, agriculture alone may be insufficient to provide sustainable livelihoods for most rural people (Rigg et al. 2016). Yet too often, enclosure of land, increasing landlessness, the shift to cash cropping, changing consumption patterns and lifestyles, and other factors work to undermine subsistence capacities. If diversification and migration options remain inadequate, this leads to nutritional and livelihood insecurity. Here, agriculture and land-based livelihoods are entwined in a broader livelihood web. Agriculture serves as a "base for social reproduction", and "a bulwark of food (and by extension, livelihood) security through own-production" (Pritchard, Vicol and Jones 2017: 41), but on its own may provide only a semi-subsistence livelihood (Rigg et al. 2016). The implication here is that policy needs to keep in view the asset base of rural communities: effective interventions may do well to focus on supporting the subsistence capacity of regional populations, including by protecting community access to and control over land.

Studies show that many of the determinants of child undernutrition are well understood. Assistance programmes tend to focus on access to nutritious food, parenting/childcare, health care services, and clean water and sanitation (Arif et al. 2020). Such programmes can make critical contributions to addressing these issues. However, from this scenario analysis, we suggest that established health and nutrition-based framings of food security may be inadequate on their own. Research and policy also need to understand and address the underlying drivers of poor nutrition in food and production systems.

The comparative case studies in Chapters 4 to 10 illustrate the insights and lessons outlined above in fine-grained detail, exploring the dynamics of poverty and prosperity across a range of crucial livelihood and agroecological production contexts. The evidence and cross-case discussions are summarised and elaborated in Chapter 15.

Notes

[1] Structural mechanisms include the relations of production and exchange within globalised value chains. This structural focus addresses the inadequacy Scoones (2015: 46) found in livelihood frameworks that missed the role of the wider political economy, institutions and policies to mediate "access to livelihood resources and defin[-e] the opportunities and constraints of different livelihood strategies".

[2] In these scenarios, social relations and class are critical to the production of vulnerability. For instance, in the Sulawesi fishing boom scenario, patrons profit from the labour of the poor. However, they also provide them with a subsistence net, in some cases gobbling up the social protection funds while also accumulating from their control over production systems and networks.

[3] Here, the "household" category in surveys is inadequate. As Vel and Makambombu (Chapter 6) found, rural Sumba in many ways works as a community economy where clan (agnatic) groups, rather than households, are the economic units that decide on the use of shared resources. They jointly invest in the education of the offspring of the clan and divide the clan's subsistence and ceremonial tasks across members living in the village and in town.

[4] We find networks of exchange and reciprocity and morality associated with kinship, neighbourhood and religious networks critical to how people face challenging circumstances. However, statistical analysis will struggle to quantify these factors, and they are often overlooked. Social relations can also make people vulnerable, ameliorate risk and even, in some scenarios, offer pathways out. This, together with subsistence capacities and the ability to diversify livelihoods into small niches within rural contexts, enables people to "shift sideways" and avoid the agrarian crisis predicted by critical accounts of the truncated agrarian transition (McCarthy 2020).

[5] At the same time nutritional security is also linked to the status of women, the age that they get married and their childcare practices (Beal et al. 2018). For instance, women suffer from much higher rates of anaemia, and the age of lactating mothers significantly affects average calorie intake at the household level, because older mothers' better understand food quality and family requirements (Srinita 2018).

[6] They make use of reciprocal social relations to moderate their insecurity. To be sure, local social relations require investment, and these can be exploitative or even exclude the extremely poor. Further, as the forms of consumption and exchange associated with these social relations are so difficult to quantify, they are overlooked by most studies. However, in all our scenarios we find they play a significant role, providing mechanisms that offer some support during times of crisis. This explains why, even in deeply challenging livelihood landscapes, we see people holding out, rather than the out-and-out agrarian crisis predicted by critical accounts of the truncated agrarian transition. As Hebinck (2018) notes, "rural people continue to live and work in the rural domain, actively (re)assembling their lives and social and natural resources to maintain the vitality of their countryside and living in accordance with locally and culturally embedded strategies". Here the forecasts of agrarian pessimists may be too bleak; most people are still able to muddle through via "moving sideways", combining agriculture work with off-farm labour, the collection of products from nature and networks of reciprocity.

References

Akram-Lodhi, A.H. and C. Kay. 2010. "Surveying the Agrarian Question (Part 2): Current Debates and Beyond", *Journal of Peasant Studies* 37: 255–84.

Arif, S. et al. 2020. *Strategic Review of Food Security and Nutrition in Indonesia: 2019–2020 Update.* Jakarta: SMERU Research Institute.

Bagchi, M. and M.S. Kato. 1998. "Conceptual and Methodological Challenges in the Study of Livelihood Trajectories: Case-studies in Eastern India and Western Nepal", *Journal of International Development* 10: 453–68.

Beal, T. et al. 2018. "A Review of Child Stunting Determinants in Indonesia", *Maternal and Child Nutrition* 14, 4: 1–10.

Bernstein, H. 2011. "Is There an Agrarian Question in the 21st Century?", *Canadian Journal of Development Studies* 27, 4: 449–60.

Blaikie, P. and H. Brookfield. 1987. *Land Degradation and Society.* London: Methuen.

Bradfield, R., J. Derbyshire and G. Wright. 2016. "The Critical Role of History in Scenario Thinking: Augmenting Causal Analysis within the Intuitive Logics Scenario Development Methodology", *Futures* 77: 56–66.

Breman, J. and G. Wiradi. 2002. *Good Times and Bad Times in Rural Java: Case Study of Socio-economic Dynamics in Two Villages Towards the End of the Twentieth Century.* Leiden: KITLV Press.

Bryceson, D.F. 2000. "Disappearing Peasantries? Rural Labour Redundancy in the Neo-liberal Era and Beyond", in *Disappearing Peasantries: Rural Labour in Africa, Asia and Latin America,* ed. Deborah F. Bryceson, C. Kay and J. Mooij. London: IT Publications, pp. 299–326.

Buchanan, I. 2015. "Assemblage Theory and its Discontents", *Deleuze Studies* 9, 3: 382–92.

De Haan, L. and A. Zoomers. 2005. "Exploring the Frontier of Livelihoods Research", *Development and Change* 36, 1: 27–47.

De Koninck, R.J. Rigg and P. Vandergeest. 2012. "A Half Century of Agrarian Transformations in Southeast Asia, 1960–2010", in *Revisiting Rural Places: Pathways to Poverty and Prosperity in Southeast Asia*, ed. J. Rigg and P. Vandergeest. Singapore: NUS Press, pp. 25–37.

Development Initiatives. 2018. *2018 Global Nutrition Report, Development Initiatives Poverty Research*. Available at https://globalnutritionreport.org/reports/global-nutrition-report-2018/.

Devereux, S. 2001. "Sen's Entitlement Approach: Critiques and Counter-Critiques", *Oxford Development Studies* 29, 3: 245–63.

Dorward, A. et al. 2009. "Hanging In, Stepping Up and Stepping Out: Livelihood Aspirations and Strategies of the Poor", *Development in Practice* 19, 2: 240–7.

Du Toit, A. and D. Neves. 2014. "The Government of Poverty and The Arts of Survival: Mobile and Recombinant Strategies at the Margins of the South African Economy", *The Journal of Peasant Studies* 41, 5: 833–53.

FAO (Food and Agriculture Organization). 2019. *State of Food Security and Nutrition in the World 2019*. Available at https://www.fao.org/3/ca5162en/ca5162en.pdf (accessed 20 Aug. 2020).

Fedele, G. et al. 2016. "Ecosystem-based Strategies for Community Resilience to Climate Variability in Indonesia", in *Ecosystem-based Disaster Risk Reduction and Adaptation in Practice*, ed. F.G Renaud et al. Cham: Springer, pp. 529–52.

Fischer, A.M. 2008. "Subsistence and Rural Livelihood Strategies in Tibet under Rapid Economic and Social Transition", *International Association of Tibetan Studies* 4, 1: 1–49.

_____. 2018. *Poverty as Ideology: Rescuing Social Justice from Global Development Agendas*. London: Zed Books.

GFDRR (Global Facility for Disaster Reduction and Recovery). 2011. "Climate Risk and Adaptation Country Profile: Indonesia". Available at http://www.gfdrr.org/sites/default/files/publication/climate-change-country-profile-2011-22ndonesia.pdf (accessed 5 Sept. 2020).

Hebinck, P. 2018. "De-/Re-agrarianisation: Global Perspectives", *Journal of Rural Studies* 61: 227–35.

IPCC (Intergovernmental Panel on Climate Change). 2019. *Special Report: Climate Change and Land*. IPCC. Available at https://www.ipcc.ch/srccl/.

Kementerian Kesehatan (Indonesia, Ministry of Health). 2019. *Laporan Nasional Riskesdas 2018* [National Report of Basic Health Research 2018]. Jakarta: Badan Penelitian dan Pengembangan Kesehatan.

Levien, M., M. Watts and H. Yan. 2018. "Agrarian Marxism", *The Journal of Peasant Studies* 45, 5–6: 853–83.

Li, T.M. 2010. "To Make Live or Let Die? Rural Dispossession and the Protection of Surplus Populations", *Antipode* 41, 1: 66–93.

_____. 2011. "Centering Labour in the Land Grab Debate", *The Journal of Peasant Studies* 38: 281–98.

_____. 2014. *Land's End: Capitalist Relations on an Indigenous Frontier.* Durham, NC: Duke University Press.

McCarthy, J.F. 2020. "The Paradox of Progressing Sideways: Food Poverty and Livelihood Change in the Rice Lands of Outer Island Indonesia", *The Journal of Peasant Studies* 47, 5: 1077–97.

McMichael, P. 2009. "A Food Regime Genealogy", *The Journal of Peasant Studies* 36, 1: 139–69.

Moore, J.M. 2022. "Anthropocene, Capitalocene and the Flight from World History: Dialectical Universalism and the Geographies of Class Power in the Capitalist World Economy, 1492–2022", *Nordia Geographical Publications* 51, 2: 123–46.

Mosse, D. 2010. "A Relational Approach to Durable Poverty, Inequality and Power", *The Journal of Development Studies* 46: 1156–78.

Naylor, R.L. 2014. "The Many Faces of Food Security" in *The Evolving Sphere of Food Security*, ed. R.L. Naylor. Oxford: Oxford University Press, pp. 3–30.

Netherlands Ministry of Foreign Affairs. 2018. *Climate Change Profile: Indonesia.* Available at www.government.nl/binaries/government/documents/publications /2019/02/05/climate-change-profiles/Indonesia.pdf (accessed 12 July 2020).

Nooteboom, G. 2019. "Understanding the Nature of Rural Change: The Benefits of Migration and the (Re)creation of Precarity for Men and Women in Rural Central Java, Indonesia", *TRaNS: Trans -Regional and -National Studies of Southeast Asia* 7, 1: 1–21.

Nurhasan, M. et al. 2021. *Linking Food, Nutrition and the Environment in Indonesia: A Perspective on Sustainable Food Systems.* Bogor: Center for International Forestry Research (CIFOR).

Pattenden, J. and M. Wastuti. 2021. "Waiting for the Call to Prayer: Exploitation, Accumulation and Social Reproduction in Rural Java", *The Journal of Peasant Studies*: 1–22.

Pawera L. et al. 2020. "Wild Food Plants and Trends in Their Use: From Knowledge and Perceptions to Drivers of Change in West Sumatra, Indonesia", *Foods* 9 (1240): 1–22.

Peluso, N.L. and A.B. Purwanto. 2018. "The Remittance Forest: Turning Mobile Labor into Agrarian Capital", *Singapore Journal of Tropical Geography* 39, 1: 6–36.

Pritchard, B. et al. 2013. *Feeding India: Livelihoods, Entitlements and Capabilities.* Abingdon, Oxon: Routledge.

Pritchard, B., M. Vicol and R. Jones. 2017. "How Does the Ownership of Land Affect Household Livelihood Pathways under Conditions of De-agrarianization? 'Hanging in', 'Stepping up' and 'Stepping out' in Two North Indian Villages", *Singapore Journal of Tropical Geography* 38: 41–57.

Ribot, J. 2014. "Cause and Response: Vulnerability and Climate in The Anthropocene", *The Journal of Peasant Studies* 41, 55: 667–705.

Ribot, J. and N.L. Peluso. 2003. "A Theory of Access", *Rural Sociology* 68, 2: 153–81.

Rigg, J. 2006. "Land, Farming, Livelihoods and Poverty: Rethinking the Links in the Rural South", *World Development* 34, 1: 180–202.

Rigg, J. et al. 2016. "Between A Rock and a Hard Place: Vulnerability and Precarity in Rural Nepal", *Geoforum* 76: 63–74.

Rigg, J., A. Salamanca and E.C. Thompson. 2016. "The Puzzle of East and Southeast Asia's Persistent Smallholder", *Journal of Rural Studies* 43: 118–33.

Sallu, S.M., C. Twyman and L.C. Stringer. 2010. "Resilient or Vulnerable Livelihoods? Assessing Livelihood Dynamics and Trajectories in Rural Botswana", *Ecology and Society* 15, 4: 1–33.

Scheyvens, H. and B.R. Shivakoti, eds. 2019. *Asia-Pacific Landscape Transformations – Solutions for Sustainability.* Hayama, Japan: Institute for Global Environmental Strategies.

Schneider, C.Q. and C. Wagemann. 2006. "Reducing Complexity in Qualitative Comparative Analysis (QCA): Remote and Proximate Factors and The Consolidation of Democracy", *European Journal of Political Research* 45, 5: 751–86.

Scoones, I. 2015. "Sustainable Livelihoods and Rural Development". Rugby, UK: Practical Action Publishing.

Sen, A. 1981. *Poverty and Famines: An Essay on Entitlement and Deprivation.* Oxford: Clarendon Press.

Srinita. 2018. "Relationship between Maternal, Household, and Socio-Economic Characteristics and Household Food Security in Aceh, Indonesia", *International Journal of Human Rights in Healthcare* 11, 3: 192–203.

Steffen, W. et al. 2015. "Planetary Boundaries: Guiding Human Development on a Changing Planet", *Science* 347, 6223: 736–46.

Sugihardjo, J. et al. 2018. *Dynamic Models of Farmers' Adaptation to Climate Change (Case of Rice Farmers in Cemoro Watershed, Central Java, Indonesia),* IOP Conference Series: Earth and Environmental Science 142, 012051: 1–6.

Taylor, M. 2015. *The Political Ecology of Climate Change Adaptation.* London: Routledge.

Torlesse, H. et al. 2016. "Determinants of Stunting in Indonesian Children: Evidence from a Cross-sectional Survey Indicate a Prominent Role for the Water, Sanitation and Hygiene Sector in Stunting Reduction", *BMC Public Health* 16, 669: 1–11.

Valesova, L. et al. 2017. "The Nexus between Food Insecurity and Socioeconomic Characteristics of Rural Households in Western Indonesia Identified with Food and Nutrition Technical Assistance's Approach by USAID", *Agronomy Research* 15, 3: 921–34.

Van der Ploeg, J.D. 2018. "From De- to Repeasantization: The Modernisation of Agriculture Revisited", *Journal of Rural Studies* 61: 236–43.

Watts, M.J. and H.G. Bohle. 1993. "The Space of Vulnerability: the Causal Structure of Hunger and Famine", *Progress in Human Geography* 17, 1: 43–67.

World Bank. 2007. *World Development Report 2008: Agriculture for Development*, Washington, DC: World Bank.

CHAPTER 3

Social Protection and the Challenge of Poverty in Indonesia

Andrew McWilliam, John F. McCarthy, Gerben Nooteboom and Naimah Talib

Introduction

Over the past two decades, the Indonesian state has embarked on a large and ever-growing social policy agenda to help the poor. Social assistance has evolved from simple distribution of rice and food packages to the electronically based provision of food rations, and from basic income support to the introduction of the expanding conditional cash transfers. The government has also extended education subsidies and provided health cost coverage for the poor.[1]

This chapter builds on research in 14 locations across seven agro-ecological production zones in rural Indonesia. We focus on the provision of state-based social assistance, especially food assistance through the Raskin/Rastra programme (subsequently replaced by BPNT and now *kartu sembako*),[2] and the PKH (families of hope) conditional cash transfer (CCT) programme. Over the past decade, these two large programmes have reached the rural areas covered by this book. Hence, our village studies become a lens to explore the implications of anti-poverty and social assistance programmes from the perspective of recipient communities. We consider the performance and delivery of social assistance programmes "from below". In the process we critique the targeting, scoping, impact, underlying assumptions and policy settings derived from the World Bank's "social risk management model" (Jorgenson and Siegel 2019),[3] as discussed in Chapter 14.

We begin this chapter by recounting the history of social protection in Indonesia, and then follow with a summary of our findings and critical assessment of the Raskin/Rastra and PKH programmes. The discussion also provides background and scoping analysis for appreciating the regional case studies that follow.

Extending New Entitlements to Rural Indonesia

For the first time in its history, the Indonesian state is setting out to directly reduce the unacceptable levels of deprivation and inequality found in remote rural areas across the nation (TNP2K 2018). In the language of government, these policies develop "comprehensive social protection, basic service provision and sustainable strategies for poverty reduction" (Yulaswati 2018: 3–4).

In practice, the term "social protection" covers a broad set of approaches and mechanisms, while "social assistance" references a range of non-contributory transfers in cash, vouchers, or in-kind support. Some of the social assistance programmes, such as Raskin/Rastra, have old roots and draw upon historical practices of food (rice) provision, while others, such as PKH (conditional cash transfers), represent off the shelf measures taken from the international social policy shop (see, in this volume, Kutanegara et al., Chapter 12, and Sumarto, Chapter 14). Historically, Indonesia has experimented with programmes that offer different and sometimes opposing goals which draw upon variable (ideological) approaches to fighting poverty and increasing social welfare.

Research Questions and Key Arguments

The chapter critically explores the food assistance (Raskin, now BPNT [Bantuan Pangan Non-Tunai; Non-cash Food Assistance]) and conditional cash transfers (PKH) approaches to social assistance and their effects and impacts in the field. Central and local governments provide a range of other subsidy programmes, but we found that their availability was uneven. Survey participants, however, consistently recognised these two main areas of support. This makes these programmes amenable for direct comparative assessment.

In this chapter, we seek to answer the following key questions:

- Why has Indonesia taken up these policies?
- How effectively do these social assistance policies address poverty and vulnerability in rural Indonesia?
- What alternatives are available?
- What factors shape the outcomes we observe?

–   How do district level governments and informal relationships influence state–village interactions and affect the implementation of these programmes?
–   How do the programmes interface with agrarian change scenarios and address the roots of poverty?

We discuss these questions in the light of agrarian change scenarios leading to rural vulnerability discussed in Chapter 2. Further, we review the national level policy settings and overall management and implementation of programmes, drawing on perspectives "from below", namely, local people who directly experience the benefits and implementation complexities of top-down planning and decision making.

In developing a synthesis of our research, we draw on a range of complementary sources and datasets. These include insights and observations from the literature and media, statistical and qualitative data from different regions of Indonesia, as well as critical perspectives and analysis from our own field findings (see Chapter 1 for an explanation of the survey methodology and scope). In presenting this synthesis, we acknowledge that Indonesian social welfare presents a rapidly changing policy field, where assistance schemes and methods for targeting the poor and delivering benefits are continually under revision. Moreover, realities are dynamic and subject to change, as the COVID-19 induced crisis has made clear. Hence, we are wary of drawing final conclusions about the effectiveness of specific schemes and subsidies. For these reasons, our findings are provisional and designed to offer constructive observations and critical analysis of current trends, practices and the effects of social assistance policy settings and programme delivery to the designated recipients.

These preliminary remarks also introduce a set of dedicated chapters in the third section of the volume. Comprising four chapters, the contributions offer detailed policy analyses and critical perspectives on the history, design and delivery of social assistance in Indonesia. Collectively, they present complementary insights into the policy and politics of social protection, from its origins in the travelling technologies of global designs to its adaptive implementation and "continuous enhancement" across Indonesia. The work brings into sharp relief the entrenched and complex relationship between rural poverty, livelihood vulnerabilities and state-driven social assistance efforts. We conclude that current social assistance programmes undoubtedly help many of the poor survive and reduce statistical poverty headcounts. However, the present policy mix is struggling to meet its key objectives of addressing vulnerability and poverty in the countryside. Current approaches are focused on guaranteeing subsistence to the very poor when livelihoods are inadequate or fail, while supporting economic growth and productivity. However, we argue that broader, more inclusive and systematic approaches to poverty, inequality and social exclusion are required to meet Indonesia's commitments to the sustainable development goals (United Nations 2018).

Evolving Social Assistance Programmes

In Chapter 1 we discuss the growing government support for social protection policies and programmes (henceforth SPPs) for Indonesia's poor. These measures have evolved since the late 1990s into an ambitious and highly technical endeavour with national reach and expanding beneficiary funding. It is helpful to understand the historical emergence of the agenda to appreciate the factors shaping the policy landscape. In Indonesia, as in several earlier Latin American cases, an economic crisis triggered the development of explicit social policies addressing poverty (Feitosa de Britto 2004; St Clair 2009).

As the Asian financial crisis (*Krismon*) of 1997–98 spread across economies in Southeast Asia, Indonesia experienced a dramatic collapse in its currency exchange rates, rapid increases in food prices (especially rice, which remains a critical staple), high unemployment levels and a debt crisis threatening many Indonesian companies. In response, the government was compelled to accept a USD 23 billion bailout loan from the IMF and agreed to implement a World Bank structural adjustment programme (see Chapters 11–14).

The Indonesian response to poverty originated from growth-oriented development approaches enshrined in the post-Washington Consensus of the 1990s (Williamson 2004). Indonesia adopted a World Bank-promoted "liberal residual" welfare model, namely, one designed to limit state assistance to a basic safety net, principally subsidised rice, to a large cohort of vulnerable households and later, conditional cash transfers to the very poor when other avenues failed (MacGregor 2014). Indonesian welfare policy gradually embraced this agenda as the state extended assistance to millions of Indonesians during and after the *Krismon*.

During the early "Reformasi Era" from 1999, a coalition of trade unions worked with parliamentarians to push for national social protection legislation (Cole and Ford 2014). This was a critical step in the evolution of Indonesian social policy and coincided with the new policy of decentralisation and the rise of electoral politics at local levels of government, combined with a more democratically engaged constituency. At the same time, the social protection agenda also matched nicely the social safety net (SSN) approach of the World Bank, which offered a means to ease the pain of the economic reforms (World Bank 2012a). This convergence led to the rapid development of a more explicit suite of government policies directed to supporting poor and disadvantaged Indonesians in the early years. First, the state introduced Raskin, or "Rice for the Poor" (later renamed Rastra or "Prosperous rice"), and unconditional cash transfers (BLT) followed by conditional cash transfers (PKH) a few years later.

Like their counterparts in Latin America, planners rolled out the new policies to provide a safety net intended to alleviate the severe impact of the economic crisis on unemployed and low-income families. They aimed to avert social unrest and make pro-market liberalising reforms more palatable (such as withdrawing costly state subsidies on food and fuel) (Feitosa de Britto 2004; Gliszczynski and Leisering 2016; Kim and Kwon 2015). Known as the JPS (*Jaring Pengaman Sosial*) or Social Safety Net, the emergency programmes dispersed the equivalent of USD 1.4 billion across Indonesia. As well as subsidised rice allocations, the support included short-term employment creation and a range of health and education support activities implemented over a number of years.

In 2010, following his election, President S.B. Yudhoyono (SBY) set about consolidating the diverse social programmes under a National Team of Poverty Reduction Acceleration [*Tim Nasional Percepatan Penanggulangan Kemiskinan*, TNP2K]. This body was given a key role to integrate, harmonise and coordinate the range of poverty reduction programmes being implemented under different ministries (see Chapter 14).

Since 2014, President Joko Widodo's administration has revised and reformulated these policies, then promoted them as the combined *Kartu Sakti* ("power card") benefits scheme (OECD 2019). The nominally integrated system comprises access to three critical support programmes. The first is a national health insurance scheme for poor people, who are issued with a health care card (KIS—*Kartu Indonesia Sehat*—Healthy Indonesia) and entitlements to receive free health care on a broad range of health benefits and treatments. The second is an education support scheme, guaranteeing that all school children from disadvantaged families will receive regular financial assistance for education up to completing high school or vocational training. Beneficiaries receive a KIP card (*Kartu Indonesia Pintar*—Smart Indonesia). Third, the administration has gradually replaced the popular Rastra rice distribution programmes with a card, BPNT (*Bantuan Pangan Non-Tunai*), which provides a limited selection of staple foods (*sembako*) from designated, technology-enhanced retail suppliers. These programmes now reach over 15.6 million households across Indonesia (Kompas 2019). They operate as a targeted form of social assistance, where beneficiary selection involves a proxy means test evaluation developed from a complex, field-based data collection process (see Chapter 14 for details). Since 2016, the management of the poverty ranking and selection process has been the responsibility of the Ministry of Social Affairs (*Kemensos*).

Over time, the state has committed to expanding the coverage of these schemes. According to a 2017 World Bank public expenditure review for Indonesia, total social protection spending in 2016 was IDR 177 trillion (USD 14 billion), equivalent to 1.4 per cent of GDP and 15.4 per cent of total government spending (cited in OECD 2019: 131). This level is considered low for an economy the size of Indonesia, and the World Bank recommends two per cent of GDP for social welfare budgets (World Bank 2020). However, the outlays and expenditure on social protection have increased, with further expansion occurring in 2020 and 2021 in response to COVID-19 (see Chapter 14).

The Food Subsidy Programmes: From Raskin and Rastra to Financial Transfers

Although initially implemented during the Asian financial crisis, the provision of cheap rice under the Raskin programme continued old policy ideas from the New Order era and before, which were preoccupied with providing rice to curb social unrest. Moreover, the existing network of strategic rice storage arrangements and warehouses (Bulog—the Indonesian Bureau of Logistics) made rice distribution possible, although such distribution posed a major (and expensive) logistical challenge.

The Raskin programme provided rice free of charge in the early days, sometimes with eight other basic staple foods (*sembako*) including cooking oil, salt and sugar. But under the influence of the World bank and IMF, rice and *sembako* were made available at low and subsidised prices. The programme was subsequently renamed Rastra by the turn of the millennium, as part of the social compensation for the decrease of fuel and rice subsidies. However, both terms have been in common usage for years.

Rastra aimed to cover all households in the bottom 40 per cent of the estimated poor population with monthly deliveries of 15 kg per household of subsidised rice. The potential consumption benefits for poor households were significant. In 2017, for example, the market price for rice was IDR 9,200/kg (about 63 US cents), while a designated Rastra household should pay a fixed price rate of IDR 1,600/kg, nearly 80 per cent below market rates (OECD 2019: 94). This made the programmes highly attractive and welcome to recipients. Although often delivered to people who were not in dire need, the programme helped moderate the social impact of economic downturn and curbed social unrest. But it also highlighted the implementation challenges that confront social assistance initiatives.

Over many years, evaluations have critiqued rice distributions for multiple reasons (Timmer, Hastuti and Sumarto 2017). Earlier, reviews of the *Jaring Pengaman Sosial* (JPS) social safety net programme found that it had been "plagued with problems targeting beneficiaries and delivering benefits to intended groups" (Sumarto, Suryahadi and Widyanti 2004). The programmes did not reach large numbers of people suffering hardship, and a significant leakage of funds ended up in the hands of the non-poor. Apart from recurrent problems of poor quality and spoilage of stored rice, the timing of rice releases to beneficiaries has depended on irregular supplies, resulting in lengthy gaps between allocations, especially in remote areas.

Further, Bulog, the agency responsible for supply, undertakes to supply rice only to designated drop-off points for general distribution. The villagers themselves bear additional transport costs for delivery to more distant beneficiary communities. In practice, the village leadership has covered the transportation cost and recovered their expenses by sequestering a portion of the delivery by various means. The result has been that reductions in the overall allocation of Rice for the Poor have often resulted in disputes and accusations of fraudulent practice against village leaders (OECD 2019). Moreover, in some areas, villagers excluded from the programmes have demanded an equal share of the subsidised rice ("we are all poor") (Kutanegara and Nooteboom 2002). In response, village leaders have often broadened the distribution of government rice—with associated smaller allocations per household—to limit social discontent in the village.

In the study villages of our project, we found there has been little or no attempt to restrict the subsidised rice programmes to the official list of impoverished beneficiaries. Instead, the village leadership across rural areas commonly spread the available supplies widely and thinly across the whole village community, or to all those without formal jobs (OECD 2019). This practice, often described as *bagi rata* (to divide equally), in practice delivered much less "rice for the poor" than the intended 10–15 kg/month (see also Timmer, Hastuti and Sumarto 2017), but it also served to reduce social tensions and criticism of village leadership.

The follow-up non-cash food assistance programme (BPNT) has attempted to tackle this problem of the dilution of the rice distribution targeting by allocating individual recipients with a "credit card". Recipients can use this to purchase a broader range of staple foods at subsidised prices in designated shops. Beneficiaries receive a KKS card (*Kartu Keluarga Sejahtera*—Family Welfare Card) for use in authorised grocery outlets known as an e-warung. Cardholders have access to a list of authorised, essential foods (*sembako*)—principally rice and eggs—using their cashless swipe or tap card. While the BPNT programme is the newest iteration of the former widely criticised "rice for the poor" distribution schemes (Raskin and Rastra), already there are indications of problems with recipient selection, due to difficulties with maintaining the beneficiary database and with the econometric targeting methodology (see below). Moreover, it was evident during our research that the state had not yet implemented the system in many rural areas, due to logistical problems and inadequate banking infrastructure.

Conditional Cash Transfers: The Families of Hope Programme

In 2007, again with influential support from the World Bank, the Yudhoyono (SBY) administration trialled a Conditional Cash Transfer (CCT) programme, known now as "The Families of Hope Programme" (*Program Keluarga Harapan*—PKH). State policy embraced liberal forms of social welfare with highly targeted, means-tested and conditional social cash transfers made to cater for the most vulnerable.

Mexico, along with other countries in Latin America, developed earlier iterations of the cash transfer model, such as the *Prospera* and *Oportunidades* programmes, before recently abandoning the approach altogether (Kidd 2019). Early on however, the World Bank adopted the Mexican model as a "best practice" initiative. By 2014, this "travelling technology" had spread to more than 50 countries. The targeted or conditional model reflected a redefinition of the poverty policy, where social protection accorded with a concerted effort to reduce inequality, support secure livelihoods and build a more cohesive society (see Kutanegara et al. [Chapter 12]; OECD 2019; World Bank 2017a). The new model also directed policy attention to the need for improved government metrics to identify and target eligible beneficiaries.

Before the introduction of PKH, the Indonesian government had trialled an unconditional cash transfer programme (BLT—*Bantuan Langsung Tunai*). Introduced in 2005, it aimed to assist poor people suffering from the removal of fuel subsidies (World Bank 2012b). Some 19 million households benefitted in 2005, nearly one-third of all households, and a similar number during the second round in 2008. Although the dispersion of funds turned out to be complex, irregular and inefficient, assessments concluded that the programme delivered moderate benefits, at the right time, for a suitable duration and with a very lean administration due to its unconditional nature (World Bank 2012b). However, critics found evidence of corruption and the persistent inclusion of non-poor and the exclusion of some poor households. At the same time, overall, the measure did little to provide beneficiaries with pathways out of poverty (Wulandari and Baryshnikova 2019).

In 2016, the Indonesian government phased out the BLT and began the new conditional cash transfer programme, Families of Hope (PKH—Program Keluarga Harapan). PKH aims to provide direct quarterly cash transfers to poor recipients, especially mothers, with the explicit purpose of stimulating regular health check-ups, the consumption of food supplements and school attendance among children from low-income families. In the years after 2016, this programme gradually expanded; by 2018 it covered 10 million households, and 15 million in 2019. In this later stage, the programme included regular quarterly payments to the elderly and disabled, substantially expanding its scope and coverage in the process (OECD 2019). The new programme was means-tested and designed to target the delivery of benefits to poor households. PKH is now among Indonesia's most extensive social assistance programmes, costing upwards of IDR 37.4 trillion (USD 2.69 billion) with 89 per cent of funds spent on benefits (World Bank 2017b). During COVID-19 it also provided a key mechanism for distributing additional emergency funding into rural areas using existing databases of poor households.

Limits and Challenges

Media Evidence

The social protection programmes have been evaluated nationally, and have arguably contributed to poverty reduction, with poverty falling to 9.8 per cent of the population in December 2018 (Bappenas 2018). Further, the programmes have worked well as a social protection and income supplement scheme during the COVID-19 pandemic. While the 2018 figures were the lowest poverty rate achieved in Indonesia's history, a very low poverty line measure was adopted (see Chapter 2). At the same time, this "entitlements revolution" has faced a range of problems and challenges. A content analysis of 228 Indonesian-language news articles on social assistance programmes from March 2018 to October 2019 undertaken during this project reinforces this point. The search aimed to capture a broad range of topics on social protection.[4] The analysis found that the national media generally reported favourably on the roll out of programmes, with only five per cent of national articles criticising coverage and mistargeting issues. But among regional (Provincial and District level) media outlets, reporting presented a stark contrast, with 70 per cent of the sampled reporting highly critical of mistargeted distributions, including 56 per cent of regional newspaper articles dedicated to these problems. These figures indicate that journalists and the reading public in rural and regional areas of Indonesia remain preoccupied with the inadequacies of the programmes; the figures support a view that local concepts of distributional equity continue to be overlooked. The results reveal a persistent disjunction and further paradox between positive assessments of social assistance at the national level and critical views at the local level.

The most common complaint levelled against social programmes was mistargeting of benefits (see Table 3.1). The system consistently excluded many poor households, including recipients perceived to be non-poor. Some 106 articles addressed this issue, representing 47 per cent of the total reporting; they highlighted how widespread and contentious this aspect of the programmes has become. Media discussions also focused on the use of out-of-date data, unmerited choice of beneficiaries, general dissatisfaction, jealousies and contention within communities, and stigmatisation of the poor, provoking demonstrations by villages and even village heads (see Chapter 13).

Table 3.1 News reports on social protection issues

News item	Issues addressed	Weighting %
1	Data and Targeting	47
2	Socialisation of programmes	6
3	Poverty Issues in general	4
4	Transparency and participation monitoring	4
5	PKH expansion	4
6	Logistics redistribution	3
7	Transformation from Rastra to BPNT	4
8	Financing and sustainability of policies	4
9	SPP and human capital	4
10	Technical obstacles in programmes delivery	5
11	Programme evaluation	1
12	Development of SPP	2
13	Abuse of power and corruption allegations	4
14	SPP and financial inclusion	2
15	SPP and social inclusion	5
16	Best practice and knowledge sharing	1

Media commentary also reported on the lack of understanding among prospective beneficiaries due to poor awareness-raising (*sosialisasi*) (six per cent), technical obstacles in programmes' delivery (five per cent), and social inclusion issues (five per cent). Journalists described other issues at a lower frequency, including logistics and distribution of rice assistance, transparency and participatory monitoring, allegations of local elite capture, the expansion of PKH and the transformation of Rastra to the non-cash food assistance programme (BPNT).

The media analysis supports the criticism that the national government struggles to develop effective and equitable support mechanisms for the poor, despite successive reworking and constant adjustments. At local and regional levels, people are highly critical of the effects of mistargeting, and frustrated at the inability to correct perceived errors on inclusion and exclusion (see also Chapter 14).

Analysis and Findings

Overall, we find that the current policy mix is struggling to meet its key objectives of addressing vulnerability and poverty in the countryside. A fundamental problem remains: what analysts call "exclusion by design": across the social protection programmes, there remain significant gaps in the state-provided safety nets (OECD 2019). Unemployed men and non-elderly poor couples without children, for example, fall outside eligible categories and the near poor are not included in PKH, leaving many households at risk of falling into poverty and outside the safety net. At the same time, there is an implicit policy assumption that young, healthy families in all areas of Indonesia can find work to sustain themselves decently. Moreover, only a small percentage of the elderly are covered (TNP2K 2021). But the consequences of missing out on social assistance contribute to higher poverty indicators (poverty rates averaged 34.8 per cent across our case studies, see Figure 15.5). Gaps in social protection also undermine efforts to reduce the high incidence of infant stunting rates across much of rural Indonesia.

Despite sustained attempts to revise and fine-tune the policy levers and procedural approaches to ensure that the needs of the nation's poor are meaningfully addressed, further expansion of social protection is required to meet the UN objectives of a "social protection floor" with basic social protection for everybody. In the light of that challenge, we draw the following conclusions:

(1) First, social assistance programmes generally do provide income support and reduce food insecurity for a cohort of impoverished recipient households. Yet, although these programmes reduce consumption

poverty, as other reviews note (Ladhani and Sitter 2018; ILO 2017), we find little evidence that they help the rural poor move into more productive livelihoods. As subsequent chapters and data analysed in Chapter 15 illustrate, the system provides only marginal consumption gains for many beneficiary households. In short, the national goal of poverty alleviation remains unmet, and greater efforts are required to address the structural and equity aspects of persistent poverty across Indonesia. Social protection needs to extend beyond residualism or direct supplementary relief to households under stress, to encompass a range of systemic issues and transformative possibilities (Devereux and Sabates-Wheeler 2004; Haarstad and St Clair 2011). These shifts could include recognising the citizenship right to a minimum level of income when other sources of subsistence fail.

(2) Our surveys of rural communities confirm what other studies have shown (Ladhani and Sitter 2018): that econometric targeting—a social registry of the poor—even when combining field-based surveys with elements of community targeting to assess eligibility, leaves many households without support even when they are perceived as poor by local criteria (see Chapter 13). As other scholars have observed, this widespread issue generates local resentment and hostility among the excluded and undermines the otherwise broad support for the government initiatives (see Sumarto 2020; Goodin and Dryzek 2016). Reviews of both the Rastra and the PKH programmes report systemic problems with identifying beneficiaries accurately. The mistargeting failures lead to consistent errors of inclusion and exclusion (TNP2K 2018: 70). As detailed in Chapters 11–13, these failures also provoke a messy local politics of distribution. Targeting errors create social disaffection and resentment among recipient communities with what they perceive to be inequities in the distribution of benefits (McCarthy and Sumarto 2018) as well as gender disparities (Arif et al. 2011). Despite the widespread and persistent criticism of beneficiary selection processes, the government has made little progress in resolving these problems.

An illustration of the gaps between entitlement and benefit is presented in Figure 3.1. The figure presents data on the allocation of PKH distributions, based on results drawn from our village case studies. The figure is discussed in detail in Chapter 15 (Figure 15.9). Here we simply draw attention to the high levels of reported exclusion errors (poor households without PKH) and inclusion errors (non-poor households receiving PKH). These results demonstrate the widespread and entrenched nature of the problem.

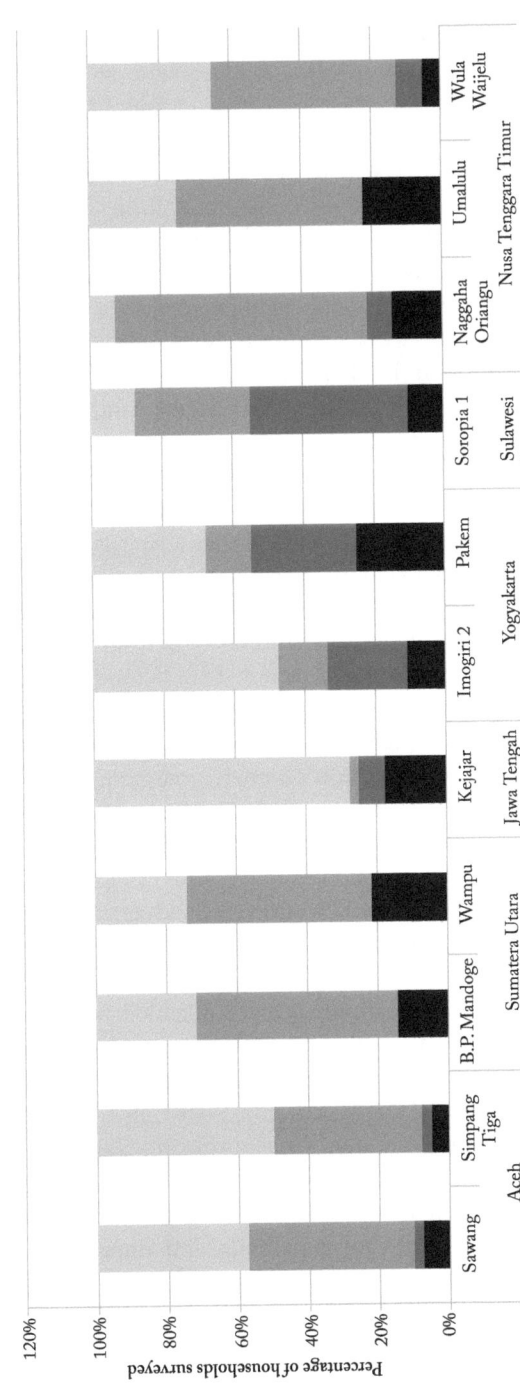

Figure 3.1 Distribution of surveyed households with and without PKH by their SoP status and survey location, 2017–19

(3)   The policy focus on technical approaches using proxy means testing and a large-centralised database involves an inevitable simplifying of the complex dynamics of poverty (see Chapters 11 and 12). This approach rests upon a particular politics of knowledge that shapes development research and practice in this field (see Chapter 11). It has proved to be impractical and costly and amounts to a form of "anti-politics" which reduces poverty to a technical problem while setting aside the underlying structural drivers of poverty (see Li 2007 and Ferguson 2015). As later chapters discuss, efforts to overcome the problems posed by these simplifications face an array of issues and constraints. These include the difficulty of implementing increasingly complex policy designs and technologies in remote and diverse rural contexts where the state has limited capacity. The effort generates an unproductive opposition between sophisticated but flawed distribution mechanisms imposed from the centre, which struggle to identify eligible beneficiaries, and the intrinsic values and expectations that shape sociality in village communities. This opposition reflects the fact that the Conditional Cash Transfer (CCT) blueprint is imported wholesale, initially as part of pro-market liberalising reforms, and then is insufficiently adapted to the Indonesian context (see Chapter 14). Behind this constraint lies a problem of path dependency, with key agencies wedded to this approach and blaming implementation mistakes, without interrogating the assumptions underlying the econometric targeting approach. We conclude that social programmes require widespread knowledge and understanding to successfully negotiate complex societies, rather than pursuing singular econometric global models. Our call for more informed approaches, directed to livelihood trajectories and agrarian scenarios as a basis for understanding and addressing regional poverty dynamics, is a contribution to that exercise.

(4)   Rural communities across Indonesia are embedded in what Stephen Gudeman has described as "high relationship economies", where strong social networks of reciprocal exchange and mutual obligation are integral to the making of material life (Gudeman 2016). But in its pursuit of administrative simplification, the social protection agenda works to discount and flatten this social reality of poverty, while denying its close-knit familial reciprocal networks and enduring clientelist ties of inter-dependency. Here, we argue for expanding and improving initiatives that build on the logics of local social life found in rural Indonesia and for drawing on the intimate knowledge of poverty in village settings to identify who is struggling and who is not.

(5)   There is a range of prospective alternative approaches to the current model. These include increasing effective community engagement in selection processes, moving towards broadening existing categories of recipients, and providing simpler delivery mechanisms such as unconditional cash transfer models (see Chapter 15; Tauchid, Damanik and Nurhadi 2021). Moving in a new direction requires experimenting with novel ways to integrate the views and logics of local social life. As recent reviews suggest, anti-poverty policy requires a systems approach to social protection through a suite of complementary programmes (Loewe and Schüring 2021). Tinkering with the technical design of social assistance programmes may improve the programmes at the margins, but a systematic approach requires ambitious coordinated policy responses. Critics of the comparative Latin America experience also support a move away from a dependence on CCTs, by adopting a wider package of measures for poverty alleviation. Examples include enhancing social and employment rights and integrating workers into the formal economy under better conditions (Papadopoulos and Leyer 2016). What is needed is real political leadership and commitment to prioritising the poor. Policies are urgently required which provide equal opportunities and access through redistribution of resources and social and economic inclusion, as well as justice and sustained economic opportunities (Roelen 2014). There is a pressing need to address entrenched structural drivers of social vulnerability, nutritional insecurity and under-employment (see also Suryahadi and Izzati 2018). An example here is the vital link between the common pool resources (CPR) that guarantee subsistence livelihoods and food security among many emplaced communities, and the enclosure and expropriation of community land during plantation development, extractive land use and resource harvesting policies. Ensuring greater protection and opportunity for poor households and rural communities, so that they benefit materially from economic development and environmental conservation, requires a sustained politics of action. The scale of the challenge is reflected in the persistent inequalities between the wealthy and the poor, between the better and less educated, rural and urban, old and young, male and female, all of which have widened across the Indonesian archipelago over recent years (Tjoe 2018).

In the following chapters, we present our regional case study findings and analyses from detailed livelihood surveys of 14 village communities in seven important production zones of rural Indonesia. The case studies offer insights into a range of rural livelihood strategies and poverty dynamics for each setting, along with the comparative impact of state-provided social protection policies and programmes (SPPs) on villagers' lives. Further analysis of Social Protection Policies development and its contribution to poverty alleviation across Indonesia is provided in Chapters 11–15.

Notes

[1] The educational and social insurance initiatives are essential pillars of social protection, but they have been extensively discussed elsewhere (OECD 2019, Agustina et al 2019) and are beyond the scope of this study.

[2] Rice for the Poor Programme; Raskin (*Beras Miskin*), later renamed Rastra (*Beras Sejahtera* – prosperous rice), then BPNT (*Bantuan Pangan Non-Tunai*–non-cash food assistance).

[3] A form of social policy that promotes public actions to improve market-based and non-market-based or informal instruments for managing risk.

[4] The search extracted Indonesian language media data from Factiva Database Press Readers (covering major newspapers) as well as Google searches. Two hundred and twenty-eight relevant news reports were collected from these sources and checked for credibility and redundancy (double counting).

References

Agustina, R. et al. 2019. "Universal Health Coverage in Indonesia: Concept, Progress, and Challenges", *The Lancet* 393, 10166: 75–102.

Arif, S. et al. 2011. *Is Conditionality Pro-female? A Case Study of Conditional Cash Transfer in Indonesia.* Jakarta: SMERU Research Institute.

Bappenas. 2018. *Inclusive Economic Growth: Reducing Poverty and Inequality in Indonesia [Press Release].* Available at https://bappenas.go.id/berita/83-inclusive-economic-growth-reducing-poverty-and-inequality-in-indonesia-L2j02 (accessed 3 Mar. 2022).

Brunberg, E. 2015. *Conditional Cash Transfers and Gender Equality: Short-term Effects on Female Empowerment. A Minor Field Study in Indonesia*, MA Thesis, Lund University.

Cole, R. and M. Ford. 2014. *The KAJS Campaign for Social Security Reform in Indonesia: Lessons for Coalitions for Social Change.* Unpublished document.

Cookson, T.P. 2016. "Working for Inclusion? Conditional Cash Transfers, Rural Women, and the Reproduction of Inequality", *Antipode* 48, 5: 1187–205.

Devereux, S. and R. Sabates-Wheeler. 2004. *Transformative Social Protection*, IDS Working Paper 232. Brighton: IDS.

Feitosa de Britto, T. 2004. *Conditional Cash Transfers: Why Have they Become so Prominent in Recent Poverty Reduction Strategies in Latin America?* ISS Working

Papers–General Series 19150. International Institute of Social Studies of Erasmus University Rotterdam (ISS), The Hague.

Ferguson, J. 2015. *Give a Man a Fish: Reflections on the New Politics of Distribution.* Durham, NC: Duke University Press.

Gliszczynski, M. and L. Leisering. 2016. "Constructing New Global Models of Social Security: How International Organisations Defined the Field of Social Cash Transfers in the 2000s", *Journal of Social Policy* 45, 2: 325–43.

Goloobi-Mutebi, F. and S. Hickey. 2009. *Governing Chronic Poverty under Inclusive Liberalism: The Case of the Northern Uganda Social Action Fund,* Chronic Poverty Research Centre Paper 150, Manchester UK. Available at https://www.tandfonline.com/doi/abs/10.1080/00220388.2010.487097 (accessed 30 May 2022).

Goodin, R.E. and J.S. Dryzek. 2006. "Deliberative Impacts: The Macro-Political Uptake of Mini-Publics", *Politics and Society* 34: 219–44.

Gudeman, S. 2016. *Anthropology and Economy.* Cambridge: Cambridge University Press.

Haarstad, H. and A.L. St Clair. 2011. "Social Policy and Global Poverty: Beyond the Residual Paradigm?", *Global Social Policy* 11, 2–3: 214–19.

Hakim, S. 2016. *Conditional Cash Transfers and Wives' Decision-making Power.* The National Team for Accelerating Poverty Reduction (TNP2K), ANU Indonesia Project Conference, Canberra.

ILO [International Labour Office]. 2017. *World Social Protection Report 2017–19: Universal Social Protection to Achieve the Sustainable Development Goals.* International Labour Office – Geneva: ILO, 2017.

Jorgenson, S. and P. Siegel. 2019. *Social Protection in an Era of Increasing Uncertainty and Disruption: Social Risk Management 2.0.* World Bank Discussion Paper 1930. Washington, DC.

Kidd, S. 2019. *The Demise of Mexico's Prospera Programme: A Tragedy Foretold.* Development Pathways, Sidcup, England. Available at https://www.developmentpathways.co.uk/blog/the-demise-of-mexicos-prospera-programme-a-tragedy-foretold/ (accessed 28 Oct. 2021).

Kim, H. and W. Kwon. 2015. "The Evolution of Cash Transfers in Indonesia: Policy Transfer and National Adaptation", *Asia and The Pacific Policy Studies* 2, 2: 425–40.

Kompas. 2019. "The Minister of Social Affairs: Beneficiaries of Non-cash Food Assistance Program Increases to 15.6 million households" [in Indonesian]. Kompas.com, 28 January 2019. https://nasional.kompas.com/read/2019/01/28/17591171/mensos-penerima-manfaat-bpnt-2019-meningkat-jadi-156-juta-keluarga (accessed 30 May 2022).

Kutanegara, M. and G. Nooteboom. 2002. "Forgotten Villages, the Effects of the Crisis and the Role of the Government in Rural Java", in *Riding a Tiger: Decentralisation and Regionalisation in Indonesia,* ed. C. Holtzappel, M. Sanders, and M. Titus. Amsterdam: Rozenberg, pp. 248–77.

Ladhani, S. and K.C. Sitter. 2018. "Conditional Cash Transfers: A Critical Review", *Development Policy Review* 38: 28–41.

Li, T.M. 2007. *The Will to Improve: Governmentality, Development, and the Practice of Politics.* Durham, NC: Duke University Press.

_____. 2009. "To Make Live or Let Die? Rural Dispossession and the Protection of Surplus Populations", *Antipode* 41 (S1): 66–93.

Loewe, M. and E. Schüring, eds. 2021. *Handbook on Social Protection Systems.* Cheltenham: Edward Elgar Handbooks in Social Policy and Welfare.

MacGregor, S. 2014. *Welfare: Theoretical and Analytical Paradigms,* UNRISD Working Paper, No. 2014–13. Geneva: United Nations Research Institute for Social Development (UNRISD).

McCarthy, J.F. and M. Sumarto. 2018. "Distributional Politics and Social Protection in Indonesia: Dilemmas of Layering, Nesting and Social Fit in Jokowi's Poverty Policy", *Southeast Asian Economies* 35, 2: 223–36.

McCarthy, J. et al. 2020. *Indonesia Assessment of COVID-19 and Food Systems Vulnerabilities,* Appendix B. ACIAR SRA Final Report *Assessment of Food System Security, Resilience and Emerging Risks in the Indo-Pacific in the Context of COVID-19: Stage 2* (CS/2020/146). Canberra: ACIAR (Australian Centre for International Agricultural Research).

McCulloch, N. and L.H. Piron. 2019. "Thinking and Working Politically: Learning from Practice. Overview to Special Issue", *Development Policy Review* 37: 1–15.

Midgley, J. and K. Tang, eds. 2008. *Social Security, the Economy and Development.* London: Palgrave Macmillan.

OECD. 2019. *Social Protection System Review of Indonesia.* OECD Development Pathways. Paris: OECD. Available at https://doi.org/10.1787/788e9d71-en (accessed 8 Aug. 2020).

Papadopoulos, T. and R.V. Leyer. 2016. "Two Decades of Social Investment in Latin America: Outcomes, Shortcomings and Achievements of Conditional Cash Transfers", *Social Policy and Society* 15, 3: 435–49.

Roelen, K. 2014. "Challenging Assumptions and Managing Expectations: Moving Towards Inclusive Social Protection in Southeast Asia", *Journal of Southeast Asian Economies* (JSEAE) 31, 1: 57–67.

St Clair, A.L. 2009. "Conditional Cash Transfers: The Need for an Integrated and Historical Perspective", *Global Social Policy* 9, 2: 177–9.

Sumarto, M. 2020. "Welfare and Conflict: Policy Failure in the Indonesian Cash Transfer", *Journal of Social Policy* 50, 3: 533–51.

Sumarto M., A. Suryahadi and W. Widyanti. 2004. "Assessing the Impact of Indonesian Social Safety Net Programmes on Household Welfare and Poverty Dynamics", *European Journal of Development Research* 17, 1: 155–77.

Suryahadi, A. and R.A. Izzati. 2018. "Cards for the Poor and Funds for Villages: Jokowi's Initiatives to Reduce Poverty and Inequality", *Journal of Southeast Asian Economies* 35, 2: 200–22.

Sutiyono, G. et al. 2018. *Indonesia's Village Fund: An Important Lever for Better Land Use and Economic Growth at the Local Level, Climate Policy Initiative.* Available at: https://www.climatepolicyinitiative.org/publication/indonesias-village-fund-an-important-lever-for-better-land-use-and-economic-growth-at-the-local-level/ (accessed 14 Jan. 2022).

Tauchid, K.Y., J. Damanik and Nurhadi. 2021. "Examining Emerging Social Policy During COVID-19 in Indonesia and the Case for a Community-based Support System", *Asia Pacific Journal Social Work and Development* 31, 1–2: 13–22. Doi: 10.1080/02185385.2020.1829499.

Timmer, P., Hastuti and S. Sumarto. 2017. "Evolution and Implementation of the Rastra Programme in Indonesia", in *The 1.5 Billion People Question, Food, Vouchers or Cash Transfers*, ed. H. Alderman, U. Gentilini and R. Yemtsov. Washington, DC: IBRD World Bank Group, pp. 265–307.

Tjoe, Y. 2018. "Two Decades of Economic Growth Benefited only the Richest 20 per cent. How Severe is Inequality in Indonesia?" *The Conversation*, April 28. Available at: https://theconversation.com/two-decades-of-economic-growth-benefited-only-the-richest-20-how-severe-is-inequality-in-indonesia-101138 (accessed 24 Sept. 2021).

TNP2K (Tim Nasional Percepatan Penanggulangan Kemiskinan/National Team for the Rapid Reduction of Poverty). 2018. *The Future of the Social Protection System in Indonesia: Social Protection for All.* Office of the Vice President of the Republic of Indonesia. Available at: http://tnp2k.go.id/downloads/the-future-of-the-social-protection-system-in-indonesia (accessed 12 Sept. 2021).

_____. 2021. *Lifecycle Social Protection Assessment: Elderly Vulnerability and Social Protection during Covid-19 Pandemic.* Jakarta: Sekretariat TNP2K. Available at: http://tnp2k.go.id/downloads/elderly-vulnerability-and-social-protection-during-covid-19-pandemic (accessed 3 Mar. 2022).

United Nations. 2018. *Promoting Inclusion through Social Protection, Report on the World Situation 2018.* ST/ESA/366. New York: United Nations Department of Economic and Social Affairs (UNDESA). Available at https://socialprotection.org/discover/publications/report-world-social-situation-2018-promoting-inclusion-through-social (accessed 3 Mar. 2022).

Williamson, J. 2004. "The Washington Consensus as Policy Prescription for Development", Lecture in the series "Practitioners of Development" delivered at the World Bank on 13 Jan. 2004. Available at https://www.piie.com/publications/papers/williamson 0204.pdf (accessed 30 Aug. 2021).

World Bank. 2012a. *History and Evolution of Social Assistance in Indonesia.* Washington, DC: World Bank. Available at: http://hdl.handle.net/10986/12259 (accessed 28 Aug. 2021).

_____. 2012b. *BLT Temporary Unconditional Cash Transfer: Social Assistance and Public Expenditure Review 2.* Available at: http://documents.worldbank.org/curated/en/652291468039239723/pdf/673240WP0BLT0T00Box367866 B00PUBLIC0.pdf (accessed 5 Sept. 2021).

_____. 2017a. *The Republic of Indonesia Social Assistance Reform Programmes.* The World Bank Social Protection and Labor Global Practice East Asia and Pacific Region. Available at: http://documents.worldbank.org/curated/en/353221496152466944/pdf/Programmes-Appraisal-Document-PAD-disclosable-version-P160665-2017-04-15-04202017.pdf (accessed 28 Sept. 2021).

_____. 2017b. *Indonesia Public Expenditure and Financial Accountability.* Jakarta: World Bank. Available at: https://openknowledge.worldbank.org/handle/10986/29820 (accessed 15 Aug. 2019).

_____. 2020. *Indonesia Public Expenditure Review, Spending for Better Results, Chapter 7, Social Assistance.* Available at: https://thedocs.worldbank.org/en/doc/23481590233776625007002 2020/original/IDPER2020Ch7SocialAssistance.pdf (accessed 10 Nov. 2021).

Wulandari, C. and N. Baryshnikova. 2019. "Did Public Cash Transfer Crowd Out Inter-household Transfers in Indonesia? Evidence from Bantuan Langsung Tunai (BLT)", *Jurnal Info Artha* 3, 2: 67–84. Available at https://jurnal.pknstan.ac.id/index.php/JIA/article/view/571 (accessed 30 May 2022).

Yulaswati, V. 2018. "Acceleration in the Implementation of the 2030 Agenda – World Without Poverty in Indonesia", pp. 1–9. Available at: https://www.un.org/development/desa/dspd/wp-content/uploads/sites/22/2018/04/ACCELERATING-IN-THE-IMPLEMENTATION-OF-THE-2030-AGENDA-World-Without-Poverty-in-Indonesia.pdf (accessed 22 May 2022).

Part Two

The Analysis and Structure of Rural Poverty

CHAPTER 4

Thriving but not Growing: Wealth, Food Insecurity and Precarity in Rural Java

Gerben Nooteboom and Pande Made Kutanegara

Javanese Villages Today

If one sits down in the early morning and watches the movement of people in a lowland, rice-producing village in Java, the roads are bustling with traffic. At six o'clock—often even earlier—hundreds of men and dozens of women ride on motorbikes to work in nearby towns and cities. On Java, isolated villages no longer exist (McGee 2009; Rotgé, Matra and Rijanta 2000). In most villages, villagers travel out to construction sites, building projects, maintenance work, or factories. Others work as security guards, drivers or service providers in the lower echelons of the urban and peri-urban economy. Women also leave the villages in lower numbers. They travel to factories or work as cleaners in clinics, schools or shops and eateries along the main roads. Around seven o'clock, dozens of youth ride on bikes or scooters, wearing school uniforms, *jilbab* and bags full of books and portfolios. Small children, in colourful uniforms, walk or bike to the primary school nearby. By eight, the villages look deserted.

Over in the fields, women and a handful of men above 50 years of age are fertilising, cleaning, preparing and weeding. Occasionally, a band of workers harvests *padi*, or collects quarry stones, logs, building materials or sand into a truck. Some villages have local industries which offer low skilled jobs in sawmills or brick, tile and furniture making, or in the production of concrete construction items such as frames, pipes and hollow blocks. Ongoing rapid economic development and improved infrastructure and electricity supply create many opportunities to start a business (Gibson and Olivia 2010: 719). Increasingly, family enterprises, often female headed, manage home businesses producing snacks, food, clothes or embroidery. Usually, each area has its own specialisation.

The Paradox of Increasing Wealth and Persistence of Food Insecurity and Precarity

Although livelihood opportunities in rural Java have improved and people are increasingly finding better paying jobs outside agriculture as a result of economic growth and urban development, rural households remain susceptible to income shocks and economic crises even as poverty is steadily declining. Moreover, nutritional insecurity remains relatively high for the rural poor, as labour outside agriculture remains precarious and insecure for them. This pattern links to wider debates on inclusive development, rural differentiation and precarity in rural areas which attempt to understand the uneven processes of rural change and the impact of diversification and migration on rural development and poverty (Hart, Turton and White 1989; Li 2014; McCarthy 2020; Rigg 2015; Rigg, Salamanca and Thompson 2016; Sunam, Barney and McCarthy 2021). How and why do rural diversification and rural-urban migration not always improve rural livelihoods, decrease poverty and lead to rural development beneficial for all?

Since 2007, poverty in Central Java and Bantul has declined by roughly a third, to 9 per cent and 10.6 per cent respectively in 2019 (BPS 2020). Yet, for many, income and nutritional insecurity are a daily reality; stunting figures remain high, with 27 per cent of all infants stunted in Bantul district (Beal et al. 2018: 3; BPS 2020). This chapter will explore this paradox of growing wealth accompanied by the persistence of poverty and nutritional insecurity. We take a multidimensional approach to understand the existence and persistence of food poverty in a context of agrarian change. What are the drivers of change, and how stable and secure are the new, urban-based sources of livelihood? How are these opportunities distributed, and which old or new inequalities and insecurities are produced? How do we account for the existence and reproduction of old and new forms of precarity in rural areas?

Over the last decades there have been broad structural changes in lowland rice-producing Central Java; "Green Revolution" investments in agriculture have generated higher production, but at higher costs. These changes, accompanied by the commodification of inputs and labour, have produced new economic and ecological vulnerabilities. Less than a third of the farmers now own the land they work on, as landownership is very unequal. The majority of the new generation of labourers has found seasonal jobs in nearby cities or urban areas and moved out of farming, or they combine agriculture with better paying but insecure jobs elsewhere. Agriculture has become a part-time activity for women and older people in Java. Javanese households face shocks and stresses and readily fall back into poverty. This is a *developmental but precarious scenario* where the poorer sections of the population, especially those dependent on one insecure source of income, or the ageing and ill, are vulnerable to livelihood and life-cycle shocks as well as economic crises such as the massive job losses caused by the 1998 Asian financial crisis or the 2020 COVID-19 pandemic.

To study these processes, we selected two hamlets in Sriharjo Village, Bantul, Central Java, called Kedung Miri and Sompok (see Figure 4.1). Our study is based on long-term qualitative and quantitative research in these two villages. In addition, in 2017–18 we surveyed 20 per cent of households in these villages about their occupations, income, livelihood and food security. The data were further elaborated and contextualised by a large study carried out in Pemalang district, Central Java.

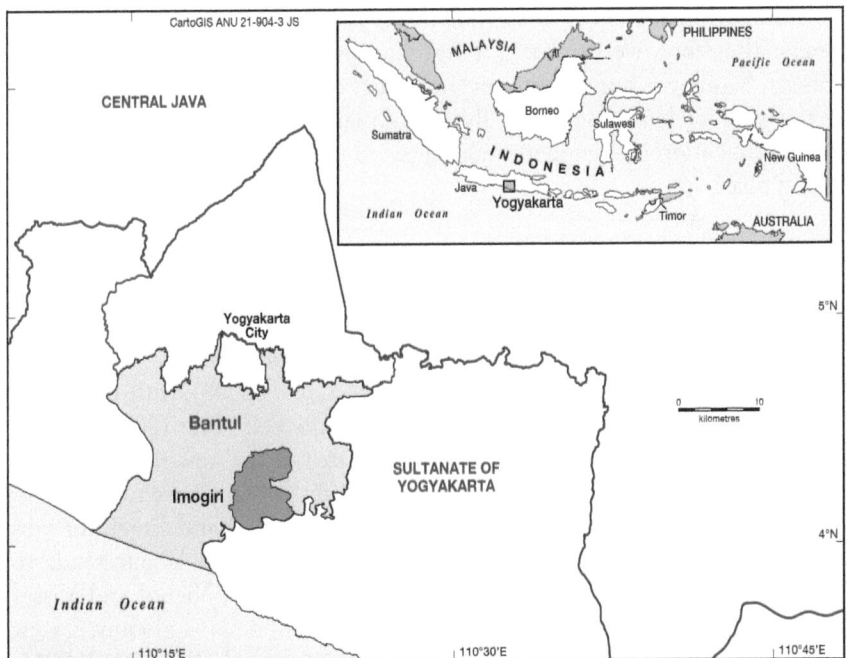

Figure 4.1 Map of Java showing subdistrict Imogiri, Bantul in which the research locations Kedung Miri and Sompok are situated

Two Villages

Sompok and Kedung Miri are situated in Sriharjo, 35 kilometres from Yogyakarta, between the hills in the southeast (Gunung Kidul) and the fertile rice plains of Yogyakarta and Bantul towards the west. Both areas have been major rice- and wood-producing regions throughout agricultural history. Until the 1990s, the villagers of Kedung Miri lived from the production and consumption of rice that they cultivated on tiny rice fields along the river or sharecropped and harvested in the plains of lower Sriharjo, supplemented by maize and cassava cultivated in the then barren, deforested hills (Singarimbun 1996; Singarimbun and Penny 1973). In Sompok, which is poorly endowed with ricefields, large proportions of villagers worked as sharecroppers in nearby villages. Both in Kedung Miri and Sompok, local production was never enough to make ends meet or surmount poverty. Lower Sriharjo is endowed with more rice fields and is situated closer to Yogyakarta and the main road, which made labour migration and trade easier. A few people owned most of the land. Sharecropping and rural labour dominated agricultural activity and poverty remained extensive and deep. In 1992, the poverty rate was over 40 per cent (Kutanegara 2017).

   Since Singarimbun's research in the 1990s, the population has remained steady. Therefore, we can make rough comparisons between the past and present. Moreover, our surveys covered issues comparable to those in studies of the past such as migration, livelihood, land ownership, sharecropping, labour, education and gender, enabling us to understand the major changes taking place.

Drivers of Change: Precarity, Agriculture, Migration and Diversification

There is a clear connection between smallholder agriculture and precarity. In line with the World Bank *World Development Report* (2008), with De Janvry and Sadoulet (2000) and with Delgado-Wise and Veltmeyer (2016: 43), we summarise the consensus in the agrarian debates of the new millennium as follows. Peasants, stuck in low-income agriculture, basically have two options: combine agriculture with wage work, or leave rural areas and search for jobs outside agriculture. As a result of this trend, agricultural labour tends to become feminised and rural areas depopulate (Gartaula, Niehof and Visser 2011; Kelkar 2006). The future of agricultural livelihoods is gloomy, a view that tends to be superimposed on rural areas in general (Rigg 2013, 2015; World Bank 2008, 2017). These commentators perceive the availability of labour opportunities in cities as positive.

This dominant perception of the gloomy future of agriculture in the global South has met with considerable criticism (Li 2014; McCarthy, Vel and Afiff 2012; Pattenden and Wastuti 2021; Rigg, Salamanca and Thompson 2016; Van der Ploeg 2008, 2010; White 2000). These authors criticise the idea that cities offer decent labour opportunities for the massive reserve of surplus labour in rural areas. In the areas under study, migration does offer a way out of agriculture. However, studies by Colfer, Ihalainen and Monterroso (2020), Elmhirst et al. (2017), Rigg, Salamanca and Thompson (2016), White (2000) and Nooteboom (2019), among others, show that wage labour outside agriculture does not lead to abandoning agriculture, although gender roles in agriculture might change. Resilience to shocks and stresses in household incomes might also improve under a changing gender balance. Peluso and Purwanto (2017) illustrate this process by showing how the (transnational) labour migration of marginalised women from a Javanese village leads to investment in rural resources from all the remittances they send back. Female labour migration enables husbands and sons to stay in the villages, thereby leading to a general "regendering" of agriculture and "remaking" of forests (Peluso and Purwanto 2017: 6). In a study of West Bengal, Schenk-Sandbergen (2018: 47) shows that women do stay in villages but do not work in agriculture anymore, as waged jobs are scarce and non-agricultural sources of income are largely absent.

The migration and precarity literature presented above is highly relevant for the analysis of labour migration and gender in rural Java. In the areas under study in Bantul, the situation is comparable in the sense that having predominantly male members working outside the village enables families to increase their household incomes. A focus on higher incomes might obscure personal and collective risks, the persistence of precarity and differential impacts for men and women. What if crises occur and people need to fall back on village-based networks of support which are poorly equipped to receive large numbers of returning labourers? This is what happened after the Asian crisis in 1997–98 (Breman 2002; Nooteboom and Kutanegara 2002), and again during the COVID-19 crisis. The outside jobs also enable villagers to continue their rural livelihoods. However, here it is women and the elderly who keep agriculture running, although men engage in occasional tasks after work and take days off during harvest and planting times.

The concept of precarity is useful as an analytical tool here, for it brings together attention to livelihood insecurity and the structural dimensions of changing labour conditions and capital in a migration context. Analysts use the concept of precarity in studying insecurities and inequalities inherent in the labour migration process, both for the workers and migrants themselves and also for family members, household livelihoods and village life. In this chapter, precarity is understood in its more general sense, referring to the social consequences of poverty and migration, most notably insecurity and vulnerability in relation to gender differences (Kaag et al. 2004; Nooteboom 2015). In other words, precarity is understood here as "a condition experienced by workers whose day-to-day existence is characterised by insecurity and instability" (Eberle and Holliday 2011: 372).

Considering the long history of migration, and of migrants supplementing their rural incomes, it is unclear if rural-urban migration improves rural livelihoods in a structural way and reduces insecurity, vulnerability and precarity as predicted by neoliberal models of rural change. In the following, we look at agrarian change, inequality, gender and precarity in the two research areas through a historical comparative perspective, as both areas are characterised by a long migration history and a long history of social science research.

Long-term Processes of Agrarian Change

Agrarian Production

Until the 1990s, the villagers of Sompok and Kedung Miri lived on the production and consumption of rice that they cultivated on tiny rice fields along the river. Besides rice, they grew maize and cassava, predominantly on the hills and the steep slopes. However, as local production never provided enough to make ends meet, poverty increased over time. In the past, as much as today, village agriculture was insufficient to make ends meet.

The poor circumstances in part derived from unequal landownership in Sriharjo. In this respect, Sriharjo is similar to other villages of Java (Hart, Turton and White 1989). In 1973, in the hamlet of Miri, 84 per cent of the 164 households owned less than a 0.20 hectare [ha], while 50 per cent owned nothing to almost nothing (less than 0.05 ha) (Singarimbun and Penny 1973: 10). Back in the early 1970s, only one third of Sriharjo villagers had enough or just enough (Singarimbun and Penny 1973: 10). In Sriharjo, a small elite of five per cent controlled 43 per cent of all village land, which included lands allocated to village officials. These percentages have remained consistent over the last four decades and reflect levels of inequality found elsewhere in rural Java (Geertz 1963; Hüsken 1989; White 1991). Communal systems, wherein many often landless villagers get access to the rice fields of richer villagers in return for harvest shares, have long existed; but the structural inequalities in land persist (Hart, Turton and White 1989: 243; Nooteboom 2015: 82–6). Today, in Kedung Miri, 30 per cent of the population have no irrigated ricefield (*sawah*) and 20 per cent own between 150 and 400 m^2

(0.015–0.04 ha). For half of the year, two thirds of the population cannot produce enough rice to survive. Only eight per cent of the villagers are completely self-sufficient in rice or able to sell rice. The 2016 survey shows that 29 per cent of all household incomes derive from farm production. In rice-field poor Sompok, the numbers are even lower; half of the population does not own any *sawah* at all. In Sompok, 19 per cent of all household income comes from agricultural production.

In the early 1970s, on average, two thirds of the Sriharjo population faced regular food insecurity and lived below the local standard of having enough (*cukupan*) (Singarimbun and Penny 1973: 14). To supplement their meagre food stocks, in the harvesting season, both men and women worked as harvesters (*derep*) on the plains of Bantul, Yogyakarta, Sleman and Purworejo, while others found work as pedicab drivers in Yogyakarta, and occasionally in construction. A small proportion of village girls and young women worked as domestic workers in Yogyakarta or Jakarta. Boys joined bands of workers in the sugarcane fields of Central Java. Dozens opted for a better living elsewhere and tried their luck as (trans)migrants in Kalimantan or Sumatra. Those who stayed in the village escaped hunger by sharecropping in the lowlands and eating *tiwul*, dried cassava, grown on *ladang* (dry fields). Cash incomes from palm sugar production or rural labour supplemented wages in kind and basic village food production. In the rainy season, those without land could sharecrop or rent *ladang* lands in the hills from richer villagers on a sharecropping basis (Singarimbun and Penny 1973: 12). This agro-ecological system started to change in the early 1990s, due to increased mobility and the rise of (peri-)urban labour opportunities.

Today, the *ladang* fields in the hills are forested, and hill land is no longer available for food production (Graaf, Nooteboom and Kutanegara 2015). Afforestation has excluded poor and old villagers from cassava planting and dry land share cropping opportunities. As incomes from urban labour enabled villagers to buy rice, this livelihood strategy is redundant. Cassava and *tiwul* had become survival foods of the past. During the last two decades, migration and government programmes have improved standards of living in the village. All houses have electricity now, and most families own or have access to a mobile phone.

Mobility

In Kedung Miri and Sompok, where labour opportunities lie almost entirely outside the village and where no public transport exists, motorbikes provide access to work and education; 74 per cent of the households have at least one motorbike, and 41 per cent of households have more than one. The poorest families, among which are elderly, single women and widows/widowers, generally lack a motorbike, which excludes them from work outside the village.

Mobility is at the centre of village life. More families have a relative working in the city than those who do not. Incomes earned in the city and remittances drive the local economy, boosting house construction, trade, transport and small-scale services. Some villagers "follow projects" and live and work for months in Java's cities before coming home "to rest" for a few weeks. Others work irregularly in one of the larger nearby cities, or they commute daily to Bantul or Yogyakarta. Long-distance migrants are mostly male. The villages have very few female migrant workers (*Tenaga Kerja Wanita*—TKW) who work abroad. Almost two thirds of the interviewed villagers who work, labour outside the village. Of these, 30 per cent are temporal migrants who stay overnight outside the village. 43 per cent of all villagers who work are in construction, while 6 per cent and 15 per cent in the two villages respectively identify as farmers, and 6.5 per cent and 13 per cent as agricultural labourers.

Remittances are crucial for sustaining the family at home. Workers who labour in the city for longer periods, and regularly send remittances home, support household expenditure on food and daily necessities, motorbikes, education and house improvements in the village. Some commuters also invest remittances in goats or cows, but few families have bank savings. In Kedung Miri, 50 per cent send remittances home and in Sompok, about 35 per cent do so. On average, these remittances amount to between IDR 0.3 and 1 million (22–74 USD) per month.

Each labour option in the city involves different engagements with the local economy. Migrants either engage in village agriculture seasonally, come home for the harvest and/or field preparation, or do some work after coming home, such as cutting grass for livestock. These options are linked to different livelihood styles, to specific combinations of local and outside earned incomes, which makes it possible to diversify incomes and risks while remaining attached to village life. As a result of these different options, vulnerabilities to shocks and stresses differ among households (see also Nooteboom 2006, 2015 on these livelihood styles). As a result of increasing jobs in the city, more agricultural tasks are left to partners or elderly members of the extended household. Today, one third of the farmers and agricultural labourers who remain working in the villages are women. The richer the households are, the less likely that women report working in agriculture. Rich landowning families tend to hire labour, or give land out for sharecropping.

Gender

In the 1990s, there was a dramatic uptake by village women, seeking a better life, by working outside the village. About 20 per cent of the women of Sriharjo worked outside the village for longer periods of time. They made up a quarter of all those migrating for reasons of labour in the 1990s. The majority of the female migrants were females aged 12–24. Next to the desire for a different and better life, this migration was born of dire need. Releasing pressure on household budgets, these women migrated to Yogyakarta and Jakarta to work as domestic helpers or in factories for a couple of years. A daughter working in the city saved a mouth to feed in the village and occasionally yielded some extra income. In the mid-1990s, of these young migrating women, 53 per cent worked as domestic helpers and 34 per cent found work in factories. The rest were engaged as babysitters, shop assistants, or traders (Kutanegara 2017). Young women came home only at the end of Ramadan, often bringing some food, presents and cash with them for their family members (ibid.). After, often delayed, marriage, most of these working women eventually returned to the village.

Three decades later, this situation has changed. Now, most young women below 20 remain at school. When women work, they work in factories, shops, trade and services rather than as domestic helpers. Today, girls are becoming better educated than boys as they stay longer at school than their male counterparts do. This has led to significant changes such as women's age of marriage, the age at which women have their first child and the kinds of jobs potentially open to women. Eighteen per cent of all women, with an average age of 25, work outside the village, but now in the region rather than Jakarta. Some also become teachers or nurses, or make it into white-collar office jobs; increasingly, they continue to live in the village. Marriage age is still rising: almost half of the working women between 20 and 30 are married. However, women workers still earn, on average, only two thirds of a male salary.

There is a paradox here. Whereas in the past, young migrant girls worked as domestic helpers in faraway cities—enjoying relative freedom before becoming "dutiful wives and mothers" once their children were born (Chan 2018: 100; see also Koning 2005)—now jobs are available nearer to the village, in shops and factories. These opportunities may occasionally support personal development and some freedoms for women, and do enable them to live in the village, where work can be combined with domestic chores and childcare. However, living in the village also forces women to comply with traditional village norms. For men, having daughters and spouses staying in the village is close to ideal. They hope to earn enough to allow their wife not to have to work at all; a wife may live the "good life" in the village where life is cheap, safe and a good place to raise a family. However, village life also means complying with village values such as sharing and reciprocity and the strict expression of Islamic values and conservative, patriarchal views on women's "decency". Higher education and sometimes owning a business can help a woman to escape the pressure of becoming merely a "dutiful wife" who takes care of the children, the house and household matters only.[1]

Less than a third of the women in the villages are able to live up to the traditional ideal of not having to work. Half of the women in the village work in agriculture to earn a little extra money, or run a little shop, business or trade. As most male workers are absent, women take on more agricultural tasks than before. About a quarter of these women have no husband, and are aged above 60. Tasks which were previously performed mostly by men are now partly or fully carried out by women. A study in Comal, Central Java lists some key tasks which were done solely by men in the past, and which are now done largely by women. These include the transport of seedlings (77 per cent of which is now undertaken by women), fertilising (37 per cent), cutting paddy (58 per cent), threshing paddy (43 per cent), and transporting the harvest (30 per cent) (Nooteboom 2019). Today, in Kedung Miri and Sompok, the percentage of female-headed households whose main occupation is agriculture is almost twice as high as the percentage of male-headed households with agriculture as the principal occupation. As incomes in agriculture are only about a third of those in urban jobs, and as women become more dependent on work in agriculture while men become dependent on irregular urban jobs, precarity remains a feature for both those dependent on wage labour and those who remain working in agriculture.

Livelihood Changes

The role of agriculture in village livelihoods has also changed dramatically as livelihoods continue to diversify (Rigg 2013, 2015; Rigg and Vandergeest 2012). In this respect, the rural transition mirrors the scenario outlined above, although Rigg's analysis does not look at changing gender roles. Increased income diversification and mobility also produce a general (re-)feminisation of agriculture.

During the 1990s, more than 40 per cent of the population was still entirely dependent on incomes from farming and farming related jobs, while just under a third combined agricultural work with non-agricultural occupations, and the remaining 28 per cent relied on non-agricultural occupations (Kutanegara 2017). A generation later, the picture has reversed. Less than 22 per cent of the heads of households in Kedung Miri and 19 per cent in Sompok identify their main occupation as agricultural; 60 per cent identify their main occupation as non-agricultural and the remaining 13 per cent are not working (mostly elderly). Of the household heads aged between 20 and 50, less than 15 per cent claim to be dependent on agriculture. Dependency on farming as a primary source of income has thus been halved in the last two decades. The average age of farmers is rising; in Central Java, it is rising even faster than the overall Indonesian average age (50 in 2014).[2] The average age of farmers (landowners and agricultural workers alike) has risen from 48 to 55 since 1992 (Nooteboom 2019). Dependence on urban jobs, and regular absences of men of working age, make it more difficult to organise collective labour activities in the village, such as house construction (*sambatan*) and village road repairs (see also Kutanegara 2017; Nooteboom 2015).

The changes in income and orientation to agriculture also affect the environment. Since the mid-1990s, landowners have taken marginal lands out of food production and planted trees which they find more profitable. The fields they use often belong to the old local elites and were previously sharecropped by landless villagers. This tree planting is also a sign of general stability in land rights and property (tree crops are considered a safe investment, and landowners expect to reap the benefits of tree planting after 10 years and for up to 40 years). The shift from perennial crops to tree crops involves a changing timeframe and might signify increased property security and trust. It also marks a break with the past that reflects a general decline in dependence on food production and an increase in dependence on other sources of income. Until the early 2000s, landless farmers could grow food crops under sharecropping arrangements, but now land is becoming the site of speculation and accumulation, the means to produce tree crops to be harvested by the landowner whenever needed. Although reforestation has some ecological benefits with regard to carbon sequestration, and the government and some NGOs herald it as an environmental success, tree planting offers a case of adverse incorporation, excluding weaker members of society from access to food and local resources and ultimately making them even more dependent on the market.

With these changes in rural areas, inequalities continue and grow. Although landless villagers now engage much more in urban off-farm labour opportunities, and many have moved (just) above the poverty line, incomes from richer families and land-owning families are rising relatively faster. Extra incomes from farming (and increasingly from wood), and the higher education of family members, enable them to earn higher wages in better jobs (the landowning families of the previous generation could educate their children for longer and at better schools). A recent study in Comal, Central Java (Kanó 2015; Nooteboom 2019) illustrates this: today, incomes are more unequal than in the past. Kanó notes that the "income disparity among sample households has not diminished, but its principal cause has shifted from the gap in the possession of agrarian resources to the gap in access to the income earning opportunity in non-agricultural activities" (2015: 33).

In the following section, we take a closer look at the impact of the changes described above, and a more detailed look at poverty and food security in Sriharjo through the findings of the 2018 food security survey.

Impact of the Agrarian Change Scenario on Poverty and Prosperity

With respect to the foregoing dynamics and the increase in income opportunities and cash incomes outside the village, we were interested in how this translates into family incomes and consumption patterns in the village. We assessed local definitions of poverty following the Stages of Progress (SoP) methodology described in the introduction of this book (and cf. Krishna 2006). In both villages, we organised discussions in separate groups of men and women. After each discussion group had finished, the outcomes from the women's discussions were presented to the men and vice versa, and the differences were discussed. Table 4.1 is a compilation of informants' responses and offers an overview of local markers of wealth and poverty as described by villagers in their own terms.

Table 4.1   Compilation of informants' responses: Poverty ranking Kedung Miri and Sompok

Men		Women	
Rich (Sugih)	*Civil servants / village officials*	*Living well (Enak)*	*Civil servants*
	Owning a car		Owning a car or motorbike
	Able to buy land, sawah or trees/wood (*kayu*)		no need to buy rice/ able to harvest enough rice, fruit trees
	Able to pay higher education for children (incl. university)		Good house, ceramics, furniture, toilet
			Owning animals (*ternak*) (cows, goats, chicken)

Table 4.1 (*cont'd*)

Men		Women	
			Always enough to eat (chicken eggs, krupuk, vegetables, fruits).
			Able to send children to school
Having all you need (Sedengan)	*Rich farmers and traders*	*Having enough (Cukup)*	
	Able to buy new motor bike		Having some animals (*ternak*)
	Pay for all schooling costs		Permanent house with tiled roof
	Invest in agricultural inputs, lease/rent or sharecrop land		Have savings
			Abe to afford transportation
Making ends meet (Pas-pasan)		*Basic but enough (Sederhana)*	
	Able to renovate the house/concrete house		Able to eat tempeh/ prawn crackers regularly
	Buy one or more cows and loan them out (gadduh)		Farmers who own, lease or sharecrop land (garap tanah)
	Able to pay credit for a cheap motor bike or buying second hand		Those who work in construction projects/ rural labourers (buruh sawah)
	Owning a number of goats		Having cattle or care for others' cattle (*nggaduh*)
			Have some gold savings (jewellery)
			Old motorbike
Have nots (Ra-nduwe (Owning nothing/not having [have not])		*Have nots (tidak punya)*	
	Owns some chickens		Own house but not enough to eat
	Eating only tempeh/ tahu as a side dish		Eating simply (local vegetables, cheap fish, tahu, local egg, sambal)

(*cont'd overleaf*)

Table 4.1 (*cont'd*)

Men		Women	
	Can afford to purchase rice		Buying cheap rice if money is available
Poorest of the poor (Ra-ndwe)		*Poor (Miskin)*	
	Eating whatever is available locally to find, such as maize, tubers, cassava		Living in a house with others (rumah numpang). House made from bamboo. Built from aid
			Receiving alms (zakat fitrah)
			No work and nobody offers work. Food is inadequate, just eating what is available
	Regularly asking neighbours to share food		Living in a house of/ with others (*rumah numpang*). House from bamboo. House of aid programme.
			Receiving alms (*Penerima zakat fitrah*)
			No work and nobody offers work Food is not enough, just eating what is available
			No animals at all, no support

The motor bike is the main distinction between being very poor and being able to cope. Those who lack a motorbike are seen as very poor and owning only one second hand or cheap motorbike is taken as a clear characteristic of being poor. People regularly commented: "Without a motorbike, it is impossible to work in the city and earn a decent income here." Having no motorbike means having no income. The SoP also shows that having sufficient food and food consumption are still major markers of being poor or less poor. The poor today do face food insecurities and are not able to meet the ideal of a proper meal: rice three times a day, with at least one meal per day when rice is supplemented with sambal, some vegetables, *tahu/tempeh*, egg, mie, fish (often dried) and occasionally chicken or meat. Women's assessments were generally more food- or consumption-focused than were men's; the male groups more often included capital goods or assets such as kinds of houses, and productive assets such as land and motor bikes. Men also focused more than women did on status symbols such as types of motor bikes, jobs and cars. Although productive agricultural assets, such as land and cattle, are still seen as a major source of rural livelihood and as distinctive of wealth and poverty, both men and women also mentioned access to urban work.

To capture the dynamics of poverty and to understand changes over time, after the SoP, participants were asked to categorise all of the households in the sample into one of four status categories, namely: A (poor then, poor now); B (poor then, not poor now); C (not poor then, poor now); and D (not poor then, not poor now) (Table 4.2; related discussion is given in Chapter 12 [Table 12.2]).

Table 4.2   Poverty ranking and categorisation of livelihood change per household in the hamlets of Kedung Miri and Sompok in Sriharjo Village, Bantul, Central Java, 1999–2018

Category		%
A	Poor then and still poor (*poor*)	25
B	Poor then, not poor now (*improved*)	65
C	Not poor then, poor now (*new poor*)	2
D	Not poor then, not poor now (*rich*)	8

Almost two thirds of the surveyed households were clearly doing better over time in the last 15 years, but a quarter remained poor. The main reasons given by respondents for livelihood improvement included better food and nutrition, improved housing conditions, improved wage-earning opportunities in the city, improved education for all children and the availability of motorbikes. The poor, unable to diversify income, rely more on agricultural incomes; some may be too old to do so. The differences between rich and poor households are striking, with wealth based both on higher incomes from agriculture and non-farm incomes. This is reflected in consumption patterns and proportions of income for each SoP category, presented in Table 4.3.

Farm-based incomes of the poor (A) and the new poor (C) have dropped, but are still significant (almost a quarter of total household income). Those able to rise out of poverty (category B) derive less than one fifth of their income from farming, and a much larger share of household income from non-farm incomes (71 per cent), which is basically wages earned in the city. They also earn the highest percentage from household and home industries

Table 4.3 Sources of income, expenditure and social assistance by household category (SoP) (2018)

Category	A (*poor*)	B (*improved*)	C (*new poor*)	D (*rich*)	Average HH income/expenditure
On-farm income	4.1	6	1.3	14.7	6.6
Non-farm income	11.3	23.8	1.6	43.5	22.8
HH industry income	6.7	10.2	1.6	15.5	9.9
Government assistance	3	3.4	0.1	0.7	2.9
Total HH income (year)	**25.1**	**43.5**	**4.6**	**74.4**	**42.1**
Food expenditure	7.7	12	13.9	14.6	11.2
Non-food expenditure	3.1	10	6.5	13.3	8.5
STR** expenditure	2	4.5	4.1	3.5	3.7
Total reported expenditure*	**12.8**	**26.5**	**24.5**	**31.5**	**23.4**
Share of government assistance (monetary and non-monetary)	20 %	12 %	4 %	1 %	10 %

Notes:
*1 USD = IDR 13,500.
**STR stands for Social Transactions and Reciprocity. It refers to expenditures for social reasons such as donations for weddings, funerals, hospital costs of fellow villagers, and reciprocal help. It includes help to family members, neighbours, and the village poor.
*** Total income does not necessarily balance with reported expenditures. In the survey, the focus was on household food production and income, and monthly monetary household expenditures. Wages in kind, such as self-grown food, harvest shares from sharecropping and wages in kind (for example padi), were calculated as monetary income at market prices. The survey did not ask about the consumption of home grown or earned food. Additionally, some under-reporting might play a role here. Large expenditures, such as on rituals (*selamatan*), cattle, motorbikes, school and hospital fees, funerals and savings, might not be mentioned by informants.

(almost one third). Families in the B category could fall back into poverty if any difficulties or household disasters occurred, such as a pandemic or other economic crisis.

On average, the improved families also receive a slightly higher amount of government support per household than the poor (this includes conditional cash transfers as well as help for house improvement(s) and entrepreneurial development). Of the 40 surveyed households in Kedung Miri in 2017, 13 per cent mentioned receiving government support of some sort; in 2018, the proportion in Sompok was almost 50 per cent. Government support basically concerns small-scale food aid (Raskin[3]), conditional cash transfers (PKH[4]), incidental help for the improvement of living conditions, house construction, sanitation, or food-for-work programmes (see Chapter 12 for a discussion of these programmes).

Food Security and Vulnerability

How do these differences in class translate into different forms of food consumption? The poor spent more than 60 per cent of their income on food (Table 4.3). As incomes in kind are hard to get for the poor, who are usually landless, they spend a higher percentage of household incomes on rice, *tahu/tempeh* and eggs (Table 4.4). They spend less on food items which are considered luxurious and not part of a poor people's diet, as indicated in the SoP. Examples of more luxurious foodstuffs are meat, vegetables and children's snacks. Although parents indicated that it was very hard to reject requests from their children for small amounts of money and snacks to take to school, this category of household spends much less on these items. The proportion of money spent on tobacco by the poor, however, is comparatively high (15 per cent).

Table 4.4 Percentage of household expenditure on key food items (2018)

Kedung Miri and Sompok	Poor	Non-poor
Rice	25%	18%
Tofu/tempeh	9%	7%
Eggs	7%	5%
Fish/meat	2%	4%
Vegetables	12%	17%
Tobacco	15%	11%
Children's snack (*jajan*)	12%	22%

The SoP and in-depth qualitative research gave more insight into the processes behind these differences. Poorer households told us they still regularly cut back on meals, from eating three times to two times a day and/or by cutting back on expensive food items such as fish or meat, vegetables and good quality rice. They never eat meat at home, and some other foods—tahu/tempeh, eggs and purchased vegetables[5]—are eaten only when they can be afforded, and on special occasions such as ceremonies (*selamatan*). Many of the poorest are women without children or widows living alone.

Household food security was also assessed, with survey data revealing that 11 per cent were severely food insecure, 4 per cent moderately insecure, 4 per cent mildly insecure and 83 per cent food secure (Figure 4.2). This correlates roughly with the 25 per cent of the villagers being poor as assessed by the SoP. It also helps to explain the high stunting figures for infants in Bantul district (27 per cent of infants).

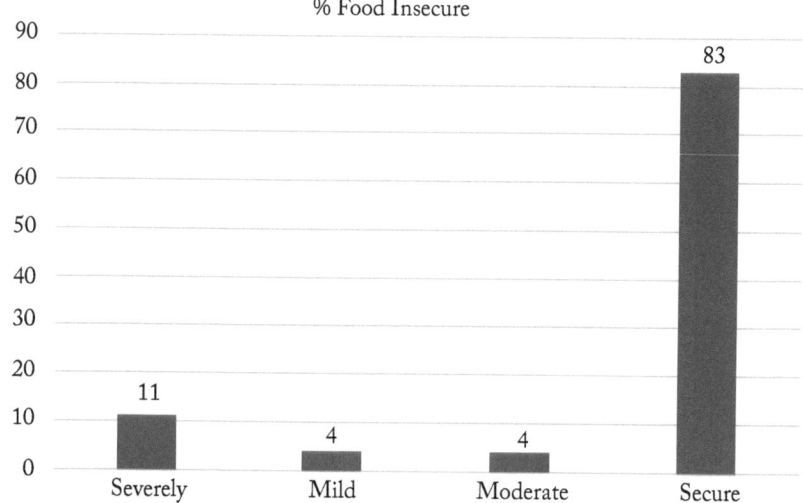

Figure 4.2   Percentages of food insecurity in Kedung Miri and Sompok (2018)

Analysis: Vulnerability and Sources of Vulnerability

Rural poverty is on the decline, but minimum wages in both industry and agriculture remain very low (IDR 1 million—1.5 million a month [USD 74–111]), with IDR 1.2 million a month being the (very low) regional poverty line in Bantul. At the same time, government poverty relief and social welfare are growing in importance.

Poverty, food insecurity and precarity can be found among four kinds of people: (1) widows, the ill and the handicapped; (2) families without assets or stable incomes; (3) outcasts; and (4) people dependent on low-paid, single sources of income. Structural inequalities in access to land and resources and the structure of unprotected and less stable jobs in the city, as well as the prospect of retirement without an income, often make life precarious for these categories:

(1) Widows, ill and handicapped people are often found in food insecure households which comprise people who do not have access to urban jobs and who do not own land. Among the most precarious cases we found, are women whose husbands had left and did not support them; usually the husband had either migrated without maintaining contact or had (re)married outside the village. These *janda migran* (migration widows), who do not (or not regularly) receive remittances, had to raise children on their own and manage their tiny farms with ever-declining returns. Others had to sell all assets to cover their husband's debts and still others live from the sparse earnings of children who have had to drop out of high school in order to work. Another category of widows living precarious lives are the aged who do not have children in the village, who do not own land and who receive little to no support from relatives or government programmes. Just by virtue of being disconnected, they have no family members or children who are benefitting from the new and abundant wage labour opportunities in the city. Although they sometimes live with other relatives, these widows or couples depend greatly on support from the neighbourhood and, increasingly, from government support. Other categories of precarious households are households with disabled children who keep parents at home, and households that have fallen into poverty because of misfortune or an accident that rendered them unable to work or forced them to sell assets.

(2) Couples and families without land or productive assets, without children, with young children, or with children who are unable or unwilling to care for them form a group which can be divided into two subcategories: (1) young couples without inherited land, with young children, dependent on a single source of income without any form of social insurance (such as occasional workers in construction). Often, incomes are irregular if the husband is still young or is unable or unwilling to work for longer periods per year in Jakarta or Surabaya; (2) older couples, over 55, too old to work outside the village, without proper assets, without children or with children unable or unwilling to support them. This also includes families in which a family member is

ill for a long period of the year, or who has been injured, for example in a traffic accident or at the workplace.

(3) Respondents identified a third category, of outcasts, referred to as "notorious" (*orang nakal*): people involved in gambling, speculative trade, drinking, promiscuous relationships, criminality and so on, as well as the mentally ill. These people are unable to save or accumulate money, are excluded from society, and are often involved in dangerous, conspicuous, or risky behaviour that can quickly deplete family resources and lead to poverty. In each village we encountered a couple of these cases and a large number of stories circulating around them. The worst cases of the *orang nakal* are pushed out of the social fabric and often forced to leave the village.

(4) The last category of precarious people consists of those who are not seen as poor at the moment, but who are potentially at risk because of being dependent on a single source of income. Entire family networks can be dependent on one individual working in irregular jobs in construction, small trade or on plantations.

This simple typology shows that ownership and control over local resources such as land, trees and cattle remain an important factor in resilience, unless households have sufficiently diversified their incomes (i.e. multiple incomes of husband and wife, savings [gold, assets], a family member working outside the village, a small pension, a little shop or trade, or living with or having supportive children with reasonably good incomes). In the event of misfortune, illness or death of a family member, these families can cover their financial problems via their own means, and usually have sufficient social networks or assets to recover.

A huge diversity exists among these populations. Being poor (and being seen as poor) depend to a large extent on whether people have access to work, land, or additional sources of income (including savings, remittances, or rent). Interviews show that having time for the children and for the household, and earning enough money in the city to raise a prosperous family in the "safe", "good" and "cheap" environment of the village, remain the ideal for many, both men and women. At the same time, those who stay in the village (especially "preferred children" who are going to inherit land, and the "dutiful daughters" who stay to care for the parents), are seen as, and feel like losers. This is the double-edged development that precarity produces. Often husbands earn enough only to sustain their family in the village; marriage and family life suffer from the long absence of spouses; and women who live the idealised life in the village feel confined, bored and frustrated.

If family members are unable to work, or if labour opportunities decline in the future, these families might easily slide back into poverty. This is especially the case for women, as not all have been able to benefit from higher education, and many lack opportunities for physical and upward mobility. Almost a sixth of the households are female-headed. Very few inspiring and suitable jobs for women exist in rural areas. Increasingly, women from poor families work in low-paid agricultural jobs or, at best, start their own businesses. Women from poorer families need to work in agriculture. The migration for low-paid jobs instead produces new forms of precarity, while some of the old forms remain. There are few alternative sources of income and when people lose jobs, have accidents, or fall ill, very few resources are left. Moreover, for women forced to stay in the village, their economic, social and moral duties and expected tasks are extensive. Aside from their responsibilities to raise a family, care for parents, run the small farm and sometimes tend the animals, their dependence on working men with single sources of income continues the risk of ending up or falling back into living precarious lives.

Thriving but not Growing

This chapter argues that despite the new labour opportunities in cities such as Yogyakarta, Surabaya and Jakarta and in neighbouring peri-urban areas, which have increased household incomes and helped families to move out of poverty, progress in the rural Javanese economy is thin and many rural livelihoods remain unstable and insecure. The available low-skilled labour opportunities for villagers do not offer permanent jobs with labour rights and social protection; rather, they can be characterised as ongoing adverse incorporation in the regional economy. This scenario highlights the precarious nature of the new labour opportunities while new and better jobs are available only to more educated, urban people.

In comparison with the early 1990s, villagers in rice-producing rural Java no longer depend solely on agriculture, but agriculture remains important and a primary employment option. Cheap unskilled labour from the villages is in high demand in the cities, and urban incomes yield much better incomes for villagers than village-based work. As most work outside the village is in nearby areas (Yogyakarta is 30–40 km maximum from home), villagers can commute or join work groups on a project basis (for example, in road and house construction), while they continue to live in their village. This reduces risk and dependency on a single family member and a single source of income. As a result of structural changes in the labour market, household incomes in the villages are rising in general, and we are seeing better access to (predominantly urban) wages and multiple sources of income for both men and women. If families own land, urban jobs are combined with local agricultural jobs; agriculture can provide an income to those who have become too old for work in the city. However, if too many people retire or fall back on the agricultural sector in the village, there will not be enough work and income for all.

All rural youth are educated now and levels of education are still rising, with young women being more highly educated than men. Due to better education and the availability of semi-skilled jobs, including those closer to or in the village, the youngest generation of women and men work only outside agriculture. For women, fewer labour opportunities close to the village are available than for men. Although women are better educated, careers for them seem stagnant.

With respect to land and the role of agriculture, we see on average a diminishing importance of agriculture for rural incomes, but increasing dependencies on agricultural incomes for specific categories of people, such as retired urban workers, female-headed households and widows. Agriculture has become more feminised, grey and exclusive, like in other rural areas in Indonesia (Colfer, Ihalainen and Monterroso 2020; Elmhirst et al. 2017). Incomes from agriculture remain important for households who are unable to diversify their livelihoods into the urban economy (Elmhirst 2011). For them, ownership of and access to agricultural land still have a key role in providing a safety net, food security and a basic income. However, such a provision remains difficult for at least two thirds of the rural population and increasingly the elderly, women and the landless poor face exclusion from agriculture as a fall-back mechanism. Next to the mounting inequality in land ownership, access to marginal lands, previously used for food production by the village poor, has also become limited. All *ladang* fields in the hills were reforested during the last two decades. While this has had some positive environmental effects, such reforestation limits agricultural opportunities for nearly landless villagers, while future incomes from wood and timber will be for the landowners and village elites.

Added to declining fall-back opportunities in agriculture, combined with a dependence on single sources of urban income, the risk of shocks and stresses adds to the persistent vulnerability of the village poor. Health and lifecycle risks, as well as economic crises (such as pandemics) can easily throw people back into poverty. Although government programmes are a great help for many individual households, village networks of exchange and reciprocity and moral economies of social support—which may be invisible to statistical analysis—are slowly being eroded as a result of migration, commoditisation of exchange relations and the individualised nature of governmental aid programmes. New lifestyles and food habits, changing consumption patterns, regular shortages of money and agricultural production systems that do not provide a stable and nutritious livelihood base conspire together to generate nutritional insecurity for a quarter of the rural households.

In conclusion, we have seen that although rural livelihoods in Java have tended to avoid the agrarian crisis predicted by agrarian pessimists, diversification into the urban economy has not brought new and stable forms of prosperity. Poverty and insecurity in rural, rice- producing Java have become more gendered as younger men continue to move out; agriculture, with its lower incomes, caters in greater proportions to women and older farmers.

In general, and as described in the introduction of this book, we see inequality in the Indonesian economy increasing in rural areas. Those with access to better jobs, multiple sources of income, new trading opportunities in the cities and/or with large quantities of land are doing well. Those who are dependent on single sources of income, or wage labour, and those less privileged in terms of health, age, gender, education or labour opportunities are sometimes facing severe income and food security issues. From a structural point of view, inequalities between lower and better educated, rural and urban, old and young have increased.

Notes

[1] Of course, this does not apply only to rural Java. Similar trends are visible in rural India, where the "good woman" ideology and patriarchal notions seem to be on the rise, undermining the life, work and freedoms of poor rural women (cf. Schenk-Sandbergen 2018: 49).

[2] In the case of female heads of household, this phenomenon is less clearly discernible because of the fact that unlike in the past, widows are seen as heads of households but do not always call themselves farmers or even mention being dependent on farming.

[3] Raskin combines the words *Beras* (rice) and *Miskin* (poor): rice for the poor. It concerns the delivery of cheap (subsidised) rice packages (usually 10 kg) to poor families.

[4] *Program Keluarga Harapan* (lit. 'hope for families' programme).

[5] This concerns vegetables which are purchased at the market, in shops or from sellers, such as cabbage, carrots, leek, onions and *pakchai*. The poor do eat locally available (leafy) vegetables, such as cassava leaves, papaya leaves, ferns, water spinach (*kangkung*), amaranth and all kinds of edible tree leaves such as *kelor* (*moringa oleifera*).

References

Beal, T. et al. 2018. "A Review of Child Stunting Determinants in Indonesia", *Maternal & Child Nutrition* 14, 4: 1–10.

BPS (Badan Pusat Statistik/Statistics Indonesia online). 2020. *Social and Population Section*. Available at https://bps.go.id/ (accessed 7 Apr. 2020).

Breman, J. 2002. *Good Times and Bad Times in Rural Java: Case Study of Socio-Economic Dynamics in Two Villages towards the End of the Twentieth Century*. Leiden: Brill.

Chan, C. 2018. *In Sickness and in Wealth: Migration, Gendered Morality, and Central Java*. Bloomington: Indiana University Press.

Colfer, C.J.P., M. Ihalainen and I. Monterroso. 2020. *Understanding Gender Dynamics in the Context of Rural Transformation Processes: An East Kalimantan Case Study* (Vol. 212). Bogor: CIFOR (Center for International Forestry Research).

De Janvry, A. and E. Sadoulet. 2000. "Rural Poverty in Latin America: Determinants and Exit Paths", *Food Policy* 25, 4: 389–409.

Delgado-Wise, R. and H. Veltmeyer. 2016. *Agrarian Change, Migration and Development*. Black Point, NS: Fernwood Publishing.

Eberle, M.L. and I. Holliday. 2011. "Precarity and Political Immobilisation: Migrants from Burma in Chiang Mai, Thailand", *Journal of Contemporary Asia* 41, 3: 371–92.

Elmhirst, R. 2011. "Migrant Pathways to Resource Access in Lampung's Political Forest: Gender, Citizenship and Creative Conjugality", *Geoforum* 42: 173–83.

Elmhirst, R. et al. 2017. "Gender and Generation in Engagements with Oil Palm in East Kalimantan, Indonesia: Insights from Feminist Political Ecology", *Journal of Peasant Societies* 44, 6: 1135–57. doi: 10.1080/03066150.2017.1337002.

Gartaula, H.N., A. Niehof and L. Visser. 2011. "Feminisation of Agriculture as an Effect of Male Out-migration: Unexpected Outcomes from Jhapa District, Eastern Nepal", *International Journal of Interdisciplinary Social Sciences* 5, 2: 565–77.

Geertz, C. 1963. *Agricultural Involution: The Process of Ecological Change in Indonesia*. Berkeley, CA: University of California Press.

Gibson, J. and S. Olivia. 2010. "The Effect of Infrastructure Access and Quality on Non-Farm Enterprises in Rural Indonesia", *World Development* 38, 5: 717–26.

Graaf, L. de, G. Nooteboom and P. M. Kutanegara. 2015. *Rural Transformation and Afforestation in Java: Understanding Farm Tree Planting in Central Java, Indonesia; its Reasons and Social Consequences*. Paper presented at the Workshop on Development and Environmental Changes, Graduate School, Sophia University, Tokyo, Japan, 9 Jan. 2015. Available at https://www.researchgate.net/publication/284028775_RURAL_TRANSFORMATION_AND_AFFORESTATION_IN_JAVA_UNDERSTANDING_FARM_TREE_PLANTING_IN_CENTRAL-JAVA_INDONESIA_ITS_REASONS_AND_SOCIAL_CONSEQUENCES (accessed 1 Apr. 2022).

Hart, G., A. Turton and B. White. 1989. *Agrarian Transformations: Local Processes and the State in Southeast Asia*. Berkeley, CA: University of California Press.

Hüsken, F. 1989. *Een Dorp op Java: Sociale Differentiatie in een Boerengemeenschap, 1850–1980.* 2nd ed. Overveen: ACASEA.

Kaag, M. et al. 2004. "Ways Forward in Livelihood Research", in *Globalization and Development: Themes and Concepts in Current Research*, ed. D. Kalb, W. Pansters and H. Siebers. Dordrecht, Boston, and London: Kluwer Academic Publishers, pp. 50–74.

Kanó, H. 2015. "Deagrarianization and Shift to a Service-based Economy: Outline of Socio-economic Change in Comal since 1990". Paper presented at the Analytical workshop on the Comal Restudy, Gadjah Mada University, Yogyakarta, March 2015.

Kelkar, G. 2006. *The Feminization of Agriculture in Asia: Implications for Women's Agency and Productivity.* New Delhi: UNIFEM South Asia Regional Office.

Koning, J. 2005. "The Impossible Return? The Post-migration Narratives of Young Women in Rural Java", *Asian Journal of Social Science* 33, 2: 165–85.

Krishna, A. 2006. "Pathways out of and into Poverty in 36 villages of Andhra Pradesh, India", *World Development* 34: 271–88.

Kutanegara, P.M. 2017. *Poverty, Crises and Social Solidarity in Sriharjo.* Yogyakarta: Percetakan Kanisius.

Kutanegara, P.M. and G. Nooteboom. 2002. "Forgotten Villages, the Effects of the Crisis and the Role of the Government in Rural Java", in *Riding a Tiger: Dilemmas of Integration and Decentralization in Indonesia*, ed. C. Holtzappel, M. Sanders and M. Titus. Amsterdam: Rozenberg, pp. 248–77.

Li, T.M. 2014. *Land's End: Capitalist Relations on an Indigenous Frontier.* Durham, NC and London: Duke University Press.

McCarthy, J.F. 2020. "The Paradox of Progressing Sideways: Food Poverty and Livelihood Change in the Rice Lands of Outer Island Indonesia", *Journal of Peasant Studies* 47, 5: 1077–97.

McCarthy, J.F., J.A.C. Vel and S. Afiff. 2012. "Trajectories of Land Acquisition and Enclosure: Development Schemes, Virtual Land Grabs, and Green Acquisitions in Indonesia's Outer Islands", *Journal of Peasant Studies* 39, 2: 521–49.

McGee, T.G. 2009. *The Spatiality of Urbanization: The Policy Challenges of Mega-urban and Desakota Regions of Southeast Asia.* UNU-IAS Working Paper. Tokyo: United Nations University Institute of Advanced Studies.

Nooteboom, G. 2006. "Styles Matter: Livelihood and Insecurity in the East Javanese Uplands", in *Ropewalking and Safety Nets: Local Ways of Managing Insecurities in Indonesia*, ed. J. Koning and F. Hüsken. Leiden, Singapore: Brill, pp. 175–98.

_____. 2015. *Forgotten People: Poverty, Risk and Social Security in Indonesia.* Leiden and Boston: Brill.

_____. 2019. "Understanding the Nature of Rural Change: The Benefits of Migration and the (Re)creation of Precarity for Men and Women in Rural Central Java, Indonesia", *TRaNS: Trans -Regional and -National Studies of Southeast Asia 7*, 1: 113–33. doi:10.1017/trn.2019.3.

Nooteboom, G. and P.M. Kutanegara 2002. "The Storm Will soon be Over? Differential Effects of the Crisis in Rural Java and the Role of the Local Government", *Moussons* 6: 3–36.

Pattenden, J. and M. Wastuti. 2021. "'Waiting for the Call to Prayer': Exploitation, Accumulation and Social Reproduction in Rural Java", *The Journal of Peasant Studies*. doi:10.1080/03066150.2021.1970540.

Peluso, N.L. and A.B. Purwanto. 2017. "The Remittance Forest: Turning Mobile Labor into Agrarian Capital", *Singapore Journal of Tropical Geography* 39, 1: 6–36. doi:10.1111/sjtg.12225.

Rigg, J. 2013. "From Rural to Urban: A Geography of Boundary Crossing in Southeast Asia", *TRaNS: Trans-Regional and -National Studies of Southeast Asia* 1, 1: 5–26. doi:10.1017/trn.2012.6.

_____. 2015. *Challenging Southeast Asian Development: The Shadows of Success*. London: Routledge. doi:10.4324/9781315686257.

Rigg, J., A. Salamanca and E. C. Thompson. 2016. "The Puzzle of East and Southeast Asia's Persistent Smallholder", *Journal of Rural Studies* 43: 118–33. doi:10.1016/j. jrurstud.2015.11.003.

Rigg, J. and P. Vandergeest, eds. 2012. *Revisiting Rural Places: Pathways to Poverty and Prosperity in Southeast Asia*. Singapore: NUS Press.

Rotgé, V.L., I.B. Matra and R. Rijanta. 2000. *Rural–Urban Integration in Java: Consequences for Regional Development and Employment*. London: Routledge Revivals Series edition 2018.

Schenk-Sandbergen, L. 2018. "De-feminisation of Agricultural Wage Labour in Jalpaiguri, West Bengal", *Economic and Political Weekly* 53, 25: 46–53.

Singarimbun, M. 1996. "Peluang Kerja dan Kemiskinan di Miri Sriharjo" [Job Opportunities and Poverty in Miri, Sriharjo], in *Penduduk Dan Perubahan*. Yogyakarta: Pustaka Pelajar.

Singarimbun, M. and D. Penny. 1973. *Population and Poverty in Rural Java: Some Economic Arithmetic from Sriharjo*. Ithaca, NY: Cornell University Press.

Sunam, R., K. Barney and J.F. McCarthy. 2021. "Transnational Labour Migration and Livelihoods in Rural Asia: Tracing Patterns of Agrarian and Forest Change", *Geoforum* 118: 1–13.

Van der Ploeg, J.D. 2008. *The New Peasantries: Struggles for Autonomy and Sustainability in an Era of Empire and Globalization*. London: Earthscan.

_____. 2010. "The Peasantries of the Twenty-first Century: The Commoditisation Debate Revisited", *Journal of Peasant Studies* 37, 1: 1–30.

White, B. 1991. "Economic Diversification and Agrarian Change in Rural Java, 1900–1990", in *In the Shadow of Agriculture: Non-Farm Activities in the Javanese Economy, Past and Present*, ed. P. Alexander, P. Boomgaard and B. White. Amsterdam: Royal Tropical Institute, pp. 41–69.

_____. 2000. "Rice Harvesting and Social Change in Java: An Unfinished Debate", *The Asia Pacific Journal of Anthropology* 1, 1: 79–102.

World Bank. 2008. *World Development Report: Agriculture for Development.* Washington DC: World Bank.

_____. 2017. *Poverty & Equity Data Portal.* Available at http://povertydata. worldbank.org/poverty/country/IDN (accessed 3 Apr. 2022).

CHAPTER 5

Progressing Sideways in the Rice Lands: Livelihood Change and Nutritional Insecurity in Aceh

John F. McCarthy, Nulwita Maliati and Shaummil Hadi

Introduction

In the aftermath of Aceh's separatist conflict (1976–2005), tsunami (2004) and peace settlement (2005), extensive development interventions focused on this province at the extreme north of the island of Sumatra. While statistical poverty has been falling since then, 15.9 per cent of Aceh's population reportedly still lived below the poverty line in 2018. Despite so much development assistance, the difficult and complex livelihood issues affecting households in the densely lowland Aceh remain. Aceh is the poorest province in Sumatra, with the highest rate of stunting (Waspada 2019).

This chapter examines patterns of rural poverty and nutritional insecurity that persist even while extreme poverty slowly falls in statistical terms. We are interested in understanding how specific drivers, structures and actors' responses come together to shape the specific scenario found in the lowlands of Aceh.

On first impression, the situation for people in the rich rice-producing lowlands of Aceh resembles what agrarian political economists have called a "truncated transition". In this scenario, the poor remain stuck between near subsistence agrarian livelihoods and employment in petty trade and services, in ways that insufficiently support them (Akram-Lodhi and Kay 2010; Breman and Wiradi 2002). Accounts of "truncated agrarian transition" suggest that agriculture is "decoupled" from the process of capital accumulation (Akram-Lodhi and Kay 2010), and poor workers are no longer required ("surplus to capital") (Li 2011). Indeed if we compare lowland Aceh to the Malaysian state Kedah, across the Malacca Strait from it (De Koninck and Ahmat 2012), it is clear that the expected linear transition from peasant agriculture to high-value agriculture and a shift into industrial labour markets remains elusive. In many respects, the situation remains remarkably similar to what De Koninck (1979) described more than 40 years ago, so much so that imagining a linear transition, even a truncated one, seems questionable. Yet, while the situation appears stagnant, a closer view reveals change at work.

To understand the hybrid trajectories of change taking place here we borrow a term from financial analysis. A sideways market is one where change does not map onto expectations for movement in a forwards-backwards direction. While there may be the great expectation of meaningful movement and while the situation appears stagnant, a closer view reveals a pattern of sideward developments. Similarly, setting aside the expectation that livelihoods in Aceh will move according to an *a priori* linear template—the teleology of the agrarian transition template discussed in the introduction—enables us to see with fresh eyes the set of changes taking place. Here the particularities of local conditions meet structural contexts to shape livelihood possibilities and produce hybrid trajectories of change.

The sideways scenario here is shaped by four specific sets of developments. First, while agriculture remains critical to nutritional security for many, there is a lack of opportunity to move into commercial agriculture and better livelihoods. At the same time, diversifying livelihoods out of agriculture is slow, difficult and hardly rewarding for most households. For a large cohort of pluriactive households (those with more than one occupation), moving sideways means cultivating land while becoming increasingly active in the non-farm economy. Households may hold together "a complex and diverse array of temporally contingent and opportunistic (though poorly remunerated) activities" (Pritchard, Vicol and Jones 2017: 51). Labour diversification and migration of some household members do occur, but for the most part do not provide a forwards trajectory. Rather, such diversification is still grounded in agriculture, collecting wild vegetables, domestic production, bartering, reciprocating and state social assistance. These help most of the poor to muddle through without attaining security. Thus, "deagrarianisation"—a delinking of livelihoods from agriculture—as far as it occurs, does so at a glacial pace.

Second, while people may not find secure work in the industrial labour market, in other ways the poor are not "decoupled" from capital. Indeed, they are subject to a range of accumulation strategies within and outside the agrarian context. Here, key structural dynamics are shaping agriculture and labour, together with patterns of consumption, socio-cultural practices and the marketing of processed food. Together these dynamics create a pattern of food poverty and nutritional insecurity, without for the most part generating an agrarian crisis.

Third, in progressing sideways, many households improve their livelihoods in terms of statistical poverty proxies used to measure poverty: they may have electricity, motorcycles and mobile phones and even renovated houses. Yet, increasing processes of commodification and patterns of consumerism also generate a trap: many households cut back on their food, principally the main source of protein (fish), during periods of seasonal scarcity, while spending significant sums on other consumption. While it may be tempting to ignore these quotidian forms of progress, for rural people they are important, especially as they enable most to evade a deep subsistence crisis. Fourth, while the state no longer seriously invests in the agricultural sector, in the absence of growth in labour markets, social assistance only softens the sharp edges of poverty for the very poor.

The site of this research, lowland rural Aceh, has a troubled and unique history marked by separatist conflict, the tsunami and aid interventions (Mahdi and Muhammad 2014; McCarthy 2014). The conflict and the tsunami had compound impacts, cumulatively deepening complex forms of vulnerability. After almost two decades, most families have reconstituted their livelihoods, most widows have long remarried and refugees have returned home. The enduring impact is from the lost ten years before 2004, when the separatist conflict disrupted and stalled rural livelihoods.

This chapter is based on research undertaken in the rich rice-producing plains extending towards the northern tip of Sumatra but not directly affected by the tsunami. Our team used each district's food security map to select survey villages around the median for poverty and food security within the same ecological-production area. The result was two contrasting cases: the first was in Aceh Besar, close to the provincial capital where opportunities to work beyond the village were more expansive; the second was a more rural village in Aceh Utara (North Aceh). This allowed for a comparison between contrasting landownership, livestock and cash cropping practices with different consumption and livelihood diversification patterns. To begin, we consider the characteristic poverty dynamics occurring here and then discuss agriculture, labour, food poverty and social assistance, before drawing our conclusions.

Poverty Dynamics and the Agricultural Question

To understand poverty dynamics in relation to farming and the link to land-based livelihoods, we undertook a wealth ranking exercise that involved requesting key village informants to analyse how households progress and to specify a poverty cut off, a point at which a household would no longer be considered poor. Respondents then jointly categorised individual households and their movements against this village-identified cut off. In the two study villages, these discussions revealed that "frugal" (*sederhana* or *sedang*) households existed below the poverty cut off (53 per cent of the sample) and "capable" (*mampu*) or non-poor households constituted the remaining 47 per cent.

Among the "frugal" (poor) households, in deliberations to work out who should receive *zakat* (alms), the village distinguishes between the "destitute" (*fakir*) and the "poor" (*miskin*), categories that correspond to degrees of nutritional and livelihood insecurity. All frugal households lacked sufficient assets and savings to face times of crisis in ways that avoided cutting back on their basic household needs. According to village elders, *fakir* may need to cook two mugs (*mok*) of rice each day, but they can afford only one. In other words, they suffer from chronic long-term or persistent forms of nutritional and/or livelihood insecurity. The village *zakat* committees classified 13 per cent of the population of the two villages as *fakir*. In contrast, the "poor" also require two mugs of rice, but only sometimes are they reduced to cooking just one. Their food poverty is transitory, and in this category they are what economists call the "occasional" or "churning" poor. *Fakir* households may have many children and a house that is considered unfit for habitation, or they may be old people, widows, or female-headed households without secure income. While they may have a garden, they usually depend on wage labour. In contrast, *miskin* households are typically tenant farmers or landowners owning less than 2 *rante* (0.8 ha) of rice land.

The highly unequal or differentiated agrarian structure remains critical to the production of vulnerability. Local people define poverty in terms of control of assets and resources, particularly land. While other aspects of livelihood remain important, land serves as both a secure basis for livelihoods and an obvious external marker of a household's situation. In the study villages, "capable" (non-poor) households are those with ownership of cattle and/or rice lands that are sufficient to provide them with elements of a secure livelihood. While capable households need to have more than two *rante* (0.8 ha) to be moving out of poverty (above the poverty cut off), a truly prosperous (*makmur*) household would own at least 6 *rante* (0.24 hectares).

Landownership varies across villages (Table 5.1). In two Aceh Besar villages visited on the west coast, the descendants of the *uleebalang* (former aristocratic elite) either owned most of the land or operated as agents for absentee landowners, while 60 per cent of farmers remained tenant farmers. An estimated ten village households owned more than 0.2 ha of rice land in the Aceh Besar village, and only two people owned more than 0.4 ha in the Aceh Utara site. Landowners on average control 0.23 ha across the two sites, but many landowners own very small plots. Fragmentation of land ownership and landlordism, processes that make so many farming households marginal, are common problems in rural Indonesia (Ambarwati et al. 2016). Indeed 37 per cent of households surveyed owned less than 0.1 hectare. Landownership is particularly fragmented in Aceh Utara, with 63 per cent of surveyed landowners owning plots of less than 0.1 ha.

Table 5.1   Rice land ownership by village (% of total households)

	Aceh Besar Village	Aceh Utara Village	Total
Land owner	30	45.2	37.8
Tenant farmer	32.5	4.8	18.3
Farmer with use right	7.5	4.8	6.1
Landowner and tenant farmer	22.5	4.8	13.4
Landless	7.5	40.5	24.4

Tenant farmers constitute 32 per cent of those surveyed, comprising more than half of Aceh Besar villagers but only about 10 per cent of villagers in the Aceh Utara site. On average, tenant farmers control 0.19 ha. Tenant farming is associated with poverty: 61 per cent of tenant farmers fell below the poverty cut off, and 60 per cent cut back on their food during the scarcity season. While on average 24 per cent of households are landless, the agrarian structure is highly uneven: 41 per cent of the Aceh Utara households are landless, but only 7.4 per cent of households in Aceh Besar village.

This area of Aceh remains a rice exporting region. While non-irrigated areas might produce only 4.2 ton/hectare, irrigated rice lands in these villages produce up to 6.8 tons per ha average production,[1] well above the national average of 4.9 ton/ha. The area represents a success for the productivist project of the green revolution. However, with so many rice cultivators poor in village terms, the irony is that, as in other rice surplus areas (Purwestri et al. 2018), for several reasons (explored below) productivist success has yet to overcome poverty in these landscapes.

There are other sources of agricultural income. In Aceh Besar, villagers use hillside land for raising cattle, with 25 per cent of surveyed households managing cows, including tenant farmers who tend cattle under profit-sharing arrangements with owners. Such means of tending cattle are the main way of saving, with households using cattle as an asset to meet a crisis, pay off debts or even to accumulate capital to buy a garden. In contrast, Aceh Utara villagers cultivate areca nut (*pinang*) palms in hilly garden areas surrounding the village, with 46 per cent of villages surveyed cultivating such gardens. Rice tenant farmers tend to have very small areca gardens, with 16 per cent of households owning or managing gardens of less than 0.1 ha. However, rice landowners typically control sufficient areas of areca palm gardens to earn on average 40 per cent of their total income in this way.

We need to differentiate those able to accumulate a surplus in agriculture from those who cannot. Landowners able to accumulate from rice production include households which, as the wealth ranking showed, had been "prosperous" for the entire 25 years. (The wealth ranking exercise found that 31 per cent of the two villages' populations had remained non-poor over 25 years.) Such households continue to accumulate from the agricultural sector, earning on average a third of their income from farming, even where on average they make 60 per cent of their income from formal sector employment. Their ability to accumulate through rice production is conditioned by farm size, their ability both to access credit and to mobilise wage or tenant labour to generate a surplus (De Koninck 1979). In this respect, capable households resemble their Thai counterparts following a pattern of deagarianisation with depeasantisation (Rigg et al. 2018).

In contrast, other landowners generate a surplus that is insufficient for them to accumulate. However, most have a sufficient degree of control over capital and debt to retain some hold over the family life cycle, investing in health and education in ways that reduce the likelihood of a downward spiral. On the other hand, the poor are not accumulating in agriculture. In the survey, only one household across the two villages progressed from the frugal to the capable category in the agricultural sector over 25 years, and they did so by investing and opening up areca gardens on the forest frontier outside the village. Hence, in line with research elsewhere (Bernstein and Oya 2014), very few households rely on agriculture alone. Indeed, only 11 per cent of surveyed households derived their incomes solely from agriculture. Across the sample only 34 per cent of households derive more than two thirds of their income from agriculture.

The major challenge for land-based livelihoods is that land ownership has diminished with the passing of each generation, ensuring that farming households have less surplus production, and less rice to eat or sell. With opportunities to expand gardens limited to a now distant forest frontier, the pressure has increased to find off-farm opportunities. As the Imam in Aceh Utara village noted, even as the percentage of people in poverty decreases over time, the total number of those impoverished has not decreased. For those stuck with one foot in farming, unlike in the Malaysian case (De Koninck and Ahmat 2012), with increasing production costs state policies have not reduced farmers' input costs or exposure to unstable markets, nor have they effectively supported the emergence of organic methods and diverse farms.

Diversification, Migration and the Question of Labour

When households diversify, or "deagrarianise", livelihoods become less reliant on agriculture. However, the literature has long debated whether or under what conditions pluriactive households that combine farming with non-farm and off-farm income, or even migrate and leave farming behind, are able to find a better future (Rigg, Salamanca and Thompson 2016).

In the two study villages, on average, both poor and non-poor households obtained approximately half of their income from off-farm activities. Moreover, of the 16 per cent of households across the total population in the two villages which had risen to become "non-poor" over 25 years, virtually all had done so by successfully diversifying outside agriculture. This involved combining personal agency and networks as well as developing some special capacity, knowledge, business opportunity or formal employment. Certainly, the returns outside agriculture can be higher and the possibilities for progress can be better for households applying their labour elsewhere. However, those who diversify require skills, acumen and some measure of good fortune to succeed; many fail, with up to 11 per cent of the two village populations we studied falling back into poverty over the 25-year period.

The possibilities for local income diversification are spatially differentiated. On the west coast of Aceh during the 1990s, villagers could take up various activities at different times, combining off-farm work within a diverse portfolio of activities (McCarthy 2006). Here, successful livelihoods tended to be opportunistic, with households diversifying and combining wage and non-wage income, subsistence and non-income activities in a variety of ways between seasons. In contrast, given the social, cultural and geographical distance of the North Aceh village from urban nodes of employment and the forest frontier, diversification opportunities for households in that village are scarce. In the village, no informants in our sample identified as having a formal sector job as civil servants, teachers, police, or office workers; while in the Aceh Besar site, located closer to the provincial capital, 17.5 per cent of respondents had formal jobs. Other opportunities were limited. Only five per cent of informants identified as making a living from trading or shop owning, with another five per cent engaged in construction work. Work is highly gendered, with males dominating agriculture and formal employment, and women carrying out household-based work, helping in the rice fields and in agricultural labour, or trading and in shop work. Consequently, a sharp gap exists between prosperous households with formal jobs and poorer households who live alongside them and are excluded from the formal sector.

In both villages, there are few opportunities for on-farm labour. In the North Aceh village, 19 per cent identified themselves as agricultural labourers, while in Aceh Besar just 10 per cent were predominately agricultural labourers. A labour survey of 12 poor families found that given their commitment to agriculture on share-cropped land during peak periods of the agricultural cycle, on average households found on-farm labour for only 40 days per year. Given the scarcity of labour opportunities, many of those existing as labourers fall into the destitute (*fakir*) group.

Migration pathways are limited, in large part due to the specific pattern of spatial and socio-ethnic integration of the Acehnese into national and regional economies. From the survey sample, 13 per cent of households had family members outside the village, typically a child working elsewhere. While remittances may well be underreported, our survey found that on average, remittances amounted to USD 140 per month, a significant amount for this rural context. The amount and frequency of remittances varied considerably: remittances ranged from 0.07 times to 4.8 times average yearly income, and were mostly received a few times a year. Only four per cent of households received more from outside than their yearly income. These seem to have been from successful children sending money back to support their elderly parents. So although households relying on remittances could avoid further marginalisation or, for some, even accumulate capital, the survey suggests that only a few households did so.

As elsewhere, youth wished to leave the land and farming (Leavy and Hossain 2014), and young, better-educated, networked and more-skilled youth could find income opportunities in the formal sector in urban areas. Interviews revealed that for most households, migration remained risky and fraught. Many leaving for Malaysia did so cheaply and even illegally. While working informally in Malaysia, they earned low wages and living expenses were high. A few found secure work in factories or the plantation sector, and given the high exchange rate, sent back a steady stream of money. For the most part, households used this cash for consumption. Some returning immigrants attempted to open small enterprises. Most families interviewed told tales of hardship. It was not unknown for families to send money to Malaysia to bring their children home. Instead, most of the youth left for less risky destinations in the regional or national capital. In the city, poor villagers often worked as petty traders or in the service sector, many barely earning enough to survive (Vignato 2018). According to the village secretary in Aceh Besar village, "it's better to stay home than go to Malaysia or Jakarta". As elsewhere, poor labourers may save too little, and rarely send money home (Nooteboom 2015). In Aceh, the fortunate ones returned with enough to pay for the bride wealth; most returned without savings.

The geography of growth shapes labour opportunities. To a significant degree, poverty is a structural outcome. We need to understand specific patterns of growth and distribution, and how they interact with subnational and spatial inequalities and social inequalities. Indeed, there are several critical structural elements shaping poverty in Aceh (Manning 2014; Vignato 2018). First, Aceh has a low level of urbanisation, with 72 per cent of Aceh's population still residing in the countryside. Just under half of all the employed population work mainly in agriculture, compared to around 30 per cent in the rest of the country (Manning 2014). These are largely self-employed farmers, where output per person is generally low. Second, the footprint of business and corporations is small: there are very few wage opportunities in palm oil and rubber plantations. The manufacturing sector is insignificant, providing only six per cent of jobs, with relatively little modern manufacturing of consumer goods. As most consumer and producer goods are sourced from Medan in one-way trade, there are very few manufacturing jobs. Third, the service sector is small (13 per cent), and there are few opportunities outside petty trade in small stalls. The sector has low productivity, only slightly above agriculture, ensuring there is little to gain from moving from agriculture into the services sector. Fourth, the off-farm sector is not able to absorb labour. As Manning notes, one third of youth are looking for work, with high levels of underemployment and part-time work, and underemployment is highest in agriculture. In other words, like many areas of outer island Indonesia, the Aceh economy is disconnected from growth poles, such as Medan and Jakarta, and persists as a place with relative spatial and social inequality.

Food Poverty and Seasonal Scarcity

Methods developed to capture experiential dimensions of food poverty enable researchers to understand intentional responses based on decisions around food sufficiency and shed light on what affected people actually do (Maxwell

1996). These methods can be combined with qualitative research to understand the experience of food poverty.

The Household Food Insecurity Access Scale (HFIAS) survey methodology provides a means to categorise households in terms of one of the main coping strategies: reducing the varieties or quantities of food consumed (Coates, Swindale and Bilinsky 2007). To gain a snapshot of coping strategies, we undertook a survey of households identified as having problems affording groceries during the maximum period of scarcity *before* the harvest. Fully 60 of the 82 households in the survey identified as experiencing difficulties paying for their groceries or other basic needs. Some 35 per cent and 42 per cent of households in Aceh Besar and Aceh Utara respectively admitted to cutting back on food consumption in various ways. Indeed, although these surveys are difficult to implement, our results indicated that 60 per cent of those classified as poor by the wealth ranking exercise were nutritionally insecure, because they regularly cut back on key types of food consumption.

Households usually avoided going hungry, but they might substitute dried fish or egg for fresh fish. However, this still required expenditure, so usually they reduced the frequency of eating fish or even vegetables, especially if they needed to sell rice to buy these staples. Fifteen per cent of the total survey population occasionally (less than ten times a month) reduced the number of days during which they ate fish or even vegetables. Another 16 per cent did so frequently (more than ten times a month), eating a monotonous diet, mostly starchy carbohydrates or other less desirable foods. Finally, nine per cent either reduced their meal size or ate foods that did not meet their food preferences, more than ten times a month.

Stunting (low height for age) among children is used as a key indicator of longer-term undernutrition. Stunting is largely due to a lack of nutrients—principally protein and micro-nutrients—often in association with poor dietary choices, maternal malnutrition or ill health (Pritchard 2016). In Aceh, other research has found that nutritional outcomes are determined by a wide range of factors, including mother's age, environmental factors such as access to safe water and sanitation facilities, and socio-economic characteristics of the household (Srinita 2018). Adequate incomes enable households to obtain more diverse diets, better health care and improved sanitation—the lack of each of these is a key determinant of undernutrition (Haddad et al. 2014). According to provincial surveys, stunting rates are 30 per cent and 43 per cent in Aceh Besar and Aceh Utara, respectively (TNP2K Aceh 2018), pointing to a significant problem of nutritional security. Interestingly, these figures mirror our findings that 35 per cent and 42 per cent of respondents across the two villages were engaging in coping behaviours that involved cutting back on key foods. As these practices entail substituting carbohydrates for protein and vegetables, many of the very poor appear overweight. As other studies suggest, obesity often co-exists with undernutrition (Usfar et al. 2010), as such practices combine with unhealthy snacking habits to contribute to poor nutrition, stunting and other health problems.

Figure 5.1   Mobile fish trader in Aceh Utara

During the scarcity period (*paceklik*) prior to harvest, when stocks from the last harvest run down, the poor resort to self-provisioning, domestic production, sharing, bartering and reciprocating to get by. They might seek work as day labourers, or if the village is close to the forest, go in search of timber or rattan and other non-forest products for sale. Surveys generally fail to capture these coping strategies and the non-market forms of provision and reciprocity. Although the poor could borrow or buy from a neighbour's family or from moneylenders or the rice mill, they would then need to pay back from the next harvest. This would be a coping strategy that in turn reduced their stock in the next season, setting them up for a more severe scarcity season the following year.

Due to anxiety about getting by, the poor had a daily sense of insecurity. In some villages, we witnessed poor women foraging and collecting wild vegetables (*sayur pakis, kangkung sawah, daun singkong* and *melinjo*), while men fished in rivers or the ocean, or went to the forest in search of timber or non-forest timber products. This reduced the need to spend money on food, or substituted for a lack of cash. Households also substituted dried fish (*ikan asin*) for fresh fish, or ate only rice with vegetables, salt and/or a bitter sauce. In many cases, villagers were reluctant to borrow too much financially, because they wished to avoid going deeply into debt or the shame of not paying back the lender in full.

Apart from temporary strategies, a household's family crisis, illness, a series of harvest failures or the need to pay for a wedding or education forces households to take more permanent responses. While it is reasonably common for villagers to sell livestock or even gardens to meet such needs, families prefer to pawn rice land rather than sell, so they still have the possibility of getting it back (see Table 5.1: 6.1 per cent of farmers had use rights, typically pawned land). Pawning land and taking out loans at high rates are damaging coping strategies that undermine long-term livelihood viability.

Even with these coping strategies, while poor households seek to avoid reducing the quantity of rice they consumed, many poor households did reduce the quality for between one and two months prior to the harvest. As the village secretary in Aceh Utara noted, "in my experience, most of the poor and frugal cut back on food, for periods of time, eating rice without much else".

When considering how food poverty is produced, we need to unpack the complex and overlapping problems. One of the proximate causes is clearly household control over rice production (see Table 5.2). The survey revealed that among farming households identified as experiencing difficulties paying for their groceries, on average they had rice stocks that lasted 4.5 months. As farmers harvest twice each year, depending on the season, over two harvest periods these families might have to survive for approximately three months with no rice stock.

A critical mechanism at work here is generating nutritional insecurity, inducing producers to sell off their rice stock. Rice is both a subsistence requirement and a cash crop sold to meet monetary needs. Even if a tenant farmer manages to store 2.5 tons behind the house, the farmer will try to meet other pressing needs by selling significant amounts of rice. In the scarcity season such farmers may even run out, forcing them to buy rice and reducing available cash for other things. This leaves them subject to food poverty. Hence, the more they store and the more diversified their incomes, the more secure the household will be. Indeed, the survey revealed that in Aceh Besar, on average farmers used 25 per cent of the harvest to repay loans to pay for production and input costs. On top of this, on average farmers sold an estimated 20 per cent of the harvest to meet cash needs.

Table 5.2   Crop production and income for owners and tenant farmers

Ton/year	Gross Ton/year	Net Ton/year	% retained after production & land rent	Income from rice (million RP)
Owner	8.7	5.5	63	25
Tenant farmer	8.0	2.5	31	11.6

Source: Maliati and McCarthy 2015.

As well as a lack of working capital to purchase inputs and pay for production, the agrarian structure (land ownership) and social relations that shape production are critical to the causes of nutritional insecurity. Tenant farmers paid 30 per cent of production as land rent. While land ownership itself does not guarantee non-poor status or act as a buffer against food poverty, for the most part landowners are more likely to be nutritionally secure because they do not pay land rents. Indeed, 61 per cent of landowners fall into the non-poor household category, and 74 per cent of landowners do not cut back on food in the scarcity season. However, tenant farmers generally expect to keep a third of their production for their own use or sale; surveys revealed more than half of tenant farming households admitted to cutting back on their food during the scarcity season. In contrast, 40 per cent of the landless or non-farming households are nutritionally insecure in these ways.

Climate

For farming households dependent on wet rice cultivation, meteorological forces and ecological factors are becoming increasingly significant, especially with climate change. As other research has found, El Nino (ENSO) events periodically delay planting of rice crops by two months or more. This extends the "scarcity season" (*paceklik*) experienced by poor rice farming households before the harvest. This delay may not be compensated by the second harvest, leaving households with smaller yields, while affecting incomes and staple food prices, with a disproportionate effect on the poor. One study even concluded that a 30-day delay in monsoon onset causes production to fall by an average of 11 per cent (Naylor et al. 2007). Studies also suggest that higher temperatures linked to climate change decrease productivity: every 1°C increase in minimum temperature during the dry season produces a 10 per cent decrease in rice yields (Naylor et al. 2007).

In the study villages, if irrigation systems were not well maintained, vital water flows could be irregular and unreliable. With the climate increasingly changeable, periods of wet or dry occur more regularly. As our interviews with village leaders (*geuchiek* and *sekdes*) confirmed, floods and drought heighten the incidence of harvest failure. When irrigation water is less available, villagers depend on rainfall for at least part of the year. If farmers have planted at the wrong time, some households face extended dry periods and even harvest failures. During the 2011 El Niño event, for example, many households experienced severe hardship.

In the study villages, these problems are compounded by occasional raids by rats, pigs, birds and infestations of insects (*wereng*). Intensive land management using chemical fertilisers and pesticides may also be reducing sawah productivity. Such reductions were exacerbated also because households had abandoned hillside cash-crop-producing gardens during the conflict. In the Aceh Utara sites these have only slowly been brought back into production.

Increasing marketisation of rice to meet production and consumer needs—a long standing rural phenomenon—is acute (De Koninck 1979). Among poor households, surveys revealed that expenditure outstripped income, confirming that for them the "net commercial balance of the farm operation is negative" (De Koninck 1979: 290). In other words, if they sold their rice rather than consumed a large proportion of it, and if labour costs are factored in, they would earn less than their costs of production. In view of this negative balance, many households exist in a state of chronic debt.

We need to understand the complex factors driving the marketisation of rice in relation to changing cultures of consumerism and basic needs. As the village head (*geuchiek*) in Aceh Besar noted, "the poor can save ... to do so sometimes they cook one cup of rice even if they could afford two.... Otherwise how would they progress?" In Aceh Besar village, interviews revealed households cutting back on food to save for cattle, fixing the roof, or paying school-related or other expenses.

With the emergence of processed food in the villages, households now buy processed snacks for their children (Table 5.3). Indeed, the survey revealed that the poor spend approximately the same amount on snacks and tobacco as they do on rice and fish. Among poor families, the large proportion of household expenditures spent on smoking and unhealthy snacks is linked to poor nutritional outcomes (Semba et al. 2007). In addition, the poor pay on credit for motorcycles, mobile phones and other commodities (over 80 per cent of households use mobile phones and have a motorbike). In the Aceh Besar village (itself not affected by the tsunami), following an upsurge of wage-earning opportunities after the tsunami, villages also aspired to improve their houses. Interviews revealed that many villagers traded off payments for consumer goods for reduced food expenditure, principally fish.

Figure 5.2   Drying areca nut (*pinang*) outside a house in Aceh Utara

Relational dynamics shape the terms of inclusion into the cash economy. Intermediate traders control access to inputs and marketing channels, and often engage in price gouging. The price for unhusked rice drops at the time of harvest and rises by 25 per cent during the scarcity season. Farmers sell unhusked rice for a little as IDR 3,000 per kilogram (about USD 0.21) at harvest time to traders from Medan, buying back milled rice at above IDR 9,000 per kilogram during the scarcity season. Farmers borrow inputs such as fertiliser and pesticides at marked-up prices from the village shop owners and middlemen during the planting season. Farmers pay back these loans after the harvest, paying a premium on the market price. If they pay in kind, they pay at the harvest price when rice is cheapest and borrow rice at inflated prices during the scarcity period.

Table 5.3 Poor households: Average amount of total expenditure on key consumption items

Rice	22%
Fish	11%
Tobacco	11%
Children's snacks	15%
Food and tobacco as percentage of total expenditure	59%

It might be assumed that integration into the market implies gradually leaving subsistence livelihoods behind, a process that had intensified during the green revolution (De Koninck 1979). As the process of commodification works its way through, the boundaries between market and non-market modes of provision shift towards the market. Gradually the role that the family or the community plays in the provision of goods and services through redistribution or reciprocity is reduced. Indeed, farming households increasingly purchase inputs and labour. The logic of intensified rice production works against labour sharing: most labour has to be paid for (De Koninck 1979). Cash payments, including from selling rice, cover mini-tractors, fertilisers and pesticides.

Households can follow pathways out of insecurity by retaining greater control over their rice production and by diversifying their income sources. Moving sideways can be a successful coping strategy when it provides a means to accumulate cash income to buy food over the scarcity period, reducing the need to sell rice to meet pressing cash needs. More than half of landless or non-farming households in the survey had diversified out of farming in ways that enabled them to overcome the sharper forms of insecurity. However, landless households that had not successfully diversified tended to be very poor, with many falling into the deeply insecure *fakir* category. Moreover, these sideward strategies are limited by increasing patterns of commodification and consumerism, which set up new insecurity traps.

Social Assistance

Practices of sharing and reciprocity amongst those short of cash continue: commodification coexists with an unevenly operating community economy of sharing, reciprocity and debt. Extended families continue to live in family complexes. Local networks can provide the first forms of social assistance, a dense network of debt and obligation involving neighbours, family, the rice mill, shops and patrons that households can call on. However, these are relations of dependence and exploitation and are particularistic. Households that borrow usually pay back from the next harvest; hence, excessive borrowing leads to scarcity in the following season. Moreover, not paying the lender back in full is both shameful as well as risky: the lender may not provide a loan the next time.

For the poor (*miskin*) households, contributions to weddings, funerals, *zakat* alms, religious and customary events are onerous but obligatory. While villagers tend to underreport these expenditures, poor respondents who answered comprehensively were found to contribute at least nine per cent of their total expenditure in this way. However, the very poor hardly donate and receive back even less in return. Indeed, very poor households try to avoid borrowing altogether. Informants noted that a key difference between "destitute" and "poor" households is that the *fakir* cannot borrow money because they are unable to repay it. Hence those who receive help during a life cycle crisis (for example birth, illness or death) tend to be those who have contributed previously to neighbours or kin who have experienced their own crises. Given their inability to invest in networks of mutual assistance, those who need assistance most—the poorest of the poor—receive least from social networks (Nooteboom 2015). Access to mutual help and local forms of social security are highly differentiated: "the poorer you are and the more support you need, the less you are protected" (Nooteboom 2015: 293). Hence, even if they borrow only occasionally, the poor usually cope by cutting back on consumption, while trying to maintain modest investments in social obligations.

Given the dynamics shaping the ability of the poor to receive assistance from the community, state social assistance for the poorest of the poor becomes important. The very poor have most to gain from effective social assistance. For them, exclusion from social assistance is extra painful: it takes away (again) potential sources of sustenance from those with little to gain from informal social safety nets other than *zakat*.

The state's social assistance programmes aim to assist the poorest in various ways. At the time of the research, the state was expanding and reforming the two key programmes aimed at helping the poor: the rice for the poor programme (*Raskin*, now renamed *Rastra*) and the Conditional Cash Transfer (CCT), or Family Hope Program (*Program Keluarga Harapan*, PKH). While the specifics of how these programmes work in this Aceh case are discussed elsewhere in this volume (see Chapter 11), suffice to say that these programmes reached the poor only to a limited degree. The rice for the poor programme distributed eight kg several times a year to the poor, with rice distribution occurring irregularly. At the time of the survey, before the expansion of PKH, we found that beneficiaries of the conditional cash transfer programme received on average 1.08 million rupiah (USD 76) per year. The programme provided assistance to 14 per cent of poor households identified by the wealth ranking exercise, and 29 per cent of the severely food-insecure households.[2]

Thus the social assistance programmes provide a means of helping the poor in a limited way. State social assistance is appreciated by the villagers who receive it, with very poor households stating that it made a significant difference during the weeks it became available. Indeed, consumption surveys revealed that poor households on average receive state assistance of 1.19 million rupiah (USD 83.72), or 5.4 per cent of their total cash expenditure. If we include *zakat* alms and other community contributions, social assistance amounts to around eight per cent of total expenditure.[3] As these benefits contribute to the wide range of sources of livelihood that the poor rely on, they soften the sharp edges of poverty. However, the benefits are too small to make a substantial difference to food-insecure livelihoods across the season, let alone provide pathways out of poverty.

Conclusion

From the above discussion, we can identify three processes structuring the sideways scenario: processes associated with agriculture; processes pertaining to diversification and migration; and processes surrounding changing needs, consumption and food practices. We will consider these in turn, before making some final observations.

First, we need to understand the processes and mechanisms at work in agriculture. The "green revolution" offered the prospect of a productivist solution to rural underdevelopment, with increasing rice yields leading to sufficient basic cereal stocks, additional rural incomes and, if paired with industrial and urban development, the prospect of pathways out of poverty. This seems to have worked in the neighbouring rice lands of peninsular Malaysia studied by De Koninck and Ahmat (2012). However, even while the intensification projects of the green revolution succeeded in lowland Aceh in many respects, the reproduction of food poverty has continued.

The agrarian structure is critical to the ongoing generation of nutritional insecurity. As we have seen, land ownership shapes who gets to keep the rice surplus. When tenant farmers (up to half of all villagers) pay land rent, they lose control of a third of their rice production. From the remaining rice stock they may need to pay a range of costs.

Social and class differences are long established and play a key role in the reproduction of poverty in agriculture. Other literature has found that the green revolution worked to the advantage of those with the capital and technology, furthering socio-economic differentiation and the accumulation of land by the wealthy (De Koninck 1979). To be sure, we found no evidence of the rapid differentiation associated with accumulation by dispossession—the process reported elsewhere which leads to the poor being displaced from land and even farming. Yet this pattern of land ownership is well established. Further, the poor lack working capital, and to purchase inputs and pay for production they borrow from shop owners, mills and patrons. Once they have paid back large amounts of their harvests to clear the debts and land rent, poor households usually retain only a third of their rice production for their own use. This leads to the highly seasonal aspect of food poverty. As the surveys revealed, during the pre-harvest scarcity season as rice stocks run down, labourers and tenant farmers cut back on protein, while those who own sufficient land rarely do. For poor households, a small plot of land is insufficient to guarantee subsistence and may set them up for regular food insecurities. Caught in this cycle, large numbers of poor households remain tenant farmers and labourers over generations, poorly paid and nutritionally insecure.

Hence, in our cases, agriculture plays a paradoxical role. The surveys reveal that nutritional security for the poor is highly tied to farming and to land. Yet, very few households can afford to rely on agriculture alone: those who stayed poor over the last 25 years are neither accumulating nor ascending from agriculture, and those who ascend do so by moving out of agriculture.

A second set of processes associated with income diversification is critical both to the reproduction of poverty and to its termination. When looking at diversification and migration, analysts often argue that these processes provide the means to overcome poverty. Indeed, the wider trend is for the percentage of income from on-farm activities to decline, as villagers take up off-farm activities or migrate (Rigg et al. 2018).

In our cases, both poor and non-poor alike earn on average half their income from off-farm activities. Those who are leaving poverty are those diversifying; ascending households have members who had successfully diversified, finding formal work or migrating. Even among households that remain poor, significant numbers of households continue to diversify out of farming to reduce the sharpest forms of insecurity. As elsewhere, farming households attempt to move "one-foot sideways", to become increasingly active in the non-farm economy (Pritchard, Vicol and Jones 2017); they engage in diversification both to reduce their distress and to pursue opportunities. Yet too often diversification fits into a set of strategies that merely helps the poor get by, without necessarily eliminating their insecurity.

The key structural problem here is that Aceh exists as a left-behind periphery, with a poor relation to the nodes of growth driving Indonesia's expanding economy. Migration pathways are limited, with ethnic, cultural and economic constraints facing migrants leaving rural Aceh, even as remittances remain important to many poor families. There are also limited opportunities off-farm: valuable off-farm work opportunities are neither abundant nor well-paid, providing limited opportunities for diversifying livelihoods.

Our surveys revealed a sharp gap between those with formal work and those without. Those who do succeed tend to have the skills and acumen to access labour markets or make the most of opportunities. The disparity between those with formal work and those excluded corresponds with class differences apparent in patterns of consumption, education and opportunity. Households with networks and education for the most part have secured non-farm employment and typically have sufficient land. This upper echelon accumulates from agriculture to improve their houses, purchase cars and pay for their children's education. The upper stratum of rural Aceh (more highly visible in peri-urban areas of Aceh Besar than the more remote hamlets of North Aceh) ensures that their children can shift into middle-class occupations.

Thus, we see that diversification can lead to several distinct, even contradictory outcomes. It is simultaneously associated with ascending, with merely getting by and with staying poor. In general, diversification and migration do not guarantee nutritional security for the poor. Among the poor who obtained more than 40 per cent of their income outside agriculture, 37 per cent were still cutting back on food consumption in the scarcity season. Despite this, given that with each generation average landholdings tend to shrink as they are divided amongst heirs, opportunities to find off-farm work remain critical.

A third set of processes is related to changing household needs and nutrition practices. As the food security surveys revealed, 35 per cent and 42 per cent of villagers in the Aceh Besar and Aceh Utara villages, respectively, cut back on food (principally fish) during the scarcity season. Indeed, we found 60 per cent of poor households in the scarcity season cutting back. For the most part, people are not going hungry; rather, they are substituting protein and vegetables for carbohydrates. Given the role of socio-economic status in the generation of stunting, this goes some way to accounting for the high stunting rates in the two districts, respectively 30 per cent and 43 per cent.

A range of changing realities is also critical to the production of food poverty. In lowland Aceh, the boundaries between market and non-market modes of provision have shifted. With the reduced role of redistribution and reciprocity, and increased cash needs, farmers meet their needs by selling agricultural products, principally rice. Labour is increasingly paid for rather than exchanged, and farmers need to pay more. Farmers face poor terms of trade: selling rice does not buy much, and agricultural inputs are expensive. Distress sales of output and accrual of debt, as we have seen, mean that small farmers and sharecroppers have weak control over their rice production.

Relational dynamics are also critical here. Landowners and intermediate traders control access to inputs and marketing channels out of the village, and at times engage in price gouging, offering a low price for rice and areca (*pinang*) at harvest, while selling rice back at higher prices in periods of scarcity. Without access to independent working capital, farmers pay back loans for fertilisers after the harvest, paying a premium on the market price. If they pay in kind, they pay at the harvest price when rice is cheapest, or borrow rice at inflated prices during periods of scarcity.

Changing consumption practices and basic needs also affect food poverty. We see this with the large percentage of income spent by the poor on snacks. Interviews also revealed that poor households often make difficult choices between eating fish more often, paying credit on motorbikes, fixing the roof or paying education or other expenses.

Our analysis leads us to distinguish three broad livelihood trajectories. The first group is those who gradually accumulate capital and diversify their livelihoods, shifting onto an upwards trajectory. This group includes landowners who hire out their land to tenant farmers, retaining 30 per cent of the rice harvested from their land. If they can somehow work in other sectors, open a successful enterprise or move into better off-farm work, they may begin an ascent to join the secure, upper stratum of the village. Meanwhile, tenant farmers, the second group, face difficulties paying for production costs and tend to fall into debt. They use their rice for cash needs and to pay off loans, and they are unable to store sufficient rice to tide them over the year. Unless they can diversify, they remain stuck in food poverty. A group of these households moves crabwise, combining limited agriculture and labour opportunities to get by without progressing forwards. These households may fix their roof, invest in a cow, seal their floor and school their children, and thereby progress according to the statistical proxies used by the social assistance system to measure poverty. However, for the most part they remain insecure, and from time to time cut back on protein. Third, there are the destitute (*fakir*, 13 per cent of the sample) households, composed in many cases of female-headed households, landless or old people.

In drawing together the threads of these observations, we see six salient aspects of rural change. First, if we compare lowland Aceh today with the situation described by De Koninck (1979), there are signs of progress. Households have greater access to consumer goods such as televisions, mobile phones and motorbikes. Their children are in school, health clinics are available, the roads are sealed and the electricity grid reaches all lowland villages.

The second aspect of rural change we observe is that for the most part, there is no clear agrarian transition in rural Aceh: most households are neither moving out of farming nor migrating to the city. The context does not meet expectations that development follows an upward trajectory, with most households remaining to various degrees insecure. As migration, farming and diversification are linked to stagnation, indebtedness, survival and progress, it is difficult to read the scenario in terms of the linear trajectories suggested by many analysts.

The third aspect we find is that, except for the destitute (*fakir*), the current situation is far from an agrarian crisis. Most people are less desperate than one might expect. In local terms, most of the poor are still "getting by" (*bertahan*), even if this involves insecurity and cutting back on nutritious foods. It is true that the poor find insufficient pathways into commercial farming and industrial wage labour. Yet, households engage in a range of coping strategies, including self-provisioning, domestic production, sharing, bartering and reciprocating through kin and neighbourhood networks. These strategies remain significant contributors to household welfare.

The fourth aspect of rural change is that many of the households that cut back their food did so to meet the costs of consumer goods and changing social needs. Several factors are at work here. Perceptions of basic needs have changed and alongside it the nature of poverty (Sen 1999): motor bikes, mobile phones and a water-tight roof are now considered necessities. Further, households make difficult choices between competing needs. Too often, being "frugal" means replacing expensive protein with cheap carbohydrates. Lastly, while a lack of household income increases the probability of inferior diets, poor nutritional outcomes are affected by multiple factors, such as the massive growth of purchased and processed foods, other social practices, cultural norms and socio-economic developments that shape the choice to spend on smoking and highly processed, low-nutrition snacks (Dixon 2016).

The fifth aspect we find is that the division of labour and employment opportunities open for women affect poverty and nutritional security. Women earn wages working in the fields during the harvest and planting seasons, providing extra income for their families. The subdivision of rice land with every generation and the coming of new technologies such as tractors reduce livelihood prospects for women. Opportunities in other sectors remain relatively closed, especially for married women and mothers. Young women with low education may find urban work only in low paid retail jobs. The development of household industries, such as fisheries processing, can offer openings for married women, as technology and marketing channels are developed.

Finally, we do see accumulation occurring in this lowland landscape. Industry may not desire the labour of the lowland Acehnese, but in two senses the poor are not "surplus to capital". A range of corporate investors reaches into these areas, opening mini-markets, selling processed food ("food from nowhere"), motorbikes and mobile phones, and offering credit via mobile lenders. Moreover, at each harvest, rice wholesalers move in: the fertile Aceh lowlands continue to produce a rice surplus for consumption by the workers in the industrial areas of nearby urban centres.

Here, where statistical progress coincides with nutritional insecurity, we can identify the paradox of progressing sideways. While households may fail to move forwards into an agrarian transition, and so the situation appears stagnant, we can identify sidewards developments. By combining agriculture, growing cash crops, managing cattle and engaging in paid labour, households for the most part muddle through. Many even manage to save a little from time to time, making small investments such as fixing the house, buying a motorbike, or sending a child to school. In this respect, many households progress economically in terms of the statistical proxies used to measure poverty. Yet many of these "simple households" are considered "poor" by local criteria because they remain vulnerable and insecure, even if they are rendered "non-poor" in the state's statistical framing.[4]

Aceh is yet to develop a "networked economy where the relative prosperity of the village is based on work away from the village" (Rigg et al. 2018: 107). It is in such contexts that policy advocates have suggested that social assistance programmes can contribute (see Chapter 3). Given that, apart from the Islamic alms (*zakat*), the poor tend to fall out of community assistance, state social assistance schemes could be designed to help during periods of scarcity, such as the hunger season. To work in the city or abroad, young people require special skills to compete in the labour market. State social assistance aims to enable children from poor families to finish high school or tertiary education. While in theory they can enter the formal labour market, limited job opportunities in Aceh, high competition for vacancies, and poor social networks into the cities and abroad remain obstacles. Nonetheless, many very poor and insecure households benefit from the social assistance programmes. However, as we will see in Chapter 11, implementing these programmes in rural Aceh remains difficult, with so many poor people left excluded and unable to request social assistance.

Acknowledgements

Thanks to Dr. Saiful Mulyadi and colleagues at the International Centre for Aceh and Indian Ocean Studies (ICAIOS) at the Syiah Kuala University for hosting the research. We are also grateful to the district governments and villagers in Aceh Besar and Aceh Utara for their generous hospitality.

Notes

[1] Data from interviews with district agricultural offices.

[2] For a discussion of percentages of those excluded and a comparison of how this changed over 2017–19, see Chapter 11.

[3] This is likely to be an underestimation: respondents are reluctant to discuss their social contributions and assistance.

[4] The poverty ranking exercise (stages of progress [SoP]) used here classified 53% of the sample as "frugal" (*miskin*), below the community poverty cut off. However, according to the Indonesia Database for Policy and Economic Research database in 2013, Aceh Besar and North Aceh districts had official poverty rates of 16.9% and 20.3%, respectively.

References

Akram-Lodhi, A.H. and C. Kay. 2010. "Surveying the Agrarian Question (Part 2): Current Debates and Beyond", *Journal of Peasant Studies* 37: 255–84.

Ambarwati, A. et al. 2016. "Land Tenure and Agrarian Structure in Regions of Small-scale Food Production", in *Land & Development in Indonesia: Searching for the People's Sovereignty*, ed. J.F. McCarthy and K. Robinson. Singapore: ISEAS Publishing, pp. 265–95.

Bernstein, H. and C. Oya. 2014. "Rural Futures: How Much Should Markets Rule?", IIED Working Paper. London: International Institute for Environment and Development (IIED). Available at https://pubs.iied.org/sites/default/files/pdfs/migrate/14639IIED.pdf (accessed 6 Mar. 2022).

Breman, J. and G. Wiradi. 2002. *Good Times and Bad Times in Rural Java: Case Study of Socio-economic Dynamics in Two Villages Towards the End of the Twentieth Century*. Leiden: KITLV Press.

Coates, J., A. Swindale and P. Bilinsky. 2007. *Household Food Insecurity Access Scale (HFIAS) for Measurement of Food Access: Indicator Guide Version 3*. Washington, DC: Food and Nutrition Technical Assistance Project (FANTA).

De Koninck, R. 1979. "The Integration of the Peasantry: Examples from Malaysia and Indonesia", *Pacific Affairs* 52, 2: 265–93.

De Koninck, R. and R. Ahmat. 2012. "A State-orchestrated Agrarian Transition on the Kedah Plain of Peninsular Malaysia 1972–2009", in *Revisiting Rural Places: Pathways to Poverty and prosperity in Southeast Asia*, ed. J. Rigg and P. Vandergeest. Singapore: NUS Press, pp. 52–67.

Dixon, J. 2016. "The Socio-economic and Socio-cultural Determinatns of Food and Nutrition Security in Developed Countries", in *Routledge Handbook of Food and Nutrition Security*, ed. B. Pritchard, R. Ortiz and M. Shekar. Abingdon: Routledge, pp. 379–90.

Haddad, L. et al. 2014. *Maharashtra's Child Stunting Declines: What is Driving Them? Findings of a Multidisciplinary Analysis*. Brighton: IDS.

Leavy, J. and N. Hossain. 2014. "Who Wants to Farm? Youth Aspirations, Opportunities and Rising Food Prices". IDS Working Paper. Available at https://policy-practice. oxfam.org/resources/who-wants-to-farm-youth-aspirations-opportunities-and-rising-food-prices-315686/ (accessed 5 Mar. 2022).

Li, T.M. 2011. "Centering Labor in the Land Grab Debate", *The Journal of Peasant Studies* 38: 281–98.

Mahdi, S. and M. Muhammad. 2014. *Potret Kemiskinan di Aceh 2014 Angka dan Narasi*. Banda Aceh: BAPPEDA Aceh.

Maliati, N. and J.F. McCarthy. 2015. "Understanding Vulnerability and Food Insecurity: an Analysis of Policy Approaches to Food Security in Post-tsunami and Post-conflict Households in Rural Aceh". Unpublished manuscript.

Manning, C. 2014. *The Labor Market and Human Resources in Aceh: A Comparative Perspective*. Unpublished Report: EPRA–ACDP Education Policy Research in Aceh, Analytical and Capacity Development Partnership.

Maxwell, S. 1996. "Food Security: a Post-modern Perspective", *Food Policy* 2, 1: 155–70.

McCarthy, J.F. 2006. *The Fourth Circle. A Political Ecology of Sumatra's Rainforest Frontier*. Palo Alto, CA: Stanford University Press.

_____. 2014. "Using Community Led Development Approaches to Address Vulnerability After Disaster: Caught in a Sad Romance", *Global Environmental Change* 27: 144–55.

Naylor, R.L. et al. 2007. "Assessing Risks of Climate Variability and Climate Change for Indonesian Rice Agriculture", *PNAS* 104, 19: 7752–7.

Nooteboom, G. 2015. *Forgotten People: Poverty, Risk and Social Security in Indonesia. The Case of the Madurese*. Leiden: Brill.

Pritchard, B. 2016. "Food and Nutrition Security", in *Routledge Handbook of Food and Nutrition Security*, ed. B. Pritchard, R. Ortiz and M. Shekar. Abingdon: Routledge, pp. 1–23.

Pritchard, B., M. Vicol and R. Jones. 2017. "How Does the Ownership of Land Affect Household Livelihood Pathways under Conditions of De-agrarianization? 'Hanging in', 'Stepping up' and 'Stepping out' in Two North Indian Villages", *Singapore Journal of Tropical Geography* 38: 41–57.

Purwestri, R.C. et al. 2018. "What Explains Stunting among Children Living in a Rice Surplus Area in Central Java, Indonesia?", in *Diversity and Change in Food Wellbeing – Cases from Southeast Asia and Nepal,* ed. A. Niehof, H.N. Gartaula and M. Quetulio-Navarra. Wageningen, NL: Wageningen Academic Publishers, pp. 137–51.

Rigg, J., A. Salamanca and E. Thompson. 2016. "The Puzzle of East and Southeast Asia's Persistent Smallholder", *Journal of Rural Studies* 43: 118–33.

Rigg, J. et al. 2018. "More Farmers, Less Farming? Understanding the Truncated Agrarian Transition in Thailand", *World Development* 107: 327–37.

Semba, R.D. et al. 2007. "Paternal Smoking is Associated with Increased Risk of Child Malnutrition among Poor Urban Families in Indonesia", *Public Health Nutrition* 10, 1: 7–15.

Sen, A. 1999. *Development as Freedom.* New Delhi: Oxford University Press.

Srinita. 2018. "Relationship between Maternal, Household, and Socio-Economic Characteristics and Household Food Security in Aceh, Indonesia", *International Journal of Human Rights in Healthcare* 11, 3: 192–203.

TNP2K Aceh. 2018. *Strategi Percepatan Penanggulangan Kemiskinan Aceh* [Aceh Poverty Reduction Acceleration Strategy]. Banda Aceh: TNP2K.

Usfar, A.A. et al. 2010. "Obesity as a Poverty-Related Emerging Nutrition Problem: The Case of Indonesia", *Obesity Reviews* 11, 12: 924–8.

Vignato, S. 2018. "What is the Solution, Miss? Small Scale Mobility, Work and Unemployment for Young Unskilled Labourers in Aceh", in *Searching for Work: Small-scale Mobility and Unskilled Labor in Southeast Asia,* ed. S. Vignato and M. Alcano. Chiang Mai: Silkworm Books, pp. 91–143.

Waspada. 2019. "Ketika Aceh Bekerja Keras Tingkatkan Asupan Gizi, Turunkan Angka Stunting" [When Aceh Works Hard to Increase Nutritional Intake, Stunting Rates Decline]. Available at https://waspadaaceh.com/ketika-aceh-bekerja-keras-tingkatkan-asupan-gizi-turunkan-angka-stunting/ (accessed 3 Mar. 2022).

CHAPTER 6

Agrarian Change, Vulnerability and the Community Economy in Sumba

Jacqueline Vel and Stepanus Makambombu

Introduction

Chapter Two, in the introductory section of this book, highlighted debates about major trends in agrarian change (Li 2014; Rigg, Salamanca and Thompson 2016). It questioned whether these trends are occurring in Indonesia and, if so, under what particular circumstances. This chapter discusses processes taking place in the relatively remote and poor province of East Nusa Tenggara, and how they relate to changes in poverty, household vulnerability and extent of governmental social support. East Nusa Tenggara province has the second lowest ranking on the human development index among all Indonesian provinces (BPS 2019). The food security situation, measured in terms of stunting rates of children below five years, is alarming: nearly 52 per cent, against a national level of 37 per cent (Food Security Council 2015; Beal et al. 2018).

Our research focuses on rural change in Sumba. Here the eastern part of the island represents an agro-ecological area with low rainfall and long dry periods, and a strong local ceremonial economy. Such a long dry period (May–November) has two main consequences. The first is seasonality effects, which means that rural people's activities vary over the months of the year in response to rainfall and currents in the sea. Those depending on subsistence agriculture plant or sow their maize and rice at the start of the rainy season in December. Periods of food shortage occur annually from January to April, when the sea is too rough for fishing and the crops are yet to ripen. At this time, some people enter the forest in search of edible roots and plants, while more prosperous households keep a food stock from the previous harvest and sell tree crops such as dried areca nut, or cashew nuts and tamarind, in order to buy rice and cover other expenses. The long dry period also requires keeping stocks of food and exchange relations with people in other micro-climate areas of the island (Nugrohowardhani 2016).

The local, traditional, community economy has developed as a system of production and exchange adapted to these natural circumstances. Academic discussions about the traditional economy date back to the work of Polanyi (1944) and Sahlins (1974), which emphasised that traditional economies differ from the modern free-market economy because economic decision making is fundamentally embedded within a broader framework of (local) socio-political relations. Against expectations that traditional economies would vanish when the market economy and capitalistic relations entered the area, several authors have shown the persistence of such economies (McWilliam 2009: 174). In the context of Melanesia, the "custom economy" relates to "kinship group-based production, distribution and consumption of horticultural and marine produce, and livestock as well as other commodities of intrinsic value" (McDonald, Naidu and Mohanty 2016: 107). Normatively, common threads in various local versions of the custom economy include an emphasis on peace and harmony within the community, on restoring relationships and the use of chiefs to facilitate agreements, while the economy is characteristically based on mixed farming (Forsyth 2009: 95). An important observation is that land provides a critical sense of socio-cultural identity in Melanesia and is a key binding mechanism of family, clans and tribes (McDonald, Naidu and Mohanty 2016). Studies of the economy of aborigines in Australia have used the concept of "hybrid economy" to emphasise the linkages between market, state and customary components of the economy (Altman 2009). The hybrid economy concept was also used in a more activist way to show the indigenous way of valuing natural resources in a context where market values of land and water would be very low, thus opening up the opportunity for capitalist enclosures. The "House" economy is a well-known variant of a community economy, where "house" is a metaphor and microcosm of the economy, a place of origin of a specific community, and for "the base" that consists of shared materials and services of the community (Gudeman 2008: 28). The Sumbanese type of such a house economy has been described as the "Uma-economy" ("uma" being the word for house in the Kamberra language of Sumba [Vel 1994]).

In our research on household vulnerability, poverty and the effect of social protection programmes, it is very important to take the community economy into account because it explains choices and behaviour of community members. Production and exchange of goods and services not only serve the direct consumption needs of individual households, but also make, mediate and maintain social relationships that preserve the community's base (Gudeman 2008: 5). From the Uma economy perspective, a nuclear family comprising one administrative household unit is not the economy's core unit. Instead, the basis for production and exchange (decisions) is the Uma: a patrilineal sub-lineage connected to a main house in the ancestral kampong (Vel 1994). Loyalties lie primarily within this Uma group, which shows itself in daily life through mutual help, shared responsibility for ceremonies, generalised reciprocity, division of tasks and financial support for educating the children of this group. In the far past the members of the Uma would live in the same kampong, with some of the lower-class members living in temporary huts in the fields where they could look after the crops and graze the animals (Twikromo 2008). Nowadays, a few Uma members even no longer live in Sumba, although there are always some members remaining in the old kampong as guardians of the Uma's land, ancestors' tombs and houses. These guardians are usually the less educated, lower class and older Uma members who actually cultivate the Uma members' lands, herd the animals and often take care of the aged. Mutual help and generalised reciprocities now take place within this dispersed group. Educated and more prosperous Uma members with salaried employment usually live in town or the district capital. They do not spend their salaries on staple food but receive rice and maize from their kinsmen in the village. In return, they pay for school fees and agricultural inputs and host the school children of their village kinsmen. The urban Uma members thus take care of part of the monetary expenses of their village Uma members, while the village members produce food and ceremonial goods (horses, buffaloes, pigs, hand-woven cloths) for the Uma group, including its urban members.

Realising that the present day rural economy in East Sumba is characterised by the dialectics of community and market (Gudeman 2008), we seek to answer the common questions of this book specifically in the context of East Sumba. What are the drivers of vulnerability and insecurity? What are the effects of the main changes in society at large on these rural communities? What are the characteristic pathways into and out of poverty? How do government social protection programmes function in this context?

The short answer to the first question is that the most vulnerable people in East Sumba are those without a well-functioning social/ceremonial network, living in rural areas and depending on traditional subsistence agriculture. They do not have a regular cash income; they are vulnerable to weather and climate hazards, and there is hardly anyone to help them in times of crisis or to escape from poverty. In this chapter we present the results of our case study that have led to this conclusion.

Research in Three Villages in East Sumba

East Sumba is a large district with low population density. The landscape consists of savannah with a kilometre-wide strip of flat, slightly elevated plains along the north and east coast while in the interior we find limestone hills with dispersed settlements. The most populated part is along the main coastal road, and parts of the plains are cultivated in plantations. Small-scale subsistence food production is the main type of agriculture, with maize and cassava in dryland gardens and rice in the valleys and irrigated areas of the coastal land.

In 2017, around 30 per cent of the population (some 74,000 people) resided in the capital town Waingapu, which is the centre of government and education in East Sumba. The harbour and airport are close to Waingapu, where the standard of living is higher than the much poorer rural areas, but that difference is not visible from district statistics, which only indicate population averages. For example, the average percentage of people living below the poverty line was 31 per cent in 2017 (BPS-ST 2018a), whereas in our village research we found an average of 70 per cent. In terms of community economy we estimate that urban Uma members make up about 30 per cent of the district population.

Table 6.1   East Sumba in figures, 2002 and 2017

Indicator	2002	2017
Population size district (persons)	193,940	252,704
Population residing in urban area (percentage)	24%	29%
Size of the district in km²	7,000	7,000
District government budget (billion RP)	170	1,112
Part of district budget derived from locally generated tax income (billion rupiah)	7	98
Number of civil servants	1,356	4,979
Motorcycles (number)	3,037	23,284

Source: BPS-ST 2002, 2018a.

A huge change in East Sumba occurred with the national decentralisation policies implemented from 2001 onwards. Decentralisation dramatically increased the district government budget in East Sumba, which enabled, for example, road construction, opening access to remote areas in the district. The number of civil servants increased by 360 per cent (Table 6.1). Sumbanese regard the government as the most important economic sector of the island, providing employment and budgets for projects and development. Therefore, people's priority investment for decades has been in the education of their children with hopes for future employment as civil servants. Decentralisation and the creation of new sub-districts and villages (*pemekaran*) have brought opportunities for government employment closer to the people in East Sumba, and the local economy has improved, as attested by the huge increase in motorcycles.

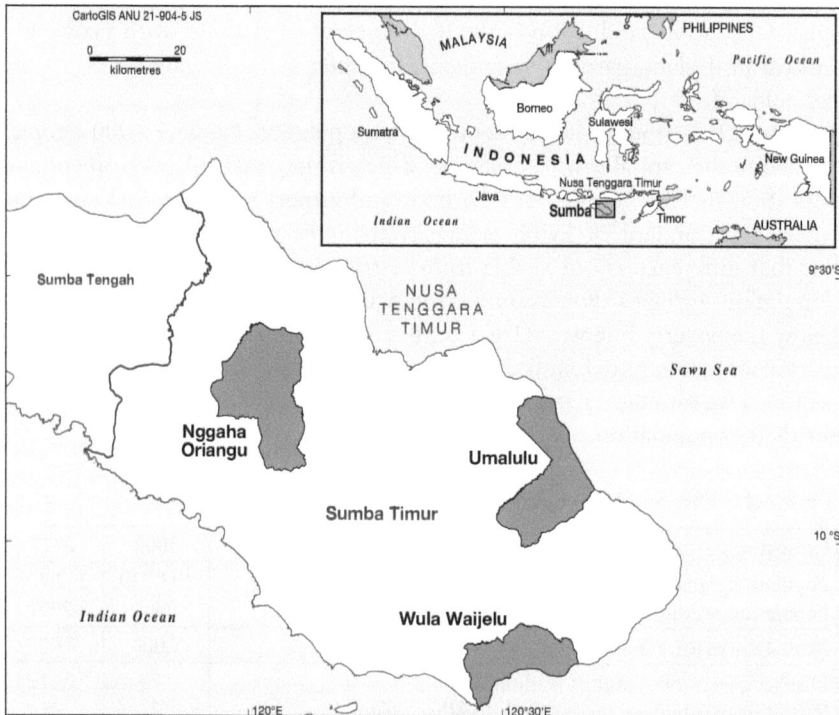

Figure 6.1   Map of case study areas on Sumba

There is no industry on Sumba that offers jobs to the local population. As a consequence, a key trend is out-migration of young people to Bali or Kalimantan for low-skilled jobs, or to pursue higher education in Waingapu, Java or the provincial capital, Kupang. International labour migration from the province East Nusa Tenggara, including Sumba, is increasing, but many are illegal migrants who are very vulnerable for exploitation and abuse (ANTARA/Floresa 2018). Often migrants' spouses or children remain in the village, creating a new category of "migration widows" and orphans. Furthermore, with out-migration, labour at home is lost and remittances are irregular and small.

To answer our research questions, we conducted field research in three villages, using the mixed methods of the comparative research project (Table 6.2). Our fieldwork took place between February 2016 and June 2018. The survey comprised 40 households per village.

Table 6.2   Three villages of the study in East Sumba, 2016 data

	Village (desa) (pseudonym)	Sub-district (kecamatan)	Number of inhabitants	Size of the village (ha)	Households (KK)
1	Desa NOA	Nggaha Oriangu	1,127	3,110	279
2	Desa WW	Wula Waijelu	1,345	9,720	248
3	Desa UM	Umalulu	2,200	6,560	357

Source: Our village questionnaires.

Our research identifies three broad scenarios of agrarian change in East Sumba. Each scenario is based on our in-depth village research and highlights specific major changes. Together the three villages capture the principal poverty and change processes occurring in Sumba, with each having different livelihood options. Two of the villages are more easily accessible, while the third is relatively remote; but all are locally regarded as poor.

Scenario 1: Dry Land, Migration and the Benefits of Decentralisation

In the village designated Desa NOA, the changes mentioned above had a clear impact. The village is situated one hour's drive east of Waingapu, in a hilly savannah landscape (*padang*) with scattered patches of dryland gardens. In the valleys there are some (rainfed) rice fields. Dryland farming here is very vulnerable to drought, as happened in 2015, when the rice harvest failed completely. Land is available for all villagers who wish to cultivate crops, but labour is the limiting factor as all agricultural work is done manually. From the savannah the villagers gather wood, fruits, wild tubers and leaves for their own consumption. Because the villagers do not measure what they gather, we could not calculate their exact annual income. Educational levels are very low: only 15 per cent of the household heads in our survey had secondary education, and 65 per cent did not finish primary school or had never been to school at all. The yields per hectare for rice and maize are low, with an estimated level of 1 ton per hectare for both rice and maize.

Local informants offered a historical reason for the basic lifestyle and high poverty incidence in the village, explaining that it has always been a poor man's settlement. It lacks the common structure of a traditional village with the leaders' houses in the centre. The villagers' origin can be traced to low class members of a traditional kingdom, who were stationed out in the fields to cultivate food gardens away from the kingdom's centre. Relatively low social status is therefore one of the characteristics of the villagers in Desa NOA, and is a structural barrier to moving out of poverty.

Selling vegetables, betel fruits and areca nuts along the main road of Sumba island provides some cash for daily expenses. The 2015 drought made rice cultivation impossible, so the villagers had to find coping strategies to earn money so that they could buy rice. A shortage of drinking water was their second problem. Relatively prosperous households could afford to buy water from a delivery service, but the poor had to walk for hours fetching water from springs. Another big problem was meeting obligations of the ceremonial economy, which means having to contribute livestock at ceremonial events. One of the solutions that apparently some people chose was stealing livestock from other households, which was a serious problem for the victims of theft (Figure 6.2).

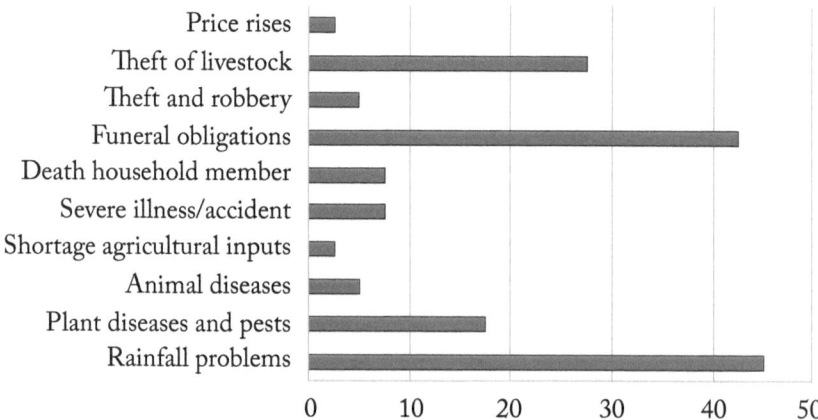

Household Problems in Desa NOA in 2015

Figure 6.2   Problems that households in Desa NOA (East Sumba) faced in 2015 (percentage of households that mentioned this problem)
Source: Our village questionnaires.

Since the village was created in 2003 as part of decentralisation efforts, government and NGO services and programmes have increased. Several respondents could move out of poverty because they managed to obtain credit or received a regular income as village government officials. Ten per cent of the households interviewed in 2016 had relatives in town or in other parts of Indonesia, but only occasionally would those labour migrants send money to their home village. Labour migration of adult household members is not an attractive option for small households that already suffer from labour shortages. Additionally, poor households cannot afford the initial costs of migrating to other areas. In one case, a man migrated to Kalimantan after being recruited for plantation labour. However, his wife had not heard from him in the eight years since he had left, and she has become a "migration widow". One positive local case concerns a man who was able to accumulate NGO assistance, a small income as the neighbourhood head, and a good position in ceremonial exchange networks. He was able to send one of his sons to Java for further education, who then obtained permanent employment in Jakarta. The son financed a new and modern house in the village, and relatives now live in the house as caretakers.

In summary, this first scenario presents the issues affecting poor dryland subsistence farmers who have limited opportunities to participate in the market economy and rely more on the community economy. Investing in ceremonial exchange is a priority to secure social relations within the community. These households are very vulnerable to hazards like droughts and animal disease epidemics, because those disasters affect the base of their livelihoods and they have few alternatives. To cope with crisis, they rely on support from the community economy networks.

Scenario 2: Food Sovereignty, Trade and Tourism

Food sovereignty, in the sense of consuming rice, maize, beans and vegetables that are grown on the communities' own land, is a basic value in the Uma economy of Sumba. Uma members who earn a salary are reluctant to use the money for buying food. Rather they cooperate with their relatives in the village as described above. The larger the biodiversity in the community's base, the easier it is to apply community food sovereignty in practice.

Such a situation is found in Desa WW, situated in a remote area on the southeastern tip of Sumba island. The village landscape is wide and diverse. From the village centre a small road bends to the famous beach with the rock formation that is one of East Sumba's official "tourist objects". To the west there are high forested hills with steep cliffs south to the sea. In the remotest part of the village, food sovereignty practices are most visible. Diverse and stable subsistence was always possible because the village is close to both the sea (fishing) and forest (gathering) and has all year agriculture on the riverbanks (*mondu*).

The riverbank gardens are private property, but without a state-issued property certificate. Instead, community rules (as part of the Uma economy) regulate use rights of this "limited base" (Gudeman 2008: 33–4). The average maize garden is 1 hectare, which yields around 400 kg of maize per year (Table 6.3). The villagers use their maize harvest for their own consumption, for generalised (barter) exchange with relatives and neighbours and for feeding chickens and pigs. Maize means food security, because it can be stored for months.

A landmark event occurred in 2010, when Desa WW was connected to the main road network, which increased trade opportunities and access to government services. From then on, people started growing cash crops and gathering forest products for sale. The spatial distribution of wealthy households indicates the link between roads and economic progress: most households that have escaped from poverty since 2010 reside along the new main road at the entrance of the village.

Trade and government services have changed the daily diet in the village. Typically, the inhabitants of this village eat two meals per day of maize and rice mixed, with the ratio depending on the availability of rice. The villagers obtain rice in two ways: as social assistance from the government or by selling or bartering other products in exchange for rice. There is a wide array of "cash products" from the forest, sea, or tree gardens, each with their own seasons for harvesting, selling and consuming. For example, shrimps and fish are available all year for those skilled in fishing. Some villagers earn money by catching lobsters and selling to a district trader. Our survey data indicate that areca nut (*pinang*) is the main cash crop. Its primary use is personal consumption, but market demand in Sumba is high and since areca is easy to dry and store, it is very suitable as a savings commodity. Whenever areca nut owners need cash, they can sell some at the local market. This means that from the perspective of the villagers gathering and selling these "cash crops", it is not really a commercial activity, but rather a way of collecting "community currency, a means to be able to fulfil a specified need (and not a marker of value in general)" (Gudeman 2008: 128).

Seasonal variation in areca market prices is high, with peaks in December–January of IDR 50,000 (USD 3.7) per kg dried nuts. Similar collecting and selling practices apply for tamarind, tobacco and betel fruit (*sirih*). From June to December some of the villagers collect sea grass (*sargesang*) from the beach. In 2016 their daily harvest per person equalled the price of 6 kg rice.

Our household survey indicated that selling pigs and chicken was the largest source of household cash income, both for the poor (42 per cent) and for the non-poor (72 per cent). Although this is not a seasonal activity, prices vary considerably due to seasonal fluctuations in market supply and demand, with peaks in the high season for ceremonies (June–August) and lowest prices in the hunger season when market supply is large. Table 6.3 provides the figures on households' annual production and share in total cash earnings. The table ends with a category of unmeasured production for own consumption, which is an essential element of the community economy.

Table 6.3   Annual production from agriculture and gathering in local market prices per household in Desa WW, East Sumba in 2016

	Poor Households		Non-poor Households	
Sources of production and cash earnings	**Rupiah x 1000**	**% of cash earnings**	**Rupiah x 1000**	**% of cash earnings**
Annual Maize production (average per household in Rupiah x 1000) (1kg=Rp 5,000)	1.727		2.224	
Real annual cash earnings from:				
agriculture and trees (no maize)	483	9	1.274	14
animal husbandry	2.115	42	6.632	72
the sea: fish, lobster, seaweed	1.367	27	1.241	13
Other (mostly gathering from forest)	1.117	22	654	1
Total measured annual production from land, forest, sea and livestock, per household per year	**6.810**		**11.435**	
Total unmeasured production for own consumption: building wood, firewood, water, roots and tubers, fruits, betel, areca nut, fish, meat, eggs, etc.	n.a.		n.a.	

Source: Our field research findings from household survey.

Another major change in this area is the development of tourism. Local tourists from Waingapu already visit the beach on Sundays. Moreover, land along the beach is targeted by real estate developers, some simply speculating on the prospect that "Sumba will be the new Bali", and others actually building tourist resorts. A government infrastructure project reached the village in 2018, providing the construction of a highway along the south coast. In 2017, the villagers wondered how tourism developments could be beneficial to themselves and their environment. During the period of our field research, tourism had not yet affected the local economy. However, in other parts of Sumba, tourism development had increased economic activity but had also caused land dispossession and conflicts between project developers and the local population (see Alvionitasari 2018).

In summary, the second scenario shows a transition from food sovereignty founded on an unlimited community resource base to a mixed system. Now, food sovereignty with a limited community base is combined with trade in livestock and tree products and supplemented with government food aid (rice). There are imminent threats to the villagers' secure access to land and sea because of the enclosure of the area for tourism development.

Scenario 3: Rice Cultivation, Climate Change and Plantations

In the coastal plains of East Sumba rice cultivation, extensive animal husbandry and fisheries have traditionally been the main sources of livelihood. Now two major changes are disrupting these practices: unpredictable and variable rainfall patterns due to climate change, and the establishment of large plantations. East Sumba district is an agro-ecological area characterised by low rainfall and long dry periods. Indeed, average annual rainfall in East Sumba was 1,045 mm in 2017 (BPS-ST 2018a), whereas in the coastal area it was 691 mm in 2016 and 851 in 2017, as shown in Figures 6.3a and 6.3b.

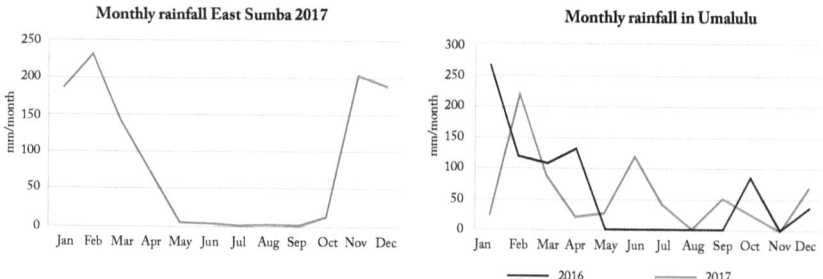

Figure 6.3 (a) East Sumba's average annual rainfall per month in 2017, (b) Rainfall in Umalulu sub-district in 2016 and 2017
Sources: BPS-ST 2018a: 40; BPS-ST 2018b: 7.

During our research, it became clear that "vulnerable to rainfall fluctuations" would be a more appropriate description of the area than "dryland", because from the end of 2015 up to January 2016, exceptional droughts occurred in the coastal Umalulu district, whereas in 2017 the same area had excessive rainfall and floods in April, which washed away part of the crops. Fishers also suffer from the consequences of climate change. Early in 2016, the coastal ocean temperature was exceptionally high and currents changed from their usual seasonal patterns. In 2017, the sea remained rough for much longer than normal, which postponed the fishing season that usually starts in June. The fishers along Sumba's east coast are vulnerable to these variables because they have only very simple equipment and no large ships that can withstand adverse weather conditions. Due to these climate change-related hazards, traditional strategies to deal with hunger periods are not sufficient anymore.

The inhabitants of the third research site, Desa UM, have been vulnerable to variations in rainfall. In our research sample, 23 per cent of the households were fisherfolk and 68 per cent rice farmers. To reduce rainfall dependency, the World Bank-sponsored development Program Nasional Pemberdayaan Masyarakat [PNPM] (National Programme for Community Empowerment) constructed an irrigation system in the period from 2005 to 2010, so that more land could be used for irrigated rice cultivation in Desa UM, resulting in an expansion from 150 ha to 560 ha. After completion of the irrigation system, there were a few years of "bumper crops" with harvests of 3 tons per hectare, twice per year. During that period, rice farmers were able to invest and could afford to send their children to town to enrol in higher education, or to Bali in search of a paid job. Among the households in our survey, 28 per cent have household members living/working in town or in other parts of Indonesia. These migrant labour relatives usually do not send regular remittances but, as village informants told us, they "help us out at when we urgently need a lot of money" (*membantu kalau ada kebutuhan mendesak*), in particular for ceremonial expenses at weddings and funerals, but also for paying fees for their siblings' tertiary education.

Unfortunately, the irrigation system in Desa UM has frequently experienced leaking pipes and long dry periods, depleting the water sources. As a temporary solution, the village government introduced a rotation scheme for irrigating paddy fields, with each field having access during half of the year. From 2013 onwards, water problems increased with the establishment of a sugar plantation, leading to a "classic story" of water grabbing (Mehta, Veldwisch and Franco 2012). The sugar plantation diverted the villagers' irrigation water to the plantation area (Vel and Makambombu 2019). Since 2014, only rain-fed rice cultivation has been possible. By 2017, a third of the respondents who had formerly cultivated rice said that they had stopped working their paddy fields altogether. Another 44 per cent continued despite the water problems, growing rice only in the rainy season. Their yields were only a third of what they had been before the establishment of the plantation.

Working for the plantation company has been an alternative source of income since 2014. Daily wages vary between IDR 61,000 for labourers to

IDR 65,000 (USD 4.5 to 4.8) for headmen (*mandor*), and all staff must bring their own food. One of the headmen commented:

> At the plantation we earn just enough to cover our daily food expenses, nothing more. But the difference is that now we can buy rice per bag for a whole month, whereas previously when food was short, we could buy only small quantities, just for a day or week.

Plantation work takes the whole day, while growing rice does not. Working for the plantation implies dependency on the market for buying food, whereas self-sufficiency in staple food used to be the norm (Makambombu 2016). Despite these disadvantages of plantation work, there has been little protest in the village against the plantation for several reasons: 35 per cent of the surveyed households depend on the plantation for employment, or work as casual labourers; they know that a critical attitude leads to immediate dismissal. Pro-plantation village leaders and the plantation company in collaboration with the district government and its security apparatus have threatened protesters. The plantation company has hired police and security forces to guard their lands and to put pressure on critical villagers.

In summary, the third scenario shows a transition from independent small-scale irrigated rice cultivation and fisheries to dependency on a plantation company for (mostly casual) labour employment and a return to rain-fed agriculture under adverse circumstances.

Poverty and Progress

After depicting the three scenarios of rural change, we will now focus specifically on the people living under these circumstances. Who are considered poor in these villages? And what are the characteristic pathways into and out of poverty?

Using the Stages of Progress (SoP) method (Krishna 2009) resulted in a differentiation between poor, less poor and relatively wealthy, according to *internal* (emic) criteria (Table 6.4). In meetings with men and women from all parts of the three villages, they specified criteria for classifying their fellow villagers' households, indicating which "stage of progress" each household had reached. SoP's opening question for generating the local stages of progress is "what is the first item of expenditure on which they would spend money? And after that....?" They made the distinctions as presented in Table 6.4.

Table 6.4   Stages of progress in three villages in East Sumba, 2016–17

Category	Stages
The very poor (*tau mila*)	1. food 2. clothes 3. shelter 4. primary education for children
Still poor but progressing	5. pigs and poultry 6. secondary education for children 7. agricultural equipment 8. kitchen equipment
Not poor (*tau peku*)	9. motorcycle 10. rice mill, maize mill, harvest equipment 11. home water reservoir 12. tertiary education for children
Wealthy (*tau wulu*)	More than 1–12

The cut-off point between poor and not poor is where households start spending money on small household investments (in this case a motorcycle), instead of on basic household needs only. The non-poor have some working capital for a small business or shop, and can afford travel costs for finding work outside Sumba as migrant labourers. "Wealthy" households also spend money on building permanent brick and tile houses in the village. Applying the SoP method in Sumba does however raise some questions. First, the poverty ranking refers to relative differences within the village community. The "non-poor or wealthy" according to SoP might be still poor according to (etic) national criteria. Second, in community economies like in Sumba—with free gathering, barter and ceremonial exchange—the methods do not capture the whole picture, because SoP is focused on monetary expenditures. However, it does indicate relative perceived poverty levels in the village community (Vel and Makambombu 2010).

Next, villagers compared the current situation of each household with the situation 10 to 15 years ago, to assess each individual household's extent of progress. In each village, a main local landmark event indicated the reference period. For scenario 1, that was the creation of Desa NOA as an independent village (decentralisation); for scenario 2, it was the village's connection to the main road (enabling trade options); and for scenario 3, it was the year before the first irrigation scheme was established. The result was that 23 per cent of the households had escaped from poverty since that time, but 70 per cent remained poor (Table 6.5).

Table 6.5 Average division of the households across three villages in East Sumba according to the Stages of Progress method

SoP Category	Percentage of total number of households in sample
Remained poor	69
Became poor	1
Escaped from poverty	23
Remained non-poor	7

The differences between the villages are considerable. In Figure 6.4 we differentiate those who have remained very poor (stages 1–4) and those who are still poor but have made some progress (up to stage 8). Particularly in Desa UM, the irrigated rice village, the poor have made considerable progress compared with the situation before the irrigation system was constructed. Another remarkable finding is that in the food sovereignty scenario, a relatively large percentage of households was able to escape from poverty after the new road was opened.

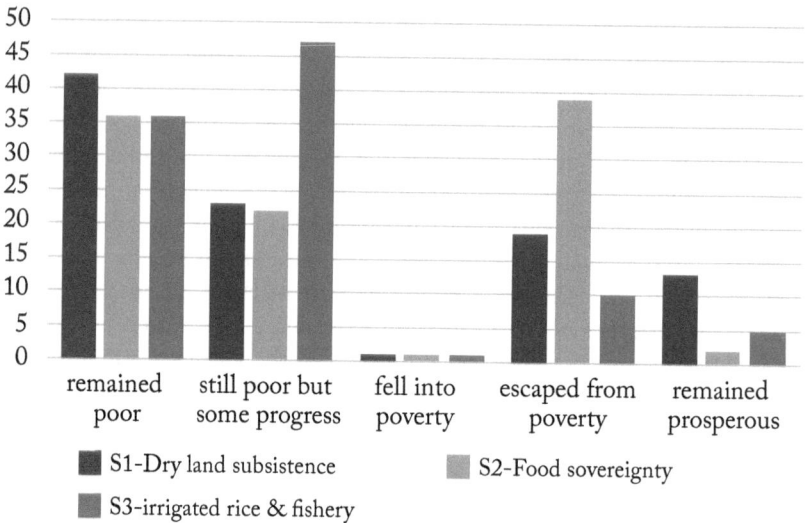

Figure 6.4 Stages of Progress division of households in three scenarios/villages in East Sumba in percentage of total number of households per village, 2016–17
Source: Results of the SoP sessions in three research villages.

The quantitative results raise questions about the people who have remained poor and the existence of characteristic pathways out of poverty when considering the people who were able to escape from poverty. Our qualitative research offered the following characteristics.

Those Who Remained Poor

People in this category have problems meeting their daily needs. Their harvest yields will provide food for only 4 to 6 months. As a consequence, they often depend on support from others; but the poorest lack good social relations with other households. Because they do not have the appropriate goods to contribute to ceremonial exchange (e.g. horses, cloths, pigs, pendants), they must either become indebted to fulfil their obligations, or accept that they are excluded from community exchange circuits and attending ceremonies. The poorest also do not have close relatives with salaried employment. Some borrow from money lenders, usually at high interest rates. Government Social support, in particular the Rastra (*beras sejahtera* [welfare rice]) programme, is very important for their food supply. Fishing, hunting and gathering from the sea and the forests are traditional sources of food security. The poor have no permanent houses but live in bamboo huts with thatched roofs. They have little or no money and cannot afford to send their children to school beyond junior high school (Sekolah Menegah Pertama [SMP]). Young couples are often in this category, because they have no capital whatsoever yet, and work as dependants of the husband's parents.

Those Who Fell into Poverty

The few households in this category have commonly lost a breadwinner, due to illness or death of a family member, or out-migration of older children. The costs of children's education and meeting *adat* obligations, animal diseases and theft deplete livestock assets. The 40 kg Rastra rice per quarter is important for these households. In one typical example, a widow received irregular small remittances from her son in Bali. She sold chickens and fruit to people working at the sugar plantation. Her house and garden are on land that belongs to her brother-in-law who works as a policeman in Bali.

Those Who Escaped Poverty

People in this category have managed to acquire household assets, including some luxury items like a television. They can afford education for their children beyond secondary school, increasing the chances that their offspring will eventually obtain a salaried job. They have chickens and pigs, and one to five horses, cattle or buffaloes. They participate in the community economy network, contributing with appropriate gifts in ceremonial exchange. This means that their social networks in the community are strong enough to borrow from fellow community members in times of shortage. However, they are not completely self-sufficient in food, but buy rice, or depend on Rastra rice. They have succeeded in escaping from poverty by running a small enterprise, selling cash crops or trading. They obtained working capital from a credit scheme or NGO aid project (Desa NOA); or bank credit or moneylenders (Desa WW); or from a few good harvests (Desa UM). Being able to access credit programmes shows they have good relations. Some people in this category perform official tasks for the village government or have become village facilitators for NGO programmes. They have enough access to land and labour to grow tree crops, such as tamarind, areca nut and cashew, and to harvest the fruits as cash crops. In Desa UM, working at the plantation has improved the household's economy for some.

Those Who Remained Non-poor

In Desa NOA, the relative number of non-poor is high compared to the other two villages, which is puzzling because from our household survey perspective, there are no wealthy people in this village, no one with a regular salary or an income-generating enterprise. The source of wealth must be in the invisible part of the economy, discussed below. In Desa UM, only two households in the survey qualified as remaining prosperous. The first belongs to a female teacher (civil servant) and her husband who occasionally works for the plantation company. The second household is a family of Savunese origin. Ten years ago, they cultivated onions as a cash crop. They also produced lontar palm sugar (*gula Sabu*) and the strong alcoholic drink locally called *peci*. Additionally, the man earned income from herding cattle for a Chinese businessman from the district capital town, in a share-arrangement that provided him with 30 per cent of each year's calves as his own property. After cattle thieves had stolen his cattle herd in 2013, the household changed to raising goats and chickens, a task which is undertaken by women and children. In 2014, the plantation company started working on the land adjacent to his house. He sold part of his land to the company for road construction and obtained employment as labour supervisor, with a monthly salary of IDR 5 million (USD 370). He could arrange plantation employment for his son and daughter as well; he regarded the presence of the plantation as "a gift of God".

Those Who Escaped the Village

Our research points to a fifth category: people who have taken the opportunity to escape from village life. The wealthiest people can stay outside the village in what they call "our own house" (*kita punya rumah sendiri*) (Vel 1994:

160–3), indicating a wide social network and access to alternative sources of income. In this category, we find the Uma members who have received higher education and now have salaried positions in town. High ranking government officials, for example, typically have three houses: one village house, one private house in town and one official residence (*rumah jabatan*). All three houses are co-inhabited by their Uma members as a way of sharing the resources of the Uma base. This category is beyond what is measured through the SoP method. From the perspective of the community economy, however, these "escaped relatives" are full members of the Uma. The closer the geographical and social distance to the village, the more important their contributions to the common pool.

Food Insecurity and Coping Strategies

With such a high incidence of poverty, and a commonly occurring annual hunger period (Van den End 1987: 579) we investigated how households in East Sumba deal with food crises. Figure 6.5 presents the overview of the remedies that households have used in times of food crisis and indicates the frequency with which each strategy was applied.

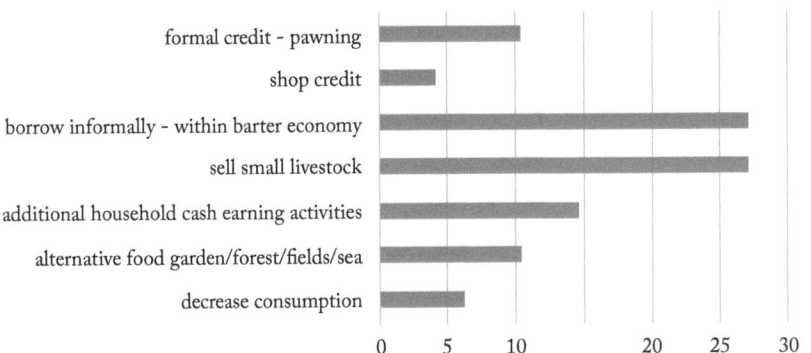

Figure 6.5   Relative importance of coping strategies in three villages in East Sumba, 2016–17 (percentage of the total number of strategies mentioned in the food security surveys)
Source: Our village food security questionnaires.

The most common strategy is to sell small livestock: chickens, piglets, dogs or goats. This is a last resort solution, because when many villagers try to sell their small livestock in the hunger period so that they can buy rice, the livestock market prices are low. Equally frequently mentioned is asking for, or borrowing money or food from relatives, neighbours and friends. This refers to the community economy which involves the mutual assistance in a long-term relationship of general or balanced reciprocity (Sahlins 1974: 193–4). In Desa NOA and Desa WW, the villagers still have the option of engaging in additional cash-earning activities, for example by selling vegetables, fruit and forest products to middlemen. Formal bank credit is minimal because the poor are generally not credit-worthy. Some people pawn their (ceremonial economy) assets. Only a few indicated they had reduced their food consumption, while 10 per cent of responses referred to gathering alternative foods like wild tubers, fish, insects or wild animals.

The coping strategies in Figure 6.5 relate to household food crises during the hunger periods. But the villagers also experience other types of problems, as indicated in Figure 6.2 above. Droughts, pests, theft of livestock and animal diseases affect the production capacity of the households. The respondents in Desa NOA indicated that for half of the problems experienced, there were no remedies at all. Their coping strategies included borrowing and obtaining help from relatives and friends and selling small livestock. For their problems related to agricultural production, the villagers hardly received any assistance from the government. The veterinary service of the government is not active in the three villages. Improved government policies to prevent livestock epidemics would enhance protection of capital (savings) in the community economy and might have more lasting effects than the social protection programmes discussed next.

Social Protection Programmes and their Effect

The government of Indonesia provides social support to citizens who qualify as recipients, based on nationally set criteria (see Chapter 3). Because the government's social protection programmes consist of cash transfers and subsidised rice to the village population, they influence the monetary and daily barter aspects of the community economy in East Sumba. Most important is the rice programme (Rastra) that provides rice to nearly all households at highly subsidised prices (around 20 per cent of market price). In Desa WW we found that for the poor households, Rastra rice accounts for a third of the total annual rice consumption and for the non-poor it is a quarter. Desa WW is different from the other two because there are no paddy fields in that village, so the villagers need to buy, get or barter all the rice they consume. Therefore, the respondents in this village could indicate their rice expenditures more precisely than in the other two villages (see Table 6.6).

Table 6.6 Rastra's annual contribution to the rice consumption of households in Desa WW, East Sumba (2016)

	Poor Households N=23		Non-poor households N=17	
	IDR	**%**	**IDR**	**%**
Desa WW East Sumba 2016 Data per household Price of rice RP 10,000/kg				
Average amount of rice aid	896,086	34	937,058	25
Annual real expenditure on rice	1,723,809	66	2,849,375	75
Total rice consumption	2,619,895	100	3,786,433	100

Source: Our field research findings from household surveys.

Village governments distribute Rastra rice every three months. In the three villages, the government decided to include all households as Rastra recipients, instead of distributing according to the official selection procedures because several obviously very poor households were missing on the official lists. Practically all households had difficulties in meeting their food requirements, even those that had more assets. This local policy of equal sharing is a way to avoid conflicts in the village, and it rests on wide consensus. In Desa WW and Desa NOA, every household received the standard amount of 30 kg per quarter. In Desa UM the government gave 50 kg to households that were on the official list, while the other households received 40 kg every 6 months. A third of the poor in our survey were apparently not on the official list, because they only received 40 kg every 6 months. None of the non-poor who received Rastra were on the official list. Although Desa UM used to be a rice producing village, our survey indicated that 40 per cent of the poor and 70 per cent of the non-poor had bought rice in 2017. The remaining 60 per cent of the poor grow their own rice or eat maize; some aged people receive rice from their children. Table 6.7 presents information about the social protection programmes that have been implemented in the three survey villages.

The number of PKH recipients in the three villages is relatively low. Two local PKH facilitators explained that many more people would qualify than those who are on the current list. Additionally, some people on the list do not meet the criteria of the programme but have had their names inserted because of interventions by the village head. Although the list should have been prepared by officials from the Central Statistics Bureau (BPS), in practice several BPS officials asked the village secretary to fill in the forms, which opened the opportunity for discretion and potential bias.

Table 6.7 Distribution of social protection programme recipients in East Sumba, 2016–17

Percentage of households per category that receive this type of social protection	Rice food aid for poor households Rastra	National direct cash transfer programme BLT	Poor students assistance BSM	National health insurance KIS	National conditional cash transfer programme – health and education PKH	Assistance for personal education expenses to disadvantaged households with school children KIP
Poor households						
Desa UM (total 30)	100	7	23	63	33	33
Desa WW	100	70	30	91	30	61
Desa NOA	97	53	63		25	
Non–poor households						
Desa UM (total 10)	80	10	20	30	0	0
Desa WW	94	38	31	75	25	50
Desa NOA	75	63	63		13	
East Sumba district % of all households in 2016 BPS-ST (2018c)	54.46				42.78	11

The cash transfers are primarily used for buying rice. BSM and PKH money is also used for school expenditures, including shoes and photocopies of schoolbooks. If there is some money left, recipients prefer to buy small livestock as a way of productively storing the money.

KIS and KIP were new programmes in these villages and not yet fully operational at the time of our survey. In Desa UM, several respondents had received KIS and KIP cards, but did not know how to use them. The former village head had distributed the cards without explanation about their use, simultaneously with distributing compensation money (*uang sirih pinang*) from the sugar plantation company, thereby associating card distribution with support for the company.

Unanswered and Invisible

This chapter has presented considerable data on the household economy, but blind spots remain.

First is the question of how to include and value the reciprocal exchanges that are characteristic of the Uma economy. In the introduction we explained how the urban Uma members pay part of the monetary expenses of their village counterparts, who produce food and ceremonial goods for the whole Uma group in exchange. However, contradicting this Uma food-sovereignty picture, the results of the household survey indicate that most village households buy subsidised Rastra and market rice. Moreover, what villagers produce for their relatives in town was not included in the survey answers about household production, because they regarded that as production for the urban relatives. Likewise, what the village households receive in return for cultivating the rice fields of their relatives is considered as (non-measured) sharing. This means not only that both production and consumption are higher than indicated by the results of the household surveys, but also that the village Uma members are often short of food for themselves.

The second issue is the (statistical) invisibility of the daily gathering and barter economy. In the food sovereignty scenario, this is a large part of the community economy. Water, firewood, materials for building simple houses, vegetables, herbs, betel, areca nut, edible insects, palm sugar, eggs and fish are all still freely available. The harvest is not counted (unless it is sold), and villagers do not regard food gathered from the forest and fields as a real meal, despite its high nutritional value. The invisibility of this part of the economy leads to undervaluation of production through surveys. It also questions the definitions of poverty that are linked to income and material assets.

A third question concerns the size of the illicit economy, which is, by definition, statistically invisible. The examples that we came across in our case study are: brewing and selling alcohol (made from palm sugar), selling eggs of protected bird species, accepting bribes from the plantation company and (alleged) embezzlement of compensation funds intended for people who offered land to the sugar plantation. The benefits of such illicit activities can be very large for some households which, for example, are suddenly able to build an expensive brick and tile house, as happened in Desa UM.

Agrarian Change and the Community Economy

Finally, we return to the questions of how major change processes relate to poverty and household vulnerability in Sumba, and how government social support programmes or mechanisms within the community economy support the resilience of East Sumba's villagers. We found three major forces at work: climate change and impacts on rainfall patterns; capitalist expansion leading to land and water dispossession and commodification of parts of the community base; and increasing state influence on village life.

In two of the three villages, the influence of climate change appeared through long drought periods followed by excessive rainfall, leading to floods washing away the crops. Because the pattern of seasons has changed, farmers wonder when to sow their crops, and what to do after floods. The traditional community coping mechanism of bartering food between relatives living in different micro-climatic zones of the island is disturbed when the harvesting periods no longer succeed each other. Harvest failure not only increases food insecurity in the villages, but also has a negative impact on the exchange relations with Uma members living in town, because the village members cannot fulfil their obligations in the community economy. Respondents in our village research did not receive any government assistance related to droughts or floods.

Irrigation systems are meant to increase resilience against drought periods and they exist in one research village. The system functioned well, until a large sugar corporation enclosed the area just upstream from the rice village and appropriated their water resources. The subsequent water shortages turned irrigated rice farmers into dry land subsistence peasants or casual plantation labourers. Land dispossession also occurs with commercial tourism investment along East Sumba's beaches. In the food-sovereignty village, an enclosure for a tourist resort development has gradually reduced the unlimited community resource base to a limited one, thus stimulating within-community competition over land and forest products.

Another effect of the emerging capitalist relations is commodification of parts of the community base. Goods that used to be gathered for free, and shared or exchanged in the ceremonial economy, are now becoming scarce. Moreover, sharing ends when property relations become individualised. The work of household members is commodified when they become plantation labourers, or labourers for wealthy rice field owners. Opening up to regional markets provides opportunities for some, as in the village where 40 per cent of the households escaped from poverty after a new road facilitated trade. However, the market economy comes with dependency on market price fluctuations. One specific impact on the community economy is that the value of livestock—horses, pigs, buffaloes—is no longer determined by the rules of ceremonial exchange (Onvlee 1980), but relates to supply and demand on the meat market in the district and eventually on Java. The consequential inflation of livestock market prices disturbs power balances between and within lineages, making ceremonial exchange unaffordable for many.

The third major force of change is the increasing influence of the state in the villages, with positive and negative effects for the village population. District and national governments facilitate capitalist expansion into the rural areas of Sumba by granting business licences for plantations or tourist resorts as mentioned above. The government prioritises economic development policies over protecting the resource base of communities. Government interventions have brought positive effects through infrastructure projects, like the irrigation scheme in one village and the connecting road in another. Villagers appreciate the increasing social support from government, in particular rice food aid, basic health insurance and child support assistance. However, government social support to individual households changes relations within the community economy and may weaken the ties between Uma members, decreasing the internal community's social support system. Considering the long-term importance of the community economy (and absence of alternatives), the government could strengthen villagers' resilience by protecting their community resource base. That would require the prevention of livestock epidemics, protection of water resources and the environment, and recognition of customary land rights.

Acknowledgements

Field research was supported by the Van Vollenhoven Institute of Leiden University. We thank our colleagues in the project and field assistants in Sumba, and in particular the residents of Desa UM, Desa WW and Desa NOA, for participation in the research and their hospitality.

References

Altman, J. 2009. "The Hybrid Economy and Anthropological Engagements with Policy Discourse: A Brief Reflection", *The Australian Journal of Anthropology* 20, 3: 318–29.

Alvionitasari, R. 2018. "Begini Kronologi Tewasnya Poro Duka di Pesisir Marosi Sumba Barat" [Here's the Chronology of Poro Duka's Death at Marosi Beach, West Sumba]. Available at https://nasional.tempo.co/read/1085044/begini-kronologi-tewasnya-poro-duka-di-pesisir-marosi-sumba-barat/ (accessed 18 October 2021).

ANTARA/Floresa. 2018. "Jumlah TKI Ilegal Asal NTT Mencapai Sekitar 100 Ribu" [Number of Illegal Indonesian Workers from NTT (East Nusa Tenggara Province) Reached around 100,000]. Available at https://www.floresa.co/2018/04/09/33756/ (accessed 20 Mar. 2022).

Beal, T. et al. 2018. "A Review of Child Stunting Determinants in Indonesia", *Maternal and Child Nutrition* 4, 4: e12617.

BPS (Badan Pusat Statistik/Central Bureau of Statistics of Indonesia). 2019. *Human Development Indices by Province, 2010–2018 (New Method)*. Available at https://bps.go.id/indicator/26/494/1/-metode-baru-indeks-pembangunan-manusia-menurut-provinsi.html (accessed 12 Jan. 2022).

BPS-ST (Statistics of East Sumba Regency) – Available at https://sumbatimurkab.bps.go.id/publication.html (accessed 12 Jan. 2022):

_____. 2002. *Sumba Timur dalam Angka* (East Sumba in Figures) *2002*.

_____. 2018a. *Sumba Timur dalam Angka* (East Sumba in Figures) *2018*.

_____. 2018b. *Umalulu dalam Angka* (Umalulu in Figures) *2018*.

_____. 2018c. *Statistik Kesejahteraan Rakyat Kabupaten Sumba Timur 2018* (Welfare Statistics of East Sumba District 2018).

Food Security Council, Department of Agriculture, World Food Programme. 2015. *Food Security and Vulnerability Atlas of Indonesia 2015*. Available at http://documents.wfp.org/stellent/groups/public/documents/ena/wfp276246.pdf (accessed 16 June 2022).

Forsyth, M. 2009. *A Bird that Flies with Two Wings: Kastom and State Justice Systems in Vanuatu*. Canberra: ANU E Press.

Gudeman, S. 2008. *Economy's Tension: the Dialectics of Community and Market*. New York and Oxford: Berghahn Books.

Krishna, A. 2009. "Subjective Assessments, Participatory Methods, and Poverty Dynamics", in *Poverty Dynamics: Interdisciplinary Perspectives*, ed. T. Addison, D. Hulme and R. Kanbur. Oxford: Oxford University Press, pp. 183–201.

Li, T.M. 2014. *Land's End: Capitalist Relations on an Indigenous Frontier*. Durham, NC: Duke University Press.

Makambombu, S. 2016. *Pembangunan Sumba Timur, Mau ke Mana? Catatan Refleksi Masuknya Investasi di Sumba Timur* [Developing East Sumba: in Which Direction? Reflection Notes on Incoming Investment to East Sumba]. Available at https://www.waingapu.com/pembangunan-sumba-timur-mau-ke-mana-catatan-refleksi-masuknya-investasi-di-sumba-timur-bagian-ii/#gsc.tab=0 (accessed 12 Jan. 2022).

McDonald, L., V. Naidu and M. Mohanty. 2016. "Vulnerability, Resilience and Dynamism of the Custom Economy in Melanesia", in *Household Vulnerability and Resilience to Economic Shocks: Findings from Melanesia*, ed. S. Feeny. London: Routledge, pp. 107–28.

McWilliam, A. 2009. "The Spiritual Commons: Some Immaterial Aspects of Community Economies in Eastern Indonesia", *The Australian Journal of Anthropology* 20, 2: 163–77.

Mehta, L., G.J. Veldwisch and J. Franco. 2012. "Introduction to the Special Issue: Water Grabbing? Focus on the (Re)appropriation of Finite Water Resources", *Water Alternatives* 5, 2: 193–207.

Nugrohowardhani, R.L.K.R. 2016. *Sabana Sumba: Kelembagaan dan Pembangunan Ekonomi Desa* [Sumba's Savannah Economy: Institutional and Economic Village Development], PhD dissertation. Salatiga: Satya Wacana Christian University.

Onvlee, L. 1980. "The Significance of Livestock on Sumba", in *The Flow of Life: Essays on Eastern Indonesia*, ed. J.J. Fox. Cambridge, MA and London, England: Harvard University Press, pp. 195–207.

Polanyi, K. 1944. *The Great Transformation: The Political and Economic Origins of our Time*. Boston, MA: Beacon Press.

Rigg, J., A. Salamanca and E.C. Thompson. 2016. "The Puzzle of East and Southeast Asia's Persistent Smallholder", *Journal of Rural Studies* 43: 118–33.

Sahlins, M.D. 1974. *Stone Age Economics*. London: Tavistock Publications.

Twikromo, Y.A. 2008. *The Local Elite and the Appropriation of Modernity: a Case in East Sumba, Indonesia*. PhD dissertation. Nijmegen: Radboud University.

Van Den End, Th. 1987. *Gereformeerde Zending op Sumba 1895–1972: een Bronnenpublicatie* [Reformed Mission on Sumba 1895–1972: A Collection of Sources]. Alphen aan den Rijn, NL: Raad voor de Zending der Ned. Herv. Kerk, de Zending der Gereformeerde Kerken in Nederland en de Gereformeerde Zendings-bond in de Ned. Herv. Kerk.

Vel, J.A.C. 1994. *The Uma-economy: Indigenous Economics and Development Work in Lawonda, Sumba*. PhD thesis. Wageningen University.

Vel, J.A.C. and S. Makambombu. 2010. "Access to Agrarian Justice in Sumba, Eastern Indonesia", *Law, Social Justice and Global Development Journal* 15: 2–22.

_____. 2019. "Strategic Framing of Adat in Land-Acquisition Politics in East Sumba", *The Asia Pacific Journal of Anthropology* 20, 5: 435–52.

CHAPTER 7

Affluence, Generational Poverty and Food Security in the Oil Palm Landscapes of North Sumatra

Henri Sitorus and John F. McCarthy

Introduction

In 1878, the Deli Maatschappij [company] initiated the cultivation of palm oil in what was then Oost Sumatra (GAPKI 2017). Subsequently, the eastern coast of Sumatra emerged as the heartland of colonial palm oil development in Indonesia. After more than a century, measured in terms of Indonesia's very modest BPS (Statistics Indonesia) poverty line, poverty rates in the oil palm districts of Langkat and Asahan in contemporary North Sumatra are comparatively low: 10.2 per cent and 10.25 per cent, respectively in 2018 (BPS 2019).[1] Yet both districts have high levels of stunting, pointing to a long-term problem of endemic undernutrition. In 2013, 55.5 per cent and 44.7 per cent of children in each district, respectively, remained stunted (Indonesian Ministry of Health 2013). Indeed, Indonesia's food security atlas (WFP 2019) demonstrates that many undernourished people live in areas where oil palm cash crop-producing landscapes predominate. Stunting levels in other centres of oil palm production, such as Riau and Central Kalimantan, remain high (TNP2K 2017).

Indonesia is a prominent exporter of estate crops, and the largest producer of palm oil globally. So the question emerges: How can adopting a high-value crop traded on international commodity markets be associated with economic growth, comparatively low poverty rates but such poor nutritional outcomes?

Oil palm is among the most researched crops globally, with Google Scholar citing 123,000 studies of oil palm issues in Indonesia. Analyses suggest that oil palm can drive rural development (Budidarsono et al. 2012) and improve rural livelihoods (Santika et al. 2019). State programmes see oil palm development as a means for socioeconomic improvement (Teoh 2010). Yet palm oil cultivation generates unsustainable livelihoods, increasing socioeconomic disparity (Santika et al. 2019), large scale deforestation and loss of land for indigenous people (Colchester et al. 2011). It reproduces and deepens poverty on a large scale (Li 2018), negatively affecting food security among low-income groups (Mendoza 2007; Sheil et al. 2009). Clearly, oil palm also has heterogeneous impacts (Krishna et al. 2017): depending upon the terms under which local people engage with the crop, both prosperity and deprivation can occur (McCarthy 2010). Yet the agrarian changes related to oil palm cultivation over more than one generation remain understudied. What are the mechanisms and trajectories of agrarian change in oil palm landscapes over the long term? How do they generate the processes producing this nutritional insecurity?

As discussed in Chapter 2, we can identify two familiar narratives framing agrarian change. Economists might expect the increase in agricultural productivity associated with a "boom crop" to increase incomes and reduce poverty and food insecurity, by offering work to poor local people and, as local enterprises take off, enabling people to diversify out of agriculture. In the medium term, we might expect absolute poverty to disappear. Yet, critical political economists might expect the introduction of this lucrative crop to lead to the emergence of a dynamic, surplus-generating class of oil palm plantations and producers who enclose land and accumulate capital. Those displaced and unable to compete will be displaced, become impoverished, migrate, or struggle to find viable forms of subsistence. Before assuming development will conform to either of these narratives, we need to study how contextual, relational and structural elements come together with actors' responses to shape specific socio-economic and environmental change scenarios.

This chapter seeks to unlock the conundrum by studying agrarian change over multiple generations, in the heartland of oil palm production. We focus on the livelihood trajectories associated with oil palm: what are the mechanisms leading to ascent and descent? How do different processes and structures come together to shape outcomes, including prosperity, poverty and nutritional insecurity?

The literature suggests two characteristic modes—insertion or adoption—taken by new entrants into the oil palm industry (Cramb and McCarthy 2016). Under the plantation mode, schemes attempt to incorporate smallholders as labourers and contract farmers under nucleus estate, smallholder out-grower schemes or lease arrangements, originally known as PIR (*Perkebunan inti rakyat*/nucleus smallholder plantation).[2] This leads to enclaves of smallholders and labourers developing within plantation landscapes dominated by corporate plantations. Second, independent smallholders adopt oil palm on their own. To investigate the processes of agrarian change associated with these two modes, we chose a site representing each scenario.

In 2019, palm oil areas in Indonesia extended over 14.6 million hectares [ha] (c. 56,000 sq miles) (BPS 2020). Seventy per cent of the country's palm oil plantations lie in Sumatra. In Langkat, district smallholders possess just 37 per cent of the land. We studied an enclave village located within a corporate plantation landscape, which, for this study, we call Wampu (the village lies in Wampu sub-district). Asahan district is a centre of smallholder production, with smallholders controlling 47.21 per cent of the land. Here we studied an independent smallholder village which we call Mandoge, in Bandar Pasir Mandoge sub-district.[3]

We carried out a household survey with a sample size of 121 respondents. The sample was selected proportionally to represent each category of households identified in the wealth ranking exercise (see Chapter 1). We also implemented the HFIAS (Household Food Insecurity Access Scale) questionnaire (Coates, Swindale and Bilinsky 2007) and a food frequency questionnaire (FFQ). The FFQ assesses the frequency with which households consume foods and food groups over a specific period, and captures how often people consume a range of foods (Dehgan et al. 2012; FAO 2018). We also interviewed key informants, including community leaders and government officials. Before discussing the two scenarios in turn, we first provide an overview of development patterns in the two sites.

Poverty Dynamics, Agrarian Structure and Food Insecurity

Most households in our case study areas live off palm oil cultivation. The representative survey (Figure 7.1) revealed that 42 per cent of respondents in Langkat (Wampu) primarily work as casual day labourers (*buruh harian lepas*); just 28 per cent were oil palm smallholders. In Asahan (Mandoge), 21 per cent work as casual day labourers, with 42 per cent cultivating oil palm. Hence Mandoge's economy is more developed and diversified, with 16 per cent of households engaged in off-farm enterprises compared with eight per cent in Wampu.

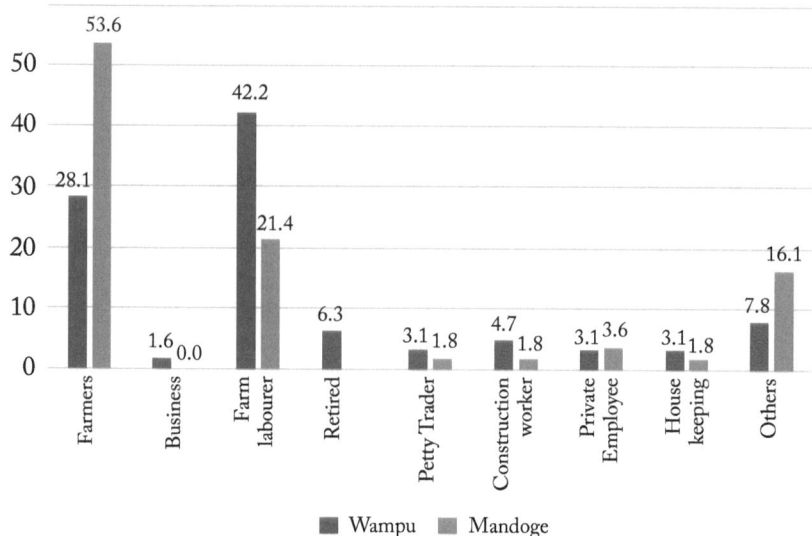

Figure 7.1   Main livelihoods of the households, 2016–17

While scholars (e.g. Glenday et al. 2016; Samosir 2017) distinguish five types of smallholders in the two case study villages, the vast majority of villagers are one type: small-scale independent farmers with small parcels (2–6 ha) of land, who sell their fresh fruit bunches (FFB) to an agent. Yet we also find a small cohort of progressive and entrepreneurial farmers (particularly in Mandoge): prosperous, newly rich farmers with up to hundreds of hectares of oil palm. Here farmer groups were once organised in cooperatives (under out-grower schemes that are now lapsed), and we do not find farmers leasing to a company under a benefit-sharing arrangement. Smallholders are neither certified (under the Roundtable on Sustainable Palm Oil [RSPO] and the Indonesian Sustainable Palm Oil [ISPO]) nor receive training or advice from plantations or mills. State extension services, such as good agriculture practices (GAP), are also minimal.

Following Sen, we can understand poverty in terms of degrees of deprivation of various basic capabilities, extending from elementary physical capacities to more complex social achievements (Sen 1995: 15). Village informants define poor (*sederhana*) households as those that can (to various degrees) meet basic food needs, support their children through school and own a simple house, usually with a wooden wall and a thatched roof and clay or timber floor, typically small in size and in poor condition. The poor are unable save or borrow. Villagers like to purchase clothes and furniture under a credit system managed by door-to-door agents. Compared to poor households, average (*sedang*) families can pay credit for motorcycles and clothes and save for their future, principally through buying cattle. *Sedang* households typically own oil palm or rubber plantations up to 2 ha (3 ha [7.4 acres] in Mandoge), possess a new motorcycle and have rehabilitated or constructed an improved (non-thatched) house. They may even have established a small business or may run a shop. Prosperous households (*sejahtera*) own farmland above 2–3 ha and may have expanded into palm oil enterprises, becoming traders and even owning a car or a truck.

Table 7.1   Stages of Progress (SoP) in Wampu and Mandoge subdistrict villages, North Sumatra in 2019

Category	
Sederhana (Poor)	• Ability to meet basic food needs of the household • Ability to support children in school • Capability to own simple house/simple motorbike
Sedang (Middle)	• Ability to purchase clothes and furniture with credit • Have cattle • Expand palm oil or rubber up to 3 ha/regular income (Wampu); up to 4 ha (Mandoge) • Purchase new motorcycle/Rehab house with better materials • Establish small off-farm enterprise/ business-shop
Sejahtera (prosperous)	• Expand farmland for more than 3 ha (Wampu)/ 4 ha (Mandoge) • Expand palm oil business, i.e. collector • Own car

The focus groups established that most households (81 per cent) remained poor in Langkat (Wampu) over 25 years. The plantation estates enclosed vast areas here. Later, landless labourers moved into the village in large numbers. As landholdings have fragmented over the decades, only a small group of people now control more than 3 hectares [ha] of land. Our survey found that 53 per cent of the sample households were landless, and another 30 per cent of households owned less than 0.5 ha. Only nine per cent of households have more than 1 ha. This enclave village is significantly different from the smallholder village: in Wampu and Mandoge respectively, 53 per cent and 37 per cent are landless.

In the early *Reformasi* period, as their trees needed replanting, a cohort of farmers sold up and moved to Riau to open larger areas, thereby avoiding the dilemma of surviving during a regeneration phase. While this reduced the total number of successful smallholders in Wampu, it helps explain the high levels of deprivation.

Table 7.2 Poverty dynamics for 25 years (1994–2019) in Wampu and Mandoge subdistrict villages, North Sumatra

Category	WAMPU (Langkat)	MANDOGE (Asahan)
Remain non-poor	5%	20%
Escape from poverty	11%	33%
Stay in poverty	81%	41%
Fall into poverty	3%	6%

N = 1,136 (households in five hamlets in Mandoge; five hamlets in Wampu).[4]

In contrast, the Asahan village reveals a more positive story: more than 50 per cent of the sample were non-poor, and after 25 years, 33.5 per cent of the households had left the poverty category. These included many families who had resided there for several generations. However, 41 per cent remained poor, primarily landless labourers who had moved into the village. The agrarian structure reflects this: 37 per cent are landless, with 28 per cent owning less than 1 ha, and 23 per cent having more than 1 ha. Yet having more than 1 ha of palm oil does not guarantee a transformation in well-being: most households who escaped poverty in Mandoge also diversified their livelihoods, finding off-farm income, including work in transportation and small shops.

Research on food security has shown that households that spend a more significant percentage of total expenditure on food are more food insecure (Indonesian Ministry of Agriculture 2013a). Wampu villagers spend 55.6 per cent of their income on food, whereas Mandoge villagers spend 35.5 per cent. Our survey showed that many respondents experienced difficulties paying for food, staples (*sembako*) and other needs. In Wampu and Mandoge respectively, 44 per cent and 39 per cent reported trouble meeting household food needs in the previous four weeks. Casual day labourers and marginal smallholders constitute the great majority of these households. Costs for *adat* (weddings, funerals, other social events) are high, and participation in these events is crucial. These obligations are reciprocal; failure to participate can lead to stigmatisation and social exclusion. Yet, these obligations are ones that the poor struggle to meet. The poor also strain to meet school expenses and support small-scale business activities.

The poor adjust their consumption, mainly the frequency and amount of protein eaten, with adverse effects on nutrition and household health (Zimmerman and Carter 2003). Nutritional insecurity and poverty are much more profound in Wampu than in Mandoge (see Table 7.3). In Wampu, the poor seldom eat fish and meat, mostly making do with rice and vegetables. Very few grow food; they often lack money to buy fish and other more nutritious food. Though the village is remote, we found at least three petty mobile traders, known as *along-along*, using motorbikes to sell fish, meat and vegetables. Hence, the problem is that, while food is available, households struggle to access it.

Table 7.3   FFQ survey among the poor households (experiencing difficulties) in 2019

Food frequency among the poor households	Asahan % (Mandoge)	Langkat (Wampu) %
Consumed salted fish more than once per day	64	10
Consumed fresh fish more than once per day	0	3
Never consumed meat over the previous 12 months	66	95
Did not consume chicken meat in the last 12 months	14	24
Did not consume tofu and *tempe/tahu* in the last 12 months	9.1	9.1
Consume tofu and *tempe* more than once per day	31	24
Consumed chicken 1-3 times per week	27	24

Villagers face a severe period of scarcity each year. Palm oil production is seasonal. Oil palm trees require rainfall or reliable access to water to support their growth, development and productivity. Drought can decrease the rate of cell division, carbon dioxide and nutrient absorption, and photosynthesis, thereby decreasing productivity (Bakoume et al. 2013). Research has found that drought can reduce oil palm productivity by 20–60 per cent, depending on the severity of the dry season (Directorate General of Plantations 2007). In addition, drought creates conditions that favour oil palm pests, such as fire caterpillars (*Setothosea asigna*), caterpillars (*Mahasena coebetti*) and large rats (*Bandicota indica*). Pest infestation and haze from forest fires also negatively affect oil palm productivity. Lack of fertiliser has also contributed to this low productivity. During the dry season or *musim trek*, which can extend for up to 6 months each year (from June to December), production of fruit bunches can decrease by up to 50 per cent. Farmers harvest around 700 kg per hectare every two weeks; however, in the *musim trek*, the harvest falls to about 400 kg per hectare for up to six months. Households surviving as casual day labourers find less work. Hence, the *musim trek* is a scarcity season (*paceklik*) when people cut back on food. Climate change is altering seasonal cycles, causing significant adverse impacts and risks for agriculture (Tollefson 2018). This includes increased intensity and frequency of storms, droughts, flooding, altered hydrological cycles and variation in rainfall (Kusumasari 2016).

Overall, climate variability clearly has implications for nutritional security; for instance, it contributes to the prevalence of stunting. The World Health

Organization (WHO) defines stunting as occurring when height-for-age is more than two standard deviations below the WHO Child Growth Standards median. Stunting is a direct physical indicator of the degree of undernutrition. However, as discussed in Chapter 2, stunting is a complex, overdetermined problem (WHO n.d.). A range of factors may affect stunting rates, including food preparation and consumption practices, women's education, motherhood age, breastfeeding practices, sanitation, hygiene and access to health care. Research has also found that a low household socioeconomic status leads to inadequate access to nutritious food, constituting a major underlying cause of stunting (UNICEF 2018). Indeed, in Indonesia, researchers have observed that stunting rates tend to be highest in the country's most deprived rural areas; this is related to food insecurity (SMERU 2015). Hence, in the two study districts, socioeconomic patterns are related to patterns of cutting back on food, which contributes to child undernourishment.

In response to these problems, Indonesia has developed various social assistance programmes (Chapter 3). Our survey undertaken in Wampu found that the conditional cash transfer programme (PKH) covers 14 per cent of those classified as poor by the community wealth ranking exercise. In Mandoge, PKH reaches only 8 per cent of the poor households. In addition to PKH the poor households also received food for the poor, known as Rastra (Beras Sejahtera) and Bantuan Pangan Non-Tunai/non-cash food assistance. However, the Rastra/BPNT food programme reached 14 per cent of households in Mandoge and 16 per cent in Wampu. Our data and interviews revealed that 30 per cent of those registered as PKH recipients were non-poor by village criteria. Villagers tend to blame the village administration for mistargeting, and excluded households often complain to the heads of the hamlets in front of village officials.

As noted in other chapters, when village forums cross-check household names on the recipient pre-list, the village administration can propose changes. However, under the centralised system, the village's proposal to change the list of beneficiaries is mainly overlooked, and the beneficiary list persists with few if any variations. While research on social protection programmes in Indonesia has claimed that error is due to elite capture during the determining of beneficiaries (Sim, Negara and Suryahadi 2015), we found no evidence of this here. During interviews, villagers preferred the inclusive approach used by the previous Rastra/Raskin system, arguing that the sharing practices were more equitable and based on a consensus among the village leaders and community members. According to these practices, the poor shared the rice allocation evenly, including among households which were not listed as official beneficiaries, but were known within the village to be in need.

To further understand the issues leading to the food poverty described above, we now analyse the two scenarios in more detail.

Oil Palm, Nutrition Outcomes and Poverty Dynamics

The Palm Oil Enclave Scenario

The Langkat village (Wampu) lies in an enclave within a sea of palm oil; this is a secluded and dusty landscape reached by an unsealed, potholed road. Rubber plantations came to dominate the Langkat landscape during the Dutch period. Colonial plantation history generated a sizeable landless, Javanese labour force here. From 1883, the Dutch imported Javanese labourers (*koeli kontrak*). By 1930, there were 260,951 workers, 90 per cent of which were Javanese (Thee 1977). When the state opened a the "Nucleus Estates and Smallholders [NES] scheme", Javanese labourers moved in, primarily fourth or fifth-generation descendants of the original Javanese migrant workers. As noted earlier, 53.13 per cent of the respondents do not own land.

At this time, state policy identified palm oil as a strategic commodity, and donor support facilitated corporate expansion into it, changing access to and control over land resources for the long term. The policy favoured a contract farming model (Baswir et al. 2009). The state company PTPN II developed an estate here in 1983, extending its operations into remaining forested areas. In the early 1990s, PTPN II changed the project into a PIR out-grower scheme. Participating farmers joined six farmers groups (*Gabungan Kelompok Tani*). This local out-grower (PIRLOK) scheme involved local farmers rather than transmigrants. It extended over 2,620 ha, with the contracted smallholders obliged to join the village cooperation (Koperasi Unit Desa, KUD). The in-migrants from Tanah Karo areas took up plots in the plasma area.

Patterns of Production

In Wampu, the former leader of the farmers' group noted that many "plasma farmers" were from outside the village. These included well-connected actors in the district who used their networks to obtain PIR entitlements. The nucleus estate held land ownership certificates as collateral for the loans granted to fund smallholder participation. After 15 years, PTPN finally transferred control of the land back to scheme participants. Hence, over this extended period, the company and cooperative, rather than the nominal landowners, controlled most of the revenue stream derived from the smallholdings.

Although PIR projects aimed to allocate land to the poor, elite actors in the village consolidated their control. The leader of the cooperative began purchasing or forcing resident smallholders to sell their land. In 2000, a large group of resident farmers sold their plots and migrated to Riau Province, and this consolidated the process. Key village actors had snapped up more than half the plasma land, with one individual owning approximately 1,000 ha.

Elite actors affiliated with local gang (*preman*) leaders use strong-arm tactics to gain monopsony control over the sale of the oil palm fruit FFBs, thereby dominating the value chain for them and other farm products. Buyers and their agents at the village level belong to this controlling elite. The key *preman* in this network sets the village level price, and producers lack alternative market channels for selling their FFBs. Hence, highly asymmetrical power relationships between producers and buyers operate, and buyers or agents dictate how the chain works, requiring producers to sell at set prices. The power of the elite figures, farmers' dependence on these patrons and the coercive power of *preman* render smallholders powerless in a captive value chain.

A critical actor also controls entertainment businesses, coffee shops, video gaming, prostitution and gambling in Wampu, while also working as a broker to consolidate and channel land transfers to other members of the elite. This pattern of control also extends to the cooperative (KUD). As the *preman* heads the cooperative, there is no transparency and accountability. However, the situation here is hardly unique: other research has described how a "mafia system" operates across Indonesia's palm oil sector, controlling land and the oil palm economy (Li 2018).

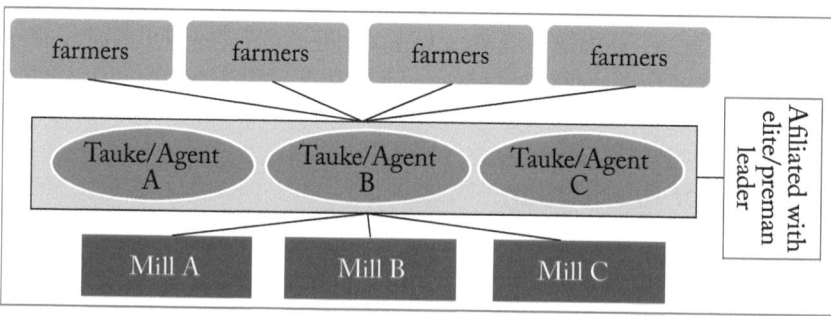

Figure 7.2   Captive value chain of FFB in Wampu

Labour

By the 1990s, PTPN II had recruited many villagers to work as casual day-wage labourers (*buruh harian lepas* or BHL). According to Sawit Watch (2015), this is a typical pattern: there are 10.5 million workers within the oil palm sector in Indonesia, of whom 70 per cent are BHL. Labour relations in oil palm plantations in Sumatra often involve outsourcing, with contractors employing BHL for activities such as weeding and harvesting (Sitorus 2015). BHL can earn up to IDR 60,000 per day (approx. USD 4), with heavy work loading a ton of FFB harvested over a single day. However, the BHL lack job security, and they work without a written labour agreement; they are appointed daily depending upon requirements. BHL are vulnerable and susceptible to nutritional insecurity due to poor pay and their work's untied, casual and insecure nature (Sinaga 2013; Siagian et al. 2011; Simanjuntak 2007).

Women living close to palm oil estates form a large part of the informal workforce, with many paid to harvest loose fruit. This group is vulnerable, given their precarious employment, lack of social security, poor access to healthcare and insurance, and lower pay. As they are more engaged in weed control involving the application of herbicides (Sitorus et al. 2017), women also face more health risks than do men (Widjayanti 2016).

An Indonesian labour law (No. 13/2003) forbids outsourcing for core plantation work, and labour arrangements have moved towards formalisation of employment. After this law, plantations ceased using casual day labourers. PTPN, the state-owned plantation company, also subcontracted management of the adjacent areas to a Malaysian company, which altered the casual employment system. While formalisation provided the plantation workforce with better wages, safety and insurance, new recruitment practices specified age and education requirements. Local villagers unable to meet education and age conditions could not apply. This regulation displaced villagers from the plantation system, further deepening the depredation found among landless households.

The focus group discussion categorised households into groups and discussed livelihood trajectories (Table 7.2). Poor villagers had remained trapped in poverty for 25 years. This category included those dependent on precarious work; those with small plots of land or low production smallholdings who obtained low FFB prices for palm oil; and those who could not supplement precarious wage work with agricultural production. For instance, Ibu Yusnita's household moved to the village in 1991. Her landless family depends upon casual work for local farmers, known as *mocok-mocok*. In addition, they farm a 2-hectare rubber garden under a revenue-sharing system (*bagi hasil*). However, due to decreasing rubber prices, their cash flow is limited.

A second cohort had fallen on bad times. This cluster included villagers who had fallen into poverty due to the exploitative business practices of the elite. In several cases, local shop owners were unable to compete and had to close. We found a cohort of households which had faced illness or other family problems, or who had lost assets due to unwise purchases or inability to pay debts.

In addition, as in other areas of Indonesia, oil palm smallholders face critical structural constraints (Cramb and McCarthy 2016). Given captive value chains, the farmers earn lower prices than nearby villages do for their fruit (15 per cent lower). There are also price fluctuations over the seasons. Farmers contend with expensive fertilisers, challenges obtaining subsidised inputs and poor agronomic practices (lack of pruning and systematic weeding). They typically have little access to financial resources.

The PIR scheme planted oil palm trees more than 25 years ago; the oil palm trees are now beyond their productive life and produce low yields. Farmers find it challenging to access high quality, certified seedlings; therefore, many end up replanting with low-yield ones. Hence, some households fall into a reproduction squeeze. Caught between limited wages and low production, expensive inputs and debt, they fall into poverty.

Yet as we have seen, a limited number of villagers can find ways to ascend from this poverty trap. These villagers have networked with key figures controlling the village, including the dominant gang families who work in the production and transportation of palm oil. Other villagers also progress by accumulating assets and savings from raising livestock or accessing the limited number of off-farm and non-farm livelihoods, for instance, opening village shops (*warung*). In this way, a limited number of families have moved out of poverty. In addition, a small group has gained more secure employment in the company (PTPN), thereby remaining non-poor.

Better-off households with formal employment tend to have secure access to the rural bank (BRI). These households borrow money with collateral, such as a land deed or a letter of guarantee from the company in the palm oil plantation. Some wealthier households also make substantial investments in cattle, getting poorer villagers to manage the livestock under a shared system.

The enclave scenario, then, is the result of several convergent processes. First, the colonial plantation system concentrated land ownership, and produced a large pool of landless surplus labourers. Second, a village elite took over around 50 per cent of the ex-plasma land, capturing the oil palm value chain and dominating the village economy. We also see the effects of structural factors that shape low production and low wages in the Indonesian smallholder sector. This includes climate change, which is having a major detrimental impact on palm oil agronomy (Paterson et al. 2017), reducing production over extended dry seasons and lengthening the scarcity season when marginal smallholders and labourers cut back on food. Fourth, the reworking of labour regulations forestalls the possibilities for landless workers to find a position in the plantation economy on better terms. Finally, we see reduced opportunities for small-scale diversification, and the weaknesses of the state plantation system. These structural and contextual processes come together to generate the pattern of seasonal insecurity and deprivation found here.

The Asahan (Mandoge) Independent Smallholder Scenario

The pleasant drive to Mandoge subdistrict follows a well-sealed, gently undulating but densely packed highway from Medan, passing the headquarters of old colonial plantations. The trip ends in the oil palm villages of Mandoge, on the border of Asahan, Toba and Simalungun Districts. While Wampu is isolated deep in the dusty (or muddy) plantation landscape, the Mandoge area links to North Sumatra's buoyant economy. Visitors can count more than 40 renovated houses with tiled rooves, satellite dishes and freshly painted plaster and brick facades along the main road. These are the houses of the *nouveaux riches*, palm oil traders, owners of chicken factories and large landowners.

Mandoge has a distinctive history. Around five generations ago, swidden farmers descended from the Toba upland to open *ladang* (swiddens) and rubber gardens here. By the late 20th century, these gardens and swiddens extended over most of the landscape. Palm oil plantations arrived in the subdistrict in 1979 with the expansion of PTPN III. By 2018, this state-owned plantation extended over 4,290.37 ha (c. 16.5 square miles). Subsequently, seven private and state-owned plantations have expanded into the area.

Earlier, during the early 1980s, district government officials invited the village to participate in a PIR out-grower scheme. After a series of meetings, the village declined, choosing to retain control over their land. Village leaders began to experiment, converting areas of rubber to palm oil. As farmers saw the higher profits from the crop, they converted their rubber gardens to oil palm, without direct support from the state schemes. Later, in-migrants moved here, attracted by the growing demand for casual labourers.

In earlier days, the Batak villagers of Mandoge established a customary tenure regime. More recently, the *adat* clan system of land control has gradually eroded, particularly after the advent of palm oil, when *ladang* areas came under permanent individual ownership. The state provided land titles through the PRONA (Program Nasional Agraria) land registration programme. This sped up changes to the land tenure regime, as families divided clan land amongst siblings according to Batak inheritance traditions.

Although now a peaceful village, the violent plantation-community conflicts found across Indonesia's oil palm sector affected the village at one time. The village head recalled that during the 1980s, a company (PTP) took over a parcel of community land (11,840 ha). The military intimidated villagers, threatening to label them as anti-development or against the government if they refused to "release" their land to the plantation. In 1996, the state granted a company an HGU ("right to cultivate") concession license over 4,434 ha encompassing land in two remote hamlets. Although the company initially tried to take over 525 ha of community land in one hamlet, villagers continued cultivating the land. In 2016, the plantation accused farmers of illegal occupation of this plantation area, effectively criminalising farming activities there. The court sentenced one farmer to four months in jail for violating the Plantation Law (No. 39/2014). The company then appropriated 1,300 ha of protected forest. Despite this, most Mandoge households remained independent oil palm smallholders. While land ownership is fragmenting with each generation, and some families have sold productive land for various reasons, most families have retained ownership of oil palm smallholdings.

Sedang (non-poor) households have smallholdings extending over at least 3–4 ha and combine their smallholdings with off-farm enterprises. As oil palm requires intermittent labour, these farmers prefer it over other crops. Smallholders usually rely on family labour for maintenance, fertilising and harvesting. As the state prioritises subsidised fertilisers for the production of food crops, farmers have limited access to subsidised fertilisers. Consequently, farmers need to purchase the fertilisers from the local market, and usually borrow capital from the palm oil traders (*tauke*) to whom they sell the harvested FFBs. To avoid debt, poor farmers frequently apply inappropriate (low) dosages of fertilisers.

Smallholders do not consistently prune their oil palms. Farmers usually know little about the technical requirements of oil palm and lack the resources for effective management. There are also significant numbers of casual day labourers (BHL) in Mandoge. The survey revealed that 37.5 per cent of respondents in Mandoge are landless and predominately live off casual labour. Although the working conditions are similar to Wampu, BHL have more opportunities in Mandoge. First, BHL find work in transportation, loading and unloading of FFBs in local mills. Second, smallholders nearby employ BHL for spraying, pruning and cleaning the "ring" surrounding palm oil trees, and most of all for harvesting. This is precarious work, given the absence of labour agreements or contracts. Local agents recruit the workers from the village on a casual basis, informing the workers on the day of work. As casual workers, they are paid in the range of IDR 50,000 to 70,000 (approx. USD 3.50–4.50) per day, earning an average of IDR 70,000 (USD 4.6). However, the hours worked per day vary enormously. Typically, a worker is paid according to a piece rate (e.g. harvesting of 1 ton FFB per day). However, BHL working for plantations are paid based on a quota/target, which means they earn the same amount irrespective of the time taken and harvesting usually requires workers to work many extra hours without overtime pay.

Casual workers are vulnerable to accidents. The company provides neither personal protective equipment nor registers them for insurance (*BPJS Ketenagakerjaan*). Due to exposure to toxic chemical substances, such as herbicides and pesticides, the workers face health risks. In addition, they have to pay for their transport. The plantation companies and smaller-scale enterprises prefer to employ daily workers because this is cheaper. A study found workers in precarious jobs working for formal companies in Indonesia usually receive 17 per cent less income than formal employees (ITUC 2014). Given the large surplus of labour found locally, daily workers have a very low bargaining position and cannot join the oil palm workers union. Union participation by palm oil workers is also paltry in general, because most trade unions in Indonesia focus on urban and industrial areas. In addition, formal workers dominate union participation, while informal workers remain non-unionised.

The case study of Johnson, a casual day labourer (BHL) in this village, illustrates this situation. Johnson Sitompul, 38 years old, works for the company without a contract. The local company agent informs him each day if he is needed. When the work is available, he earns just IDR 80/kg for harvesting. As he has three dependent sons, his wife also works as a casual worker at the company. They are vulnerable to workplace accidents, but the company does not provide them with protective equipment. As they need to find their way to the site, they maintain a motorbike for this purpose.

Workers from elsewhere have also moved to the village to find work. Ibu Noor migrated to Mandoge in 2015 from South Tapanuli, along with her husband. She works as a casual labourer two to three days per week, and her husband occasionally sells his labour to other farmers. Women labourers are more vulnerable than men are due to their more extensive work in maintenance, including pesticide and herbicide spraying, without access to adequate PPE.

In contrast to Wampu, Mandoge has a more open market governance system. Smallholders are not locked into contracts with processing crude palm oil (CPO) mills. The value chain in Mandoge is also much shorter. There are three local palm oil mills, and farmers can choose the intermediate *tauke* to whom they wish to sell. The switching costs are low, and transportation is inexpensive; hence choices tend to be governed by price. Smallholders obtain a better price with more competition among local traders (about 15 per cent higher than in Wampu).

Moreover, as *tauke* prefer repeat transactions, they develop credit linkages with sellers. *Tauke* work hard to ensure their loyalty by offering credit for fertilisers, or loans to client farmers before harvest if they face hardships. Farmers pay the *tauke* after harvesting FFBs. While this obliges farmers to sell the FFBs to their patron, farmers are free to shift traders after they meet their debt. The presence of three mills and several buyers makes this possible.

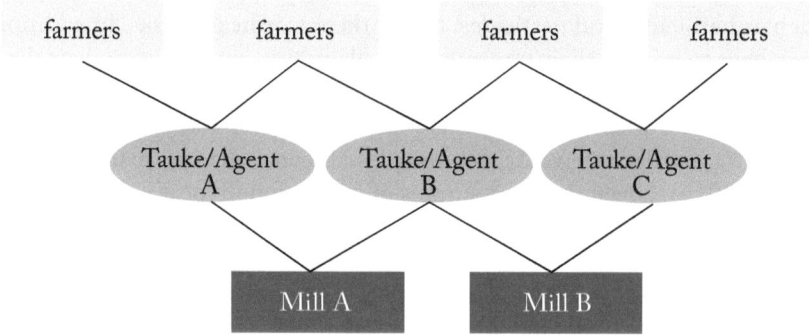

Figure 7.3   Value chain of FFB in Mandoge

Better-off households educate their family members, and their children can seek formal employment in the district or further afield. They invest in off-farm enterprises, diversifying into commercial poultry production under contracts with outside companies. In the village, there are eight large-scale chicken farms. Middle income (*sedang*) farmers also invest in cattle, which provide income and savings. Villagers also transport palm oil, operate or work in motorcycle workshops and have small shops (*warung*).

Poorer women seek extra cash, collecting *lidi* (palm fronds) to make *sapu lidi* (broomsticks). Although cutting and drying fronds is hard work, the women earn just IDR 1,000 per kg. If they work particularly hard, the poor may make about IDR 200,000 (USD 12) per month in such ways. Children also help collect palm oil branches to increase the family income.

In the smallholder village, many have moved out of the "poor" category. The presence of oil palm factories, the structure of value chains and the access to financial services make this more possible than in Wampu. Workers can work for plantations, smallholders, mills, or transportation due to the sealed roads. Moreover, a significant number of households retain ownership of their land.

Figure 7.4   Collecting *lidi* (palm fronds) to make *sapu lidi* (broomsticks)

Landowners include several wealthier households residing in the city, some of whom have accumulated over 100 ha of land. In several cases, local *tauke* have gained control of up to 30 ha. Perhaps 30 households along the main road have improved their houses, bought cars and enjoy a prosperous existence.

Successful farmers in Mandoge also have access to finance: a sub-unit of the rural bank (BRI) operates in the village centre. The bank offers IDR 50 million loans with three years of credit to farmers with 3 ha of palm oil. During an interview, BRI officials noted that about 80 per cent of the customers in the bank were oil palm farmers.

Sources of mobility are limited for labouring households: very few have moved up by working as casual labourers. Poor landless families can send their young daughters to work in factories in Malaysia; remittances from migrant workers improve incomes. However, families spend most of these remittances on consumption, such as fixing the house or paying siblings' school fees. Our surveys failed to find any poor households who had ascended through migrant labour.

In the past, smallholders could farm their way out of poverty. Most of those who escaped poverty in Mandoge converted at least 4 ha of their rubber or swidden land into palm oil smallholdings. People obtaining formal employment also enjoyed increased social and economic security and many sought to place their children in formal work. Ascending households also diversified into commercial poultry and cattle husbandry, shipping palm oil, or small enterprises. Very few had succeeded by working as palm oil collectors who channel FFBs to nearby mills. For example, the Landong Sinaga household originally owned 3 ha of palm oil. Then, the family head started a business as a FFB collector ten years ago. Today he runs FFB transportation services to the nearby mills.

Figure 7.5   Poultry farm in Mandoge

However, in Wampu a cohort of formerly prosperous households has also fallen on hard times. Households might divide the land among several siblings, leaving some in poor circumstances. Divorce, family breakdown, or drug addiction could lead to the elderly taking responsibility for children. Business failures and debt can lead to the sale of productive assets, or ambitious parents might sell land to support a child's university education.

Some households have remained stuck in a chronic poverty trap, due to a web of interacting factors. Low production, the low price of palm oil, the precarious nature of casual labour and a household's inability to save are all factors which can cut off progress. Life crises, long-term illness, limited opportunities and a lack of capital can also constrain those seeking to diversify. Here, entrenched patterns of inequality and marginalisation have hampered poorer households wishing to participate in the thriving palm oil sector.

In sum, the independent smallholder scenario and enclave scenario are very distinct. The ability of villagers to retain significant control over large land areas is critical. While structural constraints limit income, the open oil palm value chain here provides an opening. The FFB in Mandoge earned a 12 per cent higher price than in Wampu. Labour relations in the oil palm sector create a poverty trap for casual day labourers and near-landless smallholders.

Yet, oil palm cultivation and diversification have provided a large cohort of smallholders with the income to leave poverty.

Structural Constraints and Nutritional Insecurity

We now return to the questions at the heart of this study. How has oil palm transformed these rural societies over 30–40 years? What are the mechanisms and processes leading to poverty, food or nutritional security and livelihood progress that emerge from this multi-generational study? In answering these questions, we have identified two scenarios: the plantation enclave and smallholder development scenarios.

The history of the plantation system shapes the enclave scenario of Wampu. Here, land enclosure during the colonial period left a large pool of poor labourers living in enclaves amidst a sea of rubber and later oil palm. Planners initially conceived of the PIR out-grower schemes as a means of addressing smallholder poverty. During the New Order period, privately owned and state-owned plantation corporations continued to extend into forested areas of Langkat, but these now included smallholders in out-grower schemes. In this site, key actors and their relatives were able to gain control of over 50 per cent of formerly PIR land over subsequent decades.

Exploitative social relations are also critical. A local elite intimidated smallholders, manipulated cooperatives, bought up land from voluntary sales and captured control of the oil palm value chains. Here, the local elite and its affiliates accumulate value by employing landless labourers as poorly paid causal workers and by controlling captive value chains. For the landless majority, casual day labouring is the only livelihood option. The reworking of labour regulations further destabilised their livelihoods, excluding them from formal labour opportunities. Finally, the enclave context has few opportunities for diversification. These processes cumulatively turn the oil palm enclave into a poverty trap for a large pool of undernourished labourers.

The independent smallholder scenario has proceeded very differently. Here, village leaders refused the PIR Scheme, and subsequently, smallholders maintain control over virtually all the land. As they gradually transition into oil palm, producers can earn reasonable prices in a market-based governance system and a large cohort has left poverty behind. At the Asahan (Mandoge village) site, given the vibrant nature of the oil palm economy compared to Wampu, there are also more significant work and livelihood diversification opportunities.

While the contexts shape these different outcomes, the structural constraints found in Indonesia's oil palm smallholder sector also determine consequences (Cramb and McCarthy 2016). First, low-quality seedlings and inadequate fertiliser application reduce smallholder production. This is due in part to a lack of capital among farmers, including poor access to financial resources; inadequate education regarding oil palm agriculture is however also a major issue. Second, planters established oil palm over a generation ago. Productivity of oil palms falls with the age of the trees, and farmers need to replant after 25 years. However, smallholders lack the capital to replant oil palm plots, and lack alternative livelihood options to sustain them during the replanting period (Hanu and Sadjili 2013). The Indonesian Ministry of Agriculture has launched a palm oil revitalisation programme with credit and subsidised loans to facilitate replanting and rehabilitation of the old oil palm areas (Indonesian Ministry of Agriculture 2013b).[5] However, smallholders face difficulties meeting the programme's requirements.

Figure 7.6   Smallholder replanting with oil palm in Mandoge (2019)

A range of other structural mechanisms affects the patterns of exclusion and inequality that we found. Farmers have limited access to information about agronomic techniques (such as recommended dosage of fertilisers), the oil palm market and price and credit. The limited availability of extension services contributes to this problem. Despite Ministry of Agriculture Regulations (e.g. No. 395 / Kits /OT.140/11/2005), farmers obtain low FFB prices, due to their low bargaining position and relative powerlessness and fluctuations in global markets. Farmers in remote hamlets also encounter poor road conditions, making it challenging to market their fruit.

Further, buyers in the field differentiate FFBs according to the quality and age of the tree and offer different prices. There is no functional farmers' or civil society organisation to articulate the interests of smallholders during pricing, to demand better financial services or to ensure improved access to agriculture inputs. Few smallholders have the agency or capacity to affect palm oil decision making and in many settings, given their lack of power, smallholders' agency is constrained (Gillespie 2016).

In 2015, stakeholders in Indonesia's palm oil sector such as the Ministry of Agriculture and GAPKI (Association of Palm Oil Growers) advocated a productivity target of 35 tons of FFB per hectare, with a 26 per cent rate of palm oil extraction (*rendemen*), achieving 9 tons of CPO/ha each year (Saragih 2017). However, according to the Plantations Agency in North Sumatra, in 2018 producers reached only 16 tons and 21 tons per hectare [ha] in Langkat and Asahan Districts, respectively.

Conclusion

This study ties smallholder progress and nutritional insecurity, stunting and food poverty to the pattern of agrarian change occurring in the oil palm sector over the past several decades. On the one hand, the cultivation of cash crops, accompanied by livelihood diversification, underpins an ascending livelihood trajectory. Here, a large cohort in the *smallholder development scenario* has escaped from rural impoverishment. On the other hand, the enclosure of land on a large scale, the ongoing casualisation and informalisation of labour, and the adverse incorporation of marginal smallholders and labourers into the oil palm economy provide a stagnant livelihood trajectory for a large cohort of labourers and smallholders. In this *enclave plantation scenario* a large cohort of people has precarious rural livelihoods. Here, a web of exploitative social relations affects smallholders' ability to market crops, access credit and seedlings, or even buy food. For villagers in this scenario, poverty is "not just unimproved by growth or integration into (global) markets, but deepened by it" (Mosse 2010: 1161).

Here we identify three specific livelihood trajectories working across generations, suggesting a process of ongoing agrarian differentiation and increasing inequality. First, we see *smallholder development*, which fits the optimistic agricultural development thesis discussed earlier (see Chapter 2). We see a group of smallholders with access to more than two hectares of land. They utilise their production of a high-value crop to accumulate from agriculture. Their rise ("farming out of poverty") is facilitated by market governance of value chains and access to finance from rural development banks. As the rural economy develops, they can educate their children, many of whom exit agriculture and find formal employment outside it. With the emergence of new opportunities, farmers with more than four hectares of palm oil can raise livestock (cattle and commercial poultry), become palm oil FFB collectors, take up transportation services, or open village shops, thereby gaining the capability to accumulate and leave poverty behind.

At the same time, we see a *pauperisation* trajectory, which more or less fits the *truncated agrarian transition thesis* (see Chapter 1). A large pool of landless labourers lives in a chronic poverty trap, marginalised within a plantation enclave. Between corporate domination of the plantation landscape and control of land and value chains by local elite actors, the landless or functionally landless and labourers exist within an enclave of surplus labour. As described by Tania Li (2010), the poor struggle to subsist from agriculture and labour markets; they barely survive in the spaces left for their reproduction.

Third, we find a *moving sideways* (*jalan di tempat* or treading water) trajectory. Here smallholders possessing two hectares or fewer of land face the marginal profitability of their enterprises with small returns from palm oil production. Due to poor quality seedlings, price instability, poor access to fertilisers and other inputs, poor quality maintenance and an inability to replace aged plants, this is a low production trap. Here smallholders survive by combining cultivation with part-time wage labour. Given the land fragmentation that occurs with each generation and the impacts of climate change on oil palm production, alongside the problems of implementing supporting state policies to provide subsidies or micro-credit to enable replanting, the sustainability of the low productivity palm oil remains in question. These smallholders face increasing vulnerability. For the most part, these are the well-documented structural problems affecting an underperforming palm oil sector (Cramb and McCarthy 2016). In addition, we see a lack of functional farmers' organisations to facilitate access to services or support village cooperatives in both research sites.

Diversification and migration may seem like a panacea, another way of "moving out of poverty" (World Bank 2008). Indeed, many households have pursued complex mixed-livelihood strategies successfully. However, other households have insufficient access to land and insecure employment to provide a basis for household autonomy. For these households, the opportunity to diversify is limited to petty options such as making *sapu lidi* from palm oil leaves, or selling their labour to plantations and more successful smallholders. Under the last two trajectories, entering cash crop production and joining the labour market do not provide for an ascent.

With respect to nutrition outcomes, the poor cannot eat oil palm or forage for food in plantation landscapes. Under the second and third trajectory, smallholders may have higher cash income than the swidden or subsistence farmers in other cases in this volume. However, they have little subsistence capacity: rather than relying on their production or foraging in the landscape for at least some of their needs, they must buy all their food. Marginal farmers and labourers earn poor cash incomes, even as they face increasing food prices and requirements for cash income. This creates the conditions we found in our food surveys. Here, poor households routinely cut back on more expensive foods containing vital bio-available nutrients, such as fish and poultry, at least seasonally. This is especially pronounced during extended dry seasons, when oil palm productivity declines and the demand for casual day labour falls. This leads to the micro-nutrient deficiencies and high stunting rates we find here. Hence, while the statistics regarding average incomes suggest lower poverty levels than in semi-subsistence landscapes, the stunting statistics point to the ongoing problems of nutritional insecurity and food poverty.

Oil palm is a controversial crop. The international press associates it with clearing native forests, large-scale carbon pollution and biodiversity loss. Yet, we see a cohort of smallholders in rural Sumatra finding prosperity in the *smallholder development scenario*. Even in this more optimistic scenario, we see farm labourers and small-scale farm owners facing stagnation in poverty traps and exposed to nutritional insecurity. In the *enclave plantation scenario*, agribusiness control over land, captive value chains, poor oil palm production, and precarious and insecure labour conditions constrain opportunities. To be sure, well-intentioned policy actions are essential, including strengthening palm oil agriculture practices, enabling replanting and providing more effective social assistance. Nonetheless, for many villagers, the boom of recent decades has restructured livelihoods in ways that are yet to provide security of employment and income or, to date, the protections of an effective welfare programme. Deeper and more extended periods of drought due to the climate crisis cast a shadow over their future.

Acknowledgements

We would like to thank Mohammad Reza, Sugi Astuti and Anaesthasia Bessie for their valuable assistance and local officials and villagers in the field for their support.

Notes

[1] As noted in Chapter 1, the poverty line calculation is based on the cost of 2,100 calories per day and a small amount of non-food items. For a discussion, see Hill (2021). In September 2018, the rural poverty line was set at IDR 392,154 per month per capita (USD 27.15), which is very far below the international poverty line of USD 1.90 per day.

[2] Farmers who participated in this programme received 2 ha of plantation land and 0.5 ha of home garden (Molenaar et al. 2010). Participating farmers entered into a contract with the nucleus estate. Under the contract, the company undertook land clearing and planting before the plasma land was eventually handed over to the participating farmers. Farmers managed the smallholders after this conversion, selling fresh fruit bunches (FFB) under the contract to the plantation company under a cooperative arrangement.

[3] In North Sumatra, smallholders own 34.10% of the palm oil area, while private companies (both national and multinational corporations) hold 47.35%, and state-owned corporations hold 18.55% (Indonesian Ministry of Agriculture [2019]).

[4] The SoP process did not include the resident plantation workers living in neighbouring hamlets, which fall in the plantation areas of private company/state-owned companies.

[5] Based on Indonesian government policy, plantation revitalisation is carried out in one of two ways: (1) Partnership, by involving companies as development partners in plantation development, processing and marketing of results; and (2) Non-partnership or modes of smallholder development that are not tied to plantation estates.

References

Alwarritzi, W., T. Nanseki and Y. Chomei. 2015. "Analysis of the Factors Influencing the Technical Efficiency among Oil Palm Smallholder Farmers in Indonesia", *Procedia Environmental Sciences* 28: 630–8.

Bakoume, C. et al. 2013. "Improved Method for Estimating Soil Moisture Deficit in Oil Palm (Elaeis guineensis Jacq.) Areas with Limited Climatic Data", *Journal of Agricultural Science* 5, 8: 57–65.

Baswir, R. et al. 2019. *Pekebun Mandiri dalam Industri Perkebunan Sawit di Indonesia* [Independent Smallholders in the Oil Palm Plantation Industry in Indonesia]. Jogyakarta: Pusat Studi Ekonomi Kerakyatan Universitas Gadjah Mada.

BPS [Badan Pusat Statistik/Statistics Indonesia]. 2018. *Sumatera Utara dalam Angka* [North Sumatera in Figures]. Medan: BPS.

_____. 2019. *Direktori Perusahaan Perkebunan Besar di Kecamatan Bandar Pasir Mandoge* [Directory of Large Plantation Companies in Bandar Pasir Mandoge District]. Kisaran: BPS Kabupaten Asahan.

_____. 2020. *Statistik Kelapa Sawit Indonesia 2019* [Indonesian Oil Palm Statistics 2019]. Available at https://www.bps.go.id/publication/2020/11/30/36cba77a73179202def4ba14/statistik-kelapa-sawit-indonesia-2019.html (accessed 17 June 2022).

Budidarsono, S. et al. 2012. *Socio-economic Impact Assessment of Palm Oil Production.* Bogor: World Agroforestry Centre. Available at http://apps.worldagroforestry. org/downloads/Publications/PDFS/TB12053.PDF (accessed 7 Mar. 2022).

Coates, J., A. Swindale and P. Bilinsky. 2007. *Household Food Insecurity Access Scale (HFIAS) for Measurement of Food Access: Indicator Guide Version 3.* Washington, DC: Food and Nutrition Technical Assistance Project (FANTA).

Colchester, M. et al. 2011. *Oil Palm Expansion in South East Asia.* Bogor, Moreton-in-Marsh: Forest People Programme and Perkumpulan Sawit Watch.

Cramb, R. and J.F. McCarthy. 2016. "Characterising Oil Palm Production in Indonesia and Malaysia", in *The Oil Palm Complex*, ed. R. Cramb and J.F. McCarthy. Singapore: NUS Press, pp. 27–77.

Dehgan, M. et al. 2012. "Development, Reproducibility and Validity of the Food Frequency Questionnaire in the Poland Arm of the Prospective Urban and Rural Epidemiological (PURE) Study", *Journal of Human Nutrition and Diet*etics 25, 3: 225–32.

Dib, J.B., Z. Alamsyah and M. Qaim. 2018. "Land-Use Change and Income Inequality in Rural Indonesia", *Forest Policy and Economics* 94: 55–66.

Dinas Perkebunan. 2019. *Data luas areal, produksi dan produktivitas perkebunan rakyat komoditas kelapa sawit* [Data on area, production and productivity of oil palm commodity smallholder plantation]. Available at http://disbun.sumutprov.go.id/statistik_2019/web/index.php?r=site%2Flaporan-komoditi&tahun=2018&kabup aten=17&komoditas=2 (accessed 20 Sept. 2020).

Directorate General of Plantations. 2007. *Pedoman Umum Program Revitalisasi Perkebunan (Kelapa Sawit, Karet, dan Kakao)* [General Guidelines of the Plantation Revitalisation Programme (Palm Oil, Rubber and Cocoa)]. Jakarta: Ministry of Agriculture.

Ditjenbun. 2017. *Statistik Perkebunan Indonesia: Kelapa Sawit 2015–2017* [Statistics of Indonesian Plantation: Oil Palm 2015–2017]. Jakarta: Ditjenbun/Directorate General of Plantations, Ministry of Agriculture.

Euler, M. et al. 2016. "Oil Palm Expansion among Smallholder Farmers in Sumatra, Indonesia", *Journal of Agricultural Economics* 67, 3: 658–76.

FAO [Food and Agriculture Organization of the United Nations]. 2018. *Dietary Assessment: A Resource Guide to Method Selection and Application in Low Resource Settings.* Rome: FAO.

GAPKI [Indonesian Palm Oil Association]. 2017. *Perkembangan mutakhir industri sawit di Indonesia* [Recent development in the Palm Oil Industry in Indonesia]. Available at https://gapki.id/news/3971/perkembangan-mutakhir-industri-minyak-sawit-indonesia (accessed 30 Sept. 2020).

Gillespie, P. 2016. "People, Participation, Power: The Upstream Complexity of Indonesian Oil Palm Plantations", in *The Oil Palm Complex*, ed. R. Cramb and J.F. McCarthy. Singapore: NUS Press, pp. 301–26.

Glenday, S. et al. 2016. *Indonesian Oil Palm Smallholder Farmers: Sustainability Challenges and Recommendations for the Design of Smallholder Support Programs.* Bogor: Daemeter. Available at http://daemeter.org/new/uploads/20161105173525. Daemeter_SHF_2016_WP2_ENG_compressed.pdf (accessed 8 Mar. 2022).

Hanu, M.A. and M. Sadjili. 2013. *Market Transformation by Oil Palm Smallholders.* Bogor: Serikat Petani Kelapa Sawit. Available at https://www.spks.or.id/publikasi/market-transformation-by-oil-palm-smallholders/ (accessed 17 June 2022).

Hayati, K. and I. Caniago. 2011. "Zakat Potential As A Means To Overcome Poverty (A Study in Lampung)", *Journal of Indonesian Economy and Business* 26, 2: 187–200.

Hill, H. 2021. "What's Happened to Poverty and Inequality in Indonesia over Half a Century?", *Asian Development Review* 38, 1: 68–97.

Hutabarat, S. 2018. "Tantangan Keberlanjutan Pekebun Kelapa Sawit Rakyat di Kabupaten Pelalawan, Riau dalam Perubahan Perdagangan Global" [Challenges for the Sustainability of Oil Palm Smallholders in Pelalawan Regency, Riau in Changing Global Trade], *Masyarakat Indonesia* 43, 1: 47–64.

Indonesian Ministry of Agriculture. 2013a. *Statistik Ketahanan Pangan Tahun 2013* [Food Security Statistics 2013]. Jakarta: Ministry of Agriculture.

_____. 2013b. *Peraturan Menteri Pertanian No. 131/Permentan/OT.140/12/2013 Pedoman Budidaya Kelapa Sawit yang Baik* [Ministry of Agriculture Guide for Good Practices in Palm Oil]. Jakarta: Ministry of Agriculture.

_____. 2016. *Outlook Kelapa Sawit Komoditas Pertanian Subsektor Pertanian* [Outlook for Palm Oil Agricultural Commodities Agricultural Subsector]. Jakarta: Ministry of Agriculture.

_____. 2019. *Statistik Perkebunan Indonesia Kelapa Sawit 2017–2019* [Statistics of Palm Oil in Indonesia 2017–2019]. Jakarta: Directorate General of Estate Crops.

Indonesian Ministry of Health. 2013. *Riset Kesehatan Dasar 2013* [Basic Health Research of 2013]. Jakarta: Ministry of Health. Available at https://pusdatin.kemkes.go.id/resources/download/general/Hasil%20Riskesdas%202013.pdf (accessed 17 June 2022).

ITUC (International Trade Union Confederation). 2014. *Precarious Work in the Asia Pacific Region: A 10 Country Study by The International Trade Union Confederation (ITUC) and ITUC Asia-Pacific.*

Jelsma, I., K. Giller and T. Fairhurst. 2009. *Smallholder Oil Palm Production Systems in Indonesia: Lessons from the NESP Ophir Project.* Wageningen: Wageningen University.

Kahf, M. 1997. "Potential Effects of Zakat on Government Budget", *IIUM Journal of Economics and Management* 5, 1: 67–85.

Krishna, A. 2005. *Stages of Progress: A Community-Based Methodology for Defining and Understanding Poverty.* Available at www. pubpol. duke. edu/krishna/SoP. pdf (accessed 17 June 2022).

Krishna, V. et al. 2017. "Differential Livelihood Impacts of Oil Palm Expansion in Indonesia", *Agricultural Economics* 48, 5: 639–53.

Kusumasari, B. 2016. "Climate Change and Agricultural Adaptation in Indonesia", MIMBAR 32, 2: 243–53.

Li, T.M. 2010. "To Make Live or Let Die? Rural Dispossession and the Protection of Surplus Populations", *Antipode* 41: 66–93.

_____. 2018. "After the Land Grab: Infrastructural Violence and the 'Mafia System' in Indonesia's Oil Palm Plantation Zones", *Geoforum* 96: 328–37.

McCarthy, J.F. 2010. "Processes of Inclusion and Adverse Incorporation: Oil Palm and Agrarian Change in Sumatra, Indonesia", *The Journal of Peasant Studies* 37, 4: 821–50.

McCord, A. 2013. *The Public Pursuit of Secure Welfare: Background Paper on International Development Institutions, Social Protection & Developing Countries.* London: ODI [Overseas Development Institute].

Mendoza, T.C. 2007. "Are Biofuels Really Beneficial for Humanity?", *Philippine Journal of Crop Science* 32, 3: 85–100.

Molenaar, J.W. et al. 2010. *Analysis of the Agronomic and Institutional Constraints to Smallholder Yield Improvement in Indonesia.* Amsterdam: Aidenvironment & Global Sustainability Associates.

Mosse, D. 2010. "A Relational Approach to Durable Poverty, Inequality and Power", *Journal of Development Studies* 46, 7: 1156–78.

OECD [Organisation for Economic Co-operation and Development]. 2019. *Social Protection System Review of Indonesia (OECD Development Pathways).* Paris: OECD Publishing. Available at https://www.oecd.org/social/inclusive societiesanddevelopment/SPSR_Indonesia_ebook.pdf (accessed 7 Mar. 2022).

Paterson, R.R.M. et al. 2017. "World Climate Suitability Projections to 2050 and 2100 for Growing Oil Palm", *Journal of Agricultural Science* 155: 689–702.

Samosir, R. 2017. "Perempuan pekerja kebun sawit di Desa Bukit Agung Kecamatan Kerinci Kanan Kabupaten Siak". *Jurnal Online Mahasiswa* 4, 2. Available at https://jom.unri.ac.id/index.php/JOMFSIP/issue/view/433 (accessed 9 Aug. 2020).

Santika, T. et al. 2019. "Does Oil Palm Agriculture Help Alleviate Poverty? A Multidimensional Counterfactual Assessment of Oil Palm Development in Indonesia", *World Development* 120: 105–17.

Saragih, B. 2017. *Produktivitas Sumber Pertumbuhan Minyak Sawit Yang Berkelanjutan* [Productivity Sources of Sustainable Palm Oil Growth]. Available at https://www.iopri.org/wp-content/uploads/2017/07/I-01.-Makalah-Prof-Bungaran-Saragih-Produktivitas.pdf (accessed 17 June 2022).

Sawit Watch. 2015. "Catatan singkat akhir tahun perburuhan Sawit Watch 2015: Pelanggaran dan pengabaian hak ekonomi sosial buruh perkebunan kelapa sawit di Indonesia" [A Sawit Watch brief note at the end of 2015: Violations and ignorance of the social economic rights of palm oil plantation workers in Indonesia]. Available at https://sawitwatch.or.id/2016/02/09/catatan-singkat-akhir-tahun-perburuhan-sawit-watch-2015/ (accessed 20 Aug. 2020).

Sen, A. 1995. "The Political Economy of Targeting", in *Public Spending and the Poor*, ed. D. van de Walle and K. Nead. Washington, DC: World Bank, pp. 12–24.

Sheil, D. et al. 2009. *The Impacts and Opportunities of Oil Palm in Southeast Asia: What do We Know and What do We Need to Know?* Bogor: Center for International Forestry Research. Available at https://www.cifor.org/knowledge/publication/2792#:~:text=Oil%20palm's%20considerable%20profitability%20offers,exploitation%2C%20misinformation%20and%20market%20instabilities (accessed 8 Mar. 2022).

Siagian, S.P. et al. 2011. *The Loss of Reason: Human Rights Violations in the Oil-Palm Plantations in Indonesia - A Report based on Case Studies in Labuhan Batu, Medan.* On behalf of Lentera Rakyat. Available at https://www.brot-fuer-die-welt.de/fileadmin/mediapool/2_Downloads/Fachinformationen/Aktuell/Aktuell_22_loss-of-reason.pdf (accessed 8 Mar. 2022).

Sim, A. A., R. Negara and A. Suryahadi. 2015. *Inequality, Elite Capture, and Targeting of Social Protection Programs: Evidence from Indonesia.* Working Paper. SMERU Research Institute. Available at https://smeru.or.id/en/publication/inequality-elite-capture-and-targeting-social-protection-programs-evidence-indonesia (accessed 17 June 2022).

Simanjuntak, S.B. 2007. *Pengelolaan Perkebunan* [Plantation Management]. Medan: Fakultas Pertanian Universitas Sumatera Utara.

Sinaga, H. 2013. "Employment and Income of Workers on Indonesian Oil Palm Plantations: Food Crisis at the Micro Level", *Future of Food: Journal on Food and Agriculture and Society* 1, 2: 64–78.

Sitorus, H. 2015. "Tantangan kesejahteraan dan kondisi kerja buruh perkebunan kelapa sawit di Indonesia" [Challenges for the welfare and working conditions of oil palm plantation workers in Indonesia]. Paper Presented at Multistakeholder Workshop on Trade Unions and Palm Oil Sector, Medan.

_____, et al. 2017. "A Case Study of Drivers and Constraints for OSH in the Palm Oil Global Value Chain from Two Producing Provinces in Indonesia", in

International Labour Organisation, *Food and Agriculture Global Value Chains: Drivers and Constraints for Occupational Safety and Health Improvement.* Geneva: ILO.

SMERU Research Institute. 2015. *Food and Nutrition Security in Indonesia: a Strategic Review Improving Food and Nutrition Security to Reduce Stunting.* SMERU Research Institute. Available at https://docs.wfp.org/api/documents/WFP-0000005506/download/ (accessed 12 June 2020).

Suhada, A.T., B. Bagja and S. Saleh. 2018. *Smallholder Farmers Are Key to Making the Palm Oil Industry Sustainable.* Washington, DC: World Resources Institute. Available at https://www.wri.org/blog/2018/03/smallholder-farmers-are-key-making-palm-oil-industry-sustainable (accessed 8 Mar. 2022).

Teoh C.H. 2010. "Key Sustainability Issues in the Palm Oil Sector". A Discussion Paper for Multi-Stakeholders Consultations. International Finance Corporation, World Bank Group. Available at http://www.biofuelobservatory.org/Documentos/Otros/Palm-Oil-Discussion-Paper-FINAL.pdf (accessed 8 Mar. 2022).

Thee K.W. 1977. *Plantation Agricultural and Export Growth: an Economic History of East Sumatra.* Jakarta: National Economic Institute, Indonesian Institute of Sciences.

TNP2K. 2017. *100 Kabupaten/Kota Prioritas untuk Intervensi Anak Kerdil (Stunting)* [100 Priority Districts/Cities for Interventions on Stunted Children]. Jakarta: National Team for the Acceleration of Poverty Reduction.

Tollefson, J. 2018. "Humans are Altering Seasonal Climate Cycles Worldwide". Available at https://www.nature.com/articles/d41586-018-05780-z#:~:text= An %20analysis%20of%20decades%20of,swings%20in%20the%20northern%20 hemisphere (accessed 20 Sept. 2020).

UNICEF. 2018. *Nutrition Capacity Assessment in Indonesia.* Jakarta: UNICEF Indonesia. Available at https://www.unicef.org/indonesia/reports/nutrition-capacity-assessment-indonesia (accessed 8 Mar. 2022).

WFP. 2019. *Food Security and Vulnerability Atlas.* Indonesia. World Food Programme.

WHO. n.d. *Stunting in a Nutshell.* Available at https://www.who.int/news/item/19-11-2015-stunting-in-a-nutshell (accessed 17 June 2022).

Widjayanti, T. 2016. "Women and Palm Oil; IWD [International Women's Day] Highlights the Need to Empower Women in Agricultural Sector". Available at https://www.id.undp.org/content/indonesia/en/home/presscenter/articles/2016/03/17/-blog-women-and-palm-oil-iwd-highlights-the-need-to-empower-women-in-agricultural-sector.html (accessed 8 Mar. 2022).

World Bank. 2008. *Agriculture for Development. World Development Report 2008.* Washington, DC: World Bank.

Zimmerman, F.J. and M.R. Carter. 2003. "Asset Smoothing, Consumption Smoothing and the Reproduction of Inequality under Risk and Subsistence Constraints", *Journal of Development Economics* 71, 2: 233–60.

CHAPTER 8

Poverty, Vulnerability and Social Protection in Upland Java: The "Haves" and the "Have Nots"

Lisa Woodward

Introduction: Livelihoods in Upland Java

Java, the most fertile island of Indonesia, covers just 6.8 per cent of the country's total land area (Syuaib 2016: 172) but is home to 56 per cent of Indonesia's 260 million people (BPS 2015). Despite a decrease of 4.5 million farming households on Java between 2003 and 2013 (BPS 2013: 6), smallholder agriculture remains a significant source of work for millions on the island. In 2013, 13.4 million Javanese households worked in agriculture (BPS 2013: 6), representing approximately 50 per cent of Indonesia's total farming households[1] (BPS 2013: 6). Based on national statistics, 75 per cent of land-owning households in Java controlled less than 0.5 hectare (ha) (BPS 2013: 28–9), meaning that most farmers were *petani gurem*[2] or "marginal" and thus vulnerable to poverty (Ambarwati, Harahap and White 2016: 289).

However, in the largely unirrigated parts of upland Central Java and the Special Regency of Yogyakarta (DIY) presented in this study, fertile volcanic soil, high rainfall and intensive farming practices have facilitated relatively high horticultural productivity, enabling many smallholders to escape from the worst forms of poverty. A small number have also managed to accumulate substantial wealth by speculating in land and employing wage labourers.

Thirty years ago, Robert Hefner observed that although "absolute landlessness" was not widespread, and a middle class suppressed the gap between rich and poor, mountain villagers in Java "will quietly acknowledge that there are 'haves'... and 'have nots'... in their communities" (Hefner 1990:

154). From the 1970s, commercial agriculture developments brought "outside investors, wage labour, and new forms of social differentiation" (Hefner 1990: 157). As wealthier landowners stepped back from on-farm work to pursue more lucrative activities, new employment opportunities were created for the poor (Hefner 1990: 158). This was generally viewed as a positive development, as the poor and smallest landowners were offered alternative means to survive. However, because of smallholders'"shrinking landholdings, and [being] drawn more firmly into national markets and politics... a more class-stratified village [was] emerging" (Hefner 1990: 158).

Life has generally improved for many in upland Java since Hefner's observations, but processes and mechanisms generating inequality and poverty have intensified. The story that emerges from this study of smallholder agriculture in two mountain locations over the past 30 years is one of contrasts. On the one hand we see "the haves", wealthy villagers operating efficient, larger farms or lucrative non-farm businesses. On the other hand, we see the "have nots", villagers with little or no land or capital, whose livelihoods largely depend on labouring or informal work and local forms of social assistance to "get by".

To understand how and why these patterns have emerged in two distinct settings of upland Java, this chapter adopts a "relational approach" to poverty (Bernstein 2010: 94). Contrary to the "residual" approach which considers market exclusion to be the cause of poverty, a relational approach views the cause to be "the very terms of poor people's insertion into particular patterns of social relations" (Borras 2009: 13). It is necessary, therefore, to consider the ways in which the poor engage with wider socio-economic, political and cultural systems (Mosse 2010: 1158), including how local capitalist relations and factors of production facilitate prosperity for some and generate insecurity and poverty for others (Li 2014: 7).

To frame this chapter, I follow the line of argument that a "specific conjunction of factors" combines to shape people's lives in different ways at a particular time and place (Li 2014: 4). I explain how particular sets of socio-economic relations, political processes and environmental factors have combined to facilitate *a boom crop, agrarian differentiation scenario* in upland Java. Here, thriving horticultural industries and the multiple factors underlying them have enabled many farmers to accumulate profits; this leads to upward social mobility in each village. However, those who lose out in this scenario face the likelihood of falling into poverty. This disadvantaged group, especially young people with aspirations of becoming farmers, are "squeezed out" from owning productive resources, access to capital and inputs including fertiliser and water for irrigation. Over the past decade, thriving non-farm industries have also arisen in each village, providing alternative work prospects for the poor and the potential to "step up" or "sideways". However, each of these opportunities has its own set of challenges for overcoming structural forms of poverty, vulnerability to food insecurity and for the local environment. Increasingly, completing higher education is viewed as the best way to escape the poverty cycle.

This chapter also investigates how effectively state social protection programmes alleviate vulnerability to poverty and food insecurity. Attention is paid to the Family Hope Program (PKH), Indonesian Health Assistance for the Poor (JKN-KIS), and the Rice for the Poor (Rastra) programme. The intersection of these programmes with local social processes including the "moral economy" and perceptions of what constitutes "fairness" are also discussed. This analysis provides insights into challenges of accessibility to these programmes and the distribution of cash benefits. Every government programme is undoubtedly helpful in alleviating household financial burdens, but findings from this study highlight several social and structural challenges that undermine their efficacy in solving critical challenges of food (nutritional) insecurity and of the costs of health treatments and education. This is particularly the case for disadvantaged young people. I suggest that by paying attention to local processes and conventions of giving assistance, the PKH could be distributed in a way that complements existing notions of "fairness", thereby avoiding social tensions and maintaining the fabric of society.

An Overview of the Two Research Locations

The two selected mountain villages[3] differ in terms of size, demographics and horticultural industries. The choice of study locations was guided by their differences in agricultural production, proximity to larger centres for alternative work and education opportunities, and degrees of vulnerability and poverty. These differences allow comparisons to be made between the processes driving poverty dynamics and forms of food insecurity.

According to government figures, 8.2 per cent[4] of the population in Sleman district, the location of Kahawa village, lived in poverty (BPS Kabupaten Sleman 2017b) in 2016. For the purposes of this study with a focus on vulnerability, it is noteworthy that in 2016, 19.66 per cent of households in Sleman district were also considered "vulnerable to poverty" (BPS Kabupaten Sleman 2017a). Meanwhile, in Wonosobo district, the site of Cindaga village, a high percentage of the population (20.53 per cent) lived below the poverty line in 2016[5] (Diskominfo Kabupaten Wonosobo 2017: 137).

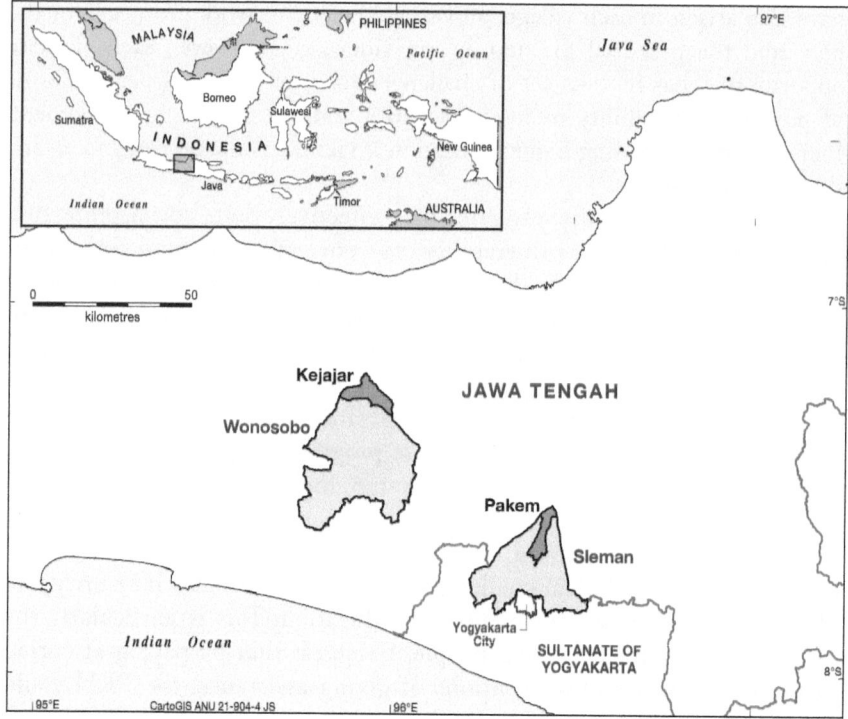

Figure 8.1   Location of Cindaga and Kahawa (pseudonyms) villages on Java

Kahawa village, population 9,369, comprises between 3,220 and 3,644 households and 16 hamlets.[6] The village is located 50 minutes by car from the city of Yogyakarta and lies between 600 and 980 metres above sea level on the southern slopes of Mount Merapi, one of the world's most active volcanoes. Merapi presents both an opportunity and a threat to villagers: fertile volcanic soil facilitates agricultural productivity and the volcanic sand provides work for labourers and traders, even as violent eruptions risk lives and livelihoods. In a 2010 eruption, 273 people across the Sleman regency lost their lives and many villagers were evacuated for up to four months. Livelihoods were severely disrupted, and villagers experienced significant damage to their homes and crops, along with food shortages. The state provided compensation in the form of goats, cows and *salak pondoh* (a variety of fruit) seedlings, to encourage market-oriented activities and improve prosperity. Other local employment opportunities include cutting and selling grass as animal fodder, milk production, tourism (driving jeeps and running small food stalls on Mt. Merapi) and small businesses (for example, hair salons, laundries and food stalls).

Cindaga village is situated in the cool climes (2,300m) of the Dieng Plateau of Central Java. It is a significantly smaller settlement than Kahawa, with a population of 1,267, comprising 344 households (BPS Kabupaten Wonosobo 2017: 41–50). Most villagers (91 per cent) nominate themselves as potato farmers, with the remaining working as farm labourers and traders, government employees and construction labourers (Santoso 2015: 66). Other crops grown include carrots, cabbage and *carica* fruit (a type of endemic papaya). From 2010, a thriving tourism industry emerged, offering new work providing supplementary incomes.

Figure 8.2   Mountains and ricefields in upland Java

Poverty and Wealth Dynamics

Villagers in both locations understand poverty, vulnerability and wealth in similar ways. Those whose livelihoods are in a state of flux are considered *"miskin"* (poor) or *"kurang mampu"* (disadvantaged). Their homes are often described as *"kurang layak"* (sub-standard), usually made of wood or bamboo with some exposure to rain, wind, or the cold night air, and they often have earthen floors and smoky open wood fires. Homes may not have piped water or their own toilet. The villagers rely on *zakat* (Islamic alms) non-state social assistance to "smooth" difficulties, particularly if they are elderly without children or widowed.

During the Stages of Progress (SoP) activity, small focus groups, representing a cross section of each community, considered the characteristics of poverty and wealth and what constitutes the "cut-off lines" for poverty and prosperity in their village. In both villages, land shortages were viewed as a key driver of poverty and vulnerability, supporting Hefner's assessment that, by limiting yield sizes, land scarcity caused poverty in upland Java (Hefner 1990: 125). The poorest farmers own or rent very small plots of land, a sign of poverty (Rigg et al. 2016: 66). Consequently, they must take on additional work as labourers, *ojek* (motorbike taxi) drivers or rely on informal assistance to "get by". In Cindaga village the poorest own or rent less than 0.1 ha (1,000m²), while in Kahawa village these areas are significantly smaller, approximately 100m² to 200m². In Kahawa, under- or unemployment was also mentioned as a key factor causing insecurity: "the most important thing is to have work" said one woman.

The "non-poor" fall into one of two categories. Those who have escaped the worst effects of poverty are described as "*sedang*", average, or "*mampu*", capable. However, within this first category there are several distinctions. While households owning or renting land between 0.1 ha and 0.25 ha, or who have supplementary incomes, may fall into this group, many are still considered "*rentan*" (vulnerable) to seasonal poverty. Crop failures, erratic returns producing insufficient incomes, personal difficulties (divorce, revolving debt, significant illness) and lack of social assistance are common triggers of household vulnerability and poverty.

In Cindaga, those considered "less vulnerable" to becoming poor typically own land between 0.25 to 0.99 ha; this is typically *tegalan* (unirrigated dryland) or *ladang/kebun* (fields/gardens). In Kahawa village, the "less vulnerable" group might have skilled employment, productive stall-fed livestock[7] or *warung* (food stalls) or engage in sand quarrying. Their houses are modest, secure from wind and rain, and made of cement and tiles. "Capable" households may have small savings and more than two motorbikes or receive additional income from adult children.

The second and most prosperous ("*makmur*") group of non-poor may have accumulated more than one hectare of land on which they employ farm labourers. In both villages the wealthiest might be professionals or government employees working outside the village or may own or operate a profitable business (for example, agricultural or sand trader, a small shop with mini petrol pump, or homestay accommodation). These investments or well-paid jobs enable them to send their children to university, attend the *haj* (pilgrimage) in Mecca, buy a car or truck or renovate their home.

The second activity involved ranking households into categories to understand wealth dynamics over time. Table 8. 1 shows that of 80 households interviewed across both villages, most (71.25 per cent) had escaped poverty or have remained non-poor over the last 25 years. Fewer households remained poor or became poor in that time. However, when combined, these categories account for nearly 30 per cent of the population, indicating that poverty and vulnerability remain problematic in these areas.

Table 8.1 Wealth ranking results for Cindaga and Kahawa (pseudonyms) villages on Java, 1991–2016

Category	Kahawa % N = 40	Cindaga % N = 40	Total % N = 80
A: Remained poor	25	15	20
B: Escaped poverty	42.5	42.5	42.5
C: Became poor	12.5	5	8.75
D: Remained non-poor	20	37.5	28.75

According to the ranking process, the same proportion (42.5 per cent) of households in both villages has escaped poverty. The similarity stems largely from the difficulty in determining whether households in Kahawa village were "poor" or "vulnerable". On balance, it was decided by locals participating in the SoP and ranking activity in Kahawa that some vulnerable households could still be considered poor in the local context because of ongoing difficulties affording school fees and food staples (*sembako*). This reflects the higher number of households listed in category A (25 per cent) compared to Cindaga village (15 per cent), where the conditional cash transfer (PKH) had been introduced earlier and significantly fewer households reported difficulties affording school fees and food.

The ranking process revealed that fewer households had fallen into poverty (5 per cent) in Cindaga village compared to Kahawa (12.5 per cent). The disparity is likely due to improved local economic conditions because of tourism development and, more recently, steadier farm incomes compared to erratic (and lower) *salak* fruit prices in Kahawa. More Cindaga villagers (37.5 per cent) had also remained non-poor compared to 20 per cent in Kahawa, suggesting that for the wealthy, income and investment opportunities have remained more accessible, lucrative and certain in Cindaga.

To understand the socio-economic and political processes driving poverty and wealth dynamics in more detail, I turn next to explaining conjunctural factors generating sharp differences in livelihood outcomes between the poor and non-poor in each village.

Kahawa Village

Deteriorating Market Conditions for Salak Fruit

The snakeskin fruit (*salak pondoh*) was introduced to the village in the 1980s and production has thrived with regular rainfall as well as access to irrigation and routine application of pesticides to avoid plant disease. Today, fierce competition among producers means that the market is flooded not only with *salak* but with other fruit including mango and watermelon, harvested at the same peak times. Returns are frequently insufficient to cover the costs of production, substantiating the argument that vulnerability and descent into poverty are often a result of fluctuating markets or a "simple-reproduction squeeze" (Bernstein 1979: 427), exemplified by "the classic case of declining producer prices with increasing input and consumption-good prices" (Ribot 1995: 120). *Salak* farmers partly blame their weak position on middlemen who come directly to the village and control the prices.

The government is also criticised for not intervening to stabilise erratic prices or for not providing effective distribution channels (Permana 2017). Erratic prices for *salak* fruit caused financial difficulties for 15 per cent of household survey respondents in the previous 12 months. During 2016, prices fluctuated from a high of IDR 10,000 (USD 0.74[8]) per kg in the dry season, to just IDR 1,500/kg (USD 0.11) during the *panen raya* (main harvest) of 2016. *Panen raya*, the season of highest production from around November to January, is the time when returns are lowest and potential financial losses are greatest. In 2017, *salak* farmers requested the district government to stabilise market prices. In response, the government stated that farmers needed to become more creative and turn their fruit into value added produce such as snacks or sweets. However, although some farmers in the village have done this, their incomes have not increased due to ongoing difficulties with marketing and distribution channels. They argue that overcoming this income stagnation requires government assistance (Permana 2017).

Alarmingly, in 2016, 60 per cent of household respondents stated that a prolonged lack of rainfall during the dry season resulted in very poor-quality fruit yields and loss of income. Unequal access to irrigation water between *dusun* (hamlets) within the village also compounds problems. In 2006, water from a local river was diverted to a reservoir built on village government land with central government funds to provide additional clean drinking water and irrigation. However, the reservoir's foundation collapsed within months after it began leaking. In 2016 it continued to leach water into the ground, severely reducing irrigation water supply for horticulturalists in three hamlets covered in this research. Although the state-owned Regional Water Supply

Company pipes enough water to homes for daily use, supply is insufficient for irrigation in the hamlets affected. For poor farmers in other areas of the village which have access to an irrigation pump, the cost of fuel, around IDR 100,000 (USD 7.40), is too expensive for daily use.

Given the challenges of irrigation access and costs causing seasonal difficulties, diverse income streams are required. By far the quickest way to supplement incomes is through manual sand mining: one man who had earned enough money from quarrying sand to send his daughter to university said "it's faster getting cash from sand compared to animals or *salak* or anything else. There's no other work like this here" (interview with household informant #21, 20 July 2017).

A Sandmining Boom

After the 2010 eruption of Mt. Merapi, government permits were issued for mining activities to extract sand, in order to normalise rivers near the village until 2014. Since then, when the sand resources were deemed by authorities to be depleted, mining without permits has been illegal in the area, especially along the river systems. However, there is confusion among villagers about the situation. Some householders stated that licences are not required on private land, while others said they should have one, but they cannot afford one and the process of organising one takes too long.[9] Compounding local confusion, a Regional Energy and Mineral Resources government official explained that although unlicensed sand quarrying is illegal, "we still tolerate sand labourers who are poor. They need to eat every day. Yes, there are some instances of heavy machinery operators being jailed but not the poor. They are given warnings" (interview at Department of Public Works, Housing and Resources Energy, Yogyakarta, 18 Aug. 2017).

Despite being illegal, manual sand quarrying is the quickest way to earn cash, and many villagers are willing to risk being caught or fined. Indeed, 55 per cent of participants in the household survey stated that they work as sand labourers. The industry also provides financial benefits to landowners and the village government. Owners can rent their land to sand traders, usually truck owners who employ local labourers who then on-sell the sand to construction companies or private buyers. In 2017, 500m^2 could earn a landowner IDR 45 million (USD 3,333) in rent. The price is dependent on the quality and quantity of sand available, and the landowner and miner bargain on an agreed price. Usually, 500m^2 provides work for between one and two years, depending on the number of orders. However, if there are many orders from construction companies, sand could run out within six months.

The village government can also earn IDR 2 million (USD 148) per day in funds (referred to as "retribution"), paid by drivers who are charged IDR 48,000 for each truckload (USD 3.55) of sand. It is unclear how the revenue raised from sand mining is used by village government. Findings from this study suggest that it is not used for improving access to water sources or irrigation infrastructure. However, ensuring long term sustainability of the horticultural industry, issues of land rehabilitation and water security require urgent attention by government authorities and the community.

It seems that vested interests drive unsustainable land use practices and undermine local water security. When I asked a key informant why he thought illegal sand mining was not stopped, he replied emphatically, "it is not possible to stop the sand mining. The village government won't stop it. From normal people to the local, regional, police in the field [who fine offenders who are caught], everyone knows about sand mining. Everyone gets [a share of the] money" (interview, 21 July 2017). This has negative implications both for the local environment through erosion and for struggling producers whose water security is increasingly compromised.

There are signs that social attitudes towards sand quarrying could be changing. One 21-year-old male who had completed a trade qualification and secured full-time work outside the village remarked that "sand quarrying is fast money, but it runs out and can't be passed on [to the next generation]. It's a job for lower educated people and youth" (youth interview #15, 20 July 2017). His views suggest that educated young people or those concerned with sustainability issues will be less inclined to choose this form of work.

Cindaga Village

A Potato Crop Boom

After decades of growing tobacco, corn and Chinese cabbage with comparatively poor income returns, resulting in high to extreme poverty levels, potato farming was introduced in Cindaga village in the early 1970s. Struggling farmers embraced the opportunity to participate in the competitive market economy, supplying potatoes for an increasingly "modern" consumer society in the cities. By the 1980s, the potato had become an established "boom crop" (Santoso 2015: 12). From the 1980s to the mid-1990s, because of high productivity and strong prices, it became possible for some village households to hire labourers, accumulate significant profits for investment in more land, improve homes and undertake the haj.

Since the mid-1990s however, state development policies promoting intensive farming practices and chemical inputs have degraded soil quality and caused potato yields to drop significantly. A key informant stated that between 1979 and 1990, 1 kg of seed potatoes yielded up to 30 kg of potatoes. Today the same number of seed potatoes produces only between eight and ten kilograms, inducing precarity, particularly if prices drop or crops fail. To make more income, most farmers choose to plant and harvest three potato crops per year, not allowing enough time for the land to recuperate. Consequently, to produce more potatoes on a limited supply of land, and despite the cost, farmers remain on the "pesticide treadmill", applying large quantities of chemicals and fertilisers, reducing soil quality and threatening the long-term future of potato production in some areas, as well as consumer safety.

Paradoxically, potato farmers commonly complain about the increased cost of agricultural inputs (fertilisers, pesticides, insecticides), contending that they do not benefit from state subsidies. Traders of these inputs subsequently blame expensive transport and delivery costs and pass them onto producers. Smallholders, particularly those without savings and poor harvests, become caught between the increasing production costs and diminishing returns. At this juncture, strong social relations are critical for vulnerable farmers: they depend on loans from family or neighbours and farm labouring work from other villagers to get by until their next successful harvest.

Progressive farmers are diversifying by planting *carica* fruit trees and engaging in tourism activities, indicating a willingness to diversify to reduce dependence on potato farming. Despite this, potato farming is still widely viewed as the best way to "get ahead". The aspiration to accumulate agricultural land to escape vulnerability was summarised by a young (21-year-old) woman who works as a farm labourer and, together with her husband, rents a small *warung* selling meatball noodle soup: "I want to be a farmer and employ other people to help us. We have a future if we have land" (interview, 20 July 2017). Her husband elaborated: "our incomes are uncertain, it's difficult to buy land, it's too expensive. We need access to credit from the government".

Their views indicate that owning enough land (at least 0.25 ha) for intensive farming ventures is still an aspiration harboured by the poor, a step towards upward social mobility in Cindaga village. However, this is becoming increasingly difficult, as local land prices have risen exponentially in the last decade because of tourism development.

A Tourism Development Boom

Since 2010 a thriving tourism industry has emerged in Cindaga, attracting up to 2,000, mostly domestic, tourists on weekends. Tourists come to view the "Golden Sunrise" across the surrounding mountains of the village. Many visitors, particularly the young from large cities, enjoy camping in tents on the shores of the local lake, while others stay in large, rather ostentatious homestay accommodations built by prosperous villagers and which stand in stark contrast to the homes of the much less wealthy.

The tourism industry has paved the way for new business opportunities, with successful potato farmers investing their profits in cafes, homestays and small shops. New opportunities have also arisen for poor villagers, including driving *ojek*, operating petty food stalls, busking and selling entry tickets to the national forest. Nevertheless, because these forms of work are irregular and incomes fluctuate, they are typically viewed as supplementary to potato farming and insufficient to "escape poverty". In some cases, this work may expose struggling farmers to new problems, exacerbating inequalities between "the haves" and "the have nots". For example, a household informant (#15) with a tiny (160m²) land plot hoped to supplement his farm income by renting a *warung* where he sells noodles, *nasi goreng*, tea and coffee. However, he and his wife were struggling to turn a profit and were running out of money to purchase stock. He told me that "getting capital is my biggest problem. I started with nothing, but I can't go beyond because I lack capital" (interview, 19 Sept. 2016). By May 2018, as he was unable to afford IDR 5 million (USD 370) in stock because his last potato crop had failed, I heard he had closed his business. His story differs markedly from successful business owners who, with profits from farming and greater access to capital, have established lucrative eateries and homestays.

Tourism development has intensified pre-existing problems of waste disposal and poor sanitation around water resources used for drinking, washing and irrigation. An inefficient waste management system and poor public infrastructure (toilets, camping grounds) pose sustainability challenges and a risk to villagers' health. For workers with limited assets and who lack social assistance, any significant downturn in tourist numbers due to public health concerns will likely trigger significant household difficulties. As one villager intent on accumulating profits from his *warung* told me: "I will be poor if my stall shuts. I don't have insurance or receive any social assistance" (household #3 interview, 22 Sept. 2016). Undoubtedly, this scenario played out when the COVID-19 pandemic forced the closure of Cindaga's tourism industry in early 2020.

Food and Nutritional Insecurity

A second smaller survey was conducted to provide a snapshot of the level of food vulnerability during the period of greatest seasonal scarcity, known as the *paceklik* (food scarcity) in Indonesia.[10] 24 households participated (12 from each village). Respondents were invited to participate if they had experienced significant household difficulties during the previous twelve months, particularly related to costs of affording agricultural inputs, food and the costs of health and education. It is important to note that the small sample is not representative of the whole population in each village and that not all respondents were poor. Thus, results provide only an indication that a small cohort, comprising both poor and non-poor households, had experienced some level of food insecurity during the *paceklik* period.

Additionally, the villages experience different *paceklik* seasons, which exemplifies the complexity of comparing upland livelihoods and consumption patterns and also alerts us to the danger of generalising about livelihoods in rural communities across Indonesia. In Cindaga, the peak period of seasonal difficulty occurs during the wet season (particularly December–March) when potato yields are typically smaller or may fail because of heavy rainfall and high winds. In Kahawa, although *salak* prices are higher during the dry season months from around May to July, small scale farmers who cannot afford or do not have access to irrigation[11] had experienced particularly heavy crop failure and low yields.

In Kahawa, an extended dry season and water access problems in 2016 caused significant declines in fruit yields. However, while the respondents found life more difficult at this time, this does not seem to have translated into deep food insecurities, largely because they had alternative incomes or assistance from family. During that period, five of the 12 respondents (42 per cent) in the small sample remained food secure and a further 42 per cent experienced mild insecurity. This meant that although they ate a monotonous diet they did not cut back on quantity. Meanwhile, two households in this small sample experienced greater levels of food insecurity, sometimes reducing the quality or quantity of food during the *paceklik* period. Instead of eating protein they ate less favoured or less-satiating replacements; as one older woman (household respondent #8) said, "we can always find some food in the garden" (interview, 5 Oct. 2016). This indicates that while cutbacks resulting in severe hunger are unlikely, not all villagers can afford what they would ordinarily prefer.

In Cindaga village, three of the 12 (25 per cent) respondents experienced no food difficulties during the *paceklik* period, however four households (33 per cent) indicated mild levels of insecurity. One respondent said that while his household is not hungry, they often lack cash to buy a variety of foods and that his family's diet is "*kurang bergizi*" (not so nutritious) (interview with household respondent #35, 23 Sept. 2016). They would like to eat more meat and green leafy vegetables, but the costs are too high.[12] With fewer opportunities available to make "fast money" to cover cash shortfalls during the *paceklik* period, as well as the need to repay loans for agricultural inputs, several of the small group of respondents experienced a greater depth of food insecurity. Three of the 12 (25 per cent) could be considered moderately food insecure while another two (17 per cent) experienced a severe level of food insecurity, regularly reducing their food portions or number of meals to cope. This likely helps to explain the fact that the stunting rates (defined as "low height for age" [Rokx, Subandoro and Gallagher 2018: 4]) in Wonosobo district are very high.

In Wonosobo district, the 2013 stunting rate of 41 per cent was significantly higher than the national stunting rate of 37 per cent (Rokx, Subandoro and Gallagher 2018: 16). This result led to Wonosobo district being included as one of one hundred regencies prioritised for a national stunting intervention in 2017–18 (TNP2K 2017). Beside insufficient food, stunting rates in children are linked to poor sanitation, sickness and unclean water (Rokx, Subandoro and Gallagher 2018: 20). Qualitative evidence from this study suggests these are causal factors in Cindaga village. For example, a young mother and her 40-day-old baby, who appeared underweight and undernourished, had been unwell with diarrhoea, requiring medical treatment. According to the mother, the water in the village is unclean and diarrhoea and typhoid occur regularly especially during the dry season (youth interview #17, 28 July 2017). This is especially the case for those who use public amenities because they do not have a toilet or piped water to their homes. Because the young family does not receive the conditional cash transfer (PKH), and because neither mother nor baby had been included on the father's health assistance card (KIS), they had been forced to pay all the medical costs themselves. Just five days before I spoke to the young mother, she had sold a ring to pay for the baby's medicine.

When I asked the young mother how she would cope if they became sick again, she replied, "I don't have anything else to sell. Next time I will borrow money from my family". She did not understand why she could not access free health assistance. According to the PKH *Pendamping* (Facilitator), however, the couple had probably not updated their Family Card (KK) or Resident Identity Card (e-KTP) after their marriage two years earlier, or after the birth of their baby. These are pre-requisites for gaining access to all social assistance programmes. A village official explained "if there is a mistake in the name, a change in the ID Card or Family Card, people go to the Village Office to fix and update it" (follow up telephone interview with Head of Dusun, 10 July 2018). However, young people in the village commented on the slow government process for arranging the cards and uncertainty about the costs. According to one 30-year-old man, "not everyone has a family ID card, and the government provides little help. It's a slow process [to arrange]" (interview, 28 June 2017). This indicates that structural processes undermine access to formal social assistance for eligible households.

Borrowing money, usually from family or neighbours, but sometimes through credit institutions (even if typically avoided due to high interest rates), is a common coping mechanism. Over the previous 12 months, 48 per cent of households borrowed money from neighbours because unseasonal weather and pest or plant disease caused crop failure, with the expectation that it would be repaid after the next successful harvest. Survey results suggest remittances play a role in alleviating poverty for non-poor households in Kahawa. Here, 20 per cent of households received some assistance from family members living and working outside the village. Of those, five were households that had ascended from poverty and two had remained non-poor, indicating that remittances are an effective coping mechanism. Just one poor household received outside remittances and the total amount was very small, only IDR 100,000 (USD 7.40) received "occasionally" during the year. For the remaining seven households, remittances were received regularly, ranging from IDR 200,000 (USD 14.80) to IDR 5 million (USD 370) per annum, the median remittance being IDR 1 million (USD 74) per annum. By contrast, in Cindaga village just one poor household received occasional outside remittances from family members,[13] suggesting that local social assistance and diversified work options within the village are preferred ways of coping there.

Consumption and Expenditure Patterns

Household expenditure patterns suggest that the consumption of healthy food is compromised in favour of cigarettes and *jajan* ("snacks for children"). As a proportion of expenditure on food and household consumables (which makes up 44.2 per cent of total spending), poor households spend considerably more on *jajan* than fish and meat, with 23 poor and 57 non-poor households spending 16 per cent and 14 per cent, respectively, of their total expenditure on snacks for children.

Concerningly, field observations indicate that *jajan* is not particularly nutritious and potentially harmful; it usually comprises sugary or deep fried foods. Poor households also spent more on cigarettes and tobacco (9.2 per cent) than rice (2.2 per cent), fish and meat (1.1 per cent). It should be pointed out that no women involved in this study were smokers, indicating that men's social habits have high opportunity costs: "money spent on tobacco is money not spent on basic necessities, such as food, transportation, housing, and health care, thus increasing the risk of adverse health outcomes for pregnant women and their fetuses" (WHO 2013: 22). While public policies to raise awareness of the costs of smoking are required, effective social assistance programmes are critical to reduce the likelihood that precarity and inequality between the rich and poor will grow (Rigg et al. 2016: 66). This highlights the need and opportunity for an effective social transfer system.

An Analysis of Social Protection Programmes

Government Social Assistance

One objective of the research was to understand how well state social protection programmes (SPPs) meet the needs of the poor. This section will pay attention to two key programmes: first, the subsidised rice programme, Rastra, and second, the Family Hope Program (PKH) conditional cash transfer. At the time this research was undertaken, in 2016–17, the total PKH annual benefit per household was IDR 1.89 million (USD 140), paid in quarterly instalments.

The survey results show that Rastra (Rice Social Assistance) was well distributed to poor households in both villages: 96 per cent of poor households received the benefit. However, 42 per cent of non-poor households also received Rastra at various times, some monthly, indicating programme leakage. Despite this, household respondents did not complain about the targeting of Rastra,[14] suggesting that villagers were satisfied with how the programme is targeted. Nevertheless, the rate of Rastra distributed to non-poor households suggests that poor households received insufficient entitlements: the average annual value of subsidised rice received by poor households was approximately IDR 350,000 (USD 26), around 19 per cent of total government assistance received. This is considered very low, as Rastra is supposed to deliver rice worth IDR 110,000 (USD 8) to poor households each month. The state hopes that the new non-cash food assistance programme *Bantuan Pangan Non-Tunai* (Non-Cash Food Aid), rolled out via the integrated welfare *Kartu Keluarga Sejahtera* card, will reduce programme leakage and deliver better quality rice and other nutritional food commodities to the neediest households (Sundaryani 2017).

The PKH programme was introduced to Kahawa village in late 2016, and at the time of the household surveys, no PKH payments had been received. By August 2017, beneficiaries in the village had received two payments. However, some of the PKH beneficiaries told me the benefits were not enough for their households' needs, particularly if they had a child attending kindergarten or high school[15] who did not receive education assistance (KIP), or their husbands' incomes were irregular. By contrast in Cindaga village, where the PKH had been introduced earlier, 60 per cent of PKH beneficiaries participating in the household survey stated that it had enabled them to increase either the frequency of meals or the size of their food portions.

Of the 23 poor households in 2017, 17 (74 per cent) benefited from the PKH. This seems quite positive. However, given inclusion and exclusion errors, there is still room for improving the targeting and selection process: 15 of 57 (26 per cent) non-poor households were receiving the PKH, while five of the six excluded poor households were eligible to receive the programme, according to the state's criteria (which include pregnancy; children attending pre-school or school and old age [70+]). Indeed, women at PKH meetings in both villages commented that the targeting and selection process was unfair, because there were households who ought to receive the assistance but did not. For example, a poor, elderly man living alone in Cindaga had not been included in the programme. Consequently, several women shared some of their own PKH benefit with him. In the same village, several disadvantaged households, comprising young parents, babies and toddlers, were not included in the programme either, although they too could surely benefit from the assistance.

The following example highlights how the Proxy Means Test (PMT[16]) used to select PKH beneficiaries has caused disappointment and some tension in Cindaga. When the PKH Facilitator took over the job in the village in early 2017, locals informed her that two recipient households were considered "*sudah mampu*" (already capable) and should not receive the PKH. She visited the households and found that both owned cars, a proxy for "prosperity", as reflected in the SoP activity explained earlier. She deleted them from the programme, causing both households to become disgruntled. Nevertheless, the Facilitator followed community expectations. According to her, however, other poor households cannot replace the two deleted households until the central government approves additional beneficiaries for the village.

This situation highlights several points. First, it demonstrates the importance of cooperation between the community and the PKH Facilitator to monitor beneficiaries to ensure transparency and accountability of the programme. Secondly, it underscores the need to improve the selection and feedback process, so that other eligible households can be included if existing beneficiaries are subsequently deleted. Thirdly, it suggests the need for a transparent appeals process through which households can make the case for their ongoing inclusion before being excluded. Finally, it demonstrates a weakness of the PMT targeting the poor and vulnerable, because it fails to account for dynamic fluctuations in household incomes, consumption and composition (Kidd, Gelders and Bailey-Athias 2017: ix).

In 2017, women at PKH meetings in both villages said they believed that the allocation of benefits was fair, because the national government had changed the system so that all recipients received the same amount of cash benefits four times a year, regardless of individual household needs. In this way, they said, no household benefitted more than another; in the local context that was perceived as equitable. One beneficiary in Cindaga village remarked that "the programme is not fair for those who don't receive the PKH but it is fair if everyone gets the same amount so there is no jealousy".[17] Others agreed. This perspective highlights two points: first, a state social protection system may conflict with locally accepted selection and distribution processes. Secondly it points to the importance of following not only an open and transparent selection system but also a distribution process that is based on local understandings of equity and fairness to minimise social problems (Kidd, Gelders and Bailey-Athias 2017: 18).

In 2019 the central government introduced changes to the PKH. Now, beneficiary households receive higher, but different amounts of up to IDR 9 million (USD 666) per year depending on their family's burdens. Social Minister Agus Gumiwang Kartasasmita reportedly stated that a household may receive benefits for a pregnant woman, the elderly and disabled, and for elementary school children (up to four components), but "if there are still high school students, we will not add to it" (Ashari 2018). Based on the 2017 interviews with PKH beneficiaries for this research, the 2019 distribution changes are likely to be considered unfair by mountain villagers in Java, particularly if eligible households continue to be excluded while non-poor households are included. It remains to be seen how these changes to the programme will play out in the village.

Informal Social Assistance

In contrast to concerns regarding the PKH selection method, survey respondents made no complaints about who received *zakat*[18] assistance. Local mosque leaders use eight broadly inclusive criteria, based on instruction from the Koran, for determining *zakat* eligibility. *Fakir* and *miskin* (destitute and poor) households are said to be prioritised. Other beneficiaries include religious instructors at the *Taman Pendidikan Al Qur'an* (TPQ) or *madrasah*, households with children who study at *pesantren*, *madrasah* and TPQ (with a focus on the poorer households), people studying Islam and members of the Zakat Committee. This explains why the benefit is quite widely distributed, either as rice, cash, or a combination of both.

Of 80 surveyed households, 59 per cent received *zakat*. Of the 23 poor households, 19 (83 per cent) had received the benefit, while proportionally fewer, but still nearly half of the non-poor households,[19] had also benefited from *zakat*. This suggests that more poor households could benefit if fewer non-poor were excluded; however, as the Koran states, eight different groups of Muslims can receive *zakat*, which includes the non-poor.[20] Locally, this system is normatively accepted by villagers, with amounts distributed in line with Islamic beliefs, values and local understanding of fairness.

Like Rastra, however, average *zakat* rice benefits are low, just IDR 167,000 (USD 12), indicating they are also short-term benefits which do little more than smooth household consumption during difficult periods. *Zakat* cash benefits are, on average, slightly higher at IDR 215,666 (USD 15.90). Although some households receive larger amounts of *zakat* than others, respondents did not complain about its targeting or distribution, suggesting a greater level of acceptance in the way it is distributed compared to state social protection programmes, or perhaps reticence to criticise local Islamic institutions and risk social ostracisation. This suggests, then, that wider sharing of benefits contributes to social solidarity between villagers, an aspect of life that continues to be valued in both locations.

Expenditure patterns show that there is a strong culture of assisting other households by giving rice or cash donations at occasions such as births, deaths and marriages.[21] On average, poor households spent up to 24 per cent of their total expenditures on social, traditional and religious donations, and non-poor households spent around 22 per cent. Some poor households indicated that giving money or rice to others strains their own budget; nevertheless one informant from Cindaga said: "we are obliged, we must give. If not, we will be embarrassed with the neighbours" (interview #18, 20 Sept. 2016), indicating that the "moral economy" remains strong in the mountains but is conditioned by Islamic beliefs and social pressure to "belong" or "conform" to local expectations. Another informant (interview #40, 4 July 2017), whose family was struggling with the costs of living after their father had passed away a year earlier, said "[community assistance] helps, but is not enough", highlighting that for the poor, this kind of help cannot radically alter their situation or enable them to escape poverty, but is important for maintaining social relations and "smoothing" difficulties.

Conclusions

It is true that many households in both villages have escaped the worst forms of poverty over the last 30 years, but it is indeed apparent that the social and agrarian changes in upland Java, noticed by Robert Hefner, continue to produce the "haves" and the "have nots". Conjunctural factors including strong competition for limited land resources, difficulties accessing capital, erratic weather, expensive inputs and unstable returns on production have shaped livelihood outcomes in different ways. I have characterised the rural economy here as a *boom crop, agrarian differentiation scenario*, where thriving horticultural industries, and the multiple factors underlying them, have enabled many farmers to accumulate profits, leading to upward social mobility in each village. At the same time, those who lose out in this scenario face the likelihood of falling into poverty. These same processes also impact negatively on local ecologies, exacerbating environmental challenges and compounding difficulties for horticultural producers.

Nevertheless, many smallholders are reluctant to leave the mountains, and despite their adversities, they "cling on" to their tiny tracts of land, while looking for other ways to make money. Remittances, loans from neighbours and local forms of assistance, while insufficient for overcoming structural forms of poverty, remain important mechanisms for smoothing seasonal difficulties and promoting social solidarity and the "mountain way of life". Since the COVID-19 pandemic began and work from tourism-related activities has dried up, it is highly likely that these kinds of informal coping mechanisms, along with farm work, have become even more important for sustaining the mountain way of life in both villages. The main point this research makes is that although villagers welcome state assistance programmes such as the PKH, they do not want what is seen as an unfair targeting and selection process to generate animosity or erode the social fabric within their mountain communities. Perhaps by harnessing these critical insights and building on well-established local mechanisms for distributing assistance in a socially acceptable way, government social assistance programmes could one day be viewed in a similar way to informal ones.

Acknowledgements

Research for this chapter was made possible with financial support from the Australian Research Council (DP140103828: *Household Vulnerability and the Politics of Social Protection in Indonesia*: Towards an Integrated Approach), and an Australian Postgraduate Award Scholarship. I am grateful for the research assistance of Ngabidin (Cindaga village) and Hilya (Kahawa village), and to the residents and local officials who welcomed my presence in each location.

Notes

[1] According to the 2013 Agriculture Census there were 26.14 million farming households across Indonesia (BPS 2013: 5).

[2] *Petani gurem* are farming households that own or control less than 0.5 ha.

[3] Pseudonyms have been used for both villages in this study.

[4] Poverty line as IDR 334,406 (USD 25) per person per month (BPS Kabupaten Sleman 2017b).

[5] IDR 297,422 (USD 22) per person per month (Diskominfo Kabupaten Wonosobo 2017: 139).

[6] Two different household figures (3,644 and 3,220) are provided by the district government (BPS Kabupaten Sleman 2016: 7). Therefore, population data obtained can only be an approximate guide. Four key *dusun* (hamlets) were selected with input from local community members to capture a representative sample and cross section of the village. Total population of these four hamlets is 2,927 and total number of households is 1,028.

[7] Typically, six or more goats or two or more cows for dairy and meat production.

[8] Average exchange rate of IDR 13,500 to USD 1 between 2009 and 2021.

[9] The politics of mining is an ongoing source of uncertainty for local miners across Indonesia (Robinson and Erb 2017). The state allows for *UU Mineral Batubara or UU Minerba* ('People's Mining' in Mining Law) No. 4/2009, provided they have authorisation or a permit from the district head to exploit minerals on local land. However, this is not clearly defined in Indonesian legislation and "uncertainty surrounding these miners' status leads to around 90 per cent of them being regarded as 'illegal'" (Lahiri-Dutt 2017). The subsequent Law No. 23/2014 on Local Government mandates the provincial government to issue 'Type C' licences for sand mining activities; however none of the miners interviewed for this research had one.

[10] This study adopted the Household Food Insecurity Access Scale (HFIAS) (Coates, Swindale and Bilinsky 2007) methodology.

[11] However, *salak* farmers also complained of income losses during the *panen raya* (large harvest) in the wet season from around December to March, when prices fall significantly due to high competition in the marketplace driven by oversupply. Thus, small *salak* producers commonly supplement agricultural incomes all year round.

[12] A variety of nutritious vegetables is not grown in large quantities in Cindaga village but is instead brought in and sold by motorcycle vendors. Cost is a prohibitive factor for poorer households.

[13] Localised assistance was of greater importance to poor households than outside remittances in Cindaga village.

[14] Informants from Kahawa village government stated that Rastra is distributed according to local needs, which are decided at monthly local government meetings, while officials from Cindaga village claimed that Rastra is distributed only according to mandated government procedures.

[15] *Sumbangan Pembinaan Pendidikan* (monthly educational donations) range between IDR 75,000 (USD 5.55) to IDR 150,000 (USD 11) per month at senior and vocational high schools. Fees are paid to schools where government funding allocations are insufficient to cover all costs. Poor students should be exempt from SPP, but the cost of schoolbooks, transport, and uniform is onerous without KIP assistance.

[16] Household assets and education are used as "proxies" for wealth; for example, highest level of schooling completed, home and land ownership, number of motorbikes or vehicles and participation on the haj pilgrimage.

[17] PKH meeting, Wonosobo village, 21 Aug. 2017. In attendance were 48 PKH beneficiaries and the PKH Facilitator.

[18] *Zakat* is a 2.5 per cent tax paid on accumulated wealth.

[19] 28 of the 57 (49 per cent) of non-poor households across both villages had received *zakat*.

[20] Cf. the Koran 9:60: *Zakat* may be given to the poor, the needy, *zakat* administrators, new Muslims and friends of the Muslim community, those in bondage (slaves and captives), those in debt, in the cause of God, and the "wayfarer" (travellers or stranded with few resources).

[21] This is reflective of the SoP results, discussed earlier, which showed that households will spend on social assistance before saving money for themselves.

References

Ambarwati, A.R., S.I. Harahap and B. White. 2016. "Land Tenure and Agrarian Structure in Regions of Small-scale Food Production", in *Land & Development in Indonesia: Searching for the People's Sovereignty*, ed. J. F. McCarthy and K. Robinson. Singapore: ISEAS, pp. 265–94.

Ashari, M. 2018. "Bantuan Program Keluarga Harapan Dihitung Datar Mulai 2019" [Family Hope Program Assistance will be Calculated from a Flat Rate Starting 2019], *Pikiran Rakyat*, 13 Dec. 2018. Available at https://www.pikiran-rakyat.com/nasional/2018/12/13/bantuan-program-keluarga-harapan-dihitung-datar-mulai-2019 (accessed 24 Mar. 2022).

Bernstein, H. 1979. "African Peasantries: A Theoretical Framework", *The Journal of Peasant Studies* 6, 4: 421–43.

_____. 2010. "Rural Livelihoods and Agrarian Change: Bringing Class Back In", in *Rural Transformations and Development – China in Context: The Everyday Lives of Policies and People*, ed. N. Long, Ye J. and Wang Y. Cheltenham: Edward Elgar, pp. 79–109.

Borras, S.M. 2009. "Agrarian Change and Peasant Studies: Changes, Continuities and Challenges – an Introduction", *The Journal of Peasant Studies* 36, 1: 5–31.

BPS (Badan Pusat Statistik/Statistics Indonesia). 2013. *Laporan Hasil Sensus Pertanian 2013* [Agricultural Census Report 2013], Badan Pusat Statistik Indonesia [Central Statistics Agency Indonesia]. Available at https://st2013.bps.go.id/st2013esya/booklet/at0000.pdf (accessed 24 Mar. 2022).

_____. 2015. *Distribusi Persentase Penduduk menurut Provinsi, 2000–2015* [Population Percentage Distribution by Province, 2000–2015]. Badan Pusat Statistik Indonesia [Central Statistics Agency Indonesia]. Available at https://

www.bps.go.id/dynamictable/2015/09/07/843/distribusi-persentase-penduduk-menurut-provinsi-2000-2015.html (accessed 12 Dec. 2021).

BPS Kabupaten Sleman. 2016. *Statistik Daerah Kecamatan Pakem 2016* [Statistics of the Pakem Sub-District 2016]. Badan Pusat Statistik Kabupaten Sleman [Central Statistics Agency Sleman District]. Available at https://slemankab.bps.go.id. (accessed 24 Jan. 2022).

_____. 2017a. *Banyaknya Kepala Keluarga dan Keluarga Miskin per Kecamatan di Kabupaten Sleman, 2016* [Number of Household Heads and Poor Families per Subdistrict in Sleman District, 2016]. Available at https://slemankab.bps.go.id/statictable/2017/11/09/116/banyaknya-kepala-keluarga-dan-keluarga-miskin-per-kecamatan-di-kabupaten-sleman-2016.html (accessed 24 Mar. 2022).

_____. 2017b. *Kemiskinan Kabupaten Sleman, Tahun 2010-2016* [Poverty in Sleman Regency, 2010-2016]. Available at https://slemankab.bps.go.id/statictable/2017/06/07/77/kemiskinan-kabupaten-sleman-tahun-2010-2016.html (accessed 14 April 2018).

BPS Kabupaten Wonosobo. 2017. *Kecamatan Kejajar dalam Angka 2017* [Kejajar Sub-District in Numbers 2017]. BPS Kabupaten Wonosobo [Central Statistics Agency Wonosobo District]. Available at https://wonosobokab.bps.go.id/publication/2017/09/26/3dc5b4bd61b89e7ec622941c/kecamatan-kejajar-dalam-angka-2017.html (accessed 24 Nov. 2020).

Coates, J., A. Swindale and P. Bilinsky. 2007. *Household Food Insecurity Access Scale (HFIAS) for Measurement of Food Access: Indicator Guide (V3)*. Washington, DC: Food and Nutrition Technical Assistance Project.

Diskominfo Kabupaten Wonosobo. 2017. *Indikator Statistik Pembangunan Daerah Wonosobo 2017* [Statistical Indicators of Development in Wonosobo District 2017]. Dinas Komunikasi dan Informatika Wonosobo [Department of Communication and Information Wonosobo]. Available at https://wonosobokab.go.id/website/data/Statistik/Indikator%20Statistik%20Pembangunan%20Daerah%20Tahun%202017.pdf (accessed 20 Nov. 2020).

Hefner, R. 1990. *The Political Economy of Mountain Java: An Interpretive History*. Berkeley and Los Angeles: University of California Press.

Kidd, S., B. Gelders and D. Bailey-Athias. 2017. *Exclusion by Design: An Assessment of the Effectiveness of the Proxy Means Test Poverty Targeting Mechanism*. Geneva: International Labour Organisation, Social Protection Department.

Lahiri-Dutt, K. 2017. "Mining the Land, Mining People", *Inside Indonesia*. Available at https://www.insideindonesia.org/mining-the-land-mining-people-3 (accessed 25 Sept. 2019).

Li, T.M. 2014. *Land's End: Capitalist Relations on an Indigenous Frontier*. Durham, NC and London: Duke University Press.

Mosse, D. 2010. "A Relational Approach to Durable Poverty, Inequality and Power", *The Journal of Development Studies* 46, 7: 1156–78.

Permana, S.I. 2017. "Salak Pondoh Sleman Tak Semanis Lagi Harganya" [The Price of Sleman's Snake Skin Fruit is No Longer as Sweet], *detikNews*. https://news.detik.com/berita-jawa-tengah/d-3556942/salak-pondoh-sleman-tak-semanis-lagi-harganya (accessed 4 June 2022).

Ribot, J.C. 1995. "The Causal Structure of Vulnerability: Its Application to Climate Impact Analysis", *GeoJournal* 35, 2: 119–22.

Rigg, J. et al. 2016. "Between a Rock and a Hard Place: Vulnerability and Precarity in Rural Nepal", *Geoforum* 76: 63–74.

Robinson, K. and M. Erb. 2017. "Mining – Who Benefits?" *Inside Indonesia*, 19 Oct. Available at https://www.insideindonesia.org/mining-who-benefits-3 (accessed 25 Sept. 2019).

Rokx, C., A. Subandoro and P. Gallagher. 2018. *Aiming High: Indonesia's Ambition to Reduce Stunting*. Available at http://documents.worldbank.org/curated/en/913341532704260864/pdf/128954-REVISED-WB-Nutrition-Book-Aiming-High-11-Sep-2018.pdf (accessed 4 Aug. 2020).

Santoso, H. 2015. *Bertani itu Berjudi: Ketika Mekanisme Pasar Bias Spekulasi* [Farming is a Gamble: When the Market Mechanism is Speculative], PhD Thesis, Faculty of Cultural Science Anthropology, Gadjah Mada University, 2015.

Sundaryani, F. 2017. "Logistics Agency Questions New Role in Non-cash Rice Distribution Program", *The Jakarta Post*, 14 June. Available at http://www.thejakartapost.com/news/2017/06/14/logistics-agency-questions-new-role-in-non-cash-rice-distribution-program.html (accessed 15 June 2018).

Syuaib, M.F. 2016. "Sustainable Agriculture in Indonesia: Facts and Challenges to Keep Growing in Harmony with Environment", *Agricultural Engineering International: CIGR Journal* 18, 2: 170–84.

TNP2K. 2017. *100 Kabupaten/Kota Prioritas untuk Intervensi Anak Kerdil (Stunting)* [100 Districts/Cities for Child Stunting Intervention], ed. Tim Nasional Percepatan Penanggulangan Kemiskinan [The National Team for the Acceleration of Poverty Reduction]. Available at http://www.tnp2k.go.id/downloads/100-kabupatenkota-prioritas-untuk-intervensi-anak-kerdil-stunting-volume-3 (accessed 22 June 2019).

WHO (World Health Organisation). 2013. *WHO Recommendations for the Prevention and Management of Tobacco-Use and Second Hand Smoke Exposure in Pregnancy 2013*. Available at https://apps.who.int/iris/handle/10665/94555 (accessed 24 Mar. 2022).

CHAPTER 9

Between the Sea and a Hard Place: Fisheries Degradation and Livelihood Precarity in a West Bali Coastal Community

Carol Warren

Introduction

This chapter examines the impact of environmental decline on local livelihoods in a west Balinese coastal community, as a case study of the precarity arising from resource degradation affecting many rural communities in Indonesia and beyond (Rigg et al. 2016). Alongside vulnerability to life cycle crises of illness, death and disability, precarity for the population of Perangkat (pseudonym), a fishing community in the district of Jembrana, west Bali, arises from a number of serious anthropogenically induced environmental challenges, leaving villagers with limited prospects of a "sustainable" future to support livelihoods in their home community. More broadly, this case study is a harbinger of longer-term vulnerabilities, exploring the under-recognised looming threats to food security and economic development posed by natural resource degradation. The new precarities are starkly evident in the fisheries sector, but represent a wider issue driven by unsustainable production practices in agriculture and other sectors of intensified natural resource extraction. The paradox in these cases is that the same market expansion and capitalist accumulation processes that underpin "development" trajectories are ultimately undermining them.

The fishing village of Perangkat was officially classified as a *desa tertinggal* (left-behind village) during the Suharto Era. The progression out of poverty over the 1990s and early 2000s and the subsequent unravelling of the local economy as a consequence of the collapse of the Bali Strait fishery since 2010 do not fit neatly into conventional agrarian transition models or stages of poverty scenarios. The primary focus of this chapter is on the impact of resource decline and the complexity of interpreting questions of poverty, food security and social protection in settings where an ambiguous sense of "precarity" poses so many shades of grey in the measurement and assessment of community and household livelihood trajectories, presenting a scenario of reversal precipitated by resource degradation.

Local Concepts of Poverty and Precarity

Concepts of poverty in Balinese villages have been shaped by dramatic shifts in economic and environmental conditions over the past four decades and by the relativities of material and other personal circumstances among fellow villagers in the present. Bali's economic base has changed dramatically since the 1970s, shifting from agriculture to tourism and transforming the island from one of the poorest to one of the highest income provinces in the country. But this transformation is heavily concentrated in what might be considered the "overdeveloped" southern tourist enclaves (Warren and Wardana 2018), leaving remote and primary producing districts with substantial pockets of poverty.

There is consensus on a rough chronology of poverty, livelihood improvement and then decline among villagers in this relatively remote fishing community, and a general perception that material poverty (but relative equality) had characterised villagers' socio-economic status until the late 1990s. As one fisher and leader of a local fishers' cooperative expressed it:

> In general, from those days until now, we were more or less equal
> here. The only really poor now are old people that can't work and
> widows. Because of the strong idea that we should be equal, the fishers'
> [cooperative] group is concerned to find a way to free those members
> with remaining debts to local traders… [The irony is that] previously
> our poverty was due to lack of alternative markets or access to credit.
> We caught lots of fish that were worth little then. Now credit and
> markets are easy, but there aren't enough fish. (Interview, I Budiarna[1],
> 11 July 2017)

Today, material differentials are increasingly evident but unevenly distributed over time, space and economic sectors. Furthermore, fisheries have very different patterns of seasonal variability and productivity compared to agricultural production cycles, making this case study distinctly different in several respects from the agricultural cases covered in this book, where declining resource bases, cropping patterns and market values, though analogous, present a different mix of challenges and time frames.

The inequalities traditionally characterising lowland rice-growing Balinese villages—based on land ownership and differential status—have not been significant in this village. Perangkat does not have an aristocratic or large land-holding class. Dryland ownership was limited, and did not confer economic advantage compared to fishing until tourism and real estate development spurred speculative investment and drove up land prices across Bali from the late New Order "developmentalist" period of the 1990s (Warren 1998; Warren and Wardana 2018). Only with that recent increase in land values and the sudden decline in the Bali Strait fishery, both driven by poor governance and overdevelopment,[2] did some villagers find themselves significantly better off than others. To date in Perangkat, however, what substantial socio-economic differentials exist relate primarily to employment in the upper echelons of the modern economy outside the village. That said, almost all villagers have customary (*adat*) rights to residential land, and therefore pay no rent, a major cost for those seeking migrant labour opportunities away from their home village.

Discussions regarding villagers' concepts of poverty and well-being elicited a commonly held set of criteria for categorising socio-economic groupings, not dissimilar to state-established models. Villagers associated the characteristics outlined in Table 9.1 with three categories: poverty/disadvantage; well-being/sufficiency and prosperity/wealth.

Table 9.1   Villagers' criteria for assessing livelihood categories of poverty, well-being and prosperity in Desa Perangkat

Poverty / disadvantage – *miskin / kurang mampu / pra-sejahtera, lacur (B)*[3]
• unable to eat rice regularly; depend on cassava or corn as staple or rice supplement
• impermanent housing (bamboo walls, dirt floors, thatch roof)
• too many dependent children; or elderly without income or support from adult children
• children unable to continue beyond primary school
• no health protection or emergency savings
• renting or indebted for small outrigger boat (*jukung* - B) and fishing equipment
_____ *Poverty line* _____
Well-being / sufficiency – *sejahtera / mampu / madia (B)*
• eat rice and fish daily
• own some livestock (cow, chickens)
• own their own outrigger fishing boat (jukung) with small engine or have steady moderate-wage employment
• own a motorbike and mobile phone

(cont'd overleaf)

Table 9.1 (*cont'd*)

• refurbished home of cement and tile construction
• schooling children to middle and upper high school (SMP and SMA)
• have small savings
_____ *Prosperity line* _____
Prosperity / wealth – *makhmur / sejahtera plus, sugi (B)*
• own profitable business or commercial purse seine boat (*selerek*)
• own more than one hectare of irrigated land or several hectares of dryland and a substantial number of livestock
• post-secondary schooling for children
• own a car or truck
• have large savings and/or able to carry big debts

The apparent neatness of classification, however, belies the reality of mixed fortunes and cross-category assets, as well as the difficulties of classifying marginal households. Owning a motorbike or shifting to wage labour, for example, does not guarantee livelihood security, or indicate that a household will be able to afford to keep children in school or to save in the face of crisis. The largest socio-economic cohort among survey households for this research comprises the group that straddles both sides of the poverty line.

A lineal developmentalist chronology of clear-cut "stages" of escape from poverty to well-being, implied in "agrarian transition" and "stages of progress" (SoP) frameworks, therefore, does not fit comfortably the experience of the fishers of Perangkat. Nor for that matter does either of the conventional modernisation or political economy of development trajectories prove an adequate approach to understanding contemporary precarity. Neither of these dominant approaches to development studies takes adequate account of the impacts of environmental degradation on living standards and levels of (in-) security. Nor do these approaches tend to credit reciprocal social relations with a significant role in modulating the impacts of livelihood insecurities. The prevailing neo-liberal models of resource management and economic development in particular ignore the relevance of mutual aid networks and say nothing about the looming precarities faced by even apparently secure households in responding to the already formidable challenges of environmental degradation and economic transformation.

The people of Perangkat had bought into the developmentalist agenda of government rhetoric, and had no difficulty establishing criteria that reflected material improvement in their lives since the early days of "poverty" prior to the 1990s. What is problematic in classifying household socio-economic status is the complexity of using material assets as markers of a prosperity that did not prove sustainable. Indeed, such asset accumulation tended to disguise the fact that the very productivity-increasing drivers that brought higher incomes were also the cause of decline. The disproportionate role of capitalist markets as structural drivers underpins the counter-developmental *natural resource degradation scenario* represented in this case study.

Villagers describe an experience of transformation from poverty[4] to prosperity and then precipitous deterioration in incomes and security, as the decline of their fisheries impacted all those directly or indirectly dependent upon this previously rich natural resource. Outlined below are villagers' descriptions of the three periods of economic and ecological transformation that appear to undercut developmentalist modernity's promise of ever-increasing well-being.

(1) Poverty: Prior to the Late 1980s

Those old enough to remember the economic situation before the 1990s describe the village as poor. Some used the term *lacur* (*Balinese [B]*: destitute) to describe life in seasonal low-yield fishing periods (*paceklik*) before markets, credit, alternative employment opportunities, health, education and infrastructure development contributed to substantial improvements. In the 1970s, Perangkat was an isolated community, with little access to markets for artisanal fishers. Reciprocity and gleaning provided for subsistence food needs in lean *paceklik* months, and houseyard gardens produced vegetables, groundnuts and tubers to supplement or replace rice. Nonetheless, these were described as difficult times by all villagers: "We are never now as food insecure as we were years ago when we could go days without eating rice, relying on cassava greens and tubers" (I Budiarna, #15). "30 years ago, during *paceklik*, fishing households could have days with only one meal, no rice or fish. In primary school, I had no uniform and went to school without shoes" (I Weta, #19).

Slow changes came with economic diversification and expansion of animal husbandry as a dietary supplement and economic insurance. One of the hamlet leaders specifically dated moves toward village-wide diversification in response to *paceklik* vulnerability from the 1980s, when the former village head encouraged villagers to rear animals as a safety net for bad times (Interview, Kadus Ledang, 29 August 2016). Today the average household of 3.3 persons in Perangkat owns 1 cow, 0.58 of a pig and 3.2 chickens (RTRW and Renstra 2016: 23–4).

From the late 1970s to the mid-1990s, new opportunities began to open up when several fish processing factories were established across the river in Pengambengan to exploit the rich Bali Strait sardine fishery (ACIAR Report 2011). A commercial purse seine fleet serving the new factories began to anchor in the river at the time. Most of the owners and crew were from nearby Muslim villages. Although the establishment of a commercial fleet was initially opposed by Perangkat small-scale outrigger (*jukung*) fishers, expansion of commercial operations over the following decades offered opportunities for occasional labour—as crew on the sardine fishery purse seine vessels (*selerek*)—and brought supplementary cash income to *jukung* line fishers.

Until the 1990s most homes were still impermanent structures with dirt floors, woven bamboo walls and no toilets. Few families owned motorbikes, and children stopped studies before middle school (SMP). Only four children, including one who became the current village head, went on to senior secondary school (SMA) before the 1990s. By comparison, 657 villagers had graduated from senior secondary school (SMA) in 2015, with an additional 43 completing post-secondary studies (RTRW and Renstra 2016: 26–7).

(2)   Prosperity: 1990s–2009

Economic diversification accelerated with the construction of a bridge across the river to the district capital, cutting travel time in half. With opportunities for work and education beyond the village, also expanded by the availability of motorcycles on cheap credit, Perangkat was no longer a remote or "left behind" community by the late 1990s. Permanent houses of brick and tile began to appear, initially in those households where a member had temporarily left the village to take on wage labour. But even fishing families that remained village-based began to renovate some of their dwellings. Household shrines were carved and painted, replacing bamboo and tin with wood and expensive black thatch roofs as markers of prosperity and gratitude to the ancestors.

The years of economic crisis in 1997–98 paradoxically accelerated the period of economic prosperity for Perangkat fishing households, when the devaluation of the Indonesian currency brought the international market closer to the village. The price of fish rose dramatically as a result.[5] Villagers refurbished their houses and large numbers of children began to study to the end of secondary school (SMA). Most households came to own motorbikes. In addition to finding better paying work as crew on the purse seine fleet, young unmarried men and a few women began to seek work further afield in Denpasar, Jakarta and beyond. District policies in the early decentralisation period were also an important stimulus for improved welfare. The district government facilitated what seemed a natural new employment opportunity for work on cruise and cargo ships.

The district health system, established in the early Reform Era under Jembrana's innovative District Head (*Bupati*) Winasa, was undoubtedly the most significant improvement in household well-being through public policy in the early 2000s (Rosser and Wilson 2012). But when Jembrana's ambitious *Bupati* lost office and was jailed on maladministration charges, his reforms were quickly unwound. The loss of what villagers regarded as a major contribution to livelihood security, due to the perverse politics of decentralisation in the post-Suharto period, was widely remarked upon in interviews. One villager complained that since Winasa's district health card system was replaced by provincial then national health care programmes, their household hadn't received any health card at all, despite repeatedly submitting the required paperwork (I Sukada, #2).[6]

By the early 2000s, signs of precarity arising from human-induced environmental decline impending at local and global levels simultaneously were already setting in. Some villagers sold residential land to a Japanese–Balinese partnership along the coast as erosion became an increasing problem; others lost their homes to the forces of nature and had to buy land on slightly higher ground. Capture fisheries decline, mangrove destruction, shrimp farm degradation, the crackdown on the turtle trade and beach erosion[7] all contributed to the sense of slow and relentless economic reversal that began to take hold.

(3) Decline: 2010 to Present

The sudden collapse of the Bali Strait fishery in 2010–12 marked the decline of the local economy along with the depletion of the marine resources upon which villagers had depended for generations. Nonetheless, in 2015 the number of fishers in the village was officially reported as 615, still involving on average one family member in half of its 1281 households (RTRW and Renstra 2016). The Pengambengan official landing and auction site (TPI) provides the statistical data which can be used to trace the rise and fall of the commercial sardine fishery in the Bali Strait (Figure 9.1).

Recorded landings of fish at the Pengambengan TPI, where only the commercial purse seine fleet sell their fish, had risen from 6.6 million kg in 2005 to 21.8 million kg at the height of productivity of the sardine fishery in 2009, but dropped dramatically to 11.6 million kg in 2010, and 2.7 million at its lowest point in 2012, 12 per cent of the record breaking catch three years before. In 2014 the total catch landed at the TPI rose again to 9.4 million, but now with significantly different composition.

Instead of the larger *lemuru* sardines, catch statistics since 2010 are dominated by smaller, less valuable juvenile class sardines (*protolan*) and other pelagic species such as skipjack tuna (*tongkol*) that are the main target of small-scale fishers (see Warren and Steenbergen 2021).

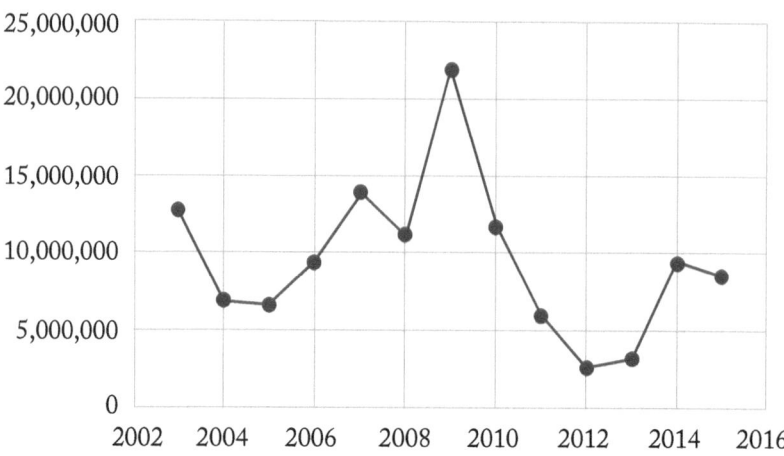

Figure 9.1   Annual fish landings by weight (kg) at Pengambengan TPI: 2003–15

Pengambengan canneries were already reported to be operating at only 60 per cent of capacity when an Australian government research centre study investigated the state of the fishery (ACIAR 2011). The few Balinese who had invested in the commercial purse seine *selerek* boats in the boom years went bankrupt in the aftermath. The wealthiest commercial boat owner from a neighbouring village was operating only half of his 24-vessel fleet on a much-reduced schedule after 2010. Crew from the grounded purse seiners turned to small-scale fishing, putting further pressure on artisanal *jukung* fishers, who in turn were increasingly seeking day work in construction outside the village to make ends meet.

In addition to the impact of global warming and other environmental factors (IPPC 2019), capture fisheries decline was also the result of poor governance, which allowed overfishing, overcapacity and illegal technologies to continue unchecked. The ACIAR (2011) study of the Bali Strait sardine fishery notes that by 2010–11, catches in the fishery were already at an historic low (ACIAR 2011: 2). Nonetheless, the Bali Strait sardine fishery was "considered to have the attributes that could lead to successful management strategies" (ACIAR 2011 Appendix 2.6: 2). A UNESCO-funded management plan had been drafted 30 years before and a Memorandum of Understanding between the districts of East Java and Bali was signed in 1992 to restrict the number of commercial purse seine units at the two sites to 190 and 83, respectively. But this limit was not enforced, and boat size and numbers grew over the years to take advantage of what many assumed to be a limitless resource (interview, TPI official, 12 July 2017). The commercial sardine fishery became a classic example of Illegal, Unreported and Unregulated (IUU) practices driving the resource degradation scenario.

Aside from failure to implement fleet size restrictions, illegal fishing methods undoubtedly contributed to the collapse. Purse seine net mesh sizes of 1 cm (instead of the requisite minimum 1 inch) meant that juvenile fish were scooped up by the growing commercial fleet to be sold for low-value fish meal. The purse seine boats, when unsuccessful with their target sardine catches, also fished illegally in near shore waters zoned for artisanal fishers. Boats that were built to carry 50 tonne maximum catch by then were reported to be landing an average catch of three tonnes (ACIAR 2011).

The ACIAR research team estimated that with a 50 per cent fishing effort reduction, the overexploited Bali Strait sardine fishery could become sustainable (ACIAR 2011, Appendix 2: 3). Simbolon, Nurfaqih and Sala (2017: 842) similarly conclude that reduction of fishing pressure, through enforcement of restrictions on mesh sizes and fishing vessel numbers, is essential to the viability of the Bali Strait fishery. Their study of Bali Strait sardine hauls in February and March 2015 found that 91 per cent of the catches sampled comprised illegal undersized sardines.

To date, the size and quantity of the fish caught in the Bali Strait sardine fishery have declined dramatically, and TPI reports since 2014 now classify most sardine catches as *protolan*, about half the size and value of the standard *lemuru* sardine class (~>12 cm). There seems little prospect of recovery in the Bali Strait fishery in the short term. The total catch levels that have been possible to maintain comprise these low-value small sardines and smaller takes of higher value pelagic fish that are the primary target of artisanal fishers.[8]

Environmental Decline and Livelihood Precarity

The combination of direct impacts from the collapse of the commercial sardine fishery and its indirect effects on the small-scale fishing sector has been substantial, and prospects for improvement are not good. Despite the introduction of hard-line policies on Illegal, Unregulated and Unreported (IUU) fishing under then Minister for Marine Affairs and Fisheries (2014–19) Pujiastuti, primarily applied to foreign vessels fishing illegally in Indonesian waters, the political clout of the domestic commercial fishery sector has to date protected its short-term interests. During the period of this research, there were no signs of implementation of controls on the commercial purse seine fleet or its use of illegal nets,[9] despite several visits by the Minister to the District.

The effects of resource decline have been felt across the village and beyond fishery-dependent households. Apart from direct income lost to fishers in 16 survey households (down from 22 fishing households among the same 40 surveyed in 2010), fish traders and cannery workers in another seven households, together comprising 58 per cent of the 2016 sample, as well as village small businesses and vendors, have also been severely affected. Ni Nuri, who runs a mobile phone recharge kiosk, said "I can measure its impact by the money people spend on credit for their mobile phones. Over the last couple of years that has dropped by half—No, more even than half" (interview, 3 Aug. 2016). I Tiarsa (#35), a mechanic who owns a small business repairing motorbikes and boat engines, estimated a similar income decline affecting his business.

In former times (pre-1990s) there was poverty and food insecurity in Perangkat. Fishers' families remember days when there was only one meal and no rice in the then shorter *paceklik* periods. In contrast, there are different categories of need and vulnerability in the present. All agree that government poverty-line standards are no longer adequate measures of contemporary needs. What appear as markers of well-being or prosperity in the classifications elicited in the village (Table 9.1) are now complicated by new sources of precarity. While there was general agreement among villagers on the assets and situations that marked states of poverty, sufficiency and prosperity, complex conditionalities and an increasingly unpredictable resource base make it difficult to be definitive regarding the side of the poverty line on which particular households should be situated. Much of the local debate about national social protection policies is fuelled by the growing sense of marginality and ambiguity of classification that triggers government supports. As Ni Nuri told us:

> What was poor before was a house of bamboo and earthen floors; not being able to afford rice, which was often mixed with cassava or corn; being afraid to go into debt; and having to take children from school when we couldn't make ends meet. Now the bar is higher. I would say only a quarter of those listed as "poor" really are. That is the cause of a lot of conflict. There are households on the list for social support who have a car! (Interview, 3 August 2016)

The high costs of health and education, the need for mobility and communication, and risks of personal crisis put a large proportion of the population in states of insecurity in the short term, compounded by resource degradation that haunts the indefinite future. I Budiarna struck a pessimistic note:

> What if the decline in the fishery continues and there are no fish to share? ... How can we small *jukung* fishers make a living when the fish are all gone? ... If the Fisheries Department doesn't do something about regulating this, the next generation won't even know the names of these fish—because there won't be any left. (Interview, 26 August 2010)

In earlier times, the term *paceklik* referred to the seasonal low-catch periods of scarcity in the capture fishery in February–March and July each year. These periods have now lengthened and become more unpredictable. Today the prolonged and deeper lean periods due to fisheries decline exacerbate inevitable life-cycle pressures. As one young *jukung* fisher reported:

> Household income improved, and then declined over the last 10 years. In between, we could save and upgrade the house. For our household the main reason for the decline compared to a decade ago is the long scarcity period (*paceklik panjang*) as well as my father's death ... Since marrying, I now have more dependents, a wife and two children that I didn't have then. (I Suardi, #10).

In Suardi's case, as for most of those who fell into states of marginal precarity despite their location on the well-being side of the poverty line, life circumstances (illness, death, indebtedness) against the background of income decline put livelihoods in proximate jeopardy. Due to his father's illness and death, the costs of medical treatment and funerary rituals wiped out their savings from the prosperity period, forcing them to sell their livestock and leaving them in debt to the village development fund (*BumDes*) for 3 million rupiah (USD 222). This added to his longstanding debt of 5 million rupiah to a local fish trader (*pengepul*) to pay for his small outrigger. Although their household received customary (*suka-duka*) contributions from other villagers to support funerary rituals, the community cycles of mutual obligation meant similar amounts were received were also given out over time.

Suardi's household economic decline has not put his family below the income thresholds that trigger significant government subsidies. In fact, the rice subsidy benefit that they previously received as support for his elderly parent ceased. His father's death had a double negative impact on their household economy since it involved both loss of income from his father's fishing as well as the loss of government *Raskin* rice supplements, compounding the effects of indebtedness and fisheries decline.

An indication of the importance of even the modest government subsidies for mitigating adverse livelihood impacts is evident in the 40-household survey data. The data in Table 9.2 demonstrate the contribution which government subsidies make to the income level of poor households.

Table 9.2 Comparison of average annual household earned income and average government assistance for poor and non-poor survey households

	Poor (n = 6)	Non-Poor (n = 34)	HH income of poor represented as a % of non-poor incomes
Average earned income per annum (per household)	15,233,333	41,495,000	36%
Average government assistance per annum (per household)	9,617,500	2,589,853	371%
Total annual income (per household)	24,850,833	44,084,853	56%
Per capita daily income (USD)*	$1.20	$1.86	

* *Note*: Per capita calculations are based on average household size of 4.2 persons for poor and 4.8 persons for non-poor households among 2016 survey respondents, using the project average exchange rate of IDR13,500 to the USD.

Clearly, government subsidies have had some impact in raising the incomes of the poor from just over a third to above half the average income of non-poor households, but still below the international poverty line for per capita daily income set at USD 1.90.[10] It is also the case that many non-poor household incomes are not substantially above the poverty line figure. In the 2016 project survey, six households were classified as poor and needy according to community norms, but an additional seven of the 40 respondent households (together representing a third of those surveyed) reported facing significant economic difficulties. These additional households were only marginally classified as non-poor (*pas-pasan*—just making do) by virtue of mixed criteria including assets such as motorbikes, motorised outriggers and mobile phones. The inclusion of a substantial number of marginal households on the non-poor side of the poverty threshold, by virtue of assets accumulated during the prosperous period of the fisheries, mutes the extent of the livelihood divide.

The growing sense of precarity arising from the fisheries crisis is indicated by survey responses to identical questions in 2010 and 2016 concerning difficulties covering costs of basic needs in the areas of education, health or food expenditure. In 2010, immediately following the high point of sardinella catches, 20 per cent of respondents indicated that they experienced difficulties in one or more of these three areas of household consumption. By comparison, 48 per cent of respondents in the 2016 survey reported difficulties covering some basic need(s).

Further complicating the picture is the limited advantage of the "transition" out of the fishing sector for ordinary fishing households. Numbers of small-scale fishers sought alternative work, mainly in construction, which was rarely full-time. They had average incomes of IDR 45,000 (USD 3.33) per day, but some worked only one in four days. Those mainly young villagers who secured ongoing jobs in local tourist villas earned an average of IDR 39,000/ day (USD 2.89). These two main occupations available to those remaining resident in the village were low paid and often unstable. Neither offered better average incomes than those reported by fishers for the same period.

Monetary income and survey expenditure statistics, of course, do not tell the whole story. The survey did not capture well the under- or un-calculated "income" from coping strategies that blur the margins between poor and non-poor, leaving a much larger vulnerable category that hovers above and below the margin between impoverished circumstances and getting by.

Invisible Economies—Reciprocities and Domestic Piecework

An important coping feature of rural life in Indonesia has been the resilience of aspects of the traditional moral economy. This has been a somewhat counter-transformational phenomenon, but consistent with findings elsewhere in Southeast Asia, and especially evident during the 1997–98 Asian economic crisis (De Koninck, Rigg and Vandergeest 2012). The continuity and forms of village-based reciprocity and redistribution remain an understudied dimension of the age of precarity (cf. Li 2014: 150–64), and with the exception of formal customary (*adat*) obligations, proved predictably difficult to quantify for this study. In a similar vein, the poorly remunerated but essential contribution of women's casual home-based piecework sometimes supplied the only cash available during *paceklik* periods, and was also generally under-reported in the survey. The large discrepancy our survey found in comparing the percentage of reported expenditures to income—39 per cent above estimated income for poor households, compared to 3 per cent below income in non-poor households—can be explained at least partially by these low commercial-value and often invisible contributions to local livelihoods, which tend to be taken for granted and which patch together the household response to precarity deficits and bridge some of the inequalities evident in Table 9.2.

If security of food, health and education are minimum measures of the well-being threshold, then these informal and under-reported spheres of exchange underwriting subsistence through everyday coping strategies must be taken into account, despite the difficulties of capturing them statistically.

Moral Economy

Alongside the range of categories of household expenditure and supports documented through the 40-household survey, extended interviews and observations revealed the ongoing significance of informal exchanges that were largely uncalculated. Acts and expectations of generalised and balanced reciprocity continue to fit the classic economic anthropological models of gift-giving and redistributive and balanced provisioning, more or less invoked according to the relativities of social proximity and basic need set out by Sahlins (1972). These remain pivotal to managing the day-to-day vagaries of the local fishing economy, and continue to tide households over the lengthening *paceklik* lean periods. Gift/request, labour offer/exchange and informal borrowing were the coping relations most frequently observed and referred to in conversations and extended interviews.

The daughter-in-law in I Weten's [#11] large marginal-income household said she didn't spend money on clothes. It was enough to ask (*ngidih*) when she needed some. The family estimated that only IDR 500,000 (USD 37) were spent annually on clothing (compared with an average IDR 3.2 million spent on school-age children's snacks per household, per year across survey households. I Suwenda [#18], a retired fisher from an exceptionally large undivided house compound of 52 people in 21 households, said he never bought clothes, and just asked (*ngidih*) for whatever he needed from his large extended family. His wife occasionally worked in the largest of the Pengambengan fish factories, but rarely for more than five days a month recently and had had no work at all in the month we surveyed their household. Nonetheless, Suwenda says he never has to buy fish, because he can always go down to the beach to "*nujur*" *(B)*– to help other fishers carry the *jukung* outriggers and equipment to and from the sea (see photograph in Appendix, Figure 9.3), when he would always be given fish.

N[g]ujur, to offer casual labour assistance in return for in-kind food or other gifts, was widely availed by women in the village. Ni Resi [#4], an elderly widow who lived with her mentally ill, unemployed son and grandson, often stopped in at neighbours' homes to help with light work that needed doing. *Nujur* was the term also used for the small army of mostly women who cleaned the scrap fish from purse seine nets after the main haul had been dropped at the TPI (see photograph in Appendix, Figure 9.4). Like gleaners of padi fields (*munuh* [B]), they kept all of the scrap fish collected.[11] Indicating the extent to which various forms of redistribution and in-kind exchange represented a significant proportion of even the commercial fish catch, the 2009 ACIAR fieldtrip report notes that "about 25 per cent of total catch is categorised as 'lost', dispersed to various people involved in the catching and unloading of the fish. These include *Penguras* (boat scrubbers/cleaners), *Pengisi* (fish unloaders), *Pacokan* (fish porters), *Pakelaut* (ferrymen), and *Nujur/Curi* (people who gather around the vessels during unloading to clean the nets or take/steal fish)" (ACIAR 2011, Appendix 2.6, Trip Report 30/10/09).

Ngebon/bon, the widespread short-term borrowing, mainly of rice, from small home-based *warung* (villagers' kiosks selling snacks and basic supplies) should be included as an extension of reciprocity in the local moral economy, since these exchange arrangements are without interest and depend upon ongoing personal relationships. I Marsa (#5) said his family regularly borrowed IDR 10–20,000 (USD 0.74–1.48) worth of rice from the local *warung* and would make small repayments with no interest, which my Denpasar-based research assistant concurred was common practice everywhere in Bali. This practice is essential in the day-to-day provisioning of rice in non-agricultural communities where this staple needs to be bought. Borrowing with elastic limitations on the amount of debt that can be accumulated and on the length of time in which repayment is expected is typical of balanced forms of small-scale exchange. These flexible loans of rice on credit, that are strongly influenced by social distance and need, arguably constitute a form of balanced reciprocity significantly different from other forms of indebtedness. Also distinguishing this small-scale borrowing from more substantial and formal kinds of indebtedness are the attitudes of Perangkat villagers, who generally regard the latter with anxiety and reluctance, while *ngebon* (credit) from the *warung* or *nyelang* (loan) from family and friends refer to common and essential borrowing in which strong family, neighbourly or friendship ties and relations of trust are involved.

Notably, fish for consumption was not commonly among the commodities purchased by fishing families, being typically subject to *ngidih-ngasih* and *nujur* gift-giving and redistributive relations rather than relations of *ngebon*, which involves the obligation to return an explicit cash payment when able. These relations worked across both the commercial and artisanal fisheries with which Perangkat villagers engaged. Even though I Budiarna's brother had good luck with an 8 kg catch on the day we happened to be discussing reciprocities, he was still given two sardines by a friend who worked as crew on the purse seine fleet (I Budiarna, Interview, 22 July 2015). Gift-giving of fish remains a subtle and widespread practice, although the almost casual passing of small strings of fish by successful *jukung* fishers and purse seine crew is undoubtedly declining in scale and frequency with the resource.

Women's Domestic Low-income Piecework

Another perhaps predictable point to be made is that surveys generally did not capture sufficiently well the labour-intensive and casual supplementary household income sources that characterise most women's cash earnings in Perangkat. It was mainly qualitative observation that revealed the wide range of very small-scale incremental income-generating activities that represent supplementary cash sources availed mainly by women to support their households. These domestic income sources were of disproportionate importance in dealing with uncertainties of fishing incomes and played a critical role in bridging gaps that kept children in school, paid for medicines, created small savings or repaid small loans that keep households afloat.

The example of Ni Sudianti in the household where I stayed over several years of periodic research in Perangkat illustrates the difficulty of tracking casual supplementary home-based incomes earned by women, and of converting these into meaningful figures. Every year I found Sudianti engaged in different activities, often previously unmentioned, to supplement household income. Only as I observed these activities over the years of periodic stays did queries yield some sense of their scale and importance, despite the low income-to-labour time ratio they typically represented under low rural opportunity cost conditions.

In the long *paceklik* season of 2013, I found Sudianti, along with other women of the village, collecting seagrass,[12] weaving dried palm leaf ritual offering containers, and collecting and drying frangipani flowers to be sold for incense and perfume manufacture. In 2014, tamarind processing had taken over as slightly more rewarding supplementary labour during fruiting season. In 2015 it was again massive quantities of simple woven palm leaf ritual offering holders (*porosan*) to be sold in Denpasar that absorbed quiet hours of evening socialising in the household, sometimes involving both men and women. In 2016, thanks to sewing machinery skills she had learned when working in Denpasar before marriage, Sudianti was doing piecework embroidery on a machine loaned by a trader, which brought in much higher piece rates compared to most other domestic income-generating activities at IDR 35,000 (USD 2.60) for an embroidered blouse. She could complete two or three in an (atypically) uninterrupted day's work. Throughout the fishing season she also supported her husband and four other related households at the lowest level of the local fish trade pyramid, providing ice and on-selling their small catches in the local market supply chain. She earned IDR 1,000–4,000 (7 to 30 US cents) per day for one or two hours' work on 15 days in a good fishing month.

Women's supplementary income was generally limited by time devoted to their other domestic duties, and by the erratic market conditions of casual piecework. Prices for dried frangipani flowers, for example, reached such low levels in 2016–17, at IDR 5,000/kg (roughly 37 cents), that most women stopped collecting and drying them (#4 Ni Resi, 2 Sept. 2016). The 13 households that reported these kinds of small-scale home-based women's income in our survey indicated average incomes of IDR 6,500/day, equivalent to a 48 US cents contribution to their daily domestic budgets, enough to cover less than the cost of a kg of rice (IDR 10,000/kg) or a litre of petrol (IDR 7,000/ltr) for the day's fishing.

Nonetheless, women's small-scale home-based piecework, as well as their work involved in running small general supply kiosks and coffee shops, petty trading, and rearing animals has been crucial for maintaining a basic living standard for households in this village. From these mixed sources of income, Sudianti (possibly over-) estimated her income at an exceptional 15 million rupiah or USD 1,111[13] out of their IDR 39 million total family income for the survey in 2016. That would average USD 3.04/day for the relatively high proportion of annual household income she contributed (approximately 38 per cent of the household income that year). In earlier years, the savings from this supplementary work, combined with some surplus from her husband's fishing, enabled them to renovate their home and accumulate 19 million rupiah in banked savings that were wiped out by one hospitalisation in 2011. Their joint household income of 39 million rupiah for 2016, supporting three people now that their older daughter had married out of the household, meant this family was comfortably in the non-poor category with IDR 13 million per capita income that year, or ~USD 2.60 per household member, per day. Above the World Bank USD 1.90 per day income per capita poverty line, the Budiarna/Sudianti household sat in the middle-income range for this village. But that did not mean they lacked a strong sense of the precarity of their economic situation.

Accumulated Assets and the Masking Effects of the Prosperity Period

Most villagers have accumulated a store of material assets and social capital in the form of better education, diversified employment experience and improved housing and transportation that are carry-overs from the prosperity period. In consequence, the village today appears relatively prosperous. Typically, Balinese house compounds (comprising a large range of single to multi-household extended families) have at least one brick and tile dwelling, piped water, electricity, more than one motorbike, and one or more mobile phones. A few villagers now own a car and a computer and have a family member with post-secondary education, often enabled by remittances from short- or long-term work migration.[14] Remittances reported in the 2016 40-household survey ranged from a half-million rupiah to 12 million per annum (USD 37–889), averaging IDR 7.9 million among the eight recipient households, roughly equivalent to USD 73 annually per household. A few households in Perangkat benefit from financial contributions from family members married to foreigners they had met when working in the tourism sector outside the village.

Village-wide statistics and the project survey show a significant rise in education levels and possession of potentially productive assets including motorcycles and mobile phones. But almost all respondents indicated apprehension regarding future prospects, because of the declining state of their natural resource base and the uncertainties of alternative income sources. As noted above, only 6 households of 40 sampled (15 per cent) were classified as poor and needy by community criteria set out in Table 9.1. But an additional 7 of the 40 respondent households reported difficulties with education, health and everyday living costs, and were only marginally classified as non-poor. These were typically placed in the non-poor group by virtue of mixed criteria including assets such as ownership of motorbikes, a motorised outrigger and mobile phones.

For the substantial marginal group of households hovering above the poverty line as well as those classified as "poor", everyday life is focused on basic necessities. For many of these, formal classification by any simple fixed poverty line was experienced as arbitrary. Targeting social protection policies in such circumstances, where at least a third of the survey respondents were marginal enough to be considered or to consider themselves worthy of some subsidy and safety net provisions, is inevitably fraught. The difficulty of calculating the economic contribution of informal redistributive supports and of low-paid casual domestic work to degrees of subsistence precarity and the masking effect of social, educational and material assets gained during the now fading prosperity period explain why the issue of social protection policy provokes such controversy. The strong sense of entitlement combined with a similarly strong sense of precarity pits balanced (equity-based) against generalised (need-based) reciprocity principles. Efforts to bundle supports, such as through the Family Hope Program (PKH) scheme, may exacerbate the situation by failing to address the food, health and education needs of more differentiated populations at risk.

For Balinese, higher costs of living across the province, due to tourism development, as well as the expense of customary *adat* ceremonial obligations— an average of six million rupiah (USD 444) per survey household in 2016— make the international poverty line figure an inadequate measure of the pressures experienced by those working outside global economic sectors.

Environmental Precarity and Social Protection Policies

State policies aimed at addressing rural vulnerability and precarity will undoubtedly need to take greater account of the specificities of locality and resource sectors in the delivery of short- and long-term policies aimed at social protection. Safety net, fuel subsidies, credit and insurance provision, storage and marketing improvements, and value-adding through downstream processing are among important government initiatives that are undoubtedly essential to developing effective outcomes for supporting the small-scale fishery sector. These are particularly important for women who are typically the local fish traders and processors in resource-dependent communities such as Perangkat (Stacey et al. 2019). At the same time, development policies must provide for sustainable stewardship of marine resources. Indonesia remains committed to productivity-increasing development as the primary solution to poverty alleviation. Government grants for technological improvements have been aimed at encouraging small-scale fishers to go further out to sea, by providing larger, more powerful fibreglass boats and equipment. But these also introduce new precarities that may increase risks of economic debt and fish stock depletion in the absence of equally serious commitments to reversing resource decline.

The diversity of causes, impacts and options for social protection and poverty alleviation means that if, as De Koninck, Rigg and Vandergeest argue, "there cannot be a general theory of poverty or impoverishment" (2012: 36), there cannot be a simple strategy for social protection either. This is all the more the case when faced with the vagaries of the fishing industry where resource abundance and incomes are notoriously erratic (Béné, Macfadyen and

Allison 2007), and where the effects of climate change and poor governance are increasingly felt.

Over 17 consecutive days in the middle-income Budiarna-Sudianti household where I stayed in September 2016 (when a normal *paceklik* period would in the past have broken), I Budiarna fished 13 days, with no catches on four occasions. Non-fishing days were due to bad weather and ritual events. Over the nine "successful" outings he brought in a total of 117 kg, but his worst and best daily hauls varied from less than 1 kg to a substantial 60 kg. The total income from his fishing activity for this 17-day period averaged IDR 62,000/day. Subtracting estimated costs for petrol and equipment, the net cash income from fishing, at IDR 42,000 or USD 3.11 per day, without other supplementary income, would have pulled their family of three below the international poverty line—lower still, if their now married daughter were still a dependent. Budiarna did not have debts; he was able to work in the regional capital through in-law connections if he had to; and his wife, as we have seen, had skills that substantially cushioned their family budget. This was not the case for many of the other village households that lacked connections and specialist skills to give them a repertoire of possibilities to increase their own life chances and those of their children.

None of the Perangkat respondents admitted to serious food insecurity, although a few regarded themselves as "poor" and many more as "needy" in terms of government social protection policies. Certainly, the women of household #1 who had lost all but occasional days of work in the fish factory, and the four families affected by loss of the primary breadwinner or by disability and mental illness (households #4, #26, #35, #40), fell clearly into the generally recognised "poor" category. While it may be relatively easy to identify those at the top and bottom ends of the poverty-to-well-being spectrum, assessing and responding to the long-term needs of the much larger numbers facing precarity due to resource decline are more difficult matters. This "produced" situation (Rigg et al. 2016) compounds vulnerability to life cycle and other crises. The effects of climate change and environmental deterioration will only exacerbate these impacts and make social protection policies more complex and difficult to target in the *resource degradation scenario* represented in this case.

Purwaningsih, Widjaja and Partiwi (2011) predict that the Bali Strait will be fished out by 2040, with the loss of 15,000 jobs for fishers and processors based at Muncar, the site of the other important purse seine fleet on the East Java side of the Bali Strait. Muncar and Perangkat fishers—indeed all of the estimated 2.5 to 3.7 million coastal villagers in Indonesia dependent on capture fisheries (CEA 2016: 4)—face the prospect of an "End to Fish" analogous to the depressing scenario presented for upland farmers in Tania Li's *Land's End* (2014).

Because the fishers of Perangkat live near the district capital on an island that is a global hub of the tourism industry, the immediate fate of most village households is being cushioned by the diversification that Rigg and Vandergeest (2012) and Rigg et al. (2016) see as the positive side of globalising processes. Yet as Li's (2014) study shows for remote rural communities, and as numerous critics of unbridled capitalist economic frameworks argue on a global scale (for example, Stiglitz 2010; Standing 2014; Piketty 2014;[15] Monbiot 2017; Brooks 2017), precarity is a feature of late-capitalist development that is eclipsing the concept of a proto-proletariat once thought to be on the path of progressive "transition". In the absence of radical structural transformation through a politics of distribution put forward by Li, the imbalances in the global economy coupled with the end of the resource frontier—which together produced financial and natural resource debits contributing to the economic and environmental crises of 1998 and 2008—appear destined to reproduce indefinitely a world of de-capitalised and insecure jobless, self-employed and underemployed populations in countries of both the global north and south. As Li (2014: 184–5) concludes, "Too often movements are derailed by restatements of the transition narrative that counts on growth to solve most of the problem and envisages distribution as a 'safety net' reserved for residual cases. The hard realities of jobless growth, and the uneven distribution of the costs and rewards of growth, are left out of the account."

In contrast, De Koninck, Rigg and Vandergeest (2012: 36) argue that the pessimistic projections of development scholars and practitioners regarding the prospects for rural transformations may over the last few decades have been "more wrong than right". That has been the case in a much wider context of massive economic expansion over the late 20th century, but with a heavy environmental sting in the tail that has yet to work its way through local and global economies. Without considering the massive effects of mobility and remittances, and the capacity for development strategies to "freeload" on the formerly expansive and renewable natural resources of land and sea, it is difficult to conclude that the positive side of the ledger can be projected with any degree of confidence into the future of a resource-depleted world.

Both perspectives recognise the fault-line in narrowly growth-dependent strategies and seek ways forward that depend respectively upon one, the other or some combination of livelihood diversification (Rigg) and distributional politics (Li). But we have still to take more serious account of the complex ways in which economic and environmental policies that underpin both agendas find themselves at odds—at least in the short term, and in the absence of genuinely foresighted policies. As Brooks puts it bluntly in *The End of Development*, "When policymakers attempt to embrace the untidy issue of global environmental change, they are inevitably hamstrung by the reality that capitalist development and environmental preservation are incompatible" (2017: 186).

Acknowledgements

Alongside the villagers and local officials of Perangkat, without whom this research would not have been possible, I wish to acknowledge the invaluable research assistance of Denik Puriati and staff of Yayasan Wisnu, the sponsorship of the Bali Peace and Democracy Institute and support of colleagues at Udayana University.

Appendix

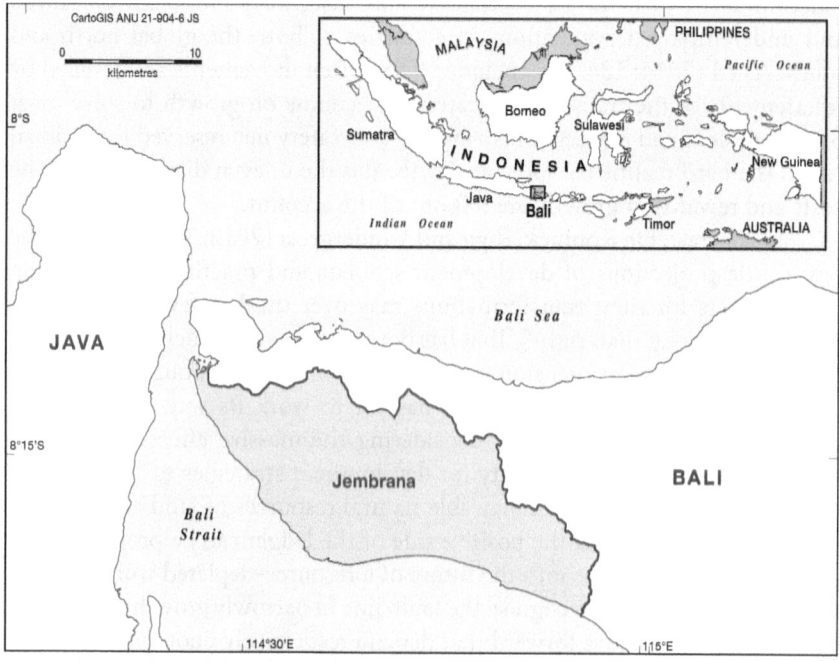

Figure 9.2 Map of Desa Perangkat

Figure 9.3 *Nujur* – mutual assistance among *jukung* fishers, 2011 (author's personal collection)

Figure 9.4 *Nujur* – gleaning (cleaning) nets from purse seine *selerek*, 2006 (author's personal collection)

Figure 9.5   Two classes of sardine: *Lemuru* (bottom) and *Protolan* (top) (ACIAR 2011)

Figure 9.6   A good day's catch, 2016 (author's personal collection)

Figure 9.7   A poor day's catch, 2016 (author's personal collection)

Notes

[1] Throughout this chapter, pseudonyms are used for informants' names. Where numbers are indicated, the information was recorded in the context of responses to the 2016 40-household survey questions. Where no number is provided, citations refer to open-ended interviews conducted separately. The formal titles "I" and "Ni" are polite forms of reference to Balinese male and female individuals of non-aristocratic rank.

[2] "Overdevelopment" refers to the disproportionate and inequality-generating investment in certain market-driven sectors linked to global capital flows in tourism, real estate and the infrastructure that supports these industries. For glaring examples in the tourism heartland of Bali and Lombok, see Warren (2013) and Warren and Wardana (2018).

[3] Terms labelled (B) are in Balinese language; otherwise, italicised words refer to Indonesian terms. Interviews took place in both languages.

[4] Those in the 2016 project random sample survey who were identified as "poor" (*miskin, kurang mampu, lacur*) through the SoP exercise fell into this category largely through personal circumstances, such as illness or death of the primary income earner. The vast majority of the community considered themselves in a position of precarity in the present directly or indirectly due to the decline of their traditional resource base, now compounding lifecycle and seasonal vulnerabilities.

[5] The price of sardines (*lemuru*) recorded at the Pengambengan fish landing and auction house (TPI) rose from IDR 225 (USD 0.10) per kg in 1993 to IDR 6,000 (USD 0.44) in 2016. Over this period the currency devalued by approximately 300%, although the

cost of living did not change so rapidly. In this chapter an average exchange rate of 2,200 rupiah to the US dollar is used for the period 1990–97; 10,000 rupiah to the US dollar for 1998–2013, and 13,500 rupiah to the US dollar from 2014 to the present (cf. https://tradingeconomics.com/indonesia/currency).

[6] There was considerable criticism in the village of outdated central government lists of poor households upon which benefit distributions were based. Our survey found 13 of 40 households (33%), including five of the six households locally classified as "poor" received rice subsidies. 15 of 40 households (38%) received education subsidies, only six of which held education subsidy cards (KIP) at the time of the survey. One of these card recipients (#9) had not received any student subsidies to date, however.

[7] Bali's coastline has been suffering serious erosion as a consequence of lax enforcement of setback regulations and climate change. This was exacerbated in 2012 when the loss of income from fishing drove villagers to a mass harvest of seagrasses along their coast, with damaging environmental consequences. Over the period 2010–15, 60 ha of Perangkat coastal land were lost due to erosion (Warren 2016).

[8] 2012 TPI records began to distinguish between the two sardine classes: *lemuru*, which were priced at IDR 6,000/kg, and low-value *protolan*, which brought only about IDR 3,000 per kg (see Appendix, Figure 9.5). See also Warren and Steenbergen (2021) for more detail on compositional changes in commercial catches over this period.

[9] See Ministerial Decrees Peraturan Menteri Kelautan dan Perikanan No.02/MEN/2011, and No.02/MEN/2015.

[10] The international poverty line is set using the 2011 Purchasing Power Parity conversion rate of IDR 9,864.7 to the USD.

[11] See Appendix, Figure 9.4 showing women cleaning purse seine nets of residual scrap fish. At the time of the photograph in 2006 these fish were valued at only IDR 250/kg compared to IDR 2,000/kg (USD 0.03 to 0.15) that was the going price for standard sardines.

[12] Gleaning seagrass flowers had been a traditional seasonal activity. But in 2012 the decline of the fishery drove villagers to a mass harvest of seagrasses along their coast, to supply outside traders, with damaging environmental consequences (see Warren 2016).

[13] This compares to an average (also probably under-reported) domestic piecework income of 3.9 million rupiah (USD 288) per household in the 2016 project survey, the differential being largely due to Sudianti's embroidery and local fish-trading, but undoubtedly also reflecting a lower level of prompted survey data on this work for other households.

[14] Of the 40 households surveyed, 12 currently had a family member working in other parts of Bali (8), elsewhere in Indonesia (2), or overseas (2). Many more individuals had previously worked away from home for short periods both to seek adventure and to improve personal and family circumstances.

[15] Ironically, Piketty devotes only a few pages to the climate change issue, which he nonetheless rates as "the world's principal long-term worry" (2014: 567).

References

ACIAR (The Australian Centre for International Agricultural Research). 2011. *Project Annual Report FIS/2006/142. Developing New Assessment and Policy Frameworks for Indonesia's Marine Fisheries, including the Control and Management of Illegal,*

Unregulated and Unreported (IUU) Fishing. Prepared by Ron West, ANCORS, University of Wollongong for ACIAR.

Bené, C., G. Macfadyen and E.H. Allison. 2007. *Increasing the Contribution of Small-scale Fisheries to Poverty Alleviation and Food Security*. Rome: UN Food and Agricultural Organisation.

Brooks, A. 2017. *The End of Development: A Global History of Poverty and Prosperity*. London: Zed Books.

CEA (California Environmental Associates). 2016. *Indonesia Fisheries: 2015 Review*. Prepared for The David and Lucile Packard Foundation.

De Koninck, R., J. Rigg and P. Vandergeest. 2012. "A Half Century of Agrarian Transformations in Southeast Asia, 1960–2010", in *Revisiting Rural Places: Pathways to Poverty and Prosperity in Southeast Asia*, ed. J. Rigg and P. Vandergeest. Honolulu: University of Hawai'i Press.

Erdmann, M.V. and J. Pet. 1999. "Krismon & DFP: Some Observations on the Effects of the Asian Financial Crisis on Destructive Fishing Practices in Indonesia", *SPC Live Reef Fish Information Bulletin* 5: 22–6.

Indonesian Ministry of Fisheries and Marine Affairs Regulations Nos. 02/2011, 56/2014 and 2/2015.

IPCC (Intergovernmental Panel on Climate Change). 2019. *Special Report on the Ocean and Cryosphere in a Changing Climate* (SROCC), Chapter 5, "Changing Ocean, Marine Ecosystems and Dependent Communities". Available at https://www.ipcc.ch/srocc/home/ (accessed 9 Mar. 2022).

Li, T.M. 2014. *Land's End: Capitalist Relations on an Indigenous Frontier*. Durham, NC: Duke University Press.

Monbiot, G. 2017. *Out of the Wreckage: A New Politics for an Age of Crisis*. London: Verso.

Piketty, T. [2013] 2014. *Capital in the Twenty-first Century*. Cambridge, MA: Harvard University Press.

Purwaningsih, R., S. Widjaja and S.G. Partiwi. 2011. "The Effect of Marine Fish Stock Reduction to Fishers' Revenue (A case study of sardinella lemuru fisheries in Bali Strait)", *IPTEK Journal of Technology and Science* 22, 3: 166–76.

Rigg, J. 2016. *Challenging Southeast Asian Development: The Shadows of Success*. London: Routledge.

Rigg, J. et al. 2016. "Between a Rock and a Hard Place: Vulnerability and Precarity in Rural Nepal", *Geoforum* 76: 63–74.

Rigg, J. and P. Vandergeest. 2012. *Revisiting Rural Places: Pathways to Poverty and Prosperity in Southeast Asia*. Honolulu: University of Hawai'i Press.

Rosser, A. and I. Wilson. 2012. "Democratic Decentralisation and Pro-poor Policy Reform in Indonesia: The Politics of Health Insurance for the Poor in Jembrana and Tabanan", *Asian Journal of Social Science* 40: 608–34.

RTRW (Rencana Tata Ruang Wilayah) and Renstra. 2016. *Dokumen Rencana Tata Ruang dan Rencana Strategis Desa [Perangkat], Kecamatan Jembrana, Kabupaten Jembrana, Bali Tahun 2016–2028*. Samdhana Institute, Yayasan Wisnu, Komunitas Sunda Kecil, Maluku, Delta Api.

Sahlins, M. 1972. *Stone Age Economics*. London: Tavistock.

Simbolon D., L. Nurfaqih and R. Sala. 2017. "Analysis of Oil Sardine (*Sardinella Lemuru*) Fishing Grounds in the Bali Strait Waters, Indonesia", *AACL Bioflux* 10, 3: 830–43.

Stacey, N. et al. 2019. "Enhancing Coastal Livelihoods in Indonesia: An Evaluation of Recent Initiatives on Gender, Women and Livelihoods in Small-scale Fisheries", *Maritime Studies* 18: 359–71. Available at https://doi.org/10.1007/s40152-019-00142-5 (accessed 9 Mar. 2022).

Standing, G. 2014. "Understanding the Precariat through Labour and Work", *Development and Change* 45, 5: 963–80.

Stiglitz, J. 2010. *Freefall: America, Free Markets and the Sinking of the Global Economy*. London: Allen Lane.

Warren, C. 1998. "Tanah Lot: The Political Economy of Resort Development in Bali", in *The Politics of Environment in Southeast Asia: Resources and Resistance*, ed. P. Hirsch and C. Warren. London: Routledge.

————. 2013. "Legal Certainty for Whom? Land Contestation and Value Transformations at Gili Trawangan, Lombok", in *Land For The People: State Policy And Agrarian Conflict In Indonesia*, ed. A. Lucas and C. Warren. Athens, OH: Ohio University Press, pp. 243–73.

————. 2016. "Leadership, Social Capital and Coastal Community Resource Governance: the Case of the Destructive Seaweed Harvest in West Bali", *Human Ecology* 44, 3: 329–39.

Warren, C. and D. Steenbergen. 2021. "Fisheries Decline, Local Livelihoods, and Conflicted Governance: An Indonesian Case", *Ocean and Coastal Management* 202, 1: 105498. Available at https://doi.org/10.1016/j.ocecoaman.2020.105498 (accessed 9 Mar. 2022).

Warren, C. and A. Wardana. 2018. "Sustaining the Unsustainable? Environmental Impact Assessment and Overdevelopment in Bali", *Asia Pacific Journal of Environmental Law* 21, 2: 101–25.

CHAPTER **10**

Sustaining Livelihoods from the Seas: Sama Bajo Vulnerabilities and Resilience

Andrew McWilliam, Nur Isiyana Wianti and Yani Taufik

Introduction

Indonesia is the largest archipelagic state in the world, with the fourth largest population (260 million). It is therefore unsurprising that the fisheries sector is a vitally important segment of the national economy. Over six million people are engaged directly with inland and wild-caught marine fishing and fish farming (FAO 2014). The majority of small-scale operators utilise low technology equipment and vessels (<10 gross tonnes). All remain tied in varying degrees to seafood-based trading and consumption to sustain their livelihoods. But many more Indonesians are dependent on the fisheries catch for their sustenance, with fish and seafood consumption now providing 50 per cent of the national protein supply, and per capita consumption rising over fourfold, from 10.6 kg/year in the 1970s to 46.49 kg/year in 2017 (CEA 2018). In addition to freshly harvested fish, an important proportion of the catch (eight per cent) is also consumed in dried, salted, smoked and fermented forms (FAO 2014). Urbanisation is one of the driving forces underlying the trend of growing demand (Foale et al. 2013).

Increased fish protein consumption is nutritionally beneficial (Bennett et al. 2018), but rising demand for seafood products, most of which are harvested and consumed domestically,[1] results in major increases in the seafood catch across a wide range of important fish species[2] (CEA 2018; Ariansyach 2019). Indonesian government policy has been to increase seafood production, accompanied by gradual improvements in marine management and the enforcement of regulations. Priority has also been given to substantially increasing aquaculture production to boost supply (Phillips et al. 2015). But, with many important pelagic and demersal marine species already reaching or breaching sustainable catch limits, the longer-term viability of wild-caught fisheries is under increasing pressure. Deleterious impacts include marine pollution and habitat destruction, especially of mangroves for (often short term) shrimp production; overfishing and unsustainable fishing techniques (undersize catches, bottom trawling, reef bombing and bycatch losses); and illegal, unreported and unregulated (IUU) fishing (e.g. foreign boat incursions, shark finning and cyanide fishing for the live fish trade to China). The combined effects of these destructive activities place growing pressure on thousands of Indonesian coastal and maritime-based communities, all of which remain highly dependent on inshore waters for their subsistence livelihoods and are vulnerable to reduced availability of fish stocks.[3]

This chapter reports on the research findings from two Sama Bajo fishing villages in Southeast Sulawesi, both of which are oriented to specialised sea-based livelihoods (fishing, sea farming and reef foraging). Our study focuses on the livelihood dynamics that shape Sama Bajo fishing fortunes as they negotiate the localised impacts of these broader trends affecting the fisheries sector. Their experiences resonate with wider populations of Sama Bajo fishing communities that are demographically well represented across the Indonesian archipelago (Stacey et al. 2017). Although there is growing evidence of over-fishing and pressure on existing fishing stocks, southeast Sulawesi coastal waters remain consistently productive. They support an array of high value seafood industries marketing their catch to destinations across Indonesia and internationally, including Hong Kong and Taiwan. In the agrarian context we characterise the region as a *fishing boom scenario*, one that continues to attract significant investment interest while supporting the livelihoods of large numbers of small-scale fisher communities.

Findings from the two study communities reveal three relatively clear and interconnected livelihood trajectories among resident households. These trajectories can be characterised as follows: (1) prosperous accumulative; (2) economically aspirational; and (3) precarious on the margins. Each of these livelihood trajectories finds expression in the embodied practices of the constituent households within the two communities.

(1)   The first of these trajectories is observed in the livelihoods of established fish traders and creditors who have accumulated significant investment capital and maintain strong links to market supply chains. The heads of these households use their accumulated capital and connections to invest

in fishing ventures on a larger scale. They typically sustain their incomes via networks of client fishers and crew, via extension of credit and loans in return for their labour and loyalty.

(2) A second livelihood trajectory is reflected in the practices of economically aspirational fisher households, able to take advantage of high value seasonal fishing and or to acquire productive assets like fish traps or floating grow-out pens, and thereby generate lucrative market returns. This livelihood approach enables practitioners to avoid falling into debt and to benefit from the risks they take to secure fishing incomes.

(3) A third trajectory is one characterised by near subsistence incomes and an inability to move beyond the poverty trap. This category includes widows and female-headed households whose capacity to generate income is highly constrained because of their reduced circumstances. Poor fisher households also suffer during the annual downturn in fishing production driven by the southeast monsoon and adverse integration into debt arrangements.

The dynamic relational properties of these three livelihood trajectories often intersect and generate a range of inter-dependencies and constraints that work both to perpetuate the status quo and to offer opportunities for productive change (see Thanh, Tschakert and Hipsey 2021).

Sama Bajo Culture: Livelihoods and Seasonality

Sama Bajo language communities are a regional subset of similar maritime-oriented groups across Insular Southeast Asia. There is an estimated resident population of some 200,000 spread across eastern Indonesia, most of whom live in dispersed stilt house settlements, in "water villages" and intertidal zones or crowded onto low-lying islands and islets across the archipelago. Historically, they have been a highly mobile population (Fox 1977), and often poorly legible to state authorities, who for decades have pursued policies of sedentarisation and re-settlement of these communities in permanent dwellings along the coast.

The great majority of Sama Bajo engage in seasonal fishing activities as a primary source of household income. All are practising Muslims[4] and livelihood roles are strongly gendered, with men typically active in sea-based fishing pursuits, while women focus more on home and shore-based activities, including fishing, gleaning and food processing, together with small-scale trading of fish and marine products in local markets. Along the coasts of southeast Sulawesi, the principal forms of fishing activity include team-based operations for tidal fish traps (*sero*) and longline fishing techniques (*rawé* and *tonda*) for pelagic species (tuna, mackerel, shark, trevally), typically using single-hulled wooden and fibreglass boats powered by single or twin inboard petrol engines (*bodi motor, katintin*). There is also current interest in using floating pens (*keramba*) and submerged fish cages (*bubu*) employing compressed air diving, to gather lobster and wrasse/grouper (*sunu*) for sale into the lucrative live fish trade. Low technology inshore fishing, spearfishing and reef gleaning provide other vital sources of additional income and sustenance, particularly for poorer households (see Foale et al. 2013).

Figure 10.1   Saponda Laut village scene (photo: Andrew McWilliam 2019)

Sama Bajo are very enterprising and tend to be highly sensitised to market trends and price signals. The harvest of fish and other marine products (shellfish, lobsters, stingrays, octopus, squid, cuttlefish, sea urchins and crabs) is channelled into local and regional markets daily and on-sold to domestic consumers or larger scale fish trading companies. Sama Bajo domestic economies are in this respect closely integrated into diverse commercial and export value chains of Indonesian fishing produce. They have been active in these pursuits over generations of opportunistic practice. Their marine knowledge and capacity to target specific marine species have enabled them to sustain their commercial connections and marine-based livelihoods in a constantly shifting economic and marine environment (Deswandi 2011; see Gaynor 2016 for historical perspectives).

At the same time, Sama Bajo livelihoods are also shaped by and highly vulnerable to changing environmental conditions. Pollution and overfishing, combined with the marked seasonality of the monsoon weather patterns, have variable and often deleterious impacts on the fishing household economies. The southeast monsoon blowing out of Australia (June–September), for example, brings strong winds and high seas (*musim selatan/tenggara* – southern/southeast season). These winds can severely constrain fishing activity (*gagal melaut*), particularly for fishers operating low technology boats and equipment, who risk being swamped or blown out to sea by the conditions.[5]

Most Sama Baja households associate this time with food shortages and reduced incomes. Families rely on a processed form of dried *sago* (known as *sinolé*), rather than more expensive hulled rice, to accompany whatever seafood they can glean along the coastal reefs and inshore waters. The period of high wind is also a time when people accrue debts and obligations to neighbours and shop-owners in order to maintain adequate household consumption. In this context of uncertainty, a characteristic feature of Sama Bajo fishing livelihoods is an enduring pattern of patron-client relationships that represents a key enabling livelihood element for fishing and seafood marketing. This model of political and economic relations thrives in contexts where formal financial and regulatory arrangements are constrained or underdeveloped. It represents an age-old mode of economic relations in Indonesia and a potent alternative to regulated economic markets and banking. Sama Bajo refer to this relationship as *punggawa–sabi* (patron-client). The phrase *punggawa* has a complex derivation,[6] but carries the general sense of patron or *bos*, while *sabi* refers to a dependent client. The distinction is also translated as "boat captain and crew", reflecting the historical reality that most Sama Bajo households have relied on patron-client networks to sustain their fishing and maritime livelihoods over time.

Many *punggawa* are ethnically Sama Bajo themselves and often locally resident in the coastal communities where they provide a flow of credit and capital to their *sabi* clients.[7] The relationship expresses the idea of an informal economic safety net, but also a form of market-based inter-dependency (*baku pegang*), founded on debt that requires recompense in the characteristic style explored by James Scott in his work on the moral economy of the peasant (1976). This chapter foregrounds the crucial role of patron-client relations in Sama Bajo communities.

Bokori and Saponda Laut: History, Resettlement and Change

The two Sama Bajo village communities that agreed to participate in the stages of progress (SoP) household surveys were Bokori (579 people in 147 households) and Saponda Laut (764 people in 152 households).[8] They form two of the constituent villages of the sub-district of Soropia and the wider district (Kabupaten) of Konawe in Southeast Sulawesi. The choice of the villages was guided by their contrasting comparative situations. Bokori is a coastal settlement situated on the Sulawesi mainland, with a sealed road connecting the village to the markets of the bustling Provincial city of Kendari (population 300,000+) some 12–15 kilometres away. Saponda Laut occupies an offshore sand island with an extensive sea territory and lies around 40 minutes off the coast by boat and 42 kilometres away from the ports of Kendari. The marked discrepancy in household population size between the villages, with Saponda nearly 30 per cent higher, is likely to reflect age differences between the sites. Bokori has larger numbers of older households and widows living on the mainland.

Historically, the populations of the villages originate from the eponymously named Bokori Island, lying just offshore (400 metres) from the present location of Bokori Village. In 1976, the Provincial government relocated the population and refashioned the island as a tourist and recreation park. In response, some of the people moved to the largely uninhabited Saponda Island further offshore. The remainder resisted moving to the mainland until 1984, when, under pressure from government, they accepted the offer of new housing and relocation assistance. Many found the social housing away from the sea unsuitable and gradually established a series of coastal settlements in the intertidal zone across from Bokori Island with direct access to the sea.[9]

Since then, the population of affiliated families has continued to grow and prosper, creating a series of contiguous residential settlements mostly built on stilts over the tidal flats around the edge of the shallow bay. As a result of successive processes of administrative division (*pemekaran*), there are now nine closely related but administratively separate villages representing the Bajo population of the former island inhabitants. The mainland settlements form a line of closely built houses that extends into the inter-tidal zone. The great majority of households continue to pursue fishing and fishing-related activities as their primary livelihoods, combining inshore fishing, reef gleaning and mariculture grow-out pens (lobsters and groupers/cod and threadfin trevally also known as "ikan putih").[10] More extended expeditions in motorised *perahu* (*bodi motor*) are also taken as far as the richer fishing grounds of Labengki Island and Salabangka, four hours sailing to the north.

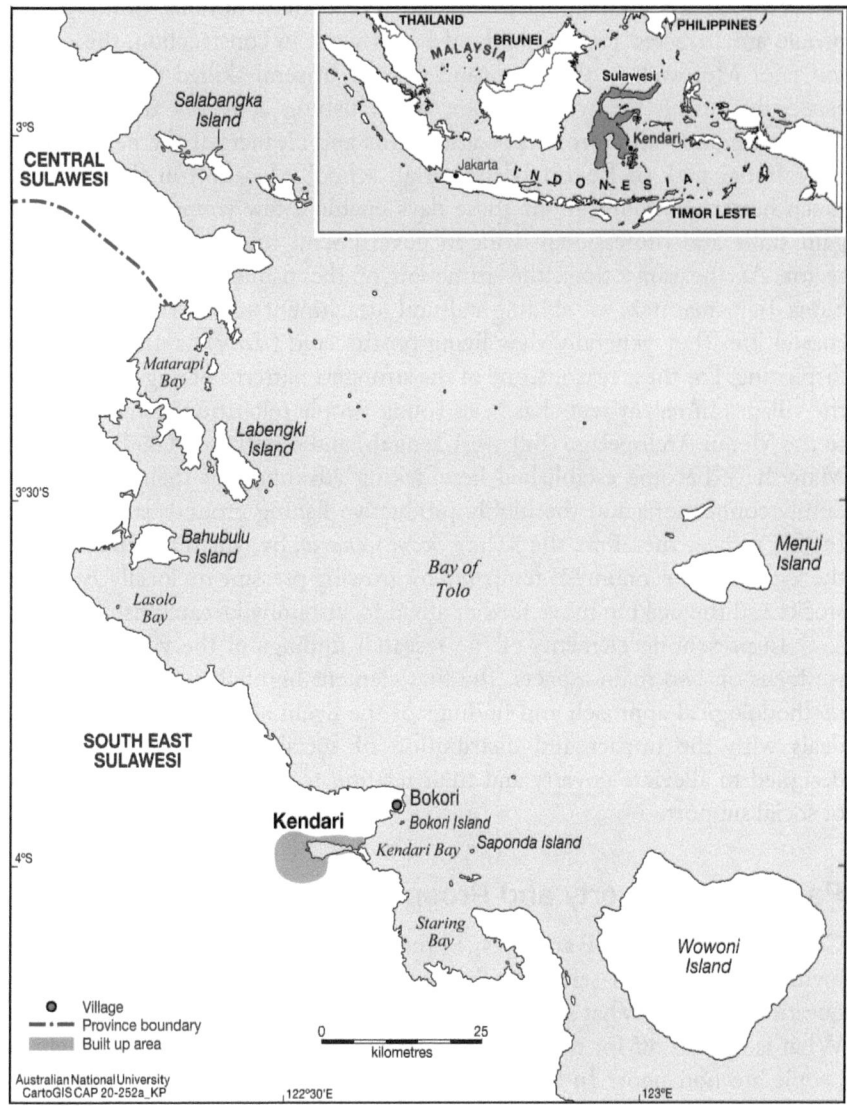

Figure 10.2   Map of the study area

The Sama Bajo population of the area shows a tenacious commitment to their maritime-based livelihoods. But livelihood diversification and migration out of the area are emerging as alternative economic options. Some young people are attracted to periodic land-based work in construction, the nickel mines of Morowali in the north and a range of semi-skilled work in town, especially during the windy season when fishing activities are restricted. Local women work on rosters as attendants and cleaners at the nearby busy recreational park of Bokori Island. High school education in the city and much better communications these days enable a few younger residents to gain skills and professional work in government, teaching and the health sector. At the same time, the attraction of the fishing life is strong, and Sama Bajo maintain an abiding cultural attachment to the rhythms of the coastal life. They generally view living on the land (*darat*) as unhealthy and dispiriting. For these reasons, one of the strongest patterns of migration out of the villages in recent years has been young people relocating along the coast to the Menui Archipelago (Sulawesi Tengah) and especially Masadian Island. Many have become established here, taking advantage of their Sama Bajo family connections and the highly productive fishing grounds still on offer. In this respect therefore, the *fishing boom scenario*, by which we characterise the local village economy, is tempered by growing pressure on locally available stocks and the need to move further afield to sustain wild-catch fish harvests.

In presenting elements of the research findings of the village surveys, we focus on two main aspects. The first element highlights the comparative methodological approach and findings of the livelihood surveys. The second deals with the impact and distribution of social assistance programmes designed to alleviate poverty and their relation to existing informal patterns of social support.

Patterns of Poverty and Prosperity

Consistent with the SoP approach, in the first poverty assessment exercise, we invited a group of self-selected village residents (male and female) to consider questions such as: What are the characteristics of the very poor in the village? What is the cut off for the local poverty line (*garis kemiskinan*) above which people are non-poor? In both Sama Bajo villages, once the purpose of the exercise was clear, the local group became enthusiastic participants; within a short time there was agreement on a clear ranking of well-recognised local indicators of poverty. As expected, fishing-related indicators and associated assets were prominent, given the nature of the community's livelihood focus. Land and productive land-based assets are notably absent in the lists.

Community members' perceptions revealed strong consistencies between the two villages (see Table 10.1). They well appreciated the perceived gap between the characteristics of those who are "poor" (I [Indonesian]: *miskin*; SB [Sama Bajo]: *sengsare*),[11] and those who are "managing" (I: *mampu*, SB: *sugi*) or non-poor. Both communities also recognised a "line of prosperity" (*garis kemakmuran*) above which households were regarded as comparatively well off. This emphasis on a threefold distinction is, we believe, a reflection of the stratified nature of both communities, where wealthier patrons/boat owners (*punggawa*) are long-term residents and form an integral part of the community and the broader moral economies of the settlements.

Poor households in both communities shared the following characteristics: they had (1) insufficient means to ensure adequate food security, and (2) a need to seek (modest amounts of) credit to make ends meet in times of need. Their status was also reflected in (3) poor quality housing, and (4) the inability to purchase or acquire larger motorised fishing boats (*bodi motor*). Poor households sometimes describe their standard of living as *pas pasan* (just getting by). They make do with small paddle canoes (*lepa lepa*) or (5) work as fishing crew (*sabi*) on the boats of others.

Table 10.1 Poverty ranking of households (hh) in Bokori and Saponda Laut

Desa Bokori hh = 40

Poor Households	Eating 1 time per day Dilapidated house / falling down Working as a crew (sabi) on a boat Owing small amounts of debt Small perahu (lepa lepa), small motor.	Poverty Line (*garis kemiskinan*)
Non-Poor Households	Long line fisher (*rawé / tonda*) (larger boat) Cement rendered house with metal roof Owner of kiosks and in shore fish traps (sero) Some savings.	Prosperity Line (*garis kemakmuran*)
Prosperous Households	Owner of large fish trap (*sero*) Owner of grow out pens (lobster and grouper)/ rumpon Large house / Large motorboat/s (*bodi motor besar*) Large debts (*punggawa*).	

Desa Saponda Laut = 40

Poor Households	Use firewood to cook Have to borrow for daily needs Only access to dugout canoe for fishing Crew/ passenger on other boats Own small outboard boat but still carry debt	(*kura sugi = poor*) ↑ Poverty Line (*garis kemiskinan*)

(*cont'd overleaf*)

Table 10.1 (*cont'd*)

Non-Poor Households	Have their own house (not living with parents) Use gas bottles to cook Own / raise goats Own motor boat (*bodi motor*) Own a kiosk/ own fish/lobsters pens	Prosperity Line (*garis kemakmuran*)
Prosperous Households	Own large modern house Own large boat (over 7m and 30hp engine) Have live fish business and substantial investment capital Have undertaken pilgrimage to Mecca.	↓ [*sugi* = has resources)

Note: For an island completely composed of sand, Saponda Laut supports a large number of goats that forage around the settlement grazing on a wide range of food scraps and refuse, which seem to do well despite the absence of grass. Goats are raised by a minority of households as a store of wealth and for the Idul Adha (Feast of slaughter) celebration in the Muslim calendar.

By contrast, the profiles of those who are non-poor have the following qualities. They tend to (1) own/control their own fishing boats (*bodi motor, katintin*) and gear (or own them with limited debt). (2) They have their own house and cook with gas bottles (*komfor*) instead of firewood. (3) They may own a kiosk attached to their house, and a smaller fish trap (*sero*) or grow-out pens (*keramba*) for fish or lobster. (4) They usually have some savings or a buffer against misfortune. At higher levels of prosperity and wealth, well-off people (*kaya*) possess multiple large boats, substantial capital for investment, large investment loans, diversified fishing businesses and the wherewithal to undertake the pilgrimage to Mecca (*naik haji*).

Poverty and Prosperity Pathways over Time

The second stage of the SoP involves classifying households in the village sample into categories that represent changes in household economic status over time. For comparison, the year 2000 was adopted as the benchmark for the comparative period in question. In the exercise we asked the village reference group to categorise all the households in the sample into one of four status categories: A (poor then, poor now); B (poor then, not poor now); C (not poor then, poor now) and D (not poor then, not poor now). The people we interviewed managed this exercise with ease and strong agreement, revealing in the process an intimate knowledge of their neighbours' economic standing and history and an openness to discuss their relative financial status.

The results of the two village assessments (see Table 10.2) reveal a degree of consistency regarding the relative weighting between categories. The main difference is that Desa Bokori has higher numbers of households that had either remained poor (A) (42.3 per cent compared to 29 per cent) or fallen into poverty (C) (14 per cent versus 8 per cent) over the interim period compared to Saponda Laut.

Conversely, a significantly greater number of households—double the percentage—in the Saponda Laut sample had moved out of poverty (B), compared to Bokori (52 per cent versus 25.8 per cent). Saponda Laut lies some distance offshore and much further from markets than for those people living in Bokori on the mainland, with easier access to the Provincial capital, Kendari. The reasons for these differences are multi-layered, but likely relate, first, to greater returns and more regular fishing success over time for households operating offshore out of Saponda Laut, with direct access to healthy fishing grounds. Secondly, Bokori residents frequently complain about competition, over-fishing and pollution effects in the waters around Bokori village, which probably contribute to reduced fishing yields over time.

Table 10.2   Pathways into and out of poverty in Bokori and Saponda Laut (2018)

(1)	Bokori [N = 85, 40hh = 47% sample of village]		
A	Poor then, still poor now	=	36 (42.35%)
B	Poor then, not poor now	=	22 (25.8%)
C	Not poor then, poor now	=	12 (14.1%)
D	Not poor then, not poor now	=	15 (17.46%)

(2)	Saponda Laut [N = 112, 40hh = 37.5% sample]		
A	Poor then, still poor now	=	30 (29%)
B	Poor then, not poor now	=	59 (52%)
C	Not poor then, poor now	=	9 (8%)
D	Not poor then, not poor now	=	11 (10%)

A further point to highlight is that between 10 and 17 per cent of the households maintained their "non-poor" (D) status over the relevant period. These households include the "patrons" and boat captains (*punggawa laut*) with capital in the community,[12] some of whom have very substantial assets and exert considerable influence over the conduct of village affairs.[13]

The poverty ranking exercises provided a robust comparative methodology for identifying patterns of poverty based on respondents' intimate understanding of domestic household economies. What is evident in the village case studies is that there are two general categories of households that are more likely to be poor: female-headed households and household heads who work as crew (*sabi*) on other people's boats.

Female-headed Households

The poorest households in categories A (remained poor) and C (not poor then, now poor) in both Bokori and Saponda Laut are those headed by women who were either widows (*janda*) or divorced. In Bokori, for example, of the 24 households categorised as poor, 41.6 per cent were female-headed households. In Saponda Laut the comparable figure is seven households out of 16, or 43.7 per cent of the poor families in the sample. Although there are many reasons why any specific household might fall into poverty (illness, misfortune, gambling and so on), it is clear that in Sama Bajo communities, when women lose their husbands' support, the burden they bear is more significant because they lose access to their principal and vital source of cash income: fishing. For women, and mothers in particular, the loss of her spouse frequently means that they fall rapidly into poverty, because their remaining resources and assets need to be sold down to sustain the household. There are few alternative options in Sama Bajo society. The main income sources for these women are reef gleaning, mixed with small-scale trading (of *nasi kuning*, *jajan* sweets, ice, *kue*), or offering labour services to other households (cleaning, childcare, cooking). But since the returns from these activities tend to be meagre, many poor women rely on their immediate families and close relatives for assistance in times of need. It is common for neighbours to provide food and labour support for aged and widowed relatives, especially those struggling to raise dependent children. This group is also usually most in need of social assistance but their social marginality means that they are often overlooked.

Crewing as a Livelihood

The second essential category designated as poor by local Bajo encompasses those with the status of "*sabi*" (*sawi*) or crew on local fishing boats. These individuals usually do not have the means to own a more significant (7–9m) motorised fishing vessel (*katintin or bodi*) and are therefore reliant for their incomes on the returns they garner working on the boat of their *bos* (*punggawa*). Men working as crew are usually wholly dependent on their *punggawa* to gain a position in the boats and provide the necessary provisioning (fuel, fishing gear, food, drinks and cigarettes) to cover their needs over the intended fishing period. Their bargaining position is weak, and this dependency is reflected in the returns they receive for their labour.

To give a sense of the relative returns possible from fishing and the benefits devolving to crew (*sabi*), we highlight one common distribution pattern among those earning marine-based incomes. Fishing practices in these villages are based around a nominal cyclical period of fishing (15–20 nights), associated with the bright phase of the moon, followed by a period of rest (*turo*) during the dark phase, when fishing in shallow waters is less rewarding. During the active fishing period, the boat crew pursues high value fish species, returning each morning to offload their catch with their *bos/punggawa* or one of his assistants (*pengumpul*).[14] The fish are packed into iceboxes (*gabus*) with catch weight and species recorded,[15] and every few days the *punggawa* sends his larger boat loaded with fish to the markets in Kendari. Here the fish are off loaded, weighed again and then sent to auction or sold directly into the markets at the port. All local *punggawa* maintain client relations with their land-based patrons (*punggawa darat*)[16] who provide credit for fishing boats and take a portion of the value of the catch.

Crews and client/indebted fisher households are paid by their *punggawa/ bos* during the *turo* (rest) phase (also known as closing the books, *tutup buku*) when the last catch has been delivered and sold. Payment is calculated on a portion of the monetary value of the fish catch. In cases where an investor has financial interests in the fishing operations (e.g. providing credit for boats), they take 10 per cent of the value off the top. Then the boat owner makes a deduction for operating and associated expenses, including ice, fuel, crew provisions, fishing gear and bait fish (*umpan*), amounting to around 30 per cent of the value or the so-called "shared costs" (*ongkos bersama*). The remaining profit is divided by the boat owner into two equal beneficiary portions: one portion to himself[17] and one portion for the crew as a group.[18] Putting this another way, if the operation earned IDR 10 million (USD 1,000) throughout the *turo*, and 10 per cent was deducted for the land-based patron with operating costs at 30 per cent, then the *punggawa* takes USD 300 and the three crew receive USD 100 (IDR 1 million) each from the remaining portion. This is a bare minimum wage, and needs to be supplemented with inshore fishing with lines and nets, or working the traps (*sero*) secured in the inter-tidal zone at strategic locations.[19] Even so, client fishermen remain conscious of their allegiance to their *punggawa*, and any fish of size (>3 kg) will be taken directly to their *bos* in the first instance.[20] *Sabi* are usually not in a position to reject these arrangements or seek work and trading opportunities elsewhere. As one *punggawa* commented, it would be like "we planted the crop and others harvested it". In return, however, *sabi* expect and receive continuing support and assistance from their *punggawa* to recognise their loyalty and view them as a source of support in times of need. The position of the *punggawa* in this context is thus a powerful one that strongly shapes the capacity of *sabi* households to gain access to boats and benefit from the bounty of the sea (Ribot and Peluso 2003).

These days, however, the crewing system (*sabi*) applies to a minority of Sama Bajo households. Far more commonly, male household heads seek to operate their own boats, many of which are secured through loans from local *punggawa*. These clients are then tied to their respective "bosses" (*punggawa*) by paying off their loans and are often then obliged to sell them their catch. Still, they do so on their own terms and receive a discounted market price for their fish. In this respect the crew (*sabi*) are directly dependent on their *punggawa* patrons, while the indebted independent fisher is only indirectly so, and is therefore usually better off.

It is also the case that the nature of fishing in these places results in more young men being interested in pursuing a fishing livelihood than there are boats or opportunities to do so. Consequently, numerous fishing support activities provide small or subsistence-level incomes for some householders. Examples include sharing the use of fishing boats, cleaning and securing returned boats for their owners, crewing on boats transferring fish to markets, tending and feeding live fish in grow-out pens (especially giant trevally [*caranx ignobilis*]) catching and selling baitfish (*umpan*), and repairing nets and lines. There are always livelihood jobs to be completed in a Sama Bajo fishing village. Remuneration for these ancillary tasks is usually modest in cash terms,[21] and collectively referred to by the phrase *jamé jamé*. The practice can be observed at the Kendari fish market wharf, when *perahu motor* arrive laden with fish-filled iceboxes (*gabus*) in the early morning. As each box is opened and unloaded, one of the leading crew members takes a double handful of fish, setting it aside on the deck to be divided later among the crew as payment for their transport services.

Food Insecurity and Seasonality

The reality of poverty for Sama Bajo households is heightened during the annual southeast monsoon (June–September in eastern Indonesia). During this time (*musim angin*), strong prevailing winds flowing out of Australia create big ocean swells and choppy seas, and fishing opportunities are typically dramatically reduced (along with incomes) because of the twin problems of hazardous weather conditions and much increased sea water turbidity.[22] Poorer households working as crew (*sabi*), or as sole operators of smaller boats with low freeboard (e.g. 7m single engine *bodi perahu*), are forced to limit their fishing excursions to calmer days closer in-shore, or spend time floating over nearby reefs, foraging for seafood and hooking shark (*hiu*) or stingrays (*pari*) which are sliced up and dried for sale. In Saponda Laut, another defining feature of the windy season is the marked drop off in visits to the island from mainland traders, due to the rough seas. For most people, this means the absence of fresh fruit and vegetables and limited supplies of other basic domestic goods for some months.

One component of the village case studies included a complementary set of interviews focused on food security and undertaken in both Bokori (16 hh) and Saponda Laut (18 hh) during the period of scarcity (*paceklik*) in July 2018. Household selection drew on respondents from the earlier surveys who mentioned that they experienced food shortages during that time. For the most part these households were from categories (A) and (C).

Tables 10.3 and 10.4 summarise the responses to the survey interviews. The main point to highlight is the high numbers of people who worried about not having enough food for their households (Bokori 81.8 per cent and Saponda Laut 94.4 per cent). They worried about this issue "sometimes" and "often" during the period. The data illustrate that 39 out of 80 survey households (48.7 per cent), or half the villages, were concerned about their food security during the season of scarcity. To address these concerns, the majority of respondents said that they would reduce portions or amounts of food for consumption (Bokori [100 per cent], Saponda Laut [83.3 per cent]). A substantial group also admitted to occasionally going to bed hungry when food resources were depleted, having ensured that children were fed. These kinds of seasonal food stresses experienced by poor households highlight some of the factors that underlie the districts' high infant stunting rates (45.1 per cent in Konawe [Kementrian Kesehatan 2015]).

Table 10.3 Responses to household food security survey during the period of shortages (2018)

Questions	Bokori	Saponda Laut
Number of Respondents	16 hh	18 hh
Worry about not having enough food 1: rarely, 2: sometimes, 3: often	100% [2 & 3]	94.4% [2 & 3]
Worry they could not afford enough to eat	68.7% [1 & 2]	77.7%
Reduce amounts or portions of food.	100% [2]	83.3% [1 & 2]
Had to eat poor quality food	31.25% [2]	50% [2]
Reduce meals	68.7%	66.6%
Store food	93.7% [3]	88.8%
Went to sleep hungry	43%	50% [1 & 2]

Table 10.4 Degrees of food insecurity during the season of winds

Villages	Not food insecure %	Moderately food insecure %	Severely food insecure %
Bokori	60	10	30
Saponda Laut	60	15	25

Note: Figures approximate the methodology of Household Food Insecurity Access Scale (HFIAS).

Another commonly adopted strategy for a great majority of households (Bokori [93.7 per cent], Saponda Laut [88.8 per cent]), is to prepare for this time by storing food in their houses as a reserve against scarcity. There is a general pattern to these practices, reflecting a long-term accommodation to the seasonal constraints. During the primary fishing season (November–April) people take advantage of the relative abundance of fish to salt and preserve their catch, selling some[23] and saving a portion. In the months leading up to the season of scarcity (*paceklik*), households also begin to stockpile quantities of processed sago.[24] These can be stored for many months and then sun-dried, crumbled and heated (with water and shredded coconut) to produce a fragrant grain-like food (*sinolé*) that is eaten frequently with fish during the season. In the food security survey, the meal most commonly reported in July 2018, by a significant margin, was a combination of fish (either fresh or salted), boiled rice and servings of *sinolé*. When asked about food consumed the previous day, 26 households of the sample (74.6 per cent) reported this combination. Others ate variants such as rice and fish, *sinolé* and *tetehe* (sea urchin roe),[25] shellfish species, instant noodles and vegetables. The survey also found that non-poor households purchased over twice as much rice as their poorer neighbours and spent around 70 per cent more on discretionary items, including fuel, clothes, mobile recharge, and snacks (*jajan*) for children.

A further feature of the social dynamics over the windy season, June–September, is that many households resort to credit and taking on small loans from neighbours and local kiosk owners or fishing patrons (*punggawa*) to finance their consumption. This is a widespread strategy among the poor, and respondents spoke of cycles of debt and repayment that result in them never accumulating sufficient savings to improve their situation substantially. One man described the cycle as akin to digging a hole of debt during the season of scarcity (*paceklik*), and then filling it up with repayments throughout the following fishing season. In this respect, falling into debt during the layover months is a significant factor in perpetuating dependency and poverty over time. Conversely, avoiding obligations at this time of stress is a key to avoiding sliding into poverty.

Figure 10.3 Drying fish for storage and sale

Ironically, although the windy season is generally associated with restricted incomes and limited fishing opportunities for poorer households, for a minority of non-poor Sama Bajo fishers it is also the season when migratory schools of pelagic Spanish mackerel (SB: *Tinambu;* I: *Tenggiri* [*Scomberomorus commerson*]) are running. Fishers actively seek these fish for domestic and export markets. *Tinambu* are typically caught using hand-held, steel troll lines (*tonda*) with handmade lures (one lure, 5 hooks), from larger size *perahu* (9m+) with twin inboard engines (20 hp). Although sea conditions are hazardous during this season, those with the means, skill and courage to head out fishing at this time can obtain some of the most lucrative returns available.[26]

In July 2018, ten fishermen from Saponda Laut travelled in their own boats, provisioned and supported by local *punggawa* "D", four hours north to the fishing grounds of Salabangka following news that the *tenggiri* were surfacing (chasing schools of bait fish). Fishers sell direct to the *punggawa* on water from their boats (at IDR 65,000/kg) and the catch is then packed on ice and stored. When the *punggawa*'s three tonne fiberglass boat is full (500 kg), his crew makes the 3–5 day round trip to the Kendari markets, offloading the catch and returning loaded with ice. Gross returns on one trip for the *bos* D, are up to IDR 50,000,000 (500 kgs x IDR 100,000/kg) (USD 5,000), from which he makes various deductions and distributions while ensuring a healthy margin. One fisherman interviewed recalled that he had made over IDR 3,000,000 (>USD 300) from his mackerel fishing exploits over two weeks. The ability of fishing households like his to take advantage of these lucrative, albeit risky seasonal pelagic fishing opportunities is an essential factor in the ability of some households to rise above poverty and avoid the debts that constrain households less able to participate. We find support for these findings of income disparities in the analysis of household survey data from the two villages.

Table 10.5   Annual incomes by category (Bokori and Saponda Laut combined)[27]

Category	A (poor)	B (not poor)	C (poor now)	D (not poor)
Income (IDR)	6,715,360	47,510,572	3,985,000	61,040,000
% total income	5.6	39.8	3.4	51.2

Table 10.5 shows the relative annual incomes generated by different categories of household. Leaving aside the difficulties of obtaining precise income numbers (given the often, non-monetised nature of poor household incomes), there are striking differences between poor and non-poor households. Non-poor households, namely 50 per cent of the village, secure up to 90 per cent of overall income, while neighbouring poor households make do with much less and many depend on the goodwill of relatives and neighbours to make up the shortfall.

Social Assistance Programmes and Impacts

One of the main objectives of the household surveys was to investigate village respondents who received government social assistance benefits and to consider whether the coverage was consistent with their economic status. This proved to be a less than straightforward exercise, for a range of reasons. Some programmes had discontinued or were transitioning to new arrangements under different names and with varying implementation schedules. While this situation rather neatly reflects the complexity of the policy context of social assistance more generally, it also highlights the fast-changing landscape of the programmes and their differential impacts across Indonesia. In this section we focus on two of the main (national level) subsidies that have a strong presence in the study communities: the discounted rice subsidy programme, *raskin* (*beras miskin* – rice for the poor), and the conditional cash transfer programme (Program Keluarga Harapan – families of hope).[28]

The rice subsidy programme aimed to provide 15 kg per month to poor households, using an allocation from a government agency, Bulog, responsible for stocking and distributing rice in every district (Kabupaten). Recipients would pay a heavily subsidised price for their allocation (40 per cent of average market price). The programme was well received across the country but was one that has constantly underperformed its stated objectives. Two significant recurring problems are worth highlighting. One is the issue of rice distribution. Bulog has a limited capacity to deliver stocks beyond a small number of designated supply points. As a result, many village communities must find their own means of transporting the "rice for the poor" to their settlements. For island communities like Saponda Laut, these additional imposts have usually reduced the allocation of rice available to poorer households to help defray transport costs.[29] More significantly, a widespread response to the concept of government-supplied rice across Indonesia has been to set aside the beneficiary list altogether and to allocate an equal portion to all households in the village irrespective of wealth status (Timmer, Hastuti and Sumarto 2017). Referred to as *bagi rata* (to divide evenly), the practice reflects a compromise solution in the face of disputes and jealousies driven by households that resent missing out. Arguably, it also forms part of a long-standing expectation that Indonesian government funds directed to supporting communities are best distributed evenly for the most significant benefit, an informal principle known as *pemerataan* (equalisation).

These dynamics operate just as strongly in the survey villages. Over 90 per cent of food-insecure respondents to the household surveys reported having access to subsidised rice. But they did so as part of an open-access arrangement for the whole village that inevitably marginalises those it aims to assist.[30] In recent years, the government has sought to move away from subsidised rice distributions in favour of a card-based system known as BPNT (*Bantuan Pangan Non-Tunai* – Non-cash food assistance). The approach links food assistance to a designated recipient, who can use their card at an authorised "e-warung" to purchase from the prescribed nine basic foods (*sembako*).[31] There were no such facilities in the two study villages; the challenge to secure assistance still works against the poor, and as of late 2019, the old system of *Raskin* distributions remained in place.

The PKH programme is the latest iteration of a conditional cash-based assistance programme. It supports the poorest households with infants and school age children by offering quarterly cash payments, redeemable through government operated post-offices (*Kantor Pos*).[32] In the Sama Bajo survey, many of the food insecure households were also beneficiaries of the PKH programme (Bokori 50 per cent and Saponda Laut 94 per cent of households meeting the criteria). These were widely welcomed supplements and made essential contributions to limited household budgets. The large discrepancy between Bokori and Saponda Laut recipients is likely to be due to two factors. First, there were higher numbers of ageing widows (*janda*) in the Bokori sample compared with Saponda Laut, most of whom had no dependent children and hence were not eligible to receive the support at the time. Second, the introduction of the PKH programme was relatively new in 2017, and delays in implementation may have shown up in the survey data for Bokori village.

One of the interesting findings from Saponda Laut was that for eligible households among the 40 hh sample (those with infants or school age children), 31 per cent of the locally identified poor households received the cash support. Still, more than twice that many (69 per cent) of the eligible poor missed out. By contrast, among households identified as non-poor in our survey (Category B), a surprising 85 per cent received the subsidy. The skewing, in this case, provides an instructive example of the widely reported inclusion and exclusion errors in the poverty assessment process and problems with the changing status of individual households over time. The complexity of the PKH entitlement system means that while recipients may lose access to benefits over time, due to changes in their family status, there is no standard mechanism to include new households on the recipient list. This results in some recipients benefitting significantly from more generous new allowances, while eligible but non-recipient households miss out altogether.

These exclusionary effects for poor households may be contrasted with the comparative example of the annual distribution of *zakat* (obligatory Islamic tithes levied on the faithful) in Saponda Laut. All residents are obliged to contribute a *zakat* payment to the local mosque, according to their capacity. The donations are then collected and re-distributed to households regarded as impoverished or needy. In 2017 the *zakat* payments in Saponda Laut revealed a very different pattern from the government PKH allocations. In the judgement of a local committee of residents, a relatively large proportion, 70.4 per cent, of identified poor households received a *zakat* contribution and only 22.7 per cent of the designated non-poor families were recipients. The differences between social assistance schemes and *zakat* distributions are stark: they point to real weaknesses in identifying and supporting poor households under current government-funded welfare programmes. They also highlight the various structural factors of exclusion that marginalise the very poor.

Conclusion: Debt, Vulnerability and the Moral Economy

The findings from the case studies of Bokori and Saponda Laut highlight three relational livelihood trajectories reflected in the fishing communities. They can also be described as intersecting relations of poverty and prosperity. These trajectories combine to generate the *fishing boom scenario* in Southeast Sulawesi, where conditions are such that fishing productivity remains viable and rewarding even as increasing pressures on fish stocks and marine ecologies are all too evident.

The three livelihood trajectories identified in the study broadly reflect the socio-economic status divisions in the communities, namely: (1) prosperous households with significant productive assets; (2) non-poor and economical aspirational households; and (3) impoverished households. These categories are porous to a degree, but the SoP surveys indicate that the relative proportions of poor and prosperous households have remained relatively constant over 20 years, while the larger movement is within that group of households escaping poverty, namely the economic aspirationals.

The livelihood trajectory that reinforces subsistence level incomes and the dispiriting experience of poverty includes most widows, female-headed households and poor Sama Bajo households with little productive capital, or whose fishing incomes tend to collapse during the annual southeast monsoon when high winds and seas make venturing out hazardous and unrewarding (*gagal melaut*). Among Sama Bajo households, the loss of male breadwinners has immediate and damaging impacts on family finances. Most widows and female-headed households struggle to generate sufficient income to cover their costs and rely significantly on reef gleaning and support from neighbours to get by. Within this grouping also are poor male-headed fisher households which lack the equipment and capital to undertake lucrative offshore fishing and which focus their efforts inshore and foraging on reefs. Seasonal turbidity of coastal waters reduces fishing success and generates marginal returns on effort. These households have few options, other than going into debt to local patrons to fund the consumption needs. Over continuous annual cycles of debt and repayment, these households fail to make economic headway and so remain poor.

Some Bajo households manage to avoid the debt trap and find ways to prosper. For these non-poor economically aspirational households, the pathway to prosperity is gradual and made up of incremental steps that build on a combination of fishing success, risk-taking and what Bajo call *dalé* or good fortune[33] (I: *rejeki*). These qualities include heading out to sea when conditions are rough to chase high value pelagic fish species or investing in floating grow-out pens and raising sought-after plate-size trevally (*ikan putih*) for the local market. Their abiding orientation to commercial options and integration into wider capitalist value chains help ensure success and the means to maintain their maritime-based livelihoods.[34]

The economically aspirational households highlight a livelihood approach that is replicated in multiple Sama Bajo settlements across the Indonesian archipelago to varying degrees. In the process, these Sama Bajo fisher households reveal themselves to be highly adaptive and opportunistic in the face of environmental and economic uncertainty, and thereby continue to sustain their engagement with the seas. As a generalised set of cultural and economic preferences, this approach has proved highly durable over many generations. But its very viability is also built on the critical economic role performed by the third identified livelihood trajectory group, namely the prosperous co-resident patrons (*punggawa*).

The *punggawa*'s personalised networks of influence and credit with financial brokers and traders in the city and their capacity to deliver regular supplies of high-value fish catches to market ensure their continued success. In their wake, they enable otherwise economically marginal fishing households in their communities (clients) to sustain themselves and even prosper when conditions are propitious. Collectively, we might say that these home-grown and hybridised community/market economies, which shape local *patron-client* relationships, also underwrite the sustainability of Sama Bajo maritime settlements. In this respect, they reflect what anthropologist Stephen Gudeman has described as the different interactive principles of community and market economies: community economic relations sustained for their own sake, and market-based economies ordered around short term self-interest. Both are inevitably and variably informed through interactive (dialectic) tension. The patron-client relationship is a specific cultural expression of this complex interactive economic field (Gudeman 2008).

However, these relationships, as we have sought to demonstrate, are not based on notions of equality, altruism, or principles of social justice *per se*, although the highly personalised nature of the relationships may allow the possibility for these elements to emerge over time. Instead, they reflect a combination of mutual interests and degrees of co-dependency to achieve desired outcomes. But the consequence of these long-term interactions between patrons and clients is that inequality and marked differences in levels of household prosperity remain a striking and continuing feature of Sama Bajo settlements. In other words, the *punggawa* patron is both an architect of debt and economic vulnerability, even exploitation among their erstwhile clients (*sabi*), and at the same time a dependable source for the means to overcome hardship (credit and access to boats) and household needs in times of crisis. *Punggawa* represent a reliable, albeit highly constraining source of informal local social assistance in circumstances where, until recently, there have been few other options. In this respect, the patron-client relationship is also a contemporary example of the "moral economy" articulated by James Scott in his studies of Southeast Asian peasant societies (1977). The moral economy expresses a regime where the well-to-do peasantry legitimate their prominent social positions by deploying their resources in ways that meet the broadly defined welfare needs of villagers (Scott 1977: 41). In return, they attain growing prestige and wealth and the support of a grateful clientele.[35] Such patterns of co-dependency and "soft domination" (see Reeves 1995)[36] inform contemporary social relations in Sama Bajo settlements and generate the operating conditions that characterise the *fishing boom scenario* for this region.

As a framework and mechanism for social resilience in the face of uncertainty and the vagaries of maritime-based fortunes, the *punggawa–sabi* relationship has proved its value over hundreds of years. However, as a form of economic interdependency, it comes at the cost of autonomy and freedom to pursue alternative choices that could offer more attractive economic returns. This understanding suggests a second point of conclusion, namely the extent to which state-funded social assistance policies, in particular the rice subsidy programmes (*Raskin/Rastra*) and the conditional (now non-cash) transfers (PKH), provide adequate independent support for the poor. The answer we think is a mixed one. For impoverished households with limited resources and uncertain prospects, any additional assistance is welcome and provides a significant impact on their well-being; this is a fact borne out by analysis of the household data. Government assistance also directly offsets indebtedness to local lenders or family members and to this extent provides a valuable supplementary economic and social buffer. However, there are also multiple deficiencies in the delivery of these programmes, and growing criticism of the government about the rising costs, as well as significant exclusion and inclusion errors occurring for eligible beneficiaries (Sim, Negara and Suryahadi 2015; McCarthy and Sumarto 2018).

Our main point of difference here is that Indonesia's current approach to social assistance follows a model of nominally, objectively defined parameters and a standardised non-discriminatory distribution of resources. No matter how much improvement might be coaxed out of the poverty alleviation programmes, they can never overcome specific human communities' interpersonal, political and status dynamics. As the examples of the *punggawa* patron-benefactors highlight, ideas of support, mutual obligations and social assistance are woven into the cultural fabric, power relations and dispositions of the maritime Sama Bajo communities. Ignoring these and other realities of a local sense of fairness and transactional obligations means that national poverty alleviation programmes distributed from on high will, perhaps inevitably, miss their mark.

Acknowledgements

We thank our colleagues and field assistants from the State University of Halo Oleo (Kendari, Southeast Sulawesi) and the residents of Bokori and Saponda Laut for their participation in the research and their hospitality.

Notes

[1] Indonesia is also an important exporter of commercially valuable, high end, wild-caught fish species, such as blue fin and skipjack tuna, Spanish mackerel, grouper/wrasse and lobster (CEA 2018).

[2] The wide marine biodiversity found in Indonesia's tropical waters is also reflected in the composition of the catch: as many as 90 species make up 90 per cent of capture fisheries production (including tuna, scad, mackerel, catfish, grouper, shark, squid and bivalves) (CEA 2018: 46).

[3] Current trends in marine resources and fisheries management in Indonesia (CEA 2018) indicate that the ability of capture fisheries to contribute to food and nutrition security will be significantly compromised in the future by overfishing, pollution, climate variability over the ocean and associated declines in fish catches (CEA 2018: 18; see also Foale et al. 2013).

[4] Beliefs and practices associated with the Bajo ancestral religion are also expressed through protective mantras and sailing techniques on the open seas.

[5] Sama Bajo do not use (nor can afford) safety gear such as life jackets or emergency responders. The now widespread availability of mobile phones has provided a major benefit, particularly for families waiting at home for their fisher men to return.

[6] The term may derive from the Bugis language of South Sulawesi (Pelras 1996: 332) and is variously associated with the title of military leader or ship's captain. Bugis seafarers have had close and long-term linkages with Sama Bajo groups, who operated as client traders and allies for powerful Bugis rulers. According to Sopher (1977: 151, 268) during the nineteenth century, the headman of each Bajo group held the title of *punggawa*.

[7] Also known as ABK – *Anak buah kapal* (crew/dependants).

[8] *Soropia dalam Angka 2015* (BPS: Sulawesi Tenggara).

[9] 125 households moved to Mekar in 1984 and another 110 in 1986. In 1987 a further 90 households relocated to establish Desa Leppe. It was not until 1995 that the ancestral remains from the cemetery on the island were relocated to the village of Leppe.

[10] Also known locally as "Ikan Putih" ("white fish", *Alectis ciliaris*), the threadfin trevally grows rapidly in sea pens with supplementary feeding and provides an important source of income for Sama Bajo households when sold into local markets.

[11] Evidently an Indonesian language borrowing from *sengsara*, meaning poor, wretched, destitute.

[12] *Punggawa darat* (land Patrons) are often larger scale financiers and investors, such as Chinese traders in the main towns who deal in fishing supply chains and export industries. *Punggawa darat* are also financial backers of *punggawa laut*, providing larger scale credit to purchase boats and equipment in return for a hefty percentage of the income.

[13] Haji A, whom I interviewed on Saponda, exemplified this category. He has a large house in the village and well-stocked kiosk run by his wife. He owns and operates two 10m twin engine powerboats which he uses to buy freshly caught fish from local fishermen, usually while they are out at sea, and then trades into the main fish markets of Kendari.

[14] Depending on their means, *punggawa* may send one of their own boats out to sea to purchase and store the fresh-caught fish directly from local clients.

[15] Fishing boats sometime return with small but high value, live fish caught and held in a section of the boat containing seawater. These fish are recorded and then transferred to floating grow-out pens for future sale.

[16] These contacts include *pengumpul* (stockpiler/ wholesaler) or *bos lelang* (controllers of fish auctions).

[17] There are also some female *punggawa* who have parleyed their resources into larger scale operations.

[18] Unlikely as it sounds, the current division of fishing income has improved the fishing returns to crew. A generation ago, *punggawa* boat owners would take 75 per cent (one portion to the owner, one portion to the engine, and a third portion to the boat). The greater availability of boats and cheaper engines has allowed more young men to pursue more independent fishing pursuits.

[19] Here they follow a similar system where the owner (*bos* or *punggawa*) of the fish traps receives the majority of income and the *sabi* crew receives a smaller portion, based on the value of the fluctuating yield.

[20] In fact, there is a beneficial logic to this practice. The patron (*bos*) pays good prices for larger fish, and sells them on for profit in the markets. The alternative of selling locally in the community attracts a much lower premium and the fish would have to be cut into smaller pieces to attract buyers.

[21] The role of transporting fish to the market attracts a collective 50 per cent share of remuneration paid to active members of the fishing crew.

[22] Octopus fishing is an important component of Sama Bajo seasonal fishing during calmer weather (November through April), when some households concentrate on this fishery.

[23] Dried and preserved shark, octopus and stingray find a ready market in villages and inland towns where refrigeration is uncommon.

[24] Sago is much more economical than rice. A 20 kg bag (*karong*) costs around USD 5 and can feed a family of four for up to a month.

[25] Sea urchin gonads (SB *tetehe* / *Bulu babi*) are widely consumed and nutritionally beneficial (see Wiralis et al. 2017) but regarded as a low-quality food.

[26] Skipjack (*tongkol* : *Katsuwonus pelamis*) and bonito (*cakalang*) are other species caught with long line trolling.

[27] By way of comparison, an estimate of the minimal needs of a household of four in Bokori was made in 2017 using local knowledge of costs and needs including tobacco, food and payments for basic services. The analysis came to IDR 1 million or about USD 100 per month. Earning less than this amount meant that the household had no buffers or safety nets should there be any shortfall.

28 Two other widespread support programmes are subsidised (free) health insurance (KIS: *Kartu Indonesia Sehat*) for the poor and a scholarship programme for school children (KIP: *Kartu Indonesia Pintar*).

29 Transport payments for Raskin distributions are normally paid in cash and up front, a sum of money that is usually covered by village heads either personally or from village funds, which can raise suspicions and accusations of impropriety or misuse of government funds.

30 The rice subsidy programme is designed to provide allocations of rice every month. But due to logistical and seasonal factors, especially for small island communities, these distributions are often delayed.

31 By 2019 the programme planned to provide support for 5.6 million poor (Ministry of Finance Director, pers. comm.).

32 Under the new iteration, a poor family received support for pregnancy and infants [2.4 million], children at school [Sekolah Menengah Atas (SMA) – High School, 2 million; Sekolah Menengah Pertama (SMP – Junior High School) 1.5 million; SD (primary school) 900,000] up to four children; severe disability [2.4 million] and old age [2.4 million]. The overall allocation to PKH has also increased significantly, showing the Jokowi government's commitment to social protection.

33 As one woman commented, "everything really depends on *dalé* (good fortune) for both men and women".

34 It was also the fishery that suffered the biggest immediate downturn when the COVID-19 pandemic arrived in the province in 2020.

35 Well to-do villagers avoid malicious gossip only at the price of an exaggerated generosity (1977: 41). The relationship reflects what Scott identified as two practical principles of peasant society, namely "the norm of reciprocity and the right to subsistence" (1977: 167).

36 Reeves, citing Bourdieu's notion of "soft domination", describes a condition where material and political advantage are translated into virtue and piety and thereby disable and deflect resistance (1995: 307).

References

Ariansyach, I. 2019. "Fisheries Country Profile: Indonesia, Southeast Asian Fisheries Development Centre (SEAFDEC)". Available at: http://www.seafdec.org/fisheries-country-profile-indonesia/ (accessed 29 Jan. 2019).

Bennett, A. et al. 2018. *Contribution of Fisheries to Food and Nutrition Security: Current Knowledge, Policy, and Research*. NI Report 18-02. Durham, NC: Duke University. Available at http://nicholasinstitute.duke.edu/publication (accessed 28 Sept. 2019).

CEA (California Environmental Associates). 2018. *Trends in Marine Resources and Fisheries Management in Indonesia: A 2018 Review*. Available at https://www.ceaconsulting.com/wp-content/uploads/Indonesia-Report-2018. Full-Report. Interactive.pdf (accessed 18 Jan. 2019).

Deswandi, R. 2011. "Understanding Institutional Dynamics: The Emergence, Persistence, and Change of Institutions in Fisheries in Spermonde Archipelago,

South Sulawesi, Indonesia", PhD Thesis, Leibniz Centre for Tropical Marine Ecology, Bremen, Germany.

FAO (Food and Agriculture Organisation of the United Nations). 2014. *Fisheries and Aquaculture - Fishery and Aquaculture Country Profiles - The Republic of Indonesia.* Available at https://www.fao.org/fishery/en/facp/idn?lang=en (accessed 6 May 2022).

Ferguson, J. 1990. *The Anti-Politics Machine: Development, Depoliticization, and Bureaucratic Power in Lesotho.* Cambridge: Cambridge University Press.

Foale, S. et al. 2013. "Food Security and the Coral Triangle", *Marine Policy* 38: 174–83.

Fox, J.J. 1977. "Notes on the Southern Voyages and Settlements of the Sama-Bajau", *Bijdragen tot de Taal-, Land- en Volkenkunde* 133, 4: 459–65.

Gaynor, J.L. 2016. *Intertidal History in Island Southeast Asia: Submerged Genealogy and the Legacy of Coastal Capture.* Ithaca: Cornell Southeast Asia Publications.

Gudeman, S. 2008. *Economy's Tension: The Dialectics of Community and Market.* New York: Berghahn Books.

Kementrian Kesehatan. 2015. *Gambaran Konsumsi Pangan, Permasalahan Gizi dan Penyakit Tidak Menular di Sulawesi Tenggara (Sultra)* [Description of Food Consumption, Nutrition Problems and Non-communicable Disease in Southeast Sulawesi]. Badan Penelitian dan Pengembangan Kesehatan, Kementerian Kesehatan RI.

Krishna, A. 2005. *Stages of Progress: A Community-Based Methodology for Defining and Understanding Poverty, Version 2.0.* Available at https://sites.duke.edu/krishna/files/2013/06/SoP.pdf (accessed 9 Jan. 2019).

_____. 2006. "Pathways Out of and Into Poverty in 36 Villages of Andhra Pradesh, India", *World Development* 34, 2: 271–88.

McCarthy, J. and M. Sumarto. 2018. "Distributional Politics and Social Protection in Indonesia: Dilemma of Layering, Nesting and Social Fit in Jokowi's Poverty Policy", *Journal of Southeast Asian Economies* 35, 2: 223–36.

McWilliam A., N. Wianti and Y. Taufik. 2021. "Pathways to Poverty and Prosperity among Sama Bajo Fishing Communities (Southeast Sulawesi)", *The Singapore Journal of Tropical Geography* 42, 1: 132–48. Available at https://doi.org/10.1111/sjtg.12349 (accessed 14 July 2021).

Pelras, C. 1996. *The Bugis.* Oxford, UK; Cambridge, MA: Blackwell.

_____. 2000. "Patron-client Ties among the Bugis and Makassarese of South Sulawesi", *Bijdragen tot de Taal-, Land- en Volkenkunde* 156, 3: 393–432.

Phillips, M. et al. 2015. "Exploring Indonesian Aquaculture Futures". Penang: World Fish Program Report, pp. 2015–39.

Reeves, B. 1995. "Power, Resistance, and the Cult of Muslim Saints in a Northern Egyptian Town", *American Ethnologist* 22, 2: 306–23.

Ribot, J.C. and N.L. Peluso. 2003. "A Theory of Access", *Rural Sociology* 68, 2: 153–81.

Scott, J.C. 1977. *The Moral Economy of the Peasant: Rebellion and Assistance in Southeast Asia*. New Haven: Yale University Press.

Sim A., R. Negara and A. Suryahadi. 2015. *Inequality, Elite Capture and Targeting of Social Protection Programs: Evidence from Indonesia*. Jakarta: The SMERU Research Institute.

Sopher, D. 1977. *The Sea Nomads: A Study of the Maritime Boat People of Southeast Asia*. Singapore: National Museum.

Stacey, N. et al. 2017. "Impacts of Marine Protected Areas on Livelihoods and Food Security of the Bajau as an Indigenous Migratory People in Maritime Southeast Asia", in *Marine Protected Areas: Interactions with Fishery Livelihoods and Food Security*, ed. L. Westlund, A. Charles, S.M. Garcia and J. Sanders. Rome: Food and Agriculture Organisation of the United Nations, pp. 113–26. Available at http://www.fao.org/policy-support/resources/resources-details/en/c/853709/ (accessed 3 Oct. 2021).

Timmer, P., Hastuti and S.J. Sumarto. 2017. "Evolution and Implementation of the Rastra Program in Indonesia", in *The 1.5 Billion People Question, Food, Vouchers or Cash Transfers*, ed. H. Alderman, U. Gentilini and R. Yemtsov. Washington, DC: IBRD World Bank Group, pp. 265–307.

Thanh, H.T., P. Tschakert and M.R. Hipsey. 2021. "Moving Up or Going Under? Differential Livelihood Trajectories in Coastal Communities in Vietnam", *World Development* 138. https://doi.org/10.1016/j.worlddev.2020.105219.

Wiralis, T. et al. 2017. *Edukasi Gizi untuk peningkatan kualitas menu anak balita dengan konsumsi gonad bulu babi sebagai sumber protein alternatif pada keluarga etnis Bajo Soropia* [Nutrition Education to Improve Quality of Menu for Children Under Five by Consuming Sea Urchin Gonads as a Protein Alternative for Bajo Families in Soropia]. *GIZI INDONESIA: Journal of the Indonesian Nutrition Association* 40, 2: 69–78.

Part Three

Social Protection

CHAPTER 11

Are Conditional Cash Transfer Policies Implementable? Social Cash Transfers and Emergent Patterns of Entitlement in Rural Aceh

John F. McCarthy, Shaummil Hadi and Nulwita Maliati

Introduction

Following the emergence of the social protection agenda over two decades ago, the Indonesian state has considerably expanded the scope of its activities to protect the poorest Indonesians. This has created new sets of entitlements to social benefits. Research has found that conditional cash transfers (CCTs) and other targeted programmes have positively impacted school enrolment, access to health care, maternal mortality and child nutrition (e.g. Satriawan 2016; Cahyadi et al. 2018). At the same time, local newspapers catalogue a litany of problems, including the unmerited choice of beneficiaries leading to widespread dissatisfaction, jealousy, contention within communities and even demonstrations by villages and village heads (see Chapter 3). This chapter examines this disjunction in more detail with reference to the Aceh context (presented in Chapter 5 above).

Over recent decades, scholars have observed that a politics of knowledge shapes development research and practice. Development practice depends upon specific disciplinary modes of knowing. Here, specialist expertise, principally development economics, generates knowledge modalities from specific theories with their methodologies, biases and normative assumptions. While this provides ways of translating policy aims into specific intervention logics, the deployment of these development technologies also has constitutive

279

governance effects (Dahler-Larsen 2012; Vetterlein 2012; Merry 2011). For objects that are contested and difficult to measure, how they are quantified shapes the realities they focus on, guiding practical action and "defining the social realities of which they are a part" (Dahler-Larsen 2012: 173). To be sure, the uses of indicators and measurement produce "a more or less orderly view of an otherwise disorderly reality" (Dahler-Larsen 2014: 976). However, this involves simplifications (Scott 1999). When decisions are made based on statistical information, understandings that are less amenable to quantification can be left aside. Moreover, this conceals biases based on normative assumptions embedded in specialist decisions; the practical knowledge required for effective interventions and negotiating pathways to better outcomes may be marginalised (Scoones 2009).

A more comprehensive body of literature notes the "anti-political" nature of such processes that convert development problems into technical problems. Processes of "rendering technical" (Li 2007) that "economise the social" (Vetterlein 2012) appear to depoliticise distributional processes. Yet, politics has been described as concerned with "who gets what, when [and] how" (Lasswell 1936), so allocating social cash transfers is inherently political. As the transfers are conditional, the CCT targeting modality is highly selective and residual. In aiming to assist only the very poor, it provides a level and quality of protection that generates patterns of inclusion and exclusion at the village level. At this level, as we will see, villagers have a well-developed sense of entitlement. Ironically, when studied at this level, processes that appear highly technical and apolitical—providing a seemingly "objective" process of selecting beneficiaries according to technical criteria—involve informal relational processes that primarily occur off-stage. These processes also provoke an animated political discussion around inclusion and exclusion. Discussions regarding social cash transfers involve distributional choices (who gets included and who gets excluded), and "must answer to some idea of the proper, of the just, of the 'rightful'" (Ferguson 2015: 184).

Social cash transfers, in other words, pose questions of entitlement and enfranchisement. The former pertains to the "broader domain of well-being and advantage" (Watts and Bohle 1993: 117), the capacity of the poor to obtain assistance. However, poverty involves more than a lack of income and material resources; it encompasses a lack of power, physical and social autonomy and social respect. Hence, development programmes pose questions concerning the enfranchisement of the poor: the ability of the poor to make demands on the state, for instance, during periods of seasonal or life-cycle vulnerability. In other words, they provoke questions regarding the rights of the poor and their marginal capacity to influence decision-making about entitlements. Hence, in evaluating the effects of social cash transfers on the poor, we can also consider the constitutive effects on who can obtain assistance and to what degree recipient communities and the poor play a role in providing entitlements.

The critical dilemma at the heart of this chapter and the case studies presented above is the contradiction between two different distributional logics. Village households exist within networks of reciprocity and mutual dependence, where access to benefits depends upon relationships. Here, individuals live as clients as much as citizens; they invest in social relations with the expectations of redress during times of crisis (Benda-Beckmann, Benda-Beckmann and Marks 1994; Berenschot and van Klinken 2018). Equity and inclusion emerge as critical concerns, but as the state builds a governmental apparatus to provide benefits to the poor, efficiency may be a higher priority (Hanna and Olken 2018). The key questions from this economic perspective include: does the system efficiently deliver the limited revenue available for social assistance to those who need it most? Does it provide welfare gains to the poorest households in a way that reduces poverty?

This chapter focuses on how the politics of knowledge associated with CCTs works through a governance apparatus for implementing the CCT model and village social relations to generate the practices and social realities of social cash transfers in rural Indonesia. Here we are concerned with two questions. First, how are shifting CCT designs translated into the processes that shape emergent patterns of entitlements and enfranchisement? Second, what are the formative effects of these knowledges and practices on how social cash transfers work out?

We argue that the social cash transfer programme depends upon policy models that utilise specific technologies that fit with predominant disciplinary and professional hierarchies, and that this has critical constitutive effects. First, although the programme's methodology appears to be apolitical, as it shapes who gains the *capacity to obtain assistance*, and this provokes a highly uneven and contested distributional politics. The system works at odds with the logic of reciprocity and redistribution found in the study villages. This poses unresolved questions of appropriateness, legitimacy and distributional justice. Further, although CCTs used metrics that appear to structure the messy reality of poverty into legible forms for actionable policy, they generate significant errors. This in turn engenders a never-ending process of re-contextualising poverty technologies, introducing technical processes developed elsewhere into the rural context. The allocation methods tend to be opaque in terms of decision processes, conforming to neither a clientelist nor an econometric targeting logic. The process leaves a cohort of households unable to make effective demands on the state for social cash transfers. It reveals wicked policy dilemmas at the heart of this "liberal-residualist" targeting model.

This paper discusses the evolution of the social cash transfers, exploring their effects in the two villages in Aceh Besar and Aceh Utara (discussed earlier in Chapter 5) between 2015 and 2019. First, we consider the emergence of poverty targeting for social protection, the shift from purely econometric targeting methods to a programme that attempts to hybridise the proxy means testing by bringing in elements of community-based targeting. Given that the non-cash food assistance (*Bantuan Pangan Non-Tunai*) programme had yet to reach this area of Aceh at the time of this research, the discussion here focuses on the conditional cash transfer programme (PKH).

Emergence and Implementation: Poverty Targeting in Aceh

The Indonesian government began to embrace social protection programmes (principally assistance in kind and social cash transfers) after the East Asia crisis in 1997. Following the structural adjustment programmes of this period, national policymakers made use of donor expertise. As in other cases, the national context influenced the desirability of these policy ideas, the incentives of state managers and what was considered practicable (Bebbington, Guggenheim and Olson 2004). A donor model emerged as the favoured approach, specifically the CCT Oportunidades-Prospera programme pioneered with the World Bank's assistance in Mexico and the Bolsa Familia (family purse) programme in Brazil. In Mexico the "Washington consensus" agencies had developed the conditional cash transfers (CCTs) model, described as a liberal-residual conception of social welfare. This model provides for modest means-tested benefits only to the very poor, emphasising targeting, poverty reduction, human welfare investments and conditionalities (Leisering 2019). The model corresponds to a particular politics of development where highly targeted programmes using the proxy-means testing methodology progressively substituted unconditional entitlements based on need, food subsidies and help-in-kind (see Chapter 3). In Mexico and Indonesia, albeit in different ways, macroeconomic changes accompanied the rolling out of CCTs, as planners worked to cement a social consensus around structural changes by pairing unpopular macro-economic reforms with policies that aim to assist the very poor (Peck and Theodore 2015).

Earlier iterations of Indonesia's social protection programmes faced considerable difficulties. During the early years of the *Raskin* (rice for the poor) programme, *Raskin* sought to transfer 15 kg of rice per month to the poorest households, targeted following national criteria and classifications of households developed using statistical data. If the village leadership followed state lists, they would exclude many who felt entitled to benefits. Consequently, village heads adjusted distribution processes. Avoiding tensions and disputes, they distributed the subsidised rice according to village agreements, and responded to targeting errors by dividing rice allocations equally. For instance, at the time of fieldwork in one of the survey villages in Aceh Besar, the state had identified 35 households as deserving recipients of 15 kg of rice according to the state's criteria. Still, the village head distributed benefit to 95 households, with each getting an equal 5 kg.[1] The rice distributions also did not occur regularly, and although the poor were happy to receive benefits, the distribution made only a small contribution to livelihoods.

Critics of *Raskin* pointed to poor coverage, inclusion and exclusion errors, irregular transfers, and problems of speculation, fraud, loss and poor quality (Hastuti et al. 2008). They advocated moving to a more effective, econometric targeting system, which would sort those deemed deserving of assistance from the others based on survey data, thereby moving the allocation of social benefits beyond elite capture and clientelism, while reducing corruption, prejudice and the arbitrary power of elites.

Here, two key technical aspects of the conditional cash transfer programme model, favoured by the World Bank and state planners, become apparent. First, planners needed to develop a social registry of the bottom 40 per cent to target those most deserving of assistance. The Social Protection Programme (SPP) system needed statistics, data on the status of households, which were ultimately derived and harmonised from a series of door-to-door surveys. Second, the system used an algorithm derived from statistical models to determine which households were the most worthy of assistance. Planners needed to identify proxies and attach a weighting to them, "depending on the strength of their correlation with consumption or income" of the households, which are then given scores and ranked from poorest to richest (Kidd and Bailey-Athias 2020: 8; see also Stoeffler, Mills and Ninno 2016).

Interviews with Aceh Besar and Aceh Utara officials during 2015 revealed considerable difficulties in implementing this approach. Officials in the district planning office (*Bappeda*) estimated that at least 30 per cent of those who would have met the criteria for inclusion were overlooked, with a similar proportion erroneously included. Villages who deemed themselves deserving but left off the list complained about the process. Jealousy and blame-shifting abounded. District-level statistics officers responsible for surveying spoke of villagers protesting outside statistics offices and coming to their houses to complain. Disgruntled villages pressured village heads and visited sub-district and district offices to lobby for their inclusion (Sumarto 2020). When villagers attempted to get on the list, officials and facilitators explained that the data came from a central agency (TNP2K [the National Team for the Acceleration of Poverty Reduction]). Nothing could be done until the beneficiary list was reviewed and renewed.

Involving Community Leaders

After World Bank research found that involving the community in targeting improved community satisfaction (Alatas et al. 2019), borrowing from the Mexican programme, state agencies developed a hybrid approach that combined elements of community-based targeting (CBT) with econometric targeting (PMT). Village leaders would participate in a process known as "updating the single registry for social aid recipients" (Pemutakhiran Basis Data Terpadu or PBDT). Rather than devolving authority to locally elected village governments, the system allowed village leaders to modify the existing pre-list. To reduce errors, they would check for excluded low-income families and included affluent households. Those overseeing the process would also cross-check poor informants for excluded low-income families. Following this process, ideally, the state statistics agency would re-survey all those on the edited beneficiary register to create a corrected PBDT list.

Interviews with village informants and district officials revealed the verification process's dynamics, pointing to the "emotional" considerations, "field risks" and "political nuances" affecting the process. In some villages visited during our research, the leadership carried out deliberative meetings as a formality. A sub-district official recalled that the administration could come to a strong consensus regarding who should obtain benefits. With strong leadership, he argued that the agreement would stick, allowing them to exclude those deemed unworthy of benefits. However, in the two study villages, the deliberative meeting was considered unnecessary. The village leadership argued that they knew who was poor. To avoid complaints from those excluded, they evaded stirring up this recurrent, chronic problem by allowing the "government programme" to continue as usual. District officials told stories of excluded people physically threatening village heads and making allegations of corruption to higher authorities. When village heads made decisions about the pre-list without deliberative meetings, district officials discreetly allowed this to occur.

Villagers compare social cash transfers to *zakat*, the obligatory Islamic alms that the village community provides to the poor. In rural Aceh, *zakat* amounts to a tax under precise rules, whereby leaders of the village mosque organise a committee to oversee the calculations and payments, strategically managing and distributing assistance to the poor based on notions of fairness and deservedness. This process set out to avoid giving some deserving recipients too much, allocating *zakat* to those not considered worthy of help, or providing other deserving recipients with too little (Alfitri 2005). During this process, the committee overseeing the *zakat* system used well-established concepts of need used in the stages of progress methodology described in Chapter 1. This differentiated between poor (*miskin*) and indigent (*fakir*) households and allocated twice as much assistance to the latter (see Chapter 5). Village heads noted that, unlike the *zakat* system, the government pre-list process lacked a clear "cut off" concept, defining in local terms at what point a household should be considered non-poor. This feature and the wish to avoid decreasing other social assistance to the village meant that village leaders included as many people as possible in the pre-list, including many who might not be deemed worthy of *zakat* assistance.

During interviews, village heads said they included people on the list whom the village head held to be "deserving" of assistance after considering poverty levels, assets, land, housing and the number of children. However, it was an open secret that the list included relatives and others close to village leaders, increasing their chance of obtaining benefits. Some informants speculated that village-level selection might exclude villagers who failed to participate in village activities, those considered undeserving or lazy, or perhaps who opposed the village head during elections. Field-level social affairs officials (*Tenaga Kesejahteraan Social Kecamatan* or TKSK; responsible for overseeing several social programmes across dozens of sub-district villages) have noted that the prevalence of these dynamics of nepotism and cronyism will depend on the personal character of decision-makers. One TKSK estimated that 15 per cent of villages chronically experienced these problems. Earlier World Bank research suggested that, while those holding formal leadership positions are more likely to receive benefits, this leads to small welfare losses (Alatas et al. 2019). However, there are significant social impacts and emotional reactions among excluded villagers who observe better-off and better-connected villagers accessing benefits (Cameron and Shah 2014).

Village heads pointed to "village" accountability mechanisms shaping their behaviour. One village head admitted that "family factors" played a role, but that this was insignificant, and argued that "five from a hundred choices would have a family nuance". While the list of potential beneficiaries was a secret, villagers would notice who received benefits, including those they deemed unentitled. This would become a focus of discussion and resentment, with negative gossip undermining the position of the village head during village elections. It is undoubtedly possible for village heads to enter some family members onto a list, but such recipients needed to be from modest households to avoid drawing too much criticism. In Aceh, a village head who flagrantly abused his position would not survive long in it.

Surveying the Poor

After the finalisation of the pre-list, during the PBDT process, enumerators surveyed households. Interviews with officials revealed how "field risks" discussed in earlier reports shaped the survey (SMERU 2012). Earlier research has suggested that measurement processes lead those governed by them to change their behaviour to enhance their scores (Merry 2011). Hence, respondents wishing to maximise the chance of getting listed as poor may overlook assets and mask their true economic status. More savvy villagers could field questions well, but the poor might inadvertently imply they owned assets which they rented or managed.

Enumerators had limited incentives for doing the survey well and faced few sanctions if they carried out the surveys poorly. The programme paid enumerators a flat fee per village and transport costs. If people were away, enumerators would need to revisit remote hamlets several times. They also faced constant criticisms from those excluded from the earlier beneficiary list. At a certain point, the task became too demanding and it was not worth going door-to-door. For example, in Aceh Besar, a TKSK recalled seeing the enumerator sitting filling out the survey forms with the village head. In Aceh Utara the village secretary provided information while the enumerator filled in a large pile of documents.

Several informants suggested that surveyors, even if recruited from the village, lacked the competency, authority or discernment to do the survey well. In the Aceh Besar village, the village head selected a young unmarried woman to carry out the survey. A villager complained that she was "too close" to the village head and simply "accepts it when he proposes several people". Some informants who had seen key villagers guiding the completion of forms suspected that this shaped the pre-listing. Another informant questioned whether she was confident enough to press older, recalcitrant male interviewees to answer questions truthfully or otherwise to induce them to provide accurate information. Once the system had excluded poor households, they faced considerable difficulties getting on the list, as the system failed to include poor and excluded eligible households retrospectively. For this reason, poor households remained desperate for inclusion and bitterly contested their exclusion.

Econometric Targeting

To identify the poor, village data are subject to the proxy means testing methodology. This econometric targeting applies a statistical model, using indicators derived from statistical analysis of these household survey datasets, to calculate a household's level of welfare relative to other households. Given the problems of measuring household income and consumption, assets and other "stable" characteristics like education levels are proxies for household welfare. The process selected indicators because visiting enumerators could easily observe them, thus producing real simplification problems.

Villagers and district officials quickly recognised the difficulty of using assets as a proxy for welfare. As one observed, "people may have a poor house but extensive gardens or rice paddy; alternatively, a house may have tiles and a good floor, but the family may have a poor income". The messy survey process confounded this problem. While enumerators may easily observe house characteristics, assets are less easy to evaluate. Some indicators may also mislead, for instance, the survey can get an affirmative answer to a question whether a household owns a motorbike, but in many cases, motorbikes are purchased on credit. More complex welfare indicators that are difficult to survey would need to be considered and many argued that the survey provided a superficial understanding of household welfare.

The literature regarding proxy means tests confirms these concerns. First, households accumulate assets from past work, and assets are "often a poor indicator of present income". Since livelihoods are highly dynamic, the accuracy of PMT assessments degrades rapidly (Kidd, Gelders and Bailey-Athias 2017). As a household improves its circumstances, it can become an "inclusion error" in future years, particularly given the difficulty of "graduating" those deemed no longer poor. On the other hand, people who have fallen into poverty between surveys may remain excluded, even if they are re-surveyed, because their proxies suggest they are still wealthy. Second, critics have raised transparency concerns with the method and formula being too complicated, poorly explained, or kept secret; those on the ground may misunderstand targeting methods (Brown, Ravallion and van de Walle 2016). Interviews with district officials revealed that those administering the programme lacked an understanding of how beneficiaries were selected. Third, analysts observe that econometric targeting tends to overestimate living standards for the poorest and underestimate them for the richest, tending to exclude the poor as well as the non-poor (Brown, Ravallion and van de Walle 2016). One study concluded that "the majority of households identified by the mechanism as being in the poorest 20 per cent of the population are, in fact, in the poorest 40 per cent" (Kidd, Gelders and Bailey-Athias 2017: 18). However, these authors also note that "when a programme is targeted at the poorest 10 per cent [such as in Indonesia], the in-built design exclusion error tends to be around 60 per cent (in other words, around 60 per cent of the target group are excluded from the scheme)". In theory, as the programme expands, this reduces such exclusion errors.

Outcomes

This research used a survey of 82 villagers from two villages to analyse outcomes, applying a stratified proportional random sampling approach. We compared those receiving benefits with the classifications of households derived from community wealth-rankings (Table 11.1). According to the villagers' own criteria, the wealth-ranking exercise classified 43 families (52 per cent of the sample) as poor. Twenty-two of these households (27 per cent of the sample) also met the PKH demographic criteria, screening as potential recipients. The survey revealed that 22 per cent of the group identified as poor and meeting PKH criteria received CCTs. Concerning inclusion, we found that 50 per cent of those receiving benefits were "capable" or "non-poor" households according to the community wealth-ranking exercise. Comparing this result with those receiving alms under Islamic practices, we found that the *zakat* provided benefits to 30 households (37 per cent), comprising 70 per cent of those identified as poor by village wealth-ranking. The local community provided *zakat* to six households considered non-poor by community standards (17 per cent of total *zakat* recipients); these non-poor recipients included the committee, which the *zakat* system paid for overseeing the alms-giving. A comparison of the PKH recipients with the food security survey revealed that 17 per cent of food-insecure households obtained CCT benefits, while 56 per cent of food-insecure households in our sample received *zakat*.

Triangulating these outcomes with informants revealed that the excluded poor included people who had fallen into poverty after the survey or whose proxies led them to be misidentified, along with young and poor households whom the registry (PBDT) had never listed. Those mistakenly enlisted included economically modest households somehow identified as poor, and poor households which had become prosperous. Many of these could use strong personal ties to leverage enlistment. For example, in Aceh Besar village, the mother of the TKSK official, who owned her rice-land, received benefits. We also found a member of the village council listed. In Aceh Utara village, we discovered a preacher in the Islamic school, several hamlet heads and the family of the village secretary receiving CCT benefits. All these were modest (non-wealthy) households, but "capable" or non-poor by village criteria. As one village head noted, the system provided conditional cash transfers "to many people who are worthy of help, but often not to those most in need".

By 2019, the system had revised the beneficiary list, following the implementation of the verification process (PBDT). The number of recipients among those surveyed had increased from 14 per cent to 21 per cent of the sample. Methods of validation had improved the targeting: conditional cash transfers now reached 23 per cent of those classified as poor and meeting PKH criteria. However, 44 per cent of those receiving benefits were still considered non-poor. There was a path dependency at work here. We found 15 per cent of PKH recipients in our 2015 survey cohort had graduated (they no longer met PKH demographic criteria), while 85 per cent still received benefits in 2019. Rather than being elevated out of poverty by the CCTs, most recipients categorised as poor in 2011 remained poor. As district officials noted, once the system registered a household as poor and deserving of assistance, their names tended to be locked in. In theory, the community meeting entrusted with modifying the pre-list could exclude those deemed unworthy of assistance, and recipients should graduate after five years. However, district officials observed that village heads, wary of creating lifelong enemies, avoided signing forms indicating that a household was already "capable" and the disparity with those left out persisted.

Table 11.1 Poverty targeting across the two cases: Share of poor and non-poor receiving PKH

Category	% of total sample	Explanation
% of sample receiving PKH	14	Increased to 22% in 2019
Poor (by SoP)	52	
Poor & fit PKH criteria	27	52% of poor households
Poor & get PKH	7	22% of those classified as potential PKH beneficiaries (23% in 2019)
Non-Poor & receive PKH	7	50% of PKH recipients are non-poor by SOP/local criteria; falls to 44% in 2019
Zakat recipients	41	
Poor & get Zakat	37	70% of those considered poor by SOP

Response

Policymakers have changed the mechanisms for collecting and verifying data, launching a Verification-Validation Mechanism for Social Welfare Information System (SIKS-NG), now under the Ministry of Social Affairs. As one brochure noted, difficulties had emerged due to a "traditional, manual and partial" data management system (Kementrian Sosial RI 2016). The ministry doubled down and introduced this more technically advanced system for re-surveying recipient populations.[2]

Yet the state capacity issues that beset earlier iterations of the programme remained. A social affairs official (TKSK) in each sub-district supervised the process. The Aceh Utara subdistrict contained 39 villages. With strict deadlines to meet, so many villages to survey, and wishing to avoid community complaints about targeting, TKSK rarely met villagers directly. Still, they enlisted the village apparatus to revise pre-lists and surveys.

Interviews with village leaders and TKSK revealed a predicament associated with the hybrid PMT-CBT system. By allowing village leaders to vet the pre-list, the revised system aimed to improve the selection of beneficiaries. However, econometric targeting ultimately chose the beneficiaries. Even if village heads and TKSKs selected poor households for inclusion, they could not guarantee the inclusion of the poor or the exclusion of better-off villagers. Afraid of being accused of creating programme inaccuracy, they avoided consultative meetings to revise the pre-lists or going to people's homes to carry out surveys. As the SPP problem had continued for so long, they were "fed up" with the system. One hamlet head explained that, as he "knew his people", he could complete the survey in secret; if errors occurred, villagers would see the mistakes as coming from the central government.

Conclusion: Constitutive Effects of CCT Knowledge

As we have seen, Indonesia's CCT programme rests upon a specific politics of knowledge that legitimises current approaches. The CCT model uses econometric targeting to make poverty legible, effectively defining what poverty means, how to measure it and how to respond to it. The model uses codified, systematically expressed, quantified and documented forms of information, institutionalising a technical approach focused on fiscal effectiveness and rationing benefits to those deemed eligible. This is a "blueprint" approach where planners map out the expected causal pathways from inputs to desired outcomes in detail at the outset. The model involves complex administrative criteria and targeting methodology and amounts to a process with strong upward accountability mechanisms under a powerful central authority. The process has the advantage of providing a legible, scalable and administratively convenient format for actionable policy. Along the way, the approach irons out the messy reality of poverty as experienced by measuring and modelling. In doing so, "phenomena which are otherwise polyvalent and rich in meaning" are subdued and reduced to more straightforward dimensions (Dahler-Larsen 2014: 976). However, this process of simplification compounds the errors involved.

Several factors condition how this apparatus works. First, the opaque and complex process described above necessarily involves making approximations based on generalisations and assumptions embedded in econometric models.

This necessarily involves simplifications that generate a certain level of error. Second, as we have seen, given fiscal constraints and political decisions, the programme needs to be highly selective, aiming to target the bottom 10 per cent. However, given limited state capacities at the district level, the state agencies entrusted with implementing the programme have limited resources at their disposal and this affects implementation. Third, this highly centralised system struggles to incorporate the non-codifiable, contextually embedded knowledge required for accurate targeting. Fourth, although the programme appears to provide a sophisticated, highly technical approach to selecting beneficiaries, it takes on a relational aspect at the district and village levels. The process involves a broad array of actors who take up roles overseeing processes, developing pre-lists, surveys and data entry and facilitating social protection programmes. As the programme recruited local personnel in its methods of pre-listing and surveying, it also remained subject to field risks, social relationships and village politics. It resulted, at its best, in a patchwork apparatus for knowing and governing the poor.

As a result, all the development knowledge and practices deployed have several formative effects on how social cash transfers work out. In the first place, they influence the behaviour of villagers and village leaders, provoking a village-level politics of distribution around the allocation of resources, of who is entitled to receive them and why. As respondents highlighted during surveys, they attempt to manipulate their answers, hiding assets or otherwise seeking to increase their chances of ending up on the beneficiary list.

To maximise the chance of inclusion, villagers attempt to make use of social relationships. All villagers in rural Indonesia exist within elaborate networks of reciprocity and mutual dependence, systems that encompass both reciprocal and generalised reciprocity. In terms of social welfare, villagers relate to the state more as clients than as citizens. In other words, access to state programmes depends on social relationships that are accessible only for those who invest in maintaining them. All but the very poor can try to use such relationships to win inclusion on SPP pre-lists. However, the CCT process works according to a different logic: it does not map onto local notions of fairness or concepts of entitlement and villagers find to their cost that local clientelist networks cannot assure inclusion.

Village leaders also respond strategically to the apparatus for implementing the CCT model. As this is an allocative system where the resources available need to be rationed, the model requires village leaders to edit the pre-lists, setting out who is poor and excluding those deemed less eligible. Yet village heads are embedded in local social fields characterised by clientelist relations. Many villages have a sense of entitlement to state resources, expecting their leaders to respond to their moral demands. Village leaders themselves may hope to win re-election or avoid complex conflicts while maintaining village cohesion. During interviews, it became clear that village leaders sought to prevent openly excluding people. Earlier, when villages had discretionary power over the allocation mechanism (under the *Raskin* programme), they redistributed social benefits across broad sections of the village.

When it came to administering the PKH programme, village leaders initially sought to distribute benefits broadly. However, in setting out to place the allocative system beyond elite capture and clientelism, even after including elements of community-based targeting, the proxy means test makes the final decision. Once the village heads oversee the pre-listing and data collection, opaque econometric targeting and state implementation processes take over and determine who obtains benefits. Even if village leaders add people to the list, there is no guarantee they will receive benefits. The village apparatus avoided open meetings to prevent being closely associated with the system and disappointing or embittering residents left off the final list. Their role in checking pre-lists or helping with the surveys occurred off-stage, outside village forms of accountability and transparency.

Another set of constitutive effects pertains to the constant re-contextualisation of this poverty technology. Given these targeting errors, the CCT system is constantly updating, introducing technologies from elsewhere, and the latest "patch" to the system always seems to be about to resolve these problems. This never-ending process of improving the technology and systems of collecting data to obtain better and more reliable data has its effects (Freistein 2016). Downloading the latest technical "patch" will leave the assumptions and methodological issues behind these formative effects untouched. Further, local officials and village informants tend to be confused, as the acronyms proliferate and data collection methods, selection and checking practices shift.

The CCT programme model also shapes an emergent pattern of entitlements and enfranchisement. The process of providing entitlements—the capacity to obtain assistance during times of need—tends to be opaque, erratic and uneven. Villagers can't understand why the system includes one family and excludes another. Poor households who face household deprivation due to a shock cannot seek social cash transfers. Households who have gained the capacity to access benefits include both poor and non-poor. Indeed, comparing the community poverty ranking exercise with the PKH recipient list revealed that 23 per cent of those classified as poor and meeting PKH criteria received conditional cash transfers, while 44 per cent of those receiving benefits were considered non-poor by the village wealth-ranking exercise. This has created the distributional politics so heatedly discussed in village coffee shops and local media.

Overcoming poverty ideally involves processes of enfranchisement, where the communities and the very poor might gain some discretionary authority over decision-making. Given that community members have a role in vetting pre-lists, the process is not purely econometric targeting. However, as village heads lack control over allocative decisions, neither is it a clientelist system. Here village leaders avoid the blame of being openly involved in implementation. Hence, from a village perspective, decision-making processes tend to be unclear, occurring off-stage and via unaccountable processes. The current system runs up against village structures and practices engrained in culture, political and social expectations and behaviour. To some degree, communities maintain reciprocal and redistributive practices that bind together village sociality; this depends upon ingrained notions of fairness, responsiveness to expectations of inclusion and moral claims. Yet this residual system involves differentiating the eligible from the ineligible according to a techno-administrative standard and process. As communities discuss whether those receiving benefits are "deserving", this leads to cycles of stigmatisation. Local government officials now place "poor household" stickers on the front of PKH households, shaming households into withdrawing from the programme unless they can face the views of excluded neighbours regarding whether they are more entitled to benefits. In this way, critics of residual CCT systems argue that they lead to segmentation, creating a distance between the poor and other citizens left out of social provisions even if they remain vulnerable (Fischer 2018).

In prioritising efficiency over equity, the econometric analysis used in programme design and evaluation overlooks this important cultural-political insight: exclusion from benefits in rural Aceh is taken as an entitlement failure and has impacts on social cohesion and a household's sense of inclusion in the community. Excluded villagers may shirk participation in village meetings and mutual assistance (*gotong royong*) and bitterly resent village leaders (McCarthy and Sumarto 2018). Villagers prefer a more inclusive approach over a highly targeted system that leaves so many poor people out.

Poverty programmes require wrestling with questions of social values and goals and making normative political decisions regarding how society should address poverty and inequality and who is entitled to assistance. However, only experts understand the metrics, measurements and targeting processes that resolve who gets what assistance: a firewall of technicality conceals the political questions at the heart of poverty, inequality and food security (Merry 2011; Li 2007). Hence, public discussions of poverty in parliament focus on what has become the main challenge: ensuring CCTs are well-targeted and reach the poor (DPR 2019). This displaces discussion of how best to address the causes of poverty, or how growth might be more inclusive and how labour or agricultural commodity markets might work for the poor.

At the heart of this lies a wicked distributional dilemma: a highly selective, residual and conditional system necessarily needs to work out who might be entitled to assistance. The challenge involves categorising households relative to some standard of deprivation, either a state-provided one or the community's standard. But proceeding with either a state-provided or community-based approach may ultimately be unsatisfactory and reflects a central dilemma. As a member of the local legislature noted, there is "no way for statistics to get an accurate reckoning of who is poor and who is not; and without village deliberation, there is no way to validate data". At the same time, "if only the village elite makes the decision, then 'political nuances' are not overcome". This suggests a choice between the state's inaccurate selection or a selection process governed by village elites that many accounts allege is affected by clientelism. In other words, as research has suggested, no optimal targeting mechanism exists (Devereux et al. 2017). As discussed in Chapters 3 and 16, there are other approaches that may ameliorate this dilemma to some degree by moving beyond the liberal-residual approach to social assistance.

In a 2004 article, David Mosse asked, "is good policy implementable?". In answering this question, he provocatively suggested that policy is "good" if it effectively generates mobilising metaphors that, while concealing ideological differences, allow for compromises, enable the enrolling of interests and the development of coalitions around a policy idea, and justify the flow of resources. However, he argued that while the ideas that make "good policy" effective may perform well in legitimising and mobilising political and practical support, "good policy" is often a poor guide for action. This is usually revealed during implementation when "good policy" ideas bump into institutions, social relations and vested interests. Hence, while all the development knowledge behind the idea of conditional cash transfers "successfully" supports a set of development practices and sustains a set of interpretations, it may not be implementable in any easy, straightforward, or unambiguous way.

Notes

[1] There is an extra 50 kg, which could not be accounted for during the interview, possibly due to irregularities in how this system works.

[2] Another mechanism, *Mekanisme Pemutakhiran Mandiri*, would be used to verify data.

References

Alatas, V. et al. 2019. "Does Elite Capture Matter? Local Elites and Targeted Welfare Programs in Indonesia", *AEA Papers and Proceedings* 109: 334–9. Available at DOI: 10.1257/pandp.20191047 (accessed 10 Mar. 2022).

Alfitri. 2005. "The Law of Zakat Management and Non-Governmental Zakat Collectors in Indonesia", *The International Journal of Not-for-Profit Law* 8, 2. Available at https://www.icnl.org/resources/research/ijnl/the-law-of-zakat-management-and-non-governmental-zakat-collectors-in-indonesia (accessed 10 Mar. 2022).

Bebbington, A., S. Guggenheim and E. Olson. 2004. "Exploring Social Capital Debates at the World Bank", *Journal of Development Studies* 40: 33–64.

Benda-Beckmann, F. von, K. von Benda-Beckmann and H. Marks, eds. 1994. *Coping with Insecurity: An "Underall" Perspective on Social Security in the Third World.* Yogyakarta: Pustaka Pelajar.

Berenschot, W. and G. van Klinken. 2018. "Informality and Citizenship: the Everyday State in Indonesia", *Citizenship Studies* 22, 2: 95–111.

Brown, C., M. Ravallion and D. van de Walle. 2016. "A Poor Means Test? Econometric Targeting in Africa". World Bank Policy Research Working Paper 7915. Washington, DC: World Bank. Available at https://openknowledge.worldbank.org/handle/ 10986/25814 (accessed 11 Mar. 2022).

Cahyadi, N. et al. 2018. "Cumulative Impacts of Conditional Cash Transfer Programs: Experimental Evidence from Indonesia", TNP2K Working Paper 4–2018. Jakarta, Indonesia. Available at http://tnp2k.go.id/downloads/cumulative-impacts-of-conditional-cash-transfer-programs:-experimental-evidence-from-indonesia (accessed 11 Mar. 2022).

Cameron, L. and M. Shah. 2014. "Can Mistargeting Destroy Social Capital and Stimulate Crime? Evidence from a Cash Transfer Program in Indonesia", *Economic Development and Cultural Change* 62, 2: 381–415.

Dahler-Larsen, P. 2012. "Constitutive Effects as a Social Accomplishment: A Qualitative Study of the Political in Testing", *Education Inquiry* 3, 2: 171–86.

_____. 2014. "Constitutive Effects of Performance Indicators: Getting Beyond Unintended Consequences", *Public Management Review* 16, 7: 969–86.

Devereux, S. et al. 2017. "The Targeting Effectiveness of Social Transfer", *Journal of Development Effectiveness* 9, 2: 162–211.

DPR (Dewan Perwakilan Rakyat/House of Representatives). 2019. "PKH Harus Tepat Sasaran" [National Family Hope Program has to be right on target]. Available at https://www.dpr.go.id/berita/detail/id/25124/t/javascript (accessed 20 Aug. 2020).

Ferguson, J. 2015. *Give a Man a Fish: Reflections on the New Politics of Distribution.* Durham, NC: Duke University Press.

Fischer, A.M. 2018. *Poverty as Ideology: Rescuing Social Justice from Global Development Agendas.* London: Zed Books.

Freistein, K. 2016. "Effects of Indicator Use: A Comparison of Poverty Measuring Instruments at the World Bank", *Journal of Comparative Policy Analysis: Research and Practice* 18: 366–81.

Hanna, R. and B.A. Olken. 2018. "Universal Basic Incomes versus Targeted Transfers: Anti-Poverty Programs in Developing Countries", *Journal of Economic Perspectives* 32, 4: 201–26.

Hastuti et al. 2008. *The Effectiveness of the Raskin Program.* Jakarta: SMERU Research Institute.

Kementerian Sosial RI (Ministry of Social Affairs of the Republic of Indonesia). 2016. *Aplikasi Sistem Informasi Kesejahteraan Sosial* [The Application of Information Systems to Social Welfare]. Jakarta: Kementerian Sosial Republik Indonesia.

Kidd, S. and D. Bailey-Athias. 2020. "Hit and Miss: An Assessment of Targeting Effectiveness in Social Protection with Additional Analysis". Working Paper: June 2020 Development Pathways, London, UK.

Kidd, S., B. Gelders and D. Bailey-Athias. 2017. *Exclusion by Design: An Assessment of the Effectiveness of the Proxy Means Test Poverty Targeting Mechanism.* ESS Working Paper No.56, International Labour Organization and Development Pathways. Available at https://www.ilo.org/global/topics/dw4sd/WCMS_568678/lang--en/index.htm (accessed 10 Mar. 2022).

Kwon H-J. and W.R. Kim. 2015. "The Evolution of Cash Transfer in Indonesia: Policy Transfer and National Adaptation", *Asia & the Pacific Policy Studies* 2, 2: 425–40.

Lasswell, H.D. 1936. *Politics: Who Gets What, When, How.* New York: McGraw Hill. Rpt. Auckland: Papamoa, 2018.

Leisering, L. 2019. *The Global Rise of Social Cash Transfers: How States and International Organizations Constructed a New Instrument for Combating Poverty.* Oxford: Oxford University Press.

Li, T.M. 2007. *The Will to Improve: Governmentality, Development, and the Practice of Politics.* Durham, NC: Duke University Press.

McCarthy, J.F. and M. Sumarto. 2018. "Distributional Politics and Social Protection in Indonesia: Dilemmas of Layering, Nesting and Social Fit in Jokowi's Poverty Policy", *Journal of Southeast Asian Economies* 35, 2: 223–36.

Merry, S. 2011. "Measuring the World Indicators, Human Rights, and Global Governance", *Current Anthropology* 52, 3: S83–S95.

Mosse, D. 2004. "Is Good Policy Unimplementable? Reflections on the Ethnography of Aid Policy and Practice", *Development and Change* 35, 4: 639–71.

Papadopoulos, T. and R. Velazquez-Leyer. 2016. "Two Decades of Social Investment in Latin America: Outcomes, Shortcomings and Achievements of Conditional Cash Transfers", *Social Policy and Society* 15, 3: 435–49.

Peck, J. and N. Theodore. 2015. *Fast Policy: Experimental Statecraft at the Thresholds of Neoliberalism.* Minneapolis: Minnesota University Press.

Satriawan, E. 2016. "Evaluating Longer-term Impact of Indonesia's CCT Program: Evidence from a Randomised Controlled Trial". Paper presented at JPAL SEA Conference on Social Protection, Jakarta.

Scoones, I. 2009. "The Politics of Global Assessments: The Case of the International Assessment of Agricultural Knowledge, Science and Technology for Development (IAASTD)", *The Journal of Peasant Studies* 36, 3: 547–71.

Scott, J.C. 1999. *Seeing like a State.* New Haven, CT: Yale University Press.

SMERU. 2012. *Rapid Appraisal of the 2011 Data Collection of Social Protection Programs (PPLS 2011).* Jakarta: SMERU Research Institute. https://smeru.or.id/en/content/rapid-appraisal-2011-data-collection-social-protection-programs-ppls-2011.

Stoeffler, Q., B. Mills and C. del Ninno. 2016. "Reaching the Poor: Cash Transfer Program Targeting in Cameroon", *World Development* 83: 244–63.

Sumarto, M. 2020. "Welfare and Conflict: Policy Failure in the Indonesian Cash Transfer", *Journal of Social Policy* 50, 3: 1–19.

Vetterlein, A. 2012. "Seeing Like the World Bank on Poverty", *New Political Economy* 17, 1: 35–58.

Watts, M.J. and H.G. Bohle. 1993. "Hunger, Famine and The Space of Vulnerability", *GeoJournal* 30, 2: 117–25.

CHAPTER 12

The Arrival and Implementation of Conditional Cash Transfers in Indonesia

Pande Made Kutanegara, Gerben Nooteboom and Michelle Pols

Introduction

This chapter focuses on the political pathway and logic of the introduction of the PKH[1] programme (conditional cash transfers—CCTs) in Indonesia, and offers local insights into its implementation in the village of Sriharjo, central Java. We study the local and national impacts of travelling global poverty eradication ideas and their accompanying technologies (targeting, proxy means testing and implementation). We argue that a specific politics of knowledge, which underpins the CCT methodology globally, generates high inclusion and exclusion errors and a myriad of unintended consequences on the ground in Indonesia.[2] Some key unintended consequences are social unrest and jealousy among households, a general weakening of local leadership and governance structures, materialistic, individualised and income-focused poverty thinking, weakening social welfare and solidarity at the village level, depoliticisation of poverty and inequality, a focus on consumption and income and a neglect of production and redistribution at the local level.

Over the last decade, the Indonesian government has embarked on an ambitious, large-scale social protection agenda to fight poverty. This consists of four key policies: national health insurance (JKN[3]); education for all (KIP[4]); food assistance to the poor (RASTRA and BPNT[5]), and a conditional cash transfer programme (PKH) for the poor (Sumarto 2017). Typically, the programmes consist of the development triangle *health*, *education* and *nutrition*, common in WHO, UN and World Bank programmes (Glewwe and Miguel

2007). The PKH programme complements the other three components, and offers conditional, regular transfers of money via ATM.

In order to receive the quarterly cash transfers, recipients have to pay regular visits to health clinics, send their children to school and take part in family development workshops, with the obligation to spend a large part of the received cash on basic food in state-run e-shops[6] (*e-warung*).[7] The PKH programme also offers food supplements for children and pregnant mothers.

Since its introduction, the programme has gained popularity among policymakers and recipients (Gabel and Kamerman 2013; Kwon and Kim 2015). In 2016, six million Indonesian households received PKH via a series of, initially irregular, payments. In 2018, the programme was improved and extended to 12 million families (est. 40 million people) who received 1.8 million Rupiah (USD 133 at 2018 prices) per year. In 2019, Indonesia embarked on yet another massive increase in payments to provide regular cash transfers to 15 million households. During the COVID-19 pandemic, the PKH programme was one of the backbones of the government's mitigation and support programmes (World Bank 2021). Already before the pandemic, the PKH programme represented Indonesia's first comprehensive attempt at full coverage of the poorest 10 per cent of society and at targeting poverty on an individual basis. As such, it also entailed a paradigm shift from welfare and social security, with a focus on labour and entitlements (mostly for working men), to social protection, while addressing vulnerability (especially for women and children) and universal rights.

Conditional Cash Transfers (CCT) as a Global Model

The Indonesian model largely follows the global model of conditional cash transfers, designed to break the cycle of intergenerational poverty via investments in health, education and nutrition (Lomeli 2009: 167). Following their initial popularity in Latin American countries (especially Brazil and Mexico) and in Africa, the model gained momentum in Asian countries such as Cambodia, the Philippines and Indonesia (Gliszczynski and Leisering 2016; World Bank 2012). The World Bank has been influential in its spread and actively propagates the model following positive results from early evaluations.

CCTs are supposed to be complementary to existing social welfare arrangements. However, they are often believed to be magic bullets, single solutions for complex and variate problems (Nooteboom and Rutten 2012). St. Clair makes the point that "CCTs cannot be ends in themselves or a major anti-poverty measure; rather they are a means—a temporary solution for specific circumstances" (St. Clair 2009: 178). Despite this disclaimer, CCTs were quickly adopted by major institutional donors and have become the dominant approach to ameliorating complex poverty conditions in many countries. Once introduced, they tend to be hard to wind back or transform.

The CCT model has been extensively reviewed, but not much is known about programme implementation, local interactions and mediation processes of policy in different cultural contexts. Indonesia is an interesting case study, because it had never previously had nation-wide fully institutionalised welfare programmes (Koning and Hüsken 2006). When the CCT programme was implemented in 2007, almost a decade after the first programmes in Latin America, there was already ample evidence highlighting targeting problems and the failure of CCTs to eradicate poverty. The CCTs also proved to be unsuited as replacements for insurance programmes (Barrientos and DeJong 2006; Feitosa de Britto 2004; Farrington and Slater 2006). These lessons however, have not played a major role in the adoption and selection of CCTs as a prioritised anti-poverty instrument in Indonesia. More important was the pragmatic social and electoral need to continue welfare as part of the social safety net approaches of the IMF and the World Bank following the Asian Financial Crisis, and now as a pivotal programme in dealing with the adverse effects of the COVID-19 crisis.

The Making of a Model

The first CCT-programmes were initiated in the 1990s and early 2000s— including Mexico's PROGRESA and subsequent *Oportunidades* programme, and Brazil's *Bolsa Escolar* and *Bolsa Familia*—and these have been studied intensively (Shibuya 2008; Fernald, Gertler and Neufeld 2008; Ramírez 2016; Gliszczynski 2016). CCT programmes were brought onto the global agenda by two papers by the World Bank in 2004 and 2006, and quickly gained popularity in the international development arena (Sugiyama 2011).

After being depoliticised as an anti-poverty strategy, belonging to neither the camps of the left or right (Gardner and Lewis 2015: 105), CCTs became attractive for populist politicians and state bureaucracies globally. They also replaced traditional welfare programmes, food and fuel subsidies, and social safety nets, which were subsequently critiqued as part of patronage politics, vote buying and for their poor financial reputation. Governments of both the left and right in Latin America needed new programmes; with political momentum and associated electoral benefits, Conditional Cash Transfers to the poor became the preferred model (Sugiyama 2011: 250–2).

CCTs were thus promoted as part of a democratisation process that was suited to populism and electoral campaigns between left and right economic and social policies. They turned out to be attractive and united different political agendas (pro-poor as well as market-oriented) (Papadopoulos and Leyer 2016). Politically, they adhered to the desires of the left to serve the poor and to redistribute capital (in this case direct cash), while economically they fitted right-wing political preferences (that is, for conditionality) as social policy instruments supporting a neoliberal market logic (cash stimulates markets). Paradoxically, the politics were a reaction to increased poverty and inequality caused by market solutions, but CCTs themselves thrive in a neoliberal context with their focus on investment, direct cash provision, use of markets, institutional set up (efficiency) and individual focus. External incentives offered by International Financial Institutions (IFIs) such as the World Bank, and later the Asian Development Bank, also played a role (Hunter and Brown 2000). IFIs, with their focus on evidence-based targeted interventions, measurable results and efficient interventions, became very influential in the spread of CCTs as a global poverty alleviation model (Gliszczynski and Leisering 2016).

The Popularity of CCTs as a Policy Model

Conditional cash transfers contain certain magic bullet-like characteristics that make the strategy popular. CCTs are attractive because they are intended to have both short- and long-term effects on poverty alleviation. Besides this, the themes and focus of the package of the CCT programme also help to explain its popularity (Lomelí 2008).

Eight key aspects of CCTs, loosely based on the "ten salient features" mentioned by Lomelí (2008), are typically highlighted:

(1) CCTs focus on health (especially for children) and education to break the intergenerational poverty cycle.[8]

(2) They bear the promise of ending poverty, combining short term benefits (giving cash to the poor to cover their needs and buying capacity to purchase goods) and long-term effects (changing the conditions of the poor to break the cycle of poverty and obtain jobs).

(3) The conditionality moves away from expensive and unpopular welfare programmes and fits neoliberal ideas of responsibility and mutuality.

(4) The framing of CCTs as investments in human capital means a move away from charity to neoliberal thinking in potentials and chances.[9]

(5) The focus on women, children and pregnant mothers fits the old archetype that mothers spend money "better" (for the family) than

men do. It also reproduces the image of mothers as primary agents of childcare and social development.

(6) CCTs show respect for the dignity of the poor; they are non-paternalistic in the sense that recipients are free to spend the money according to their own needs and preferences (Leisering 2009). They thus fit ideologically into agency and pro-poor approaches, as well as neoliberal approaches.

(7) They are efficient. CCTs potentially can achieve high coverage at low cost.

(8) CCTs promise to tackle multiple problems in a single policy (Feitosa de Britto 2004). Widespread inequalities in the distribution of income and opportunities have persistently excluded large proportions of the population from the benefits of economic development and CCTs.

The Politics of Travelling Models

CCT Implementation and Expansion in Indonesia

The current Indonesian CCT model is the same as that designed in Latin America, but its implementation has been shaped by local effects. Two developments coincided to create this result: On the one hand, the introduction of CCTs was a logical continuation of the IMF and World Bank social safety net programmes implemented during the Asian crisis of 1997–2003. At the same time, the introduction and popularity of CCTs in Indonesia emerged as special effects of the democratisation process in Indonesia, following the fall of Suharto in 1998.

Crucial to understanding the logic of the introduction of CCTs was the change to the election system in 2004, permitting direct presidential elections. At the same time, the popular IMF and World Bank social safety net programmes came to an end. Indonesia had by then paid off its loans, and there was budgetary space for continuation or even an extension of the programmes. Beginning from 2004, politicians started to think about how the social protection programmes could be used to build up credit and to mobilise the electorate among the poorer segments of society. In that year, Susilo Bambang Yudhoyono (SBY) won the Presidential election and had the opportunity to play a more significant role in the improvement of the Indonesian welfare system.

When Yudhoyono became President, the government was under pressure to cut fuel subsidies, a highly unpopular measure among the poor. In 2005, Yudhoyono replaced the popular social safety net programmes with four poverty reduction programmes focused on food security (*Raskin*), health (*Askes*), education (*BOS*) and a programme of unconditional cash transfers to the poor (*BLT*). Of all these programmes, only BLT (*Bantuan Langsung Tunai*—direct cash transfers) was completely new. The existing health insurance and educational programmes were extensions of earlier programmes and *Raskin* was simply a continuation of the old rice for the poor programme. In the process, all names of the social protection programmes changed as part of a strategic rebranding of social protection schemes for re-election purposes. Direct cash transfers were presented as one form of compensation for the poor for the reduction of fuel subsidies (Purwoko 2009).

In 2007, the direct cash programme BLT was replaced by the conditional cash transfer programme, PKH (*Program Keluarga Harapan*—hope for families). This was accompanied by a new approach to data collection and technical calculation of the poor, through proxy means testing which was intended to break with previous social protection schemes based on different data sets, and was carried out by a variety of government departments using a variety of approaches.

Under Yudhoyono, Indonesia's anti-poverty programmes had expanded massively. In 2008, there were more than 50 anti-poverty programmes, of which the PKH programme became the pre-eminent.[10] The package was initially IDR 1.8 million per year in four instalments. Since 2018, it has increased to IDR 2 million per year, oriented to all registered pregnant women, children under five, households who had school-going children up to senior high school (Sekolah Menengah Atas [SMA]), elderly people (formerly for people over 70, now extended to people over 60), and disabled people. Before 2018, the package consisted of a complex disaggregated measurement per eligibility factor adding up to a maximum of IDR 1.8 million, and criteria were checked. It was then simplified to the full amount of IDR 2 million if just one criterion was met, with recipients being paid in four tranches.

The presidential election of 2009 proved that the expansion of welfare programmes worked as a viable re-election policy. According to Aspinall (2010), the landslide victory of Yudhoyono was due to BLT. At least, Yudhoyono was able to claim the credit for the poverty programmes. Since then, it has become clear that a seated president can profit electorally from social protection programmes and every subsequent president is likely to promote their benefits.

The first years of the Jokowi presidency, from 2014 onwards, highlighted this pattern. The PKH programme has been extended from supporting 5 million, to supporting over 15 million families in 2019. To put his stamp on the support, Jokowi also renamed most of the other social protection programmes. He has improved and extended national health insurance, educational subsidies and basic needs provision to highlight his commitment to the programmes. The PKH programme was an important element in his re-election in April 2019 (*The Asian Post*, 5 April 2019). Most of these programmes and their extensions have been issued under presidential edict and introduced without formal ratification by the parliament. The social welfare and CCT programmes in Indonesia are likely to continue, especially in the COVID-19 crisis, when they are seen as pivotal conduits for support in the face of economic disruption.

The Politics of Poverty Data Control

When unconditional cash programmes (BLT) were hastily introduced in 2005, the Indonesian Central Bureau of Statistics (BPS) gathered general data on the social economic position of households.[11] These aggregated data were ill-suited to identifying and targeting the poorest households. Nevertheless, this dataset provided the basis of BLT and the programmes relied heavily on local governments to identify the poor (World Bank 2012). In this context, village elites were able to influence beneficiary lists and clientelist relations were a prominent feature of the early programme. Coverage was low, data grossly unreliable, distribution often problematic and money often came late or intermittently.

At the introduction of PKH, in 2008, data were collected as part of PPLS (*Pendataan Program Perlindungan Sosial* [Data Collection for Social Protection Programmes]), a special data collection incentive of the BPS using the proxy means test (PMT) implemented and propagated by the World Bank. PMT is a distribution approach that relies on statistical calculation, using survey data to predict household welfare (Stoeffler, Mills and Del Ninno 2016). It scores households against their possession of a set of proxies that are correlated with consumption and uses this to rank households and then allocate resources to beneficiaries selected according to certain criteria (Kidd, Gilders and Bailey-Athias 2017; McCarthy and Sumarto 2018). It was supposed that an independent, neutral and objective assessment of poverty could be achieved by this proxy means test, which was designed to improve targeting and avoid clientelism.

In the first decade of the 2000s, data collection and the control of specific datasets became a political enterprise in Indonesia. Each department (for example Health, Education, Social Welfare, and the Bureau of Food Security, *Bulog*) had its own dataset for social programmes. Control of these data offered political candidates the opportunity to strategically identify and support their electorate. Since his election in 2004, president Yudhoyono had tried to bring all poverty data under the Central Bureau of Statistics

(Badan Pusat Statistik [BPS]), and shift all programmes to the Department of Social Welfare, a formerly very weak and underfunded government department.[12]

In 2011, during the second term of president Yudhoyono, the poverty data were updated again and operationalised for social protection purposes. The so-called BDT data (*Basis Data Terpadu*—integrated data base), used by the special coordination body established by presidential degree (TNP2K),[13] managed the World Bank-provided proxy means test. These poverty data were collected by independent officials and executed by the social welfare department, but village elites and local governments were able to influence the list of beneficiaries. The extension of PKH, the first nation-wide conditional cash programme, was based on these data.

In 2015, a new round of data collection took place. The purpose of this second round of independent data collection was to bypass local village officials and their alleged existing networks of patronage. However, the system continued to grapple with irregularities, leading to large numbers of complaints. This time, the data were again based on the BDT held in Jakarta, and the bottom 40 per cent was targeted to identify the lowest 10 per cent of the poor in Indonesia using the proxy means test. The survey was initially planned for 2014, but postponed to 2015 because of the 2014 elections. The new data were unified and monopolised under a direct programme of the department of social welfare and when the new data collection method was adopted, completely in line with World Bank instructions, local elites and village officials could no longer influence the list of beneficiaries. This policy shift had various unintended effects, including the inability of local officials to correct assessments and targeting mistakes.

Based on the new BDT dataset, a total of six million households were targeted in 2017, raised to 12 million in 2018 and further extended to 15 million in 2019. From 2015 onwards, an official village forum was launched ostensibly to correct and evaluate the collected data, but complaints continued as the feedback process was slow and complicated, leading to unsatisfactory results. Our own study shows a mismatch in targeting of at least 30 per cent in rural areas. Nevertheless, the BDT data continue to be refined and utilised for all poverty reduction programmes in Indonesia.

Shortcomings and Critique of CCTs

Despite their quick and ready adoption in Indonesia, CCTs have been widely criticised as a development tool. In relation to gender objectives, for instance, the transfers are geared to women in households, with benefits going directly to women rather than the household heads (mainly men). Behind this strategy is the persistent idea that women in the family spend money more responsibly than men do. According to some critics, this reproduces gender stereotypes and the role of women as prime providers of care and as responsible for the health, nutrition and education of children. Arguably, the process also takes responsibility away from men: "The design of the programmes may contribute to perpetuate [*sic*] gender inequalities and cultural bias against people living in poverty" (Medrano 2016: 505). Further, the focus on children as a means of breaking the intergenerational poverty cycle may be criticised in that it sees children as agents of change. Notwithstanding these concerns, the strategy has helped in mobilising support for social policies and welfare expenditure and added to the popularity of the PKH programme.

There has also been much discussion about the conditionality of the programmes, where people in real need are excluded because they cannot meet conditions. Many programmes in poor and remote areas also still lack the required facilities including a health post, school, or ATMs to enable the receipt of benefits. According to some critics, these conditionalities are expensive, unnecessary and contradictory to the right to self-determination (Nagels 2016; Barrientos and DeJong 2006; Barrientos 2007). Veit-Wilson (2009) questions the authority of those who set the conditions underlying the conditionality in relation to reciprocity, human rights and social inclusion. There is a relation of reciprocity implied in the CCT-programmes, but the question is: who owes what to whom? According to Veit-Wilson, conditionality is often contrary to human rights and limits people's free choice; he argues for more direct influence from the target population (Veit-Wilson 2009).

Often, conditionalities are simply imposed for political reasons, to make programmes acceptable for political opponents such as conservative political parties and for those in the middle class who reject the idea of "free money" to the poor. This also reveals an important blind spot in CCTs: due to conditionality requirements, vulnerable groups such as homeless people and people with addictions and poor mental health, who might most need the programme, may be overlooked or not meet the required conditions and are therefore excluded. International and Indonesian experience shows that the programmes are often riddled with errors of inclusion and exclusion.

Technologies of implementation of CCTs are criticised by Feitosa de Britto (2004). International pressure plays a major part in policy choices around CCT-programmes (together with electoral concerns and technical advice); not all aspects however can be thought out before implementation. According to economists, the weakness of CCTs is their focus on the supply side: it has effects on only consumption, not production (Farrington and Slater

2006), provoking widely disparate reactions and raising a number of political, financial and operational challenges for governments, donors and NGOs.[14] Lomeli (2008) adds that reforms are needed so that state institutions have to provide basic public services. Ghosh (2011) acknowledges the potential positive aspects of CCTs, but argues that they should not work as replacements for public services. CCTs fight some key symptoms of poverty, but obscure the attention to structural and multidimensional social economic, cultural and political drivers of poverty.

In relation to education support, there is no attention given to the quality issues inherent in education and school facilities.[15] Sending children to school does not help much if the schools are substandard, if teachers are absent, poorly motivated, of low quality and poorly paid. Schooling can also reproduce (class) inequalities and class differences (Bourdieu 1986; Willmott 1999). The same criticism can be extended to the focus on health and nutrition. There are deeply rooted and persistent ideas that healthy, well-fed children learn better (see for instance UNICEF 2019), but these improvements do not help much if schools remain substandard.

Finally, although CCTs have been extensively reviewed, not much is known about the context in which programmes are implemented, the interactions and mediation processes of policy implementation in different cultural contexts, or the specific conjuncture of adoption and interpretation at local levels. Ramirez (2016) points to the importance of the relationship between front-line officers and participants in the Oportunidades/Prospera programme in Mexico. However, in Indonesia, there is little literature on the relations between the officials who run programmes locally and the participants in the programmes, and therefore little feedback on the well-being of the participants. The appeal and persistence of these ideas may blind policymakers to the potential social and economic limitations of CCT-programmes, such as structural sources of inequality and intra-community tensions. CCTs may depoliticise social problems of poverty and inequality (Ferguson 2015). With these diverse critical commentaries in mind, we turn to a description of our field experiences in central Java.

Programme Outcomes at District and Village Level: The Case of Sriharjo[16]

In Sriharjo (central Java), one of the eight villages (*desa*) of Imogiri sub-district, 23 per cent of all households received PKH in 2018 (see Table 12.1). This translates as 14 per cent of all PKH recipients in Imogiri. This relatively high number fits with the size of the village and its poverty levels. Sriharjo is a large *desa* with 9,467 inhabitants (2018) and consists of 13 neighbourhoods or sub-villages. Desa Sriharjo combines fertile, productive rice plains with dryland areas, which are the poorest sections of Imogiri subdistrict. The case study areas—the sub-villages of Kedung Miri and Sompok—are situated in the poorer, eastern part of Sriharjo.

Table 12.1   Number of recipients of PKH in Imogiri subdistrict, April 2018 (DepSos Kabupaten Bantul)

	Number of recipient households	Percentage of all recipients in Kec. Imogiri
Girirejo	258	6%
Imogiri	234	5.4%
Karang Tengah	420	9.8%
Karangtalun	241	5.6%
Kebon Agung	341	7.9%
Selopamioro	1012	23.5%
Sriharjo	602	14%
Wukirsari	1192	27.7%

In 2018, rural poverty was roughly 12 per cent in Central Java province and 13 per cent in the special region of Yogyakarta (BPS 2020). Regional poverty in Bantul district declined from 17.3 per cent in 2011 to 12.9 per cent in 2019 (BPS 2019). The official poverty rate in Sriharjo in 2018 was 13.7 per cent. Sriharjo typically takes a middle position in terms of socio-economic and ecological conditions. The centre of the village lies in the western part of Sriharjo, close to the main road, and is well connected to Yogyakarta. The western part has fertile rice plains and densely populated *kampung*; its poverty levels are equal to the average of Bantul district (comparable to average poverty rates of rural Yogyakarta and rural central Java). Western Sriharjo residents call themselves *wong ngare*, lowland people, while people from the east are known as *wong gunung*, mountain people. These are deeply rooted stereotypes; the latter, *wong gunung* comes with connotations of being backward, poor, less refined, syncretist and traditional. They have fewer rice fields, infertile drylands and higher poverty levels (see Chapter 4 [Figure 4.1]).

While 23 per cent of all families in Sriharjo received PKH in 2018, this varied by sub-village; in Sompok, the poorest sub-village of Sriharjo, 34 per cent of all households received the assistance. Percentages of villagers in Kedung Miri were almost the same as those in Sompok.[17]

Organisation of PKH

The PKH programme in Sriharjo is a replication of the national, and subsequently international, model. Selected families receive IDR 2.0 million (2019) in four instalments of IDR 450,000 every three months on a special account that can be accessed by an ATM. Conditionalities are school participation, regular check-ups at the health clinic and taking part in meetings focused on the development of family skills. PKH officials (*pendamping*) check if conditionalities are met. They are also available for consultation, sometimes give information on available government credit programmes for business development (KUBE) and they organise the family skills development workshops. Over the years, these *pendamping* have become influential figures, as they can get names off the list of recipients—in 2019, they were authorised to list new names.

Local beneficiaries of welfare payments are selected through the complex statistical analysis undertaken at the national level. Lists of approved beneficiaries are then conveyed to civil servants from the Department of Social Affairs at the district level (*kabupaten* Bantul), who approach the beneficiaries directly and, in the process, bypass subdistrict and lower levels of government. In Sriharjo, as discussed above, village officials no longer have a role in or influence over government social welfare programmes and they cannot decide who should be a beneficiary. This remains a continuing source of complaint and resentment as will be explored in the next section.

Programme Implementation at Sriharjo

Programme Problems

In Sompok and Kedung Miri, many problems are reported around the organisation, targeting and execution of the PKH programme. Contrary to previous social programmes and the rice distribution (Raskin) programme which are channelled from the centre into the villages through hierarchical networks of control, PKH data come straight from the social department at the *kabupaten* (district) level. Village officials, no longer authorised to participate in the beneficiary selection, complain that the Departemen Sosial (DepSos) field staff do not have the time, capacity or skills to survey large numbers of households and undertake a proper data analysis. Local officials feel incapable of resolving the social unrest occurring within their communities due to the perceived welfare payment mistargeting problems.

To study and understand the local effects of targeting, we assessed local ideas of poverty by using Krishna's Stages of Progress (SoP) methodology

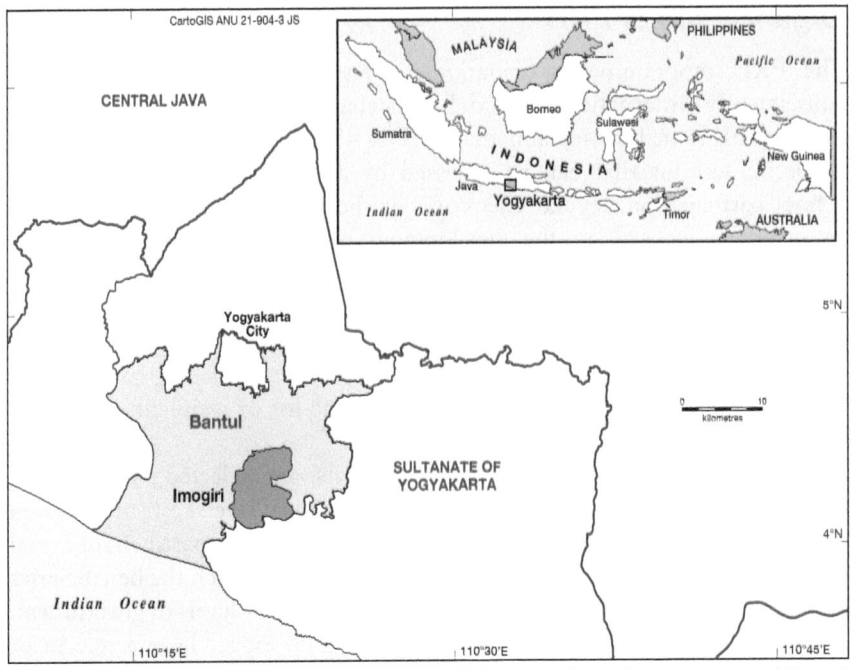

Figure 12.1 Map of Kecamatan Bantul. Sriharjo village lies in the middle of subdistrict Imogiri

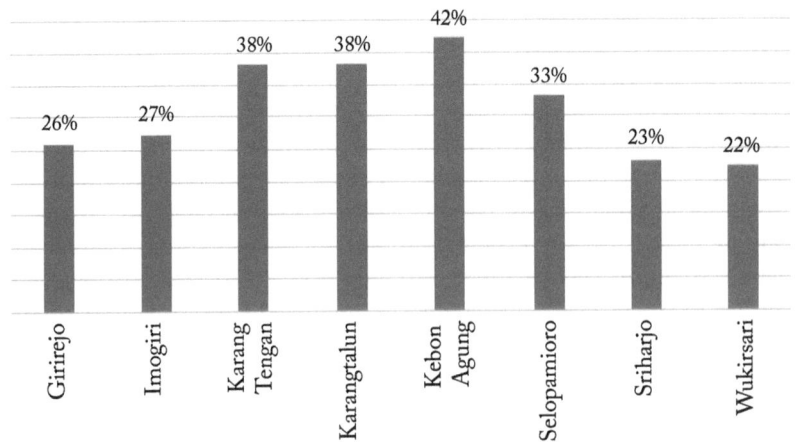

Figure 12.2 Percentage of households per village receiving PKH in Imogiri, 2018
Source: BPS Kabupaten Bantul, kecamatan Imogiri.

(2006). In Sompok and Kedung Miri, we executed four wealth ranking exercises, one in each neighbourhood (Rukun Tetangga [RT]). In addition, we surveyed 20 per cent of households (N = 160). Kedung Miri was surveyed in 2016[18] and Sompok in 2018. In each selected household, the household head (husband or wife),[19] was interviewed. For the purpose of the analysis in this chapter, we assessed poverty levels and potential PKH recipients based on the SoP and the household survey (Table 12.2; related discussion is given in Chapter 4 [Table 4.2]). In Sompok, about one quarter of the villagers was defined as poor according to local standards as formulated in the SoP. These households were, according to local poverty standards, all eligible as PKH recipients as they had low incomes, poor health, poor diets, low income earning capacity and no or almost no assets such as land, cattle or a motor cycle. Age and the ability to earn money in the city remain important criteria for being seen as poor or otherwise. The average age of those seen as poor is 65.5 years old, while the non-poor are on average 48.4 years. Among the poor, almost no-one worked in the city for a wage.

We found that the programme aided only 44 per cent of the potential PKH recipients. Of the non-poor and specifically the category just above the poverty cut off one third (23 per cent of the total number of households) did receive PKH benefits. While the PKH programme does not explicitly aim to assist the nutritionally insecure, approximately 60 per cent of the PKH recipients were food secure and not especially poor, according to our wealth ranking exercise and food security surveys. However, only half of the severely food insecure households received PKH, suggesting that the distribution missed many households (the poorest of the poor), in addition to reaching only a third of the moderately food insecure. The proxy means testing thus failed, to a large extent, to identify the neediest households.

Table 12.2 Poverty ranking and categorisation of livelihood change per household between 1999 and 2018 in Sriharjo (SoP)

Category	Percentage
A Poor then and still poor (*poor*)	25
B Poor then, not poor now (*improved*)	65
C Not poor then, poor now (*new poor*)	2
D Not poor then, not poor now (*rich*)	8

In Figure 12.3, we first look at the percentage of the population receiving Raskin (PBNT); this is followed by details of PKH recipients (Figures 12.4 and 12.5).

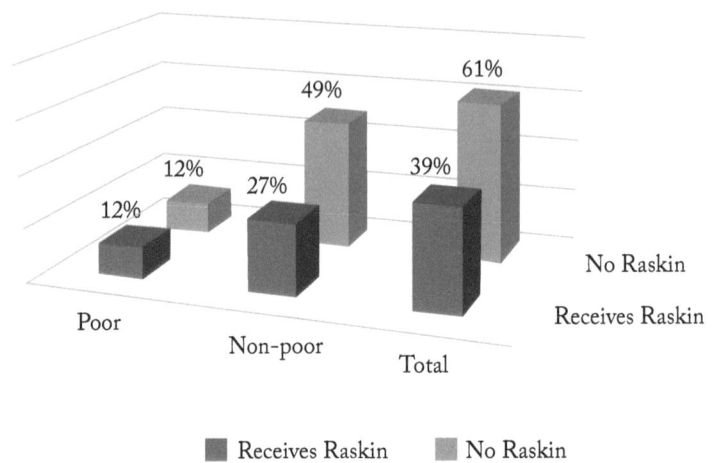

Figure 12.3   Percentages of poor and non-poor receiving Raskin (PBNT) in Sompok
Source: 2018 survey.

Recipients receive a debit card enabling them to buy rice and/or eggs at the local *e-warung*. Often, the rice received is shared with neighbours or families, as such sharing is part of an important ethic in the village (see Kutanegara and Nooteboom [2002] for the cultural importance of *bagi rata*, equal sharing of government dole outs, in Sriharjo). In Sompok, in 2018, 39 per cent of the population received Raskin (PBNT), which officially should amount to IDR 150,000 in rice per month. Half the poor, and a third of the non-poor, received Raskin. On average, each receiving household reported only IDR 110,000 worth of rice per month that year, which was consistent with previous years. The average age of those receiving Raskin was 67.4 for the poor, and 63.6 for the non-poor.

In Sriharjo, 34 per cent of the population received PKH assistance; only a third of total PKH money flowing into the village reached the poor. Only 41 per cent of the poor received PKH, while 32 per cent of the non-poor also received PKH. 59 per cent of the poor did not receive PKH assistance, although they should receive it according to local standards defined in the SoP. 37 per cent of the poor did not receive any anti-poverty benefit at all.[20] This means that the mismatch in targeting in both Raskin and PKH is tremendous, when compared to the local understanding of poverty. This turned out to be a major source of dissatisfaction and tension among villagers.

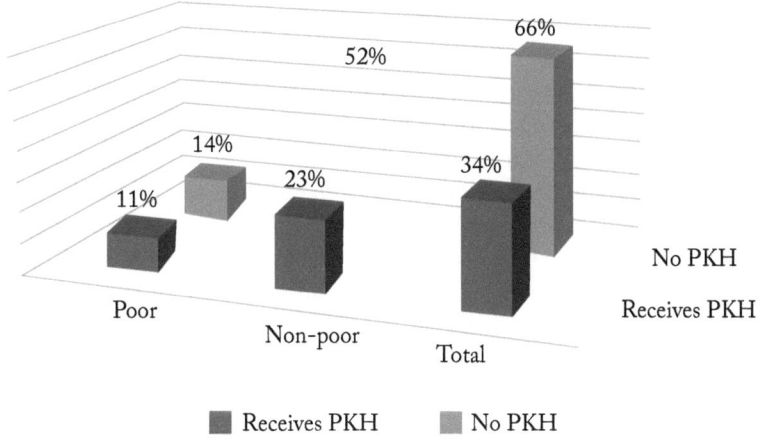

Figure 12.4   Percentages of poor and non-poor receiving PKH in Sompok
Source: 2018 survey.

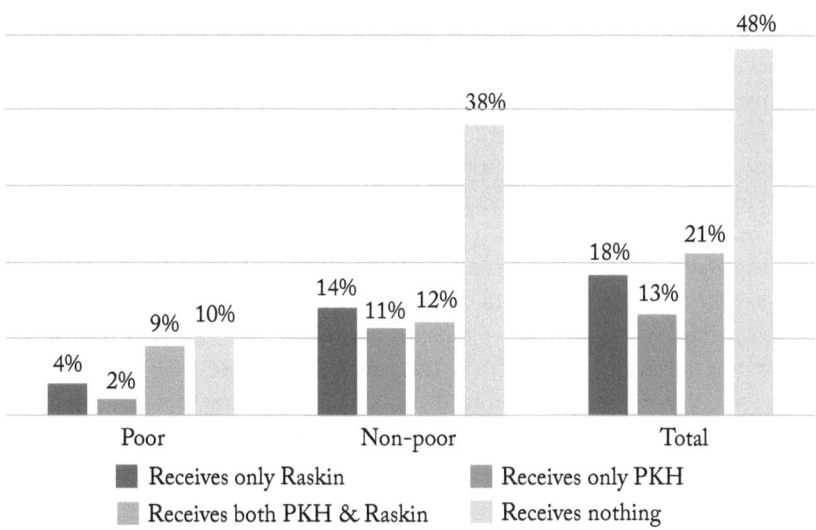

Figure 12.5   Recipients of Raskin and PKH as percentage of total population of Sriharjo
Source: 2018 survey.

Experiences on the Ground

In general, the recipients of PKH are very positive about the programme. From the recipient's perspective, it is a lot of money. People who get PKH mostly also get BPNT, but those who receive BPNT do not necessary get PKH. While BPNT is seen as bonus in the eyes of those who receive PKH benefits, this programme really addresses some of their key problems: lack of income, purchasing power for the elderly and help in the costs of schooling. Data from our earlier village surveys in Sriharjo show that children and especially boys often drop out of school to help earn money. Also, children of poor parents often do not want to go to school; children of poor households sometimes cannot afford uniforms, pencils and money for snacks. The hope is that this will change with programme support. Indeed, according to parents and teachers, school dropout rates have declined substantially since the programme's introduction. Unfortunately, the quality of many schools in rural areas remains substandard, even as the quality of education in Sriharjo is clearly rising.

Villagers try to become part of BPNT, and especially PKH, by any means; they have become very sensitive to surveys in the village. One interviewed beneficiary mentioned: "This money is very important, in the first place to send my child to school [she has three children]. But the money is also used for other things which are needed in the household such as food and clothing". In some cases, however, the support from PBNT and Raskin is felt to be superfluous: "I receive rice and eggs, but for what? We have them already". Some of the poor benefit from multiple programmes. Their food lifestyles have improved a great deal. Respondents said: "It releases stress, but it does not substitute income from work"; "It is not enough, but it helps". People with PKH continue working, and we did not encounter nor find indications that the support induced "laziness". At the same time, those who receive PKH have become very dependent on it. "I cannot imagine how to make ends meet without this support", one beneficiary commented.

The programmes are intended to last three years. After that, families are supposed to be able to stand on their own feet. If they improve their living conditions prior to the end of the programme, they are supposed to leave it earlier. According to a PKH official in Imogiri, only a minimal 3–4 per cent of the beneficiaries in Sriharjo have worked themselves out of poverty and become exempt from the programme because of their success.

People also feel "safer" and "secure" because of PKH, and a couple of informants said they have gained self-confidence (*lebih percaya diri*). This increased confidence was visible in their consumption and spending behaviour, as they spent more money on food, eggs, vegetables and chicken than in the past. PKH recipients also took on more debt. As a couple of informants said: "We dare to take debts now and we have more courage to look people in the face" (*Lebih berani untuk berhutang, lebih berani melihat orang*). This is recognised by local shopkeepers, who told us that PKH enables recipients to take on more credit. The *warung* (local shop/stall) owners know who receives PKH and who does not, and they perceive PKH recipients as safer for credit. "They have something in the back. We can feel it. They gain self-esteem from PKH. They have better lifestyles. If villagers have PKH, they are good now" (*Mereka punja sesuatu di belakang. Sangat terasa. Dapat PKH, lebih berani, lebih gaya. Gaya mereka lebih baik. Kalau dapat PKH, dia enak*).

Distance does matter though. Since 2018, the PKH money and the PBNT rice need to be collected at an ATM and an e-warung, respectively, far from the village. Since 2018, the PBNT money can be spent only at specific shops, namely the e-warung. Sriharjo has only one e-warung, which is about 8–10 km away from Sompok and Kedung Miri. For villagers without a (motor)bike, and for the elderly, this can be a large burden. They have to ask others to go the e-warung and buy rice or food items for them, or go to the ATM to get the money. A villager told us that "Often, they need to pay a percentage of the money in return for the service (*potongan*), and in some sub-villages, the heads tried to collect a local tax from PKH beneficiaries". When we crosschecked, we came across *potongan* rates of sometimes 10 to 20 per cent to be paid to the person who collects the money, or to heads of the sub-village.[21] Sometimes, the e-warung is out of stock and another trip is needed. The e-warung of Sriharjo must prepare rice and food items for more than 100 households. They also must go far to transport the rice from the Bulog warehouse, but the e-warung is thriving; it makes large profits from the programme.

Rising Tensions and Dissatisfaction

As a result of the PKH programme, tensions and social dissatisfaction in Sriharjo have been rising. Since the beginning of 2018, the programme has been enlarged; this becomes visible at the village level. People talk a lot about the programmes and especially about the "mysterious" (mis)targeting. The inclusion of better-off households has led to gossip, jealousies and conflict, and local community leaders express their frustration at not being able to correct the data collection. The social distinction between those who receive benefits and those who do not is not fair and consequently people who are "near poor" feel disenfranchised.

PKH programmes are seen as individualistic and not (always) a good cultural fit. The money comes directly to the account, making it less visible and open to demands for sharing. People who do not have the programme are jealous, because in the past they shared the money. Now it is more individual, because it is hidden money and can be spent individually.

Village officials in particular are not happy with the programme. They complained about it each time we visited them. They do not know who receives benefits, what the procedure is, or how to propose changes to the recipient list, such as new names. Villagers come to them complaining about not getting their payments, or to ask for help accessing the programme, which the village officials cannot do. They feel bypassed and overlooked. In the past, officials knew exactly who received government aid. Now they have lost control and power as well as influence over village affairs and social welfare, at the expense of the new PKH officials. This damages their power base and has an impact on village and national elections as rural voters are increasingly resistant to influence.

In 2016, our research informants often talked about delays in payments. This caused considerable extra work and sometimes major extra costs for the beneficiaries. One informant told us that a woman had to call her husband who works on a construction project in Kota Gede (40 km away). He took his wife to the bank and helped organise the money. His daily wage is IDR 80,000 (USD5.9) and he lost a day's wages to secure her payment. Since 2018, the 3-monthly transfers have arrived more regularly, and financial services have become more reliable. Nevertheless, delays cause panic and feelings of insecurity. "A delay can be for several reasons and I start to worry about it. Maybe I missed a meeting at the local health post (*posyandu*), maybe my baby was not weighed or the score was not noted down, maybe my child missed too many days at school, or the bank made a mistake". Recipients often know when the money is coming and inform each other. "They have their own WhatsApp group", a PKH official informed us.

Conditionality and the Role of Officials

The spending of the CCT money is often not as free as in other global CCT programmes. In rural Indonesia, over the years, conditionality has become tighter and the PKH officials (*pendamping*), often from middle class families, have become more paternalistic about how to behave. There are moral and social pressures on *pendamping* to improve and shape the lives of the poor according to middle-class values. Conditionality is an important element of the PKH programme and *pendamping* play a key part in the process. While these officials are unable to include new people on the list of beneficiaries, since 2019 they have been able to nominate new names to replace beneficiaries who no longer meet the criteria. Most of their power, however, turns on their capacity to delete names from the list.

Beneficiaries are divided into groups of about 30 households. One official is responsible for about 300 households and officially needs to visit all of them every three months to assess whether the people in their group still meet the conditions. The checks concern issues such as: if the beneficiaries are attending the health check programme (*posyandu*), if children are going to school and if their grades are improving. Imogiri has 14 Departemen Sosial (DepSos) field staff, of whom 12 are female and only two are situated in Sriharjo. Some officials take their role less seriously and only check numbers from schools and health posts. Others try to empower and help recipients to improve their lives. Some are rather passive, while others regularly organise monthly Family Development Sessions where knowledge, skills and values are transferred. Some officials even check receipts to see if recipients spend their funds in the right way, such as on shoes for children, healthy food and milk powder. According to some recipients, officials can be quite pushy, including urging higher grades from the children; in this way, they go well beyond the intended goals of the health and educational conditionalities. Moreover, they take away agency from poor people, a key element in the positive literature about CCT programmes.

If parents do not fulfil the conditions, funds can be held back. If the situation does not improve, beneficiaries can be dropped off the beneficiary list. According to the coordinator of officials in the city of Yogyakarta, 300 beneficiaries—out of 11,000—had been removed from the list for transgressive behaviour, such as parents/fathers who drink and/or spend money on alcohol or drugs, situations of domestic violence, parents who are absent and regularly leave children with a grandmother or grandparents, or children who are truant.[22]

However, there is a great variation between officials in terms of commitment to PKH beneficiaries. In Sriharjo, for instance, one official helped a woman to start her own business as a food seller and created a website for her. She used her first cash transfer to buy food and equipment to start her food stall. Now she makes so much money that she is no longer eligible for support and does not need the programme's money. Other officials become brokers of information and knowledge, help to fix technical problems, and offer advice on accessing other programmes and support, such as health clinics (to arrange a hospital bed), or (family) counselling. Some become real brokers of money, information and power. One official told us confidently that he would certainly be elected to the local government if he became a candidate in the next election.

Three officials quit their job in the first year because they found their work too demanding, with all the commitments they are expected to fulfil. The work is seen as emotionally difficult, the poverty problems are extensive and complex, beneficiaries are often much older than the official and cutting allowances is a complex and emotionally challenging decision. Many officials are recruited locally and it is hard for them to be strict with people in their community. "I cannot advise the department to throw out my own neighbour from the programme", an official commented. Due to the workload and expectations of the positions, the field staff find the work stressful and often leave the occupation if they can get something better. In addition to the other stressors, the officials are contract workers and the status of the job is not particularly high and offers limited career prospects. Moreover, although many officials have backgrounds in languages, agriculture and even ICT, they are generally not trained social workers and often lack the necessary communication skills, conflict resolution skills and sometimes empathy. They also bring in their own—sometimes biased—ideas about poor people, and can adopt patronising attitudes and patron-like status for poor clients.

Analysis and Conclusions

Over the last decade, the government of Indonesia has embarked on large social projects to fight poverty. Many of these programmes focus on health, school education and social assistance to the poor. The programmes are based on travelling policy models and are accompanied by technologies of measurement, implementation and evaluation. Although the programmes appear politically neutral, they obscure complex political dimensions (growing inequality) on the ground and produce paradoxical social effects (conflicts, self-blame and disciplinary measures for the poor), as they reveal implicit assumptions about the nature of poverty, governability and (market-based) solutions. These aspects have become visible in this study.

The programmes also produce multiple unintended consequences on the ground such as social unrest and jealousy; a general weakening of local leadership and governance structures; materialistic, individualised and income-focused poverty thinking; weakening social welfare and solidarity at the village level; depoliticisation of poverty and inequality; a focus on consumption and income, and a neglect of production and redistribution at the local level.

As a policy model, the PKH programme obscures the political and structural dimensions of inequality and poverty, by rendering developmental problems into technical issues. As such, Indonesian social policies reflect dominant ideas and technologies from mainstream development thinking propagated by global development agencies today. These ideas favour decentralised, efficient, pro-poor and market-based solutions. They also come with specific technologies of implementation, including targeting, statistical algorithms and distributions. Social issues such as inequality, social justice and the redistribution of wealth are rendered technical in the process of targeting and implementation.

The PKH programme in Indonesia is a good example of how global development models travel in an increasingly multi-polar world. Although these programmes are pushed as a new and neutral model for social policy, political reasons for adoption are just as important as the drivers and donors behind these programmes. The travelling CCT model thus challenges traditional North–South thinking, where developmental ideas do not typically travel from North to South only (CCTs travel from South to South), but are also actively sought and adopted by governments in the South. However, the technicalities of the PKH programme, such as the proxy means testing and specific politics of knowledge, very much follow the CCT global blueprint. PKH has all the elements that the global model prescribes: a focus on women and children; conditionalities for education, health checks and nutrition; maternity care, and even the additional package of mandatory family development meetings—all embedded in a wider scheme of social welfare programmes. A further comparison shows similarities in the technicalities of targeting (and the inherent mismatches) and popularity and support of the CCT idea among (populist) political leaders who expect electoral benefits and bureaucratic reforms—all embedded in the opaque, neoliberal, idea of making people independent actors who take responsibility for their own future.

While technologies of implementation, targeting and measurement travel alongside the policy models, these technologies lead to specific local outcomes. In the case of the proxy means test, for instance, the simplified and technological way of measuring poverty based on large datasets leads to an enormous mismatch in identifying the poor and needy. Experiences on the ground demonstrate that faith in centralised, quantitative data methods can lead to serious mistakes in targeting. The result is the familiar refrain that many poor families are excluded from the programme even though they are poor and food insecure, but better off neighbours are included. Some neighbourhoods receive much more help than others, leading to resentment and acrimony. But, by excluding local leaders from the process, the complaints of villagers can be addressed neither by village leaders nor by government officials at local levels and the lack of effective feedback and timely reporting mechanisms appears to be a major weakness of programme implementation.

CCTs can be a solution for the consequences of poverty, rather than the causes. CCTs treat the symptoms of poverty only, thus obscuring the structural and multi-dimensional drivers of inequality and poverty in Indonesia. Many CCT programmes are financially unsustainable (Leisering 2009), but in Indonesia, due to the electoral benefits in (presidential elections) and the COVID-19 pandemic, CCTs are likely to stay.

In this chapter, we have studied the local and national impacts of travelling global poverty eradication ideas and their accompanying technologies. We argue that a specific politics of knowledge underpins the CCT methodology, generating high inclusion and exclusion errors. This system is yet to meet local expectations of shared benefits even as it weakens local social cohesion. It also generates a complex and messy politics of distribution in many areas of rural Indonesia. We note that the Social Protection Programme (SPP) system could provide a cash floor on which most marginal people could depend. However, at present the CCT system involves gross simplifications of poverty, which serve immediate political interests more than the long-term interests of the poor.

Our analysis suggests that the structural forms of poverty will be softened by social protection, but structural inequality will not be changed as a result of these policies. We see this at work through depoliticising technologies such as the proxy means test, (e)banking for the poor, and the household lifeskills workshops. All these obscure the structural (and political) dimensions of poverty. This raises the question of whether these approaches are suited to deal with the entrenched dimensions of poverty. Despite the contributions that CCTs schemes make to helping some of the poor and to reducing poverty headcounts, we find that agrarian-based forms of poverty, food insecurity and precarity may well persist unless other far-reaching strategic changes are also deployed.

Acknowledgements

Fieldwork for this research was made possible by the Australian Research Council, the Netherlands Organisation of Scientific Research (NWO-Wotro) and by travel grants from the Moving Matters Research Group (MoMat) of the University of Amsterdam. We warmly thank Monika Swastyastu for Javanese translations and for assisting and coordinating the survey in the field. The research would not have been possible without the help of students and research assistants from the University of Amsterdam (UvA) and Universitas Gadjah Mada, Yogyakarta: Merel van Andel, Caroline Astipranatari, Evi Gusti, Galeh Prabowo, Aditya Rizki Pratama and Monika Swastyastu. Last but not the least, we would like to thank all informants and villagers who so kindly welcomed us and cooperated in this study.

Notes

[1] The *Program Keluarga Harapan*, the hope for families programme.

[2] The study is based on an extensive literature review of conditional cash transfers and on fieldwork between 2016 and 2018 in Sriharjo.

[3] The JKN, the *Jaminan Kesehatan Nasional* or *Jamkesnas* (National Health Insurance Scheme) has been administered by the BPJS, the *Badan Penyelenggara Jaminan Sosial* (the government body of Social Insurance Administration) since 2011. The BPJS consists of two programmes: the BPJS *Ketanagakerjaan*, the former formal sector insurance (*Jamsostek*) for employees; and of the newly formed BPJS *Kesehatan*, simply called KIS (*Kartu Indonesia Sehat)* (Indonesian Health Card), which aims to cover all self-employed, informal sector workers as well as the poor.

[4] The *Kartu Indonesia Pintar* (KIP) (Smart Indonesia Card) guarantees that all school-aged children from disadvantaged families receive financial assistance for education up to high school/vocational school.

[5] The food programmes consist of monthly rice donations of 10kg for poor families, known as *Rastra* (*Beras untuk keluarga sejahtera*) (rice for family welfare), previously called *Raskin* (*beras miskin*) (rice for the poor – or poor rice) and BPNT (*Bantuan Pangan Non-Tunai*) non-cash food assistance (usually non-rice food aid such as eggs, flour or cooking oil). The semantics of programme name-giving and changing are significant. They often carry an optimistic, political and family-focused message.

[6] Since 2018, the cash has been distributed by banks and made available on a bank card which can be used only in certain shops, the so-called *e-warung* referring to the electronic payment.

[7] For elderly or poor families without children, conditions comprise regular visits to health facilities and joining meetings around the distribution of food supplements and family development skills.

[8] This expectation is highly problematic both empirically as theoretically, as we will see later.

[9] At the same time, conditionalities can also become problematic as avenues for new forms of paternalisation, stigmatisation and inequality through the (unconscious) reproduction of ideas about the poor being dirty, lazy and unsuited to enter modern society on their own.

[10] Februany (personal communication): "there was a lot of criticism of BLT, which was seen as a strategy to quickly win votes". According to Februany, the PKH programme was politically even more attractive. Kwon and Kim reflect: "The government intended to introduce CCTs for some time because they knew those programmes would be politically popular. Nevertheless, it would take time to develop the necessary administrative systems, so they introduced a smaller scale of UCTs first, which did not require sophisticated administrative set-ups" (2015: 433).

[11] PSE ([*Pendapatan Social Ekonomi*], Social economic data collection).

[12] Since Jokowi's presidency, starting in 2014, this process has continued, and all social welfare and anti-poverty programmes are now administered by the department of social welfare, with strong Presidential oversight.

[13] *Tim Nasional Percepatan Penanggulangan Kemiskinan* (The National Team for the Acceleration of Poverty Reduction).
[14] See, for instance, Leisering (2009) on conditionality being counter-productive.
[15] Papadopoulos and Leyer (2016) emphasise the lack of infrastructure for schooling in many countries.
[16] Sriharjo is part of Imogiri subdistrict, Bantul. Background information on Sriharjo can be found in some of our previous publications: Singarimbun and Penny (1973); Kutanegara (2017); Singarimbun (1996); Nooteboom and Kutanegara (2003); Kutanegara and Nooteboom (2002) and Indiyanto et al. (2006).
[17] Comparable figures on PKH coverage in Kedung Miri are missing as the village was surveyed in 2016 and revisited only in 2018.
[18] This turned out to be problematic for comparison, and Kedung Miri has been left out of the statistical analysis. In 2016, the PKH programme had not been rolled out completely in Kedung Miri and the name of the programme was very unclear to people, who confused it with BLT. Also, the conditionalities were unclear or people were completely unaware of them. In 2018 and 2019, qualitative fieldwork was undertaken in both villages, and these data were used in the description and interpretation of the findings.
[19] In total, one third of the informants was female, and two thirds were men.
[20] It should be noted, however, that the line of calibration between poor and non-poor in Sriharjo is fine. Many villagers live just above the poverty line.
[21] During fieldwork we gathered stories from villagers about cards pawned to money lenders in return for a cash advance. We received several reports of people who organised collecting funds in groups and of brokers who sourced the money for elderly people. Of course, these services are rarely free and beneficiaries are expected to pay transportation costs and food and/or cigarettes. In 2016, in Kedung Miri, heads of hamlets also asked for a percentage of the money as a contribution to the village community. Also, other villages mentioned other levelling mechanisms and social taxes to skim incomes from individual beneficiaries.
[22] Research in the villages showed that very few people were actually taken off the list.

References

Aspinall, E. 2010. "Indonesia in 2009: Democratic Triumphs and Trials", *Southeast Asian Affairs 2010*, ed. Daljit Singh. Singapore: ISEAS Publishing, pp. 103–25.

Barrientos, A. 2007. "Understanding Conditions in Income Transfer Programmes: A Brief(est) Note", *IDS Bulletin* 38, 3: 66–8. doi:10.1111/j.1759-5436.2007.tb00380.x.

Barrientos, A. and J. DeJong. 2006. "Reducing Child Poverty With Cash Transfers: A Sure Thing?" *Development Policy Review* 24, 5: 537–52. doi:10.1111/j.1467-7679.2006.00346.x.

Bourdieu, P. 1986. "The Forms of Capital", in *Handbook of Theory and Research for the Sociology of Education*, ed. J. Richardson. New York: Greenwood Press, pp. 241–58.

BPS (Badan Pusat Statistik). 2019. Kabupaten Bantul, kecamatan Imogiri. Available at www.bantulkab.bps.go.id (accessed 11 June 2022).

Farrington, J. and R. Slater. 2006. "Introduction: Cash Transfers: Panacea for Poverty Reduction or Money Down the Drain?" *Development Policy Review* 24, 5: 499–511. doi:10.1111/j.1467-7679.2006.00344.x.

Feitosa de Britto, T. 2004. "Conditional Cash Transfers: Why Have They Become so Prominent in Recent Poverty Reduction Strategies in Latin America?" *ORPAS - Institute of Social Studies*, no. 390: 61.

Ferguson, J. 2015. *Give a Man a Fish: Reflections on the New Politics of Distribution.* Durham, NC and London: Duke University Press.

Fernald, L.C.H., P.J. Gertler and L.M. Neufeld. 2008. "Role of Cash in Conditional Cash Transfer Programmes for Child Health, Growth, and Development: An Analysis of Mexico's Oportunidades", *The Lancet* 371 (9615): 828–37. doi:10.1016/S0140-6736(08)60382-7.

Gabel, S.G. and S.B. Kamerman. 2013. "Conditional Cash Transfers (CCTs): A Child Policy Strategy in Asia", in *Economic Stress, Human Capital, and Families in Asia*, ed. W.-J. J. Yeung and M.T. Yap. Dordrecht: Springer, pp. 197–220.

Gardner, K. and D. Lewis. 2015. *Anthropology and Development: Challenges for the Twenty-First Century*. London: Pluto Press.

Ghosh, J. 2011. "Cash Transfers as the Silver Bullet for Poverty Reduction: A Sceptical Note", *Economic and Political Weekly* xlvi (21): 67–71.

Glewwe, P. and E.A. Miguel. 2007. "The Impact of Child Health and Nutrition on Education in Less Developed Countries", *Handbook of Development Economics* 4: 3561–606.

Gliszczynski, M. von. 2016. "Social Protection and Basic Income in Global Policy", *Global Social Policy: 2015–7*. doi:10.1177/1468018116676706.

Gliszczynski, M. von and L. Leisering. 2016. "Constructing New Global Models of Social Security: How International Organizations Defined the Field of Social Cash Transfers in the 2000s", *Journal of Social Policy* 45, 2: 325–43. doi:10.1017/S0047279415000720.

Hunter, W. and D.S. Brown. 2000. "World Bank Directives, Domestic Interests, and the Politics of Human Capital Investment in Latin America", *Comparative Political Studies* 33, 1: 113–43. doi:10.1177/0010414000033001005.

Indiyanto, A. et al. 2006. "Close Encounters and Distant Violence: Local Experiences of Indonesia's 'Total Crisis'", in *Indonesian Transitions*, ed. H. Schulte-Nordholt and I. Hoogenboom. Yogyakarta: Pustaka Pelajar, pp 23–74.

Kidd, S., B. Gilders and D. Bailey-Athias. 2017. *Exclusion by Design: An Assessment of the Effectiveness of the Proxy Means Test Poverty Targeting Mechanism*. Geneva: International Labour Office.

Koning, J.B.M. and F. Hüsken. 2006. *Ropewalking and Safetynets: Local Ways of Managing Insecurity in Indonesia*. Leiden: Brill.

Krishna, A. 2006. "Pathways Out of and Into Poverty in 36 Villages of Andhra Pradesh, India", *World Development* 34: 271–88.

Kutanegara, P.M. 2017. *Social Security in Sriharjo, Central Java*. Nijmegen: University of Nijmegen, Department of Anthropology.

Kutanegara, P.M. and G. Nooteboom. 2002. "Forgotten Villages, the Effects of the Crisis and the Role of the Government in Rural Java", in *Riding a Tiger. Decentralisation and Regionalisation in Indonesia*, ed. C. Holtzappel, M. Sanders and M. Titus. Amsterdam: Rozenberg Publishers, pp. 248–77.

Kwon H. and Kim W. 2015. "The Evolution of Cash Transfers in Indonesia: Policy Transfer and National Adaptation", *Asia & the Pacific Policy Studies* 2, 2: 425–40. doi:10.1002/app5.83.

Leisering, L. 2009. "Extending Social Security to the Excluded: Are Social Cash Transfers to the Poor an Appropriate Way of Fighting Poverty in Developing Countries?" *Global Social Policy* 9, 2: 246–72. doi:10.1177/1468018109104628.

Lomelí, E.V. 2008. "Conditional Cash Transfers as Social Policy in Latin America: An Assessment of Their Contributions and Limitations", *Annual Review of Sociology* 34, 1: 475–99. doi:10.1146/annurev.soc.34.040507.134537.

_____. 2009. "Conditional Cash Transfer Programs: Achievements and Illusions", *Global Social Policy* 9, 2: 167–71.

McCarthy, J. and M. Sumarto. 2018. "Distributional Politics and Social Protection in Indonesia: Dilemma of Layering, Nesting and Social Fit in Jokowi's Poverty Policy", *Journal of Southeast Asian Economies* 35, 2: 223–36. doi: 10.1355/ae35-2g.

Medrano, A. 2016. "CCTs for Female Heads of Households and Market Citizenship at State-Level in Mexico", *Social Policy and Society* 15, 3: 495–507. doi:10.1017/S1474746416000099.

Nagels, N. 2016. "The Social Investment Perspective, Conditional Cash Transfer Programmes and the Welfare Mix: Peru and Bolivia", *Social Policy and Society* 15, 3: 479–93. doi:10.1017/S1474746416000105.

Nooteboom, G. and P.M. Kutanegara. 2003. "The Storm Will Soon Be Over? Winners and Losers during the Economic Crisis in Java", *Moussons* 6: 3–36.

Nooteboom, G. and M. Rutten. 2012. "Magic Bullets in Development: Assumptions, Teleology and the Popularity of Three Solutions to End Poverty", in *Re-integrating Technology and Economy in Human Life and Society: Proceedings of the 17th Annual Working Conference of the IIDE, Maarssen, May 2011. Vol. I*, ed. L. Botes, R. Jongeneel and S. Strijbos. Maarssen: IIDE, pp. 103–20.

Papadopoulos, T. and R.V. Leyer. 2016. "Two Decades of Social Investment in Latin America: Outcomes, Shortcomings and Achievements of Conditional

Cash Transfers", *Social Policy and Society* 15, 3: 435–49. doi:10.1017/S1474746416000117.

Purwoko, B. 2009. "Social Protection Rebuilding in Indonesia: Process and Challenges", *Paper Presented on GTZ Conference of Growth Quality on Social Protection Systems Held in New Delhi 2009.* Conference proceedings, pp. 14–8.

Ramírez, V. 2016. "CCTs Through a Wellbeing Lens: The Importance of the Relationship Between Front-Line Officers and Participants in the Oportunidades/Prospera Programme in Mexico", *Social Policy and Society* 15, 3: 451–64. doi:10.1017/S1474746416000129.

Shibuya, K. 2008. "Conditional Cash Transfer: A Magic Bullet for Health?" *The Lancet* 371 (issue 9615): 789–91. doi:10.1016/S0140-6736(08)60356-6.

Singarimbun, M. 1996. "Peluang Kerja Dan Kemiskinan Di Miri Sriharjo", *Penduduk Dan Perubahan.* Yogyakarta: Pustaka Pelajar.

Singarimbun, M. and D. Penny. 1973. *Population and Poverty in Rural Java: Some Economic Arithmetic from Sriharjo.* Ithaca, NY: Cornell University Press.

St. Clair, A.L. 2009. "Conditional Cash Transfers: The Need for an Integrated and Historical Perspective", *Global Social Policy* 9, 2: 177–9. doi:10.1177/1468018190090020106.

Stoeffler, Q., B. Mills and C. del Ninno. 2016. "Reaching the Poor: Cash Transfer Program Targeting in Cameroon", *World Development* 83: 244–63.

Sugiyama, N.B. 2011. "The Diffusion of Conditional Cash Transfer Programs in the Americas", *Global Social Policy* 11, 2–3: 250–78. doi:10.1177/1468018111421295.

Sumarto, M. 2017. "Welfare Regime Change in Developing Countries: Evidence from Indonesia", *Social Policy & Administration* 51, 6: 940–59. doi:10.1111/spol.12340.

UNICEF. 2019. "Growing Well in a Changing World: Children, Food and Nutrition", *The State of the World's Children 2019.* Available at https://www.unicef.org/reports/state-of-worlds-children-2019 (accessed 30 Mar. 2022).

Veit-Wilson, J. 2009. "Who Sets the Conditions? Conditionality, Reciprocity, Human Rights and Inclusion in Society", *Global Social Policy* 9, 2: 171–4. doi:10.1177/14680181090090020104.

Willmott, R. 1999. "Structure, Agency and the Sociology of Education: Rescuing Analytical Dualism", *British Journal of Sociology of Education* 20, 1: 5–21

World Bank. 2012. *BLT Temporary Unconditional Cash Transfer. Social Assistance Program and Public Expenditure Review 2.* Jakarta/Washington: World Bank.

_____. 2021. *Indonesia COVID-19 Observatory.* Available at www.worldbank.org/indonesia/covid19monitor (accessed 30 Oct. 2021).

CHAPTER 13

Village Politics, Ritual Deliberation and the Problem of Beneficiary Mistargeting in Central Java

Katiman

Introduction

Social assistance programmes involve political commitments to helping particular categories of people. One of the critical challenges for these programmes is uneven coverage due to either the design or implementation of the programme (Leisering 2020). As earlier chapters have noted, Indonesia's social protection programmes have struggled to overcome problems of exclusion and inclusion. When this leads the programme to neglect households facing acute financial distress or include households deemed less "deserving", it generates social difficulties, tensions and jealousy between households (TNP2K 2015) and can result in social conflict (Sumarto 2020).

Policymakers have sought to address this problem by involving communities (Yamauchi 2010). Assuming that communities have more accurate information regarding who is eligible for assistance, researchers have argued for decentralising the selection of beneficiaries (Alderman 2002; Faguet 2004; Yamauchi 2010). The World Bank has supported including community deliberation to increase accuracy (Subbarao et al. 1997).

Following the realisation that the proxy means-test (PMT) alone tends to be inaccurate (Coady, Grosh and Hoddinott 2004; McCarthy and Sumarto 2018; other chapters in this volume), policymakers in Indonesia began to include community deliberation (*musyawarah desa* [*musdes*]). If state planners fully embraced community-based targeting, the state would allow the community, or some part of it (such as local leaders), to select beneficiaries (Alatas et al. 2013). However, before COVID-19, the social welfare system involved such community deliberation (*musdes*) only partially: the state still applied the econometric targeting (Proxy Means Testing or PMT) to lists approved by the *musdes* to create beneficiary lists. Here Indonesia followed the example of Mexico's *Progresa* project, which pioneered this hybrid approach, reportedly achieving relatively greater success (see Skoufias, Davis and De La Vega 2001).

This chapter will examine how the Indonesian state has used such deliberation (*musdes*) to address the exclusion problem. Integrating community deliberation into the targeting is meant to offer four main benefits. First, if the state embeds *musdes* in the programme design, *musdes* can be deployed consistently across Indonesia. Second, the *musdes* would provide "space" for communities to express their concerns. Third, the *musdes* would act as arenas where villagers can present arguments over who should be eligible to receive assistance. Fourth, incorporating these *musdes* processes into decision-making processes would be more aligned with existing village practices.

This chapter discusses how villages conduct *musdes*, considering how *musdes* and deliberation processes occur; what patterns are evident; and how and why deliberation works out in particular ways. The chapter also considers how social relations, power dynamics and accountability processes affect social welfare distributional processes.

Before we proceed further, we need to consider the different elements of the targeting system. While the Ministry of Social Affairs (MoSA) managed both the Rastra Program and PKH (the Program Keluarga Harapan [Family Hope Programme]), and although both programmes used the UDB (Unified Data Base) to identify eligible recipients initially, the two programmes have different mechanisms for updating their recipient lists. Specifically, the Rastra Program employs the *musdes* to update its lists of beneficiaries, while the PKH gives the task of updating its recipient lists to PKH programme facilitators at the local (village, sub-district and district) levels. In contrast, the verification and validation of the UDB using the *musdes* are conducted only once every three years, depending on state budget allocations.

This chapter argues that the attempt to involve communities has neither overcome unfair processes of beneficiary selection nor resolved the mistargeting of welfare. Instead, the overcomplicated and centralised design of the social welfare system and the intense pressures that hold village government accountable upwards have circumscribed the scope for deliberation. Consequently, the *musdes* works as a ritual or rubber-stamp forum that legitimises the pre-list of beneficiaries provided from above. Hence, it cannot effectively help the welfare system identify the most eligible welfare recipients. At the same time, village social relations create pressures for accountability and inclusion, which in turn lead the village government to organise more authentic forms of deliberation, using village-based surveys and village funds to arrange compensatory social assistance for excluded households.

This study took place in three villages in Kebumen district, Central Java Province. It set out to understand how deliberation processes are applied to distribute social assistance in the field. The study uses pseudonyms for three villages: Tambak, Tudung and Tani villages. After discussing the design of the two *musdes* in each case, the chapter examines how the *musyawarah* worked out in the three study villages; including a discussion of how deliberation processes occurred, how accountability mechanisms work in the process and how local and community governments overcome the issues resulting from mistargeting.

Village Decision-making: Updating the Social Assistance Recipient List

Musdes Rastra in the Three Study Villages

Central government guidance specifies six steps to update the list of beneficiaries of the Rastra Program (see Figure 13.1). The key step involves the village government holding a *musdes* to discuss required changes to the list of Rastra beneficiaries, including removing recipients who, according to the guidelines, are no longer eligible and proposing adding recipients. The *Dinas Sosial* (Social Service office) at the district level approves the list of recipients and submits the lists to *Dinas Sosial* at the provincial level and the MoSA.

The *Musdes Rastra* and UDB are part of centralised processes and organisational structures within which the village-level coordinating team is responsible for distributing social assistance and conducting a *musdes* to update recipient data for the Rastra Program. According to the guidelines issued by a higher level of government, the headman selects the chair of the coordinating team, and the chair should be responsible to the village head. In practice, the centralised design of social assistance targeting circumscribes the role of *Musdes Rastra*, with two consequences.

First, the centralised process leads to the *musdes* being a relatively "exclusive" process. This exclusivity was apparent in all three villages. The village governments invited only selected community representatives (mostly village leaders), actors from outside the village, such as TKSK (district facilitators) and sub-district officials and district government agencies. Consequently, the forum usually does not provide opportunities for ordinary villagers to participate in the deliberations. In this context, equitable deliberation cannot occur.

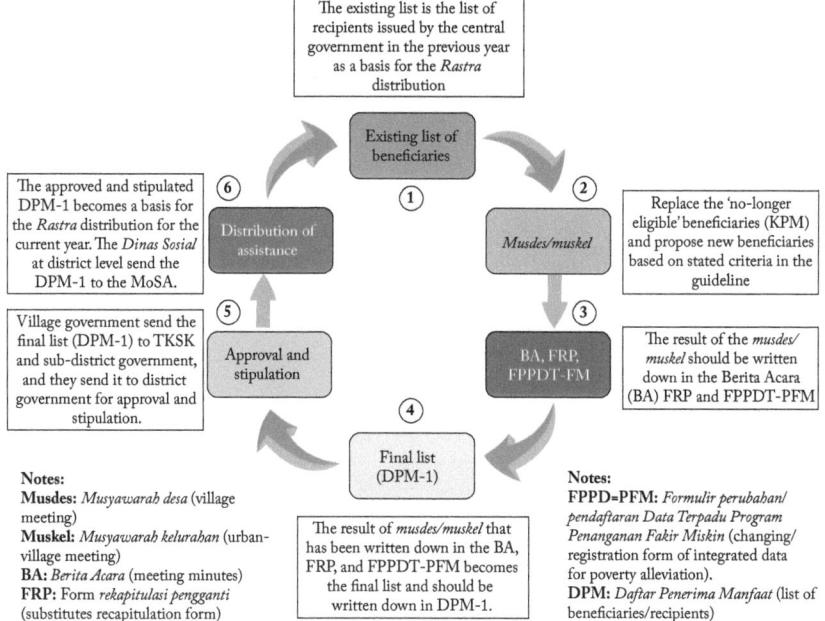

The existing list is the list of recipients issued by the central government in the previous year as a basis for the *Rastra* distribution

Existing list of beneficiaries

Replace the 'no-longer eligible' beneficiaries (KPM) and propose new beneficiaries based on stated criteria in the guideline

Musdes/muskel

The result of the *musdes/muskel* should be written down in the Berita Acara (BA) FRP and FPPDT-PFM

BA, FRP, FPPDT-FM

The result of *musdes/muskel* that has been written down in the BA, FRP, and FPPDT-PFM becomes the final list and should be written down in DPM-1.

Final list (DPM-1)

Village government send the final list (DPM-1) to TKSK and sub-district government, and they send it to district government for approval and stipulation.

Approval and stipulation

Distribution of assistance

The approved and stipulated DPM-1 becomes a basis for the *Rastra* distribution for the current year. The *Dinas Sosial* at district level send the DPM-1 to the MoSA.

Notes:
Musdes: *Musyawarah desa* (village meeting)
Muskel: *Musyawarah kelurahan* (urban-village meeting)
BA: *Berita Acara* (meeting minutes)
FRP: Form *rekapitulasi pengganti* (substitutes recapitulation form)

Notes:
FPPD=PFM: *Formulir perubahan/ pendaftaran Data Terpadu Program Penanganan Fakir Miskin* (changing/ registration form of integrated data for poverty alleviation).
DPM: *Daftar Penerima Manfaat* (list of beneficiaries/recipients)

Figure 13.1 Updating process of the list of beneficiaries of Rastra Program through Musdes
Source: Pedoman Umum (general guideline) of Rastra Program 2017.

However, the level of exclusivity of the *Musdes Rastra* varies: some village heads try to be inclusive. The headman of Tudung village wanted to show that under his administration, the village government was focused on being transparent and participatory in decision-making. The headman, Pak Rekso, wanted to distinguish his administration from that of his predecessor. Ensuring that a wide range of stakeholders "owned" any decisions reached would also reduce the risk of the headman being blamed if a decision went wrong (Interview with secretary of Tudung village, April 2018). The Tudung headman also wanted to avoid the negative experience of previous decision-making regarding poverty support funds. During the implementation of the *BLSM* (*Bantuan Langsung Sementara Masyarakat/* Unconditional cash transfer) programme, when the headman was assigned as an enumerator to collect data for the programme's targeting, someone threw a stone at his house and broke the glass door. He was concerned that the culprit was someone who did not receive assistance (*bantuan*) from the BLSM. That event led the headman to become very cautious when dealing with poverty data. During his administration, he has focused on transparency to avoid tensions among villagers and maintain harmony in the village.

Figure 13.2 shows the door of the headman's house following damage by an unidentified member of the village. The headman decided not to repair the door to remind himself about the "bad" day and always be careful when making decisions concerning poverty data.

Figure 13.2 The broken door of the Tudung headman's house following damage caused by a rock

Second, due to the centralised design, state actors tend to dominate the process. However, unequal power relations between actors are at work here: village governments defer upwards to higher-level governments and make decisions that focus on the perceived needs and administrative requirements of these levels, rather than on the needs of village communities. The tendency of headmen to focus on being accountable upwards served their interests in several ways. First, the headmen were motivated to maintain "good relations" with sub-district and district officials. The headman perceives that if officials at the district level know him and think of him well, there may be a higher likelihood of receiving information, offers and support from district officials regarding additional programmes, particularly infrastructure projects which are too expensive for the village government to afford alone (Interview, November 2017). Good relations with officials in higher-level governments can also strengthen a headman's political networks and support, both from the village and from actors outside the village (i.e. political support from the heads of sub-district and district agencies). The headmen hope that because they are consistently accountable to upper levels, the state will continue to provide sufficient Rastra Program assistance to the village.

For several reasons, headmen avoid changing pre-lists. For instance, village headmen are tempted to blame-shift, deflecting criticism from themselves and the village level government to higher levels of government. Village governments are also aware that if they remove names from the pre-list so that the overall total number of households on the revised list is lower than before, the overall Rastra budget for their village will decrease. The general perception among headmen is that receiving a lower Rastra budget would damage their reputation and reduce the community's trust in the village government, which would not be conducive to the re-election of the headman.

However, retaining the entire list of (unchanged) recipients for the Rastra Program also creates problems, particularly among villagers who had fallen into poverty and had expected to receive assistance. Pak Wira, secretary of Tudung village and the head of Tani village, admitted that villagers who deemed themselves eligible but were excluded often complained to the village government. In Tani village, these concerns were heightened because the list of Rastra Program recipients included the headman's parents. Mistargeting issues often lead to jealousy and associated conflicts. For example, in Tudung village, such jealousies affected the tradition of mutual assistance (*gotong royong*) (Interview, February 2018). Households which deemed themselves eligible but which were excluded had less motivation to join voluntary community service activities (i.e. *Krigan* or *Kerja Bakti*).

The centralised design involves lengthy accountability procedures. To report any changes to the data, those concerned need to follow long and complicated procedures involving protracted data updating (Interview, July 2018). This entails drawn-out and costly policy coordination, and is vulnerable to human error, for instance. Interviews revealed that, although officials reported the result of *Musdes Rastra* to the provincial office, the ministry (*Pusdatin* in the MoSA) never received the data from the Central Java Province. As a result, the national team at the Ministry (MoSA) assumed that there were no changes to the pre-list of recipients in the Central Java province. After they investigated, the head of the division for social protection found that the data operator had forgotten to send the recapitulated data from the *musdes* to the MoSA.

Consequently, the data from the village and district level were incomplete. An official in MoSA admitted that, as some local governments fail to send their revised data to MoSA, the Ministry used the previous year's data. The officials also often fail to send the updated Rastra data to the official responsible for updating the UDB. For such reasons, the data regarding the recipients of Rastra from villages and the UDB often do not match (Interview, February 2020).

In the study villages, officials noted that, despite their efforts to develop updated lists, the final list of recipients for Rastra received from higher government had remained unchanged for three consecutive years. The Tambak headman said that the village government now viewed the *Musdes Rastra* as useless for addressing mistargeting issues. Pak Miskam, a village official in Tambak village, reported that this had embarrassed him and the village headman. They had promised villagers who were included in the new list that they would receive assistance; when the same list emerged, this did not occur. The villagers blamed the village government for these continuing mistargeting problems (Interview, December 2017). Hence, in later years the three village governments conducted a *Musdes Rastra* simply "as a formality" to fulfil the administrative requirements from higher-level governments. This dissatisfaction leads village officials to submit the same pre-list.

The unchanged lists impacted villagers experiencing poverty who were unable to receive support; in other words, excluded villagers who deem themselves eligible express intense disappointment. The government of Tambak village, for example, received many complaints about mistargeting. However, village officials claimed that they could do nothing other than attempt to calm down the villagers. Village officials blamed officials at the district level, such as *dinas sosial*, for the negative impacts of mistargeting. In one case, a village official even accused an excluded villager. In Tambak village, Pak Yono, a village official said:

> When there was a complaint about mistargeting, I told villagers that those who received assistance were those willing to donate (*bersedekah*) to others. According to Islamic thought, if you give more, you will

get more. Thus, those who received the *bantuan* (assistance) must be those who had shared more with other villagers. I also told them that it would be better and more dignified if we could earn money by ourselves rather than expecting social assistance from the government (Interview, August 2018).

Alternatively, village officials could choose to ignore mistargeting issues and associated complaints from excluded villagers, arguing that paying attention to complaints could increase social tensions and disputes. In Tambak, village officials considered it easiest to "turn a blind eye" to mistargeting issues, as long as there was no overt tension. Revising the list would mean excluding several households, and this would create social tensions as no households would voluntarily surrender their entitlement. While they chose to leave the pre-list unchanged from previous years, Tambak officials told villagers that they did not know why the pre-list excluded households who should be eligible, but included other better-off households. Pak Yono explained:

> We [village government] are aware that some beneficiaries of the Rastra or PKH have experienced improved economic status and should be no longer eligible to get social assistance. Some villagers have protested to the village government about this. However, we decided that we could not do anything to respond to the protest. The higher-level government has never acknowledged our proposal to revise the existing list. We have [in previous years] sent an updated list of the Rastra Program's recipients, yet the list of beneficiaries at the national level remained unchanged. In the end [in subsequent years], we decided that as long as there were no significant social tensions in the village due to the mistargeting issue, we would not do anything further to revise the list (Interview, July 2018).

Village officials faced difficulties excluding better-off households. In Tambak village, for example, if officials forced such families to withdraw, those affected might blacken officials' names, and the headman's reputation would suffer. Attempts to remove households from the pre-list led to resistance from those households, creating problems that were "inconvenient" for village officials. The Tudung headman was not brave enough to issue a *Surat Keterangan Tidak Miskin* (*SKTM*/a-not-poor letter) stating that those recipients were no longer considered eligible to receive assistance.

Hence, in the three study villages the *musdes* functioned as a "rubber stamp" process, to meet administrative requirements from the central government and to ensure that the existing quota of Rastra Program funds for villagers in each village was not decreased or lost. The process of *Musdes Rastra* in each of the three study villages followed relatively similar patterns.

In each of the study villages, village officials and elites dominated the *Musdes Rastra*, and ordinary villagers had little opportunity to participate in the decision-making process; village headmen however did seek to accommodate dissatisfaction with the Rastra distribution and respond to demands from villagers. For instance, Tambak and Tudung villages conducted their own surveys. The villages surveyed all villagers listed in the UDB (BDT) using a BPS questionnaire and modified it to fit the village's condition. The village government used the village budget to finance data collection and processing, paying enumerators and data entry staff (Interview, December 2017). The village then assisted excluded villagers using the village budget.

Moreover, the village headmen sought to address the unfair inclusion of non-poor households employing personal, cultural and religious approaches. For example, the headman of Tudung village summoned Pak Yani to come to the village office to have a face-to-face discussion. Pak Aji, the headman, reported:

> I explained to him that his family was not eligible to receive the assistance anymore, and he should return his entitlement to other eligible villagers. In the beginning, he refused, and told me that the *bantuan* (assistance) was a right from the government to which he was entitled. Once the government had selected specific target/recipients, no one could take this support away from them. I convinced him that the programme is only for those in need, and that there are a lot of villagers who should receive the assistance, yet for some reason, they do not receive the entitlement. We had an intense discussion and finally he agreed to return the entitlement: with one condition. He chose his parent (his mother) who lived separately in the village and was in a poor economic condition. I had no choice other than to agree with his terms. At least he decided to return the entitlement (Interview, July 2018).

Consequently, in conducting *Musdes Rastra*, upwards accountability relations are stronger than the pressures that hold village governments accountable downwards. The village headman in three villages had *Musdes Rastra* as a formality to meet the requirements of higher-level governments. Substantive deliberation could not occur as the village government used the forum as a rubber stamp. Yet village governments also respond to pressures that hold them accountable to the ordinary village. Attempting to diffuse the resentments arising from mistargeting, the village government uses village budgets to allocate assistance to excluded households, reducing jealousy and social tensions.

Musdes UDB (Unified Data Base) in the Three Study Villages

Every three years or so, the central government requires local government to oversee a second *musdes* to update the data regarding poor households in the database (UDB) that serves as the basis for the econometric targeting (PMT) method employed by the social welfare system (Bah et al. 2019).[1] First, the central government prepares a pre-list of families based on the previous year's data. Then village governments conduct a *musdes* to verify, amend if required and validate the pre-list data, and to identify the poorest 40 per cent of households. According to the guidelines (*panduan umum*) for updating the UDB, the *musdes* should invite community leaders, heads of neighbourhoods, village police (*Babinsa*), and representatives of villagers/communities. A survey team will use this revised list when collecting data about the listed households. After the survey results are submitted, a data management team in Jakarta uses the PMT (proxy means-test) to update the list of the poorest 40 per cent of households. These updated UDB data become the source of information to distribute all social assistance. Figure 13.3 shows the process of updating the UDB.

As shown in Figure 13.3, the role of village governments in the targeting system is minimal; this is by design. Village government is involved only in the preparation and implementation of the *musdes*, while the central government designs and defines the updating system, prepares the pre-list, conducts the home surveys, processes the data from the *musdes* and surveys to decide the final list at the central level.[2]

We consider how this works in practice in three villages. In Kebumen, villages were reluctant for several reasons to conduct *musdes* for updating the UDB database. The Bupati instructed village governments to use villages' budgets to conduct *Musdes* UDB. Yet, the village governments allocated their budget to finance village programmes as stipulated in their plans (*RPJMDes* and *RKPDes*) (Interview, July 2019). Moreover, the data remained unchanged for several years, and this led villages to hesitate. Only after numerous reminders did the village governments conduct the *Musdes* UDB.

Tambak village held the *Musdes* UDB merely as a formality to meet state-level requirements and to demonstrate its support for the district government. Tudung village held *Musdes* UDB to execute the village programme in its village plan (*RPJMDes*) and in the hope of achieving better

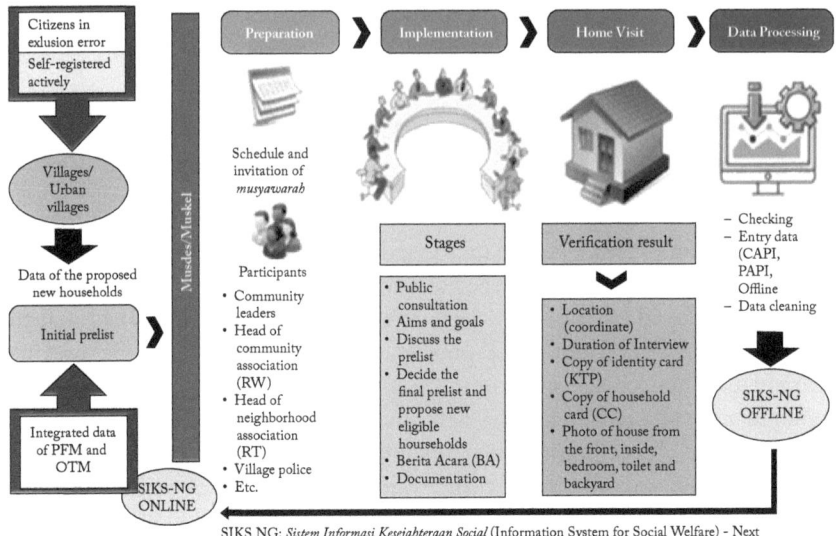

SIKS NG: *Sistem Informasi Kesejahteraan Sosial* (Information System for Social Welfare) - Next Generation)

Figure 13.3 Integrated data verification and validation activities at local level
Sources: Pusat Data dan Informasi Kesejahteraan Sosial (Pusdatin), Ministry of Social Affairs.

Figure 13.4 *Musdes* verification and validation of the BDT (UDB) in Tambak village in February 2019

targeting. However, Tani village chose not to revise the pre-list irrespective of any changes to villagers' eligibility, as the village did not want to lose the existing quota for state assistance.

In Tambak and Tudung villages, the village governments also conducted *musyawarah* at RT (*rukun tetangga* or neighbourhood association) levels, allowing ordinary villagers to participate. In these cases, neighbourhood fora identified households that needed to be surveyed further, recognising villagers listed in the initial list (pre-list) but now considered to have improved their economic conditions. Substantial deliberation occurred due to the village intention to avoid tensions and disputes (maintaining village harmony) and to respond to protests from villagers. In this sense, the village government demonstrated its responsiveness to local concerns. The village secretary in Tudung village emphasised that poverty data is a sensitive issue, hence involving communities will reduce social tensions. He also stated that if there were a protest from villagers in the future, the village government would have a stronger argument and justification; communities cannot blame the village government for the mistargeting problems based on deliberation (Interview, July 2018). In contrast, the Tani village government preferred to conduct the *Musdes UDB* without involving *musyawarah* at RT (hamlet) levels. The Tani village government considered involving RTs that would take additional time and complicate the overall process.

To summarise, while there was no actual deliberation in *Musdes Rastra*, during the *Musdes* UDB more substantial forms of deliberation occurred at the hamlet level in two of the study villages, particularly to assess the pre-list and to draw up a final list. Two of the village governments responded to village voices concerned with mistargeting while also meeting state accountability requirements.

Discussion

Policymakers envisaged that involving communities in decisions about the delivery of social programmes would lead to a range of benefits. Hence the state requires village governments to hold a *musdes* to update the data. However, in the three villages examined in this study, the meetings were merely a formality to meet these obligations. In the *musdes*, participants readily agreed to retain the pre-list. As others have found, this is ritual rather than authentic decision-making (Tanasoca and Sass 2019), and for several reasons, the deliberative process tends to work in this ritual fashion.

It is often assumed that elites dominate village deliberation processes. Village governments invite participants of the *Musdes Rastra* and UDB based on the central government's written guidance. Participants take part in the meeting only if the village government has invited them. Here, we observe power working through agenda-setting and domination of the processes (Lukes 2005). These are structural barriers to participation related to established social hierarchy and class systems within the villages; village governments tend to extend *musdes* invitations only to villagers who possess economic status, strong networks and social relationships (Fox referenced in McCarthy et al. 2014: 229) and political capital (Birner and Wittmer 2003: 298). Deliberation in the *musdes* tends to be dominated by participants who appear well-informed and capable of producing arguments for judgement, regardless of whether these participants can be a voice for those excluded.

The critical problem is that the centralised design of the *musdes* process circumscribes the deliberation processes. The agencies involved in the targeting process intended the updating procedures to provide an accountability mechanism to prevent elite capture at the local level. Accountability mechanisms aim to offer a democratic means to monitor and manage government conduct, including balancing power, and to enhance the learning capacity and the effectiveness of public administration (Bovens 2007; Aucoin and Heintzman 2000). However, the higher-level government experienced issues during the updating process of the recipients of the Rastra Program. High-ranking officials from both the TNP2K and MoSA admitted during this research that the village-level results from *Musdes Rastra* had not, up to that time, been used to update the UDB data, even though the UDB is the primary source of data for identifying legitimate recipients of the programme (Interview, December 2020) and its accuracy should therefore be paramount.

There is a second issue here: even in cases where the central government uses the *Musdes* UDB to revise the UDB list for a particular village, this does not guarantee that the village will receive assistance as per the list they submitted. This is because the central government uses econometric targeting (PMT) to decide on the final list of the 40 per cent poorest households. Therefore, there is a possibility that villagers included in the village-level UDB list will be removed from the final list of eligible individuals, following the modelling results.

A key issue here is communication between government levels. The higher-level government appears not to have communicated effectively to villagers about why the final lists are different from the revisions submitted by the village. Similarly, the higher-level government appears to be unaware that this issue has led village governments to decide that there is no point submitting revisions, and that instead, *musdes* should be conducted merely to keep up the "appearance" of meeting state-level requirements, while not making any actual changes to the pre-list.

Another issue derives from the complicated nature of the system. The mechanism remained problematic, with lengthy and over-complicated mechanisms proving error prone. An official from the *TNP2K* admitted that there are problems with integrating and updating data using the results of the *musdes*, including issues with the completeness of data and concerns about consistency and reliability of the data, given that village governments may conduct the *musdes* in various ways. In many cases, the official responsible for implementing the Rastra Program, in the MoSA, did not share the updated data with the division in charge of information and data. Therefore, during this time (2014–16), the MoSA sent the same pre-list of Rastra recipients to villages as they had received the previous year, without accommodating any changes.

Despite villages repeatedly proposing changes to the process, village administrators see the same unchanged recipient data returning. Villages doubt that conducting *musdes* will solve the mistargeting issues: village leaders wish to avoid the embarrassment and the resentment amongst villagers aspiring to be included. Distrusting the higher-level governments' capabilities, villages hold the *musdes* to avoid administrative sanctions from them. But rather than substantial deliberation, *Musdes Rastra*, as simply "ritual deliberation" (Tanasoca and Sass 2019), became a process used by villages by which pre-determined decisions were legitimised. Following the procedures set out in the state guidance regarding *musdes*, they proceed without a sincere intention or expectation of fixing the mistargeting issues; indeed, the villages often chose to submit lists unchanged from the pre-list. Hence low levels of trust and low expectations regarding the benefits of a state programme led to a low commitment to participation in decision-making.

The three villages in this study demonstrated different levels of accountability in the *musdes* processes. While "voice" is here defined as the capacity of people to express their interests to those in power, "accountability" is defined as the capacity and will of those who set and implement a society's rules to respond to community voices and needs (O'Neil, Foresti and Hudson 2007). Voice and accountability can only be present when citizens have sufficient knowledge and power to make requests and demands. Those in positions of power have the capacity and will to respond in ways that accommodate citizens' voices. In Tambak village and Tudung village, communities' concerns could hold village leaders to account, but this did not occur in Tani village. The village governments in Tambak village and Tudung village responded to villagers' voices concerning mistargeting problems, while the government of Tani village did not. The Tambak and Tudung village governments responded, for example, by explaining that errors regarding the target lists had been made at the higher-level government level and initiating village-funded social programmes. At the same time, they responded to pressures from above by supporting the implementation of the programmes to the extent that they held *musdes*, even if they did not submit the revisions that emerged from the process.

In response to concerns from those unjustifiably excluded, the headmen attempted to take action. One approach is to "force" those no-longer considered eligible to give up their entitlements. For example, the headman of Tudung village led the *musdes* and requested villagers with improved economic conditions to surrender their entitlements. However, when a village headman and village officials delete a person's name from the list, villagers argue strongly in the *musyawarah*. The TKSK interviewed during this study noted that, since the time he became a TKSK nine years earlier, only one recipient of the Rastra Program had cancelled his entitlement because his economic conditions had changed and he no longer felt eligible (Interview, April 2018). The targeting system thus struggles to deal with mistargeting issues at the community level. As a work-around, the headman also summoned villagers who refused to surrender their entitlement to persuade them to accept withdrawal from the list during face-to-face discussions.

Moreover, we saw much a higher degree of deliberation in two villages, particularly at the neighbourhood (RT) level during the *Musdes* UDB, where ordinary villagers participated in discussions. In Tudung village, the village government also gathered its data regarding poor households, distinctly different from the pre-list data issued by the central government. In this *Musdes* UDB, the village elites, particularly *Ketua RTs* [neighbourhood or hamlet chairmen], identified the mistargeting problems as they interacted with and communicated directly to villagers in their everyday life. The villagers are closer to *Ketua RTs* and could voice their complaints regarding programme implementation. The village government used its data from a village survey to make a strong argument in the deliberation process. Pak Wira explained the process:

> The *Musdes* BDT (UDB) aimed to decide the final pre-list and select recipients on the list who had better economic conditions. In our village, from the total 281 households in the initial pre-list, we agreed to select 70 families that, according to our observations, now had improved livelihoods and did not need assistance. We used input and views from participants, primarily *Ketua RT* who observe the villagers

daily in their neighbourhood, to select the households. In the *musdes*, several *Ketua* RT also proposed new additional families that, according to them, were now eligible for government assistance. In the following steps, the joint team (*Tim bersama*) will survey the 70 households and additional new households to inform their decisions and finalise the data revisions for updating the BDT.

This approach also responded to district-level initiatives. Poverty is a sensitive issue in Kebumen district. Pak Mari, the head of the *Bappermasdes* (the local community and village empowerment agency*)*, confided his reservations about the accuracy of the official poverty figures for Kebumen district, given that they had remained stagnant over five years, despite the district government implementing several poverty reduction programmes over that period. He also recommended that the district conduct its local surveys to obtain accurate data, rather than relying on the BPS data. To this end, *Bappeda* (the regional development planning agency) requested each village to conduct a village-level survey and census of poor households that had been listed in the BDT, so that these could be compared to the BPS data and, if necessary, used to counter them. The *Bappeda* also used these data from the local targeting as a basis for formulating a poverty reduction programme at the district level.

The Kebumen district government's frustrations with inaccurate data, the misclassification of households and the high degree of mistargeting led to the initiative of the *petugas lapangan* (field officer) to place a sign on the households receiving *Raskin/Rastra* assistance. The sign stated that the household promised that it was indeed a poor household; each recipient household was obliged to display it publicly (see Figure 13.5). This initiative was an effort to "publicly shame" current recipients who were sufficiently well off to be ineligible for the funds and thereby encourage them to return their entitlement willingly. As it involved stigmatising poor households, it was controversial, leading to harmful impacts in several villages, as the head of *Bappermasdes* later communicated. Specifically, several households across several villages cancelled assistance as they felt so embarrassed—even though they were eligible to receive assistance. This outcome, and the associated village tensions, led to two village headmen handing in their resignations.

In an attempt to resolve the mistargeting issues in both programmes, village governments responded to local dissatisfaction. Tambak and Tudung allocated a portion of the village budget to finance local social protection programmes. The effort aimed to fill the mistargeting gap. For example, both village governments introduced a "housing for the poor programme" and a "cattle assistance programme" (*bantuan ternak*), with the same mechanisms of programme delivery that the central government initiated. While the

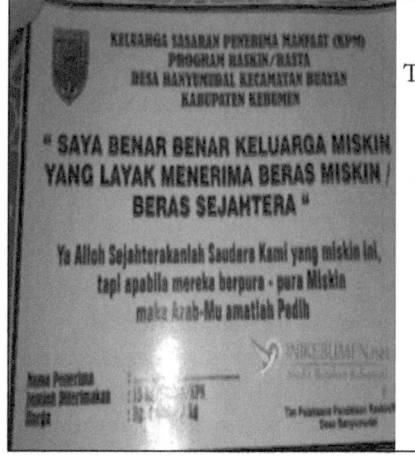

[Translation of the signboard]

Targeted household of Raskin/Rastra Program village Banyumudal, sub-district Buayan, Kebumen District.

"I AM TRULY A POOR FAMILY WHO DESERVES TO RECEIVE RICE FOR THE POOR/RICE FOR PROSPERITY"

"Ya allah, make this poor household prosperous. Yet if they are just pretending to be a poor people, indeed your punishment is a great hurt"

Figure 13.5 Signboard for the recipients of *Rastra* in one of the villages in Kebumen District

Figure 13.6 Regular meeting of PKH recipients in Tani Village

amount of funding provided by these village-level support programmes is less than would be available from the national programmes, these village-level programmes helped maintain village harmony while preserving the "good" image of leaders and the village government.

In some cases, mistargeting problems affect social values and collective action in the village. As stated in the programme guidelines, recipients of the PKH receive benefits from all social assistance programmes, such as the *Rastra*, health and education benefits. As a result, recipients of PKH have received assistance from four of five programmes at the same time. This practice caused many protests and jealous feelings, generating tension in the village. Pak Kliwon, an official of Petanahan sub-district, revealed that all villagers wanted to get *bantuan* (assistance) regardless of their economic condition. They had participated in *kerja bakti/gotong royong*. They found it unfair when only selected villagers received assistance (Interview, July and August 2018).

In response, some villages encourage the sharing of assistance among those in need. For example, in Tambak village, one of the recipients of the PKH gave a proportion of the Rastra benefit to other poor households in the village. According to the TKSK, the practice of recipients sharing assistance occurred quite often, as a means of maintaining social relationships and village harmony. However, the amount of assistance from the Rastra Program is relatively smaller than that of the PKH. In 2017 when the government replaced in-kind (i.e. rice under the Rastra programme) with direct transfer of cash (under the BPNT programme), the practice of equal distribution (*bagito* or *bagi roto*) became rare.

Conclusion

Indonesia has followed the policy prescription that suggests that community involvement in poverty targeting can improve the delivery of social assistance (Narayan and Pritchett 1999; La Ferrara 2022; Subbarao et al. 1997; Conning and Kevane 2002). State efforts to use the two *musdes* as fora resonate with the ideal of "empowered participatory governance" (Fung and Wright 2003), where ordinary villagers are included in the decision-making process through reasoned deliberation. However, as this study concludes, the deliberation processes have proved inadequate to meet this aspiration for several reasons.

First, the deliberative processes tend to be controlled by village government and village elites. The central government instructions require the village government to invite only representatives of communities and village leaders, not "ordinary" villagers. This requirement consolidates the structural barriers that limit the participation of ordinary villagers in deliberative processes. As other research has found, only local village leaders and other authorities tend to attend the *musdes* to finalise the list of Raskin recipients (Alatas et al. 2013). Yet, elite control is not the same as elite capture: although the elite dominates the *musdes* processes, for the most part, we do not see elite capture of social assistance. This research found that village headmen, officials and village leaders avoided influencing the targeting process to ensure that they and their families would become programme beneficiaries. Instead, they used elite control to maintain social cohesion and village harmony, thereby protecting their reputations as leaders. This corroborates previous observations that local elite control does not always translate into elite capture (Dasgupta and Beard 2007). Undeniably, in the three study villages, the headmen's interests and community pressures shape leaders' actions. For instance, in dealing with mistargeting issues, headmen were motivated by their interests in maintaining village harmony, avoiding social tensions, responding to villagers' protests and maintaining their political and social reputations.

Second, we find that the predominant form of deliberation is ritualistic. The primary reason for this derives from the highly convoluted and centralised social welfare system, which is complex and error prone. Despite villages repeatedly proposing changes to the list of beneficiaries, village administrators often see the same unchanged list of recipients returning due to problems in the data management system. Subsequently, unfair beneficiary selection and mistargeted distribution corrode community trust towards village government. Some villages blamed the headman and village officials. Others alleged that the headman and officials encouraged and pressured them to surrender their programme entitlement due to personal animosities rather than fair and objective consideration of their economic condition and actual eligibility for programme support. Further, when the data come back unchanged, the headman is embarrassed and disappointed. Facing these heated issues, village leaders tend to avoid social tensions and maintain their reputations.

Hence, as villages primarily neither conduct the *musdes* nor send the result to the central government, the central database is incomplete. This and other errors in the data management system mean that the state cannot utilise the data derived from the *musdes* to decide on the final list of recipients. Hence the data tend to return from the national level unchanged from year to year. The econometric modelling approach makes the final decision, contributing to the gap between village lists and the definitive list of beneficiaries. As a result, rather than promoting social integration and avoiding social exclusion, mistargeted benefits escalate social tensions in villages, leading to jealousy among those who deem themselves eligible for assistance, and even stimulating multifaceted conflict in communities (Sumarto 2020).

However, village governments are held accountable upwards by state administrative arrangements. Further, headmen have interests in maintaining good relations with higher levels of the state. Hence, higher-level governmental power "forces" village governments to conduct the *musdes*, imposing administrative sanctions on villages if they fail to support the central government programmes. Faced with this dilemma and disappointed with the unchanged beneficiary data, villager leaders conduct *musdes* merely as a formality. Hence the headmen instructed village officials to just go through the motions of performing the *musdes*. Third, the range of processes and pressures to some degree make village leaders downwardly accountable. Village leaders find work-arounds, undertaking more authentic deliberative processes to redress the problems caused by unfair and exclusionary selection processes. Local and village governments' anxiety concerning the central government and fear of village discord compel local leaders to respond. Faced with resentment, social pressure and threats to their reputation, local and village governments search for remedies. The district agencies observed in this study carried out their own surveys to produce more valid and reliable poverty data for local planning. District governments also initiated local social protections programmes, funded by local budgets.

Similarly, the three village governments in this study funded surveys and allocated funds for social assistance from village budgets. Even at the village level, the village headman and officials employed personal, cultural and religious approaches to reduce tensions related to mistargeting issues in their communities. To this end, village governments also arranged informal redistribution of assistance. They suggested that villagers who received the social assistance should share their benefits with eligible villagers who were excluded.

The inability of the formal *musdes* to provide space for actual deliberation to occur, and hence the *musdes'* lack of capacity to help improve targeting, contributed to a second process. This study found that more authentic deliberation could still occur during the *musdes*, especially during the *Musdes* UDB at the neighbourhood level despite elite control and domination. Here, ordinary villagers have an equal opportunity to participate in the forum. In this sense, the requirements for ideal deliberation, such as free and equal access and opportunities (Bohman 1998), are fulfilled. However, the research found actual deliberation in the *Musdes* UDB at Tudung village, but not in Tambak and Tani villages. This genuine deliberation happened because the *musdes* reflected a discursive practice that has both deliberative and democratic features (Tanasoca and Sass 2019), including proper procedures, clear goals and reflected sincerity of participants in the reason-giving processes. Here, village deliberators could make well-reasoned arguments because they have valid data from their village surveys and daily observations of villagers' economic situations.

Further, the officials in Tudung village have the task of data updating according to the village development plan. However, the actual deliberation may fail to provide better targeting of social assistance. In the end, the decisions regarding who is considered eligible to be a beneficiary of the programmes lie in the central government's hands.

This chapter concludes that this way of involving communities in distributing state welfare has not achieved the oversight and corrective mechanisms required for inclusive state welfare programmes. The overly complex centralised design of the system circumscribes the roles of *musdes* and together with strong upward forms of accountability structures the process. These factors lead village governments to conduct *musdes* as a mere formality, with village governments tending to use *musyawarah* as a ritual process (ritual deliberation). Responding to informal forms of accountability, local and village governments react by searching for ways to resolve unfair and exclusionary welfare distribution problems. In other circumstances, *musdes* can provide an accountable forum to ensure legitimacy and to achieve consensus. Yet, in the conditions created by a centralised and unwieldy welfare system with dominant upwards accountability, deliberation cannot address the main problems leading to problematic distributional outcomes. The villages react by going through the motions of conducting *musdes* merely to meet administrative requirements, build good relations with higher-level governments and maintain village harmony. The implication is that new social welfare designs are required to address the problems of unfair beneficiary selection and mistargeted distribution. These need to be based on a more sophisticated understanding of local realities.

Notes

[1] In 2015, the government introduced the UDB, which is managed by the TNP2K. In 2017, the President appointed a *Pusat Data dan Informasi* (*Pusdatin*–Data and Information Center), under the MoSA, to lead the updating of the UDB in coordination with the TNP2K and BPS (central statistics agency). In 2018, The MoSA changed the name of the *Basis Data Terpadu* (UDB) to DTKS (*Data Terpadu Kesejahteraan Sosial*–Integrated Data for Social Welfare). This chapter focuses on the updating process of the UDB before the MoSA changed the name to the DTKS.

[2] In 2018 the MoSA developed an application to speed up the updating of the list and disseminate information more efficiently between government and village levels— the SIKS-NG (*Sistem Informasi Kesejahteraan Sosial*-Next Generation/Social Welfare Information System-Next Generation). With this application, the government hopes that

any data changes at the village level will be communicated directly to the data operator at the central level. However, at the time of this fieldwork, the application was not yet in general use, as the MoSA required more time to train the TKSK and data operator at local levels to use the application. Hence at the time of writing, the reporting mechanisms still involved paper-based reporting.

References

Alatas, V. et al. 2013. "Does Elite Capture Matter? Local Elites and Targeted Welfare Programmes in Indonesia", Harvard Kennedy School Working Paper No. RWP13-008. Available at https://www.hks.harvard.edu/publications/does-elite-capture-matter-local-elites-and-targeted-welfare-programs-indonesia (accessed 11 Mar. 2022).

Alderman, H. 2002. "Do Local Officials Know Something We Don't? Decentralization of Targeted Transfers in Albania", *Journal of Public Economics* 83: 375–404.

Aucoin, P. and R. Heintzman. 2000. "The Dialectics of Accountability for Performance in Public Management Reform", *International Review of Administrative Sciences* 66: 45–55.

Bah, A. et al. 2019. "Finding the Poor vs. Measuring Their Poverty: Exploring the Drivers of Targeting Effectiveness in Indonesia", *The World Bank Economic Review* 33: 573–97.

Birner, R. and H. Wittmer. 2003. "Using Social Capital to Create Political Capital: How do Local Communities Gain Political Influence? A Theoretical Approach and Empirical Evidence from Thailand", in *The Commons in the New Millennium: Challenges and Adaptation*, ed. Nives Dolšak and Elinor Ostrom. Cambridge, MA: The MIT Press.

Bohman, J. 1998. "Survey Article: The Coming of Age of Deliberative Democracy", *The Journal of Political Philosophy* 6: 400–25.

Bovens, M. 2007. "Analysing and Assessing Accountability: A Conceptual Framework", *European Law Journal* 13: 447–68.

Coady, D., M. Grosh and J. Hoddinott. 2004. *Targeting of Transfers in Developing Countries*. Washington, DC: World Bank and IFRI (International Food Policy Research Institute).

Conning, J. and M. Kevane. 2002. "Community-Based Targeting Mechanisms for Social Safety Nets: A Critical Review", *World Development* 30, 3: 375–94.

Dasgupta, A. and V.A. Beard. 2007. "Community Driven Development, Collective Action and Elite Capture in Indonesia", *Development and Change* 38: 229–49.

Faguet, J.-P. 2004. "Does Decentralization Increase Government Responsiveness to Local Needs?", *Journal of Public Economics* 88: 867–93.

Fung, A. and O.E. Wright. 2003. *Deepening Democracy, Institutional Innovations in Empowerted Participatory Governance.* London: Verso.

Goodin, R. E. and J.S. Dryzek. 2016. "Deliberative Impacts: The Macro-Political Uptake of Mini-Publics", *Politics & Society* 34: 219–44.

La Ferrara, E. 2002. "Inequality and Group Participation: Theory and Evidence from Rural Tanzania", *Journal of Public Economics* 85, 2: 235–73.

Leisering, L., ed. 2020. *One Hundred Years of Social Protection: The Changing Social Question in Brazil, India, China and South Africa.* London: Palgrave MacMillan.

Lukes, S. 2005. *Power: A Radical View, Second Edition, London:* Palgrave Macmillan.

McCarthy, J. and M. Sumarto. 2018. "Distributional Politics and Social Protection in Indonesia: Dilemma of Layering, Nesting and Social Fit in Jokowi's Poverty Policy", *Southeast Asian Economies* 35: 223–36.

McCarthy, J.F. et al. 2014. "Dilemmas of Participation: The National Community Empowerment Program", in *Regional Dynamics in a Decentralized Indonesia*, ed. H Hill. Singapore: ISEAS, pp. 233–59.

Narayan, D. and L. Pritchett. 1999. "Cents and Sociability: Household Income and Social Capital in Rural Tanzania", Policy Research Working Paper No. WPS1796. Washington, DC: World Bank.

O'Neil, T., M. Foresti and A. Hudson. 2007. *Evaluation of Citizens' Voice and Accountability: Review of the Literature and Donor Approaches.* London: [UK.Gov] Department for International Development.

Skoufias, E., B. Davis and S. De La Vega. 2001. "Targeting the Poor in Mexico: An Evaluation of the Selection of Households into PROGRESA", *World Development* 29: 1769–84.

Subbarao, K. et al. 1997. *Safety Net Programs and Poverty Reduction: Lessons from Cross-country Experience.* Washington, DC: World Bank.

Sumarto, M. 2020. "Welfare and Conflict: Policy Failure in the Indonesian Cash Transfer", *Journal of Social Policy* 1–19.

Sumarto, S. and S. Bazzi. 2011. "Social Protection in Indonesia: Past Experiences and Lessons for the Future", *The 2011 Annual World Bank Conference on Development Opportunities.* Paris.

Tanasoca, A. and J. Sass. 2019. "Ritual Deliberation", *Journal of Political Philosophy* 27: 139–65.

TNP2K 2015. *Raskin: The Challenge of Improving Programme Effectiveness.* National Team for the Acceleration of Poverty Reduction (TNP2K), Republic Indonesia.

Yamauchi, C. 2010. "Community-based Targeting and Initial Local Conditions: Evidence from Indonesia's IDT Program", *Economic Development and Cultural Change* 59: 95–147.

CHAPTER 14

Conditional Cash Transfers, Global Politics and the Development of Indonesia's Social Protection Policy

Mulyadi Sumarto

Introduction

This chapter uses PKH (the *Program Keluarga Harapan*—Family Hope Program) as a case study to explore how global ideas have shaped current Indonesian nation-state social protection policies for socio-economic development. Specifically, I investigate how the Indonesian government adopted global social investment ideas under policy diffusion driven by the World Bank. There have been very limited studies on this issue in Indonesia, but scholars have conducted studies in many countries across Asia, Africa and Latin America (Jenson and Nagels 2018; Mendoza 2019; Ogamba 2020; Razak 2015; Sugiyama and Hunter 2020; Reininger, Villalobos and Wyman 2019).

First, the paper reviews the concept of social investment. I then trace its uptake in Indonesia from the East Asia financial crisis (1997) onwards, discussing the evolution of social assistance programmes from the targeted, rice-based social assistance *Beras Sejahtera* (Rastra) programme, to the inception and implementation of conditional cash transfers (CCTs) in Indonesia. The paper argues that the current impasse in Indonesian social policy results from a process of institutionalisation that lacks indigenous ideas of appropriate social policy models. This process represents the unquestioning adoption of the social investment concept with ineffective guidance from a global institution.

To explore the evolution of social protection in Indonesia, I draw on primary data from in-depth interviews conducted in Jakarta between 2015 and 2018 with high-level national government officers, politicians, international donor representatives and the directors of global non-governmental organisations (NGOs). An examination of secondary data, previous studies, government documents and World Bank archives supports the analysis.

Social Investment and Political Issues in Global Policy Diffusion—A Conceptual Review

Global politics affects the local–national process of policy adoption of CCTs in the Global South. Global politics refers to transnational political activity (Lyon 2013) that sees power relations and dynamics having an important impact on a number of global issues and processes (Kitchen and Mathers 2019). The concept of global politics covers global policy diffusion, global ideas regarding social investment and liberalisation shaped by global institutions.

Many countries in the Global South have implemented CCTs, which emerged as a tool for a global agenda to disseminate social investment ideas (Gliszczynski and Leisering 2016; Mahon 2019; Nagels 2016; Nelson and Sandberg 2016; Papadopoulos and Leyer 2016). The term "social investment" refers to a policy in which the government uses spending to invest in and develop citizens' skills and knowledge (Dräbing and Nelson 2017: 129). Social investment, therefore, is a strategy for developing and protecting human capital to improve the socio-economic conditions of citizens, families and economies (Hemerijck 2017: 19). The investment is sometimes seen as a "panacea", with the expectation that government expenditure on social policy increases labour productivity to achieve high economic growth. In this context, "productivism" is viewed as a crucial underlying idea of social investment to achieve such growth. As a result, several authors (Barbier 2017; Zehavi and Breznitz 2018) believe that social investment is closely associated with the concept of neo-liberalism, with its enthusiasm for deregulation, competition and market mechanisms to shape the economy.

The agenda of social investment in the Global South arose simultaneously with the diffusion of the CCT concept. The CCT initiative emerged in Brazil and Mexico but then some global institutions, mainly the World Bank, replicated and applied the programme across the Global South (Béland et al. 2018; Borges 2018). Policy diffusion refers to an "interdependence of states and/or regions and its effects on policy adoption" (Vagionaki and Trein 2020:

308). Global diffusion may involve neoliberal ideological transfers (Béland et al. 2018) and, in a narrower sense, the diffusion may include more practical ideas such as CCT programmes (Borges 2018). Global policy diffusion is a "transfer of policies from one national jurisdiction to another" (Béland et al. 2018: 463). Policy diffusion refers to the spread of innovation from an innovator to the policy learner and emulator (Weyland 2017).

Many researchers propose that policy diffusion includes policy learning, emulation, competition and coercion (Gilardi and Wasserfallen 2019; Vagionaki and Trein 2020; Weyland 2017). The term "learning" here represents an effort to raise the level of socio-economic achievement. At the same time "emulation" denotes an attempt to follow and imitate a constructive prototype exercised by a peer group or other country. In contrast, "competition" indicates an actor's interest to contest resources for position and status, while "coercion" refers to an asymmetrical relationship between the actors involved in the policy diffusion (Weyland 2017). In this view, coercion in policy diffusion carries political-ideological interests, which may cause complicated political issues. Powerful countries or authoritative global institutions, such as the World Bank, enforce (at some points), provide and promote hegemonic policy ideas that can influence and drive policy change (Gilardi and Wasserfallen 2019). As other chapters in this book also note (see Chapters 3 and 12), and as explored further below, Indonesian policymakers also had reasons for adopting this model.

The Development of Social Protection for the Poor in Indonesia

In 1998, the Indonesian government developed a widespread programme known as JPS (*Jaring Pengaman Sosial*—social safety net) targeted to support the poor. The World Bank designed JPS to reduce some of the risks resulting from resistance to or unintended consequences of the political-economic reforms under the Structural Adjustment Program (SAP) and associated social unrest (Sumarto 2017). In some respects, however, the JPS programmes failed to protect the poor from economic austerity. A 2006 evaluation conducted by the World Bank on poverty issues and social protection programmes in Indonesia found several failures. It noted that:

> The continued social safety net [JPS] programs address a diversity of issues, but are low in coverage, institutionally fragmented and are not managed as one umbrella system. ... They [the JPS programs] were designed and implemented by a wide array of government agencies,

> with limited budgetary resources and little coordination. ... Clearly, the
> JPS programs are failing to operate as an effective safety net for most of
> the poor (World Bank 2006: 164).

Despite criticisms that the SAP failed to improve the Indonesian political-
economic situation (Sumarto 2017), the government expanded the JPS
programme, now renamed the "Poverty Reduction Programme". This
enlargement of social protection programmes led to a rapid rise in government
funding for social welfare. Figure 14.1 shows the programme's expansion from
2005 to 2017, when government spending increased more than ten-fold.

The Indonesian poverty reduction programme subsequently included
a Kecamatan (sub-district) based programme, PNPM (*Program Nasional
Pemberdayaan Masyarakat*/National Programme for Community Empowerment), also based on the advice and support of the World Bank. In 2010,
soon after his re-election in the 2009 presidential election, President S.B.
Yudhoyono began consolidating the dispersed poverty reduction programmes
under the TNP2K (National Team for the Acceleration of Poverty Reduction).

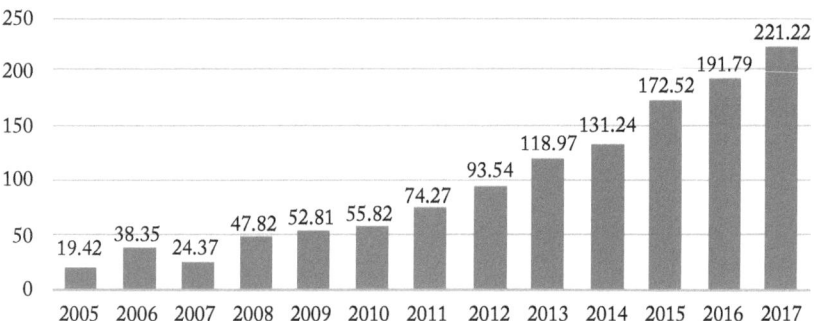

Figure 14.1   Government expenditure on Social Protection Programmes, 2005–17
Source: Unpublished data from the Ministry of Finance (McCarthy and Sumarto 2018).

The Indonesian government depended heavily on the World Bank's policy
designs and agenda during the design and introduction of targeted social
assistance. Before the East Asian Financial Crisis (1997), the Indonesian
government had not planned to implement targeted social assistance for the
poor. When the crisis struck, the government accepted the JPS and World
Bank advice regarding social assistance models, including the design and
technical arrangement of the JPS (Sumarto and Kaasch 2018).

During the COVID-19 pandemic, the Indonesian government provided
JPS, which covered several types of social assistance. These are targeted to the
poor, unemployed workers, low-wage workers and small enterprise owners.

The JPS basically aimed to help the poor and low wage workers deal with the economic hardship caused by COVID-19. It also supported the national economic recovery by providing social supports for newly-unemployed workers to re-enter labour markets and for people running small enterprises to develop their businesses. To finance the JPS, the government uses three financial sources: the national government budget, global bonds and a World Bank loan (Sumarto and Ferdiansyah 2021).

The Rastra Programme

The Rastra programme is discussed here as this programme may serve as a lens to understand the administrative issues and social impact of PKH in communities. Rastra is one of Indonesia's oldest targeted social assistance programmes, with the highest government budget allocation and numbers of recipients (Timmer, Hastuti and Sumarto 2018). However, there is a wide gap between the number of eligible recipients of Rastra and its actual recipients (Table 14.1). The gap represents a significant inclusion error, with Rastra reaching on average just 50.3 per cent of eligible recipients. Complicated administrative issues rooted in inaccurate household data have led to the mistargeted distribution, which in turn has generated social jealousy and latent conflict (Sumarto 2013).

Table 14.1   Monthly allocation of Rastra and the number of Rastra recipients

Period [1]	Monthly allocation of rice (kg/ household)* [2]	Number of recipients		
		Eligible recipients (million)** [3]	Recipients (million)** [4]	% of non-poor included as beneficiaries*** [5]
1998	10 or 20	n/a	n/a	n/a
1999	20	n/a	n/a	n/a
2000	20	n/a	n/a	n/a
2001	15	n/a	n/a	n/a
2002	20	9.8	20.9	53.11
2003	20	8.6	22.5	61.78
2004	20	8.6	19.5	55.90
2005	20	8.3	22.9	63.76
2006	15	10.8	24.5	55.92
2007	15	15.8	29.4	46.26
2008	10 or 15	19.1	30.5	37.38

(cont'd overleaf)

Table 14.1 (*cont'd*)

Period [1]	Monthly allocation of rice (kg/ household)* [2]	Number of recipients		
		Eligible recipients (million)** [3]	Recipients (million)** [4]	% of non-poor included as beneficiaries*** [5]
2009	15	18.5	30.2	38.74
2010	13 or 15	17.5	31.0	43.55
2011	15	17.5	32.6	46.32
2012	15	17.5	33.2	47.29
2013	15	15.5	32.8	52.74
2014	15	15.5	33.4	53.59
2015	15	n/a	n/a	n/a

Sources: *: Table 7.4; **: Figure 7.5 (Timmer et al. 2018); ***: Author's calculation, using the formula: ([4] – [3]) : [4] x 100%.

During the 1997 Asian financial crisis, the JPS programme initiated special market operations—the *Operasi Pasar Khusus* (OPK; later renamed Raskin and subsequently, Rastra) programme. OPK aimed to assist the poor to access staple food (rice) at an affordable price. After experiencing several changes, in 2018, the government eventually reformed the Rastra programme, shifting from subsidised rice to providing 10 kg of free rice per month to every poor household in Indonesia. The government also replaced Rastra with a Non-cash Food Assistance programme, *Bantuan Pangan Non-Tunai* (BPNT), seeking to overcome the mistargeting problem that was causing widespread community discontent. As a result, Bulog (the Indonesian Bureau of Logistics) is no longer a key player for supplying welfare rice to relevant outlets.

BPNT provides electronic-based cash assistance to poor households for staple foods, primarily rice and eggs. Each poor household is entitled to an allocation of IDR 110,000 per month (USD 7.50), which the government transfers to the recipient's electronic card. The card is called the Prosperous Family Card—*Kartu Keluarga Sejahtera* (KKS)—and is equipped with an identifying electronic chip. The problem is that most of the poor do not generally use banking services, so the government has requested that the banks—most of which are state-owned enterprises appointed by the government—support the BPNT programme by setting up bank accounts for recipients. Once this is in place, the recipients can use the KKS to buy rice and eggs at an e-warung (shop, cooperative, or small and micro enterprise) in their neighbourhood. The e-warung provides an allocation of rice and eggs under the BPNT programme. A district coordinating team for food assistance appoints and authorises the e-warung. The district head is responsible for coordination, and these teams manage all technical and institutional aspects of the BPNT distribution process.

While the BPNT is more sophisticated than its predecessors in that it uses electronic-based technology, this feature is also a significant limitation on its current effectiveness: the BPNT programme cannot be provided in all districts across Indonesia, due to limited technological capacity and banking facilities in remote districts. Indonesia's 514 districts (regencies and cities) have very different levels of infrastructure. Some districts, particularly those in remote areas outside Java and in eastern Indonesia, have minimal technology provision, including a lack of access to electricity, which precludes these districts from providing the electronic-based banking services to residents. The wider point, however, is that even if the technical aspects of the new programme could be overcome, the mistargeting problem for beneficiaries remains. This indicates that the deeper problem lies with the econometric/hybrid model promoted by the World Bank.

PKH History

Few scholars have discussed the history of PKH in Indonesia. Documents published by the World Bank and the Indonesian government show that the efforts of the World Bank over a very short period led to the introduction of CCT to Indonesia. After the success of CCT programmes in Brazil and in Mexico, the World Bank disseminated the model to many developing countries across Africa and Asia (Béland et al. 2018), including Indonesia (Sumarto 2014).

A 2006 World Bank report on poverty reduction programmes in Indonesia clearly articulated the idea of the PKH in Indonesia for the first time. In the same year, the PKH programme began. The World Bank stated optimistically that a pilot programme would begin the following year and would be scaled up gradually at the national level. No formal Indonesian documents had ever mentioned the term PKH until the programme commenced in 2007, when a technical paper first used the term "PKH". Prior to this point, it was not mentioned in Indonesia's 2007 national budget document nor the country's medium-term development plan (*Rencana Pembangunan Jangka Menengah Nasional 2004–2009* [mid-term 5-year plan]).

The timeline outlined above regarding the implementation of the PKH, without previous reference to the initiative in state planning documents, shows that the Indonesian government had no independent planning for the PKH. When the World Bank approached the Indonesian government with the idea of piloting the PKH in 2006, Indonesia accepted and implemented the idea immediately. This highlights two important points. First, Indonesia lacked a systematic plan for including CCT in its social assistance policy. The World Bank prepared the PKH, working closely with Indonesian planning agency, Bappenas, for about one year (2006–07). Second, the rapid onset of PKH demonstrated the persuasive influence of the World Bank in shaping Indonesian social policy.

As the World Bank had earlier advised their client countries in Latin America and other middle-income countries, it was essential that the CCT programme be trialled in each country. In 2007, a pilot project in seven provinces in Indonesia (out of a total of 33) introduced PKH in 48 regencies and cities (out of a total 440 regencies and cities). From this trial, the World Bank pushed to expand the project to the national level.

The trial occurred in the shadow of the Indonesian government's disappointment with the first BLT programme (*Bantuan Langsung Tunai* [direct cash assistance]), which was rolled out in 2005–06, a year before the initiation of the PKH. The 2005 BLT programme generated substantial social conflict and social unrest due to the perceived inequity in the selection of recipients (Sumarto 2013, 2021). In response to this poor reception, the Indonesian government and the World Bank decided to replace the BLT with PKH (World Bank 2006). However, the PKH could not simply replace the BLT, because the two programmes were based on different premises. The BLT was intended to compensate households for fuel subsidy reductions that had largely benefitted the middle classes, while PKH is intended as a tool for social investment. BLT payments were issued in 2008, 2013 and 2015 explicitly as compensation for reducing fuel subsidies (Sumarto 2021).

The legal arrangements of the PKH remained straightforward. The Coordinating Minister of Social Welfare in a 2007 decree (No. 31/ Kep/Menko/-Kesra/IX/2007) provided the technical team tasked with implementing the PKH. The decree itself, however, did not mention "PKH". This legal arrangement leaves the PKH legally and politically vulnerable to a sudden policy change. If a new government no longer supports the PKH programme, it may be readily cancelled or its form and scale modified. In contrast, the JKN (Jaminan Kesehatan Nasional—National Health Insurance) legal arrangements and position under the social security law are very stable. This may be because the design of the PKH was initially intended to be a small pilot project, covering a few regions with a limited budget and recipients. In this context the government may not have considered the legal arrangements to be a high priority.

As seen above, the Indonesian government introduced and implemented the PKH before the government had developed the understanding or capacity required to create its social protection policy. This occurred for two main reasons: first, the government had limited experience managing social assistance policy and practice; and second, the PKH was an imported model, emerging from a global policy diffusion by a global institution, for which Indonesia lacked the expertise and experience. In this context the adoption of the PKH is an example of the unequal relations between influential authorities (in this case, the Indonesian government) and a powerful global institution with large scale, low interest financial resources.

Current Developments of the PKH

The PKH aims to achieve five important goals: (1) improving poor households' living standards through increasing access to education, health and social welfare; (2) reducing household expenditure and increasing household income; (3) enhancing household economic sufficiency; (4) reducing poverty; and (5) introducing financial services to poor households (Kemensos 2019a). These objectives imply that the PKH is a cash benefit, which is used to supplement income. After people receive the benefit, the assumption is that recipients will see improved household incomes, living standards and economic self-sufficiency, leading to poverty reduction. However, the logic here is questionable, as the cash benefit is not for income generation and productive purposes. In practice, households simply spend the cash to send children to school and access primary health services.

The PKH has grown and expanded over time, and has seen increased Indonesian government expenditure and growing numbers of recipients covered. Figure 14.2 shows the extent of PKH expansion. From 2007 to 2019, government annual allocations increased by more than 67 times the original amount, from IDR 508 billion to IDR 34,239 billion. This has dramatically boosted the number of PKH recipients. In 2007, PKH beneficiaries totalled just 390 poor households but in 2019 this had increased to 10,000 households. Following this dramatic increase, as demonstrated in Figure 14.3, although the amount of the PKH budget remained smaller than the budget for the former Rastra and JKN programmes, the proportion of government spending and the numbers of PKH recipients have risen dramatically.

The government funded the PKH through the state budget and via soft loans from the World Bank. In 2017 the World Bank disbursed a USD 200 million loan (24.7 per cent of the 2017 national budget) to help the Indonesian government finance the PKH between 2017 to 2021 (World Bank 2017). The government used this budget to finance all technical-administrative expenditures required for the programme as well as PKH fund disbursements.

Since 2007 the programme has adjusted the coverage and actual amounts paid to beneficiaries. Table 14.2 depicts the types of benefits and the differences in relation to the range of the benefits between 2007 and 2019.

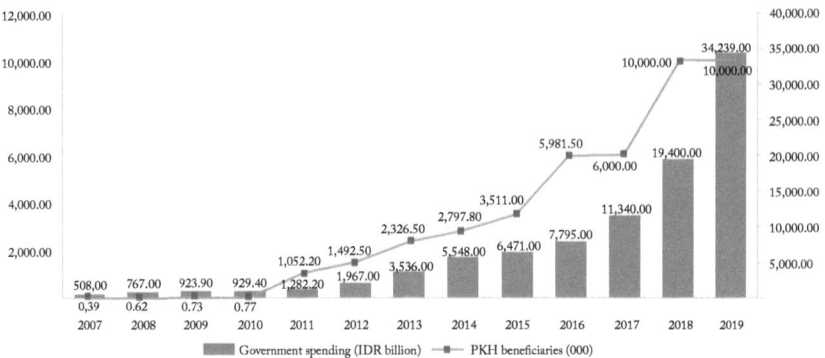

Figure 14.2   Government spending for PKH and PKH beneficiaries, 2007–19
Source: Kemensos 2019a.

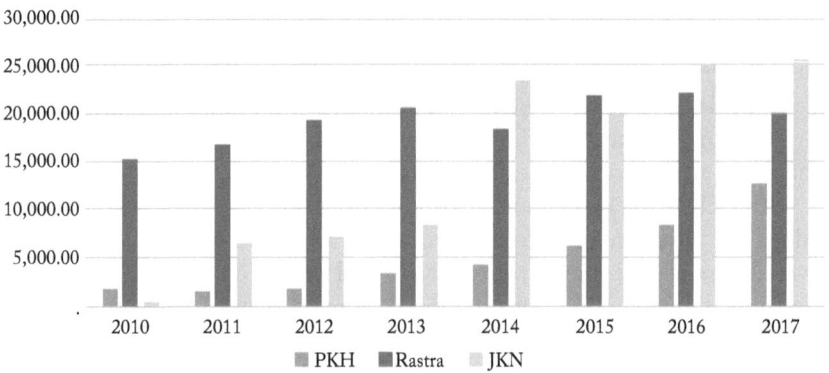

Figure 14.3   Government spending for PKH, Rastra, and JKN, 2010–17
Source: Unpublished data from Indonesian Ministry of Finance, 2019.

To obtain the PKH benefit, recipients must go to one of numerous banks selected by the Indonesian government to support the distribution. Beneficiaries receive their benefits through electronic banking transfers into their bank accounts. This means that, as with the BPNT discussed above, every recipient must have a bank account. However, poverty, low education levels and other factors mean that most people who would be otherwise eligible for the PKH, do not use banks and do not know how to use them. As for the BPNT, the government now requires the banks to create bank accounts for eligible recipients. The government gives each recipient a bank account and an associated account identification card using KKS, the same card used for the BPNT food allocation programme. The recipients claim the benefit at their bank by showing their personal KKS. Through these efforts, the government is also seeking to meet the final objective of the PKH, namely introducing financial services to poor households.

Table 14.2 Types of benefit and amount of benefit per household annually, 2007 and 2019

Types of benefit		Amount of the cash benefit (IDR thousand)	
		2007	**2019**
1.	Primary benefit Regular PKH	200	550
2.	Primary benefit Access PKH	n/a	1,000
3.	Pregnant /lactating household member	800	2,400
4.	Child (0–6 years old)	800	2,400
5.	Child studying at primary school	400	900
6.	Child studying at junior high school	800	1,500
7.	Child studying at senior high school	n/a	2,000
8.	Disabled household member	n/a	2,400
9.	Elderly household member	n/a	2,400
Maximum amount which can be received by recipient		2,200	10,150 (regular PKH)
			10,600 (access PKH)

Source: 2007: Kemensos 2007; 2019: Kemensos 2019b.

Soon after receiving PKH benefits, all beneficiaries need to undertake three obligations. First, beneficiaries who are pregnant or with children under seven years old must visit a health service to obtain services related to the pregnancy or the children. Second, PKH recipients with children must send them to school. Attendance rates of at least 85 per cent are required for the benefit to be continued. Lastly, PKH recipients who receive the benefit for disabled and elderly household members are required to bring their disabled and elderly members to access health services and activities specifically designed to support the disabled and elderly. Beneficiary households that do not access the relevant services promptly may be penalised through delay or discontinuation of the PKH benefit. However, these conditions are hard to enforce in practice, and programmes allow for several warnings before benefits are withdrawn. Many households still received full payments despite non-compliance (Hanna 2019).

Mistargeting Selection and Distribution Methods

Over the last two decades, the Indonesian government has sought to improve the accuracy of its selection process for beneficiaries of social assistance. As earlier chapters have noted, the selection of eligible beneficiaries has moved from using purely econometric targeting (PMT—Proxy-Means Testing), to a hybrid approach that (conceptually at least) combines PMT and community-based targeting (CBT) methods (McCarthy and Sumarto 2018). The hybrid approach combines the PMT and CBT methods and is known as *Pemutakhiran Basis Data Terpadu* (PBDT [Integrated Database Updating]), which was conducted in 2015. The hybrid approach involved several steps, as set out in Figure 14.4. Unfortunately, as earlier chapters have shown, the continued use of the PMT has led to the inevitable replication of targeting errors.

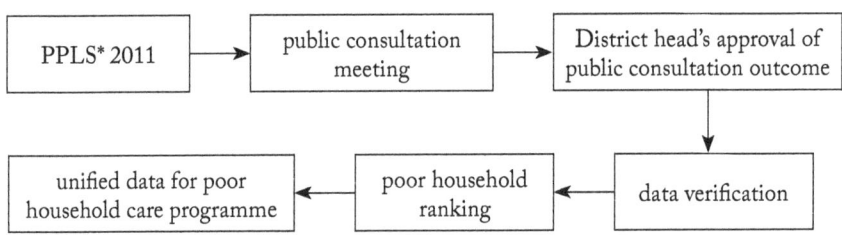

Figure 14.4   Stages in updating of the unified database of the Poor-Household Care Programme
Note: *PPLS: The Social Protection Program Survey (*Pendataan Program Perlindungan Social*).

Recently the programme implementation design has shifted again, as the government has updated the household poverty data using a Self-Updating Method, the *Mekanisme Pemutakhiran Mandiri* (MPM; Figure 14.5). The MPM relies heavily on the support of the poor and the local-district government for effective implementation. In the MPM, all the poor who consider that they are entitled to receive the targeted social assistance may register their names for it at their local village office. This involves a process of checking those who register to assess their eligibility to receive benefits. The system lists applicants deemed eligible under this initial assessment and who are subject to the next step for data verification and validation, conducted by a verifier recruited at the level of the district/municipality government. During the data verification and validation process, the verifier examines the households' socio-economic status using PMT indicators. The district/municipality government takes responsibility for these steps.

Under the MPM, all district/municipality governments throughout Indonesia need to conduct this process of verification and validation twice a year. After the agencies verify the data, these are submitted to the central agency TNP2K, to be ranked using the PMT algorithm. The ranking produces a national list of poor households eligible for social assistance. The final stage of the MPM is an endorsement of the national list of poor households via the issuing of a ministerial decree signed by the Social Affairs Minister (Working Group for Unified Data of Poor-Household Care Programme 2016).

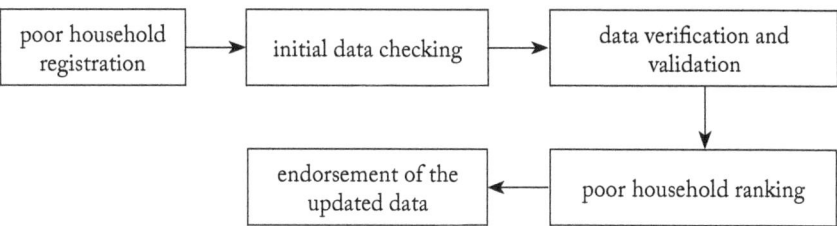

Figure 14.5   Stages in the self-updating method

The MPM is currently under the control of the Ministry of Social Affairs (Kemensos). The authorisation of Kemensos for MPM follows an institutional reform initiated in 2016, when the government shifted responsibility for conducting the MPM from TNP2K to Kemensos. This reform occurred when the government enacted a law entitled *Penanganan Fakir Miskin* (Care of the Poor). The law states that the management of data of poor households, including updating of these data, was to be delegated to Kemensos. Prior to this shift, the Ministry had no experience conducting national surveys or using community-based data to update social assistance data.

During the COVID-19 pandemic, the government continued using MPM to update the beneficiary data of PKH and of other COVID-19 JPS programmes. This commitment, however, generates additional and more problematic mistargeting for several reasons. First, people's intention to receive COVID-19 JPS is high because the government provides greater social assistance compared to the regular BLT programme. For instance, in the regular BLT, the government provides cash of IDR 100,000 per month, but during COVID-19 this was increased significantly to IDR 600,000 per month. Second, socio-economic activity restrictions, which were enforced by the government to reduce the spread of the pandemic, lessened the intensity and quality of the beneficiary registration and data validation process. Third, when COVID-19 struck, the MPM system had not been fully established, particularly in many districts outside Java where further development work was needed. Finally, the attraction of the JPS funding, combined with inaccurate poor household data, exacerbated the intensity of public complaints and protests from households who missed out (Sumarto and Ferdiansyah

2021). In the face of this widespread surge of discontent, many village leaders reverted to the default response which was to redistribute the increased JPS funding broadly in the village without considering the socio-economic status of the recipients.

PKH's Socio-Political Issues in Communities

The well-intentioned expanded financial assistance disseminated under the emergency COVID-19 JPS programme highlighted the increased capacity of the Indonesian government to use social assistance beneficiary lists for swift delivery of financial benefits in times of stress. But the complex process of identifying eligible poor households and ranking them according to levels of poverty proved entirely inadequate to the task; widespread social discontent and division ensued across the social landscape. The process simply reinforced the perception that mistargeting remains an endemic weakness in the social assistance policy.

Mistargeting takes place for technical and socio-political reasons. This includes the inaccuracy of beneficiary selection methods, even after the government had switched to using the self-reporting (MPM) selection method. There are three key underlying reasons for such inaccuracy. First, Kemensos has limited capacity to manage the database and its updating requirements. The Centre for Data and Information—*Pusat Data dan Informasi* (Pusdatin), a small division within Kemensos—is responsible for data updates under the MPM. However, Pusdatin has insufficient staffing and financial resources. Previously when TNP2K carried out data updates, Pusdatin was given a narrow scope of work; it was limited to documenting and managing information on Kemensos' programmes. Pusdatin has few employees, with relatively limited expertise. At the same time, Pusdatin (like TNP2K) lacks a structural network with district-level agencies and this lack creates coordination difficulties and complexity with the local government. Pusdatin has conducted data updating through a process of verification and validation twice a year in 83,344 villages across the archipelago. The task requires high technical capacity, a strong organisational network and consistent high-quality data, all of which were lacking.

Second, many autonomous district governments (*Kabupaten*) have limited staffing and technical capacity. Some districts/municipalities can manage social assistance policies, but many districts have limited expertise in this area, particularly in remote parts of the archipelago. It is unlikely that many district agencies could manage the data verification and validation bi-annually in remote areas, resulting in poor quality information which lacked verification.

Third, some verifier staff also have limited training to implement this work. The programme requires verifiers to understand a myriad of local issues among the village communities in which they work. When the local governments recruit local people as verifiers, few skilled applicants apply; inevitably, districts select and train verifiers who lack the competency for the role. These factors and the demands placed on verifier staff for limited remuneration mean that many of the verifiers across the 83,344 villages are unlikely to conduct verification and validation processes according to the pre-defined standardised procedures and instead resort to short cuts to achieve their target numbers.

The Indonesian government may have assumed that the inclusion of public consultation meetings might ensure that the aspirations of all community members would be represented (McCarthy and Sumarto 2018). Conceptually, this additional step may lead to lists of eligible PKH recipients being updated correctly, after a fair and open discussion in which participants critically review and update the list. However, (as discussed in Chapter 13), there are numerous issues surrounding deliberation in rural areas and which act as obstacles to consensus regarding village-based lists of approved beneficiaries. The result, too often, is perceived mistargeting, leading to social jealousy and latent conflicts within Indonesian communities (Sumarto 2021).

Earlier research has found that jealousy and latent conflict have plagued the Rastra and BLT programmes from their inception (Sumarto 2013, 2021). In the case of the BLT, public conflicts emerged among community members, between community members and community leaders and between village heads and their political rivals. These intense disagreements led to unrest and protests, damage to public facilities and in some cases physical injuries. In these circumstances, higher value social assistance attracted more intense conflicts because the stakes were higher, a feature that has continued to be a focus for social discontent as benefits are increased.

In 2015, for example, the BLT benefit equated to 19.3 per cent of monthly earnings (given the poverty rates at the time). Rastra provided a subsidy amounting to a mere 7.2 per cent. At the maximum level, the government provided an annual 2007-PKH benefit for each household of IDR 2,200,000, while the yearly maximum amount of the 2019-PKH benefit saw a fivefold increase to IDR 10,600,000 (see Kemensos 2019b). Based on the poverty lines at these times, the 2007-PKH assistance equated to 31.2 per cent of the monthly income poverty line, while the 2019-PKH cash was equivalent to 52.8 per cent. This means that the potential of the PKH to generate jealousy, leading to social conflict, was dramatically higher for PKH than the Rastra and BLT programmes. The higher benefit distributed under the PKH represents a current and ongoing problem for the programme, unless the government manages the risks of social jealousy associated with targeted social assistance. This begs the question: what alternative approaches might be designed and deployed to improve coverage and effectiveness?

Conclusion

Returning to the questions posed in the introduction, this chapter comes to three conclusions. First, the Indonesian government has transformed the JPS programmes into a national social protection policy, with heavy guidance from the World Bank. In this situation, the Indonesian government depended on the World Bank to develop the policy. The institutionalisation of the programmes lacked indigenous ideas around policy governance and policy directions. Second, the guidance of a global institution was not effective; it resulted in chronic failures and weaknesses in the dissemination of social assistance such as the PKH, which continues to be plagued by a range of technical and socio-political problems. Like the precursor targeted social assistance programmes, such as Rastra and the BLT, PKH is rife with poor and contested targeting of beneficiaries. Third, the Indonesian government adopted a World Bank social investment model without sufficient understanding of the social investment concept and the challenge of its application in a complex country like Indonesia. The result was that in developing a national social protection policy, the local authority remained submissive to the global driver (the World Bank) with its global liberalising policy diffusion agenda.

These three problems reflect the complicated process of adopting targeted social protection policies, resulting from global diffusion, under the guidance of the World Bank. The concept of guidance here denotes a process whereby the Indonesian government learns from the World Bank. However, the discussion in the previous sections reveals the World Bank's poor track record in guiding the implementation of these assistance programmes.

When the Indonesian government first adopted Rastra and other JPS programmes, it had little choice but to accept the World Bank's advice. At the time, the conditionalities for receiving the World Bank's SAP loan included accepting the JPS programme as part of a package, which aimed to liberalise the economic system through privatisation and price liberalisation. Later, despite the unresolved technical-administrative and social issues with Rastra and other targeted social assistance, the Indonesian government adopted PKH. Initially, the government's decision to adopt the policy was not autonomous and it was under coercion to accept the conditionalities. Later, the World Bank may not have coerced the government to take up PKH; without its own policy models, however, Indonesia remained under the hegemonic influence of World Bank ideas. In subsequent years, the World Bank continued to promote the liberalisation of Indonesian social policy. CCTs represent a social investment idea loaded with productivist and market-oriented agendas. Productivism is one of the tools of neoliberal ideology to achieve economic growth using the mechanism of the market.

The local-national process of social policy adoption, therefore, reveals the lopsided nature of global politics. The global actor diffuses global ideas, covering social investment and liberalisation with forceful or hegemonic policy advice. The local-national government submissively accepts the advice for two reasons: the global institution's conditionalities, and later, the local-national government's limited knowledge and capacity to implement social policy.

References

Barbier, J.C. 2017. "'Social Investment': With or Against Social Protection?", in *The Uses of Social Investment*, ed. A. Hemerijck. Oxford: Oxford University Press, pp. 51–8.

Béland, D. et al. 2018. "Instrument Constituencies and Transnational Policy Diffusion: The Case of Conditional Cash Transfers", *Review of International Political Economy* 25, 4: 462–83. DOI: 10.1080/09692290.2018.1470548.

Borges, F.A. 2018. "Neoliberalism with a Human Face? Ideology and the Diffusion of Latin America's Conditional Cash Transfers", *Comparative Politics* 50, 2: 147–67.

Dräbing, V. and M. Nelson. 2017. "Addressing Human Capital Risks and the Role of Institutional Complementarities", in *The Uses of Social Investment*, ed. A Hemerijck. Oxford: Oxford University Press, pp. 128–39.

Gilardi, F. and F. Wasserfallen. 2019. "The Politics of Policy Diffusion", *European Journal of Political Research* 58, 4: 1245–56. DOI: 10.1111/1475-6765.12326.

Gliszczynski, M. von and L. Leisering. 2016. "Constructing New Global Models of Social Security: How International Organisations Defined the Field of Social Cash Transfers in the 2000s", *Journal of Social Policy* 45, 2: 325–43.

Hanna, R. 2019. "New Research Busts the Myth of Welfare Dependency". World Economic Forum. Available at: https://www.weforum.org/agenda/2019/08/golden-truth-behind-welfare-dependency (accessed 8 Nov. 2021).

Hemerijck, A. 2017. "Social Investment and Its Critics", in *The Uses of Social Investment*, ed A. Hemerijck. Oxford: Oxford University Press, pp. 3–39.

Jenson, J. and N. Nagels. 2018. "Social Policy Instruments in Motion. Conditional Cash Transfers from Mexico to Peru", *Social Policy and Administration* 52, 1: 323–42.

Kemensos (Ministry of Social Affairs). 2007. *Pedoman Umum: Program Keluarga Harapan* [PKH guidelines]. Jakarta: Tim Penyusun Pedoman Umum PKH.

————. 2019a. *Pedoman Pelaksanaan Program Keluarga Harapan, Tahun 2019* [Guidelines of the Family Hope Program, 2019]. Jakarta: Kemensos.

————. 2019b. *Sosialisasi Penyaluran Bantuan Sosial Program Keluarga Harapan, Tahun 2019* [The 2019–PKH Socialisation]. Jakarta: Kemensos.

Kitchen, V. and J.G. Mathers. 2019. "Introduction", in *Heroism and Global Politics*, ed. V. Kitchen and J.G. Mathers. London: Routledge, pp. 1–20.

Lyon, A. 2013. "Relational Representation: An Agency-based Approach to Global Justice", *Critical Review of International Social and Political Philosophy* 16, 2: 233–48.

Mahon, R. 2019. "Broadening the Social Investment Agenda: The OECD, the World Bank and Inclusive Growth", *Global Social Policy* 19, 1–2: 121–38. DOI: 10.1177/1468018119826404.

McCarthy, J. and M. Sumarto. 2018. "Distributional Politics and Social Protection in Indonesia: Dilemma of Layering, Nesting and Social Fit in Jokowi's Poverty Policy", *Journal of Southeast Asian Economies* 35, 2: 223–36.

Mendoza, E.N. 2019. "Are Conditional Cash Transfer Programs for Women? Engendering the Philippine Pantawid", *Asian Social Work Policy Review* 13, 1: 78–86. DOI: 10.1111/aswp.12158.

Nagels, N. 2016. "The Social Investment Perspective, Conditional Cash Transfer Programmes and the Welfare Mix: Peru and Bolivia", *Journal of Social Policy* 15, 3: 479–93.

Nelson, M. and J. Sandberg. 2016. "From Perspectives to Policy Contingencies: Conditional Cash Transfers as Social Investments", *Global Social Policy* 17, 1: 21–37. DOI: 10.1177/1468018116633560.

Ogamba, I.K. 2020. "Conditional Cash Transfer and Education under Neoliberalism in Nigeria: Inequality, Poverty and Commercialisation in the School Sector", *Review of African Political Economy* 47, 5: 1–10. DOI: 10.1080/03056244.2020.1771298.

Papadopoulos, T. and R.V. Leyer. 2016. "Two Decades of Social Investment in Latin America: Outcomes, Shortcomings and Achievements of Conditional Cash Transfers", *Social Policy and Society* 15, 3: 435–49.

Razak, O. 2015. "Beyond Poverty Reduction: Conditional Cash Transfers and Citizenship in Ghana", *Journal of Social Welfare* 24: 27–36.

Reininger, T., C. Villalobos and I. Wyman. 2019. "CCTs and Conditionalities: an Exploratory Analysis of Not Meeting Conditional Cash Transfer Conditionalities in Chile's Families Programme", *Journal of Poverty and Social Justice* 27, 1: 95–114.

Sugiyama, N.B. and W. Hunter. 2020. "Do Conditional Cash Transfers Empower Women? Insights from Brazil's Bolsa Família", *Latin American Politics and Society* 6, 2: 53–74.

Sumarto, M. (under the name of Mulyadi). 2013. *Welfare Regime, Social Conflict, and Clientelism in Indonesia*, Canberra: Australian National University. Unpublished PhD thesis.

_____. 2014. *Perlindungan Sosial dan Klientelisme: Makna Politik Bantuan Tunai dalam Pemilihan Umum* [Social Protection and Clientelism: the Political Meaning of Cash Transfer Programmes in Presidential Elections in Indonesia]. Yogyakarta: Gadjah Mada University Press.

_____. 2017. "Welfare Regime Change in Developing Countries: Evidence from Indonesia", *Social Policy and Administration* 51, 6: 940–59.

_____. 2021. "Welfare and Conflict: Policy Failure in the Indonesian Cash Transfer", *Journal of Social Policy* 50, 3: 533–51.

Sumarto, M. and F. Ferdiansyah. 2021. "Indonesia's Social Policy Response to Covid-19: Targeted Social Protection under Budget Constraints". *CRC 1342 Covid-19 Social Policy Response Series, 28*. Bremen: CRC (Collaborative Research Centre) 1342.

Sumarto, M. and A. Kaasch. 2018. *New Directions in Social Policy: Evidence from the Indonesian Health Insurance Programme*. UNRISD Working Paper, no. 2018–9. Geneva: UNRISD.

Timmer, P., Hastuti and S. Sumarto. 2018. "Evolution and Implementation of the Rastra Program in Indonesia", in *The 1.5 Billion People Question: Food, Vouchers, or Cash Transfers?* ed. H. Alderman, U. Gentilini and R. Yemtsov. Washington, DC: World Bank, pp. 265–310.

Vagionaki, T. and P. Trein. 2020. "Learning in Political Analysis", *Political Studies Review* 18, 2: 304–19.

Weyland, K. 2017. "Autocratic Diffusion and Cooperation: The Impact of Interests vs. Ideology", *Democratisation* 24, 7: 1235–52.

Working Group for Unified Data of Poor-Household Care Programme. 2016. *Pedoman Umum Mekanisme Pemutakhiran Mandiri* [Guidelines for Self-Updating Method]. Jakarta: Working Group for Unified Data of Poor-Household Care Programme.

World Bank. 2006. *Making the New Indonesia Work for the Poor*. Jakarta: World Bank.

_____. 2012. *Targeting Poor and Vulnerable Households in Indonesia*. Jakarta: World Bank.

_____. 2017. *International Bank for Reconstruction and Development Program Appraisal Document on a Proposed Loan in the Amount of US$200 million to the*

Republic of Indonesia for a Social Assistance Reform Program, Report No: 112703-ID. Jakarta: World Bank.

Zehavi, A. and D. Breznitz. 2018. "The Neoliberal Targeted Social Investment State: The Case of Ethnic Minorities", *Journal of Social Policy* 48, 2: 207–25. DOI:10.1017/S004727941800034X.

Part Four

Conclusions

CHAPTER 15

Agrarian Change and Social Assistance Outcomes

John F. McCarthy, Andrew McWilliam, Gerben Nooteboom,
Pande Made Kutanegara, Rudy Purba, Henri Sitorus, Jacqueline Vel,
Carol Warren and Lisa Woodward

This chapter draws together our findings on poverty dynamics and social assistance.[1] First, we consider the predominant patterns of rural change: what is the character of poverty and nutritional security in contemporary Indonesia? Second, we discuss the significance of social assistance programmes: what are the patterns of inclusion and exclusion, and what processes shape these outcomes?

Escaping Poverty

Our study uses community-based concepts of poverty—using the Stages of Poverty (SoP) methodology (see Krishna 2004, 2006 and introductory Chapters 1–2)—derived from the experienced realities in each socio-economic milieu. Given this method's emic dimension, and the reality that social needs and expectations as well as the understanding of poverty change over time, we need to be cautious about comparing across contexts. By way of overview, we do see significant numbers of people leaving poverty behind (Figures 15.1 and 15.2). In six of our cases, participatory assessments indicated that, according to locally constituted markers of poverty, more than 30 per cent of the population has moved out of poverty over the past 20–30 years. However, the proportion of people following specific livelihood trajectories varies across cases, and what works in one case may fail in another (see Figure 15.1).

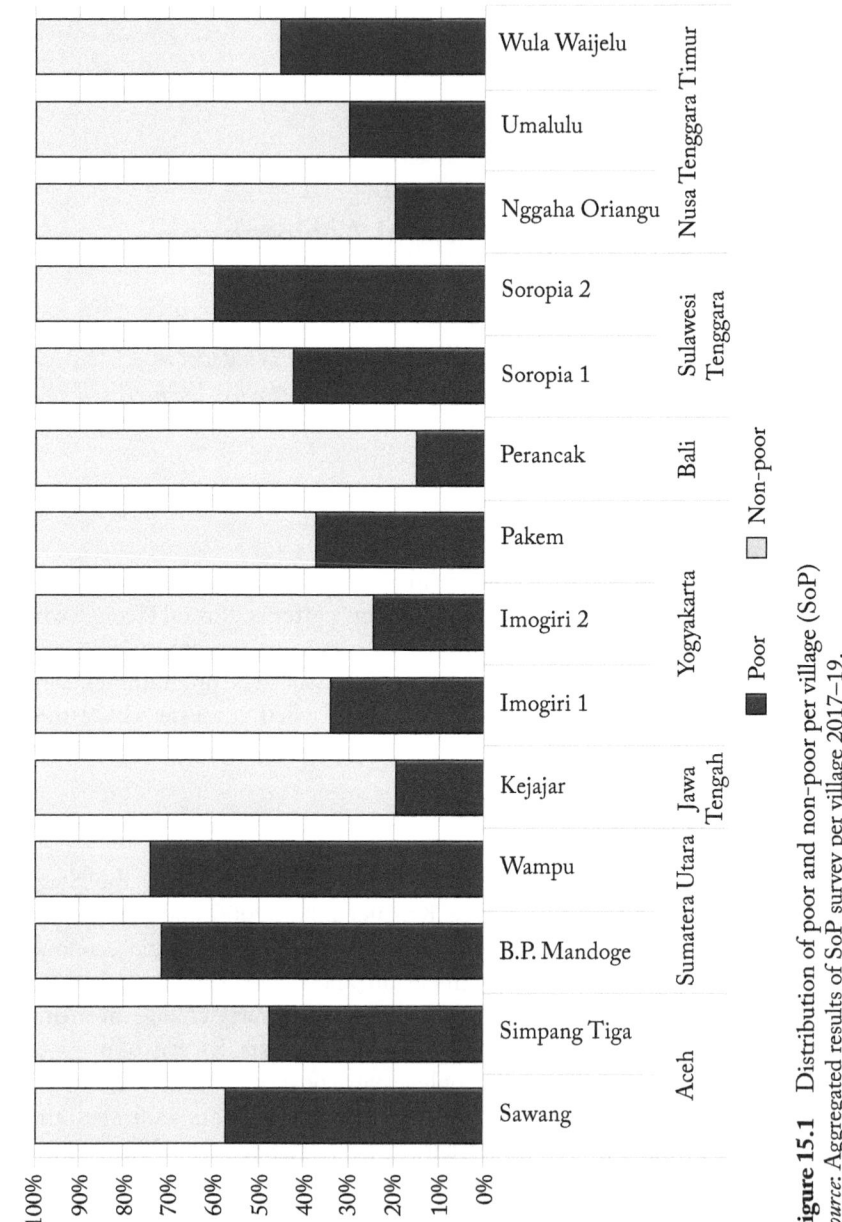

Figure 15.1 Distribution of poor and non-poor per village (SoP)
Source: Aggregated results of SoP survey per village 2017–19.

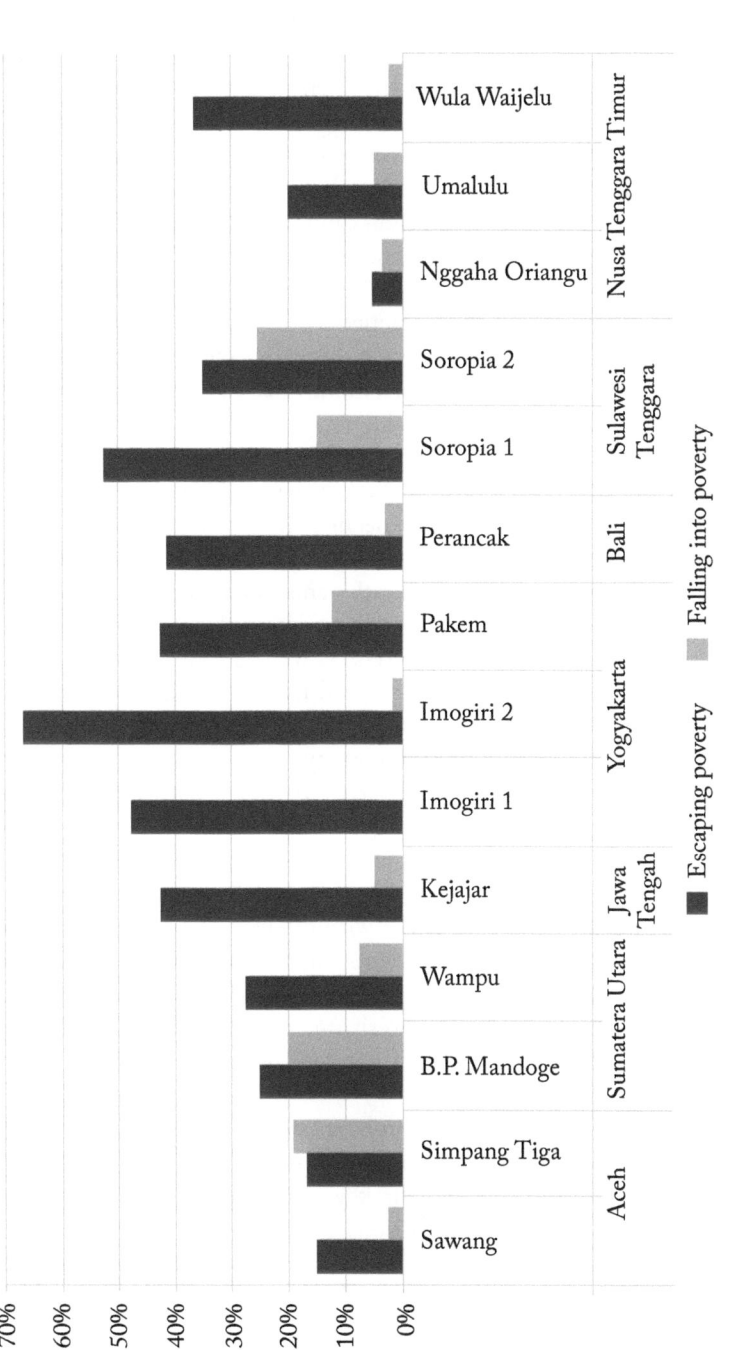

Figure 15.2 Moving in and out of poverty over 20–30 years
Source: SoP results.

Historically, researchers and policymakers have argued that inclusive agricultural growth with appropriate state support could be powerfully pro-poor and provide a means of raising the smallholding poor out of poverty (Haggblade, Hazell and Reardon 2010; Wiggins, Kirsten and Llambí 2010). This view sees a virtuous circle of increasing agricultural productivity, with higher incomes and flow-on effects that reduce poverty and food insecurity. Actors with access to the market, sufficient capital and technology can respond to new market opportunities, thereby accumulating resources in fishing or agriculture. Supportive state policies have been critical for this shift as farmers (or fishers) intensify or extend their practices.

We see evidence of a farming and fishing trajectory out of poverty in three scenarios. In the upland Java *horticultural boom scenario* (Chapter 4), many households boosted potato production using land and capital under their control. Many families also moved out of poverty via enhanced fisheries production in the Bali marine degradation scenario (Chapter 9) before fish stocks have more recently fallen into decline. In the *fisheries boom scenario* (Southeast Sulawesi, Chapter 10), households have improved their livelihoods. Key drivers included increased domestic and international demand for seafood, access to ice, the emergence of fish traders with capital and networks in the community and into urban markets, as well as widespread availability of improved boat technologies that enhanced fish harvesting and marketing success. The capacity of some small-scale fishers to reap dividends in pelagic fisheries has facilitated pathways out of poverty.

In the *precarious developmental scenario* (Bantul, Central Java), farmers who engaged in intensive (rice) farming, combined with extensive livestock rearing and the afforestation of marginal lands using valuable wood trees such as teak and Malay ebony, also progressed. However, the key to such an advance involved combining agriculture with off-farm work in nearby cities. Over time, men shifted from agriculture to construction or other jobs, which supported a feminisation of agriculture (Nooteboom 2019; Pattenden and Wastuti 2021). Similarly, in the Sulawesi *fisheries boom scenario*, women are more highly engaged as traders in fish markets and we see a sharpening of gendered labour roles.

Some scenarios resonate with a broader body of research: under certain conditions, combining different sources of income (farming, on-farm and off-farm, including migration) provides the key to progress (Haggblade, Hazell and Reardon 2010). Different proportions of actors in each scenario move out of fisheries and agricultural livelihoods altogether, either by diversification off-farm, migration, or education. These options include construction workers (*tukang bangun*) in Java, who subcontract their land and collect land rents while diversifying into other activities. Similarly, a cohort of actors in Aceh gave their land over to sharecropping or hired seasonal labour to work the land while putting most of their efforts into off-farm activities.

In the *horticulture boom scenario* (Java, Chapter 4), a younger generation, including the majority of children from families who previously farmed, predominantly found work outside agriculture.[2] In Bali's *marine degradation scenario* (Chapter 9), villagers accumulated a store of assets, attained education, diversified employment experience and improved their housing and transportation during the prosperity period. Some households diversified into other sectors, while fishers earned higher prices. While very few found employment in tourism, educated family members were able to take up employment opportunities beyond the village. Even in the comparatively stagnant, low-growth Sumba *semi-subsistence scenario*, a number of people with kin-based support could invest in their education beyond the village and follow migration and non-agrarian trajectories. This enabled some to obtain government jobs and send money to their families.

Superior trajectories emerge where households combine diversification and intensification. In the Sumatran *smallholder development scenario* (Asahan), we see rapid progress where people can accumulate in oil palm production by control of land, generating sufficient capital to diversify outwards and making use of the province's diversified economy to consolidate these gains. Even in places where we see minimal movement, we can identify mechanisms for progress for some. In the Aceh *sideways scenario*, a small number of families used off-farm or other opportunities to rise above poverty while sharecropping their land and extracting rents. In Sumba, where opportunities to move forward are even more difficult, some households accumulated capital by selling crops, engaging in wage labour on sugar and other plantations, opening small enterprises and becoming traders, especially where new roads enhanced access.

In many scenarios, progress appears to be cyclical, where bust follows boom and returns to bust, and continues onwards. The Bali *marine degradation scenario* provides a salutary lesson, where gains over decades were wiped away by over-accumulation, mismanagement and over-extraction of fisheries, all exacerbated by anthropogenic climate change. We see a similar boom-bust dynamic and ecological degradation in the Java potato *horticultural boom scenario*.

In both these scenarios, *ecological pressures and squeezes* threaten progress. Actors are forced into distress diversification or more intensive production following the end of a commodity or agricultural boom. For instance, over-capitalisation and over-exploitation in the purse seine fishery have led to falling production, and fishers in the large and small-scale sectors moved backwards after the boom ended. Similarly, potato farms in upland Java, stuck on the pesticide treadmill and engaging in soil mining, now face production insecurities due to an increasingly unstable climate.

It is also likely that progress in the Southeast Sulawesi *fisheries boom scenario* could be wiped out, due to competition and over-exploitation of these open-access resources combined with the impact of environmental degradation and poor government regulation. These cases highlight the familiar cyclical nature of commodity booms and busts, described, for example, in Li (2014), and the historical "cycles of commercialisation and accumulation" described for central Java by Hüsken (1989), as well as new harmful trajectories from forms of over-exploitation not seen before.

Table 15.1 Moving up (based on comparative analysis)

Java Lowland *precarious developmental scenario*	**Diversification:** taking on one of the many job opportunities outside agriculture (e.g. construction, wage labour, rural industries, services); **Combining wage labour outside agriculture** with part-time farming on small owned or leased plots (often relations are gendered, women engage more in farming); **Migration and de-agrarianization** plus remittances, education and family/home-based micro-enterprises.
Aceh *sideways scenario*	**Diversify** out of agriculture while giving over rice land to sharecropping and extracting land rent; **Minimising labour inputs into agriculture** while also diversifying.
Sumba *semi-subsistence scenario*	**Diversification within the village:** accumulate by selling cash crops, opening a small enterprise or become traders; **Migration and deagrarianization plus remittances:** investing in their children; e.g. bartering services with urban Uma members who provide access to education. Children escape from agriculture, obtain a government job and provide for family in the village.
Java Upland *horticultural boom scenario.*	**Intensified agriculture based on control of land labour and capital:** intensive potato farming with high inputs; **Diversification** into tourism or other businesses and work; sand mining, cattle; **Education** and obtaining formal employment in government.
North Sumatra *smallholder development and enclave plantation scenario*	**Accumulate:** through sufficient control of oil palm land (integration into high value agriculture); **Diversify outwards** given the highly developed economy of North Sumatra.

Table 15.1 (*cont'd*)

Bali marine degradation scenario	**Diversification:** moving into employment in the tourist sector outside the village; deagrarianization as HH members take on wage labour outside the village;[3] **Diversification** within the village: e.g. expansion of animal husbandry; **Intensification of fishing effort** following partial integration of artisanal fishers into the international market, but reversal with over-exploitation and decline of the resource.[4]
Southeast Sulawesi fisheries boom scenario	**Intensification of fishing effort:** avoiding debt during the scarcity season (*musim paceklik*); participating in high value fishing during the monsoon (*musim angin*) as client of patron or independent supplier; **Diversifying income sources** across different target species, use grow out pens, tidal traps and small-scale trading. Using patronage to connect to markets and centres of power and protection.[5]

Staying poor and moving sideways

As other research has found, poverty is dynamic and there is a great deal of churning: even as some people move out of poverty, others fall back (Krishna 2004, 2006). Analysts here distinguish between the chronic and the transient poor (Jalan and Ravallion 2000). In all our scenarios, some households become poor, typically due to lifecycle crises such as divorce, illness, death of a spouse, or growing old and being unable to work. Others become poor after unsuccessfully trying to diversify or taking on too much risk. Newly married couples may fall into poverty after starting a family before obtaining a stable domestic economy. Indeed, studies have found that adolescent women who become pregnant and younger women are more vulnerable and have a higher risk of having stunted children (Beal et al. 2018).

Across our cases, we also find that many people remained poor over the period of comparison. Around 43 per cent of the total surveyed who were poor two decades earlier remained poor by local criteria (Figure 15.3), with 6 out of the 14 cases having around half the population staying poor in local terms. Stuck and insecure households include those in debt to patrons or caught in poorly paid wage labour or tenant farming. These include, for example, sharecroppers in Aceh who pay for production costs and fail to retain sufficient control over their rice production to avoid debt. These "scissor effects", which combine declining farm size, rising cash needs, problems accessing inputs and credit at low interest rates, environmental decline and falling state assistance, all affect smallholders (Mahmood et al. 2014). Likewise, fishers need to borrow to make it through the scarcity season (*paceklik*), entering into long-term debt cycles with patrons. There are thus few signs of the classic "agrarian transition" for many households across most of our sites. Yet even while the mechanisms vary considerably and the widespread reproduction of poverty is evident across most scenarios, we do not see an agrarian crisis. Villagers for the most part muddle through, escaping hunger if not nutritional insecurity.

On average, we found higher levels of poverty where larger proportions of the population remained engaged in agriculture. Indeed, state statistics suggest that poverty in rural areas is double that of cities, and highest in more remote rural areas, where most of the population remains in agriculture (*Jakarta Post* 2018). In each scenario, particular sets of structural factors work to keep people poor. For instance, land is relatively abundant in the Sumba *semi-subsistence scenario*, but labour is constrained and seasonal variability with frequent crop losses is increasingly common as environmental conditions become more severe. Sharing food and borrowing money within the larger community economy are the primary ways of coping with seasonal food shortages. Selling small livestock is the second most common option when household conditions deteriorate.[6]

Some of the agricultural scenarios resonate with the classical agrarian political economy narrative of political and economic marginalisation. In Aceh, the poor tend to be landless or those with minimal land and work as tenant farmers. Even if yields are high among tenant farmers, their returns are meagre once they pay land rent and production costs. Similar patterns are visible in lowland Java for those who are "stuck" in small scale rice production. In upland Java, we see insecure access to irrigation and subjection to market forces (e.g. lower prices at harvest). The unsustainable ecological basis of the potato boom has compounded this pattern. In upland Java, fertility is declining, with soil mining causing potato yields to drop significantly since the mid-1990s. In Aceh and Java, the squeeze on agriculture leaves farmers caught between increasing production costs and unstable or diminishing returns. The role of intermediaries who engage in price speculation and the lack of state policies to prevent price gouging aggravate such factors.[7]

In several scenarios, social relations play a crucial role in the constitution and reproduction of poverty. In the Sulawesi *fishing boom scenario*, the poor are locked into a production system and social relations that effectively deny their economic mobility. Crew members obtain only a limited share of fish production and most cannot save sufficiently during the fishing season. As they borrow from their patron and fall into seasonal debt, most cannot accumulate adequately in the season to move forward. At the same time, independent fishers can access markets through the same patron networks and benefit from higher prices. In summary, as set out in Table 15.2, we identify the contextual and structural processes coming together to shape how people fall into poverty or stay poor.

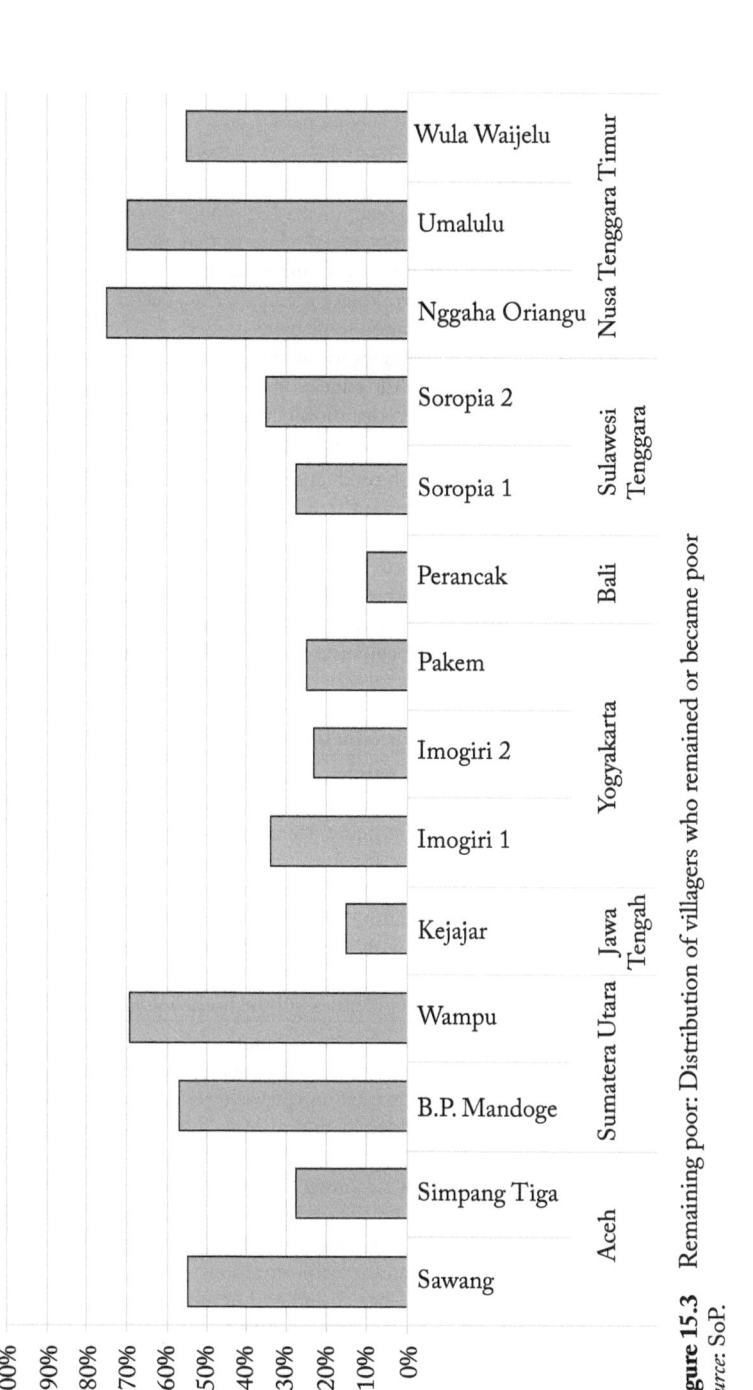

Figure 15.3 Remaining poor: Distribution of villagers who remained or became poor
Source: SoP.

Table 15.2 Becoming or staying poor (based on comparative analysis)

	Falling into poverty or staying poor
Java Lowland *precarious developmental scenario*	• **Landlessness:** Highly unequal access to land and productive resources; • **Reproduction squeeze:** increasing production costs and unstable or diminished returns, social relations that are exploitative compounded by insecure access to land; • **Life cycle risks:** workplace accidents, the general precarity of the wage-labour migration remittance model; • High social pressure on social obligations, **uncertain returns of investments** in the education of children, reproduction of inequality through education/business failure.
Aceh *sideways scenario*	• **The political economy of production:** structures of land ownership and high production costs, commodification of inputs including labour, tenant farmers borrow and pay land rent, lead to reduced control over rice surplus with patterns of stunting and food insecurity; • **Structure of labour markets:** limited integration into regional labour markets, few opportunities for diversification or migration; • **The emergence of consumptive lifestyles and integration into the market:** high expenses have detrimental impacts on food security. • **Life cycle debt or production crisis.**
Sumba *semi-subsistence scenario*	• **Semi-subsistence nature of agriculture:** Climate and agroecology are unstable due to low rainfall and prolonged dry periods, as well as extreme fluctuations; droughts and floods, lack of household labour for expanding gardens or engaging in other income-generating activities with high levels of stunting;[8] • Water grabbing leading to decreasing rice yields; • No close relatives with salaried work who can help in times of shortage; • Livestock disease epidemics kill the households' savings.
Java Upland *horticultural boom scenario*	• **Reproduction squeeze:** increasing production costs and unstable/diminished returns exacerbated by state policies; associated with insertion into the market on adverse terms; exploitative social relations compounded by diminishing land sizes; limited access to irrigation; • **Structural factors:** declining soil fertility from intensive farming and sand mining and the pesticide treadmill. Subject to erratic weather, extended dry season or prolonged heavy rainfall and floods, landslides and volcanic eruptions; • **Life cycle risks**, ill-health and cost of medical treatment leading to debt; cost of high school education such as accommodation and transport.

Table 15.2 (*cont'd*)

North Sumatra *Smallholder development and Enclave plantation scenario*	• **Rising costs** for consumption and production among smallholders, unstable prices, combined with low or reduced crop production with aging tree crops; locked into captive value chains; • **Fragmentation of land;** lifecycle crisis or debt crisis forcing the sale of land; • **Seasonal scarcity of labour opportunities;** precarious and low-paying work, leading to nutritional insecurity deepening during low production periods in oil palm estates.
Bali *marine degradation scenario*	• **Life cycle crises** due to circumstances (illness, death, indebtedness); • **Anthropogenic environmental stresses** from the collapse of the Bali Strait fishery and competition between commercial and small-scale fishery—driven by poor governance and overdevelopment; • **The decline of the natural resource base** makes some households more vulnerable, leading to distress diversification and differentiation; • **Customary (*adat*)** ritual and social obligations time consuming and affect the capacity of households to accumulate capital; but they also underpin the moral economy and residential land rights.
Southeast Sulawesi *fisheries boom scenario*	• **Falling into debt** during the layover months is a significant factor in the rise of dependency and poverty over time; • **Death of breadwinner:** women lose their fisher husband's support through divorce or death and access to their principal and vital source of cash income from fishing, leading to crisis sale of assets; • **Life cycle crises:** illness, misfortune, gambling, divorce.

To sum up our findings on poverty dynamics, we find a significant cohort of households across scenarios moving out of poverty as defined by local criteria. The proportions vary across scenarios, along with the mechanisms and processes at work (see Figures 15.1–15.3). In the most successful diversification scenarios, such as Bali (Chapter 9) and Java (Chapter 4), progress is still insecure for many of these successful households, due to the uncertain or precarious nature of household integration into the economy, and because this occurs on adverse terms. In our three boom scenarios, over-exploitation and climate change threaten to wash away the gains of recent decades. In most scenarios, we see also the reproduction of poverty on a large scale. The processes that reproduce poverty vary. Yet, in most scenarios, the structure of labour markets, agricultural value chains and land ownership and the combined workings of exploitative social relations, life cycle risks, environmental factors and debt in individual cases render people vulnerable.

Food Poverty and Nutritional Insecurity

We found significant patterns of seasonal scarcity, especially in regions with high stunting rates. Stunting is a chronic nutritional problem characterised by a child's failure to grow and develop optimally due to the cumulative and ongoing effects of malnutrition. Stunted children are very short for their age. High stunting rates provide evidence of extensive food poverty and nutritional insecurity. In Aceh, Southeast Sulawesi, upland Java, North Sumatra and Sumba, we see pronounced patterns of seasonal insecurity combined with high stunting rates (see Figure 15.6 below). The scarcity season typically involves replacing proteins with carbohydrates and reducing the purchase of vegetables while relying on common coping strategies. Nutritional insecurity coincides with temporal shortages of food or limited capacity to access nutritionally rich food, one of our study's key areas of investigation.

If poverty statistics provide an indirect measure of vulnerability and deprivation, stunting offers a direct and comprehensive multidimensional poverty indicator (Setboonsarng 2005). The literature on the nutritional status of children in Indonesia points to three categories of problems that help explain high levels of stunting. First, analysts describe a set of proximate factors related to specific behaviours and deficiencies. These include women marrying young; households drinking untreated water and having poor sanitation (Semba et al. 2011); poor breastfeeding practices and exposure to infectious diseases (Torlesse et al. 2016; Bardosono, Sastroamidjojo and Lukito 2007). Second, research points to a broader set of community and societal factors, such as communities lacking access to adequate health care services (Anwar et al. 2010; Bardosono, Sastroamidjojo and Lukito 2007) and good quality health care providers (Torlesse et al. 2016). Third, the socio-economic status of households, including poor maternal knowledge of nutrition, is related to poor access to specific micronutrients (Rachmi et al. 2016). The prevalence of many of these problems in rural areas is associated with a higher likelihood of stunting (Rachmi et al. 2016; Sandjaja et al. 2013). Most significantly for this study, low income and unemployment are associated with stunting (Bardosono, Sastroamidjojo and Lukito 2007; Ramli et al. 2009). Children from the lowest wealth quintile are much more likely to be stunted (Torlesse et al. 2016).

Econometric analysis of the relationship between poverty (Susenas 2018) and stunting (Riskesdas 2018) in Indonesia found a significant positive relationship and concluded that "the higher the proportion of poor people, the higher the proportion of stunting". However, we need to avoid measuring food security in terms of calories. When caloric requirements are deployed as the chief metric, the range of acceptable foods emphasises simple carbohydrates,

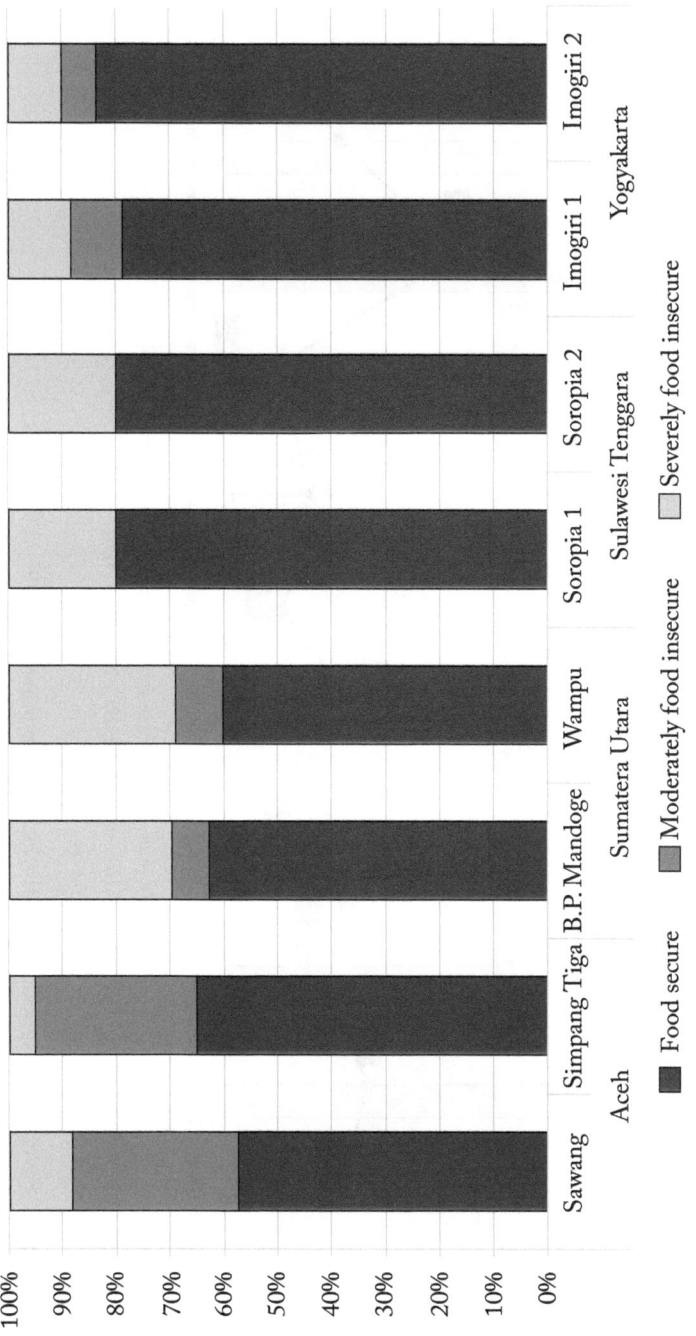

Figure 15.4 Patterns of food insecurity in a selection of our cases, 2017–19
Source: Food security survey.

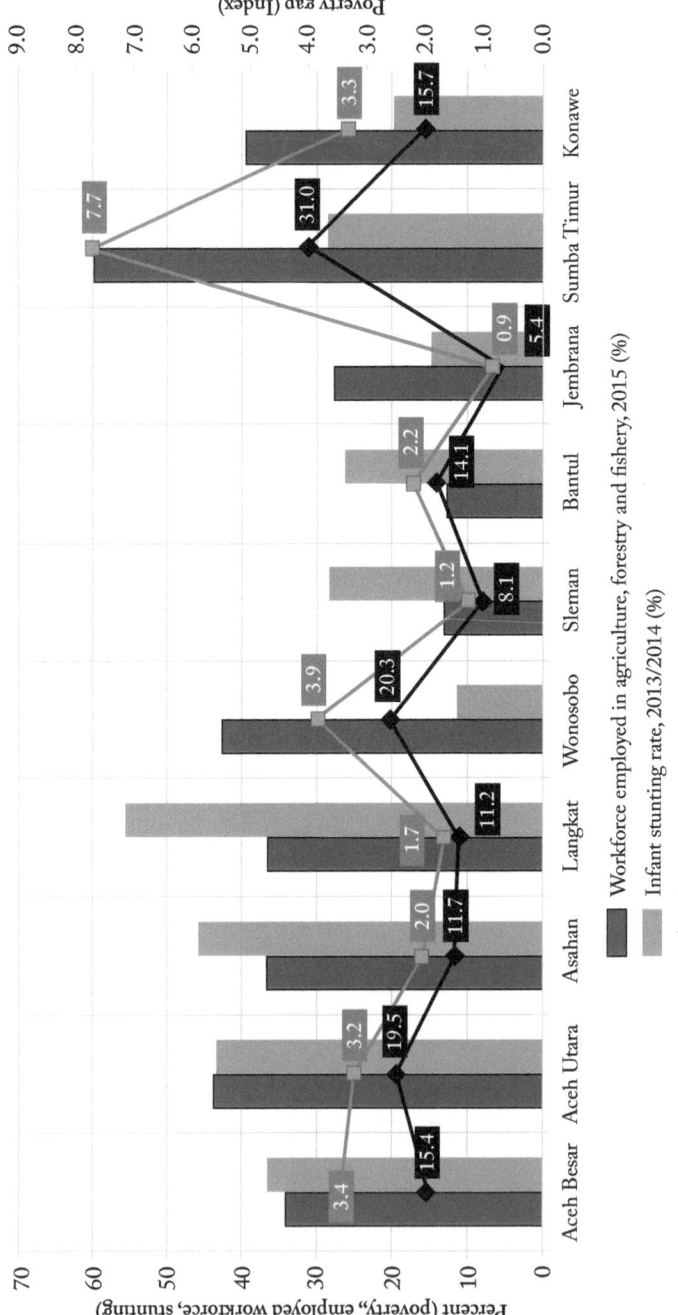

Figure 15.5 Poverty rates, agricultural employment and stunting, 2017–19

Source: BPS (Badan Pusat Statistik/Statistics Indonesia).

fats and sugars. In contrast, when nutrient security becomes the principal metric, proper diets need greater diversity, emphasising fruits, vegetables and a range of proteins. Village coping strategies that involve moving to high carbohydrate foods and cutting back on protein have negative nutritional outcomes.

Remarkably, stunting does not always or only correlate with high poverty levels; some areas with quantitatively higher cash incomes, such as palm oil-producing areas (Asahan and Langkat), can also have high stunting rates. Similarly, the movement out of agriculture may not reduce stunting: areas where fewer people are engaged in agriculture (rural Yogyakarta/Central Java), may also retain high stunting rates. Food preferences and cultures (i.e. snacks known as *jajan*; distaste for fish; *tahu/tempe*) also affect nutritional outcomes. Hence, we need to recognise the diverse causes of poverty and malnutrition.

In recent decades, food systems have changed. Corporate supply chains now penetrate remote villages, providing affordable access to cheap, highly processed and packaged foods with high concentrations of fat, sugars and additives. As "calorie rich foods provide a greater 'bang for the buck' in terms of satiety" (Dixon 2016), rural households which are increasingly dependent on low-wage work and less reliant on subsistence agriculture (self-provisioning of food) or foraging, now rely on the market to access cheap processed foods, including snacks (*jajan*) marketed specifically to the young.

In the Sumba (Chapter 6) *semi-subsistence scenario*, where the depth of poverty is most significant, the variable climate, poor production and lack of financial assets are long-term structural problems. Here only six per cent of villagers decreased their food consumption but changed their diet, from eating rice unmixed to mixing it with corn and cassava. Ten per cent also gathered alternative foods, such as wild tubers and insects, hunted animals, and sourced mushrooms from the forest and fish from the sea. Traditional strategies to deal with hunger periods, including reciprocal relations with neighbours and relatives, continue to shape farming in these seasonally dry uplands. Here, analysis of income and consumption based on statistics or our surveys provides only limited insights and, in these scenarios, subsistence capacity, the ability to subsist on one's own production, is critical to nutritional outcomes (Fischer 2008).

Subsistence strategies often also complement market integration. This points to a methodological problem that emerged in our analysis: surveys incompletely capture the dimensions of wealth in subsistence aspects of rural livelihoods, such as those found in Sumba and, to varying degrees, in the Aceh, Bali and Southeast Sulawesi cases. As Fischer notes, "there is considerable wealth generated and stored in subsistence-based rural economies" that conventional household income measures poorly capture (2008: 18).

In the Aceh *sideways scenario*, the authors found that those with little subsistence capacity lacked control over rice production. Here it is not the level of food production *per se* that matters, but rather how the poor are integrated into the rice production system and the broader economy. Those who suffer scarcity tend to be sharecroppers or landless farmers with few assets. Low cash incomes combine with poor subsistence capacity to deepen nutritional insecurity, particularly if people also have insecure cash-earning work opportunities. Here, labour and production social relations are exploitative and sharecroppers or functionally landless households just do not have enough left from their harvests to tide them over. Cultural issues also came into play. Our research found that poor households expressed shame if they sent their children to school without sweet snacks (*jajan*), and insecure households tended to trade-off buying nutritious food against other purchases, including fixing a roof or paying for school needs.

By contrast, in the *smallholder development and enclave plantation scenario*, even though the data suggest that the population is less poor in statistical terms, stunting data show that they are nutritionally insecure. We suggest that this is because they have higher income in cash terms, but less subsistence capacity in oil palm landscapes. The dispossession of land assets during earlier processes of enclosure has undercut the subsistence basis of rural livelihoods. Many households in Langkat remain dependent on food markets, while poorly paid and insecure work reduces their ability to feed their families. These contrasting scenarios contradict the hypothesis that entering the labour market and leaving subsistence agriculture behind will provide pathways out of poverty. Due to continuing casualisation of lowly paid and insecure labour, and adverse incorporation in the booming oil palm sector, market integration across generations has re-worked the nature of vulnerability for these households. This supports the observations in Rigg, Salamanca and Thompson (2016), in a different context, that families move from vulnerabilities associated with older cash crop (rubber) and swidden systems into new forms of precarity created by processes of plantation development. However, the nutritional implications of this shift may be missed, where the older subsistence-orientated livelihoods in rural Indonesia offered more diverse and nutritious diets (Mehraban and Ickowitz 2021).

In the Javanese district of Wonosobo *horticultural boom scenario*, we see a high rate of employment in agriculture and relatively higher stunting. In contrast, in the Sleman and Bantul *precarious development scenario*, we see lower rates of work in agriculture and still relatively high rates of stunting. While we need to be cautious about extrapolating from the statistics, we note that non-agricultural households do not access food from family production. In other words, many farmers have low subsistence capacity. In some cases, families may earn high amounts of cash income but spend more on food and in these landscapes the cash incomes cannot be supplemented by foraging or self-provisioning. In short, the transition out of agriculture may lead to more cash income and households moving above the poverty line in statistical terms, while remaining (or even becoming more) nutritionally insecure. In lowland Java, these deagrarianisation dynamics are most apparent where poverty rates have gone down as people earn more cash, but the poverty rate of 25 per cent remains similar to the stunting rate.

We also find nutritional insecurity within what appear to be agricultural livelihoods. In the *smallholder development and enclave plantation scenario*, households primarily cultivate or labour in the oil palm sector, and there are higher stunting rates than in rice-growing Java. Here, those who cultivate ever-smaller plots of oil palm, those whose oil palm trees are now too old or unproductive, or those who rely on insecure paid labour, tend to be those falling back into poverty. Again, there is a correlation between a low subsistence capacity and households that are nutritionally insecure.

The mechanisms at work in the fishing cases seem to be quite different. In the Bali *fisheries scenario*, reciprocal relations modulate the effects of seasonal and general declines in the fishing industry. Here, we attribute better nutritional security to the redistribution of subsistence fish, even in scarcity periods, as much as to the relatively high protein content of a fish diet. However, the emergence of consumer lifestyles has combined with insecure integration into the market to deliver detrimental impacts on nutrition.

In the Sulawesi *fishing boom scenario*, the majority are still poor and food insecure, unable to produce and save enough over the fishing season to tide them over during scarcity. They need to repay debts to support consumption during the windy season when they are unable to go to sea (*gagal melaut*), and this leads them inevitably into another cycle of cutting back during the following scarcity season. In response, poorer households resort to subsistence level reef gleaning and the consumption of sago (*sinolé*) as a substitute for rice and vegetables (due to lower prices and difficulty accessing the latter) and as a proven means of getting by.

Subsistence and Consumption

Globally, the highly efficient production of cheap "quick energy" foods is associated with over-consumption and the global obesity epidemic (Joint WHO/FAO 2003; Chou, Grossman and Saffer 2004; Drewnoski and Specter 2004). The emergence of new markets for industrialised and processed food has had significant negative impacts on nutrition (Scott-Villiers et al. 2016).

Across our sites, the poor continue to spend a large part of their income on staple food items, typically above 50 per cent of their total expenditure (see Figure 15.6). Poor families also spend significant amounts on tobacco, carbohydrates and sugar-rich cheap snacks (*jajan*) found in village shops (*warung*). In the Aceh *sideways scenario*, village women explained that children expect to take *jajan* to school and will pester their parents to pay for it. Surveys revealed that households may well spend more cash money on these snacks and on cigarettes than on protein (meat, fish or soybean products). However, in the Sumba villages, families do not spend money on meat; rather they raise livestock and poultry or receive a share of meat from ceremonial events. Similarly, in Sulawesi, fishing households rarely need to purchase fish or seafood for consumption. These forms of production and consumption are not well captured in surveys.

In many areas of Indonesia, rural people are net food buyers, with two out of three farmers in the country classified as "net consumers" (Costa 2020). Food prices have remained high over several years. According to one report, consumers have paid between 50–70 per cent higher prices for rice in Indonesia than in other Southeast Asian countries; prices for protein and nutrient-rich foods such as poultry, fruits and vegetables have also been higher (Asian Development Bank 2019). The high and rising cost of staples impacts family budgets; analysts have argued that the larger the percentage of income spent on food, the lower the prosperity of the household. Low-income groups spend, on average, 55 per cent of their income on food (Kaufman et al. 1997).[9] In almost all of our cases, households spend at least 50 per cent of their income on food and while cash incomes are higher in some areas, this does not mean that stunting rates are lower.

Subsistence capacities can be crucial to nutritional security. In several scenarios in our research, although households earn more and are less poor in statistical terms, they lack self-provisioning opportunities from farming and foraging, especially following the enclosure of common-pool resources and land alienation by large scale plantations. This leads to persistent nutritional insecurity. Specific food preferences and food cultures also play a role here. Research has found that inappropriate dietary intake, high consumption of unhealthy snacks (Savitri et al. 2017), and parental smoking (Best et al. 2008) are all linked to increased risk of child stunting in rural Indonesia. Hence, while households may leave behind semi-subsistence agriculture, this does not guarantee nutritional security; thus the association between economic growth and an escape from food poverty is not that clear: households can be better off in monetary terms but still food poor.

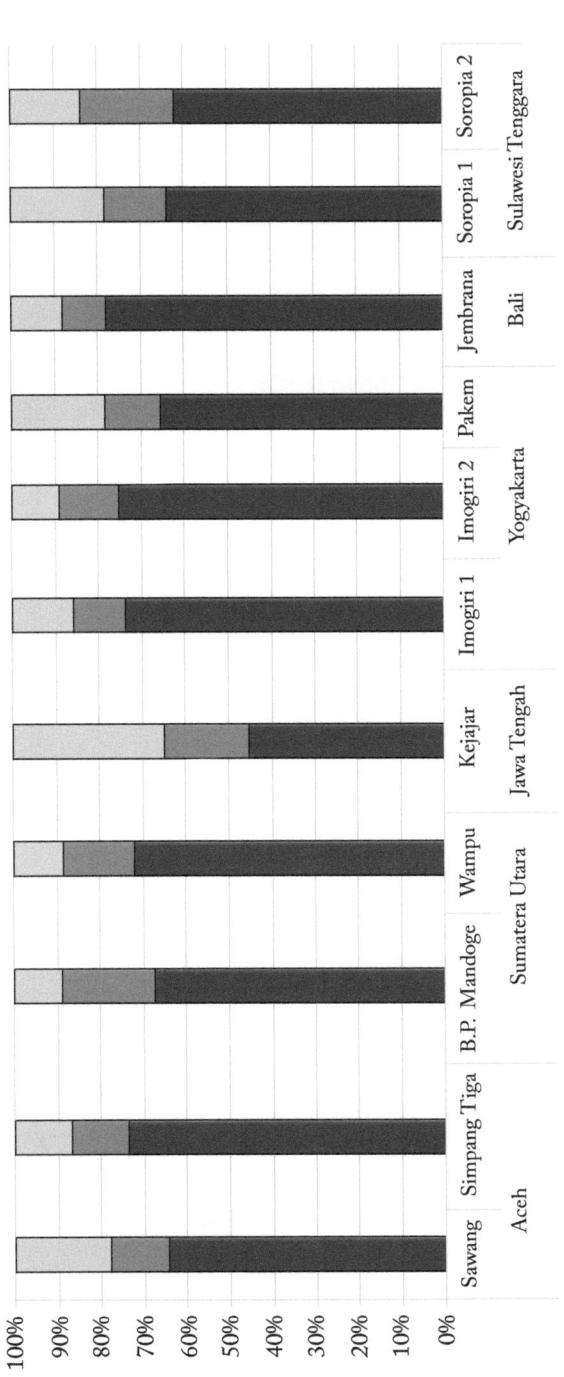

Figure 15.6 Food consumption, tobacco and snacks (*jajan*) of poor households, 2017–19
Source: survey.

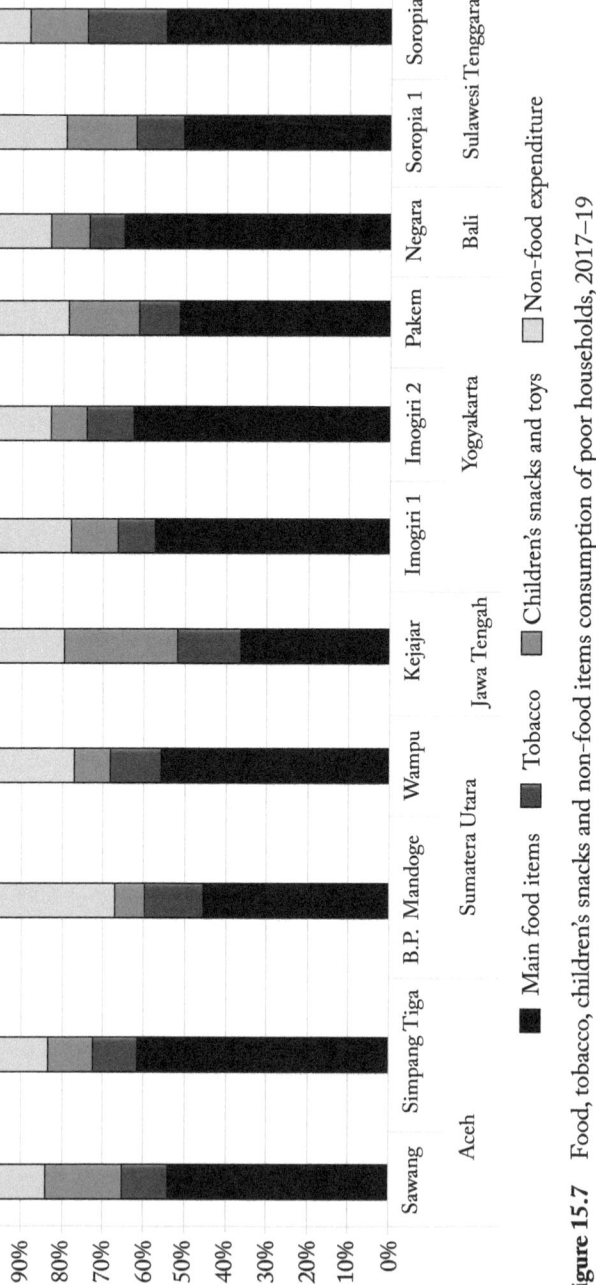

Figure 15.7 Food, tobacco, children's snacks and non-food items consumption of poor households, 2017–19

Poverty and Nutritional Security Dynamics

In summary, first, we see a significant shift (in local, emic terms) out of poverty in most cases. Yet, the mechanisms and processes vary. Even successful diversification trajectories tend to be fragile and integration occurs on uncertain or adverse terms.

Second, we also see the reproduction of poverty on a large scale. The structural processes include the semi-subsistence nature of agriculture, land shortages due to enclosure or fragmentation, environmental decline and climate change, and the structure of labour markets that provide scarce opportunities for diversification or migration. These combine with contextual drivers in specific cases to produce debt traps, life cycle crises and unsuccessful diversification.

Third, our research points to continuing and deep patterns of seasonal insecurity and scarcity. Food poverty, the inability to access a nutritious meal at times during the year, continues for complex reasons across scenarios. Rural households need to pay for labour and agricultural inputs and shifting social needs; much of their surplus income is used to fund consumption linked to changing lifestyles. This and evolving cultural food practices all contribute to new forms of nutritional insecurity.

When compared to the picture offered by a simple reading of poverty statistics, this analysis points to a distinctly different experience of poverty on the ground. Economic and nutritional accounts of stunting describe the proximate factors that affect outcomes, including income, maternal health, dietary practices, the age of women when they give birth, health services and sanitation. These approaches underpin policy interventions including cash transfers, nutritional supplements and education on nutrition. Such interventions aim to remedy the proximate causes of undernutrition, but often ignore the underlying drivers of nutritional insecurity. They also tend to overlook how processes of agrarian change co-produce nutritional outcomes and, more specifically, how livelihood dynamics within change scenarios drive food poverty. In the following section, we review the outcomes of state policies and responses that deal with poverty and nutritional insecurity. How effectively have such policies provided a remedy for rural poverty?

Findings of the Field Studies on the PKH Programmes

Indonesian policymakers tend to view social protection programmes (SPPs) as the primary instrument to address food insecurity, natural hazards, the Covid-19 pandemic, and even climate change related vulnerabilities. This volume sets out to understand how, and to what extent, existing forms of social assistance address critical forms of vulnerability among the Indonesian rural population of 120 million people. In rural areas, despite sustained economic growth at the national level over recent decades, nearly half the population still lives with degrees of endemic poverty and vulnerability.

A range of studies argues that policy approaches which integrate political economy viewpoints and the knowledge, values and experiences of populations and institutions are more likely to result in better outcomes than top-down planning processes (Carothers and de Gramont 2013; McCulloch and Piron 2019; Teskey 2017). Hence, there is a pressing need for policy-relevant research focused on the potential of existing forms of "informal" social security and existing institutions to provide effective forms of social protection.

Based on our grounded investigations, the analysis here aims to complement statistical analysis by showing the processes that shape pathways into and out of poverty. It thus aims to bring this analysis of poverty generating processes into systematic relation with existing social assistance practices. The question here is how well do pre-eminent forms of social aid enhance resilience and reduce vulnerability to poverty traps? In the following account, we note that social assistance programmes are constantly evolving. Our analysis is thus a snapshot taken over one period, highlighting underlying issues rather than surface aspects of programmes that change rapidly.

In Indonesia, the official poverty line is based on the official National Socio-economic Survey (Survei Sosial Ekonomi Nasional [Susenas]), which records household expenditures rather than incomes and considers people below the poverty line if their average spending is estimated to be below IDR 11,000 (USD 0.81) a day, well below the moderate poverty line of the World Bank. Indonesia's conditional cash transfer programme (PKH) uses the proxy means test (an estimated level of consumption based on household characteristics) to identify beneficiaries. In contrast, our study used a participatory poverty ranking exercise (SoP), to determine who was considered poor based on local standards. We then compared this with the list of people receiving PKH benefits (see Chapter 1). This is the basis for our discussion of PKH-related outcomes below. As discussed in Chapter 2, these approaches reflect distinctly different methodologies and sets of assumptions. Nonetheless, we argue that the poverty ranking exercise provides a reliable and strongly grounded point of comparison with the proxy means testing method.

In the following section, we sum up our conclusions regarding the benefits and distribution of the PKH system: how significant the benefits are; who is included or excluded, and why. We then assess what shapes the process and why the programme tends to be so fraught and conflicted from our informants' perspectives, particularly in remote rural areas. Figure 15.8 illustrates the relative distribution of PKH payments recorded during surveys in the study villages before COVID-19. The comparative figures reveal that while PKH contributions provide a welcome supplementary financial benefit to recipients, they make a relatively modest contribution to total household budgets among the poor.

Even as the scale of benefits has increased and broadened since our surveys (from 2016–18), the current social transfers are still too low to assist poor households escape poverty. In 2018, just 18 per cent of 0 to 6-year-olds in the bottom 40 per cent of households had access to PKH, while older people had the lowest coverage of all non-contributory social protection, at 1.7 per cent of the same grouping (TNP2K 2018: 82). Since 2017, older people have been included in PKH arrangements and have gained a critical supplementary benefit.

Figure 15.9 highlights the proportion of poor households (as categorised by local poverty criteria) which receive PKH payments. The findings and percentages vary widely across the village sites and, in most cases, significant numbers of poor households reportedly missed out on payments. In the three case study villages, the programme included numerous non-poor families (23–45 per cent). These findings provide further evidence of the legitimation crisis affecting the conditional cash transfer programmes. The lack of confidence in the administrative functions and institutions over-seeing the programmes which we observed during our research is also reflected in the local media reporting (see Chapter 3).

At the same time, this CCT programme needs to account for households which move above and below the poverty line (sometimes repeatedly) as their circumstances change. The Asian economic crisis of 1998, the global financial crisis of 2008–09 and the effects of the pandemic in 2020, as well as panel data, illustrate the continuing problem of vulnerability among a large cohort of rural households (Booth, Purnagunawan and Satriawan 2019). We also note that communities in different survey sites have distinct ways of thinking about what constitutes poverty and the level of welfare considered poor or non-poor. Hence, we cannot simply compare a single notion of "poverty" across all cases. This point highlights the challenges of introducing one government-funded, off-the-shelf solution to benefit all poor households in Indonesia.[10]

In rural Sumba (Chapter 6) there were reports of significant difficulties in targeting and accessing financial services through which CCT funds are transferred. Local conditions confounded efforts to deliver support to the poor. In upland Javanese communities (Chapter 8), people expressed their gratitude for receiving the CCT assistance, which was used mostly to increase

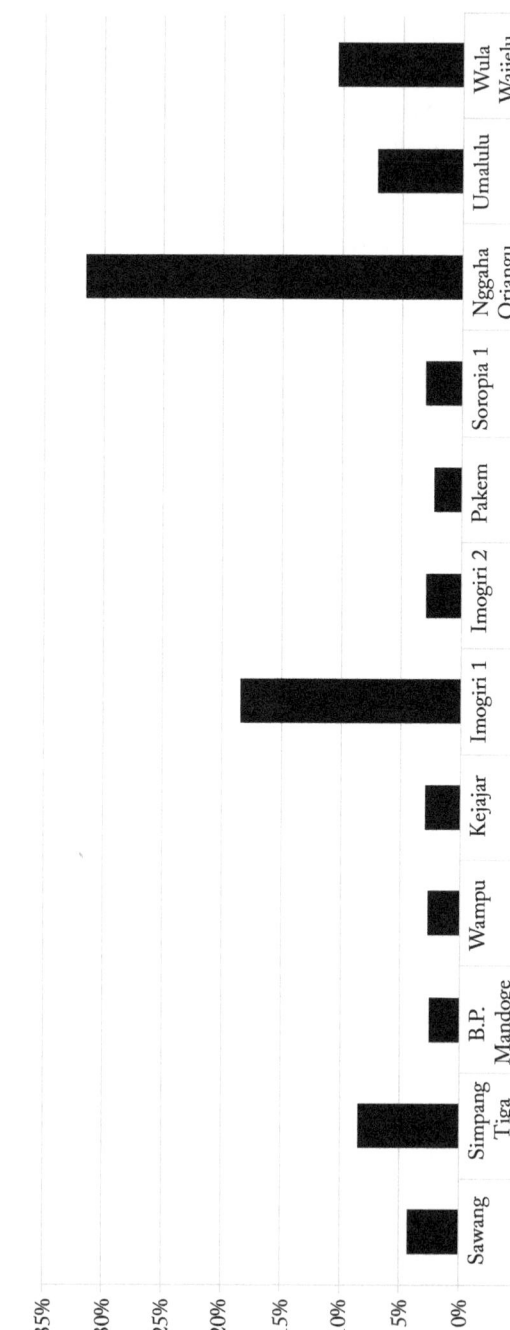

Figure 15.8 Conditional cash transfers as a percentage of household consumption among poor households, 2017–19

Note: Soropia 2 was receiving BLT (unconditional cash transfers) at the time of our surveys and so is not included in the figure. It was evident that poor households were comparatively better served by the BLT than the PKD conditional cash transfers. PKH had also not been implemented in Bali at this time. The tables do not include foraged or hunted food resources that may be consumed but not accurately measured. This is particularly the case in Sumba, where people mostly produce their own food, freely gathered from the fields, forest and coastal waters. The same can be said of Sama Bajo fishing communities (Soropia) in Sulawesi Tenggara. Measures of total consumption in these cases therefore are only approximated.

Source: survey data.

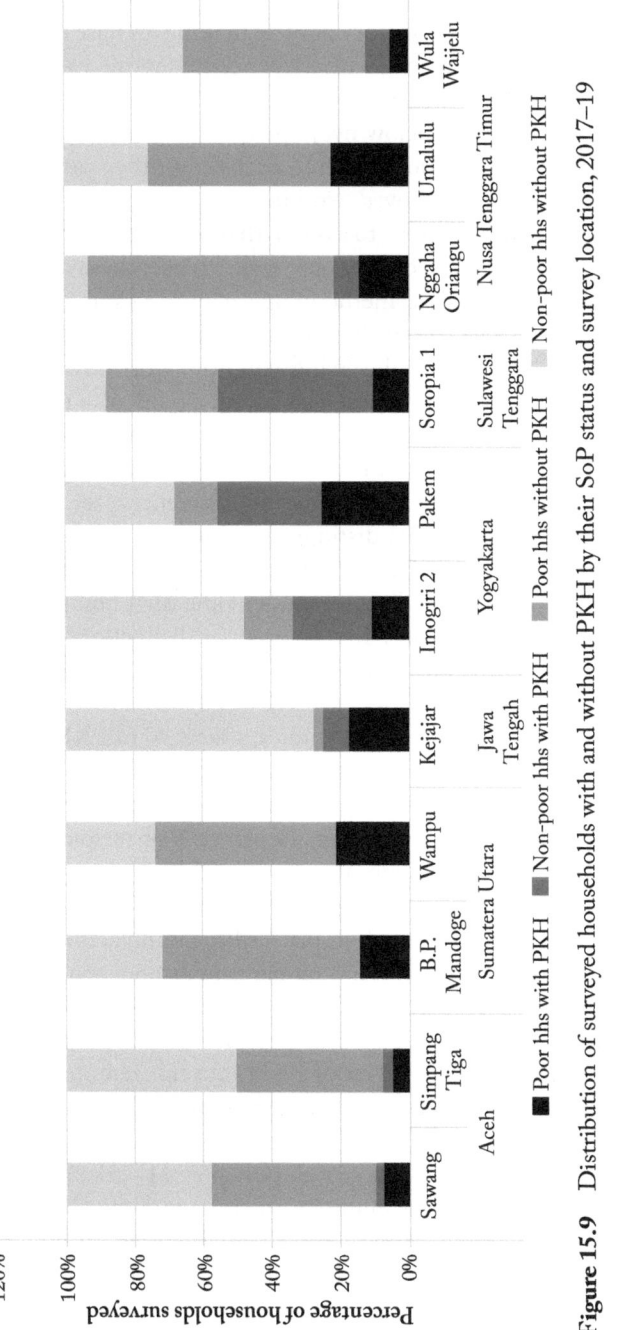

Figure 15.9 Distribution of surveyed households with and without PKH by their SoP status and survey location, 2017–19

household food portion size and frequency of meals. Here, village households assessed as poor by the participatory poverty ranking exercise (SoP) accounted for 74 per cent of the recipients, with 26 per cent identified as non-poor.

PKH, by its nature, focuses on young families with young children (*balita* [bawah lima tahun/ below five]), pregnant women and children going to school (below high school [SMA]), excluding other categories of poor households such as unemployed working-age men and families without children. The programme seems to assume that most healthy young men who are heads of households have access to work. Hence, these are precisely the families that the programme methodology may not rank as poor. In rural Java, for example, there are large numbers of people on or close to the poverty line (Chapter 13). However, the living conditions of those just above the poverty line barely differ from those just below, a point also demonstrated in the Bali fisheries community study (Chapter 9). Given the churning nature of poverty, the proxy means test in the verification process cannot differentiate between these minor, but locally significant, differences (see Chapters 9 and 12). But when PKH payments distinguish these minor differences through preferential payments, especially when households repeatedly cross the two sides of the statistical poverty line, resentment and discontent emerge at local levels (see Chapters 10, 12 and 13). These finer distinctions and conditions apply across the sites under study, including central Java and the coastal Sulawesi case studies.

In the Southeast Sulawesi case studies, a skewing of PKH cash subsidies to non-poor households is also discernible, with only 52 per cent of low-income families (by community standards) reporting regular cash payments from the government. The remaining 48 per cent of recipients of the cash payments were non-poor by community standards (Figure 15.9). However, these figures represent an averaging of the two case study samples, which masks contrasting results. In the Soropia 2 village sample, the process classed 31 per cent of recipients as poor and 69 per cent as non-poor. In contrast, in Soropia 1 village on the mainland, 72.7 per cent of the recipients were poor households and 27.3 per cent were non-poor. In the latter case, at the time of research, given delays in the rollout of PKH into this remote area, recipients were still accepting BLT (unconditional cash payments), which afforded more significant levels of coverage.

In the Aceh case, McCarthy et al. (Chapter 11) calculated how many poor households (by local community standards) met the PKH criteria and compared this list with those receiving PKH. The exercise found that only around a quarter of these potentially eligible households (poor by village standards and meeting PKH criteria) had received benefits.

Returning in 2019, the research team looked at how the benefit distributions had changed following the implementation of the centralised 2015 PBDT method (revising the social registry following a new community vetting of beneficiary lists, surveying and proxy means-testing to fix the problem). As a result of these changes to the programme, the number of recipients in the sample increased from 14 per cent to 21 per cent, and the number of poor and eligible recipients had increased by only a few per cent. However, 44 per cent of those receiving benefits were non-poor according to the village wealth-ranking exercises. These figures are by no means unique; surveys in the North Sumatra case (Chapter 7) revealed that only 14 per cent and 8 per cent of the poor within the two village cases were covered by PKH, while 30 per cent of the those included as recipients were non-poor by local standards.

To resolve the problems of mistargeting, local officials have sometimes tried to shame wealthier recipients into leaving the programmes by using identifying marks such as paint or stickers to identify beneficiaries' houses. The idea behind this approach is that more affluent families will feel embarrassed to be labelled as poor. But this tactic is often demoralising for the genuinely poor and creates feelings of humiliation and shame among publicly identified households. The media has reported these practices widely, noting that many PKH beneficiaries withdrew from the programmes in protest at having their status displayed on their house (*Banjarmasin Post* 2019; Kompas 2018, 2019). This stigmatisation is also found elsewhere across a range of other social protection systems.

In the Bali case, well-to-do villagers in one hamlet signed a letter requesting that they be removed from the Rastra distribution list and that their shares should be transferred to others more in need. Despite this request, no formal correction had been made as of 2019, although informal redistributions of rice supplements have occurred. With the shift to the BPNT non-cash food supplement system, the distributive mechanism became less transparent than the Rastra and this impeded informal redistribution.

Our studies show that social protection provokes a local politics whereby village actors lobby for inclusion. Here, village heads, afraid of conflict with their constituents, prefer to avoid making allocative decisions that exclude and alienate villagers. To avoid social jealousy and conflict, they choose to redistribute benefits in an inclusive manner, or otherwise avoid taking responsibility for the programme, while distancing themselves from community deliberations to improve targeting. We found that village and district governments frequently used their budgets for programmes such as housing for the poor (*bedah rumah*) and scholarships for the poor (*beasiswa miskin*) to deliver assistance to those otherwise excluded (see Chapter 13). Besides attempting to maintain social harmony, such initiatives sought to include villagers left out of central SPP programmes, if those households were considered eligible for support according to village/district perceptions and criteria.

In the case study communities where Islam is the predominant religion, the system of informal cash distributions to the poor is undertaken annually through the institution of *zakat* or an obligatory annual 2.5 per cent tax on accumulated wealth. Among the sample households, relatively high rates of poor households received *zakat* payments (Aceh 70 per cent), Upland Java (83 per cent) and Southeast Sulawesi (70.3 per cent), while non-poor households were also beneficiaries to a varying degree (Aceh 17 per cent, Upland Java 49 per cent and Southeast Sulawesi 22.7 per cent). When comparing the *zakat* distributions relative to the PKH targeting of poor household beneficiaries, the case study examples reveal marked discrepancies. The comparisons indicate that local *zakat* systems are much more effective at identifying poorer households than the centralised PKH programmes (see Chapters 10 and 11). As members of *zakat* distribution committees are very familiar with local households' economic conditions and the distributive mechanisms are relatively flexible, this result is perhaps unsurprising. However, it highlights the value of local knowledge.

The aspiration to provide timely and standardised benefits across the great diversity of socio-political, geographical and technological conditions in Indonesia presents logistical challenges, particularly if benefits are to be strictly rationed and targeted. Sophisticated beneficiary systems require sufficient state capacity, but in the remote rural areas where most of our research took place, the state faces additional challenges to the implementation of regular services; these are challenges which it has not overcome. To date, many areas have been allocated only one social welfare field officer (TKSK) to cover an entire sub-district, with inadequate budgets for surveys and operational expenses (Chapters 12 and 13).

National policymakers consider that most of the perceived and reported problems of the present system are due to implementation and capacity constraints in regional areas. Policymakers argue that the solution lies in improving the process of identifying the poor via more regular updating of lists and better targeting and delivery of services (see Timmer, Hastuti and Sumarto 2016: 33). The government also remains committed to this policy direction, as policymakers direct much of their efforts to fine-tuning the implementation constraints of beneficiary selection, review and reporting processes at district and local levels. However, our analysis points to a broader critique, highlighting endemic and persistent weaknesses in the current design and its implementation, as well as problems to do with insufficient coverage.

Conditional cash transfers are designed to empower women. However, in many cases, the decision-making power still lies with the husband as head of household and giving cash to women does not automatically empower them (Arif et al. 2011). At best, women have limited bargaining power in decision-making over issues like domestic needs and children's welfare (Brunberg 2015; Hakim 2016). Hence, the PKH programmes may have underestimated how gendered norms and roles in the household and society reinforce structural barriers to empowerment and may lead to or perpetuate entrenched inequality (Cookson 2016: 1201). For instance, PKH mandates a community-based development activity called Family Development Sessions (FDS) and obliges mothers in households to participate at least once a month (Kompas 2018). Despite its positive goal of empowering women through knowledge-sharing and training, FDS can be a burden on the time-use of women. As well, banks are scarce in many rural areas such as rural Sumba or island Southeast Sulawesi and travelling long distances frequently to collect government cash takes a lot of time and energy, especially for women with children.

In rural areas of South Sulawesi, women who are recipients of the government's social support programmes are usually required to attend FDS-related gatherings three to five times a month, including "follow up meetings"/forums where they are given "group homework" on top of domestic chores, child-rearing and, in some cases, also "paid work" responsibilities. FDS modules focused on parenting, cash management, children's education and nutrition, women's sexual and reproductive health and the general well-being of the family can be patronising if not well designed or delivered, and often impose an additional responsibility on women to be held accountable as primary caregivers. The programmes reinforce the idea of responsible motherhood. Of course, there are positive outcomes generated from the FDS, but policy design needs to consider the gendered nuances, to avoid undermining the very empowerment objectives it seeks to achieve (see SMERU 2013).

Social Assistance Outcomes

Across Indonesia, the rollout of conditional cash transfers assists many vulnerable households. Helping the poor is a long-term objective of reformist policymakers and social movements supporting social justice and human emancipatory ideals. The rollout of social cash transfers on a modest scale is a step towards providing income support sufficient to cover basic needs and resolve hunger and inadequate nutrition among the poor. This is a residual model: the state aims to help the neediest and the very poor (the bottom ten per cent), those unable to help themselves through the market or to receive help from relatives. These developments establish a building block for developing enfranchised alternatives to a system that currently leaves many people unsupported and without genuine assistance. Under prevailing conditions, agrarian-based poverty, continuing nutritional insecurity and household precarity are likely to persist.

Despite the impression of success indicated by econometric studies, the concerns raised by the informants in our research show that the system consistently disappoints established social expectations. Villagers time and again question the justness of the distributional outcomes of the programmes, querying the programmes' appropriateness and legitimacy, particularly when some poor households facing a similar (or greater) degree of hardship as included recipients are left out. As the chapters across this volume demonstrate, even after recent improvements, the econometric approach generates systemic errors.

The proximate reasons for implementation difficulties include complex data management and the logistical issues of effective identification and delivery processes in remote areas, including insufficient resourcing and a lack of adequate human capacity to manage the programmes effectively. Observers have noted the sheer complexity and fragmentation of the policy and the associated regulatory, bureaucratic landscape (OECD 2019). Our studies extend this criticism by arguing that current targeting problems, under-coverage and systemic inclusion/exclusion errors all derive from an overly technical and depoliticising approach based on flawed analytical simplifications (see Chapters 11 and 12). In attempting to enumerate poverty realities, the system struggles with the variegated social reality, where observed assets are not necessarily an accurate index of poverty status. The poverty experience is dynamic and complex, with people moving into and out of vulnerable conditions. These econometric approaches focus on individual household metrics, ignoring the reality that households exist within close-knit relational exchange networks and enduring clientelist ties of obligation and co-dependency (Chapter 10).

In studying these outcomes, we have noted the prevalence of a particular politics of knowledge shaping poverty measurement and the allocation of benefits. Poverty targeting requires actionable knowledge, measurable indicators and quantification. Econometric knowledge fulfils these requirements for rationing limited budgets. The problem is that when poverty is framed in purely economic terms, complex social learning from local-level cultural practices—which is essential to improving policy design—is left aside (Vetterlein 2012). As Benda-Beckmann, Benda-Beckmann and Marks (1994) have noted, different social relationships and layers of sociality affect how actors achieve social protection and interpret, manipulate and modify frameworks to suit their interests. Current programmes appear to bump up against local structures and cultural processes, derailing and undermining the technical procedures set out in policy blueprints.

This politics of knowledge derives from the CCT blueprint, a travelling World Bank policy model, imported wholesale from Mexico into the Indonesian context, but without substantial inclusion of Indonesian policy ideas and social realities (see Chapter 11). Prevailing political motivations shaping programme design and development provide a safety net for the desperately poor and thereby reduce poverty headcounts. But the approach leaves aside the underlying dynamics that sustain the inequalities of the economic system at large, and avoids substantial wealth redistribution (Li 2014). Other scholars have made the related point that, while the policies have "helped the poor to maintain positive real consumption growth", they are insufficient to propel them above subsistence levels (Suryahadi and Al Izzati 2018: 210). Ironically, in response to ongoing problems, policymakers engage in a never-ending process of re-contextualising poverty technologies from elsewhere, introducing technical ideas for updating, revising policy settings and priorities, sharpening programme formats, benefit arrangements and acronyms, but without fundamentally addressing the underlying problems (Chapter 13).

A further thorny issue facing policymakers is inherent in the difficulties of collecting and updating poverty information, as existing data quickly become out-of-date and inaccurate (Gazeaud 2020). This problem undermines the utility of econometric targeting, requiring state planners to embark on continuous attempts to update the data. Efforts to implement a real-time monitoring programme to track beneficiary lists and increase reliability have proved to be impractical and too costly (Chapter 12). Similarly, the government-sponsored community-based deliberations over recipient lists have provided opportunities for eligible poor people to receive benefits, but field implementation has been messy and complex, with central agencies retaining control over final decisions (Chapters 7 and 13).

Overall, we note how remarkable the social protection programmes are. For the first time, the state has systematically set out to provide social cash transfers and other direct benefits to the poor. Yet, we also note that the current system is opaque: decisions are made about entitlements in a rather unclear, offstage and unaccountable way. While this may reduce concerns about and opportunities for clientelist capture, it is yet to provide the poor with an effective mechanism to seek assistance when they face a sudden economic crisis, or to gain redress if they are unjustifiably excluded. The result is social segmentation, creating a distance between the poor recipients and other citizens left out of social provisions, even as they remain vulnerable (Fischer 2018). While the advent of the current approach represents significant progress, it is still a long way from a system that offers comprehensive coverage, accords with established social practices and expectations that might be more inclusive, reduces jealousies, promotes solidarity and provides more effective distributional outcomes.

Notes

[1] Our conclusions derive from the mixed-method, sequential explanatory design (Tashakkori and Teddlie 2008), which combined quantitative and qualitative data, and the development of our scenario heuristic and related causalities.
[2] In Java, being non-poor depends on access to networks which can provide a job for at least 3–4 months outside the village or having a family member working outside. Over two thirds of the surveyed families had a family member working outside.
[3] The promised transition to tourism development has not occurred, as the village remains too far from tourist centres in the south of Bali. Coastal land purchase by foreigners is mainly speculative and the few villas built are for private residents and offer little and poorly paid employment.
[4] The Bali community studied here shifted from an isolated community with little access to markets, to the accumulation of some material assets and social capital, education and diversified employment over the 1990s and early 2000s, after which incomes fell due to resource decline. Forms of reciprocity and moral economy are still very strong and work against the shocks and stresses of the seasonal economy of fishing; alternative livelihood opportunities tend to be low income and casual.
[5] Diversification: The Sama bajo do not diversify much beyond the fishing sector but reproduce their livelihoods by expanding their settlements.
[6] The triggering factors appear to be largely specific to each scenario, e.g. in upland Java where both regular water shortages and prolonged rainy periods caused production problems (i.e. *salak* in mid-slope Sleman suffering from regular water shortages and potatoes in upland Dieng harmed by excess rains in other periods of the year). Climate and agro-ecology are also critical in the NTT (East Nusa Tenggara) case. Dryland Sumba is characterised by low rainfall and long dry periods and people there are vulnerable to these extreme fluctuations.
[7] Cf. in Aceh the roles of middlemen, gouging and price speculation are important as is the cost of transportation to remote villages, all of which have an impact on prices and production costs.
[8] Farming remains a semi-subsistence activity with households in or close to extreme poverty, but land rather than labour is in surplus—still also a strong ritual economy shaped by cultural needs producing for ritual and marriages etc it has both a subsistence and a cultural meaning—so political economy accounts have limited purchase. Dependence on a relational economy is not necessarily stable.

[9] Since households may not include food for personal use grown in individual gardens and farms as income, the food share in these tables may understate the value of food consumed in households with significant home food production.

[10] We undertook most project surveys before the programme expanded the benefit categories to include older people in 2018. Accordingly, at the time of our surveys, the programme excluded significant numbers of aged respondents with no children. This was the case in Southeast Sulawesi and Bali.

References

Anwar, F. et al. 2010. "High Participation in the Posyandu Nutrition Program Improved Children Nutritional Status", *Nutrition Research and Practice* 4, 3: 208–14.

Arif, S. et al. 2011, "Is Conditionality Pro Women? A Case Study of Conditional Cash Transfer in Indonesia", Jakarta: SMERU Research Institute.

Asian Development Bank. 2019. *Policies to Support Investment Requirements of Indonesia's Food and Agriculture Development During 2020–2045*. Manila: Asian Development Bank. Available at https://www.adb.org/publications/indonesia-food-agriculture-development-2020–2045 (accessed 16 Mar. 2022).

Banjarmasin Post. 2019. "Pemkab HST ungkap fakta sebenarnya saat disebut abaikan salah satu warganya di desa Pandanu" [The district government of HST reveals the actual fact when suspected of ignoring a Pandanu village resident]. Available at https://banjarmasin.tribunnews.com/2019/03/13/pemkab-hst-ungkap-fakta-sebenarnya-saat-disebut-abaikan-salah-satu-warganya-di-desa-pandanu (accessed 2 Nov. 2020).

Bardosono, S., S. Sastroamidjojo and W. Lukito. 2007. "Determinants of Child Malnutrition During the 1999 Economic Crisis in Selected Poor Areas of Indonesia", *Asia Pacific Journal of Clinical Nutrition* 16, 3: 512–26.

Beal, T. et al. "A Review of Child Stunting Determinants in Indonesia", *Maternal & Child Nutrition* 14, 4: 1–10.

Benda-Beckmann, F. von, K. von Benda-Beckmann and H. Marks, eds. 1994. *Coping with Insecurity: An "Underall" Perspective on Social Security in the Third World*. Yogyakarta: Pustaka Pelajar.

Best, C.M. et al. 2008. "Paternal Smoking and Increased Risk of Child Malnutrition Among Families in Rural Indonesia", *Tobacco Control* 17, 1: 38–45.

Booth, A., R.M. Purnagunawan and E. Satriawan. 2019. "Towards a Healthy Indonesia?", *Bulletin of Indonesian Economic Studies* 55, 2: 133–55.

Brunberg, E. 2015 "Conditional Cash Transfers and Gender Equality: Short-term Effects on Female Empowerment: A Minor Field Study in Indonesia", Master Thesis, Lund University, Sweden.

Carothers, T. and D. de Gramont. 2013. *Development Aid Confronts Politics: The Almost Revolution*. Washington: Carnegie Endowment for International Peace.

Chou, S., M. Grossman and H. Saffer. 2004. "An Economic Analysis of Adult Obesity: Results from the Behavioral Risk Factor Surveillance System", *Journal of Health Economics* 23, 3: 565–87.

Cookson, T.P. 2016. "Working for Inclusion? Conditional Cash Transfers, Rural Women, and the Reproduction of Inequality", *Antipode* 48, 5: 1187–205.

Costa, F. 2020. "Harga bahan pokok di Papua melambung" [The prices of staples in Papua have soared]. Available at https://kompas.id/baca/nusantara/2020/04/01/harga-bahan-pokok-di-papua-melambung/ (accessed 2 Nov. 2020).

Dixon, J. 2016. "The Socio-economic and Socio-cultural Determinants of Food and Nutrition Security in Developed Countries", in *Routledge Handbook of Food and Nutrition Security*, ed. B. Pritchard, R. Ortiz and M. Shekar. Abingdon, Oxon: Routledge, pp. 379–90.

Drewnoski, A. and S.E. Specter. 2004. "Poverty and Obesity: The Role of Energy Density and Energy Cost", *The American Journal of Clinical Nutrition* 79, 1: 6–16.

Fischer, A.M. 2008. "Subsistence and Rural Livelihood Strategies in Tibet—under Rapid Economic and Social Transition", *Journal of the International Association of Tibetan Studies* 4, 1: 1–49.

_____. 2018. *Poverty as Ideology: Rescuing Social Justice from Global Development Agendas*. London: Zed Books.

Gazeaud, J. 2020. "Proxy Means Testing Vulnerability to Measurement Errors?", *The Journal of Development Studies* 56, 11: 2113–33.

Haggblade, S., P. Hazell and T. Reardon. 2010. "The Rural Non-Farm Economy: Prospects for Growth and Poverty Reduction", *World Development* 38, 10: 1429–41.

Hakim, S. 2016. "Conditional Cash Transfers and Wives' Decision-making Power", Paper presented at the ANU Indonesia Project Conference, Canberra.

Hüsken, F. 1989. "Cycles of Commercialization and Accumulation in a Central Javanese Village", in *Agrarian Transformations: Local Processes and the State in Southeast Asia*, ed. G. Hart, A. Turton and B. White. Berkeley: University of California Press, pp. 303–31.

Jakarta Post. 2018. "Combating Poverty". Available at https://www.thejakartapost.com/academia/2018/07/20/combating-poverty.html (accessed 12 Aug. 2020).

Jalan, J. and M. Ravallion. 2000. "Is Transient Poverty Different? Evidence for Rural China", *Journal of Development Studies* 36, 6: 82–99.

Joint WHO and FAO Expert Consultation. 2003. *Diet, Nutrition and the Prevention of Chronic Diseases Technical Report*. Geneva: World Health Organization.

Available at https://www.who.int/dietphysicalactivity/publications/trs916/en/gsfao_introduction.pdf (accessed 17 Mar. 2022).

Kaufman P. et al. 1997. *Do the Poor Pay More for Food? Item Selection and Price Differences Affect Low-Income Household Food Costs*, Agricultural Economic Report. Washington, DC: U.S. Department of Agriculture. Available at https://www.ers.usda.gov/webdocs/publications/40816/32372_aer759.pdf?v=3133.1 (accessed 15 Mar. 2022).

Kementerian Kesehatan (Ministry of Health). 2019. *Laporan Nasional Riskesdas 2018*. Jakarta: Badan Penelitian dan Pengembangan Kesehatan.

Kompas. 2018. "Presiden Jokowi: mereka tidak mengerti kita punya PKH" [President Jokowi: they don't understand we have the Family Hope Program]. Available at https://nasional.kompas.com/read/2018/12/13/13464261/presiden-jokowi-mereka-tidak-mengerti-kita-punya-pkh (accessed 2 Nov. 2021).

————. 2019. "TKN: Ma'ruf Amin siap jelaskan jika ditanya defisit BPJS saat debat" [National Campaign Team: Ma'ruf Amin ready to explain if asked about deficit in Social Health Insurance Administration Body in the debate]. Available at https://nasional.kompas.com/read/2019/03/13/16265301/tkn-maruf-amin-siap-jelaskan-jika-ditanya-defisit-bpjs-saat-debat (accessed 2 Nov. 2021).

Krishna, A. 2004. "Escaping Poverty and Becoming Poor: Who Gains, Who Loses, and Why", *World Development* 31, 1: 121–36.

————. 2006. "Pathways Out of and Into Poverty in 36 Villages of Andhra Pradesh, India", *World Development* 34, 2: 271–88.

Li, T.M. 2014. *Land's End: Capitalist Relations on an Indigenous Frontier*. Durham, NC: Duke University Press.

Mahmood, H.Z. et al. 2014. "Re-Examining the Inverse Relationship", *The Journal of Animal & Plant Sciences* 24, 5: 1537–46.

McCulloch, N. and L-H. Piron. 2019. "Thinking and Working Politically: Learning from Practice. Overview to Special Issue", *Development Policy Review* 37: 1–15.

Mehraban, N. and A. Ickowitz. 2021. "Dietary Diversity of Rural Indonesian Households Declines Over Time with Agricultural Production Diversity Even as Incomes Rise", *Global Food Security* 28, 100502: 1–9.

Nooteboom, G. 2019. "Understanding the Nature of Rural Change: The Benefits of Migration and the (Re)creation of Precarity for Men and Women in Rural Central Java, Indonesia", *TRaNS: Trans -Regional and -National Studies of Southeast Asia* 7,1: 1–21.

OECD. 2019. *Social Protection System Review of Indonesia*, Paris: OECD Publishing. Available at https://doi.org/10.1787/788e9d71-en (accessed 16 Mar. 2022).

Pattenden, J. and M. Wastuti. 2021. "Waiting for the Call to Prayer: Exploitation, Accumulation and Social Reproduction in Rural Java", *The Journal of Peasant*

Studies 1–22. Available at https://www.tandfonline.com/doi/full/10.1080/03066
150.2021.1970540 (accessed 16 Mar. 2022).

Rachmi, C.N. et al. 2016. "Stunting, Underweight and Overweight in Children aged
2.0–4.9 Years in Indonesia: Prevalence Trends and Associated Risk Factors",
PLoS ONE 11, 5: 1–17.

Ramli, K.E. et al. 2009. "Prevalence and Risk Factors for Stunting and Severe Stunting
among Under-fives in North Maluku Province of Indonesia", *BMC Pediatrics* 9,
64: 1–10.

Rigg, J., A. Salamanca and E.C. Thompson. 2016. "The Puzzle of East and Southeast
Asia's Persistent Smallholder", *Journal of Rural Studies* 43: 118–33.

Riskesdas. 2018. *Laporan Hasil Riset Kesehatan Dasar (Riskesdas)*. Badan Penelitian
dan Pengembangan Kesehatan. Available at https://www.litbang.kemkes.go.id/
laporan-riset-kesehatan-dasar-riskesdas/ (accessed 21 June 2022).

Sandjaja, S. et al. 2013. "Food Consumption and Nutritional and Biochemical Status
of 0·5–12-year-old Indonesian Children: The SEANUTS [Southeast Asian
Nutrition Survey] Study", *British Journal of Nutrition* 110: S11–S20.

Savitri, A.I. et al. 2017. "Ramadan during Pregnancy and Birth Weight of Newborns",
Journal of Nutritional Science 7, 5: 1–9.

Scott-Villiers, P. et al. 2016. *Precarious Lives: Food, Work and Care after the Global
Food Crisis*. Brighton: IDS (Institute of Development Studies) and Oxfam
International.

Semba, R.D. et al. 2011. "Consumption of Micronutrient-Fortified Milk and
Noodles is Associated with Lower Risk of Stunting in Preschool-aged Children
in Indonesia", *Food and Nutrition Bulletin* 32, 4: 347–53.

Setboonsarng, S. 2005. "Child Malnutrition as a Poverty Indicator: An Evaluation
in the Context of Different Development Interventions in Indonesia". ADB
Institute Discussion Paper No.21. Asian Development Bank Institute. https://
www.adb.org/sites/default/files/publication/156773/adbi-dp21.pdf (accessed 17
Mar. 2022).

SMERU. 2013. *Is Conditionality Pro-women? A Case Study of Conditional Cash
Transfer in Indonesia*. SMERU Research Institute. Available at http://www.
smeru.or.id/en/content/conditionality-pro-women-case-study-conditional-cash-
transfer-indonesia (accessed 16 Mar. 2022).

Suryahadi A. and R. Al Izzati. 2018. "Cards for the Poor and Funds for Villages:
Jokowi's Initiatives to Reduce Poverty and Inequality", *Journal of Southeast Asian
Economies* 35, 2: 200–22.

Susenas. 2018. "Statistik Kesejahteraan Rakyat" [People's Welfare Statistics], *Badan
Pusat Statistik*. Available at https://www.bps.go.id/publication/2018/11/26/

81ede2d56698c07d510f6983/statistik-kesejahteraan-rakyat-2018.html (accessed 20 Aug. 2020).

Tashakkori, A. and C. Teddlie. 2008. "Quality of Inferences in Mixed Methods Research: Calling for an Integrative Framework", in *Advances in Mixed Methods Research*, ed. M Bergman. London: Sage, pp. 101–19.

Teskey, G. 2017. "Thinking and Working Politically: Are We Seeing the Emergence of a Second Orthodoxy?", Governance Working Paper Series No.1. Abt Associates. Available at https://www.abtassociates.com/insights/publications/white-paper/thinking-and-working-politically-are-we-seeing-the-emergence-of (accessed 15 Mar. 2022).

Timmer, P.C., Hastuti and S. Sumarto. 2016. "Evolution and Implementation of the Rastra Program in Indonesia", MPRA Paper 81018. University Library of Munich. Available at https://mpra.ub.uni-muenchen.de/81018/1/MPRA_paper_81018.pdf (accessed 13 Mar. 2022).

TNP2K (Tim Nasional Percepatan Penanggulangan Kemiskinan/National Team for the Rapid Reduction of Poverty). 2018. *The Future of the Social Protection System in Indonesia: Social Protection for All.* Office of the Vice President of the Republic of Indonesia. Available at: http://tnp2k.go.id/downloads/the-future-of-the-social-protection-system-in-indonesia (accessed 12 Sept. 2021).

Torlesse, H. et al. 2016. "Determinants of Stunting in Indonesian Children: Evidence from a Cross-sectional Survey Indicate a Prominent Role for the Water, Sanitation and Hygiene Sector in Stunting Reduction", *BMC Public Health* 16 (669): 1–11.

Vetterlein, A. 2012. "Seeing Like the World Bank on Poverty", *New Political Economy* 17, 1: 35–58.

Wiggins, S., J. Kirsten and L. Llambí. 2010. "The Future of Small Farms", *World Development* 38, 1010: 1341–8.

CHAPTER 16

Conclusions and Implications: Paradoxes of Agrarian Change and Social Protection

John F. McCarthy, Andrew McWilliam and Gerben Nooteboom

In this volume, we have set out to understand rural change in all its complexities. We have sought to comprehend why rural poverty and nutritional insecurity persist despite the decline in extreme poverty. How is the nature of poverty changing and what are the implications for agrarian change and social protection policy?

To answer these questions, we wish to move beyond the "big-D" view of Development. According to Hart (2001), the "big-D" approach builds on paradigms of modernisation. The "big-D" framing is set out in narratives of structural transformation, national development and agrarian transition (truncated or otherwise). The approach helps frame rural development as an object for direct intervention ("how to bring economic development to the countryside" or "how to provide pathways out of poverty"). Paradigmatically, a common "big-D" view holds that economic growth, predicated on production for national and global commodity markets and greater integration with labour markets, will provide opportunities and pathways out of poverty for a bourgeoning rural workforce. Such global narratives, based on large scale analysis of the relationships between key variables, present statistical approaches that provide the "big picture". However, they involve numerous assumptions and simplifications and remain flat and uniform compared with the highly variegated rural experiences we study here. As a result, they offer insufficient understanding of the intermediate and lower-level drivers and experiences of insecurity within agrarian society (see also Bakker and Nooteboom 2017; Hart 2009; Lewis 2019).

Little-d development, on the contrary, concerns itself with understanding processes of change. It entails "the critical study of development *processes* as historical and endogenic processes that produce contradictory outcomes shaped by and creating social relations of inequality and social in/exclusion". Little d-development views development as an "*unintentional practice*" and focuses on immanent development processes. The little d-development approach thus brings relational, unintended and bottom-up factors into the development process, things that "big D-development" may either seek to control or ignore (Bakker and Nooteboom 2017: 63).

Qualitative studies complement analyses that may be more statistically robust, by providing a deeper understanding and a stronger grasp of causality. This volume builds on "little-d" approaches, developing a scenario heuristic to better appreciate endogenous processes of change. In its raw form, rural change is "geographically uneven", a "profoundly contradictory set of historical processes" (Hart 2001: 650). "Little-d" development constitutes the space where poverty and insecurity are located and reproduced (see Venugopal 2018) and where quotidian forms of progress occur (McCarthy 2020). Here, we distinguish the mechanisms and causal relationships working from below through analytical rather than statistical generalisation. In applying this approach, we contribute to the literature in several ways.

The scenario approach (see Figure 2.1) looks for patterns among the compound, non-linear interactions of contextual, relational and structural processes that vary over time and space. It involves exploring the links between specific patterns of vulnerability, emplaced agricultural practices, ecological resource dependencies and livelihood choices that include income diversification and seasonal or long-term migration. The approach enables us to put global narratives in their place as phenomena within a broader spectrum of local and regional scenarios. This entails a bottom-up, empirically based approach, starting with empirical findings and regional variety before moving up analytically. This enables us to go beyond accounts based on the historical experiences of the global north that have dominated the field of agrarian studies for many years. Using the scenario approach to reflect on decades of agrarian change and its regional varieties in Indonesia, our volume has highlighted a series of complex, contradictory outcomes and concluded that the nature of change presents a series of enduring paradoxes. We identify a paradoxical form of progress in most of our scenarios. While more than 30 per cent of the total village populations moved out of poverty—by local criteria—in at least half our cases, we also see the reproduction of poverty on a large scale. In eight of eleven cases, half of the households remain poor in local terms, despite "big-D development" narratives, social investment policies and significant expenditure on social assistance.

Of course, we are not the first to observe that "big-D" narratives do not seem to work for the many. Large-scale studies also note that inequalities between the less and better educated, rural and urban, old and young and male and female have widened across the Indonesian archipelago over recent years (Tjoe 2018; World Bank 2015; Gibson 2017). Like other middle-income countries, Indonesia has attained a level of economic development that provides jobs and prosperity for a growing middle class. Yet the country simultaneously confronts a widespread problem of undernutrition and stunting (Arif et al. 2020). Many households are moving out of poverty and achieving higher incomes in statistical terms. However, families also face reduced dietary diversity and less subsistence capacity; hence they progress without becoming nutritionally secure. Therefore, we witness the persistent issue of undernutrition exemplified by the stunting data.

In the literature, we can identify a few predominant explanations. First, the inadequacy of current poverty metrics leads to a statistical anomaly. The Indonesian poverty line is just too low to represent poverty accurately. As others have argued for similar reasons, poverty statistics that apply concepts of basic need based on calculations of what is required for subsistence generally "underestimate the reproduction of poverty over time" (Fischer 2018: 258). Second, economists have suggested that the price of the essential staple, rice, is just too high, consistently well above the international market price (ADB 2019). The income of rural people is not keeping up with the cost of food, especially given that so many people are now net food purchasers. Third, poor nutrition is due to the consumption choices of poor households to consume cheap calories and spend their income on other priorities; higher incomes do not translate into better nutrition (Banerjee and Duflo 2011). Each explanation suggests its own set of solutions: redefining poverty concepts; reworking food policy to reduce food prices, for example by allowing for cheap imports; and providing the poor with a "nudge" towards making "better" choices through incentives, education and nutrition supplements offered via conditional cash transfers.

In contrast, we argue that the very processes of agrarian change, rooted in causal mechanisms that elude statistical generalisation, produce the paradoxical forms of progress and nutritional insecurity that we see across rural Indonesia. Our approach suggests that poverty is not a single phenomenon. By seeking the reasons for poverty in critical livelihood landscapes, we find that outcomes emerge from the complex ways in which contextual, relational and structural processes come together with people's adaptations and strategies to form scenarios of change. The resulting agrarian paradox takes different forms because poverty arises and is reproduced according to the change dynamics in each scenario (see Chapter 2 for a summary of scenarios). This suggests that "one size fits all" technical approaches may be bound to fail: policy responses require specificity. For example, anti-poverty remedies for oil palm smallholders and labourers in Sumatra are different from those needed to assist a fishing household in Eastern Indonesia. Nonetheless, despite this variation, we do identify patterns, and in drawing together our analyses, we identify the following trends:

1. In our scenarios, the poor are embedded within social relations of mutuality that affect how they access land, finance and livelihood opportunities. In scenarios where households depend upon tight reciprocities within kinship and village-based exchange networks and patron-client arrangements, village social relations can provide households with opportunities to get by. Somewhat paradoxically, village-based networks of debt and obligation subject poor households to dependence and exploitation, tying some households into chronic patterns of scarcity and precarity. In many cases, social relationships—such as those shaping tenant farming, access to finance, labour markets, or patronage relationships—keep the poor vulnerable by constraining their ability to obtain sufficient incomes or resources. Migration or livelihood diversification can offer a way out. However, in most scenarios, a cohort of poor households remains unable to save sufficiently to sustain them during periods of vulnerability, seasonal scarcity or life-cycle crises. During these periods, which can last for months, the poor usually cut back on protein, resulting in nutritional insecurity and debts.

2. In Indonesia, a nutrition transition has occurred alongside a livelihood transition. In a generation, households have moved into commodified livelihoods with shifting social needs and aspirations. Households make different choices, as the marketing of instant and deliverable food and other consumer goods has penetrated the most remote corners of the archipelago. Village conceptualisations of what constitutes a good life have also shifted. In many parts of Indonesia, households now deem a dirt floor and thatched roof unacceptable, and they need a mobile phone and motorbike for work, leisure and family reasons. They pay for school expenses, health costs, farming inputs, internet vouchers and so on, which are now deemed necessities. Hence, poverty is constituted and experienced in relatively different ways compared to those in the past. As poor households are forced

to make wicked choices between these various perceived needs, they often cut back on nutrient-rich foods.

3. Global market integration has proved to be paradoxical and contradictory. It provides many with a trajectory for leaving poverty, as households diversify and move into labour markets. Yet, with agrarian differentiation, too many families remain integrated on adverse terms. Leaving subsistence agriculture behind and entering the labour market can represent either personal progress or simply a pathway into precarity. Hence, migration and diversification are linked not only to survival and progress, but also to stagnation and indebtedness. Similarly, leaving behind semi-subsistence agriculture is no guarantee of nutritional security. In some scenarios, such as palm oil production centres and scenarios involving urban wage labour, incomes are higher than in poorer areas. Still, stunting may be more significant than in statistically poorer areas due to lost subsistence opportunities, changing consumption patterns, and poor and precarious labour conditions.

4. In all boom scenarios, recent progress has built on the overexploitation of nature. This extractive pursuit of profit, together with associated increasing seasonal variability, threatens to dismantle recent gains. While the capacity to secure additional food and nutrition from shared resources, foraging and hunting is advantageous, in many scenarios, the poor face declining subsistence capacity; they have less ability to exist from their production. New ecological fragilities also generate multidimensional insecurity, mainly where land enclosures and appropriation—deforestation, mangrove destruction, depleting soil fertility, soil erosion, overfishing and environmental pollution—shrink subsistence alternatives and undermine the local and ecological basis of livelihoods.

5. Multiple technical, medical and economic factors lead to nutritional insecurity and stunting, including parenting and childcare practices and inadequate access to nutritious food, health care services, clean water and sanitation. State strategies that prioritise the stunting issue focus on these factors; before COVID-19, there was some evidence of positive impact (Arif et al. 2020). However, we argue that food poverty also emerges from patterns of agrarian change. These patterns encompass processes of adverse market integration, changing social needs and cultural food practices, all of which contribute directly to food poverty. Hence, alongside paying attention to the proximate determinants of child undernutrition, as state programmes do, food and rural policies need to be integrated into broader social policy and development strategies

which address the root causes and structural inequalities within rural change scenarios.

6. Poverty measurement that utilises a basic needs approach, calculating household poverty according to the affordability of a basket of basic goods, and methods that rely on econometric modelling applying asset-based income analysis provide critical insights for anti-poverty interventions. However, these models make many assumptions and they may overlook factors that are difficult to enumerate, leading to simplifications and blind spots. Unless triangulated with extra-economic forms of analysis, survey-based approaches can mask primary forms of insecurity and overlook fundamental mechanisms causing poverty. Relying on technical econometric analysis can also lead to a form of anti-politics, where poverty becomes a technical question of how to target the poor, rather than a problem emerging from the operation of political economies and requiring political remedies and distributional reforms. Moreover, policy needs to address the drivers of deprivation and to consider how distributional policies might best do this.

7. Across our scenarios, we see most households muddling through. A large cohort moves sideways, combining agriculture, off-farm labour, collection of products from nature, forms of reciprocity and remittances. Here we find statistical improvement (registered by poverty statistics and econometric analysis) and quotidian forms of progress. Even if people often remain insecure, most avoid a livelihood crisis. The extensive social protection programmes of the government are a great help in this process, preventing recipients from sliding back into poverty. At the same time, we do see a fluctuating proportion of households in each scenario that are chronically poor: usually female-headed households, tenant farmers, landless and the aged, as well as less capable families who have faced livelihood crises.

Social protection programmes (SPPs) have emerged as the key instruments to deal with chronic poverty, food insecurity and vulnerability (Devereux and White 2010; Holzmann and Sipos 2009). We advance several findings related to social protection:

1. Social assistance programmes continue to alleviate some of the harshest aspects of poverty and disadvantage in Indonesia. But, as we have highlighted in our regional studies, there is considerable scope for improving design and implementation.

2. While we see the application of ever more technically sophisticated models for measuring poverty and implementing social programmes,

these efforts overlook local socio-cultural norms and sociality, not to mention broader politico-economic structural factors critical to village livelihoods. Moreover, they convert the politics of distribution into a technical question of policy design and, in the process, displace critical questions of entitlement and enfranchisement and provoke a fraught local politics of entitlement and disenchantment.

3.   We argue that social protection programmes also present a paradox: welfare programmes are finding more complex ways to assist and include the poor, leading to new forms of exclusion. Many poor people are left out because limited funding leads to a rationed, highly targeted programme which is combined with policy design inadequacies and implementation mistargeting. Also, their individualised nature might weaken existing arrangements of social support and mutual help and protection. As other research has found (Kidd 2017; Leisering 2019), for significant numbers of rural poor left behind and omitted from beneficiary lists, the rollout of social assistance sharpens their sense of exclusion.

Implications and Alternatives

In this closing discussion, we explore several possibilities and strategic directions to address the needs of the poor better and to reduce the costs and inefficiencies that bedevil the current system.

Building subsistence capacities: Research has designated household access to sufficient land and healthy ecological systems as the basis for more diverse diets and better nutritional outcomes (Nurhasan et al. 2021). Land ownership and common pool resources provide subsistence capacities, principally the capacity to grow food and engage in foraging from common-pool resources. These amount to forms of informal social protection, buffers against vulnerability and nutritional insecurity, and provide an empowering sense of cultural identity. This provides a strong reason to retain the asset base of rural communities as far as possible (Ickowitz et al. 2016). By avoiding reckless natural resource extraction, enclosures and landscape transformations that undermine livelihoods and subsistence capacities, policymakers can provide a necessary form of resource insurance that supports nutritional security and reduces environmental pressures.

Recent assessments have identified nutritional diversity as a critical challenge (Arif et al. 2020). There are opportunities for improving integration across regional planning to promote diversification of livelihoods and diets. Policy could seek to avoid extensive monocultures and support measures to enhance the sustainability of fisheries, the heterogeneity of agroforestry and the benefits of diverse production systems, including home gardens and livestock ownership. There is significant scope for promoting more sustainable and productive fisheries, agroforestry and agricultural livelihoods via strong integrated policy commitments and better regulatory oversight.

Social fit: Networks of exchange, reciprocity and moral economies enable people and communities more broadly to cope with or adapt to change to varying degrees. If combined with subsistence capacities, these informal relations of mutuality enhance the ability of people to manage in the face of constant pressures and episodic stresses. However, coping strategies and local moral economies are invisible to statistical analysis and official poverty assessments overlook them. Consequently, given that limited coverage entails the rationing of benefits under this residual approach, and the significant errors of exclusion and inclusion of eligible beneficiaries, current social programmes generate jealousy and conflict. This undercuts village solidarities and reciprocities that are also necessary forms of social protection.

Chapter 3 noted that social protection (*perlindungan sosial*), which national-level discussions promote as a highly successful set of policies and programmes, is mired in controversy and discontent at local levels. It follows that welfare programmes need to build on a richer understanding of local cultural values and practices.

Seasonality: As we have seen, many rural people remain subject to regular periods of scarcity. Policymakers could incorporate an understanding of rural patterns of seasonality and food shortages into policy, including those derived from scenario analysis, to design specific development policies that address mechanisms of exclusion, indebtedness and inequality. Policymakers could develop social assistance measures that address specific patterns of vulnerability, such as rolling out assistance precisely when local people and local communities are most insecure. Examples include the precarious months before the main food crop harvest, or during downtimes in the agricultural cycle when extra work can significantly boost incomes. There is also a vital role for local government authorities here, drawing on their local knowledge, who could provide targeted temporary assistance, including employment schemes, during these periods of hardship. The result could be a more effective use of state resources, but it requires moving away from a "one size fits all" approach to poverty alleviation.

Social assistance programmes help Indonesian households by providing safety nets, supporting school enrolments, contributing to consumption, public health insurance and offering a basic level of security to a growing number of grateful beneficiaries. The value of these benefits was evident when the COVID-19 pandemic dramatically impacted employment, market prices and mobility. Yet social assistance programmes obscure the reality that the state under-invests in production or value creation in rural areas. Questions remain around the stability of support programmes over time. The challenge continues to be one of developing genuinely redistributive ways to address critical forms of vulnerability and depredation. Policy innovation is required to move beyond depoliticising technical solutions and to build genuinely redistributive structures and institutions to address the insecurity of rural people.

The Conditional Cash Transfer (CCT) blueprint operates and provokes issues in a similar way as it travels the world (Olivier de Sardan and Piccoli 2018; Ladhani and Sitter 2020). Scholars researching CCTs in Latin America have described similar patterns. For instance, the evaluation literature on Mexico's programme deemed it highly effective in alleviating poverty and diminishing inequality (Tomazini 2019; Masino and Niño-Zarazúa 2020). Yet researchers also found significant patterns of inclusion and exclusion, the inaccuracy of surveys carried out to assess eligibility, problems of resentment and hostility in the local communities, difficulties with involving communities in hybrid targeting, the disempowering impacts of conditionalities on the poor, the inability of CCTs on their own to overcome poverty over the long-term, among other issues. Reviews also suggest that social assistance programmes work as a means to both contain unrest and establish ongoing political support while keeping public spending down (Van Gils and Yörük 2017).

Moving beyond imported travelling blueprints, Indonesia could develop bespoke socially appropriate responses, work with the logic of rural institutions and address the structural inequalities and contextual triggers generating poverty. In comparison, sub-Saharan African cash transfer programmes tend to be either categorically targeted or unconditional. China also abandoned efforts at conditionalities and rapidly moved to a targeted but unconditional programme, while Mexico has also recently moved beyond the CCT model (Sarah Cooke, personal communication). Similarly, Indonesia might overcome the divergence between national and local perceptions by considering alternative ways of delivering social protection to needy households and of increasing the depth and breadth of the programme. There is room here for methodological experimentation, of the kind that we have demonstrated, to build poverty measures that incorporate indigenous/local practices and notions of vulnerability and poverty.

Alternatives: Several studies have responded to this persistent dilemma by exploring options for improvement within the existing paradigm of social assistance and poverty measurement (see, for example, Kim and Kwon 2015; Suryadama and Yamauchi 2013; Tohari, Parsons and Rammohan 2017; Alatas et al. 2016; Hardjono, Akhmadi and Sumarto 2010). These studies may lead to greater efficiencies and better targeting of programme funding. But they also highlight the entrenched and unresolved problems that linger below the smooth promotion and well-intentioned aspirations of Indonesia's poverty alleviation mission.

What are the alternative approaches? There is growing evidence that when social safety nets engage with communities, local groups and NGOs to identify and assist the poor, this improves outcomes (Subbarao et al. 1997: 87). Many discussions analyse alternative ways of giving effect to this consultative approach (Narayan and Ebbe 1997; Robb 1999; Conning and Kevane 2002; McCord 2013: 21). Indeed, Katiman (Chapter 13) demonstrates considerable policy learning in some districts. As he shows, local governments have worked around the shortcomings of existing programmes, developing approaches to support those excluded from social assistance and left out of the integrated social welfare registry (the Data Terpadu Kesejahteraan Sosial). For example, villages use the well-resourced "Village Fund" (*Dana Desa*) to provide cash transfers (Bantuan Langsung Tunai [BLT], Dana Desa) to those omitted from the flagship programmes or to distribute material contributions to housing renewal projects for locally identified and eligible village households. Yet community-based approaches have limitations (Conning and Kevane 2002), including the expense and complexity of expanding to a national scale. McCarthy, Hadi and Maliata (Chapter 11) emphasise that selection processes for assistance take on a highly relational form at the district and village levels. As a broad array of actors plays a role, these systems are inevitably subject to local village politics and the perennial concern that entrenched patterns of clientelism will shape the outcomes. Devereux et al. (2017) conclude that no optimal targeting mechanism exists. Hence, as Chapter 11 points out, proceeding with either a state-provided, community-based, or hybrid targeting may be ultimately unsatisfactory. There is a choice between the state's inaccurate selection procedures, village elites' selection with the inevitable accusations of bias, or a messy compromise between the two. Alternatively, policymakers may find it better to move beyond this dilemma, especially in locales where state capacity is weak.

An alternative approach involves categorical targeting of particular groups with higher than average degrees of vulnerability, supporting them with regular, unconditional cash distributions. For example, payments could be delivered to widows and female-headed households, the aged and infirm, families with disabled members, or targeted occupation categories with high numbers of impoverished members. This might include casualised workers, landless labourers, smallholder farmers living on minimal land areas or farming in marginal conditions, or fishers without boat assets and in high debt during the off-season. This mechanism is suited to areas with high concentrations of poverty, and it is administratively inexpensive. Such an approach may reach higher percentages of the poor, even at the expense of including an inevitable level of non-poor households. Such methods also avoid stigmatising the poor, shifting the focus towards entitlements and citizen rights to social assistance, rather than grudging forms of welfare and conditionality for the extremely poor (see Gaarder 2012; Ferguson 2015). It is important to note that poverty refers to the lack of income and other material resources and involves lack of power, physical and social autonomy and social respect. Hence, this alternative system can also address the disempowerment and lack of autonomy experienced by impoverished women (Franzoni and Sánchez-Ancochea 2016).

Another way of viewing social protection focuses on its development role: how social assistance is integrated within more comprehensive development strategies. This approach involves moving back to sustained structural investment in people, jobs and redistribution, granting equal access to resources and income. Critics argue, with some justification, that the history of previous attempts at multifaceted integrated development approaches reveals a pattern of crippling loss of focus with overly complex objectives and programmes leading to diminishing returns (Barrientos 2014). Yet, it has long been clear that programmes narrowly focused on targeting the poor with limited cash payments, in and of themselves, provide only a limited remedy (Cook, Kabeer and Suwannarat 2003). In terms of Sen's entitlement approach (1981), interventions need to focus on production, labour and exchange entitlements as well as social transfers. A systematic approach will seek to integrate broader economic, social and political objectives into social policy and economic development (Schüring and Loewe 2021; World Bank 2012).

Debates around applications and expansion of social cash transfers, on a social protection floor, and unconditional cash transfers, fit with a broader discourse focused on expanding the scope of social policy objectives and redefining dependency on the state for financial and other forms of social protection (Devereux 2009; Gaarder 2012). For example, Ferguson (2015: 24) has argued that, rather than seeing new regimes of social cash transfers as forms of state charity or welfare, we might reframe them as a rightful share of national prosperity, based on one's status as a citizen.

The inadequacy and exclusionary nature of residual schemes move the politics of distribution to the centre of national policy debates. Experiments with Universal Basic Income (UBI), designed to provide a guaranteed minimum income and generalised safety net for all citizens, are consistent with the expanded notion of unconditional cash transfers. Examples of these kinds of blanket payments to households facing immediate financial stress have been implemented as emergency and temporary measures during the COVID-19 pandemic in several countries. But in general, and as a mainstream approach to social policy, these initiatives remain prohibitively expensive and face solid political resistance as anything other than interim or emergency measures. Yet a more inclusive approach to assistance is in accord with the reciprocal and redistributive practices that bind together the social fabric of village life. Acknowledging cultural values, normative behaviour and political expectations must be a cornerstone for effective social assistance policies.

Our discussion suggests that this space requires more than a technical focus on policy design: innovation here requires a nuanced understanding of the political and economic context that shapes rural vulnerability and policy responses to it. Policymakers need to see around the corners of the highly sophisticated but non-specific datasets provided by econometric analysis. More sentient approaches can work with local political, cultural and economic dynamics, developing tailored, flexible and adaptive strategies, rather than fixed "masterplans" or "blueprint" style interventions (Andrews et al. 2012; Algoso and Hudson 2016). There is scope for significant improvements. Yet it remains to be seen how civil society actors and decision makers can develop fairer and more effective ways of addressing the needs and interests of the poor.

References

ADB (Asian Development Bank). 2019. *Policies to Support Investment Requirements of Indonesia's Food and Agriculture Development During 2020–2045*. Manila: Asian Development Bank. Available at https://www.adb.org/publications/indonesia-food-agriculture-development-2020-2045 (accessed 1 Apr. 2022).

Alatas, V. et al. 2016. "Self-Targeting: Evidence from a Field Experiment in Indonesia", *Journal of Political Economy* 124, 2: 371–427.

Algoso, D. and A. Hudson. 2016. "Where Have We Got to on Adaptive Learning, Thinking and Working Politically, Doing Development Differently Etc? Getting beyond the People's Front of Judea", *From Poverty to Power* (blog), June 19.

Andrews, L. et al. 2012. "Classic Grounded Theory to Analyse Secondary Data: Reality and Reflections", *The Grounded Theory Review* 11, 1: 12–26.

Arif, S. et al. 2020. *Strategic Review of Food Security and Nutrition in Indonesia: 2019–2020 Update*. Jakarta: SMERU Research Institute. Available at https://smeru.or.id/en/publication/strategic-review-food-security-and-nutrition-indonesia-2019-2020-update (accessed 31 May 2022).

Bakker, L. and G. Nooteboom. 2017. "Anthropology and Inclusive Development", *Current Opinion in Environmental Sustainability* 24: 63–7.

Banerjee, A. and E. Duflo. 2011. *Poor Economics: Rethinking Poverty and the Ways to End it*. New York: Public Affairs.

Barrientos, A. 2014. "Social Protection", in *International Development: Ideas, Experience, and Prospects*, ed. B. Currie-Alder, R. Kanbur, D.M. Malone and R. Medhora. Oxford: Oxford University Press, pp. 188–203.

Conning, J. and M. Kevane. 2002. "Community-based Targeting Mechanisms for Social Safety Nets: A Critical Review", *World Development* 30, 3: 375–94.

Cook, S., N. Kabeer and G. Suwannarat. 2003. *Social Protection in Asia*. New Delhi: Har-Anand Publications.

Devereux, S. 2009. *Cash Transfers – To Condition or Not to Condition?* Brighton: Institute of Development Studies (IDS).

Devereux, S. et al. 2017. "The Targeting Effectiveness of Social Transfers", *Journal of Development Effectiveness* 9, 2: 162–211.

Devereux S. and P. White. 2010. "Social Protection in Africa: Evidence, Politics and Rights", *Poverty & Public Policy* 2, 3: 53–77.

Ferguson, J. 2015. *Give a Man a Fish: Reflections on the New Politics of Distribution*. Durham, NC: Duke University Press.

Fischer, A.M. 2018. *Poverty as Ideology: Rescuing Social Justice from Global Development Agendas*. London: Zed Books.

Franzoni, J.M. and D. Sánchez-Ancochea. 2016. "Achieving Universalism in Developing Countries", UNDP Human Development Report. New York: United Nations Development Programme.

Gaarder, M. 2012. "Conditional Versus Unconditional Cash: a Commentary", *Journal of Development Effectiveness* 4, 1: 130–3.

Gibson, L. 2017. *Towards a More Equal Indonesia: How the Government can Take Action to Close the Gap between the Richest and the Rest*. Oxfam International Briefing Paper. Available at https://www.oxfam.org/en/research/towards-more-equal-indonesia/ (accessed 1 Apr. 2022).

Hardjono, J., N. Akhmadi and S. Sumarto. 2010. *Poverty and Social Protection in Indonesia*. Singapore: Institute of Southeast Asian Studies.

Hart, G. 2001. "Development Critiques in the 1990s: Culs de Sac and Promising Paths", *Progress in Human Geography* 25, 4: 649–58.

Hart, T. 2009. "Exploring Definitions of Food Insecurity and Vulnerability: Time to Refocus Assessments", *Agrekon* 48, 4: 362–83.

Holzmann, R. and S. Sipos. 2009. "Social Protection and Labor at the World Bank: an Overview", in *Social Protection and Labor at the World Bank: 2000–2008*, ed. R. Holzmann. Washington, DC: World Bank, pp. 1–10.

Ickowitz, A. et al. 2016. "Forests, Trees, and Micronutrient-Rich Food Consumption in Indonesia", *PLoS ONE* 11, 5: 1–15.

Kidd, S. 2017. "Social Exclusion and Access to Social Protection Schemes", *Journal of Development Effectiveness* 9, 2: 212–44.

Kim W. and Kwon H. 2015. "The Evolution of Cash Transfers in Indonesia: Policy Transfer and National Adaptation", *Asia and the Pacific Policy Studies* 2 , 2: 425–40.

Ladhani, S. and K. Sitter. 2020. "Conditional Cash Transfers: A Critical Review", *Development Policy Studies* 38, 1: 28–41.

Leisering, L. 2019. *The Global Rise of Social Cash Transfers: How States and International Organizations Constructed a New Instrument for Combating Poverty.* Oxford: Oxford University Press.

Lewis, D. 2019. "'Big D' and 'little d': Two Types of Twenty-first Century Development?", *Third World Quarterly* 40, 11: 1957–75.

Masino, S. and M. Niño-Zarazúa. 2020. "Improving Financial Inclusion through the Delivery of Cash Transfer Programmes: The Case of Mexico's Progresa-Oportunidades-Prospera Programme", *The Journal of Development Studies* 56, 1: 151–68.

McCarthy, J.F. 2020. "The Paradox of Progressing Sideways: Food Poverty and Livelihood Change in the Rice Lands of Outer Island Indonesia", *The Journal of Peasant Studies* 47, 5: 1077–97.

McCord, A. 2013. "Community-Based Targeting in the Social Protection Sector". Working Paper 514. Overseas Development International. Available at https://odi.org/en/publications/community-based-targeting-cbt-in-the-social-protection-sector/ (accessed 1 Apr. 2022).

Narayan, D. and K. Ebbe. 1997. *Design of Social Funds: Participation, Demand Orientation, and Local Organisational Capacity.* World Bank Discussion Paper No. 375. Washington, DC: World Bank. https://doi.org/10.1596/0-8213-4019-0.

Nurhasan, M. et al. 2021. "Linking Food, Nutrition and the Environment in Indonesia: A Perspective on Sustainable Food Systems". Bogor: Center for International Forestry Research (CIFOR). Available at https://www.cifor.org/knowledge/publication/8070/ (accessed 1 Apr. 2022).

Olivier de Sardan, J.P. and E. Piccoli. 2018. *Cash Transfers in Context: An Anthropological Perspective.* New York: Berghahn Books.

Robb, C.M. 1999. *Can the Poor Influence Policy? Participatory Poverty Assessments in the Developing World.* Washington, DC: World Bank.

Schüring, E. and M. Loewe, eds. 2021. *Handbook on Social Protection Systems.* Cheltenham: Edward Elgar.

Sen, A. 1981. *Poverty and Famines – An Essay on Entitlement and Deprivation.* Oxford: Clarendon Press.

Subbarao, K. et al. 1997. *Safety Net Programs and Poverty Reduction: Lessons from Cross-country Experience.* Washington, DC: World Bank.

Suryadarma, D. and C. Yamauchi. 2013. "Missing Public Funds and Targeting Performance: Evidence from an Anti-Poverty Transfer Program in Indonesia", *Journal of Development Economics* 103: 62–76.

Tjoe Y. 2018. "Two Decades of Economic Growth Benefited Only the Richest 20%. How Severe is Inequality in Indonesia?" Available at https://theconversation.com/two-decades-of-economic-growth-benefited-only-the-richest-20-how-severe-is-inequality-in-indonesia-101138 (accessed 13 Aug. 2020).

Tohari A., C. Parsons and A. Rammohan. 2017. *Does Information Empower the Poor? Evidence from Indonesia's Social Security Card.* Discussion Paper Series. Bonn: IZA Institute (Forschungsinstitut zur Zukunft der Arbeit) of Labor Economics. Available at https://docs.iza.org/dp11137.pdf (accessed 1 Apr. 2022).

Tomazini, C. 2019. "Beyond Consensus: Ideas and Advocacy Coalitions Around Cash Transfer Programs in Brazil and Mexico", *Critical Policy Studies* 13, 1: 23–42.

Van Gils, E. and E. Yörük. 2017. "The World Bank's Social Assistance Recommendations for Developing and Transition Countries: Containment of Political Unrest and Mobilization of Political Support", *Current Sociology* 65, 1: 113–32.

Venugopal, R. 2018. "Ineptitude, Ignorance, or Intent: The Social Construction of Failure in Development", *World Development* 106: 238–47.

World Bank. 2012. *The World Bank's Social Protection and Labour Strategy: 2012–2022.* Washington, DC: World Bank. Available at https://documents1.worldbank.org/curated/en/443791468157506768/pdf/732350BR0CODE200doc0version0REVISED.pdf (accessed 1 Apr. 2022).

_____. 2015. *Indonesia's Rising Divide.* Washington, DC: World Bank. Available at http://documents1.worldbank.org/curated/en/885651468180231995/pdf/101668-WP-PUBLIC-Box394818B-Executive-Summary-Indonesias-Rising-Divide-English.pdf (accessed 1 Apr. 2022).

CHAPTER 17

Epilogue: The COVID-19 Pandemic, Changing Agrarian Scenarios and Social Assistance[1]

John F. McCarthy, Andrew McWilliam, Carol Warren,
Vania Budianto, Shaummil Hadi, Pande Made Kutanegara,
Nulwita Maliati, Stepanus Makambombu, Gerben Nooteboom,
Henri Sitorus, Jacqueline Vel, Yunita Winarto and Lisa Woodward

As we finalised this volume, the COVID-19 pandemic bore down on Indonesia and disrupted the picture of declining rural poverty discussed in earlier chapters. To reflect on the implications for rural livelihoods and the scenarios we identified, we conducted interviews and reviews of available reports. Here we offer some preliminary thoughts on the impacts of the pandemic and consider how COVID-19 has triggered changes within the scenarios outlined in Chapter 2. We also reflect on the role of social assistance during this crisis.

The scenario approach applied in this volume understands rural transformation as a diachronic process, where contextual and relational mechanisms interact dynamically with political, institutional, economic, social and environmental structures and social relations to produce discernible patterns of agrarian change over time. A path dependency is at work in each scenario: as proximate and relational processes have converged with structures to shape a scenario over historical time, these patterns work causally, setting the conditions for possible outcomes into the future. However, change is not predetermined. When a contingent event occurs, such as a pandemic, it may reinforce pre-existing patterns, reproducing or deepening the effects. Yet, the contingent event may also trigger reactions and changes that can shift livelihood trajectories in new directions. As we will argue below, the pattern of change will depend upon how the contingent trigger (for example, a pandemic) plays into processes and structures characteristic of the specific scenario. In this epilogue, then, we set out to explore how the COVID-19 pandemic works as a contingent trigger exerting pressure on existing patterns of rural change, and intensifying the insecurity of the most vulnerable, producing both winners and losers.

COVID-19 Impacts on Our Scenarios

Our analysis points to two salient challenges posed by COVID-19, especially during the early months of the pandemic, challenges that other studies have also documented (HLPE 2021). First, COVID-19 led to considerable market disruption. In rural areas, agri-food products pass through multiple processing and marketing stages, managed by different actors. COVID-19 disrupted these complex value chains, with shutdowns, social distancing and restrictions on labour movements affecting transportation and supply logistics. These disruptions affected wet markets in particular, but also impacted the distribution of fresh food products. Second, the pandemic disrupted labour markets. As millions lost their jobs in the cities and overseas, migrant labourers returned to their villages for support and opportunities for off-farm work declined along with remittances. Consequently, as other studies across the global south have shown, the pandemic led to widespread loss of income and livelihoods, widening social inequalities, with higher and uneven food prices (Clapp and Moseley 2020; HLPE 2021). However, as we will see, these outcomes have been highly varied.

Initially, the crisis appears to have been even deeper outside Java, where smallholder incomes are highly dependent upon the production of globalised agricultural commodities (World Bank 2020). Poor households in the *smallholder development* and *enclave scenarios* (Chapter 7), for example, typically depend on growing a single cash-crop if they are labourers working in plantation monocultures. Hence, they are structurally exposed to fluctuations in global value chains. Moreover, subsistence farming opportunities are seldom available, given land shortages in these estate monoculture landscapes and forest transitions have reduced foraging and other options for accessing resources from nature. Hence, farmers in oil palm landscapes (especially Sumatra) were highly vulnerable to local and global value chain supply shocks. In the early months of the COVID crisis, producer prices for some commodities, such as rubber, coffee and oil palm prices, fell precipitously (by up to 40–50 per cent), creating welfare crises for some growers and labourers (McCarthy et al. 2020).

However, these commodity markets are dynamic, and by 2021 they had bounced back. The harvest and sale of oil palm returned to normal, with fresh fruit bunches earning higher returns. Prices for crucial staples remain somewhat inflated but stable, as livelihood activities resume. As the Delta variety of COVID began to penetrate Indonesian villages in 2021, residents began to fall ill. Those suffering COVID symptoms might continue to work, albeit for shorter hours. Villagers preferred to keep their distance from each other, and movements outside the villages remained limited due to community restrictions imposed through PPKM (*Pemberlakuan Pembatasan Kegiatan Masyarakat* / Community Activities Restrictions Enforcement [CARE]) that continued to hamper economic life. State agencies responded to mistargeting of conditional cash transfers (PKH) by once again attempting to update the social registry. Central, provincial, district, village governments and oil palm companies all rolled out social assistance on a large scale.

The broad structural features of the fisheries sector also left it particularly exposed to the pandemic. The rapid expansion of the commercial fisheries sector in Indonesia has meant that fisheries are highly integrated into global markets. Severe disruptions of fisheries value chains in the early days of the pandemic made it difficult to transport this highly perishable product to markets in a timely way (Amnifu 2020; Orlowski 2020; DPP KNTI 2020). In early 2020, fish export volumes crashed by as much as 70 per cent (Campbell et al. 2021), with global market prices for high-value fresh fish dropping dramatically (FAO 2021). The closure of restaurants, caterers and hotels compounded this contraction in demand. Fishers in many areas faced an oversupply of fisheries products, leading to prices falling by 50–75 per cent (Amnifu 2020). Many fishers reduced their fishing efforts, seldom going to sea or shifting to other occupations. From April 2020, prices for staple foods and vegetables increased significantly, putting pressure on already-reduced household fishing incomes. Many small-scale fishers elected to consume their catches and barter fish for rice (McCarthy et al. 2020).

Among Sama Bajo fishing communities (Chapter 10), the pandemic upset *the fishing boom* scenario and resulted in a significant, if temporary, disruption to livelihood trajectories. Poor households took up a seasonal *paceklik* mode, reducing consumption of purchased staples including rice, and switching to eating sagu (*sinolé*), foraging for seafood on exposed reefs and accommodating themselves to reduced cash incomes. The seasonal southeast monsoon from June 2020 restricted fishing opportunities further. This meant that many Sama Bajo expanded food-sharing practices and went further into debt to local patrons to meet household consumption needs (Wianti, personal communication).

In the Bali *marine resource depletion* scenario (Chapter 9), fishing markets also contracted, reducing the ability of households to live off fishing incomes. Here, communities which had diversified into the tourism labour market were now exposed to the collapse of tourism, which was among the worst-hit industries and which forced work-migrants to return to their home villages. The construction industry was also decimated, with day labour opportunities dropping to as little as ten days a month. Households planted vegetables in house gardens, intensified animal husbandry and engaged in village exchange relations. Many households now fished for subsistence and stretched rice and cash subsidies further. The government provided direct cash transfers to bolster livelihoods (e.g. Bantuan Sosial Tunai—Cash Social Assistance Programme [BST] and Bantuan Langsung Tunai—Dana Desa/ Village Direct Cash Transfers [BLT DD]) (Wianti and Wayan Adi, personal communications). But while recipients of cash transfers and food packages received increased support, they continued to complain that they "still face[d] the fact that the data from central government is incorrect and causes jealousy in the community" (Wayan Anom, personal communication).

As the months proceeded, market chains gradually recovered in both the fisheries scenarios, but food security pressures persisted, especially during the seasonal periods of low fish abundance. As restaurants opened up and market demand for local fish supplies recovered, Sama Bajo households were able to re-establish their fishing patterns and substantially rebuild their sea-based incomes. Reciprocity and redistributive practices remain remarkably resilient. In response to the challenges of COVID-19, in Bali, internet-savvy returnees took up diversification and value-adding strategies, launching start-up experiments marketing home-produced fish-based snacks.

In the *subsistence-orientated scenario* (Chapter 6), remoteness, poor infrastructure and climate and the ecology of Sumba impose structural limitations on the production of marketable commodities. These constraints mean that producers are less tightly dependent upon markets. As they primarily produce for consumption, we might expect some level of protection from the COVID-led market disruption. However, even before COVID-19, during a cycle of aggressive agro-industrial and commercial expansion, land enclosures and water appropriation for plantations, food estates and tourism projects curtailed community access to essential resources across many areas (Vel and Makambombu 2021). The disruptive effects of the pandemic have worked with climate variability to impact producers; floods, droughts, storms and variable rainfall, pests and infestations of animal disease (e.g. swine flu) and post-harvest losses deepen multidimensional insecurity. The pandemic disrupted value chains, affecting the ability of communities to trade in markets. These factors exacerbated existing vulnerabilities associated with the more marginal forms of agriculture found in rain-dependent areas.

Yet, in this scenario, farmers have highly diversified agricultural portfolios and engage in reciprocal exchange relationships coordinated through extended kinship networks (Vel and Makambombu 2020). The networks often stretch across rural and urban areas, or between areas with different harvesting periods, to spread the risk and help people get by. While many farming households remain vulnerable, they are also resilient. In late 2020, the market began to recover, and farmers enjoyed bumper harvests in 2021. When the Delta variety spread across the island during 2021, households even in remote locations received Village Direct Cash Transfers (BLT DD).

In central Java, many workers are structurally integrated into labour markets in urban centres, relying mainly on casual construction and service sector work. This precarious integration into labour markets leaves many Javanese households structurally exposed to shocks and downturns. This has given a particular inflection to the livelihood impact of the pandemic. Many of those dependent on informal labour markets lost casual jobs in the early months of 2020. At this time, restrictions on movement shut down kiosks selling snacks and food, particularly impacting women working in these sectors. As labourers working overseas or in the city lost their jobs, newly unemployed urban labourers had little choice but to return to their home villages in rural areas (Woodward 2020). Increased unemployment flooded the rural labour market with workers seeking employment, reducing opportunities for income diversification (Campbell et al. 2020).

Many rural families whose livelihoods depend on labour markets and income diversification in Java are net food buyers. With decreased opportunities for income generation during the pandemic, households had less cash available for meeting daily needs, including nutritious food. As a coping strategy, poorer households reduced expenditure and chose to keep more of their harvest for home consumption (World Bank 2020). As a result, nutritional diversity fell, as women focused on providing meals to fill the stomachs of family members.

In the *developmental-precarity scenario* described for rice-producing Java (Chapter 4), the impact appears to be less severe than expected. In lowland Java, households with diversified livelihood portfolios retained a foot in agriculture. Families who produced food to some degree avoided the deleterious impacts on nutrition. Rice farmers with small plots continued to grow food to meet household needs. Moreover, labour markets and marketing channels have gradually reopened, and the negative impacts on livelihoods have gradually declined. The pandemic-generated disruption has also had less impact on construction work and agricultural labour markets, and demand for farm labour and low skill construction has increased. However, rice farmers still face growing challenges from climatic variability associated with the El Niño-Southern Oscillation (ENSO), with late rice planting and irregular rainfall affecting harvest cycles.

While the spread of the Delta strain of the virus in 2021 led to a rise in mortality, the Indonesian government continued with social assistance in wide-ranging ways. With social assistance expanding to target up to 60 per cent of the population, some households have obtained benefits even if their incomes were scarcely affected by the downturn. With the banning of ceremonies and rituals that involve the reciprocal exchange of rice and cash, households have had reduced expenditures and therefore more money to spend on family needs.

The pandemic disrupted the marketing of horticultural crops (Chapter 8), which particularly affected vegetable farmers. Although marketing channels for these crops later reopened, climate variability has also affected planting cycles and, together with pest infestations, this has impacted yields. Commercially-oriented smallholders engaging in entrepreneurial farming in the *horticultural boom scenario* were more exposed. Fluctuating prices for horticultural commodities due to market disruptions and the manipulation of fertiliser prices by actors responsible for distributing subsidised fertilisers affected the capacity of farmers to buy the inputs needed for production (Paramashanti 2020). Even when horticultural products were relatively scarce after the dry season harvest, households had less disposable income, demand remained low and farmers earned less. These impacts and the disruption to fragmented value chains compounded other vulnerabilities. Some horticultural producers sold goats, cows and timber, while others adapted by directly marketing their goods using online applications.

In a similar fashion to the Javanese lowland, in lowland Aceh agricultural production appears to have been insignificantly affected by the pandemic (Chapter 5) and it has continued as usual. The opening of new rice mills over the years preceding the pandemic changed the marketing system for rice. While this displaced intermediate traders, farmers directly sold wet rice for cash rather than storing dry rice for consumption during the scarcity season, as they had done in the past. As marketing chains for rice are very short, the pandemic did not disrupt rice sales. Rising prices of essential commodities, especially in the early months, provided limited benefits to farmers.

In Aceh's *sideways scenario*, the structure of land ownership and labour markets produces economic stagnation and the poverty trap experienced by tenant farmers and landless labourers. Here, arable land and seasonal labour opportunities remain the primary anchor for insecure households who need to diversify to get by. In Aceh's rice lands, women from low-income families comprise most of these farm labourers. Over the previous three years, the expanded use of mechanical harvesters reduced the demand for labour. During the pandemic, work opportunities for the poor have been scarcer. Farmworkers need to seek seasonal work in adjacent areas or rely on seasonal work in dryland gardens. The pandemic has made labour migration difficult, and many migrant workers have returned to their villages to become farm labourers. Families send money to migrant labourers stuck overseas without incomes, to help meet their daily needs. The demand for construction workers has also fallen due to the tightening and refocusing of government budgets for infrastructure projects towards social assistance.

As the delta wave of the pandemic swept into rural Aceh, there were higher numbers of deaths. Usually, the community will make condolence visits, bringing modest donations (typically rice) for the bereaved family. As the number of mortalities grew, increasing social costs affected the savings of farming families.

Increases in food prices in the early months of the pandemic reduced access to food among the poor. While respondents report that hunger due to rising goods prices and other factors during the pandemic remains uncommon, families reduced the types of food consumed, as usual during scarcity periods, spending less on children's snacks.

Changes to labour markets, migration opportunities and higher social costs provoked by the pandemic have increased the dependency of the rural poor on state welfare programmes. In Aceh, at least six social assistance schemes now reach out to more than 900,000 families, well above the 195,000 households classified as poor and previously targeted for assistance (Info Aceh 2020). The rolling out of social assistance on this scale has changed the social discourse. With more generous welfare and less mistargeting, village leaders report less social jealousy and a decrease in community complaints to village heads about social assistance policies. However, with several overlapping programmes, unsurprisingly, "welfare rent-seekers" were obtaining benefits from more than one social assistance programme during the pandemic. On a positive note, village leaders reported that some families could convert the social assistance funds into livestock ownership, providing a capital asset and one step towards climbing out of the rural poverty trap.

Prior research has revealed pre-existing patterns of nutritional insecurity: 95 per cent of Indonesians do not consume enough fruit and vegetables for good health, 16.3 per cent of children under five are underweight, around 30 per cent are stunted and about half of pregnant women suffer from anaemia (Bodemaev and Tuwo 2020). While stunting rates were falling prior to the pandemic, at least in part due to social assistance programmes, COVID-19 has reversed these trends (UNICEF et al. 2021). There is evidence of a shift to detrimental livelihood and food consumption strategies, deepening the forms of insecurity identified in this study. World Bank (2020) research revealed that 32 per cent of the Indonesian people faced food shortages, and 54 per cent of farming households surveyed experienced income loss. Another survey found that "half of all households (51.5 per cent) have no savings upon which to fall back. More than one-quarter (27.3 per cent) were pawning possessions to survive. A quarter (25.3 per cent) were borrowing money informally from family or friends" (UNICEF et al. 2021: 6). With almost a third of surveyed households worried they could not feed their families, affected households coped with these shocks by reducing their non-food and food expenditure. However, as the discussion above suggests, food supply chains and rural labour markets have gradually been recovering and economic activities have resumed. While the impact of the pandemic worsened during the middle of 2021, by late 2021 there were indications that rural populations were bouncing back.

Discussion and Conclusion

Historically, analysts considered a "peasant" to be a farmer who combined subsistence agriculture, for consumption in the household, with petty commodity production. As earlier chapters have noted, greater market integration has provided many village households in Indonesia with upward livelihood trajectories. Analysts who now discuss "smallholders" tend to accentuate the degree to which farming households participate in markets. One FAO report noted that "smallholder" participation in markets is vital for improved food security and poverty reduction (Arias et al. 2013: 5). Yet—and we are not the first to note this—the shift from the "peasant way" into commercial smallholding and labour markets is not without risks, pitfalls and reversals. Earlier chapters pointed to the perverse implications of market expansion and adverse incorporation, particularly with ever-present possibilities for reversing progressive accumulation due to economic and political pressures, environmental degradation and negative feedback loops. Hence, progress remains insecure and subject to setbacks. Even in the better scenarios studied in this volume, people remain exposed to the severe effects of the lifecycle, production, fiscal labour and other multivariate shocks, such as the massive demand and supply disruptions triggered by the COVID-19 crisis.

We notice a paradox at work here. With its diverse and complex impacts on production and market systems, the pandemic demonstrates how greater integration into markets (e.g. higher dependency) can leave households open to contingent events that deepen the agrarian patterns that produce vulnerabilities. At the same time, we also witnessed that rural communities pursuing rain-fed agriculture, such as horticultural producers in Java and semi-subsistence farmers in Sumba, were badly exposed to climate variability and market shocks during the pandemic.

Across several scenarios, resource degradation also works to compound these rural vulnerabilities. For instance, the *resource depletion scenario* (Chapter 9) charts the rapid decline of the previously rich Balinese commercial sardine fishery due to market-driven expansion and poor governance. Combined with a crisis in labour markets, these communities lacked sustainable ecosystems to fall back on. As in other scenarios, the economic, demographic and social processes driving intensified production are eroding agriculture, fishing, forestry and other natural resource bases. Given the tight linkage between socio-economic and environmental transformations, we notice that degradation, depletion and loss of access to productive resources increase instability and uncertainty. The *semi-subsistence scenario* (Chapter 6) points to the cascading impacts of increasing climatic variability on dryland agriculture in Sumba. Climate change works to trigger or multiply structural and relational drivers of vulnerability, deepening existing insecurities. In the years ahead, the challenge remains to address the structural and relational drivers of vulnerability, which now work with climate variability to coproduce poverty and nutritional insecurity.

While statistical analysis can reveal monetarised livelihoods, semi-subsistence farming, non-market practices and forms of mutual assistance remain critical. Poverty and development metrics have undervalued or overlooked these livelihood and cultural aspects even though they are vital to people's ability to get by (see Chapters 6, 9 and 10). Rural communities appear to be tightly knit, and neighbourhood and village forms of mutual assistance help people get by. Rural people depend upon diversified livelihood portfolios and natural resource systems that are difficult to quantify and are opaque to quantifying methods. This is relevant to our discussion of the pandemic's impacts.

When families faced disruptions in labour and commodity markets during the pandemic, they turned back to older agricultural, natural resource dependencies and reciprocities. This pandemic confirms the advantages of livelihood diversification and access to alternate productive resources or income streams. Maintaining a foothold in primary production and having access to common-pool resources also represent essential livelihood strategies that enable households to build resilience and a capacity to recover from economic shocks. The importance of these practices is enhanced, even if they are not necessarily adequate for dealing with a deep crisis or helping all the poor in a community

Our analysis above suggests then that the impact of the pandemic on food and nutritional security is highly uneven, evolving and dynamic, varying considerably across crops, commodities, gender and location. Consequently, and as earlier chapters identified, agricultural and food policies need to be flexible to develop approaches that account for the specificity of each scenario.

As community practices and coping mechanisms are often insufficient for helping all of the very poor or sustaining those affected by long-term unemployment or resource decline, the new entitlements offered by social protection systems become critical. Indonesia's adoption of particular social assistance programmes during the East Asia crisis and beyond represented a critical juncture, when state policymakers made decisions that have proved causally decisive for later institutional development. As the state has institutionalised these programmes, social assistance has become increasingly vital to how rural households navigate crises. Despite their shortcomings, these state policies geared to stabilising staple food prices and providing social assistance and credit to the poor appear to have softened the pandemic's impacts.

Initially, the issues identified in earlier chapters that affected social assistance remained prevalent during the pandemic response, namely high inclusion and exclusion errors and inadequate flexibility. The government's response to the pandemic was to reallocate existing budgets to expand targeted programmes such as PKH and the Sembako [food staple] (formerly Raskin/ Rastra/BPNT) programmes (Sumarto and Ferdiansyah 2020). However, the centralised system struggled to assist unregistered households, which fell through the cracks. These included: returned migrants; those considered non-poor but now fallen into poverty because of the virus; those rendered vulnerable due to falling income; and those dependent on adult children who had lost their jobs. Reports suggested that the system struggled to avoid overlap between programmes and to include all households rendered vulnerable by the crisis. A 2020 report concluded that 46 per cent of households in the bottom 40 per cent, and 44 per cent of newly unemployed had yet to receive any social assistance (World Bank 2020). These programmes were insufficient to cover all the poor (Sumarto and Ferdiansyah 2020). Moreover, planners grappled with developing a system that fits the local socio-cultural and institutional context (Chapters 3 and 13).

During the COVID-19 crisis, Indonesian state planners moved beyond the residual system that targets the very poor and those recognised as fitting officially designated categories. The government acknowledged the limitations of the centralised beneficiary list and, as in the 1998 crisis, the state turned to regional and village governments to implement and fast track social assistance. During 2020, it introduced the Village Direct Cash Transfer

(BLT DD) scheme, which uses community targeting to include unregistered and overlooked households. Under this scheme, villagers excluded from the PKH, Sembako or BST programmes receive social assistance, with villages empowered to nominate villagers for inclusion in the social registry. In addition, village governments and community self-help groups also provided food, quarantine houses and ambulances to vulnerable community members, including returning migrants and infected households. Despite these efforts, the gap between the needs of the poor and state-provided social cash transfers has continued (Yuda, Damanik and Nurhadi 2021). In rural areas, 24.2 per cent of the poorest households in the bottom 40 per cent "did not receive any cash assistance", including from the village distributed funds (BLT-DD) (UNICEF et al. 2021: 6).

It remains to be seen whether this turn away from the residual econometric targeting approach to social cash transfers represents a second critical juncture. Will the state institutionalise these changes and support the development of a more inclusive or universal approach to social assistance as it continues to change the way it manages social assistance?

Nutritional security and social protection remain fundamental conditions for well-being in the coming decades. With climate change deepening rural vulnerabilities, there is a compelling need to bring social support to rural communities by moving further towards a social protection floor. Policies need to protect the natural resource bases of rural communities more effectively. This objective requires a significant and renewed commitment to redistribution, investing in diversified rural development and downstream processing, price supports, improved management of market chains, conservation and sustainable resource management.

Note

[1] This epilogue draws heavily on the analysis undertaken in J.F. McCarthy et al. 2020.

References

Amnifu, D. 2020. "Distribution Disruption Hurts Thousands of NTT Fishermen", *The Jakarta Post*, 8 May 2020. Available at https://www.thejakartapost.com/news/2020/05/08/distribution-disruption-hurts-thousands (accessed 20 Jan. 2021).

Arias, P. et al. 2013. *Smallholder Integration in Changing Food Markets*. Rome: Food and Agriculture Organization of the United Nations. Available at https://www.fao.org/3/i3292e/i3292e.pdf (accessed 18 Mar. 2022).

Bodamaev, S. and A.D. Tuwo. 2020. *Indonesia Covid-19: Economic and Food Security Implications.* World Food Programme, Indonesia Country Office.

Campbell, S. et al. 2020. "Impact of COVID-19 on Small-Scale Coastal Fisheries of Southeast Sulawesi, Indonesia", *Research Square* 1–22.

Clapp, J. and W.G. Moseley. 2020. "This Food Crisis is Different: COVID-19 and the Fragility of the Neoliberal Food Security Order", *The Journal of Peasant Studies* 47, 7: 1393–417.

DPP KNTI (Indonesian Traditional Fisherfolk Union). 2020. *Covid-19 Outbreak: Socio-economic Impact on Small-scale Fisher and Aquaculture in Indonesia.* Available at https://focusweb.org/covid-19-outbreak-socio-economic-impact-on-small-scale-fisher-and-aquaculture-in-indonesia/ (accessed 27 Aug. 2020).

FAO. 2021. "The Impact of COVID-19 on Fisheries and Aquaculture Food Systems, Possible Responses". Information Paper. Food and Agriculture Organization of the United Nations. Available at https://doi.org/10.4060/cb2537en (accessed 18 Mar. 2022).

HLPE. 2021. "Impacts of COVID-19 on Food Security and Nutrition: Developing Effective Policy Responses to Address the Hunger and Malnutrition Pandemic". HLPE Issues Paper. Committee on World Food Security High Level Panel of Experts on Food Security and Nutrition. Available at https://www.fao.org/3/cb1000en/cb1000en.pdf (accessed 18 Mar. 2022).

Info Aceh. 2020. "Amankan Jaring Pengaman Sosial Aceh: Rp. 2,3 Triliun Bansos Sudah Disalurkan ke Aceh" [Safeguard Aceh's social safety net: IDR 2.3 trillion social assistance has been distributed to Aceh], *Info Aceh*, 5th Edition 3rd Year.

McCarthy, J.F. et al. 2020. "Covid-19 and Food Systems in Indonesia", in *Covid-19 and Food Systems in Indo-Pacific: An Assessment of Vulnerabilities, Impacts and Opportunities for Action*, ed. L. Robins et al. Canberra, ACT: Australian Centre for International Agricultural Research ACIAR Technical Report 96, pp. 41–92.

Orlowski, A. 2020. *Small-scale Fishermen Suffering Significantly from COVID-19 Pandemic.* Available at https://www.seafoodsource.com/news/supply-trade/small-scale-fishermen-suffering-significantly-from-covid-19-pandemic (accessed 27 Aug. 2020).

Paramashanti, B.A. 2020. "Challenges for Indonesia Zero Hunger Agenda in the Context of COVID-19 Pandemic", *National Public Health Journal* 15, 2: 24–7.

Sumarto, M. and F. Ferdiansyah. 2020. *Indonesia's Social Policy Response to Covid-19: Targeted Social Protection under Budget Constraints.* CRC [Collaborative Research Centre] 1342 Covid-19 Social Policy Response Series. Bremen: CRC 1342 Global Dynamics of Social Policy.

UNICEF, UNDP, Prospera and SMERU. 2021. *Analysis of the Social and Economic Impacts of COVID-19 on Households and Strategic Policy Recommendations for*

Indonesia. Jakarta: UNICEF. Available at https://smeru.or.id/en/publication/analysis-social-and-economic-impacts-covid-19-households-and-strategic-policy (accessed 21 June 2022).

Vel, J. and S. Makambombu. 2020. *Covid-19 Mitigation Measures Compound an Economic Crisis in Sumba.* Available at www.newmandala.org/covid-19-mitigation-measures-compound-an-economic-crisis-in-sumba/ (accessed 15 June 2020).

————. 2021. *Surviving Four Disasters in Sumba.* Available at https://www.newmandala.org/surviving-four-disasters-in-sumba/ (accessed 13 Sept. 2021).

Woodward, L. 2020. *Coping with the Economic Fallout of Covid-19 in Upland Java.* Available at www.newmandala.org/coping-with-the-economic-fallout-of-covid-19-in-upland-java/ (accessed 18 June 2020).

World Bank. 2020. *Indonesia: High-frequency Monitoring of Covid-19 Impacts.* Washington, DC: World Bank.

Yuda, T.K., J. Damanik and Nurhadi. 2021. "Examining Emerging Social Policy during COVID-19 in Indonesia and The Case for a Community-based Support System", *Asia Pacific Journal of Social Work and Development* 31, 1–2: 13–22.

List of Contributors

Vania Budianto, PhD researcher, Crawford School of Public Policy, Australian National University, Canberra, Australia.

Shaummil Hadi, Senior Lecturer, Department of International Relations, FISIP [Faculty of Social Sciences and Political Science], Universitas Al-Muslim, Bireuen, Aceh, Indonesia.

Katiman (PhD, Crawford School of Public Policy, Australian National University, Canberra, Australia), Senior Official, Coordinating Ministry of Human Development and Culture (Kementerian Koordinator Bidang Pembangunan Manusia dan Kebudayaan), Indonesia.

Pande Made Kutanegara, Associate Professor, Department of Anthropology, Senior Researcher, Center for Population and Policy Studies, Gadjah Mada University (UGM), Yogyakarta, Indonesia.

Stepanus Makambombu MSc is a PhD scholar, Development Studies, Satya Wacana Christian University, Salatiga, Indonesia.

Nulwita Maliati, Senior Lecturer, Program Studi Sosiologi, FISIP [Faculty of Social Sciences and Political Science], Universitas Malikussaleh, Lhokseumawe, Aceh, Indonesia.

John F. McCarthy, Professor, Crawford School of Public Policy, Australian National University, Canberra, Australia.

Andrew McWilliam, Professor of Anthropology, School of Social Science, Western Sydney University, Sydney, Australia.

Gerben Nooteboom, Associate Professor, Department of Anthropology, University of Amsterdam (UvA), The Netherlands.

Michelle Pols, Graduate Student, Social Sciences, University of Amsterdam

Rudy Purba, Consultant, Data Analytics.

Henri Sitorus, Associate Professor, Department of Sociology, University of North Sumatra, Medan, Indonesia.

Mulyadi Sumarto, Assistant Professor, Department of Social Development and Welfare and Senior Researcher at the Center for Population and Policy Studies, Gadjah Mada University (UGM), Yogyakarta, Indonesia.

Naimah Talib was a Research Officer in the Crawford School of Public Policy at the Australian National University, Canberra, Australia and is currently undertaking a PhD at the University of Melbourne.

Yani Taufik, Lecturer, Faculty of Agriculture (Pertanian), Halu Oleo University, Kendari, Indonesia.

Jacqueline Vel, Senior Researcher, Van Vollenhoven Institute, Leiden Law School, University of Leiden, Leiden, The Netherlands.

Carol Warren, Associate Professor, Asian Studies, Murdoch University, Perth, Australia.

Nur Isiyana Wianti, Lecturer, Faculty of Agriculture (Pertanian), Halu Oleo University, Kendari, Indonesia.

Yunita Winarto, Professor, Lecturer and Researcher, Anthropology, University of Indonesia.

Lisa Woodward completed a PhD (2020) in the Asia Research Centre, Murdoch University, Perth, Australia.

Index